Phenomena-Driven Inquiry

A STRATEGY TO EXPLORE AND EXPLAIN

PHENOMENA USING THE POQIE MODEL

By Dr. Vince Mancuso

Phenomena-Driven Inquiry

Copyright © 2017 By Dr. Vince Mancuso

ISBN# 978-0-9989330-0-9

Library of Congress Control Number: 2017953727

For permission requests, email to the publisher, "Planet Magic Publishing" addressed "Attention: Permissions Coordinator,"

Phone: 585-703-0128

Email: vince@discrepantevents.com

Website: phenomenadriveninquiry.com

Twitter : @discrepantevent

"Planet Magic Publishing"

Printed in the USA

For my amazing wife, Nancy, and for my remarkable son and daughter, Nick and Cara.

My inspiration, my life, my love, my all.

My world turns because of you.

TABLE OF CONTENTS

INTRODUCTION: ENGINEERING THE UNEXPECTED

The most beautiful thing we can experience is the mysterious. It is the source of all true art and science.

Albert Einstein

A discrepant event and a magic trick both result in the same emotions- shock and disbelief. You and your students are about to experience the *magic* of discrepant event phenomena.

Imagine that a magician has just performed the most amazing card trick you have ever seen. Consider the levels of engagement that follow. What occurs in the seconds immediately following its conclusion? First, there is a visceral, startling reaction. Next, you question how the trick happened and ask, "how did you do that?" Then, you request to "see" the cards. You feel compelled to hold them in your hands and investigate the deck. And, you don't want to do it tomorrow. You want to do it now, while your interest and curiosity is piqued; while your understanding of how the world operates has just been jarred! In his book *Strong Magic*, Darwin Ortiz refers to this sequence of emotions as "intrinsic progression." This is precisely the range of emotions that we should hope our students experience following a discrepant event demonstration in our science classrooms.

The initial visceral, startling emotion that follows discrepant event phenomena is deeply, personally moving. The cognitive contradiction that it produces causes us to question the experience. In the science classroom, these emotions ignite the process of inquiry, foster investigation, and cultivate learning.

An audience members request to "inspect the cards" is tantamount to a student's request to hold, manipulate and examine the materials involved in a demonstration. We want our students to be startled and deeply puzzled. We want their belief system to be shaken. We want them to question their personal experiences. We want students to feel compelled to discover answers and explanations of their own volition. This is true engagement. Authentic inquiry embodies these emotions. Phenomena sparks them.

The critical difference between magic and a discrepant event demonstration lies in their objectives. Magicians hope to confound and amaze, but never encourage discussion or explanation. They aim to maintain wonder shrouded in puzzlement. Science teachers present discrepant events to confound and captivate, but encourage discussion leading to explanation. They aim to elucidate the world by developing an understanding for science concepts and principles. The science teacher always follows the event with an open invitation for inquiry.

Magic tricks leave us with emotions of awe, curiosity, and disequilibrium. We should strive for our students to experience the same. We should target and cultivate these emotions in our classrooms.

The discrepant event lessons included in this book are founded on naturally occurring phenomena- not magic tricks. Although they will undoubtedly confound and amaze, they will ultimately stimulate and educate.

The natural world around us is our magic show, and science offers the secrets to the tricks we encounter. Our primary objective in the science classroom should be for our students to eagerly *want* to unlock the *secrets* of the world around them! In your classroom, embrace the *magic* and discover the science!

This is *Phenomena-Driven Inquiry*!

WELCOME TO PHENOMENA-DRIVEN INQUIRY

Innate curiosity sparked by natural phenomena.

The primary objective of this book is to equip educators with a detailed, comprehensive, practical strategy that will position itself as a powerful, valuable resource in their practice.

Across the United States, the way in which science education is delivered and experienced is at a pivotal point. *A Framework for K-12 Science Education* (National Research Council, 2012) and the *Next Generation Science Standards** (NGSS, Lead States 2013) are prompting us to reconsider the ways in which students learn, understand, and *do* science. Strongly supported by research, this movement targets objectives that guide students towards the development of knowledge and skills necessary to engage in the *process* and *discussion* of science. Driven by a shift from memorizing facts, to actively making sense of our natural world, current educational reform establishes significant emphasis on phenomena-driven learning. Phenomena has been positioned as a central focus of educational strategy, practice, and curricular expectation.

This book presents one instructional strategy, or model, to strengthen your curriculum by aligning your practices closer to current standards, reform recommendations, and learning theories, and to ultimately enrich the learning experiences of your students through a sense of curiosity and wonder for the natural world around them.

The NGSS establishes a priority for making sense of phenomena in the science classroom. The focus of this book centers on a specific strategy for students to do just that. In these pages, we'll learn to combine the power of phenomena-driven learning with the effectiveness of learning through inquiry, to develop *Phenomena-Driven Inquiry*. Here you will discover an educational strategy to engage your students in rewarding learning experiences, specifically through discrepant events. In this book, you will discover how phenomena can be purposefully used in a manner to anchor the lesson and drive the learning.

Effective educators utilize a variety of pedagogical styles and teaching techniques in their classrooms. This book presents one specific strategy for the science classroom, called the Predict-Observe-Question-Investigate-Explain (POQIE) model. Specifically, the model focuses on the role of discrepant event demonstrations in the science classroom as a powerful tool to launch rewarding, student-led, inquiry-based investigative experiences. Its primary objective is to guide students as they make sense of cognitively stimulating, naturally occurring phenomena.

The POQIE model has its roots in the POE (Predict, Observe, Explain) and the 5E models. Alone, these strategies present valuable tools to educators. The POQIE model incorporates features from both, but also includes the significant addition of several unique features. The result is a powerful tool for science educators and the learning experiences of their students.

---

*Next Generations Science Standards is a registered trademark of Achieve. Neither Achieve nor the lead states and partners that developed the Next Generation Science Standards were involved in the production of this product, and do not endorse it.
https://www.nextgenscience.org/

Representing the culmination of 15 years of research and field testing, Phenomena-Driven Inquiry and the POQIE model has its origins in my Masters work. Continuing this research through my doctoral studies, it was the focus of my dissertation. The model was fully developed, and named, through subsequent post-doctoral research conducted in my classroom over several years Fifteen years of research has yielded great insight into the learning potentials of discrepant event demonstrations, their effectiveness as instructional strategies, and their capacity to generate thoughtful and rewarding student-designed investigations.

The spotlight, weight, and emphasis on phenomena in current reform represents a revolutionary approach and charge in education. Discrepant events, which embody phenomena, are positioned at the core of Phenomena-Driven Inquiry and the POQIE model. The discrepant events included in this book involve naturally occurring phenomena that contradict beliefs and expectations. Instilling cognitive conflict, they present a powerful tool for educators. Through Phenomena-Driven Inquiry, you will discover how discrepant event phenomena can be used as pedagogical tools, presenting an unparalleled opportunity for engagement and learning.

The POQIE model capitalizes on student-generated questions caused by the startling, unexpected phenomena observed during discrepant event demonstrations. Leveraged by this curiosity and wonder, students conduct investigations to more deeply explore the phenomenon. Through reflection, discourse and argumentation, teacher and students collaboratively construct an understanding for the scientific concepts and principles that underlie the observed phenomenon.

This book is packed with an extensive array of over 100 exciting discrepant event demonstrations, involving 120 concepts from every discipline of science. Designed to be integrated in a purposeful manner into your curriculum, each has been developed into a complete and independent lesson. Able to accommodate any curriculum, they serve to guide students as they make sense of and explain the embedded phenomena.

The lessons capitalize on the educational value of the unique characteristics of each discrepant event. Although some may appear familiar, the addition of distinctly unique and novel features has reshaped each discrepant event, to achieve very specific objectives within each lesson. The demonstrations are presented in unique ways that have not been seen before. Their structure and presentation establish optimal disequilibrium and cognitive impact. Each demonstration is specifically designed as a springboard to launch into meaningful, authentic inquiry experiences.

Although this book does not discuss *how to do* inquiry, it does examine its significance, role, and strong connections to Phenomena-Driven Inquiry and the POQIE model of instruction. Through the lens of authentic inquiry, the book details how to implement rewarding phenomena-driven investigations. Guided and self-directed inquiry is clearly and distinctly positioned within the framework of each lesson. You will learn how discrepant event demonstrations utilized within the POQIE model can help you develop a strong inquiry-based, student-centered classroom.

I truly believe that you are about to discover an amazing new strategy for your classroom. Science demonstrations involving phenomena can anchor the lesson and lead to remarkably rewarding classroom experiences. Supported by research and our current understanding of how we learn, *Phenomena-Driven Inquiry* presents a valuable model for your students to build deeper understanding for their world through personally meaningful discovery.

I hope the pages that follow inspire you to launch more student-led investigations of phenomena, and that this book presents a springboard from which to do so. I hope the book provides guidance and support to develop a richer curriculum and learning experience for your students. Ultimately, I hope this book serves as a useful and practical resource as you develop your art, your curriculum, and your students learning objectives.

Above all, I hope that *Phenomena-Driven Inquiry* and the POQIE model spark wonder and foster a passion for learning in your classroom, as they have done in mine. The world around us is continually fascinating, mysterious, and inspiring. Studies of natural phenomena instill awe and wonder, generating curiosity and igniting the desire to learn. Through the lens of discrepant events, the mysterious, natural phenomena that endlessly surrounds us has the power to transform the ordinary into the extraordinary. Deliver the wonder of *phenomena* to your classroom and ignite the spark!

Welcome to *Phenomena-Driven Inquiry*!

ALIGNMENT TO STANDARDS

The goal of science is to construct explanations for the causes of phenomena.

Science and Engineering Practices in the NGSS, Appendix F, p. 11

The *Next Generation Science Standards* (NGSS, Lead States 2013), requires that classroom experiences involve rigorous, student-generated question that can yield explanations for phenomena observed in the natural world around them.

The NGSS document represents a major shift in the approach to science education. It will influence science education across the country.

The Foundations of the NGSS

In 2012 the *National Research Council* (NRC) published *A Framework for K-12 Science Education.* Identifying the science that all K-12 students should know, and grounded in the most current research at the time, this document was central to the development of the *Next Generation Science Standards* (NGSS). Managed by Achieve and released in April 2013, twenty-six states acted as lead partners in the development of this document. The objective of the NGSS is to prepare students for college and careers. The document, also grounded in the most current research, outlines science standards by discipline and grade level. Based on the NRC's *Framework* and Project 2061's *Benchmarks for Science Literacy* (AAAS, 1993), among other documents, the *Next Generation Science Standards* (NGSS) is founded on three dimensions: Science and Engineering Practices, Cross-Cutting Concepts, and Disciplinary Core Ideas. An integration of these three dimensions is paramount. The synthesis of these three dimensions drives content and practice in concert.

Both the NRC and the NGSS strongly advocate that science students have the opportunity to learn through inquiry. Although they do share in the fundamental aspects of inquiry, there are distinct and critical differences between the two documents regarding philosophy and approach.

Phenomena

Merriam-Webster defines a phenomenon as:

> Something (such as an interesting fact or event) that can be observed and studied and that typically is unusual or difficult to understand or explain fully.

http://www.merriam-webster.com/dictionary/phenomenon

Phenomena are, without a doubt, one of the most prominent features of the NGSS. It's importance to the educational approach outlined in the NGSS is critical. There are a number of instances when the National Science Education Standards (NRC, 1996) does refer to phenomena and the important role it might play in the classroom. But the NGSS advances the role of phenomena to a much more significant status in science education.

In particular, the NGSS document establishes a very direct and very prominent objective throughout: students should be clearly engaged in science and engineering practices to design solutions or make sense of phenomena. It states:

"The goal of science is to construct explanations for the causes of phenomena"

Science and Engineering Practices in the NGSS, Appendix F, p. 11

The NGSS establishes a strong emphasis on phenomena-driven learning, supported by research and our current understanding of how we learn. Although the idea of *discovering* science through the observation of natural phenomena had its roots well before the publication of the NGSS, here it becomes positioned as a central focus of educational practice.

There is a stark contrast between the National Science Education Standards (1996) and the NGSS with regards to the educational approach and significance towards the use of phenomena in the classroom. Phenomena plays a significant role, a commanding focus, in the educational strategy and expectations within the NGSS. Learning experiences involving phenomenon are prominent, distinctly defined, and clearly outlined. The use of phenomena assumes a central learning strategy throughout the document. Rather than the suggestions made by the NRC, phenomena-driven learning becomes expectation in the NGSS.

<u>Inquiry</u>

The National Science Education Standards (NRC, 1996) promoted a clear change in the direction of instruction from one with "less emphasis on activities that demonstrate and verify science content" to one with "more emphasis on activities that investigate and analyze science questions" (p.113).

The document *recommends* inquiry as a central strategy in the science classroom and states:

> *Inquiry into authentic questions generated from student experiences is the central strategy for teaching science. Teachers (should) focus inquiry predominantly on real phenomena, in classrooms, outdoors, or in laboratory settings, where students are given investigations or guided towards fashioning investigations that are demanding but within their capabilities.*

National Science Education Standards, NRC 1996, p.31

You will notice that the NRC recommendation does place some emphasis on inquiry guided by "real phenomena." In the next section, we'll discuss this *recommended* use of phenomena by the NRC, as well as the subsequent more direct and prescribed approach in the NGSS.

Advocating that teachers integrate inquiry into their curriculum, the National Science Education Standards (NSES) describes the inquiry experiences students should have:

> *Students in all grade levels and in every domain of science should have the opportunity to use scientific inquiry and develop the ability to think and act in ways associated with inquiry, including asking questions, planning and conducting investigations, using appropriate tools and techniques to gather data, thinking critically and logically about*

the relationships between evidence and explanations, constructing and analyzing alternative explanations, and communicating scientific arguments. (p.105)

The document specifically, addressed the need for students to question, discover, and be creative by suggesting that teachers:

1. Select science content and adapt and design curricula to meet the interests, knowledge, understanding, abilities, and experience of students (p.30).
2. Focus and support inquiries while interacting with students (p.32).
3. Orchestrate discourse among students about scientific ideas (p.32).
4. Encourage and model the skills of scientific inquiry, as well as the curiosity, openness to new ideas and data, and skepticism that characterize science (p.32).
5. Structure the time available so that students are able to engage in extended investigations (p.43).
6. Create a setting for student work that is flexible and supportive of science inquiry (p.43).
7. Nurture collaboration among students (p.46).
8. Structure and facilitate ongoing formal and informal discussion based on a shared understanding of rules of scientific discourse (p.46).
9. Model and emphasize the skills, attitudes, and values of scientific inquiry (p.46).

Among this list are some of the most pronounced features of inquiry. Missing from this list, but recognized in a number of other instances throughout the document, is the importance for students to experience and explain natural phenomena. The NRC *Framework* (2012) would later reinforce this educational approach and value in guiding students to *"demonstrate their own understanding of the implications of a scientific idea by developing their own explanations of phenomena" (p.68)*. In fact, the word "phenomena" appears over one hundred times in the *Framework* (2012). Certainly, the *Framework* prioritizes science education that guides students to make sense of phenomena, noting its potential for conceptual change. But, it was the NGSS that would eventually elevate student-derived explanation of phenomena as one of the most significant principles of inquiry in the classroom. The document accomplishes this by providing direct philosophy, integration into curriculum, and both teacher and student expectations regarding natural phenomena in the science classroom. In the NGSS, the experience of phenomena and the constructed explanations for it are unequivocally positioned at the forefront of science education.

In addition to the *Framework,* Project 2061's *Benchmarks for Science Literacy* (AAAS, 1993) and *Inquiry and the National Science Education Standards: A Guide for Teaching and Learning* (NRC, 2000) each firmly supported and advocated that inquiry be a staple of science classrooms. The National Science Teachers Association (NSTA) has also aggressively asserted a focused commitment that teachers maintain cultivate and nurture inquiry in their classrooms. In its 2004 Position Statement on Scientific Inquiry, the NSTA recommended that teachers at every grade level embrace scientific inquiry with the goal to foster students to "question and explore their natural world" and to "make it the centerpiece of the science classroom" (p.1).

The NGSS document emphatically strengthens and supports the significant role of inquiry, naming it as a central student learning objective. But there is one major distinction regarding the approaches to inquiry between the NGSS and the documents preceding it. Prior to the NGSS document, the National Science Education Standards (NRC, 1996) included inquiry as separate from content standards. For example, the scientific method was taught as a separate unit, or idea, from the concepts being studied. However, the NGSS embeds curricular concepts around the framework of inquiry; built into the classroom experience- a way to learn, rather than an idea to know.

The NGSS does not suggest inquiry be included in curriculum. Rather, it mandates inquiry by ensuring it as practice. This is a stark contrast to previous state and national standards which outlined separate, individual inquiry and content goals. In the NGSS, *content* and *inquiry* are no longer two separately delivered ideas that students experience independently of one another. Instead, they are both experienced in one carefully designed approach. The process of inquiry is inextricably tied to classroom experience.

Inquiry, centering on student performance through engagement, is a critical feature of the NGSS. As states adopt, and districts implement the core ideas of the NGSS, inquiry will play a central role in the development of their curricula.

Argumentation and Discourse

Argumentation is a hallmark of science. It is a process of justification by which evidence and reasoning is used to support or explain a scientific claim. Discourse involves the persuasive communication of that claim.

The National Science Education Standards referred to the importance of discourse when they called for "less emphasis on private communication of student ideas and conclusions to (the) teacher" and "more emphasis on public communication of student ideas and work to classmates" (p.113).

The NRC (2012) later asserted that argumentation should comprise a fundamental role in the science classroom, based on its authentic utility in science and engineering:

> *Scientists and engineers use evidence-based argumentation to make the case for their ideas, whether involving new theories or designs, novel ways of collecting data, or interpretations of evidence. They and their peers then attempt to identify weaknesses and limitations in the argument, with the ultimate goal of refining and improving the explanation or design. (p.46)*

A Framework for K-12 Science Education also addresses the importance of argumentation in the science classroom. It places emphasis on the structured development of argument-based lessons in K-12 curriculum and identifies that by grade 12 students should be able to:

1. Construct a scientific argument showing how data support a claim.
2. Identify possible weaknesses in scientific arguments, appropriate to the students' level of knowledge, and discuss them using reasoning and evidence.
3. Identify flaws in their own arguments and modify and improve them in response to criticism.

The NGSS provide a detailed vision for argumentation with defined *expectations* for K-12 curriculum:

Grades K–2	Grades 3–5	Grades 6–8	Grades 9–12
Engaging in argument from evidence in K–2 builds on prior experiences and progresses to comparing ideas and representations about the natural and designed world(s). Identify arguments that are supported • by evidence. • Distinguish between explanations that account for all gathered evidence and those that do not. • Analyze why some evidence is relevant • to a scientific question and some is not. • Distinguish between opinions and evidence in one's own explanations. • Listen actively to arguments to indicate agreement or disagreement based on evidence, and/or to retell the main points of the argument. • Construct an argument with evidence to support a claim. • Make a claim about the effectiveness of an object, tool, or solution that is supported by relevant evidence.	Engaging in argument from evidence in 3–5 builds on K–2 experiences and progresses to critiquing the scientific explanations or solutions proposed by peers by citing relevant evidence about the natural and designed world(s). • Compare and refine arguments based on an evaluation of the evidence presented. • Distinguish among facts, reasoned judgment based on research findings, and speculation in an explanation. • Respectfully provide and receive critiques from peers about a proposed procedure, explanation, or model by citing relevant evidence and posing specific questions. • Construct and/or support an argument with evidence, data, and/or a model. • Use data to evaluate claims about cause and effect. • Make a claim about the merit of a solution to a problem by citing relevant evidence about how it meets the criteria and constraints of the problem.	Engaging in argument from evidence in 6–8 builds on K–5 experiences and progresses to constructing a convincing argument that supports or refutes claims for either explanations or solutions about the natural and designed world(s). • Compare and critique two arguments on the same topic and analyze whether they emphasize similar or different evidence and/or interpretations of facts. • Respectfully provide and receive critiques about one's explanations, procedures, models, and questions by citing relevant evidence and posing and responding to questions that elicit pertinent elaboration and detail. • Construct, use, and/or present an oral and written argument supported by empirical evidence and scientific reasoning to support or refute an explanation or a model for a phenomenon or a solution to a problem. • Make an oral or written argument that supports or refutes the advertised performance of a device, process, or system based on empirical evidence concerning whether or not the technology meets relevant criteria and constraints. • Evaluate competing design solutions based on jointly developed and agreed-upon design criteria.	Engaging in argument from evidence in 9–12 builds on K–8 experiences and progresses to using appropriate and sufficient evidence and scientific reasoning to defend and critique claims and explanations about the natural and designed world(s). Arguments may also come from current scientific or historical episodes in science. • Compare and evaluate competing arguments or design solutions in light of currently accepted explanations, new evidence, limitations (e.g., tradeoffs), constraints, and ethical issues. • Evaluate the claims, evidence, and/or reasoning behind currently accepted explanations or solutions to determine the merits of arguments. • Respectfully provide and/or receive critiques on scientific arguments by probing reasoning and evidence, challenging ideas and conclusions, responding thoughtfully to diverse perspectives, and determining additional information required to resolve contradictions. • Construct, use, and/or present an oral and written argument or counter-arguments based on data and evidence. • Make and defend a claim based on evidence about the natural world or the effectiveness of a design solution that reflects scientific knowledge and student-generated evidence.

			• Evaluate competing design solutions to a real-world problem based on scientific ideas and principles, empirical evidence, and/or logical arguments regarding relevant factors (e.g., economic, societal, environmental, ethical considerations).

Science and Engineering Practices in the NGSS, Appendix F, p. 13

Through argumentation, it is expected that students construct evidence-based explanations for observed phenomena. Arguments should involve justification through scientific reasoning to support claims through the use of models, especially in their ability to illustrate relationships and the connected nature of variables. Students should also develop the skills and techniques to evaluate arguments and assess the validity and reliability of empirical evidence. It is encouraged that students be provided the opportunity to communicate and constructively critique arguments individually and in groups.

In the NGSS, argument and discourse are positioned as a strong centerpiece of constructed learning. One of the most central elements of the NGSS, they are critical and essential to authentic science. As such, they situate as equally essential to the experiences of science students.

The *Framework* summarizes the scientific practices of argumentation and collaborative discussion used to explain natural phenomenon:

> In science, reasoning and argument are essential for identifying the strengths and weaknesses of a line of reasoning and for finding the best explanation for a natural phenomenon. Scientists must defend explanations, formulate evidence based on a solid foundation of data, examine their own understanding in light of the evidence and comments offered by others, and collaborate with peers in searching for the best explanation for the phenomenon being investigated. (NRC 2012, p.52).

Due to the authentic nature of phenomena and their key role in scientific investigation, the *Framework* supports argumentation specifically involving the explanation of phenomena:

> The goal for students is to construct logically coherent explanations of phenomena that incorporate their current understanding of science, or a model that represents it, and are consistent with the available evidence. (NRC 2012, p.52)

In the NGSS, argumentation is central to the explanation of phenomena. It asserts that students are expected to engage in clear, cohesive, and persuasive argument when investigating a phenomenon or constructing a model intended to support an explanation:

Argument based on evidence are essential in identifying the best explanation for a natural phenomenon.

Science and Engineering Practices in the NGSS, Appendix F, p. 13

Both the *Framework* and the *NGSS* clearly define scientific argumentation as central to the construction of knowledge. In current science reform, there is an increased focus on the skills involved in the construction and evaluation of argument, discourse, and critical thinking. A clearly developed growth of importance, implementation, and philosophy for argumentation expressed in the standards over time has led to overarching objectives in the NGSS for these core processes of science.

NGSS *Practices*

The NGSS outlines practices, cross-cutting concepts, and disciplinary core ideas. Together, they form an approach called 3-Dimensional Learning, with the primary objective to design solutions to problems or explain phenomenon.

In the *Framework*, eight essential science and engineering *practices* are identified as integral components to a K-12 science curriculum. They represent the dimensions of involvement that real world scientists and engineers engage in throughout their work. They are:

1. Asking questions
2. Developing and using models
3. Planning and carrying out investigations
4. Analyzing and interpreting data: this includes the identification of significant features and patterns from data
5. Using mathematics, information and computer technology, and computational thinking
6. Constructing explanations
7. Engaging in argument from evidence
8. Obtaining, evaluating, and communicating information

(NRC, 2012, p.42)

Notice here that asking questions is a *practice*. So is argumentation. The term "practices" used by the NGSS is modeled after the *Framework*. In these documents, the term is used to encompass both skill and discipline-specific knowledge; each an essential feature of scientific investigation. In the NGSS document, the term "practices" can actually be translated into "inquiry."

When students are simply following a prescribed process or lab procedure to answer a question, they are not involved in the *practices* as defined by the NGSS. The document makes this very clear. Instead, for students to be involved in the *practices* as set forth by the NGSS, they must be "trying things out." They are not following procedural steps provided by the teacher. And their objective is not to answer a "question." Rather, engaged in thoughtful manipulation of equipment and resources, their objective is to learn more about some natural phenomenon.

Models

The development and use of models is one of the eight essential practices in the *Framework*. The document explains the importance of models in science education, as they:

> *...help develop explanations about natural phenomena. Models make it possible to go beyond observables and imagine a world not yet seen. Models enable predictions of the form "if...then...therefore" to be made in order to test hypothetical explanations. (p.50)*

The NGSS further defines the critical role of models in the science classroom. They explain:

> *In science, models are used to represent a system (or parts of a system) under study, to aid in the development of questions and explanations, to generate data that can be used to make predictions, and to communicate ideas to others.*
>
> Science and Engineering Practices in the NGSS, Appendix F, p. 6

The NGSS directs that science students develop and use models with clearly defined objectives. First, models should be used to represent systems. They should have identifiable variables. Models should reveal cause and effect and illustrate relationships within the system. They should provide the opportunity to question and make predictions regarding the state of a system. And, most significant to our discussion, models should help explain phenomena.

The NGSS clearly establishes the expected scope of model usage in the science curriculum. It is intended that students are exposed to models and the practice of modeling each year of their K-12 education. Indeed, the expectation is that their experiences with models and modeling endure throughout each of the years, rather than during an individual unit(s). The NGSS prescribes that students develop and use models to:

- Represent relationships, processes and mechanisms within a system.
- Support explanations for phenomena.
- Make predictions.
- Make conclusions drawn from models.
- Investigate possible explanations for phenomena.
- Illustrate the relationships among variables.
- To identify the effects of changing a variable or component of a system.

You can clearly see the emphasis on phenomena. Students should be provided the opportunity to ask questions about observed phenomena, and then investigate those questions. They should be developing the skills to construct and revise models as a means to predict, question, test, and explain abstract phenomena. In fact, both the *Framework* and the NGSS maintain a very strong focus on stimulating, engaging phenomena and student interactions with them in the classroom.

POQIE Model Connections

Countless features and objectives of the POQIE model align with the NGSS 3D model of learning and the Science and Engineering Practices.

The NGSS Practices are essentially inquiry expectations for our students. But these expectations, or objectives, exceed the traditional, more commonly practiced, inquiry objectives typically found in our classrooms. For example, in most inquiry classrooms, students will test a hypothesis, attempt to uncover a relationship between components, perhaps isolate a factor that causes some occurrence, and finally report findings. Inquiry in the NGSS asks that students identify a variable, design and conduct a student-led investigation with the objective to *explain* a mechanism or phenomena, and that a collaboratively co-constructed explanatory model occurs through class discourse and argumentation. This is traditional inquiry on steroids. And the POQIE model aligns perfectly with it.

Each of the educational documents we've discussed has deemed inquiry as a valuable component to student learning. The NSTA asserts that scientific inquiry is "at the heart of how students learn" (NSTA Position Statement on Scientific Inquiry, 2004, p.1). Following the suggested *recommendation* for inquiry in the National Education Standards, the subsequent NGSS document outlined a very direct charge that students be involved in all aspects of inquiry. In Chapter Six we'll discover that each of the clearly defined characteristics of inquiry is firmly embedded within the POQIE model of instruction.

Natural phenomena, and student-derived explanations for it, are a focal point of the NGSS. The NGSS defines an "explanation" as:

> *An explanation includes a claim that relates how a variable or variables relate to another variable or a set of variables. A claim is often made in response to a question and in the process of answering the question, scientists often design investigations to generate data.*
>
> Science and Engineering Practices in the NGSS, Appendix F, p.11

In the POQIE model, students work on individual investigations of different variables. Following their investigations, the observations and findings are shared through class discourse. One of the goals here is to explain the relationship of the variables and their influence in the system under study. You'll find in Chapter Six that the POQIE model aligns perfectly with the NGSS definition, as three of the five stages of the model involve the opportunity for student explanations addressed in this specific manner.

The National Research Council (2012) advocates for instruction that "leverages the personal interests and cultural knowledge" of students by making it personally relevant and meaningful to the learner. Methods that help to achieve this objective include:

1. The development of a classroom community that values students' ideas and interests.
2. Creating problem-based learning activities that are relevant to students' culture, interests, and experiences.
3. Using apparatus that students are familiar with.

4. Developing lessons that ask students to apply new understanding to explain everyday situations and phenomena.
5. Providing students a voice in planning content, selecting activities, pursuing investigations, etc.
6. Creating open-ended opportunities for students to explore their interests.

Science Scope, March 2013, p.1

Each one of these attributes is evident in the POQIE model. To begin, the ultimate objective of the POQIE model is for students to apply new understanding gained through their investigations to explain phenomena observed in the initial demonstration. Student ideas and interests are valued when students develop their own research question. Their ideas and voices are valued during the discourse that occurs following the observed demonstration, throughout their individually developed investigations, and through the final class discourse following the investigations. The investigations are guided by individual student interest in the variable they choose to explore and grounded in the personal experience gained through observation of the demonstrated phenomena. One of the key components to the POQIE model is the use of equipment and resources that are familiar to students. The support, reasoning and value behind familiarity will be discussed in Chapter Six.

Conceptual change, discussed in Chapter Four, plays a key role in the POQIE model. One of the goals of the Explanation Phase of the model, involving argumentation, aims to promote a fertile environment for conceptual change. The NRC asserts that when students engage in the development of explanations for observed phenomena, it presents the potential for conceptual change to occur. The NRC frames the idea accordingly:

> *Asking students to demonstrate their own understanding of the implications of a scientific idea by developing their own explanations of phenomena, whether based on observations they have made or models they have developed, engages them in an essential part of the process by which conceptual change can occur.*

NRC Framework, 2012, p.68-69

You'll notice in this excerpt the attention to student-developed explanations, as we've already spoken about. But, you'll also notice that in this excerpt the explanations follow observed phenomena, specifically illustrating the significance of phenomena-based student learning experiences. As we've already seen, phenomena-driven learning is an integral feature of the NGSS, a core element deemed a valuable and rewarding learning approach. The connection to discrepant events should be obvious. Discrepant events embody phenomena. The single most important feature of discrepant events is their puzzling nature, their embedded phenomenon. They present themselves as the most valuable teaching tool to provide phenomena-driven experiences to students.

The NGSS asserts that explanations attempting to explain phenomena are constructed through student-generated, data-driven evidence. One of the primary student objectives of the POQIE model is the construction of explanations for observed phenomena. Initially, the focus of the

POQIE strategy is for students to identify a variable and investigate it. But then, the findings from each individual investigation are synthesized and contribute towards an explanation for the observed phenomena and, ultimately, a deeper understanding for the underlying concept at hand. The POQIE model shares the NGSS vision for argumentation as students engage in critical discourse of investigative findings. Students become increasingly skilled in argumentation as the concepts under study develop.

The NGSS has emphatically outlined a clear expectation that science students engage in argumentation to explain observed phenomena. It is also very clearly established that the construction and presentation of arguments follow investigation of the phenomena. Finally, the NGSS distinctly and unequivocally assert that student investigations are inquiry-based. The POQIE model fully encompasses each of these expectations and directives.

In the POQIE model, investigative findings shared through classroom discourse serve towards collaborative construction for a deeper understanding of the concept(s) underlying the phenomenon. Arguments, conducted in groups and as a class, are evaluated for their rigor and merit. They are additionally considered for any features that might contribute towards a deeper understanding for the concept or phenomenon under study. As more arguments are presented, the findings from each of the investigations are collectively synthesized to generate a scientific explanation for the phenomenon and a deeper understanding for the concept.

Phenomena-Driven Inquiry and the POQIE model offer a discourse strategy and structure that differs from the style we commonly consider in the classroom. It is a robust strategy that aligns perfectly with the NGSS 3D model of learning, specifically with the core component of Cross-Cutting Concepts. Whereas typical discrepant event demonstrations focus on one particular science concept, the POQIE model affords wonderfully rewarding opportunity to explore the connections made between different concepts, even across disciplines. This is a unique approach that most of us are unfamiliar with. But, it is one that presents an incredibly valuable strategy to illustrate conceptual connections made across the domains of science. The phenomenon exhibited in any discrepant event actually has a number of underlying concepts and principles. Because student's investigations can dramatically differ, as can the variables under study, the POQIE model provides a tailor-made strategy to address Cross-Cutting Concepts. This component of the POQIE model will be discussed at great length in Chapter Six.

The scope and detail of model use in the classroom is clearly defined by the NGSS within three attributes; components, relationships, and connections. Regarding components, models should incorporate variables within the system under study. With reference to relationships, models should act as an illustration of the relationship between the "parts" or components, specifically with the objective to help explain how or why the observed phenomenon occurs. Finally, models should maintain a connection to the phenomenon or theory that students are asked to explain or predict. The models developed by students under the POQIE model incorporate each of these three attributes. When students are asked to design their investigation, they are essentially being asked to construct "models" using the materials/equipment involved in the demonstration to study the effects of variables applied to the system in order to explain the phenomenon. This adheres to the heavy emphasis placed on models as a science and engineering practice in the NGSS, requiring that students use models to predict, test and explain phenomena.

Curiosity is a key feature of the NGSS philosophy. The three-dimensional approach embedded in the NGSS document aims to foster a sense of curiosity and wonder in our students. One of its primary objectives is to encourage and stimulate students to ask, "I wonder how…?", "How does…happen?", and "What would happen if…?" The NGSS and its three-dimensional learning places the spotlight appropriately on curiosity and wonderment. Discrepant events and the POQIE model wholeheartedly capture this philosophy. The NGSS prescribes that student-generated questions should arise from observation of phenomena or unexpected results. Discrepant events align themselves wonderfully with these recommendations. By their nature, the use of discrepant events embodies wonderment and is intended to spark curiosity in students. The POQIE model capitalizes on this spark by providing the path for students to satiate that curiosity through manipulation and investigation of the phenomena.

The strongest connection to the NGSS is, without a doubt, learning outcomes generated through the interaction and investigation of phenomena. Phenomena-driven learning is a central focus of the NGSS document. And it is the central focus of this entire book. The POQIE model combines the power of phenomena-driven learning with the effectiveness of learning through inquiry. It provides an educational strategy for your students to engage in valuable, rewarding, phenomena-driven inquiry through the use of discrepant events.

Every NGSS expectation and recommendation described in this chapter can be found in Phenomena-Driven Inquiry and the POQIE model. The NGSS states that students should:

> …predict outcomes, and … design investigations that generate data to provide evidence to support claims they make about phenomena.
>
> Science and Engineering Practices in the NGSS, Appendix F, p. 7

In the POQIE model, evidence-based explanations for phenomena are developed through inquiry, the use of models, argumentation, and discourse involving the relationships between variables. In Chapter Six we will discuss in much greater detail their involvement, relationships, and significance in the POQIE model, the construction of knowledge, and in student learning outcomes.

CURIOSITY AND SURPRISE

To mediate, prioritize and direct attention, our brains classify and filter all incoming stimulus as either novel or familiar.

Take a moment, reread that sentence, and consider its profound ramifications in the classroom. We are bombarded by millions of bits of incoming information every second. Our brains would be overwhelmed if we attended to each bit of incoming stimulus. To avoid an overload, there is a filtering system in place. We tend not to focus on events and objects that we are familiar with. Instead, our attention is guided by those things around us that we are unfamiliar with. Familiarity does not garner attention. Novelty *captures* attention.

Our attraction to novelty is termed *diversive* curiosity. This type of curiosity is powerful and unceasing. It persists as a central focus as we navigate through our daily lives. Diversive curiosity is the type that grabs our attention. When our curiosity drives us to pursue understanding, it is termed *epistemic* curiosity. This is the purposeful quest for knowledge. It involves intent and invested effort. Diversive curiosity can launch epistemic curiosity. This is a critical aspect of learning, serving as the engine that propels Phenomena-Driven Inquiry.

Human beings possess innate diversive curiosity. It's in our very nature. If you need evidence of this, simply observe the actions of an infant. Children have unbounded diversive curiosity, prompting parents to install gates in doorways and safety latches on cupboards in their homes. And although our adult response to curiosity might be more methodical than that seen in children, our spirit of curiosity is perpetual- enduring throughout our lifetimes.

As educators, the significance of novelty cannot be overlooked or underestimated. But now let's take this one step further. Let's connect the power of novelty with our understanding of schema. Imagine the power of a situation that, in addition to being novel, directly challenges our understandings and expectations of the world around us. An experience that contradicts the beliefs that form our perception of the world, and our place in it. Imagine the educational potential of that situation. This is transformative.

Clearly, novelty and contradiction can play key roles in education. Each of us makes countless observations of the world around us- every minute of every day. As we observe, we assess each of those situations, comparing and evaluating them against the cognitive schema that continues to develop and build from each additional situation. We constantly analyze and assess new experiences for either familiarity or novelty by evaluating them against prior experiences. When a situation stands out as novel, it will have a much greater likelihood to *command* our focused attention. When it contradicts what we know and believe about the world, it *demands* it.

This explains why personal experience and the schema we develop from them are critical components to the specific form of curiosity and perplexity that arise from discrepant events. It is a curiosity that emerges from what we know. It can entail the situation, phenomena, or objects involved. Existing knowledge is key to curiosity. And it has a certain hierarchical effect. When we feel that we are very knowledgeable about something, it magnifies the impact of any discrepancy regarding it and, in turn, the level of curiosity surrounding it. Curiosity, and subsequent engagement, intensify as classroom experience becomes linked to personal knowledge and beliefs.

The connection to note here is the one between knowledge and our surroundings. Our situation or environment is a paramount force from which a curious response blooms. This is a salient point repeatedly found throughout the literature on curiosity, an invaluable point when considering science education and the provocation of curiosity in our classrooms. The innate capacities for curiosity that stem from the interaction between knowledge and surroundings, paves the way for effective teaching and rewarding learning.

I would like to point out a slight distinction between the emotions of curiosity and wonder. I believe that wonder ignites curiosity. Curiosity, in turn, drives us to seek answers. Because the nature of wonderment is rooted within our own individual beliefs and understandings of the world, it is an incredibly powerful motivator that can propel us towards self-directed inquiry. Wonderment is the spark that initiates inquisitiveness. Successful and rewarding student learning experiences in the science classroom capitalize on the engagement generated by wonder. The discrepant event demonstrations used in this book are intended to promote a sense of wonder, generate curiosity, and elicit student-generated questions.

To question something, we must identify some shortcoming, reservation, or disparity within our own schema; a *gap* in our existing knowledge. We must be cognizant of our own nescience. The effectiveness of a discrepant event demonstration lies in its ability to blatantly and poignantly expose us to these flaws, or gaps, in our knowledge. They make us uncomfortably aware of what we don't know, or of what we mistakenly *think* we know. Prompting our students to confront a gap in their understanding presents purposeful learning. According to George Loewenstein (1994), a psychologist and behavioral economist from Carnegie Mellon University, curiosity arises "when attention becomes focused on a gap in one's knowledge."

These *gaps* serve as the origin of curiosity. Stimulating these gaps should become a priority if curiosity is a trait we hope to encourage, arouse, and kindle. In the traditional classroom environment, didactic lessons involving facts to be memorized and regurgitated do not foster the discovery of gaps. Students in these settings perceive that they need to "learn" these facts and ideas because they're asked to, because they're taking the class. They may have no personal desire to do so. More importantly, they may have no personal *reason* to do so. The identification of a gap in one's personal schema offers the reason, the catalyst to learn or discover. This is a critical aspect of learning that exposes a vested purpose and value. Discrepant events present this purpose.

Through contradiction of expectation, discrepant events reveal schematic gaps that spark curiosity. And, curiosity lies at the heart of inquiry. Typically initiated by an observed phenomenon, curiosity is the driving force behind the inquiry process. Curiosity ignites questions. Together, curiosity and questions launch inquiry. They comprise the fuel that drives science. Sparked by curiosity, the inquiry process aims to better understand the observed phenomenon and answer the questions that arise from it. As a method of arousing curiosity that elicits questions, the discrepant event demonstration stands out as a powerful catalyst to inquiry.

We have already learned that curiosity is triggered by novelty. But, it is also activated by surprise. The surprising, awe-inspiring nature of discrepant event demonstrations establishes a situation in which curiosity thrives. It is this inherent quality that is, without a doubt, the discrepant events most significant and valuable characteristic in the science classroom. The surprising, novel outcome of a discrepant event demonstration breeds curiosity and presents a powerful tool in the classroom.

Recent research is revealing the significant impact of surprise in the learning process. One Johns Hopkins study (Feigenson and Stahl, 2015) found that the element of surprise helps us learn. In this study, infants observed a ball rolling down a ramp and hitting a wall. Then the wall was obstructed from view so that only the top could be seen. Next, the infants observed the ball being released down the ramp again. The wall was removed, showing the ball on the other side, appearing as though it had traveled through the wall. The infants immediately wanted to inspect the ball. The researchers concluded that the element of surprise, or more specifically those experiences that challenge our expectations, helps us to learn. This holds immense implications for the strategy at the core of this book, specifically the use of discrepant events and the surprise they generate. But the surprise we are referring to is a specific type.

I'd like to distinguish between two types of surprise. The difference may appear subtle, yet incredibly important, especially for our discussion here. The first type of surprise is one that occurs due to an event that is *unanticipated* or *unexpected*. The second occurs because of *misaligned expectation*. Consider two different scenarios. In the first, you're opening your daily mail and you find that you've been sent a check. You recently purchased an item and the company you purchased from realized you were overcharged. They've sent you a refund check! You did not anticipate this. You had no idea. This was not even a consideration. This is not the type of surprise that we'll be discussing in this book. It's not the type of surprise that we'll find in our discrepant event demonstrations. In the second scenario, you place an object at the base of an incline. When you release it, the object rolls UP the incline! From all your past personal experiences, and everything you've learned about gravity, you expected and trusted that the object would remain in place at the base of the incline. Yet, the outcome contradicted your expectation, which you have now discovered was misaligned. This is precisely the type of surprise that we'll focus on in this book, found in each of our discrepant event demonstrations. This is the form of surprise that generates astounding learning opportunities in the classroom. And yes, you will actually find a demonstration in this book in which an object placed at the base of an incline, rolls up when released!

You'll notice that I did not distinguish the two types of surprise by labeling them as *unanticipated* and *unexpected*. The first scenario I presented, in which you received a refund check in the mail, could very well be termed both unanticipated *and* unexpected. You neither anticipated nor expected the check. The two words could easily represent or categorize the same situation. The word unexpected is oftentimes confused by many when regarding discrepant events. If you flip through science catalogues, you'll find many "discrepant event" demonstrations, labeled so because of their "unexpected" or "surprising" results. If you're in the market for a demonstration that is "unexpected" or "surprising" to your students, then these may be exactly what you're looking for. But, if you're looking for a demonstration that represents a genuine discrepant event, then I believe many of them do not qualify. This leads me to the definition of discrepant events, as will be adhered to in this book. There are certain qualities or traits which make an experience or demonstration a true discrepant event. This is a distinction that really must be well understood if you hope to move your students beyond surprise and into meaningful, cognitive engagement. The difference is anything but subtle. Between the two, there is dramatic contrast in the direction of the experience that follows. The demonstration that ends unexpectedly, results in the joy of being surprised, sometimes pleasantly so. The demonstration that ends with misaligned expectation results in cognitive engagement through conflict and the need for resolution. In Chapter 5 we'll discuss the specific characteristics of discrepant events and define the term as it applies to our use in this book.

In the coming pages, we will discover that surprise alone does not make an event discrepant. But, every discrepant event includes the element of surprise. Contradictory experiences can become rich fodder for learning. Novel experiences that contradict expectation lead to surprise, wonderment, curiosity, and questions. As a catalyst to these experiences, discrepant events position themselves as a gateway to knowledge.

CONSTRUCTIVISM, SCHEMA AND CONCEPTUAL CHANGE

Our experiences construct our reality.

Constructivism is one theory about how individuals learn; about how we come to know what we know. It is a central philosophy to current educational reform and is currently the predominant theory of how individuals learn. The constructivist philosophy argues that experience leads us to construct our own understandings in personally, meaningful ways. Essentially, we are the sum of our individual, cultural factors and collective experiences.

As we proceed through life, our experiences are used to construct and establish an organized knowledge base about the world around us. This is our schema. It is essentially a cognitive or mental model which allows us to adapt, organize, and navigate in our environment. Each of our individual lifetime of experiences has been used to construct our schema, a mental framework of preconceptions and expectations about how the world should work. Our different schemas are unique to each of us, as they are founded on the experiences from our individual personal lives. The central purpose of our schema is to help us understand and manage incoming information and to predict the outcomes of future events. Our schema forms the scaffolded blueprint of what we know, believe, and understand.

The reality constructed by our brain reflects much more than the mere product of incoming stimuli. Our reality of the world that surrounds us is largely based on interpretation and expectation, the product of our schema. The origins and roots of our current understandings lie in our prior experiences. Crafted from these collective experiences, our schema is used to predict future experiences. What we *see* is in part a construct of what we expect to see. As the schema formed from our past individual experiences continue to prove dependable and useful to ongoing experiences, we become increasingly reliant of them. Our schema represents the basis for the expectations we hold and the predictions we make during each experience in life. We expect certain outcomes from specific situations. We expect the natural world around us to behave in certain ways. What we perceive as reality is actually a construct of expectation formed from experience. And this perception of reality includes what we see, hear, feel and think. Through all our senses, every one of our experiences is measured against beliefs and expectations constructed from prior experiences. We have tremendous capacity to construct meaning and interpretation from incoming information. The picture below is just one illustration:

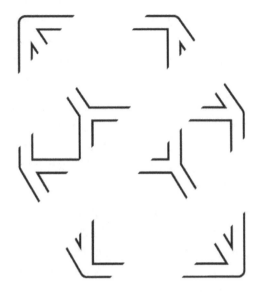

Although this is an incomplete picture, with missing information, your schema is adept at filling in the blanks and identifying an image of a box. Your prior experiences with box-shaped objects has incorporated the details of boxes into your schema. When you see the image, your mind automatically responds by drawing from its schema to evaluate and make sense of it.

Another example can be seen below. In this picture, we "see" the shape of a square, even though it isn't actually there. Again, our consistent observations of objects and shapes leads our mind to fill in the gaps.

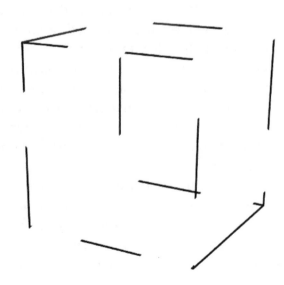

Today, educators and researchers alike agree that most people learn best by connecting what they already believe and know, to new information. New knowledge is interpreted in light of previous knowledge. New situations and experiences are interpreted through the lens of previous ones. We personally construct our own individual knowledge or understanding of the world around us through an active, continuous process; an interaction between our environment and our schema, shaping an ever-richer network of conceptual connections.

This is essentially the foundation upon which the constructivist theory is built. Knowledge is constructed by *assimilating* the accumulation of existing knowledge with newly acquired information. The individual is constantly revising and expanding his/her own meaning, interpretation, and understanding of the world through each personal experience. Knowledge is constructed in the mind of the learner.

The impact and influence on education is profound. A student's mental model, or schema, is continuously reshaped and restructured through the lens of new experience. Understanding for the world is an ever-modifying, ever-evolving construct that reflects the steady barrage of new, incoming information self-mediated through prior experiences. Meaning is continually being negotiated, and learning is an endlessly active process.

These principles of constructivism form a learning theory that align extremely well with student-centered, learner-centered classrooms. The philosophy acknowledges that students enter the classroom with pre-conceived ideas and beliefs developed through collective experiences ranging from family interactions, museums, playground experiences, and televisions shows, to mention only a few. The sources are endless. These pre-conceived beliefs, representations, and presuppositions genuinely impact a student's interpretation and understanding of their classroom experiences. Learning outcomes are influenced by prior knowledge. A student's cognitive schema of the world is actively, continuously shaped by classroom experiences and observations, all ameliorated by social interaction.

The ideological views between the traditional and constructivist models of instruction distinctly differ. The traditional, didactic model of instruction is predicated on the direct transmission of knowledge from teacher to student. It will oftentimes focus on elements external to the student. In contrast, the constructivist model of instruction involves collaborative discussion, investigation, and the construction and re-creation of ideas. It is a process of *uncovering* and *discovering*. Knowledge is constructed as the learner organizes current experiences within their preexisting cognitive schema of the world; as the individual interacts with his environment through the lens of his own understanding of it. The constructivist classroom provides and fosters actively engaging opportunities and experiences. It aims to influence learning through personal, active engagement. It places significant focus and emphasis on the internal perspective of the student. The students' individual experiences must play a role in the learning process. Research continues to show that core knowledge is a "key ingredient in driving learning forward" (Stahl & Feigenson, 2015). In the constructivist model of teaching, the student must be considered as an integral and active participant of the learning process in the classroom.

Yet, there are dilemmas rooted in the philosophy, which educators must consider. Varied interpretation is just one. Different interpretations and conclusions can be drawn amongst a group of students observing the same event, or experiencing the same lesson. There are a multitude of attributes in any given situation that can ultimately affect learning outcomes. They include a litany of factors that reside within the situation itself, such as social and cultural behaviors and transactions, and the interest level or motivation of the participants, to name just a few. And each of these factors are influenced by the differing prior experiences and schema of each participant. Tie all of this together and we begin to understand how it is possible for students in the same classroom to observe the same demonstration or phenomenon, while constructing different meaning from them. In the absence of appropriately guided, focused, critical discussion, unintended learning outcomes can persist.

But these concerns are compounded by the potential for misconception. All students walk into our classrooms with a schema. But some connections and beliefs within the framework of any schema may not be entirely accurate. Our schema can sometimes include misconceptions resulting from the interpretation of our experiences. Misconceptions are commonly referred to as naïve conceptions, preconceptions, alternative frameworks, alternative conceptions, and personal theories. Because they are based on personal experience and schema, they've also been referred to as *intelligently incorrect*. In addition to varied interpretation, students might harbor naïve conceptions due to developmental immaturity, limited personal experience, and inattention to relevant details and variables, among other reasons.

Research has shown that naïve conceptions are rigid and resistant to change through traditional forms of instruction. In fact, naïve conceptions possess their own cognitive support system and defense mechanisms (Strike & Posner, 1992). Our experiences are tempered by a confirmation bias, our tendency to actively interpret incoming information as confirmation of the existing beliefs in our own schemata. This is one of the most significant, and defiant, dilemmas that educators face in the classroom.

It can certainly prove a difficult agenda to *dissuade* firmly established, engrained misconceptions. Misconceptions can endure even under the closest guidance and direction. But, alternative conceptions present themselves as an invaluable instructional resource. Our curricula, our learning strategies, and more importantly our students learning experiences, must integrate opportunities for exposing and identifying students' existing conceptions, especially naïve conceptions.

Misconceptions can certainly influence learning in the classroom. A student's prior knowledge can interact with classroom instruction, resulting in unintended learning outcomes. The obstacle to gain insights to new experiences could potentially be rooted in fundamental misconceptions. In Chapter Six, we will discuss the significance of, and some strategies regarding, naïve conceptions.

Our schema is a critical necessity, in response to the overwhelming flow of stimuli that we are continually exposed to from the outside world. All incoming information is interpreted through our schema. Our minds would overload if we focused on each bit of minutia around us with cognitive effort and scrutiny. This is the value of being able to rely on experience and predictions that have consistently proven dependable. Our experience filled schema allows us to successfully navigate through life without having to focus on every detail around us. We make decisions and predictions, and form expectations effortlessly- by the second. As a result, we tend to focus on those situations which contradict or do not align with our schema, a phenomenon known as cognitive conflict.

The origins of cognitive conflict can be traced to Festinger (1957) and his theory of cognitive dissonance. In it, Festinger argues that because cognitive conflict, or *dissonance*, is psychologically uncomfortable, we have an inner drive to maintain harmony and avoid it. Cognitive dissonance would later become an important feature of 20th century constructivist Jean Piaget's (1970) theory of equilibration and learning (Pintrich & Schunk, 1996). Piaget believed that when new information does not fit into an existing schema, an uncomfortable state, termed *disequilibrium,* occurs. Disequilibrium leads to cognitive conflict, a force that drives us to learn and achieve a state of *equilibrium,* where there is harmony between schema and experience. Since the need to reduce conflict is such a powerful human motivator, experiencing conflict is indispensable to learning (Wise, 1996). Research has shown that deep reasoning and learning is stimulated by situations that generate cognitive disequilibrium.

When schematic conflict leads to disequilibrium, we are faced with essentially three different paths to process the contradictory information. The first is to discard the observation or experience that generated the conflict. In this scenario, we are basically disregarding the observation because it doesn't fit neatly into our belief system or our framework of knowledge. Ignorance becomes a much easier path than confronting the discrepancy and grappling with it. In the second path, we allow the incoming information to "fit" our existing schema; a process called *assimilation*. In this scenario, the new information is integrated into our existing schema. We accomplish this by selectively attending to certain features of the new information that allow us to do so. So, in this situation we are not fully acknowledging the entirety of the new information. Finally, in the third scenario, the learner feels the need to understand the discrepancy and resolve the conflict. She modifies her existing knowledge and beliefs so that the new cognitively contradictory event or experience can make sense. In this situation, she makes mental accommodations that allow this new information to replace her current understanding of the world. Either a new schema is created or an existing schema is altered to cope with the new information that does not fit; a process called *accommodation*. As a result, the individual has altered a fundamental belief about how the world works.

And this is the objective of the conceptual change model of instruction. Directly connected to constructivism, it is founded on the relationship and interactions between new experiences and existing schema. Widely accepted within education, the theory argues that conceptual change can arise when we are faced with new experiences that are inconsistent with currently held beliefs. The model acknowledges that students bring personal conceptions to the classroom, formed from their interactions with the world. The aim of the model is to promote cognitive change, thus altering the schema that it's embedded in, by establishing schematic conflict through situations which directly challenge the existing schema.

Learning sometimes requires more than just making connections of newer ideas to older ones. Learners must sometimes change the connections among the things they already know, and even discard some long-held beliefs about the world. We can be quite resistant to this type of change. Research has shown that it is oftentimes very difficult to alter the schema we've constructed. We will usually attempt to assimilate the new information first, before moving to accommodate it. If it has proved useful through our lives, why would we want to change it? It wouldn't be advantageous for us to change the approach to our world that has consistently proved adequate and practical. This is the primary challenge in conceptual change. Our schema may harbor naïve conceptions. But, if our personal life experiences have not really challenged those misconceptions, why alter them? In these situations, the most critical component is the strength of the individual's proclivity to resolve the conflict. It is essential to accommodation and conceptual change. Research by Chan, Burtis, & Bereiter (1997) substantiates this. They argue that the student must be motivated to reduce or eliminate the cognitive discomfort. The student must experience the personal need to resolve the conflict in order for conceptual change to occur.

As educators then, our objective is to create a situation in which students acknowledge the conflict *and* are compelled to resolve it. How do we achieve this? By constructing situations with the greatest potential to induce *meaningful* cognitive conflict. When the conflict is personally meaningful the rewards can be immense. But this poses an incredible challenge. Namely, differing individual experiences and schemas might easily generate conflict in one student, but not another. How do we engineer conflict with a high likelihood of "meaningfulness" to each student? In my experiences, I have found that familiarity is the key. The likelihood of successfully meeting these challenges increases when the experience is familiar to the observer. This can involve familiarity through either the equipment or the phenomenon. Even the slightest prior experience or knowledge will provide enough familiarity to cause students to be aware of the conflict between their own understanding of the phenomenon and that which they are observing. But in addition, the conflict must also be clearly discernible. So, for the most rewarding learning outcomes, the situation should involve two characteristics. The conflict must be clearly evident and the materials should be familiar. These are points that will be addressed in greater detail in Chapter Six.

Pedagogical approaches informed by the conceptual change model employ conflict as the stimulus for learning. For conceptual change to occur, we must have disequilibrium. For disequilibrium to occur, we must have an experience that challenges, or contradicts, our current belief system; a discrepancy. Therein lays the power of the discrepant event and its significance towards learning potentials.

A discrepant event must be present for learning to occur through conceptual change. The discrepant event lies at the very core of the conceptual change model. Discrepant events instill powerful cognitive dissonance by contradicting expectations rooted in a personally developed belief system grounded in experience. When experiencing a discrepant event, there is a contradiction between what we believe should occur, and what does. In these situations, we realize that both cannot be true. This is the basis for cognitive conflict and disequilibrium. The conceptual change model relies and capitalizes on the disequilibrium caused by discrepant events. They are invaluable tools towards cognitive change. In the POQIE model, students investigate the phenomenon generating the disequilibrium, establishing a prime opportunity for conceptual change.

At the very foundation of constructivism is the premise that we construct knowledge through our experiences. Our physical, cognitive, and social interactions with the world contributes towards a constantly developing understanding of it. Our experiences are the cornerstone of our schema. We have learned that our schema is essentially a network of our collective experiences; a network that acts as a cognitive "blueprint" of how we believe the world operates. Our schema guides us, providing stability and expectation as we navigate through the world. It can be thought of as a framework comprised of a unique set of structured *rules* that allows each of us to manage the world; to provide balance to it. Discrepant events upset that balance by breaking our set of *rules*. Discrepant event phenomena that does not fit into our schema is unsettling, and oftentimes shocking. The resulting disequilibrium can lead us to pause, assess, and potentially reconsider the structure of our schema.

Discrepant events present themselves as powerful learning tools, due to their inherent ability to instill uncertainty. As Dr. Beau Lotto aptly states in his 2009 TedTalk, "only through uncertainty, is there potential for understanding." Forcing us to confront our schema through contradiction of expectation, discrepant event phenomena possess transformative power. The contradictory nature of discrepant events forces us to reconsider our knowledge and beliefs in light of new evidence. Through cognitive conflict, they prompt students to question their personal understanding of the world. They ignite questions. They launch inquiry.

Phenomena that contradicts expectation lie at the very heart of education; at the very core of learning. Strategies that focus on cognitive conflict, such as Phenomena-Driven Inquiry and the POQIE model, present themselves as valuable instructional tools towards learning in the classroom. As I will show, discrepant event phenomena can certainly provide the foundation upon which conceptual change can occur and learning can emerge.

THE POWER OF DISCREPANT EVENTS IN THE SCIENCE CLASSROOM

"Perplexity is the beginning of knowledge"- Khalil Gibran

Discovering how to engineer the unexpected!

The discrepant event demonstration can be one of the most effective and valuable teaching strategies in an educator's toolbox. The power of a discrepant event lies in the specific format, strategy, and purpose of its presentation. To harness the true power and potential of discrepant events, there is much to understand and appreciate. By understanding the many facets of a discrepant event demonstration, educators can be best equipped to anchor demonstrations to lessons in ways that can meaningfully engage and significantly influence learning outcomes. This book capitalizes on the educationally valuable characteristics of discrepant event phenomena, transforming them into inquiry-based experiences offering rich learning opportunities for students.

Merriam-Webster defines a *phenomenon* as:

1. Something (such as an interesting fact or event) that can be observed and studied and that typically is unusual or difficult to understand or explain fully.

2. Someone or something that is very impressive or popular especially because of an unusual ability or quality.

https://www.merriam-webster.com/dictionary/phenomenon

Discrepant events embody phenomena. They are the cornerstone of constructivist science education. Their educational effectiveness lies in their ability to "attract and command the students' attention because they offer an immediate visual curiosity that demands explanation" (Friedl, 1991). As such, they serve as powerful learning tools in the classroom.

In this book, you will discover how phenomena can be purposefully used in a manner that drives learning. Each lesson in this book centers around a unique, inquiry-based approach that engages students in the scientific practices called for by the *Next Generation Science Standards* (NGSS, Lead States 2013). The demonstrations in these lessons have been deliberately chosen for very specific reasons. Their attributes are a critical component to their success as tools and strategies towards rewarding student learning experiences. As such, their criteria demand detailed explanation.

Let's begin by looking at the varied uses for discrepant events. Educators use discrepant events in the classroom for a number of reasons. They can be used to:

1. Demonstrate or illustrate a previously introduced concept. It can provide a concrete illustration to an abstract concept.

2. Generate engagement for an upcoming lesson or concept.

3. Grab students' attention.

4. Generate class discussion of a concept.

5. Stimulate critical thinking.

6. Stimulate curiosity and generate questions for a concept.

7. Evaluate students' understanding for a concept (includes formative and summative).

8. Reveal/address student misconceptions.

9. Assess whether students can apply a learned concept to another situation.

10. Introduce a new concept.

11. Promote further investigation to learn about the science concept involved.

But, although these are wonderful classroom objectives, I do believe that too often science teachers present discrepant events to be merely fun, engaging demonstrations. I want to be clear. In no way do I mean to discredit these demonstrations, or the teachers who use them. I use them. But, I use them at specific places in my curriculum, with specific goals in mind. Fun, engaging demonstrations certainly have a place in our curriculum. They absolutely serve a purpose and they absolutely have value. However, they simply do not serve our objectives within the POQIE strategy. The reason lies behind the specific attributes of discrepant events.

What features make an event *discrepant*? This is a critical point. To examine this issue, we need to identify the accepted definition of a discrepant event. Although it can be worded differently, the general definition for a discrepant event is:

> *An event with an unexpected result that surprises, startles, puzzles, or astonishes the observer.*

Most would agree that this definition seems to capture the key features of a discrepant event. But, it's not really an acceptable definition for our purposes. It doesn't encompass the critical attributes that define the discrepant events presented in this book. Let's discuss why this accepted definition does not meet our needs. We'll begin by outlining the operational definition for the discrepant events that offer the most rewarding learning opportunities in Phenomena-Driven Inquiry.

The most significant feature of our discrepant event demonstrations lies in their potential to generate doubt. They cause students to question and reassess their existing assumptions and beliefs about the world around them. This is a profound idea that is not captured in the accepted definition above. This attribute is paramount.

Discrepant events are novel experiences that contradict the observers existing conceptions or beliefs about the world and how it operates. They are not simply "surprising" or "puzzling."

Rather, they are *contradictive* by nature. They are counterintuitive. The outcome of a discrepant event is *inconsistent* with what one would expect. This *contradiction of expectation* is not only a key feature of an effective discrepant event, it is THE most significant characteristic. And therein lies the power of discrepant events in education.

Typically, a discrepant event is one that does not seem to follow the basic rules or principles of matter, energy, or physics. The observer realizes that prior experiences or current beliefs are inadequate to explain the situation. The result is cognitive conflict. Because it is rooted in experience bound knowledge, the conflict generated is personally meaningful to the observer, whose attempt to reconcile the situation with knowledge from prior experiences proves unsuccessful.

A discrepant event violates personal expectation. This is a salient point. The *counterintuitive* nature of discrepant event phenomena promotes cognitive conflict by contradicting the observer's expectations, which have been forged from collective experiences. This distinct feature is key to our operational definition. If you remember any one point from this chapter, this is it. A discrepant event contradicts expectation. It's not a discrepant event because it surprises. It's not a discrepant event because you've never seen it before. It's discrepant because the event differs from all the other times you *did* see it. This critical aspect of discrepant events is oftentimes overlooked. It's precisely this feature that makes the event personally meaningful. You've lived your entire life with a certain set of expectations about the world around you. You rely on those expectations to navigate, interact, and survive in the world. When you experience something that absolutely contradicts the expectations you've constructed over the years, it "breaks" the system you've relied on all your life up to this point. You suddenly are forced to reevaluate your approach and beliefs about your world. You are faced with acknowledging the possibility that the beliefs and expectations that have gotten you this far in life might actually be wrong and need revision. This is precisely what transforms the event into one that is personally meaningful. This is deep-rooted, emotional, and uncomfortable. And it's this meaningful nature of discrepant event phenomena that makes them so powerful in the classroom.

Let's compare this operational definition to an event that ends in a feeling of surprise by the observer. Consider the potato candle demonstration. In this demonstration, a tall candle is lit as the students look on. Now the teacher blows out the candle, instantly takes a bite out of its upper half, chews and swallows it! This is accomplished because the candle is actually a potato, cut in the shape of a candle. The wick is actually an almond!

If you search this demonstration online you'll find that it's commonly labeled a discrepant event. When the "candle" is eaten at the end of the demonstration, students are shocked. But they are surprised because this is not how people commonly behave with a candle. The surprise develops because the teacher's *actions* are unexpected; the event doesn't follow typical human behavior. But there is no contradiction of how the natural world operates. There is no violation of one's personal belief system. Eating the candle does not generate a cognitive dilemma by forming a barrier from which the observer cannot pass if he/she is to continue to interact with the world using their current mental model of how the world works. The experience does not impact or uproot the cognitive foundation upon which the observer relies to interact with their world. Nor does it affect how the observer interprets the world around him/her.

The outcome does not cause the observer to *reconsider* the cognitive framework, or schema, upon which similar previous experiences have been founded. Nor does it cause the observer to doubt his belief system of how the world operates. In fact, the observer can move forward in life, comfortably understanding that the candle was eaten because the teacher was "crazy" enough to do so, or that it might not have been a real candle at all; in which case, the observer simply wonders what it might have been. In this example, what is labeled as a discrepant event essentially sparks surprise or puzzlement. The observer may be "startled," but certainly not persuaded to reconsider the belief system founded on his cognitive schema. An authentic discrepant event will contradict the observer's belief system of how the world operates.

Let's consider another example known as the Oscillating Clock, Old Nassau, or Briggs-Rauscher Reaction. In this demonstration, the color of a solution formed by mixing certain chemicals together will oscillate, oftentimes from colorless to gold to deep blue. This demonstration is referred to by many sources as a discrepant event. However, I would categorize it as a *surprising* event. In no way am I minimizing the value of the demonstration. The Oscillating Clock is a wonderful demonstration if the intent is to initiate surprise and grab students' attention during a lesson. The reason that I would not classify it as a discrepant event is because the observer has not experienced the event more than once. For an event to be defined as discrepant, it must differ, or present inconsistency through repetition. If the event is being observed for the first time, there is no previous occurrence to compare. The observer may be startled or surprised, but certainly wouldn't be able to recognize any discrepancy. Surprise and discrepancy are two entirely different ideas here. Bodner (2001) states:

> Regardless of the extent to which students have been exposed to the concepts of reversible reactions, equilibria, kinetics, thermodynamics, and so on, there is nothing in their prior experiences that prepares them for a reaction that cycles between states in which the solution is colorless, then gold, and then blue. (p.33)

Consider a student who may have seen this reaction ten previous times, each producing a different color grouping display. Then, during their 11th presentation of the demonstration they observe the colorless/gold/blue color grouping for the first time. They might be *surprised*. If they were surprised, they certainly would not recognize a *discrepancy*. A true discrepancy could only be recognized if the first ten demonstrations produced a repetitive color grouping display, while the 11th produced an entirely different outcome.

There are other examples that do not qualify as true discrepant events by the definition we are using. For example, in one demonstration some steel wool is moistened with acetic acid. This is placed into a flask and the mouth is covered with an uninflated balloon. Students are asked to predict what will happen. I would venture to guess that not many students have ever experienced this sequence of actions in their life. How could they possibly have any schema or past personal experience from which to make a prediction? How can there be any cognitive conflict when there is no cognitive foundation upon which to base a prediction? This would be an outright guess, with no basis.

The words "unpredictable" and "unexpected" are often used to define a discrepant event. To a certain extent, this terminology muddles and confuses the situation. Some unpredictable and unexpected outcomes can be described as "surprise." Numerous demonstrations can be categorized as both unexpected and surprising, but they are not necessarily discrepant events. For example, the Oscillating Clock reaction can be termed unexpected, or surprising. Compare this demonstration to the Balloon Paradox in which a floating helium balloon tied to a string is held by a passenger in a car. When the traveling car suddenly stops, the balloon sways forward, toward the front of the car. Is there a difference between the Oscillating Clock reaction and the aptly named Balloon Paradox? Absolutely! The unexpected nature of the Oscillating Clock creates surprise because the observer has never seen anything like it. On the other hand, the unexpected nature of the Balloon Paradox is caused by contradiction with similar previous experiences. And this is not to say that the observer has repeatedly observed how balloons behave in this particular situation. Rather, the observer can relate her own personal life to this one particular experience. The observer knows, from personal experience, what happens when the car she is traveling in suddenly stops; her body is pushed back into the seat, a repetitive movement we are all familiar with. Hence, when the balloon responds differently, a discrepancy arises.

A key criterion for the discrepant events employed in this book is that the outcome of each firmly *contradicts* the observers understanding of how their world operates. The outcome does not simply arise from surprise. *Contradiction* expresses an entirely different meaning than *surprise*. The presence of a contradiction implies there was an expectation. Therein lies the powerful difference. This subtle, yet distinct, difference influences the way in which the observer is affected by the experience. Surprise and contradiction can both startle, but for different reasons, and with different emotive and cognitive reactions. Contradiction of expectation produces incongruity. It defies logic. It seems impossible. A discrepant event experience is always surprising, but a surprising experience is not always a discrepant event. Discrepant event phenomena impact the observer's current interpretation and understanding of their operational world; the world they exist in, forcing them to rethink that world before moving forward and possibly encountering the same type of event. The experience causes them to reconsider the cognitive framework upon which all similar previous experiences have been founded. This is a key point as we consider our objectives for the implementation of discrepant events into our curriculum.

This leads us to our main objective for using a discrepant event within the POQIE model: to generate cognitive conflict through contradiction. Not to simply surprise. There are many demonstrations found on the internet and in science catalogues that are labeled as discrepant events, yet they are not the type of discrepant event that I would categorize into our operational definition. Commonly used as attention-grabbing strategies, many of these demonstrations are simply opportunities to generate student excitement and interest. Although I do believe these types of demonstrations certainly have a place in our curriculum, there is a distinct difference between the demonstration that excites and the demonstration that instills cognitive conflict. This is an incredibly critical distinction, playing a significant role in the purposeful implementation of discrepant event demonstrations in our curriculum and the subsequent potential learning opportunities for our students.

Both surprising and contradictory outcomes might be considered engaging, yet in two distinctly different ways. One can easily imagine becoming engaged from the emotional stir of surprise or startle. But those events with contradictory outcomes could be termed "mindfully engaging." They result from perplexity. If our objective is to garner attention, then a demonstration that simply surprises, or has that "wow" factor, will meet the objective. However, if cognitive disequilibrium is our objective, then a simple demonstration that surprises will not suffice. If our goal is a cognitive restructuring of student understanding and knowledge for the natural world, then we must employ the type of discrepant event that does just that. A truly discrepant experience has the potential to ultimately lead our students toward a reconsideration of the world around them.

Discrepant event phenomena amazes because it contradicts expectation based on a belief system developed from personal experience. Indeed, we navigate through our physical world using expectation as a guide. Incoming stimuli is interpreted through our established expectations formed from the past experiences that comprise the network of our schema. This is evident, for example, as we drive in our cars. Because we have developed a set of expectations regarding common occurrences for our own behaviors as well as those around us, we are able to safely navigate the roadways. Accidents occur when situations deviate from our expectations. Without these expectations, each trip would be incredibly disorienting. Expectation is the very reason that our roads are not littered with accidents at every turn. Similarly, our students enter our classrooms with a framework of expectations and beliefs concerning the natural phenomena that comprises our world. They use this framework to construct meaning of classroom situations and experiences.

As we have learned, discrepant events present situations that generate cognitive contradiction, a discrepancy between our schema and our observations. This schematic discrepancy is rooted in expectation founded on experience. Taking this one step further, to most effectively achieve cognitive conflict, students should observe the event with only the expectations formed from personal experience. When the discrepant event is presented prior to the introduction of a concept, students must rely on prior knowledge to make sense of their observations. As a result, the discrepant event experience is best suited as an introduction to a concept. In my classroom experiences, I have consistently found this to be true.

A discrepant event demonstration is much more than simply showing students something they've never seen before. Many times, teachers confuse discrepant events for "cool" demonstrations-something they may have never observed or experienced before, intended to engage students' attention. Oftentimes, these "whiz-bang" demonstrations are somewhat fleeting. Students might be momentarily shocked. They might be momentarily excited by a surprise, such as a color change in a beaker of liquid. They might even be moved to ask the teacher to "do it again-that was cool!" These types of demonstrations can be effective tools when used for these purposes. But now consider the difference between these demonstrations and our discrepant event demonstrations. In a "cool" demonstration, student attention is *procured* by the external offbeat or unusual. In a discrepant event demonstration, student attention is *evoked* by the internal contradiction of personal belief. I think you'd agree that in the classroom, the latter is more meaningful to the student and powerful to the educator.

You won't find any demonstrations in this book that involve mixing chemicals to teach a scientific concept. This was a conscious decision. As I've mentioned, these types of demonstrations might be considered a wonderful way to momentarily engage, enhance a lesson, or emphasize a principle. But, they don't fit the characteristics of our discrepant events. Although they oftentimes generate "ooh's," "ahh's," and the ensuing "do it again!", they lack a deeper resonance with our schema. They typically don't contradict expectation born from personal experience.

Although they might engage through surprise, they lack the ability to eschew familiarity, an idea we will discuss at greater length in Chapter Six. Demonstrations that attempt to illustrate underlying chemical reactions at the molecular level, especially those that can best be explained using chemical equations and a knowledge base of the scientific concept or principle, are not inherently understood by most students who have not had prior experience with the content. Consider the Oscillating Clock demonstration, for example. The color changes may surprise and engage, but they do not necessarily contradict expectation from personal experience.

Furthermore, the scientific explanation for the series of repetitive color changes observed in the Oscillating Clock reaction are not overtly discernable. The molecular interactions aren't seen, but they manifest themselves through color changes. The results of those molecular interactions are visually evident through the color changes, but the observer cannot directly see the specific interactions at the molecular level. You can only see the effects of the reaction. The underlying chemical *mechanisms* are not visually evident or perceptually obvious. The reaction is best understood with a firm grasp of chemistry terminology and an understanding of chemical processes and equations, as shown in the following explanation:

> *Upon initial mixing of the solutions, IO_3^- reacts with H_2O_2 to produce a little HIO_2. The HIO_2 reacts with IO_3^- in the first step of the radical process (eq. 11.7). The autocatalytic radical process follows, rapidly increasing the concentration of HIO. The HIO is reduced to I^- in a reaction with H_2O_2 (eq. 11.6). The large amount of HIO reacts with I^-, producing I_2 (eq. 11.12). The I_2 reacts slowly with malonic acid, but the concentration of HIO, I_2 and I^- all increase, because reaction (11.2) is faster than reaction (11.3). As $[I^-]$ increases, the rate of its reaction with HIO_2 (eq. 11.5) surpasses that of the autocatalytic sequence of reactions (11.7) and (11.8). The radical process is then shut off, and the accumulation of reduced iodine is consumed by reaction (11.3) operating through the sequence of reactions (11.12) and (11.13). Eventually $[I^-]$ is reduced to such a low value that reactions (11.7) and (11.8) become faster than reaction (11.5), and the radical process takes over again. This oscillating sequence repeats until the malonic acid or IO_3^- is depleted.*

The equations that depict these interactions include:

$$IO_3^- + HIO_2 + H^+ ==> 2\ IO_2^\cdot + H_2O$$

$$IO_2^\cdot + Mn^{2+} + H_2O ==> HIO_2 + Mn(OH)^{2+}$$

$$Mn^{2+} + H_2O_2 ==> Mn^{2+} + H_2O + HOO^\cdot$$

$$2\ HOO^{\cdot} ==> H_2O_2 + O_2$$

$$2\ HIO_2 ==> IO_3^- + HIO + H^+$$

From: http://www1.chem.leeds.ac.uk/delights/texts/expt_11.html

The complexity of this explanation provides a wonderful opportunity to make the distinction between that which confuses and that which contradicts. The objective of a discrepant event in the classroom is not to generate confusion, but rather to generate contradiction; a contradiction between the expected and the actual. The discrepant event demonstrations included in this book are not intended to be presented as "tricks". There are a number of demonstrations listed in science catalogues as discrepant events, when in fact there is a "trick" or unobservable mechanism, typically unknown to students. There may be times in our curriculum when we do in fact want to present these types of demonstrations as a way to simply engage our students, or perhaps guide them to "problem solve" a solution to the mystery. However, neither of these are goals of the discrepant events included in this book. The objective here certainly extends well beyond mere engagement. Nor is the objective for students to "figure out" the unobservable "secret" behind the observed puzzle.

One example of a standard science catalogue demonstration that "tricks" students is often called the Sad/Happy Balls or the Bounce/No Bounce Balls. In it, two rubber balls are shown to bounce. But then the teacher is supposed to secretly switch one of the balls for another that has been hidden from the students. This ball is made of a substance that prevents it from bouncing. Now when the ball is dropped, it lands with a thud- no bounce. Sure, the students will be surprised at the outcome because it is unexpected, but that's because they are being duped. They believe that the teacher has presented an honest and accurate account of the materials used. Their surprise may not be as dramatic had they been aware of the switch made for the third ball. They would probably suggest that this ball was made of a different substance, without exactly knowing what that substance is.

I want to make two things very clear. First, I mean no disrespect to anyone who might use the Sad/Happy Balls in their classroom. Second, I am in no way de-valuing their place in a curriculum. I'm simply stating that the Sad/Happy Balls don't really fit into our operational definition of discrepant events. Allow me to illustrate how this demonstration can be modified into one that addresses the objectives of those found in this book. In our modified demonstration two balls are shown and dropped onto the floor, one at a time. One bounces, the other does not. Some students might find these "cool," but it probably won't cause any disequilibrium. The observation probably doesn't contradict student's perspective of how the world works. It probably doesn't contradict any cognitive schema. Students might easily shrug off the observation responding with "one is heavier than the other." Try to think as one of your students. They might explain it by saying, "one is hollow" or "one has rubber in it." There are a few explanations you might think of. The point is that these explanations are based on what we believe about how the world works around us. And these are a result of our past personal experiences. Whether we've encountered a hollow ball and observed how it responds when dropped, or held a rubber ball and a metal ball and seen them hit the floor, these past personal experiences have shaped what we know and believe about the world. They help us explain similar experiences. But we now continue our demonstration with a counterintuitive twist.

Students are asked to predict which of the balls will topple over a wood block, hit after being rolled down a ramp. Most students will predict that the ball that hit the floor with a thud will knock the block over. They further predict that the ball that bounces off the floor will also bounce off the block, without moving it. The balls are rolled down the ramp one at a time and the exact opposite occurs. The ball that bounces knocks the block over, not the ball that hit the floor with a heavy thud. This demonstration becomes even more counterintuitive if the ball that bounces has less mass than the ball that does not. Yes, students can mass them prior to the demonstration. When they see that one is actually heavier than the other, they almost always feel that the "heavy" ball has to be the one that knocks over the block. The Sad/Happy Balls have now become an experience that contradicts expectation. And students were fairly shown all equipment involved. This is called the Block Toppler lesson, and is described in detail on p.125. It represents the types of lesson you'll find in the following pages.

Another discrepant event commonly found in science catalogues involves abox with a funnel at the top and tubing coming from the bottom. A measured volume of liquid poured into the top of the funnel triples as it comes out the bottom. Students observing this demonstration might be challenged to try to figure out how it happens. They may even be given the necessary materials and asked to replicate the event in an attempt to uncover the "hidden mechanism" behind the puzzle. These types of demonstrations can be valuable and certainly have a place in the science classroom, but their objective is much different than those described in this book.

One of the most important qualities to look for in a rewarding discrepant event is the potential for many variables to investigate. Included in each lesson found in this book is a list of student-generated questions that lend well to empirical investigation. None of the discrepant events in the book include a list of *every* investigable variable. In fact, one of the key attributes of a valuable discrepant event is that the variables are imagined and developed by students. It isn't necessary that we, as teachers, already have a "complete" and exhaustive list of variables. A key feature of the POQIE model is that the student's direct observation sparks creativity for variables and possible investigative paths. In this sense, the student truly "owns" the investigation. Developing a complete list of potential variables and investigations is akin to providing students the procedural steps in a traditional lab.

In part, the demonstrations in this book have been chosen because of their perceptually salient investigative variables. The most fruitful discrepant event demonstrations are those in which all the components of the system are visible to the students. Nothing is hidden from view. I've found in my experiences that when the equipment and its manipulation is clearly observed, students are much more able to identify a greater number of possible variables within the system. This also minimizes the potential for students to consider the event as a magic trick, with some secret to figure out. The student is forced to accept the event as it occurred, even though they may not immediately accept it into their schema of the world.

There's also a risk that students might discredit or distrust the legitimacy of the phenomenon when it is read in text. In fact, research has shown that asking students to read about anomalous data is an ineffective instructional strategy, if the objective is conceptual change

(Mason, 2001). In the same way, verbal accounts of counterintuitive events can also lessen their credibility or lead to doubt. One can internally resolve any cognitive conflict by simply questioning and discounting the validity of what they are told. The conflict is easily resolved by imagining answers or scenarios that fit our cognitive schema and imagining aspects of the event that allow it to *fit* our schema. When we personally observe and experience the event, it becomes difficult to do this. Face to face discrepant events have the greatest impact on the observer.

In fact, even simulations and videos can be easily dismissed. The observer may be more readily apt to believe that the video or computer program contributes, in some way, to the unexpected outcome of the demonstration. Each of these methods certainly have their place in our curriculum, valuable in certain situations. However, if the intended outcome is to promote and produce potential cognitive conflict and contradiction of existing schema, the events that we experience personally have the greatest potential to do so. Phenomena should be *experienced*.

In fact, *experiences* lie at the foundation of our discrepant event lessons. We should define the word "experience" as it is used in this book. In its *simple definition* of the word "experience," Merriam-Webster.com defines it as:

> The process of doing and seeing things and of having things happen to you" or the "skill or knowledge that you get by doing something."

In its *full definition* of the word, "experience" is defined as:

> A direct observation of or participation in events as a basis of knowledge.

Or as:

> The fact or state of having been affected by or gained knowledge through direct observation or participation.

> https://www.merriam-webster.com/dictionary/experience

According to this definition, everything you interact with could be defined as an *experience*. In this book, we refer to two different circumstances that construct experience. The first refers to our individual personal experiences that form our schema of the world around us. The second are those student experiences during and following observed discrepant events. Our use of the word experience will certainly encompass the Merriam-Webster idea of "direct observation of or participation in." And the inquiry investigation that follows the discrepant event would certainly include "the process of doing" as well as the "skill or knowledge" acquired by "doing something."

But, there is one additional prominent feature that typically defines a discrepant event experience. Discrepant events exhibit phenomena that evoke emotion. The Merriam-Webster definition does include "the fact or state of having been affected by...." The term "affected" could refer to changing either your perspective or your habits because of the experience. As such, one could be "affected" without the presence of emotion. But at their core, the experiences of discrepant event phenomena stir emotion. Whereas the traditional science demonstration occurs *to* the observer, the discrepant event demonstration is experienced *by*

38

the observer. Experiences have the power to move us on a deeply personal level. Experiences are *felt*. Experiences are remembered.

Personal experience that generates perplexity, ignites curiosity that necessitates explanation, propels investigation, and drives learning. This is the objective of each discrepant event lesson found in this book. In each lesson, curiosity positions itself as the connection between prior knowledge and classroom subject matter. And in fact, research has shown that interest is an outcome of the individual's prior experiences coupled with the particular aspects within a situation (Hidi & Harachiewicz, 2000).

The lessons in this book spark genuine interest by exhibiting phenomena that surprises through contradiction. The learning potentials that arise from contradiction of expectation are now becoming strikingly evident. Research has shown that when outcomes defy our expectations, we explore the situation more, ultimately learning and better understanding it. Learning occurs when expectations are violated. (Stahl & Feigenson, 2015). When we observe phenomena that we believe to be impossible, it shakes the foundation upon which we form our beliefs about the world.

Discrepant event phenomena have the power to deeply affect us by contradicting our expectations; expectations founded on the personal experiences that form our schema of the world. A discrepant event challenges the observer's core belief system. That is the true power of a discrepant event; to engage each individual observer on a personal level by challenging their individual belief system of how the world around them operates. Discrepant events serve as an incredibly valuable springboard to inquiry as student's question, challenge, and investigate their beliefs and understandings of the world.

The following discrepant event characteristics provide the most fruitful investigations and learning opportunities for the intended objectives of the POQIE model:

1. The phenomenon involved should be clearly observable and unmistakable.
2. The phenomenon should be easily recognizable as anomalous.
3. The observed phenomenon should be unexpected, contradicting our past experiences with the natural world around us.
4. The equipment involved should be familiar or recognizable to students.
5. The observed phenomenon must be credible and unambiguous.
6. The demonstration should involve equipment with discernible potential variables.

In my classroom, I want my students to discover new experiences. I want those experiences to be personally meaningful. I want my students to experience their world in ways that they never have; experiences that have always surrounded them, but that they never knew were there. I want them to open their eyes for the first time to the mysterious world they live in. I want my students to be instilled with a sense of beauty, wonder and curiosity for the natural world around them. I want my students to look *into* the picture, not *at* it. I believe that these lessons do just that.

THE POQIE LEARNING MODEL

The mind is not a vessel to be filled but a fire to be kindled.

Plutarch (45-120 AD)

THE POQIE MODEL

Interest is the mediator of engagement. Engagement is the arbiter of understanding.

A Framework for K-12 Science Education (NRC, 2012) states that:

> *A rich science education has the potential to capture students' sense of wonder about the world and to spark their desire to continue learning about science through their lives* (p.28)

Generating a true sense of deep wonder, genuine personal interest, and an innate desire to understand the world around them are essential to the development of a rewarding science program for our students. Each of these characteristics is an objective of the POQIE (Predict, Observe, Question, Investigate, Explain) model of instruction. Through the lens of discrepant event phenomena, the model centers around students working to figure out how or why an event or behavior occurs in the natural world. Acting as the catalyst of the lesson, a discrepant event demonstration serves to launch inquiry-based investigations. Employing the POQIE model, *Phenomena-Driven Inquiry* essentially guides students as they make sense of natural phenomena, while collaboratively developing a rich understanding for their underlying scientific concepts and principles.

The chief objective of this book is to present educators with a strategy that will engage and guide students to make sense of natural phenomena by actively investigating meaningful questions. Through student-led investigations, the POQIE model engages students in the scientific practices of questioning, reasoning, investigation, explanation, and argumentation through inquiry. It empowers children to be inquisitive about the world around them by capitalizing on their natural curiosity and wonderment. The investigations that occur within this type of model align perfectly with the NGSS Science and Engineering Practices.

The POQIE model has been developed and shaped through almost fifteen years of research that began with my Master's Thesis, ultimately leading to my doctoral dissertation. It reflects the most current research on learning, especially how we learn science. Grounded in extensive research of the literature, and from my own continuous in-class action research, I continue to develop, refine, and learn from it.

I developed the POQIE Model founded on the core ideas expressed in the Predict, Observe, Explain (POE) strategy and BSCS 5E Instructional Model. Each present incredibly valuable and powerful methods of instruction and learning. As in each model, the POQIE model involves student-centered learning. However, to the POE strategy (Champagne, Klopfer and Anderson, 1979) is added the power of meaningful, student-led investigation. Students engaged in a POE are asked to observe a demonstration and then try to explain it. However, in the POQIE Model, students question and investigate prior to their proposed explanation. The observations, findings, conclusions, and collaborative class discussion of the collective investigative experiences is ultimately used to help develop and shape an explanation for the observed phenomena. To both the POE and 5E models are added the power and significance of discrepant events. This is a critical distinction that will be discussed at length in this chapter. The addition of argumentation is another key feature of the POQIE model. The construction and significance of argumentation will be detailed later in this chapter.

With its origins in the Learning Cycle (Atkin and Karplus, 1962), the BSCS 5E Instructional Model is widely credited to Rodger Bybee. Its roots can be traced back to the philosophies of Johann Herbart and the learning theories of Jean Piaget and John Dewey. The phases of the 5E Model are Engage, Explore, Explain, Elaborate or Extend, and Evaluate.

As is the 5E model, the POQIE model is grounded in constructivism. There are several significant distinctions between the BSCS 5E model and the POQIE model. First, the Engage phase of the 5E model occurs through three phases of the POQIE model. Students in the Engage phase of the 5E model are invited to connect what they already know with the learning experience that faces them. In the POQIE model, students are overtly asked to consider what they know, and the personal experiences that lead them to know or believe this, as they make predictions in the first phase and explain in the final phase. Prior experiences become powerful precursors towards anticipated outcomes through invested predictions. However, prior experiences and personal beliefs are equally considered and shared through class discourse that occurs in the Prediction, Question, and Explanation phases. As we will discuss in this chapter, exposing prior conceptions is a focal strategy employed to equally introduce, as well as to collectively develop, a concept. In this chapter, we will learn the tremendous learning benefits and rewards that can occur when prior knowledge, connected to new information, is shared and built upon.

In the first step of the 5E model, a science concept is introduced by determining prior knowledge and revealing misconceptions. In the POQIE model, attributes, features and characteristics of the concept are developed through the first four phases, the concept eventually named in the final Explain phase. In this phase, collective attributes discovered from the Investigation phase are shared, and the cumulative knowledge learned from those investigative experiences is used to shape and name the concept under study. Rather than introducing the concept and experiencing it through inquiry, it is the inquiry that introduces the concept. In the 5E model, formal labels are applied to the new concept in the third phase, whereas terminology is introduced in the final phase of the POQIE model. In this chapter, we will discuss how physical and cognitive involvement makes abstract meaningful, as well as the value of connecting new vocabulary to personal experiences already incorporated into one's schema.

In the final Explain phase of the POQIE model, the experiences and discussions encountered from each of the previous four phases form the basis for conceptual development or the introduction of a principle that accounts for the outcomes and patterns observed and discussed, oftentimes through the development of relationships. This occurs in the third phase of the 5E model. Finally, within the 5E model conceptual change is facilitated in the second phase, Exploration. In the POQIE model, conceptual change is facilitated during the fourth and fifth phases, Investigation and Explanation.

I want to be very clear that both the POE and 5E Instructional models are invaluable learning resources. I am honored to be able to use them as resources in my classroom, and towards the development of the POQIE model. I believe that the objectives and unique distinctions between these models positions them among the most rewarding strategies in any science curriculum.

The Inquiry Cycle and the Modeling Instruction approach was also an influence in the development of the POQIE model, the latter sharing an important class discussion component with the POQIE model. However, it should be noted that the Modeling Instruction typically begins with a problem to be solved. The POQIE Model incorporates distinctly unique features from each of these learning strategies. The single feature that each of these strategies does share with the POQIE model is "sense-making" by students. This is the most important overarching feature of the POQIE Model.

The most prominent features of the POQIE Model include a student-led investigation, directed by a student-developed research question generated from a discrepant event demonstration, culminating in the synthesis of a science concept through class discussion and argumentation. Through guided and self-directed inquiry, students investigate and discover the science concepts underlying the observed phenomena. The strategy involves the following phases:

Phase 1: **Predict**- The teacher presents the equipment/materials that will be involved with the demonstration. The anticipated actions/steps that will occur in the demonstration are described. Students are asked to predict what will happen when these actions are performed, and to record their individual predictions.

Phase 2: **Observe**- The students observe the demonstration as the teacher performs the anticipated actions, resulting in a discrepant event. Students record their individual observations, which are then shared out. Through discourse, past personal experiences are also shared out, providing the opportunity for connections to be made and misconceptions to be revealed.

Phase 3: **Question**- Variables are identified and shared out- either with a partner or as a class. They are each assessed for their appropriateness and investigative rigor. Students pair up with a partner to discuss and select one variable that they are interested in investigating. They must form a tentative research question involving the investigative manipulation of that variable. These research questions are shared out and the class has the opportunity to ask questions or constructively critique each question. Based on the class discussion and feedback, each group refines their research question. A procedure is designed by each group as their intended method of investigation. The groups must also identify the data they feel is integral to gather, and the method that will be used to collect that data. Each procedure and proposed data collection method is shared out with the class, which provides the opportunity for questions, critiquing, and feedback. This is followed by group revisions of their procedure.

Phase 4: **Investigate**- Following the procedures they designed, each group conducts their investigation. Observations and results are recorded. Data is collected, recorded, and compiled.

Each group reflects on and analyzes the data (measurements and observations) from which they generate evidence used to develop a claim or argument. Each group decides what presentation format(s) would best represent their data, which is then organized and presented to the class.

Phase 5: **Explain**- Each group presents their argument or claim to the class, which includes a visual presentation of their data, findings, evidence and a justification of their claim in defense of the evidence. Through discourse following each presentation, the class has an opportunity to question and critique the argument, interpretation of data and evidence, and the validity and reliability of findings. Counterarguments might be shared. Each group then has the opportunity to revise their conclusion or argument, which can be either communicated to the class, or written and submitted to the teacher. Students might also be asked to write and submit individual reports that synthesize the findings of each group within the class into a culminating paper that attempts to demonstrate a deeper understanding of the concept at hand; to develop generalizations from each individual group into a broader conclusion. The interpretation of data, and the subsequent argument formed is the keystone of scientific literacy. Evidence is used from notes taken during class presentations that should illustrate trends, comparisons, or relationships among variables tested. Students can also reflect on how they may have changed any preconceived ideas of the concept because of their experiences in this lesson.

The collective experience begins with student predictions prior to an observed demonstration. Students then design and conduct an investigation in an effort to better understand the observed phenomena and its underlying principle or mechanism. The collective experiences, findings and conclusions are shared, questioned and critiqued by the class. Students further develop and collaboratively refine their models to negotiate and construct a deeper, more coherent, connected understanding of the phenomena. The investigations and the discourse is guided by the teacher. The teacher's role, and its significance in the POQIE model, will be discussed later in this chapter.

Representing a valuable learning strategy towards collaborative, conceptual development in the science classroom, the POQIE model:

> Incorporates prior knowledge and previous experience of students throughout the lesson; as the basis for investigation, as formative assessment at the introduction of the lesson, to identify misconceptions, within classroom discourse throughout the lesson, and as a means of making connections to new information and learning outcomes.
> Is inquiry-based strategy.
> Is grounded in discrepant event phenomena.
> Makes learning engaging, personal and meaningful to students.
> Supports the development of innate capacities of students through curiosity and the self-directed pursuit of personal interest.
> Is rich in classroom communication, especially discourse and argumentation.
> Establishes a collaborative learning community.
> Involves critical thinking, science process skills and active learning.

> Establishes a student-centered classroom.
> Links content to standards.

The POQIE model begins by generating cognitive conflict through a discrepant event demonstration. It capitalizes on student-generated questions caused by the startling, unexpected phenomenon observed. Students become puzzled and curious, and are then provided the opportunity to investigate the observed phenomenon- to manipulate the very evidence that directly contradicts their world view. Their curiosity is immediately satiated by direct investigation of its very source. The demonstration positions itself as the focal point of the lesson. The observed phenomenon serves as the catalyst towards learning.

The drive to make sense of our world is an innate, universal characteristic. When confronted with counterintuitive phenomena that contradict deeply held core beliefs, students are compelled and eager to understand why or how it occurs. The inherent contradictory nature of discrepant event phenomena positions them as powerful catalysts to propel inquiry and learning in the classroom.

Using the POQIE model, these criteria of discrepant event demonstrations offer rich opportunities for student engagement and learning:

> The demonstration should arouse curiosity and establish interest by contradicting expectation.

> The demonstration should involve simple materials. This idea was introduced in previous chapters, but will be discussed in greater detail in this chapter.

> Discussion should involve examples provided by students past personal experiences. Students should be encouraged to relate the phenomenon or underlying concept to other familiar examples from their personal lives. Already touched upon in previous chapters, the significance of familiarity will be deeply explored in this chapter.

The demonstration, selected and developed by the teacher, ensures that research questions are focused on the specific science concept at hand. As a result, subsequent investigations lend themselves as fruitful and rewarding to the concept and the curriculum. Discussions become central, cohesive, and directly aligned with that concept.

As an instructional strategy, discrepant event demonstrations are most effectively implemented when they introduce a topic or concept. Using the demonstration to reinforce a concept already introduced does not generate the same level of wonderment and awe. Students would begin the demonstration with expectation, stemming from the level of conceptual understanding achieved during the instructional presentation. Essentially, when you tell the students what they will learn, or what to expect, they cannot possibly achieve the same level of wonderment as from the observation of unexpected phenomena. The inquiry model of instruction thrives from genuine wonderment. Discrepant events ignite wonder. Therefore, they are best positioned at the beginning of a lesson or unit.

Let's now take a deeper look at the components of the POQIE model.

PREDICTIONS

The importance and the power of predictions should not be underestimated. Students should be making predictions. The action causes them to become involved participants, rather than passive observers. Moreover, students become invested in the demonstration when they personally predict its outcome. They want to discover whether their prediction is correct. As a result, they remain focused and engaged.

A prediction is an expected result. It's the anticipated outcome of an experiment, typically attributed to past personal experience. This explains why students, generally quite comfortable with the personal schema they've constructed, commonly feel quite confident predicting outcomes to demonstrations.

Even though a prediction does not attribute cause, it's a valuable practice to ask students to explain their prediction once they've written it. Discourse involving prior experience is a valuable component to the collaborative development of the concept at hand. Class discussion that evolves when students share prior experiences can be incredibly rich and fruitful. When explanations are shared out, it also discourages students from guessing the most unexpected result simply because they *anticipate* a discrepant event. Some students might think that predicting is a game. They think that by "guessing" correctly, they have won the game, or look "better" than another student. They anticipate some strange result from the demonstration, so they predict an outcome that they actually would never expect, simply for that reason. Asking them to explain with as much science or past personal experience not only keeps students on a more thoughtful path, it also allows for richer discussion. Shared explanations allow fellow students to make connections to their own experiences, oftentimes connections that may not have been sparked otherwise. For these reasons, predictions and explanations should be shared before commencing the actual demonstration.

Predictions warrant and deserve calculated focus and concentrated effort. When students commit to a prediction, it establishes a foundation for learning to occur. Research has shown that conflict between prediction and observation is used as a scaffold for new and enhanced learning to take place (Stahl & Feigenson, 2015). The seemingly innocuous act of predicting actually positions itself as the precursor to learning, especially when followed by the contradictory nature of discrepant events. The value of predictions should never be overlooked.

OBSERVING

It's important to delineate observations from explanations during this phase of the demonstration. One of the objectives here is to develop and hone observation skills. Students should understand that their observations are not intended to direct them towards an attributing cause or explanation. Although some students will feel compelled to hypothesize based on these observations and past personal experiences, they should understand that the only way to confidently explain is to investigate. The simple act of observation alone does not provide sufficient support for any explanation. Discrepant event demonstrations illustrate that not all scientific reasoning, theory, evidence and understanding is derived from that which is directly observable in the natural world. These observations may, however, provide clues as to an explanation; clues that can help guide or direct an investigation towards support for the hypothesized explanation. This is precisely how research scientists approach their work. They make very careful, meticulous observations of events and phenomena and identify one variable for further study.

RESEARCH QUESTIONS AND VARIABLES

Observations should lead to a research question, investigation, and ultimately evidence-based arguments based on the results of experiments. Authentic scientific investigation begins with observations of something that is interesting or perplexing. In Phenomena-Driven Inquiry this spark is ignited by natural phenomena, encompassing observable events in our world that elicit curiosity and wonder. The POQIE model employs discrepant events, from which puzzling questions naturally arise. In this manner, the demonstration provides a context for student-generated questions.

Since scientific investigations typically stem from questions generated following personal experiences with phenomena we encounter, it becomes integral for educators to establish rich opportunities for students to experience and interact with natural, engaging, cognitively stimulating phenomena. It follows that these opportunities should involve experiences that have the greatest potential to arouse questions. Personal experience with phenomena that contradicts expectation is key to the genesis of questions. Perplexing discrepant events are incredibly powerful candidates, due to their inherent ability to contradict expectation and instill uncertainty. In his 2009 TedTalk, Dr. Beau Lotto states that "only through uncertainty, is there potential for understanding." Uncertainty through contradiction is the genesis to questions.

Since all students are observing the same demonstration, the entire class maintains a unified concept-specific focus, without actually knowing or understanding that concept. One significant feature here is that even though all students are observing the same demonstration, the subsequent investigations will vary between groups. Although students have the liberty to choose the investigation that personally interests them, these investigations are bound to the confines of the equipment used in the demonstration. This is an efficient strategy to engage students in self-directed inquiry when time is a consideration, since the focus of the investigation is directed and "limited" to the specific scientific concept and equipment underlying the observed phenomenon.

Student-derived questions are central to the POQIE model. Perhaps more important than the observed phenomena are the student-generated questions they generate. Three types of questions arise along different phases of the strategy. First, questions will spontaneously and organically arise from the observed anomaly of the demonstration itself. Through teacher guidance, these initial questions are cultivated and eventually develop into the second type of question; the research question, which ultimately lay the groundwork for the investigation to follow. Finally, student questions comprise an integral component of the explanation phase, as students critique the work and conclusions of their classmates.

Personally, meaningful questions first arise from observations made during the demonstration. Oftentimes, these questions will reveal a student's level of understanding for a scientific concept. This is valuable to the teacher who, after assessing this level of comprehension, can appropriately guide class discussion. These questions are not "answered," but rather used as fodder to enhance and direct the discussion towards the beginning of the next phase.

Students will next be asked to identify potential variables to investigate. They should identify as many variables as possible. Research has shown that students have difficulty identifying relevant variables and learning to control them in investigations (Schauble et al. 1995). Honing these skills requires teacher guidance and student practice. Students are directed to carefully consider the equipment and its manipulation prior to the demonstration. They are informed that the focus is directed on how the outcome or phenomenon might be influenced by changes within the system. Students are asked: "How can you change any of the materials, equipment, or the way it was handled in a way that might affect the outcome you just observed?" They are asked to individually brainstorm and make a list of their ideas, capitalizing on their natural enthusiasm and creativity. Once this is done, these ideas are shared out to the class. No idea is critiqued at this point; all answers are accepted. The value of their ideas is validated, and a sense of ownership is developed; students become contributors to their own education. From these ideas, students will eventually choose the variable they would like to investigate. By asking students to identify variables within the observed demonstration, the investigations that follow are more focused and manageable because they are limited to the resources you know you will have available. The experience provides students an opportunity to begin to learn how to begin an investigation, frame a research question, and manage their research.

Students should understand that a variable refers to the part of the investigation that is changed in some way to identify whether that change affects the outcome. The independent variable is manipulated to observe dependent variable responses. They should further understand that a rigorous investigation has only one variable that changes. If two variables were changed in the same investigation resulting in a different outcome, it would be difficult to determine which variable caused that outcome. Only by investigating one variable in an investigation can we begin to know how that specific variable might impact the outcome.

The identification of an independent variable is a critical one for students; it directs their investigation. A well-chosen independent variable establishes a rigorous investigation with a higher probability for a rewarding outcome. Identifying rewarding independent variables requires practice. Students will be challenged by this in their initial attempts. It is a learned skill that can be developed through a scaffolded experience. For example, in the beginning of the school year it can be helpful for students if a list is generated on the board or easel. This list is developed from those created by students while brainstorming, either individually or in pairs. This structured format provides teachers the opportunity to discuss the reasons that make some variables better candidates for research questions than others. In the beginning of the year, this can also allow for the selection of one independent variable for the entire class to investigate. If everyone in the class is focused on the same independent variable, it establishes tremendous opportunity for class discussion of the collective investigations through a common language formed from shared experiences. A shared phenomenon, experienced by all, levels the educational playing field. As they experience one common event, all students are able to discuss, contribute ideas, and share a common language. Each student acquires equal access to a common experience that positions itself as the focus of the lesson. Everyone has an equitable opportunity for involvement. The class discussion is extremely focused and equitable.

Utilizing this approach at the beginning of the year models the development of a rigorous research question for students and can serve as a scaffold towards less-structured inquiry encountered later in the year, when groups investigate differing variables. For example, as the school year and the level of inquiry progresses, the collaboratively developed list could serve as the launchpad for pairs or groups of students who select the particular variable that interests them. Although support would still be provided during the development of the list, the class begins to independently investigate a broader range of variables.

Eventually, students generate their lists, share them, and then pair up to choose a variable that they would like to investigate. A single demonstration can lead to a number of various research questions and investigative approaches. This is desirable. The intent is that through their collective investigations of variables, regardless of how these variables affect the outcome or whether they affect it at all, students begin to better understand the scientific principles that lie behind the observed phenomenon. Investigating how the phenomenon might be affected by imposed variables is a much more powerful learning tool than merely asking students to describe the events or outcome of a traditional lab.

Because each group of students potentially investigates different variables and shares their findings, there is greater opportunity for a more robust understanding of the phenomenon. This is a critical feature of the POQIE model. The objective of the lesson is not strictly focused on what the individual student might learn from his/her own investigation. Of course, that is one objective. But, keep in mind that each cooperative group of students is conducting their own investigation regarding a different aspect of the same phenomenon. Herein lies the strength of class discourse. As each group eventually shares out the finding of their own particular investigation, the entire class begins to form a deeper understanding of the phenomenon, or the science concept under study. Through class discussion, students begin to develop a breadth and depth of the concept. There is breadth through the multiple variables being studied within the one scientific principle. There is depth through the findings within each of those investigations. Each individual investigation offers the potential for a deeper level of insight and understanding. But this understanding is magnified when the findings from each investigation is shared. Students contribute a comprehensive collection of experiences that are collectively reflected upon. All students have a focused direction on the same concept, but each investigates a slightly different, yet related, aspect of that concept. The final product is additive, generative, and enriching.

As findings are shared through discourse, individual group findings and conclusions can be confirmed by the findings of one or more other groups. Groups might even hear conclusions similar to their own, yet expressed in different ways, providing confirmation and reliability to the findings. When two or more groups study the same question, it can lead to class discussions regarding validity, scientific replication, and the authentic practices used in the scientific community. This confirmation process is integral to authentic science.

The summative experience not only helps to construct a deeper insight for the concept, but also adds meaning, relevance, and significance to the contributions from each groups work. Under the guidance of the teacher, each group and each individual within that group feels the work they conducted was a valuable contribution towards the conceptual construct of the science concept. Simply put, there is greater potential for deeper insight of the scientific concept because each group investigates and shares their findings on a range of variables within the scope of the observed phenomenon.

Consider a simple pendulum experiment. We'll examine two different classroom approaches. In the first, a guided approach, students observe the action of a simple pendulum. The teacher can ask the students to form a question they might have from their observation of the pendulum in motion. One direct question might be "how long does it take for the pendulum to complete one cycle?" This answer can easily be determined without an intricately planned investigation. As a class, the time that it takes for the pendulum to complete one cycle, or period, can be determined. The teacher can now ask students to imagine the factors that might influence the time just measured. Students might respond with the length of the pendulum, the mass of the bob, the shape of the bob, or the amplitude; the angle from which the bob is released. The class chooses one of these factors to investigate. Together, with the teacher's guidance, the class develops a procedure for such an investigation. The class is divided into groups, who gather their materials, conduct the investigation, and finally report a conclusion to the class. In this example, the class discussion following the investigation would focus on the single, agreed upon factor, or variable, whether it does affect the outcome, or period, and if so, how? The collective findings contribute towards validity and support for the conclusion.

In the second classroom approach to our pendulum example, students begin by observing the simple motion of the pendulum, as in our first approach. They are asked to individually compose a list of all the factors, or variables, which could be manipulated to determine whether the change produces a difference in the observed action of the pendulum. Students are then asked to share their list with one other person and to choose one of the variables from their lists that they would like to investigate. We now have pairs of students interested in investigating the same variable, while the collective groups investigate a number of different variables. The groups gather their materials and conduct their investigations. Rather than the entire class focusing on one variable, the class is composed of a diverse range of investigations and variables, although the entire class is focused on the same initially observed phenomenon and concept. The resulting findings and conclusions form a broader picture and insight into the observed phenomenon, due to the wider scope of variables studied. The presentations from each group help to construct a deeper understanding for the concept through connections made or relationships identified. In our first example, understanding is developed for a single, chosen variable and how it influences the initial model. In the latter, the class develops an understanding for the concept, by investigating a number of variables, their collective findings contributing to a richer insight and more detailed mental model of the concept.

Once students have identified the variable they would like to investigate, the next step is to develop a research question. Scientific investigations begin with observation, not a question. Research questions are actually derived from observations, a distinction oftentimes misunderstood. The ability to develop a rigorous, investigable research question is a critical skill that is paramount to a rewarding scientific inquiry experience. This is a skill that cannot be mastered in the first attempt. It is a process that requires patience, repetition, and perseverance. Initially, students will pose questions that are not rigorous; that do not lend themselves to practical investigations. An appropriate classroom research question is one that interests the individual student, can be investigated with available materials and resources, and can be completed in the amount of class time allotted. A rigorously investigable question is addressed through systematic observations and interpretation of the data involving measurements. It should also lead to more than a one word or one sentence summative conclusion. A rigorous research question is one which involves a question that can be addressed only through lab investigation. If the research question can be answered by looking up the "answer" in a book or on the internet, it is not a quality, rigorous research question. Development of the research question should be a focused activity, since it is derived from a single variable selected for investigation. Notice that students are not developing as many research questions as possible, as they did with variables. This saves time, while allowing students terrific opportunity to devote quality time to the development of a rich research question.

The research question will shape the investigation. A rigorous research question lends to more rewarding learning opportunities. As a result, understanding how to develop them is critical. There are a number of strategies that can be used to help students develop research questions. Ultimately, we want them to generate their own rigorous questions. Students can only become proficient at this skill with practice. But, the process can be scaffolded. The first level of support can simply involve a teacher-provided research question. These research questions act as models and allow students to become familiar with good examples of rigorous questions. Direct modeling in the beginning of the year, during more structured inquiry, can become less directed as the year progresses through the continuum of inquiry.

Once students have had exposure to a few of these modeled research questions, they can be provided a less than rigorous research question with the objective to refine it into a more rewarding, investigable question. This should not be a one-time experience. Rather, students should be provided a few opportunities to refine research questions. Next, students are asked to develop a research question with a partner. This question is then presented to the class, who then engages in collaborative critiquing and refinement. Finally, following a series of these experiences, students begin to identify and construct their own individual research questions. At first, these questions might be presented to the class, who once again critiques and helps to refine the question. Eventually, student-derived research questions are entirely independent. The role of the teacher throughout is to ensure that the research questions developed involve an explicit learning goal that aligns directly with the overall goal of the lesson, the unit, and the concept.

In the beginning of the year, students might be asked to list as many research questions as possible. These are shared with the class, another partner, or in a small group. The questions are then discussed and critiqued. In addition, when students hear questions generated by their classmates, it oftentimes prompts them to come up with more questions.

Another method to support students in the beginning of the year is to provide them with a worksheet listing a variety of research questions. They are asked to identify and explain those that involve the greatest rigor. Next, they could be given a worksheet listing potential variables. Students would design rigorous research questions involving those variables.

Yet another method involves asking students to derive a question that interests them and write it on a small individual white board. Then, students are asked to find another person in the classroom who has a similar question. Once they identify that person, they are to reshape the question into a rigorous one that retains the original idea and interest of each partner.

Rather than being given a research question in one lab and being asked to generate the next entirely on their own, teachers can guide students by providing partial templates. For example, following the observation of a demonstration, students can be asked to complete the statement "What would happen to _____ if I were to change _____?" In this case students should have already had opportunities to develop their skills for identification of variables. Initially, research questions should be framed by students in their own language. Through class discussion and presentation, the teacher models the restructuring and rewording of the question. The goal is to make the research question one which has the greatest potential for rigor and investigative value. Class discussion should include the characteristics between the initial and reworked question. Students should come to identify the attributes that position a research question with greater potential for a rewarding learning experience.

Each of the suggestions just given offers valuable practice towards a deeper understanding for the rigor expected in the research questions. Rigor should be a priority since the research questions will essentially become investigations exploring possible relationships between cause and effect, dependent and independent variables, and between the variables themselves.

I've been referring to students working in groups of two, but groups could consist of 3-5 partners at the beginning of the scaffolded school year. This would promote more extensive collaboration through the development of the research question, as well as the investigation that follows. This could result in a sharpened focus on the concept. It would also limit the materials being used in the investigations. The number of participants within each group could be reduced as the year progresses and students become more proficient at research question development.

Ultimately, the classroom slowly moves towards one that is more independent and student-centered. Guided by the demonstration and the underlying phenomenon, research questions are entirely student-generated. Allowing students to develop their own research question empowers them in their own education. They become empowered to seek the answers to their own questions. In a sense, this strategy involves differentiation, since each student chooses the individual question that interests him or her. Effective education engages, involves differentiated instruction, and offers choice. Choice shifts student demeanor from one of passivity and complacency to one of involvement, caring, and creativity. Choice establishes meaningfulness. Labs involving several "parts" and potential variables are best suited for this type of differentiation.

The teacher monitors the development of the research question to ensure that the investigations are appropriate for each individual learner. This also helps to ensure that the investigations conducted offer safe, rich, rewarding learning experiences for students. Even though all students are investigating the same phenomenon, the structure and complexity of the investigations could vary due to the differing learning characteristics and skill levels of the students.

Once the variable has been identified and the research question has been written, students should create a hypothesis. This should be done prior to the design of the experiment. A hypothesis is a tentative explanation. It is not a *guess*. This is a distinction commonly misunderstood by students, who should come to understand that a hypothesis is a statement about an observation that can be tested. It considers the observation, introduces a variable, then speculates what might happen and why. It should express or describe the potential relationship between the dependent and independent variable. It describes the potential relationship between the variable and the outcome. It can connect past personal experiences or prior knowledge with new information in order to explain events. A well-developed hypothesis is articulated in an "if… then… because… "format. Some examples include:

➤ If I _____, then it will affect the system by _____ because _____.

➤ If I change the system by _____, then it will result in _____ because _____.

In the next phase, when students design their investigations, they are actually developing a model that will enable them to test their "if...then... because" hypothesis. Experiments are not conducted simply to "see what happens" or to wonder "what will happen if I…?" In the design of their experiment, students must consider how the variable will be controlled, observed, and measured; significant decisions in the construction of a well-designed investigation.

The hypothesis can be considered an extension of a prediction, sort of a prediction on steroids, since it is essentially a guess supported by reason through prior experience, observation, or established scientific knowledge. It relies heavily on past evidence. This explains why it is often called an "educated guess." But, even that is a misnomer. The hypothesis is not a "guess." It is an "educated" approach, but it is not a guess. Given these parameters, a hypothesis should only be considered acceptable if it can be founded on established evidence or prior experience.

Questions are fundamental to science. They are the foundation of all science. They initiate exploration and investigation. They surround observation, data collection and analysis, and propel further investigation. Therefore, understanding the qualities of a rigorous, investigable question, and how to develop them, is a paramount endeavor for our students. The development of rich, rigorous investigative questions is a process. Our students should not be expected to achieve a high level of proficiency after one or two classroom experiences. It should remain a highlight throughout any science student's education, providing continual opportunity to develop and refine their question posing skills.

As educators, we're oftentimes so focused on *answers* that we neglect to devote a commensurable measure of focus on student-derived, personally intriguing questions. Personal curiosity acts to spark those questions. The *answer* is not as important as the curiosity driving us towards it. The journey towards an answer is much more meaningful when it is fueled by a genuine, personal, passionate need to know. We must be genuinely interested to be genuinely engaged.

Authentic science involves an investigative direction guided by questions generated from observation(s). Because of this, demonstrations involving phenomena provide the opportunity for a rich, rewarding inquiry experience in the classroom.

INVESTIGATION

One of the most prominent features of the POQIE model is the student-led investigation. This phase provides the opportunity for students to address personally intriguing questions that arise from their observation of the demonstration. The student-led investigation is the core of the model. It establishes the underpinnings for individual and collaborative conceptual learning.

Discrepant event demonstrations foster schematic conflict; the student-led inquiry investigations that follow provide the means to resolve that conflict. The collective investigative experiences provide discourse fodder for a deeper understanding of the scientific concept underlying the observed phenomenon. *Breadth* of understanding is achieved, since groups study different variables. Synthesis of these collective experiences through class discussion provide *depth* of understanding.

A common mistake made by educators is ending the demonstration when the "demonstration" is over. In fact, the demonstration can be an exceptional launching mechanism into conceptual learning. Student engagement is elevated following a discrepant event demonstration. This is a prime opportunity to initiate an inquiry experience. The counterintuitive nature of the discrepant event acts as the catalyst to purposeful investigation.

One common misconception involving student-led inquiry-based investigations is that they are initiated by a student-generated question. In fact, a genuine inquiry-based investigation actually begins with an observation, from which a question originates. Once students have identified the variable they would like to study, they are asked to determine how they will measure the response or change to the system once the variable has been introduced.

It is not necessary that students have a formal introduction to the concept in order to investigate within the POQIE model. In fact, we will discuss the educational benefits that arise when students are introduced to the concept through the investigation. However, although no prior conceptual knowledge is necessary, it is important to recognize that students must possess some knowledge or experience for particular lab skills or techniques in order to successfully and safely conduct investigations. The teacher needs to be certain that those specific techniques have been introduced prior to each individual inquiry investigation. Each investigative process is unique and the necessary skills and techniques should be in place prior to the investigation.

Understanding how to design a sound, rigorous investigation requires a keen knowledge of scientific practices, methods, and approaches that are both effective and rewarding. As with research question development and variable identification, adeptness at investigative design demands proper instruction and consistent practice. A scaffolded approach supports students as they work to achieve a level of comfort and confidence. One scaffolded technique involves the co-construction of the lab procedure. After explaining the objective of the lab, or the question addressed, the teacher would provide the first step of the procedure. Through whole-class involvement, a student would give the next step, then the teacher, and so on. The goal is that over time there are fewer contributions made by the teacher and more by the students. In an inquiry-based setting, where time is a constraint, this approach can be a valuable instructional method. It presents as an efficient process because it presents the teacher the opportunity to monitor and adjust the level of guidance and direction. This strategy can also be used among the members of a lab group, to ensure that all members are engaged, contributing and participating.

The significance of investigation in the POQIE model is that it directly addresses the personally meaningful question generated by the student. It is also educationally powerful when the apparatus inducing the cognitive disequilibrium and sparking genuine personal interest is the exact same apparatus they get to put their hands on and investigate.

Discrepant events create amazement and curiosity because their results contradict expectations founded on experience. Outcomes can appear almost magical when they do not fit our individual belief system. In these instances, initial awe is quickly followed by questioning perplexity. Students elicit responses such as "what?", "no way!", and "how'd you do that?" Sparked curiosity provokes the desire to explain. The path towards inquiry has been paved. Allowing the opportunity for students to answer their questions through discovery establishes a prime opportunity for learning. This leads us to *inquiry*.

INQUIRY

What students learn is fundamentally linked to how they learn it.

In current science education reform, there is tremendous emphasis on inquiry-based pedagogies. The integration of inquiry into science curriculum is a key component to these efforts. The National Science Education Standards and the NGSS outline a shift towards classroom instruction emphasizing student opportunities for authentic inquiry. Each document urges educators to guide students towards the identification and construction of questions that foster opportunities for scientific inquiry. Students should be *learning* science while they are *doing* science.

Students must be provided opportunities for self-directed inquiry involving personal curiosity and interest generated from natural phenomena. Personally meaningful questions generated from discrepant event demonstrations provide the context for rewarding learning experiences in the classroom. Within the scope of a full inquiry approach, the phenomena displayed in discrepant event demonstrations establish ideal conditions to launch engaging inquiry experiences that promote critical thinking, creativity, collaboration, and communication-effectively influencing positive learning outcomes. In the context of an inquiry-based approach, discrepant events provide incredibly fruitful opportunity for students to make sense of natural phenomena.

In the science classroom, inquiry can be one of the most valuable tools for learning. Inquiry can be described as the process of investigating to better understand an observation that sparks curiosity or wonder through intrigue or surprise. An observed phenomenon stimulates a question because it does not "fit" into the observer's cognitive schema or prior experiences, initiating the personal desire to understand.

One of the central tenets of *Project 2061's Benchmark for Science Literacy* (AAAS, 1993), the *A Framework for K-12 Science Education* (2012), and *the Next Generation Science Standards* (NGSS, Lead States 2013) is the provision for an inquiry-based science program for all science students.

The NGSS explains:

> *Whether students are doing science or engineering, it is always important for them to state the goal of an investigation, predict outcomes, and plan a course of action that will provide the best evidence to support their conclusions. Students should design investigations that generate data to provide evidence to support claims they make about phenomena. Data aren't evidence until used in the process of supporting a claim. Students should use reasoning and scientific ideas, principles, and theories to show why data can be considered evidence.*

Science and Engineering Practices in the NGSS, Appendix F, p. 7

At its core, inquiry is effective because it closely models how we genuinely learn. We are all natural inquirers; eager to observe, wonder, question, and make connections. Inquiry is our basic approach to understanding the world around us. Inquiry resulting in the most rewarding learning outcomes involve direct interaction with materials that exhibit cognitively stimulating phenomena.

Inquiry in the classroom is a dynamic approach to learning and understanding through personal discovery. Through it, conceptual meaning is constructed through spontaneous interactions, situations, and circumstances emerging from the flexible, oftentimes impromptu, learning environment that unfolds. The process of inquiry involves exploration, questioning, critical thinking, and rigorous investigation followed by evidence-supported explanation. These efforts can lead to a deeper understanding of the world around us. In the classroom, it should also involve student discourse, offering opportunities to share ideas, observations, and conclusions.

The ultimate objective of inquiry in the science classroom is for students to develop their own research question, design effective data collection procedures to inform that question, conduct their own planned investigation, and construct their own conclusion. However, it takes time to achieve this level of independent inquiry. There are actually differing levels of inquiry, each involving varying degrees of teacher intervention and student involvement. They range from guided, involving the most teacher intervention, to full inquiry, involving the least. Progression towards full inquiry should be scaffolded and guided. The level of structure and guidance provided by the teacher in each phase of the POQIE model should be determined by the student's level of experience with inquiry, their research ideas, and their individual unique learning needs. The lessons included in this book are amenable to differing levels of teacher intervention and student responsibility. Throughout this chapter you will find strategies and techniques meant to move your students through the spectrum of inquiry, within each phase of the POQIE model.

Teaching science requires varied approaches and strategies; a mix between teacher and learner-centered educational strategies. Inquiry cannot, and should not, frame all our lessons. Inquiry is but one tool in our educator's toolbox. It is not the most appropriate tool for *every* instructional situation. Each lesson demands its own particular approach, or teaching strategy, based on the concept, students, teacher, and available resources. Yet, inquiry is one of the most valuable and powerful tools in the science classroom. Following discrepant event demonstrations, it positions itself as one of the most rewarding learning strategy.

Teacher guidance is the backbone of inquiry. It requires confidence in our practices and the learning potentials of our students. Rewarding inquiry in the classroom occurs under the direct guidance of the teacher. Effectively learning from inquiry experiences involves a high level of structure and direction. When the teacher has a firm grip on classroom management, the classroom is anything but chaotic. Well-managed inquiry is *orchestrated freedom*. Under the umbrella of guided inquiry, incredible student opportunity and learning potential can be established.

Inquiry is a process initiated by wonderment, curiosity, and a need to make sense of an observation or experience. Ultimately, we are motivated to investigate the circumstance in order to achieve a better understanding of the world around us. The POQIE model employs an inquiry design that broadens student exploration to include explanation and argumentation, with the intent to promote the incremental development of scientific concepts.

Indeed, it is this spontaneity that produces a challenge- even for the most seasoned traditional classroom educator. Rather than presenting prepared lectures, the educator's role is to guide students using questioning techniques and discourse strategies developed over time and through experience. When implemented, these techniques and strategies offer rewarding classroom experiences governed by the unplanned direction of interaction, woven by the students and the diversity of their personal experiences, interests, and ideas. Inquiry is a practice governed by improvisation and spontaneity. Yet, underlying it all is a controlled direction and atmosphere managed by the teacher. Experience is key in this type of environment. The inexperienced inquiry teacher will initially feel discomfort and vulnerability. But, as experience and familiarity of inquiry is established, the teacher becomes more confident and prepared for the unprepared. This is an art form. It requires absolute nurturing. It relies on an acceptance and willingness to be vulnerable. And, its benefits are immense- without doubt worth every bit of effort involved.

EXPLAIN: DISCOURSE AND ARGUMENTATION

Discourse

Phenomena-Driven Inquiry and the POQIE model offer a discourse strategy and structure that differs from the style we commonly think of when we consider discourse in the classroom. Typical books and lessons involving discrepant events for the science classroom will commonly label the one or two overarching concepts or principles that the demonstration is intended to illustrate. This traditional method of teaching allows for a concentrated focus on one specific concept. This type of approach is valuable and rewarding, and certainly has benefits to any science curriculum. But, if we look beyond the most glaringly obvious concept expressed, we will discover there are actually a range of concepts, from various disciplines, that form the underpinnings of any discrepant event demonstration. For example, a demonstration that traditionally might be used to illustrate a physics principle might just also be a wonderful method of illustrating a life science concept. This approach is perfectly suited for the POQIE model. Because of the different investigations conducted, and the diverse variables under study, the direction of discourse can encompass any of the embedded concepts. The teacher has the opportunity to choose which of these underlying concepts and principles to pursue.

At first, this may seem to be a daunting task. It may also seem to be a "scattered" approach. However, I have found through experience that just the opposite is true. To appreciate the depth of this, you only need to participate in one classroom experience as student faces light up, revealing the surprise of connections they never imagined existed, concepts they never considered to underlie the phenomenon, and the recognition that they are learning. The first time you experience these "AHA" moments, and the energy associated with them, you become fully aware of the learning power. As an educator, it is invigorating. You will find that, as discourse advances, opportunities abound to incorporate and unravel various concepts. As mentioned, this is partly due to the many different investigations conducted and variables studied, each leading to different findings, conclusions, and further questions that arise during discourse in the Explanation Phase. If we broaden our scope of the concepts and principles involved in the underlying phenomenon of any demonstration, we discover wider opportunity for ancillary concepts to evolve. Upon deeper examination, we find connections between those concepts, as well as between disciplines of science.

The ability to construct knowledge and understanding for related concepts, even though they may not be the most obvious focus of the demonstration, is a key feature of Phenomena-Driven Inquiry and the POQIE model. This is one of the powerful contributions of the model. As educators, we need to broaden our views concerning the potential concepts and principles that might be involved in not only the demonstration, but each of the ensuing, investigations.

Discourse of this manner is one of the most rewarding features of the POQIE model. Through teacher guidance, any of the science concepts involved, and their influence on other natural events and experiences, are unearthed. This is a different approach than most of us are familiar with. But it establishes the opportunity for cross-curricular and concept-to-concept connections, while broadening the range of concepts explored.

This strategy is perfectly aligned with the NGSS 3D model of learning. Conceptual connections that are made across disciplines are a very specific, core component of Cross-Cutting Concepts, one of the NGSS critical dimensions to learning science. Both the Framework and the NGSS emphasize that students should be made directly and explicitly aware of these connections, as they provide an "organizational schema for interrelating knowledge." This is a fundamental approach to current science education reform.

Every lesson found in this book includes a list of concepts and principles that are embedded in the underlying phenomenon. Identified and presented as concepts that might not be overtly considered or obvious, you'll find these lists helpful as you explore concept-concept and cross-discipline connections across your curriculum.

Argument and discourse are central to the work of scientists. Argumentation is an integral feature of the NGSS. The practice is also addressed in *A Framework for K-12 Science Education* (NRC, 2012), which states:

> *Students should have opportunities to engage in discussion about observations and explanations and to make oral presentations of their results and conclusions as well as to engage in appropriate discourse with other students by asking questions and discussing issues raised in such presentations. (p.77)*

Argumentation and discourse are critical and valuable components to science education reform, positioned as valuable practices for educators with tremendous benefits to students. Those who are most comfortable with traditional, didactic teaching methods may initially find argumentation to be an uncomfortable re-culturing process. However, through frequent opportunity and experience, comfort level with argumentation grows.

Discourse positions itself as the cornerstone of learning in the POQIE model, a key component of every phase. It occurs during the prediction-observation phases, through the development of research questions, during the investigation between partners as well as between student and teacher, and during the explanation phase, as connections are formed between the individual investigations. It accelerates learning through the co-creation of concepts based on observations, findings, and past personal experiences- all grounded in collective familiarity. This is one of the most powerful outcomes of classroom discourse; it presents a process of emergent, collective learning.

The features of discourse and argumentation embedded in the POQIE model present a forum for the generative construction of knowledge through social experience. In this social constructivist approach, the fundamental role of the teacher is to frame and navigate the learning environment towards the co-construction of knowledge. This manifests itself through exploration and discussion as the teacher guides group/class conversations that challenge perspectives and interpretation of evidence.

Discourse can present incredibly rich learning opportunities. But too often, students are reluctant to reveal their true thoughts due to lack of confidence, peer pressure, or simply because they feel it is not exactly what the teacher is "looking for." To facilitate learning, we must know what our students think, not what they feel we want to hear. In order for rewarding class discussion to thrive, the classroom climate must be a non-judgmental one; where students feel safe and comfortable to contribute and know that their ideas are valued. All ideas and comments should be encouraged and accepted during class discussion. Students are more willing to share genuine, sincere ideas when they realize they are being used to help collaboratively build ideas, rather than being assessed and evaluated. Initially, students inexperienced in the dynamics and freedom of class discussion might be unsure, anxious, or even reluctant to participate.

Strategies can be employed to encourage participation. At the start of the year, groups comprised of 3-5 students can collaborate and share out to the whole class. This would support students who might be initially reluctant or shy to share individual, personal ideas and thoughts. As the year progresses, and the students become more comfortable, the size of these groups can diminish with groups of two presenting to the class, allowing ideas to become more personally vocalized.

Rewarding discourse involves several key attributes. Guidelines for discussion should be direct and explicit. Valuable student habits include thoughtfully listening to, considering, and respecting the ideas of others. This means not interrupting others while they are speaking. Ideas put forth should not be dismissed or ridiculed. All ideas should be considered potentially valuable. Respect is a focal behavior. Students should understand that it is acceptable to criticize ideas and evidence, but not people. Furthermore, a disagreement or rebuttal must be accompanied by a counterclaim, articulated with organized thought and contrasting evidence. Students should clearly understand that the purpose of discussion is to construct and achieve common, shared learning. On the path towards that objective, students should learn to self-assess their explanations and conclusions as they compare their explanations to those of others. Through these comparisons, students learn to manage anomalous data, glean support, identify contradiction, and construct stronger arguments.

Classroom situations and environments should be carefully constructed to most efficiently foster student-generated, student-cultivated discovery. Yet, constructing these environments can be challenging for educators new to an inquiry platform. Refrain from too much participation during class discussion. Peer interaction is encouraged and necessary for rich discourse and fruitful outcomes. Student desks can be arranged in pairs, small groups, or a large circle to foster a "community" of discourse in which student interaction is promoted   The goal is for student contributions to generate student feedback, encouraging and fostering a community of learning. Your role is to guide and support, not to present. Consider asking the class to share their thoughts about an idea or response instead of presenting your own evaluation of it too soon. Students should state ideas or definitions in their own words. They should also be asked to clarify and paraphrase the ideas of others. Your role is to summarize, shape, and synthesize student comments and ideas into a scientific concept.

Provide the opportunity for students to manage the discussion as much as possible. Allow them to talk freely and learn, over time, how to respect and listen to each other. Perhaps, students can call on each other to talk. Eventually, the class will be carrying on a true discussion without raising hands. Think about a discussion or conversation you've had among a group of three, four, or five of your friends at one time. Do you all raise your hands when you want to speak? Of course not! But you do realize, appreciate, and expect some social, respectful norms within the dialogue. You know when you should begin to interject your thoughts into the dialogue. You know when it's appropriate to do so. And, you've learned this through experience. Your students can also learn these protocols through experience. Provide your students the opportunity to learn social respect and responsibility in these circumstances the same way you did- through experience.

When class discussion is introduced to students at the beginning of the year, fruitful discussion can be guided by presenting acceptable methods of contribution. For example, the following prompts can be displayed on the chalkboard or easel as suggestions for student participation:

- "I agree because…"
- "I disagree because…"
- "I do understand what _____ said, but I also think that _____"
- "I have seen something like this before in my own life when…"

As students initially begin to learn the art of collaborative discussion, framing sentences such as these can initially provide a safe, structured environment to promote participation. At the start of the year, this list can be developed and expanded from student contributions. Eventually, as students become increasingly accustomed to the dynamics of discourse, these suggested prompts are gradually removed from the display, building confidence and fostering stronger academic discourse.

Within the lesson, there are two key points that offer valuable learning opportunities through discourse. The first occurs just following the demonstration. Here, students are given the opportunity to share their ideas, questions and prior experiences relating to the observed phenomenon. This discussion is also instrumental in helping students consider the investigation ahead; what they might be interested in learning more about, and how they might approach it. The second opportunity to achieve fruitful gains through class discussion occurs once the investigations have concluded. As students share ideas, findings, and observations, this emergent conversation is intended and conducive to connection-making, conceptual development, and the association of scientific terminology.

The most meaningful connections are those identified by students. As teachers, we need to resist the urge to overtly make those connections, or *tell* students what they *should* have learned from their investigations, as commonly occurs in the didactic transmission model. Rather, we should guide students towards their own identification of connections. Sometimes, students may not even recognize that they have observed or noted a detail that is actually significant and fundamental to the concept at hand. It is the role of the educator to uncover and raise awareness of these details, and to guide students towards an appreciation for their relevance to the concept. Seemingly innocuous and unrelated ideas become meaningful and connected. Central to this lies a delicate balance of meaningful questioning and careful listening. Educators who are skilled and knowledgeable about orchestrating classroom discourse provide challenging, yet supportive questions and comments. The objective is to facilitate dialogue that promotes scaffolded, student-manifested discovery.

Posing open-ended, thought-provoking questions can encourage deeper thinking and help students make connections. These types of questions cultivate organic learning by engaging, guiding, and enlightening. Such questions can be subtle, yet powerful. They include:

- How do you know that?
- What did you discover when …?
- What did you notice when/about …?
- What is going on when …?
- How is that different from before, when you …?
- What does that suggest to you?
- When did you learn that?
- Where did you learn that?
- What makes you think that?
- How else might you say that?
- Can you identify any patterns in your data?
- Could you rephrase that?
- Where did that information come from?
- Where does that idea come from?
- So, what you're saying is…. Is that correct?
- What evidence/what have you observed that supports your explanation/argument?
- Are there other possible explanations for what you observed?
- Which argument/explanation is best supported by the evidence that we have gathered/shared?
- What do you think this means?
- What do you mean by that?
- What's the significance of that?
- Can you be more specific in your explanation?
- Can you find a way to…?
- What do you think now?
- How have your ideas changed?
- Have you ever seen this phenomenon in other situations?
- Have you thought about…?
- Can you share a little bit more about what you're thinking?
- What do others think about that idea?
- What are you thinking?
- What do you think would happen if/when…?
- How can we find out?

- How does _____ cause/affect _____?
- What is your proof?
- What does that remind you of?
- What conclusion can you draw?
- What is your interpretation of the data?
- How is _____ dependent upon _____?
- How reliable are your data?
- Do you notice any patterns emerging from the data?
- Is it possible to____?
- Have you considered_?
- What data did you find that supports that claim?
- Can you give me an example?
- If you did this investigation again, what would you do differently?
- How could you have made the investigation better? Why would that make it better?
- What could you do to increase the confidence level for your claim?
- Can anyone think of a connection between what you (we) observed and something that you may have seen or experienced in your own lives?

These types of questions compel students to rephrase answers, expand ideas, organize thoughts, and clarify understanding. Questions that elicit yes/no responses or facts do not encourage rich classroom dialogue. Questions such as these are certainly necessary, but are typically used to support arguments or clarify interpretations. However, they are certainly not as thought-provoking, cognitively stimulating, or conceptually revealing as those shown above.

Woven into classroom discourse should be the practice of asking students to paraphrase a comment or explanation just made by another student. This strategy ensures that all students are involved and focused on the discussion, while also providing you the opportunity to assess understanding. Another way to do this is to ask students to build upon the comments just made by another student. Their response will indicate whether they understand the material well enough to carry the idea one step further than the previous comment.

Within the context of discourse following their investigations, students will be inadvertently using their own words to describe observed phenomena that scientists have already identified and named. As students present their ideas, it offers a valuable opportunity to introduce and reinforce key terms. Making these connections by introducing vocabulary and terminology at these precise moments establishes incredibly fruitful learning experiences. Definitions are established as the language used by students is connected to scientific terminology, establishing the beginning of a common language in the classroom. More importantly, this terminology is attached to experience. Later in the chapter, we will discuss this idea further.

The development of concept maps or word walls can become valuable instructional tools during discourse, allowing key terms to become visuals for the class. Another strategy uses index cards. Each card would have an individual term on it. As each vocabulary word is introduced during discussion, students are given the card with that term on it. Students are later asked to create a concept map on the chalkboard or wall using the index cards. Concept maps can even be used in a more holistic way as entire concepts are related to each other to illustrate the connections that exist between the different concepts covered within the course of a year; concepts that may appear seemingly unrelated to students. Through this collaborative approach, concept maps help students recognize connections and identify patterns in the new and emerging concepts. In addition, they are instrumental in making connections to prior schema.

Some might think it more rewarding for students to have learned the vocabulary involved, prior to the lesson or the demonstration. But observations, data, and analysis gleaned through investigative experiences can provide the context for the meaningful development of terms, operational definitions, concepts, and the skills involved in scientific inquiry. The teacher's role is to facilitate the introduction of scientific vocabulary by association of experience. Terminology attached to experience is a powerful learning strategy and nuance. Once students have begun to develop an understanding for a concept through observation and tangible manipulation, vocabulary becomes useful, comprehensible, meaningful, and memorable. A common language is established for students, who can then apply it as they articulate thoughts and explanations of their investigative experiences. Vocabulary itself is abstract. Personal, physical experience ties the abstract to the concrete. The simple rote memorization of a vocabulary word does not necessarily establish an *understanding* for the term. In my experiences, I've found that many students will simply memorize a definition without really grasping an understanding for it. These students can recite the definition word for word as presented to them. But, I can't tell you how many times I've asked them to put this definition into their own words and they stumble. Definitions and concepts constructed from direct personal experience result in more meaningful learning than rote memorization. Knowledge is most enriching when it is acquired through personal experience.

Learning becomes rich when tangible, concrete experiences precede the introduction of abstract terms. Traditional instruction reverses this order, introducing concepts first, then allowing students to "observe" these concepts through either demonstration, activity, or lab. When faced with a new vocabulary term, students may be trying to integrate it into a cognitive schema that might not have a framework structured for it. The most rewarding learning occurs through connections, especially connections to experience. Tagging a new vocabulary term to an existing schema allows for deeper understanding because connections are formed to that which has already been experienced.

In my experiences, classroom discourse promotes another educational benefit that arises as students attempt to interpret observed phenomena. Namely, it oftentimes involves some connection or similarity to prior experiences. Ultimately, these shared experiences can reveal differing personal belief systems regarding the nature of our world. As these beliefs become vocal, misconceptions are sometimes revealed. Classroom discourse, which encourages and fosters the sharing of prior knowledge, cultivates an atmosphere that tends to unearth these naïve conceptions. This presents a prime opportunity to confront and address them. Student interactions of this nature, that reveal cognitive schema, provide fertile ground for identification and potential restructuring of misconceptions. As weaknesses in student understanding or continued misconceptions are exposed, the teacher's role is to guide the class towards a richer, more sophisticated understanding of the scientific concept. It is an opportunity to move student's understandings towards scientifically accepted explanations. As students communicate the findings and observations from each of their investigations, they are connected to preexisting conceptions, past personal experiences, and previously uncovered misconceptions. The learning that takes place during this reflective process is powerful as relationships between various aspects of the concept become unified and clarified. It is important to foster this valuable aspect of classroom dialogue. We will discuss the value of personal experience in the next section.

Sometimes commentary between peers can cause students to recognize that their understandings and conclusions do not have logical or scientifically sound reasoning, or that there is a conflict with other evidence presented. As ideas become articulated and compared to those of others, they can be refined. Sharing out establishes a valuable context for ideas to be challenged, strengthened, or revised in a manner consistent with the evidence.

In addition, as each group presents their data, findings, and understandings, the rest of the class has an opportunity to identify any ideas that can help strengthen, or lead to the development of more rigorous, robust future investigations. The strategy provides the opportunity for students to progressively learn how to construct lab experiences that have the greatest potential for rewarding and valuable outcomes.

The POQIE model encourages and fosters opportunities for rich, rewarding discourse in the classroom. The objective of the post-investigation class discussion is for students to develop and defend explanations for the observed phenomenon in a logical, coherent manner, founded on the evidence gathered during their individual investigation. The teacher-led class discussion of the collective results from each of the different student-led investigations, guides students towards a better understanding of the scientific concept behind the phenomenon observed in the initial class demonstration. Discourse connects seemingly disparate findings, developing a more rigorous, coherent understanding of the concept. Students learn from the collective results of each of the different investigations conducted, each focusing on concepts through different lenses. They ultimately learn that science is more than a collection of facts and data.

Argumentation

Science progresses, in large part, as a result of the scientific community's practices of critiquing research, evidence, conclusions and arguments that stem from investigative work. When students engage in opportunities to learn science in authentic ways, they acquire a deeper understanding for the construction of scientific knowledge and the development of scientific models and theories. They begin to learn that science involves skills far beyond factual knowledge and rote memorization. When they engage in authentic practices and methods, students develop a rich understanding and appreciation for the way in which scientific work is conducted and the rigorous scientific criteria it is grounded in. They begin to identify the key attributes to fruitful scientific investigation. Students should become aware that their classroom discourse practices parallel the authentic nature of science and the scientific community.

One of the paramount features of classroom discourse is that it be critical in nature. Argumentation is a central feature of discourse. The practice of argumentation, a necessary feature of authentic science, is also a critical component of inquiry. Authentic inquiry involves the construction of arguments and theories explaining mechanisms behind phenomenon with unobservable entities. It incorporates strategies to resolve inconsistencies or conflicting data from the findings of different studies. It sometimes involves building and replicating models with unobservable mechanisms. And it oftentimes involves the construction of knowledge collaboratively. Scientific inquiry should culminate with the construction and presentation of an argument. In it, the observations and data are used to support or refute a proposed explanation in a plausible and defensible manner.

Modeling the behavior of real world science, students engaged in the POQIE model share findings and observations through discussion that serve to build a conceptual model for the observed phenomena under study. Using the contributions from each group, who have studied different variables for the same phenomena, students scaffold and strengthen their understanding for the concept. The conceptual picture flourishes as evidence from each group is assessed and evaluated for its merit, after being subjected to questioning. Based upon the collective observations, relationships are established and connections are formed, founded on evidence, reason, and logical arguments.

Students are asked to organize their investigative findings into a structurally sound, rigorous format. The findings are then used to construct and defend claims. Through argumentation, students develop and communicate justification for the claims that emerge. In the context of argumentation, students use evidence and attempt to convince others of the validity of their explanations. They attempt to show why or how particular data should be considered as evidence to support the claim. Through the process, some become self-aware that their evidence is insufficient to support their arguments. Rigorous scientific arguments are founded on thoughtful reflection and analysis of collected data, and the purposeful use of that data as evidence. Students should learn to critically analyze and evaluate the rigor and merit of an argument by assessing whether the evidence and scientific reasoning supporting it is appropriate and sufficient. In other words, students should learn to evaluate the claims and arguments made by others.

This evaluation involves the art of critique, which can either help strengthen an argument, or reveal errors or instances of faulty reasoning. These outcomes can lead to a stronger argument, or a reevaluation of the investigation or the findings. Since critiquing is a skill that most students are unfamiliar with, it is important that they learn and develop appropriate critiquing techniques. Becoming adept at it requires consistent practice. This doesn't happen in a lesson, a unit, or even two units. It's incorporation in the science classroom should be scaffolded and approached as a tool. In most traditional classrooms, it is rare to see practiced critiquing being conducted, especially on a regular basis. It is much more common to see students submitting or reading their own written arguments aloud to the teacher, who in turn might critique the work. However, critiquing is a hallmark of science. If we want our students to engage in authentic science, they must learn to question and critique each other's work in a cohesive, logical manner.

For both educators and students, argumentations is a developmental process. It is a skill that requires patience, diligence, and persistent efforts. Developing an argument from evidence is a thought provoking, thought demanding process. It extends beyond "hands-on" science. The approach to argumentation should be a scaffolded one for students. Over time, they should be nurtured and encouraged to participate and become proficient in the techniques involved. Educators should learn to facilitate meaningful, equitable dialogue that establishes a risk-free environment, allowing inquiry-based learning the opportunity to flourish. Initial unfamiliarity with argumentation can be supported by offering prompts or frameworks. Some of these prompts can guide students to organize their thoughts and develop a more coherent, scientifically robust argument. Here are two examples of prompts:

- I used to think _____, but now I think_____.

- One thing I learned about _____ is _____.

To engage in scientific argument, there should be a common topic, collected data on the topic, and student tools and strategies for discourse and interpretation of data. An argument should include a question, which arises from some observed phenomenon. The question should lead to a claim, a statement which attempts to answer the question. This should be followed by justification supporting the claim, typically through logical reasoning and collected data used as evidence.

During class discussion, students need guidance to compare and identify similarities and differences between claims, evidence, and observations; to logically synthesize data, findings and evidence. As presentations are conducted, students are also encouraged to identify faulty reasoning, and even suggest reasonable alternative explanations from the evidence. Recognition of presented explanations that are both consistent and inconsistent with existing or competing models should be overt and prominent. Conducting a class discussion in this manner fosters opportunity for the identification of patterns and trends, leading to a deeper, more complex, understanding of the concept under investigation. Once again, this is another strategy that aligns wonderfully with the NGSS 3D learning model. The identification of patterns can be found in the dimension of Cross-Cutting Concepts. Rather than fielding student responses to rigid, fact-based questions, teachers should cultivate an atmosphere in which students' emerging ideas can be expressed, insights can be shared, associations made, and connections either developed or strengthened.

Connections are established as students process and verbalize the observations and conclusive ideas generated from their individual investigations. The act of verbalizing one's thoughts promotes self-evaluation oftentimes resulting in either solidification or reconstruction of those ideas. The ideas, questions, and claims of one student may support, encourage and even build upon those of another. In addition to aiding in the collaborative development of the concept, this emphasizes value on each student's investigative work, findings, and ideas. Affirmation of findings and conclusions adds value to each investigation and significance to the collaborative efforts of the entire class. The ability to identify connections becomes significant.

Engagement of this nature contributes towards the development of a student-centered classroom fostering the significance of communication. As some formulate weak arguments and others very strong ones, students begin to identify the components of effective communication. They gain an appreciation for clear, concise, persuasive communication, and the significant role it plays in the advancement of science.

As they defend their argument, students review and reflect on their investigative process and techniques. This includes collection of data, observations, interpretation of data, and conclusions. The entire investigative process becomes a holistic one in which the strength and validity of their conclusions and arguments are directly dependent upon the strength of the connections they make between each step. They are compelled to evaluate the adequacy and logic for the support they have formed as the foundation of their argument. When asked to form rational explanations of their observations, students push beyond the task of simply reporting findings, as is commonly found in traditional classrooms.

There is a critical distinction between asking students to develop arguments at the end of a unit or lesson, and developing one from a student-developed inquiry investigation. When arguments are developed following a unit, the expectation is that students will use the science covered in that unit to construct the argument. Here, science is portrayed as a set of previously established ideas in which arguments simply employ the known set of existing scientific ideas. However, development of an argument following an inquiry investigation portrays argumentation as a central component of new learning; a creative and skillful practice that leads to a deeper understanding of science. Students should understand that argumentation can, and oftentimes should, be an opportunity for knowledge building; a process under which science knowledge is constructed. In this context, students appreciate knowledge building *through* argumentation.

All too often, as educators, we focus on our own abilities to successfully communicate a conceptual idea, and overlook the even more significant opportunities for purposeful, meaningful student discourse. Deep understanding and appreciation for the full scope of a concept requires opportunity for collaborative dialogue, investigation, and reflection. Our students should be provided ample opportunity for these experiences in the classroom.

Students should come to understand that the objective of discourse and argumentation in the science classroom is to collaboratively develop a deeper understanding for observed phenomena; to make sense of a particular phenomenon through shared ideas. In the POQIE model, groups of students conduct investigations of different variables within the same phenomenon. As interpretation of findings and conclusions are shared, the class collectively generates a deeper understanding for the phenomenon or scientific concept. The structure frames a classroom culture which establishes a scientific learning community.

An integral part of science is the articulation of ideas and theories. The expression of our ideas becomes a meaningful process when investigative observations are shared and conclusions are critiqued. Engaged in processes followed by scientists in the real world, the evaluation of claims, arguments, and models presents a strategy for students to make sense of their world. Through evidence-based argumentation, students address differences and similarities among their models. As data, observations and arguments are presented, students begin to identify patterns, correlations, and relationships between variables and outcomes. As claims are defended, the opportunity is ripe to identify coherency, consistency, and conflict between findings, arguments, and evidence. Just as scientists do in the real world, students learn they can revisit and modify their ideas based on new information. They can revise and add to their understanding of the concept. As in authentic scientific processes, discourse establishes a recursive process which allows for previous conversations and ideas to be revisited. Oftentimes, students will connect their prior understandings to their new experiences. The teacher's role throughout is to guide the class towards a richer, more sophisticated understanding of the scientific concept. Any weaknesses in student understanding, or continued misconceptions, can be exposed and addressed. The learning that takes place during this reflective process is powerful.

Through this type of approach, students are guided towards an appreciation for the work involved in forming a thoughtful, comprehensive conclusion from observations and data. They begin to appreciate the significant components involved in research and how these components contribute towards the construction of knowledge for our world. Discourse should be viewed as much more than an opportunity for students to share findings and explanations. Through discourse, students "propose" explanations, subject to evaluation, with the goal of constructing, shaping, and framing science concepts. The implications of discourse are profound. Learning is not just an outcome of discourse. Rather, discourse is a process of discovery through the synthesis of collective explanation and argumentation. The educational value of discourse revolves around argumentation.

PERSONAL EXPERIENCE AND FAMILIARITY

As we learned in Chapter Four, our knowledge base or cognitive schema is formed from our individual collective experiences. The experiences provide relevance, meaning, and usefulness as we navigate through our lives. New experiences capitalize on those previously encountered. As such, new knowledge is shaped from that previously constructed. Through the lens of constructivism, new understandings and knowledge is developed from what we currently know and believe. The continual construction of knowledge is essentially built from personal experience.

Dr. Beau Lotto states that "perception is grounded in our history." We "perceive" and interpret new experience and observations of the world around us through the filter of the cognitive schema constructed from our collective past experiences. Our past personal experiences play a key role in the ongoing construction of our schema. They are critical to the shaping of our schema.

All inquiry begins with a question. The scientific inquiry discussed in this book begins with student-generated curiosities and questions regarding observed natural phenomena. Prior knowledge guides and shapes students' personal interpretation and meaning of those observations. Learning is further shaped by investigation and interactive manipulation of the materials involved in the phenomena.

Prior knowledge and its significance to learning is moving to the forefront of education. Connecting prior knowledge with new incoming information is a critical component to building concepts and generating deeper understanding. Since knowledge is constructed from experience, the anchoring of prior experience to a new one is a critical aspect of the inquiry process, and a central feature threaded throughout Phenomena-Driven Inquiry and the POQIE model. Social experiences are certainly included in those that provide valuable context for the construction of knowledge. As we discussed in the previous section, this forging and sculpting of knowledge through the shared experiences of others is a powerful strength of classroom discourse. But personal experience is also a critical, dynamic element towards the development of a hypothesis, prediction, and argument.

Using prior experiences, we consistently analyze new experiences for consistency, novelty, usefulness, and personal safety. New experiences or incoming information stands apart from that which we have previously encountered. We are constantly exposed to an incredible amount of incoming information and stimulus. Our visual system, along with our brains, has a limited capacity to process all of the input that it receives. Our brains would go into overload if it were to try to attend to each bit of information. Therefore, we have a filtering system in place. Any area of visual focus in our environment is typically surrounded by a great deal of irrelevant stimuli. To avoid overload, these systems operate by focusing on the most salient details of our environment and filtering out, even suppressing, what it deems least important.

The first priority of this system is to determine whether the incoming information presents any threat towards us. We assess this level of threat based on our experiences. We will not focus on the incoming information that has proved to be safe in the past. We will not waste valuable time or energy focusing on a situation that we have previously experienced and are comfortable in. We may have experienced the same information hundreds, or even thousands, of times before. If it has consistently proven to be safe for us, why focus on it? What we will focus on is any information that we have not previously experienced. We focus on novelty. This is our primary concern. Whether you know you are doing it or not, your brain is constantly assessing its surroundings for novelty. Since we have no background or experience of these situations to rely on, this is what our brain will focus on. We "ignore" familiarity so that we can focus on novelty. Our brain is inherently "tuned in" to novelty.

Our attention is activated by our constant evaluation for threats or novelty in our surroundings. Referred to as *immediate attention*, the identification of either potential danger or unusual phenomena is a persistent process. We are conditioned to actively assess our surrounding to be sure that we are safe in our current environment. This is a survival mechanism that is hardwired in each of us. In the hierarchy of our attention, this is our foremost priority. Our brains are always trying to determine exactly what we need to pay attention to. We feel safe when our surroundings are familiar and we know them to be safe based on past experience. When something in our environment is unfamiliar, or novel, it commands our immediate attention. This explains why novelty ignites attention. A disruption within the familiarity of our cognitive schema elicits immediate attention.

As we discussed in Chapter Five, this is precisely why discrepant events are so powerful in the classroom. They present situations that contradict our expectations based on experience. They present novelty. They demand attention. Novel situations are invaluable to education and learning.

The novelty that arises from a discrepant event is sparked by contradiction. Engaged in the demonstration, students link observations to prior experiences. Our schema, and the experiences that have formed it, lead us to certain expectations as we observe an event. When these expectations are broken, the contradiction *is* novel. This novelty generates curiosity, the most critical feature of a discrepant event demonstration. At its very core, the curiosity that stems from the novel situation is the initial driving force behind an engaging experience for students.

Novelty and surprise act as mechanisms that dictate attention. A solid body of research has shown that unique or novel sensory cues are more likely to be remembered. Results of studies regarding attention-based phenomena, such as the *novel popout effect*, indicate that "attention is rapidly drawn to the novel object in an otherwise familiar display." (Strayer and Johnston, 2000). Understanding this phenomenon explains why discrepant events are so captivating. This is a similar idea to the Von Restorff effect, the phenomenon in which an item or object stands out amongst a collection because its properties differ from the others in the group. It's the contrast of novel events framed within familiar settings that cause them to become memorable. Notice that it's important that we have familiarity with the situation and the objects involved, but for the event to be disarming we should not have familiarity with the outcome.

Piaget considered learning as the assimilation, or incorporation, of new information into a cognitive schema founded on prior knowledge. The argument asserts the significance of prior knowledge; a significance that cannot be underestimated or overlooked. Within the mechanism of learning, prior knowledge positions itself as a key, pivotal feature. Appleton (1993) has said that "A learning experience commences with some new encounter which the learner interprets and makes sense of in terms of his or her existing cognitive structure" (p.269). The extent to which something makes sense depends upon the experiences, knowledge, and schema of the individual. In other words, we interpret new experiences by relating it to previous knowledge. It is essential that students be afforded the time to make connections to prior knowledge as they acquire new information. Good and Brophy (1997) supported this idea through their research, which showed that the construction of new knowledge is more likely when learners are able to relate new information to their existing schema, or background knowledge.

In order for students to develop a more robust schema, they must evaluate their personal schema against observed experiences and phenomena. Depending on how those observed experiences align or misalign with their personal schema, the individual will choose whether to maintain, modify, or entirely abandon their current schema for a more favorable one consistent with the new incoming information. The outcome of a discrepant event may lead to cognitive conflict, and perhaps conceptual change. But, I think it's important to remember that the observer's cognitive schema was constructed and developed through personal experience. I believe that accommodating new incoming information similarly requires personal experience. However, research has consistently shown that we are quite reluctant to replace our current schema, or cognitive models, with new ones (Carey 1986; MacBeth 2000).

According to Piaget, a necessary criterion for conceptual change to transpire is the acknowledged dissatisfaction with ones existing schema. Dissatisfaction occurs when an individual realizes that their pre-conceived knowledge, or schema, directly contradicts incoming information. In **Chapter Four** we learned that when an observers understanding of the world is challenged, the resulting *dissatisfaction* can be the impetus to cognitive change. This type of dissatisfaction results in a cognitive dilemma, called disequilibrium.

Disequilibrium is only possible with familiarity. In an entirely new situation, wherein the scene involves new characteristics, circumstances and details, the observer has no prior experience- no familiarity with which to compare. Thus, there can be no cognitive dissatisfaction. This personal recognition is precisely why familiarity and past personal experiences are such critical, powerful aspects of learning as viewed through the constructivist lens of cognitive change.

Since prior knowledge is a significant factor affecting cognitive conflict, I feel that familiarity with the materials involved is one of the most critical components to a successful discrepant event demonstration. It is only through familiarity that a student has the ability to be truly puzzled or startled. Familiarity is the key to curiosity. A student unfamiliar with the materials or the manipulative procedures observed can certainly be engaged. But engagement does not necessarily evoke or induce contradiction or curiosity. It does not ensure even the slightest cognitive conflict, or disequilibrium. Engagement does not equate to contradiction.

Phenomena become powerfully meaningful when the materials involved are within the realm of the observer's personal experiences and knowledge. Familiarity must be a precursor to genuine cognitive conflict. When selecting discrepant event demonstrations, familiarity should a strongly considered criteria. Familiarity of materials and equipment can even help make connections to unfamiliar concepts. In addition, personal experiences that provide familiarity for some students can become shared experiences for all, through classroom discourse. Sometimes, shared experiences can remind others of similar experiences. Shared experiences can nurture connections to concepts as well as to other students. While one student's experiences might generate cognitive conflict during the observation phase, another student's experiences might become a valuable tool to better understand the observed phenomenon during group discussion. Each of our previous interactions with the world provide a resource based on familiarity that aids and influences meaning, interpretation, and learning. Observations made during a discrepant event demonstration are filtered through this schema-driven familiarity.

We have learned that the demonstration becomes relevant and meaningful when the phenomenon has been personally experienced in other situations. Ideally, during a discrepant event demonstration, the equipment and the situation or circumstances involved should be familiar, or recognizable. It is critical that students have had prior experience, or familiarity, with the materials involved in the demonstration in order that they are able to generate an expectation. Without expectation, discrepancy cannot occur.

The memories from our personal experiences are called episodic; different from those memories formed by factual knowledge gained from books and other forms of communication, called semantic. Students certainly don't need to know this distinction. However, they should be made aware that much of our schema, or outlook of the world, is formed from past personal experiences and the memories we have of them. When they begin to consider schema, students become aware of not only what they know, but also how they know it. This metacognitive approach, an awareness of one's own thinking, is a feature found in rich learning. A metacognitive awareness allows students to appreciate how and why each of us might have differing schemas of the world, and how alternative conceptions might arise. Conscious awareness to the development of personal schema is an effective way to begin to identify misconceptions. In the POQIE model, metacognition is encouraged and fostered through the generative opportunity for the self-expression of individual beliefs and ideas. It occurs when students share ideas and argue explanations through discourse. This metaconceptual awareness of one's own schema and beliefs is a precursor to sensing the existence of anomaly or cognitive conflict.

Metacognition plays a role in each phase of the POQIE model. In the first phase, students should be asked to directly consider prior experience when predicting the outcome of the demonstration. Oftentimes, students will view a demonstration as something that will undoubtedly produce a surprise outcome, like a magic trick. When approached from this perspective, students guess that something "magical" will happen rather than engaging in critical thinking. Rather than using experience and knowledge to make a prediction, they will instead try to consider the most unlikely outcome. This diverts from the intended objective to cause disequilibrium generated from the contradiction of experience.

Discrepant event demonstrations should not have a "trick" behind them. Nothing should be hidden from students. The "parts," or equipment should be clearly visible. Equipment should not be "secretly" introduced. The Sad/Happy Balls demonstration comes to mind, where one of the balls is secretly switched for another. The outcome doesn't occur because of natural phenomena, but rather because the observer has been tricked. To generate cognitive dissonance, the observer must believe the event to be naturally occurring and authentic. When the observer feels there is a "trick" involved, their curiosity is driven by the desire to simply "know the secret."

Magicians actually rely on their spectator's familiarity regarding physical movements and the props used in the trick. The more unfamiliar, the more suspect, and the less puzzling. Magicians will spend hours on one particular physical move, so that it appears to be a common, familiar move to the observer. Unfamiliar moves become "suspicious." Believe it or not, for educators, there is some merit in studying this philosophy. It's true that sometimes one objective for the magician is to perfect a "secret move" so well that it is imperceptible to the observer- essentially rehearsing a move so much that it remains undetected when executed. To the untrained or inexperienced this might appear that the primary goal is to "hide" a move, while performing it directly in front of the spectator. In actuality, this is a lesser objective. The greater objective is to make the move that *is* seen, to appear as a common, familiar one. This is a critical idea, especially for the purposes of our discussion. The move may be well hidden, but if the physical gesture appears to be suspect, involving movements or characteristics unfamiliar to the spectator, then the gesture as a whole will not be plausible. When the move looks unnatural, attention is distracted towards it. Familiarity allows participants to "relax" as observers. The outcome of "relaxed" familiarity is greater puzzlement because the observer expects certain outcomes from familiar actions. When the result contradicts the expectation, the observer is more deeply puzzled. The spectator's expectations result from repeated observations of a particular action followed by the same outcome. The spectator is familiar with the result due to familiarity with the action. This is the hope of the magician; that the familiarity of actions lead to expected results. When the result is contradictory, there is cognitive dissonance. And when the action is embedded and woven into an entertaining experience, the result is magical.

All of this is entirely germane to our discussion of discrepant event demonstrations in the science classroom. If our objective as educators is to cause cognitive dissonance in our students, then familiarity of materials and actions should be a strong consideration in our lesson plans. As we have already established, we want our students to be challenged through contradictory observations. If we want this contradiction to be profound, to impact the observer at a deeply personal level, then the expectation should be based on personal experience- familiarity. And when surprising or puzzling experiences are observed from personally familiar events, the contradiction becomes personal, meaningful, and educationally valuable.

Some literature argues that anomalies cannot be readily identified by students without prior "thorough knowledge" of the concept embedded in the demonstration. Supporters of this argument contend that concepts should be introduced and students should have a grasp of them prior to the demonstration. The claim is that only when the student understands the concept can the intended objective be recognized. However, when the demonstration involves a discrepant event, I would disagree with this view. I would question whether the observer must have an established understanding of the embedded concept in order for an anomaly to be identified. If in fact a student did have a thorough understanding for the concept, could an anomaly ever really exist? A truly thorough understanding implies that the student would essentially appreciate and understand the outcome. When the principles behind the discrepant event phenomenon are deeply understood, the outcome is not truly *discrepant*. There would be no anomaly to recognize.

In addition, I would contend that the impact of the discrepant event is minimized, perhaps even non-existent, with a complete understanding for the phenomenon involved. When the concept is introduced prior to the discrepant event, students readily access that newly learned information when challenged by their observations. However, if the discrepant event is presented prior to the introduction of a concept, students must rely on prior knowledge to understand their observations. Without prior instructional exposure to the concept, there is a greater likelihood to experience conceptual incongruity. Yet, we have already discussed the tremendous opportunity for anomaly identification simply due to the inherent nature of discrepant events. So, are there ideal conditions that might lead to the recognition of anomaly? What are they? Do certain characteristics of the observer lead to greater identification of anomaly?

To begin, I would argue that just as anomaly would be undetected by a student knowledgeable of a concept, the same would be true for a student lacking knowledge of the concept. A student void of understanding or knowledge for a concept would also be unable to recognize anomaly. Anomaly stems from contradiction. But this means there must be an understanding from which this contradiction arises. The most effective or opportunistic situation for anomaly identification would occur if a student had what she believed to be an understanding, based on prior experience, which was in fact a misconception, or misconstruction. The most profound identification of anomaly, would occur in the face of an individual schema formed from personal experience, thought to be valid and "correct"- essentially the recognition of misconception. The outcome of a discrepant event demonstration is powerful because the curiosity it derives is founded on the observer's personal experiences. Contradiction between these experiences and observations of the demonstration sparks genuine curiosity. Thus, the ensuing investigation becomes personally meaningful to each student.

In order to appreciate an actual discrepancy from the observed phenomenon in the discrepant event, the observer must have an already established basic "understanding" arising from familiarity of the events taking place within the demonstration. This "understanding" does not have to be accurate for the concept being demonstrated. It simply needs to be the understanding that the individual has developed within her own conceptual framework of how the world operates. This is why certain demonstrations are more effective than others at generating cognitive dissonance. This is also precisely why discrepant events that involve familiar equipment and setups most effectively generate disequilibrium.

Although the entire class is watching the same discrepant event, the experience affects each student in a different way. This is because each of those students has had their own unique set of life experiences with the observed phenomenon, or the materials involved. Thus, each has formed their own schema of the world and how it operates. Among the students in the classroom, some schema might be aligned with one another. Other, not so much. Some students might be more familiar with the phenomenon than others. Although the discrepant event demonstration is intended to startle, it is not so important to strive for a discrepant event that will ensure surprise in every student. I've discovered through experience that discourse between students with differing familiarities of an observation can be rich and incredibly valuable. As we will learn in the next section, the interaction and collaboration between students with differing schema is incredibly rich fodder for learning. The contributions made from each student's personal experiences comprise a prominent, powerful feature of the POQIE model, strongly influencing student engagement, and ultimately learning. As beliefs and ideas are shared through discourse, the collective effect is generative, formative, and exciting.

The differing schema that our students bring to the classroom might also explain why intended learning outcomes may not be achieved from traditional science demonstrations. Differing personal experiences can result in a variety of schema and beliefs that can influence the interpretation of observed events. Thus, any intended connections from science to the observed demonstration may not actually meet our expectations. When the demonstration involves a discrepant event, these varied interpretations are welcomed and encouraged.

There are three phases of the POQIE model in which collective prior experiences of students play a key role. The prediction phase specifically aims to draw from experience. Students are overtly asked to draw from experience as they predict the outcome of the demonstration. Fostering imagination is not really the objective here. This is not to say that imagination is unwarranted and invaluable in the science classroom. On the contrary. As we have already discussed, imagination and creativity are incredibly valuable student characteristics that can certainly lead to some tremendous learning. Some of the greatest benefits from imagination come during the phases of explanation and investigation. This is when we should actively promote and pursue imagination and creativity. But the prediction and explanation phases, in particular, benefit immensely from student experiences and familiarity shared through discourse.

Tremendous benefits arise when we encourage students to consider and share prior experiences. When these experiences are used in the classroom to extend and deepen the understanding for a science concept, students feel that their contributions are respected and valued. They consider themselves to be significant contributors to the process of education and learning. When prior knowledge and experience is welcomed, nurtured and respected by all students, it cultivates a classroom atmosphere of equity. This, in turn, establishes a classroom of equitable learning opportunities. As student's personal experiences become relevant in the classroom, students become producers of knowledge, rather than consumers of it; reinforcing their sense of agency. The inclusion and cultivation of prior knowledge in the classroom provides context, authenticity, and connection to both student's personal lives, the curriculum, and the concept at hand.

COLLABORATION:

Science is a social endeavor; a collaborative process. Scientists in the real world typically work within a group, or groups, collaborating towards the same objective. It is uncommon for a scientist to work in isolation. As such, if we want our students' experiences to be authentic, they should be involved in collaborative efforts. Our classroom should reflect the collaborative nature of science.

Information that is socially gathered and shared can inform individual learning and promote conceptual understanding. Although we build our cognitive schema individually, its framework is strongly affected by social conditions and interactions. Situated Cognition Theory asserts that individuals actively develop their own perceptive interpretations of a given experience, and the objects involved, as a result of their own unique prior experiences *and* the interactions with others they share the current experience with. The interrelationships that develop between those engaged in a shared experience are products of the way distinct backgrounds, beliefs, and values interact. Learning experiences through individuality and collaboration are symbiotic; mutually dynamic and generative. When students engage in a common learning objective through inquiry, their collaborative efforts produce a richer learning experience.

The interpretation of experiences and the communication of meaning can only be accomplished through negotiated dialogue; the interplay of conversation. When the objective is to uncover meaning, the most rewarding interplay involves certain characteristics. First, it should evolve through spontaneous collaborative exchange. It should also allow for interjection from others. And, the dialogue should not be limited to factual information. From a social constructivist perspective, this pedagogical approach produces a much more dynamic relationship between teacher/student and student/student than a traditional classroom. In contrast to the passive, transference of information, this model involves the construction of science through negotiation.

Refinement for our understanding of scientific principles and the construction of new representations of the world is best achieved through interaction. This interaction takes shape in numerous ways. For example, it can occur between observations made and evidence gathered. As we have already discussed, there is also a critical interaction between observations and the conceptual schema of the observer. This interaction results in the interpretation of events. In the classroom, contributions from experience, observations, schema, and interpretation intertwine to generate new knowledge, or to either challenge or reinforce that which already exists. Consider that these examples involve multiple individuals, each with unique schema and perspectives, and you begin to understand the power and rewards that can be achieved from collaboration and interaction. In the POQIE model, multiple groups are focused on the same concept. Because of collaboration and interaction, opportunities abound for multiple representations and perspectives concerning that concept.

As students are sometimes forced to refine their interpretations and understandings through discourse, they begin to realize that scientific knowledge is tentative; changing over time based on new evidence. They discover that by sharing information and ideas in a systematic, logical way, scientists revise their arguments through reflection, collaborative assessment, and a critical approach. Students should learn that scientific knowledge evolves; one of the most powerful features of the discipline. It can undergo revision in light of new evidence that arises- a set of ideas susceptible to continuous change. Students begin to recognize that a community of collaborative learners can be a powerful context for the construction and reconstruction of scientific meaning.

Using discrepant event demonstrations, the POQIE model creates a sense of classroom "community" through the collaborative energy of shared experiences involving genuine interest, mystery, and wonder. But, its effectiveness relies on continued exercise and routine praxis.

MODELS

The NGSS urges students to engage in science by modeling, designing, and analyzing; all features of the POQIE model. This type of engagement embodies creativity and critical thinking, all achieved within a framework supported by meaning through relevance.

In the scientific community, models are used to represent underlying mechanisms of structures and observed phenomena. They are used to predict *how* or *why* phenomena occur. In education, many of us consider models to be physical structures used as representation, such as a 3D model of a cell, an atom, or a planetary model of the solar system. Most students are familiar with these traditional types of models. They construct them to reinforce ideas or demonstrate their level of understanding for concepts or mechanisms. This sort of traditional classroom model is intended to be *descriptive*. As educators, we might hope that when students engage in the construction of these models they might increase, reinforce, or demonstrate their level of understanding for a concept taught by the teacher. Used for evaluative purposes, these types of models do have their place. But they are not the type we're discussing here.

The models we are referring to in Phenomena-Driven Inquiry aim for different objectives. These models are intended to be more than *descriptive*. They are constructed for explanatory or predictive purposes. Their intent is to advance an idea. They might be used to represent a conceptual mechanism relevant to evidence. They might also be used to offer an explanation to a proposed question or system. They could also be used to support a proposed prediction. And they could be used to convey interpretation of observed phenomena. In fact, in the POQIE model, the discrepant event demonstration is actually used as a model to form research questions by identifying variables, as well as to generate predictions based on their manipulation. The demonstration is also used as a model towards the development of an empirical investigation. Each of these uses has tremendous educational merit. The discrepant event demonstrations included in this book lead to student-led investigations that will both involve the use of models, as well as inform their development.

A model could be a tangible construction. But models do not have to be physical, tangible replicas. Along with the common physical representation, models can include drawings, diagrams, simulations, analogies, and mathematical representations. The model should help develop an answer or explanation concerning *how* or *why*. Essentially, modeling occurs when ideas are developed and used to help explain or predict phenomena. They comprise a set of ideas or representations about how our world operates. They should describe or represent the relationship between components or variables within a system and, in turn, these relationships should explain or account for the observed phenomena within the system. Both the development and the evaluation of models involve argumentation. Models that are used to support an argument must be consistent with, and evaluated against, empirical data used to form that argument.

The prediction and explanation phases of the POQIE model present tremendous opportunity for students to use models. Pictures and diagrams can also be used as models during the process of designing an investigation. As groups present models in the explanations that follow investigations, the teacher guides the class towards one culminating model that embodies and reflects the combined representations. Here we see the formation of the targeted conceptual model, formed *by* the class, from the contributive efforts *of* the class. This eventual model helps to explain and connect observed patterns among the groups. This is a key objective during the explanation phase of the POQIE strategy. Developed from observations and patterns, the eventual model emerging from review and revision can actually be used to help explain them. In fact, research has shown that students are more likely to recall content when they develop a scientific model, and use it to frame an explanation through discussion (Atkin and Karplus 1962; Lawson, Abraham, and Renner 1989).

Models inculcate student thoughts, ideas, and predictions. Student-derived models provide teachers an opportunity to assess understanding and uncover misconceptions. When involved in class discussion, teachers can guide their development and build upon student explanations.

The learning in our classrooms should involve models. Our students should be *using* them to interpret, demonstrate, and construct meaning from.

MEANINGFULNESS

Meaningfulness to the student is tied to the students' personal interests, curiosity, and some connection to their own personal experience.

Windschitl & Buttemer, 2000

Science education research has shown that most students learn best from instruction in which they are actively engaged, rather than passive, and when their experiences are personally meaningful. Engagement can only occur once attention is captured, so it should remain a priority to capture the attention of our students. But, ultimately we want that engagement to be personal and meaningful, and to provide experiences students will never forget. Phenomena-Driven inquiry provides us the ability to engage our students in a profoundly meaningful manner. Because the sense of wonder generated from discrepant events stems from the contradiction of a personally held belief about the nature of the world, it impacts the observer in a meaningful way. As I've already mentioned, traditional demonstrations might provide *exciting* experiences, but discrepant events provide *meaningful* experiences.

Captivating discrepant event experiences should not be followed by passive lecture that *explains* the phenomenon. Passive classrooms, such as a lecture format, generate declarative, isolated statements, ideas, and questions posed by the teacher. Consider the many questions that you might be asked in the course of a day. Many of them may not be deeply meaningful to you. Keep in mind that although the question might demand your attention and involvement, it does not necessarily guarantee meaningfulness. A passive classroom does not cultivate engagement. Once engagement has been sparked by the discrepant event, maintain it. Ride the momentum.

When students are asked to make a prediction for the outcome of the demonstration, they become invested, involved, and engaged. Engagement heightens when the outcome is observed to be discrepant. By identifying and investigating a variable that sparks personal curiosity and interest, student engagement remains active. The entire investigative journey maintains a focus on the interest forged from observations that contradict cognitive schema. Students are empowered throughout the entire process, from the moment they observe the discrepant event phenomena, to the generation of a meaningful question, investigation, and ultimately the formation of a conclusion which attempts to answer those meaningful questions. When students investigate their own variable, generated by their own genuine interest and curiosity, there is increased potential for more meaningful learning.

Meaningfulness to a student is an event that has some connection to their own personal interest, curiosity, or past experiences. Research has shown that when the content learned is not connected to prior knowledge or experience, it is less meaningful. When student's prior knowledge and experience is allowed to enter the classroom, students recognize the relevant connections between science and their lives. When students make these personal connections, classroom experiences become meaningful and engaging.

Meaningfulness and engagement is heightened when the contradiction of expectation is founded in familiarity. By using demonstrations that incorporate familiar materials, the contradictory nature of the discrepant event is greater, leading to a more meaningful experience. When the materials involved in the demonstration are familiar to students and lie within the realm of their prior experiences and knowledge, the conflict is greater and the event becomes more meaningful.

Research has shown that classroom experiences become more engaging when they are designed to connect students with their own personal interests and experiences. Prior experience is a critical feature of rewarding learning. Research has also shown that learning is deeper and students are more motivated to learn when their classroom experiences are anchored in genuine, real world problems that are personally meaningful to them. And so when the relevance of personal experiences plays a role in the classroom, science becomes more stimulating, interesting, and accessible to students (Weaver, 1998).

Ultimately, we hope that our student experiences are meaningful enough to endure. In their book *Made to Stick*, Heath and Heath make the argument that several key features will most effectively make an idea *stick* with those you communicate it to. To begin with, one of the strongest ways to make an idea stick is to pair it, when communicated, with something unexpected. This of course is the backbone of discrepant events. They add that the idea intended to stick should also be engaging. We have spoken about the engagement generated by the contradictory nature of discrepant events. For an idea to be sticky, it should also be concrete. This is achieved by presenting the idea through the expression of physical equipment and the ability to physically engage with that equipment. Physical involvement makes the abstract meaningful.

Sticky ideas are also credible. If students were to listen to an explanation of a phenomenon, without observing it directly, they might be able to discount it as unbelievable for a number of possible reasons. But when the phenomenon is directly observed, we are forced to reckon with it. Heath and Heath add that a *sticky* idea stirs emotion. In the POQIE model, this is certainly accomplished by the curiosity, puzzlement, and cognitive contradiction generated from discrepant event phenomena. The final component to a sticky idea is the ability for the receiving party to act on it. In the POQIE model, all students observing the phenomenon have the opportunity to engage with it through an inquiry investigation.

In the POQIE model the discrepant event demonstration is followed by student-centered, inquiry-based exploration towards the construction of new knowledge. Cognitive engagement is supported through the connection between captivating classroom experiences to personal, meaningful, real-life experiences of students. Students become engaged by the discovery of puzzling phenomenon contradicting their schema. With the objective to help make sense of the puzzling phenomenon, the student-led investigation becomes a meaningful experience.

The teacher's primary role is to guide students towards learning and achievement. Assessment of any successful classroom centers on these two outcomes. I believe that rather than explaining to your students how classroom content connects to their lives, they should *experience* that connection. Don't explain how content might affect them. Rather, affect them. Don't talk about how it will impact them. Instead, impact them. Don't explain content is meaningful. Establish experiences that promotes meaningfulness. *Attack* their knowledge, understanding, or belief system about the world they live in, the world they believe in, the world they've built.

Meaningfulness plays one of the most critical roles in student achievement. It plays a key role towards the influence of student engagement and learning outcomes. What I find to be so intriguing about this idea, is that meaningfulness occurs within an individual, but generates from ones surroundings. Think about that. Individual meaningfulness can be affected, developed, even scaffolded, by ones surroundings. Such a simple idea, with such a powerful message. If educators understand just how meaningfulness influences student engagement and learning through classroom experience, *and* they have the ability to manipulate the classroom experience, then educators would have a powerful tool. Through meticulous lesson planning, we have the ability to construct experiences that can be meaningful, and ultimately influence student engagement and rewarding learning.

EDUCATOR'S ROLE

As educators, it is critical to develop well-structured content that has the greatest potential to lead to positive learning outcomes. The educator's role is a critical feature of the Phenomena-Driven Inquiry and the POQIE model, influencing and guiding those learning outcomes at each phase. The objective throughout is to guide students towards the richest, most valuable learning experiences as they co-construct an explanation for the phenomenon under study and connect it to a scientific concept. Along the way, student's knowledge, ideas and scientific skills are continuously monitored to inform instruction and target conceptual change.

Every educator is fully aware of the difficulties and challenges that this path presents. One of the most critical is the vast amount of content educators must cover within a school year and the limited time to do so. This is a paramount concern that needs to be addressed through each phase of the model. Although inquiry experiences are not as rigidly structured as traditional lab experiences, this does not mean that students have unlimited time to explore. You do have a curriculum to deliver in the school year. Placing time limits on inquiry investigations establishes a boundary. It also helps to establish the idea of pacing for students as they work through their investigation. With time limits, students realize that expectations do exist in an inquiry classroom. The efficient utilization of classroom time is a priority. We need to remain mindful of it as we lesson plan.

While lesson planning, consider the grouping format, and the number of students per group, that would be most fruitful for the particular classroom experience. Grouping that is structured prior to the lesson contributes to a well-managed classroom. This maximizes learning opportunities by allowing you to focus your attention on student interactions and the investigative process. In addition, grouping indoctrinates students to value collaboration, a skill that should be woven into inquiry lesson plan objectives throughout the school year. Student grouping should also be varied throughout the year, teaching students to work effectively with different personalities and ideas, and to value the thoughts and views of others.

When selecting the discrepant event that you will present, make sure that it maintains a focus on the concept to be studied. This ensures that the research questions and subsequent investigations will maintain a focus on the concept as well. Engage students and draw them in through your language. For example, after presenting the demonstration there will be students who respond "Do that again!" or "Can I try that?" These responses indicate engagement and interest. Follow up with something like "If you don't understand how this happens, and you're curious to know how, we are about to find out! We're about to learn the science behind this (phenomenon)." I have found that students are more apt to "buy-in" and to be more engaged or motivated to learn when the lesson helps to explain a personally puzzling experience.

Sometimes, students will expect or anticipate unexpected events in a demonstration. This can especially happen over time, if students repeatedly observe unexpected outcomes. This is just one reason why demonstrations should not always be discrepant events. In this section we will discuss other reasons as well. Your language can also lead students to expect unnatural outcomes in a demonstration. We certainly may not intentionally structure our language in this manner. But, sometimes the manner in which we introduce the equipment and the demonstration will convey a surprise to come. For example, simply using the words "guess what will happen" can lead students to speculate from ideas that might be frivolous or improbable. We don't want students to view each demonstration as a puzzle, or as a "game" to determine whether they can correctly guess the surprise ending. When this happens, rather than writing their true predictions, they will instead attempt to anticipate the unexpected observation and write that down as their "prediction." They will try to "outsmart" the prediction by guessing the opposite, or most unlikely, outcome than what they actually think will happen. The prediction is not at all aligned with the prediction they would have made had they considered what they think "should" happen. What "should" happen implies a prediction based on experience or current understanding. To avoid this scenario, rephrase the initial question from "what do you think *will* happen?" to "what do you think *should* happen?" or "what *should* happen based on what you know from past personal experience?"

Throughout the lesson, educators should use questioning techniques that guide students to consider their classroom experiences through the lens of personal experience. When following predictions in the first phase and observations in the second phase, questions can personally and intimately engage students. For example, consider the Drops on a Penny lesson included in this book. A student might remark that the drops remind him of droplets on the walls of a shower, or rain on a car. This is a prime opportunity for valuable discourse. The remark should not be simply acknowledged and passed over. In fact, the follow-up should not really even be an assertive echo to the class. Restating the remark to ensure that all students hear and understand it is certainly an educationally sound idea. However, if the follow-up included the question "How many of you have ever experienced what Johnny is talking about?" Students are now drawn into the conversation as they consider each of their own past personal experiences. The classroom discussion becomes personally engaging, provoking mental stimulation. In the discrepant event experience, the observations captivate through visceral intrigue and the questions engage through deep introspect. The sharing of both observations and prior experiences in class discussion creates a leveling effect. Each student enters the classroom and approaches their classroom experiences with varying background experiences. When individual past personal experiences and recollections are shared, each student considers their own schema, and can build upon it through collective, indirect experience.

The teacher is provided a tremendous diagnostic opportunity as students attempt to explain their observations of the demonstration. Through their use of scientific vocabulary and concepts, students reveal their level of understanding and background knowledge, as well as any misconceptions they may harbor. This is a formative assessment technique that helps the teacher guide the direction of the lesson, especially discourse that follows investigation, where these misconceptions can be revisited. We need to listen carefully for misconceptions. Rather than a hindrance to the lesson, or to learning in the classroom, they become an asset. As misconceptions are identified, the teacher can address them and help students make sense of their observations. But as they form explanations of the demonstration, and later the findings from their investigations, students directly face these misconceptions. This is a valuable experience. I have observed students challenge their own ideas of how the world works by testing those ideas through their self-designed investigations. Here, misconceptions become powerful tools as students directly test their beliefs. Learning situations are established when we design experiences that cause students to personally confront misconceptions.

One of the most valuable aspects of the POQIE model is the development of research questions that arise from genuine curiosity. When students are "jolted" by a surprising phenomenon that runs contrary to their belief system, questions are a natural result. They have no difficulty coming up with a question. When developing their research questions, one of the teacher's main roles is to guide students towards those investigative directions that might prove most fruitful. As we have already discussed in this chapter, this is accomplished through discourse, by addressing the characteristics that make one research question richer and potentially more rewarding than another. The process is a collaborative one, ultimately student-driven, but closely monitored and guided by the teacher. As mentioned earlier, students become gradually more proficient at the development of research questions with time and repeated practice. Students should become informed and adept at identifying research questions that have a high level of investigative rigor. But, the teacher must remain mindful that the chosen research questions remain aligned with the learning objectives and standards for that particular unit. Ultimately, the educator's main objective is to guide students towards the development of richer, more focused questions that are more amenable to rigorous investigation, while ensuring that the student's interest remains embedded in the question.

Prior to the lesson, it is important to decide whether you want students to investigate the same variable, or a different one. This will depend on the objective, available time, and resources. The objective might be to focus on one particular aspect of a concept or phenomenon. In that case, it might prove more rewarding for students to conduct the same investigation and compare results and findings. If, however, the objective is to learn about the many characteristics of a particular concept, or to explore the NGSS Cross-Cutting Concepts, it would be more rewarding for students to investigate different variables and synthesize results.

When groups conduct varied experiments on the same concept it can contribute to an experience and appreciation for the capacities and benefits of authentic science. When results differ, students realize the need for repetitive investigation. They also come to understand how to examine and evaluate the procedure used. When results, findings and conclusions are similar, students begin to understand the power that this validation adds toward the support of their own arguments and findings. They also begin to realize the weakness of an argument which only has one study, or trial, to support it. Students also begin to realize the need for multiple trials, as they provide evidence that the results of one trial did not occur by chance, or might be skewed by error. Multiple trials can also reveal patterns, observable only through repetitive, investigative duplicity. Classroom experiences should help students realize the significance of patterns in scientific investigation and endeavor. The connections made between seemingly unrelated patterns can oftentimes lead to scientific breakthroughs and discoveries. Once again, patterns are an important feature of the NGSS Cross-Cutting Concepts. The identification of patterns can also lead to further questions and investigations. In science, patterns help us to see relationships between actions, ideas, and concepts. These relationships help to strengthen, develop, and reinforce our understanding of our world- and it begins with patterns.

Teacher-guided discourse is one of the most critical aspects of the POQIE model. One of the teacher's primary roles as facilitator during class discussion is to synthesize group findings; to guide students towards emerging patterns and connections. This requires an alertness for opportunities where connections can be made. As students communicate their findings and observations it presents an opportunity to discuss how the findings from each of the diverse investigations are connected. Relationships between various investigations will be revealed. The teacher needs to listen carefully as thoughts and reasoning develop. She listens for useful comments which can be built upon, as well as for any gaps or misconceptions. She introduces any ideas that can provide additional support, or fill in any gaps, towards the construction of the concept. And she asks questions intended to elicit and clarify ideas. The discussion should be explicit and reflective in nature.

As the discussion unfolds, the teacher guides the class, through prompts, questions, and comments intended to illustrate and identify patterns and relationships among the collective data. Together, the class begins to identify and organize what might at first appear to be seemingly disparate observations and findings into a collective, meaningful picture of the concept being studied. One of the most difficult behaviors for teachers assuming the role of facilitator in class discussions is to refrain from validating responses or providing answers. It requires a bit of time, patience, and self-monitoring for teachers to essentially become part of the conversation in this way.

One strategy that can be employed is for the teacher to listen for any keywords that might surface as students share their findings, explanations, and conclusions. These keywords are written on the board as they emerge from discussion. When the opportunity presents itself, either as a formative strategy through the class discussion, or as a summative strategy following the class discussion, these words are combined and used as a class activity to compose a final explanation, definition, or theory for the concept.

Connections can be made within individual investigations, as well as between different investigations. It is also critical that the teacher explicitly make strong connections between the phenomena observed during those investigations and the scientific concept at the focus of the lesson. Connections can also be made to familiar phenomena that lie outside the boundary of the investigations conducted in the classroom, extending classroom experiences to real-world situations. Learning evolves from connections. It is not an isolated event. When our classroom is structured to allow for connections to be made, students are immersed in potentially fruitful learning opportunities.

These objectives should be clear to students at the outset of their investigative work. Students should understand that the work in which they are about to embark is expected to be shared and that each of these contributions will help the entire class to form a more thorough understanding of the concept and the world around us. From my experience, I've found that when students understand this message, a sense of self-value is built that generates increased individual rigor, focus, and value to the investigative work. Students view their personal lab experience as significant and valuable towards a collaborative understanding for the concept.

Assessment of student practices and knowledge should also be of consideration here. We must address how our students apply scientific knowledge and skills in order to makes sense of phenomena, explain observations, develop connections, and further their understanding of concepts. Assessment can include teacher observation, teacher-student discussion, worksheets, student journals, and student portfolios. Journals and portfolios, in particular, present flexible opportunities for students to demonstrate their understanding of the material. These assessment tools provide wonderful methods to complement and balance the more traditional types of assessments. Evaluative questions can include, but certainly are not limited to:

> Are student thorough and accurate in their representation of the phenomenon or concept?

> What is the level of strength of their argument?

> Are students respectful to the ideas of others?

> Are students assuming shared responsibility for the work within their group?

We had previously spoken about the time constraints that teachers face. Another way to address this issue is for teachers to develop a system of materials management. This includes the planning, organization, and distribution of materials and equipment. This type of classroom management should be addressed *prior* to the start of the lesson- not *during* the lesson. Each investigative experience might involve a number of different pieces of equipment, acting as variables to be studied. Organization of these materials will allow you to maintain greater focus on students, rather than a scattered assortment of materials. One idea is to keep small plastic boxes in which you have organized and labeled various types of materials and resources. Students would be responsible to put their materials back into the appropriate boxes at the end of their investigation. A representative from each group could also be designated with this responsibility. The initial creation of these boxes is truly the most difficult task. Once the boxes are assembled, they are just pulled out and reused from year to year.

You might think that if discrepant event demonstrations can be powerfully effective learning tools, they should be used often in the classroom. However, I would not agree with this idea. As I spoke of earlier, with repetitive use, the pattern of unexpected phenomena becomes a recognizable one by students. Subsequently, legitimate surprises become presumptive anticipations. If everything you present to students ends in an unexpected outcome, eventual expectation replaces desired surprise. In my experience, when this occurs I've found that students become entirely focused on "guessing" the correct outcome to the demonstration. It becomes a game. Students simply speculate every possible surprise outcome, no matter how ridiculous it may seem. In fact, they sometimes try to see who can imagine the most bizarre prediction. As a result, the demonstration not only loses its impact, it loses its entire purpose for student learning. It may be true that students are engaged, but not in the way that you want them to be. With overuse, students will eventually begin to randomly guess the outcome without any critical thinking or introspect to their own personal experiences or beliefs. Throughout any curriculum, only some of the demonstrations should be non-discrepant events.

In addition, you might discover a number of discrepant event demonstrations that you think are very exciting, or very "cool." due to their visually striking phenomenon. Resist the temptation to be self-indulgent. As I mentioned earlier, we should all be including these types of demonstrations in our curriculum. But, when presented in the POQIE model through Phenomena-Driven Inquiry, demonstrations should not be presented simply for their "WOW" factor, or because you find them interesting as a science teacher. The demonstrations you present need to be selected very meticulously. The fact that you like a particular demonstration is certainly not reason enough to incorporate it into your curriculum. Each demonstration you present should meet certain criteria that we've already discussed. They should relate directly to your curriculum. Their incorporation into a lesson plan should have a specific purpose and objective. That means they should have very specific learning goals and should address very specific standards. And, of course, they should excite through schematic discrepancy. Present only those that most directly meet these objectives.

Educators thoroughly enjoy the discipline that they teach. They find so much of it exciting. This is part of what makes us effective teachers and our teaching so rewarding to our students. This is also why it is so difficult to adhere to this policy. Limiting our curriculum to only the most valuable components and not over indulging is one of the most difficult rules to follow. But, if you really consider your students learning experiences, you will agree that limitations are not only wise, they are a necessity. This is an approach that demands discipline, but is necessary to effective teaching and learning.

You may discover a number of discrepant events addressing the same scientific concept that you might consider to be effective and rewarding compliments to your curriculum. Rather than presenting more than one discrepant event for a single concept, compile a list and cycle through them each year. Incorporating more than one discrepant event demonstration that addresses the same scientific concept does not mean that your students will learn the concept deeper. In this case, more is not necessarily better. In fact, cycling through different demonstrations each year provides a fresh perspective that makes the presentation even more exciting for you, resulting in a more exciting and engaging experience for your students. When you present something that is new, exciting, and different to you, students perceive this. It affects the dynamic of the classroom, the emotions that are evoked within that experience, and ultimately the learning that occurs.

As the class engages in discourse, one of the primary roles of the teacher is to guide the collective discussion towards the development and ultimate formation of conceptual constructs. Throughout each phase of the POQIE model, student observations, findings, explanations, and arguments are synthesized and scaffolded toward a more sophisticated understanding of the concept. It becomes the teacher's responsibility to accomplish this task while ensuring that the explanations and arguments remain logical in light of the investigative observations and findings. Through questioning, the direction of discourse is navigated towards, and maintains a path on, the focus of the lesson. Above all, the teacher's primary role in Phenomena-Driven Inquiry is to guide and direct the synthesis of findings, explanations, and arguments towards the development and eventual formation of science concepts and principles.

PART 2 -

THE LESSONS

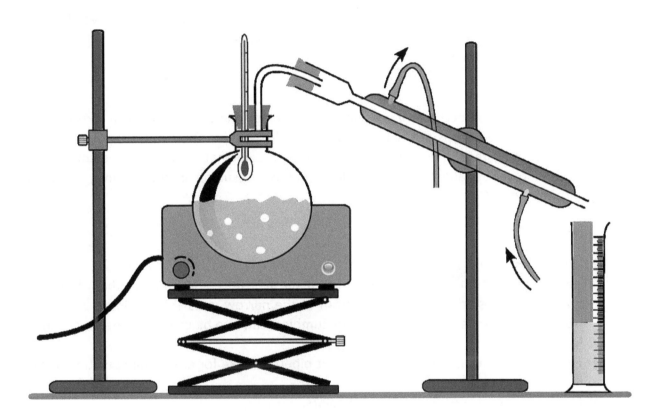

A Twist in Time

<u>Concepts Illustrated:</u> Fluid dynamics, viscosity, miscibility, properties of liquids, properties of mixtures, physical changes, volume, process of dissolving, solutions, homogeneous and heterogeneous solutions, solute, solvent, solubility, turbulent flow, laminar flow, global weather patterns, ocean currents, atmosphere of distant planets, vascular system of the human body.

This demonstration illustrates a phenomenon that looks like magic! Students will have difficulty believing it happened- even while watching it! It must be seen to be fully appreciated. It's truly an astonishing phenomenon!

<u>Paradox:</u>

Three different colors of food coloring are individually blotted into a glass of corn syrup. These three separate colored drops are mixed and smeared together. Their original colors are no longer observable. Instead, the mixture appears to be a combination of the three colors. Yet, the process is reversed and the mixed colors "unmix," resulting in the original, distinctly separate colored drops!

<u>Equipment:</u>

1) Wide glass. It must be cylindrical.
2) Narrow glass. It must also be cylindrical. It must fit into, and be taller than, the wide glass. When nested together the bottom of the narrow glass should almost reach the bottom of the wide one. Note that glass tumblers can also be used, but one must still fit into the other.
3) Pipettes. Drinking straws can be used, but pipettes make for easier manipulation of the liquid drops.
4) Food coloring- at least three different colors.
5) Corn syrup or clear liquid hand soap.
6) Four large binder clips. The size of these clips will depend on the size of the glasses used. Smaller clips can be used when using shorter glass tumblers.
7) Three small cups. Medicine cups work well.
8) Water.

<u>Preparation:</u>

It is not necessary, but if you are able to shine a light from either behind or underneath the glasses, the phenomenon is more visible and astonishing.

The setup

Birds-eye view

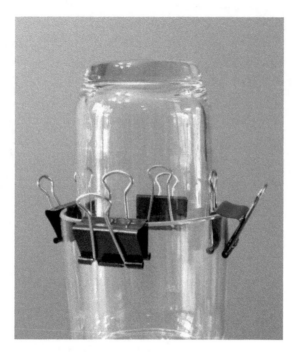

A close-up view

<u>Preparation</u>:

It is not necessary, but if you are able to shine a light from either behind or underneath the glasses, the phenomenon is more visible and astonishing.

<u>The Lesson</u>:

The demonstration will be explained using corn syrup. However, if it is not available, you can substitute clear liquid hand soap in its place.

Show the wide glass and fill about half of the glass with corn syrup. Now gently lower the narrow glass into the corn syrup. Lower this glass in slowly to avoid the formation of air bubbles. When fully nested, the corn syrup should rise to fill about ¾ of the wide glass. Fill the inner glass with water, to almost the top of the wide glass. This serves to hold the narrow glass in place by adding mass and preventing it from being buoyant. Fasten three of the large binder clips to the rim of the wide glass. Imagining the face of a clock, position the clips at 12, 3, and 6 o'clock. The fourth clip will soon be added to the 9 o'clock position. The "handles" of these clips will press against the inner, narrow glass. They serve to hold the narrow glass firmly in place, and centered inside the wider glass.

Add a small amount of corn syrup to each of the three medicine cups. Add a few drops of food coloring to each of the cups. Any colors can be used, but each cup must be a different color. Using the pipettes, stir the syrup to mix the food coloring thoroughly. Use a different pipette for each color, so the colors do not mix.

Now, using a pipette, draw some of the colored syrup from one of the cups. Try to remove air bubbles. Carefully lower the pipette into the corn syrup between the two nested glasses, at the location of the missing fourth binder clip. Squirt some of the colored syrup into the clear corn syrup, leaving a large, single, blot or drop of the color. This drop of color will remain in place. Do not tip the inner glass when doing this. Repeat this step with the other two colored liquids. Place the drops of color side by side. They should not be touching one another and should not mix. They should be clearly seen as three differently colored, indistinct drops. Add the fourth binder clip to the 9 o'clock position on the rim of the wide glass.

Now ask students to predict what will happen to the three colored drops when you twist the inner glass in one direction, and then the other. It is important that the prediction be approached in this manner. You do not want to ask students to make two separate predictions. Once they see the colors mix on the first twist, asking them to predict what will happen when twisted in the opposite direction will most likely "tip off" some students that something different than the first outcome will occur. Rather than breaking the sequence of events into two actions, address it as one. "What will happen to these three colored drops when I twist the inner glass, spinning it in one direction, and then the other?"

Once they have made their predictions, slowly rotate the inner glass in a clockwise direction. Keep the glasses as concentric as possible, without tipping them. Be careful that you do not cover the colors with your fingers as you do this. Students will notice that the colors will begin to mix and smear together, dragging along in the liquid as you rotate the glass. If you spin the glass enough, the colors will almost "disappear" from view as they dissipate within the corn syrup. You can spin the glass almost one full rotation. Stop and ask students if that is the outcome they predicted. Now act as if you suddenly remembered, if no one else does, that you said you were going to spin the glass in one direction, and then the other. You still need to spin in the opposite direction. Holding the outer glass in place, rotate the inner glass in a counter-clockwise direction. The colors "unmix" returning to their original conditions! Each individual color is back as a separate drop, side by side! This looks so much like a magic trick that you will have to assure students it is a natural phenomenon and not tricked in any way! The only way to prove it to themselves is to DO IT for themselves- and they are about to!

Possible Variables:

1. Different liquids other than corn syrup or hand soap. This can involve other viscous fluids, such as honey, vegetable oil, etc., or fluids with little to no viscosity. This can also involve different brands of corn syrup or vegetable oil.
2. Different liquids that the food coloring is mixed into. This can also involve the same viscosity or density between the colored liquid and that which fills the glass. It can also involve an investigation with a different density for each of those liquids. Additionally, it could involve each ink colored liquid having the same density, or each with a different density. Different densities can be achieved by adding salt or sugar to water. The food coloring can even be mixed with plain water.
3. Reversing the clear and color liquids used. This means adding food coloring to the corn syrup that fills the space between the glasses, while keeping the liquid added with the pipette clear.
4. The degree of rotation in each of the two spins of the inner glass. For example, the second spin can pass the original starting point.

5. The volume of colored drops.
6. The placement of the colored drops.
7. Pipetting "lines" of food coloring, or any other shape, rather than "drops."
8. The speed that the inner glass is rotated.
9. Different brands of soap that the ink is mixed with.
10. Different brands of soap that the glass is filled with.
11. Different brand of food coloring.
12. Using the food coloring directly, without mixing it with any other liquid.

Phenomenon Explained:

This amazing demonstration appears as though you are turning back the hands of time. We know from experience that color mixing is not a reversible process. Mix blue and yellow and it will produce green. Separating colors mixed from dye or food coloring is not a process we are familiar with.

A solution is one in which a solute is dissolve in a solvent. The solute is the substance being dissolved and the solvent is the substance in which the solute is dissolved. Water is called the universal solvent because it is capable of dissolving more solutes than any other liquid. Solubility is the ability of a solute to dissolve in a solvent.

Miscibility refers to the inability of two substances, typically two liquids, to mix and form a homogeneous solution. A solution that is homogeneous is the same throughout. When blended together, immiscible liquids will eventually separate into layers. An example would be oil and water.

To understand the apparent mixing and unmixing of colors observed in this demonstration, we must understand two principles of fluid dynamics, namely laminar flow and turbulent flow. Laminar flow occurs when a fluid, either gas or liquid, flows in parallel layers with no disruption between those layers. In laminar flow, the fluid flows in a well-defined, orderly manner, with rather distinct paths. On the other hand, turbulent flow describes random, chaotic flow. There is no order in turbulent flow. Instead, the fluid undergoes irregular fluctuations. Turbulent flow can be observed in streams used for whitewater rafting, where the water moves in random and erratic directions. Consider laminar flow as the opposite of turbulent flow.

We actually observe laminar flow in many facets of our lives. One example is blood flow through capillaries. Each particle in the fluid flows in a smooth path, never interfering with one another. As a result, the velocity of the fluid is constant at any point in the flow. Another example can be seen when a candle flame is extinguished. The smoke that rises straight up from the wick is in laminar flow. But, as it reaches some distance from the wick it begins to spread out, waver, and even curl around. This is turbulent flow. It is rather difficult, if not impossible, to predict the behavior of turbulent flow. Turbulent flow can be the cause of murmurs in the heart and larger arteries. Recent research on turbulent flow continues to provide new insights into global weather patterns, as well as the atmosphere of distant planets.

The smearing effect produced by the first rotation of the inner glass, is in fact different parallel layers of the viscous corn syrup. The colors actually do not mix, instead remaining in their own layers. Rather than mixing, the colored drops essentially "stretch out" or "elongate." Although they appear to be mixed, the smeared colors are actually separate streams of color layered around one another. The process is able to be reversed because there is no fluid turbulence in the laminar flow. When the glass is spun the second time, in reverse, the colored stretched out streams are essentially "compressed" to their original condition.

Viscosity is defined as a fluid's resistance to flow. Think of it as the "thickness" of a fluid. Fluids such as honey, molasses, and engine oil are highly viscous. The high viscosity of corn syrup and liquid hand soap allow for a high degree of laminar flow. Don't wait too long between the two rotations of the inner glass. After some time, diffusion might interfere with the outcome.

Standards Alignment:
Next Generation Science Standards (NGSS, Lead States 2013)

Disciplinary Core Ideas in Physical Science

PS1: Matter and Its Interactions

PS1.A: Structure and Properties of Matter

PS1.B: Chemical Reactions

Disciplinary Core Ideas in Life Science

LS1: From Molecules to Organisms: Structures and Processes

LS1.A: Structure and Function

Disciplinary Core Ideas in Earth and Space Science

ESS2: Earth's Systems

ESS2.C: The Roles of Water in Earth's Surface Processes

ESS2.D: Weather and Climate

Abandoning Gravity

Concepts Illustrated: Center of gravity, center of mass, inclined planes, gravity, normal force, mass.

This commonly known demonstration is presented here in a unique manner that begins by allowing students to gain confidence in their expectations, only to have them sharply contradicted a few moments later. In addition to the unique presentation, note the slight variation of equipment, which builds upon student expectation and adds to the contradictory outcome.

Paradox:

A series of objects are rolled down an inclined plane. Students observe the distance these objects travel from the plane. The distance is noted for common cylinders made of wood and metal, a cylinder with a disk on each end, and a bow-tie shaped object. But, no one expects what happens next when a double-cone shaped object seems to defy both expectation and gravity as it rolls UP the incline plane!

Equipment:
Details on the construction of the following objects can be found in the Preparation section below.

1. An inclined plane, created by a V-shaped track.
2. One or two cylinders, each with a length that allows it to travel on the inclined plane. Only one cylinder is necessary. The second is optional. This will be explained in the sections that follow.
3. A bow-tie shaped object.
4. A cylinder with a disk on each end.
5. A double-cone shaped object.

Preparation:

The inclined plane can be made of wood, Styrofoam, or even very sturdy cardboard. The track diverges from its lowest point to a distance typically about 10cm wide. However, this will vary depending on the size of the double cone used. The width at the top of the plane should be equal to the length of the double-cone, without the cone falling through. Another simple method of construction involves two meter sticks and a pegboard. Lay the meter sticks on their edge and place them side by side. Tape them together at one end. Spread the opposite ends apart and butt them up against the pegboard. Lift them up about 1.5cm from the bottom of the pegboard and press a thumbtack through the holes of the pegboard and into the ends of the meter sticks. The exact width of the meter sticks will need to be determined by trial and error, depending on the size of the double-cone you use.

As detailed in the Equipment section, you will need at least one cylinder. It should be made of wood. This cylinder, or dowel, can be easily modified to have a disk on each end. Do this by attaching the disks to each end of the cylinder, or dowel, using thumbtacks. These disks can easily be as simple as circles cut-out of think construction paper, or as sophisticated as disks cut out of very thin wood with a hole in the center to accommodate the thumbtack.

The second cylinder, made of metal, allows students to observe the different outcomes when two different substances, with two different masses, are used. However, this cylinder is optional. The demonstration can still proceed if resources are limited and you only have the wooden dowel. If you do add this cylinder to your demonstration, be sure that its mass allows it to travel a bit once it leaves the plane. You don't want it to abruptly stop abruptly due to its mass.

The bow-tie shaped object can be constructed a number of ways. The first way to make it is from two wooden cones. They can easily be found at local craft stores. Cut the tips of the cones off. These need to be straight cuts. Your tech department will most likely be able to help with this. Then, connect those cut ends together with either hot glue or Super Glue. The second way to construct this object is by using Styrofoam. These can also easily be found at local craft stores. Using a utility knife, cut the tips off and glue them together. The final method of construction involves two funnels. They should have relatively short stems. Place the stems facing each other. They can be connected by either using hot glue, Super Glue, or tape. Before connecting, be sure that the object is wide enough to travel down the plane.

The double-cone object can be made in the same manner as the bow-tie object, from either wood cones, funnels, or Styrofoam. The tip of the cones, or the stems of the funnels, face away from each other. The wide end of the cones, or the rim of the funnels, are connected in the same manner as the bow-tie object.

Using either paint or tape, mark two points on the plane that signify the points from which objects are released. This ensures that the objects are released from the same point in every trial. The marks should be made on the side of the arm that is facing students, so that they can clearly see that the release point is the same for every trial.

<u>The Lesson:</u>

Show the inclined plane to the students. Be sure to hold it up so they can see the entire design. Be certain to point out the angle of the plane as it sits on the table. Explain that there will be a series of predictions during this demonstration.

Show the cylinder made of metal. Ask students to predict the distance that the cylinder will travel when released from the highest point on the plane. Once they have made their predictions, place the cylinder atop the highest point possible on the plane and release it. When it comes to a stop, measure the distance from the end of the plane. Now explain that you will once again place the cylinder on the plane, but this time you will place it about ¾ of the way down the plane. This will be the cylinders new starting point. Using the previous observation and measurement, ask students to predict how far the cylinder will travel from this new point. Place the cylinder about ¾ down the plane, very close to the end of it. Release the cylinder and record its distance.

At this point, if you have a second cylinder made of wood, execute the same steps you conducted with the metal cylinder. Students would predict the distance traveled when the wood cylinder, or dowel, is released from the same two points on the plane. Be sure to release from the lowest point first. Students would be told the substance each object is made of prior to releasing it down the plane. The idea here is that students are comparing the two cylinders, each with a different mass. If you only have a metal cylinder, move on to the next step.

Next, attach a disk to each end of the wood cylinder. Explain that these disks will act as "wheels". Whereas the previous cylinder rolled directly onto the table from the plane, this cylinder will be rolling on its "wheels". Will the distance it travels change because the cylinder is no longer in direct contact with the table? Ask students to predict the distance it will travel. Then roll this dowel down the plane. It should be released from the lowest point on the plane first. The significance of this will soon become clear.

By now, students believe two things. The first is that the objective of the demonstration is to measure the distance traveled by different objects from different points on the plane. The second is to recognize that different objects will travel different distances from the plane.

Continue the demonstration by introducing the bow-tie shaped object and clearly showing its shape, and how it differs from the previous cylinders. Explain that the idea is to now examine how far differently shaped objects might travel when released down the plane. Ask students to predict the distance travelled by this new shape. Then roll it down the plane twice, again releasing it from the lowest point first. The reason for this will become apparent in the next step.

Now introduce the double-cone shaped object and explain that it will also be released from the two points on the plane. As in the previous trials, ask students to predict the distance travelled from the lowest point first. It is important that the object is released from the lowest point first because you want it to travel the farthest distance possible UP the plane. If it were released from the highest point, it would only fall back into the grooves on the arms of the plane. The greatest shock is achieved when the object travels the farthest distance, seemingly against gravity. Since each previous trial began with the lowest point, this will not stand out as different from any other part of the demonstration. Place the object at the lowest point on the plane and release it, as though you too are expecting it to roll down as the other objects did. The actual behavior creates quite a stir. Students are amazed when this object not only behaves quite differently from the others, but also appears to defy our laws of nature- travelling UP the inclined plane!

This is the behavior that is studied in the student-led investigations that follow.

Possible Variables:

1. The size of the double-cones. There are many different sizes, made of Styrofoam, which can be found at local craft stores.
2. The mass of the double-cone. To do this, students would add sand to the funnels and connect them with wide tape. The mass can be changed by the amount of sand added. The stems would need to be plugged with clay or putty.
3. The angle of the cones. Styrofoam cones of varying angles and lengths can easily be found at local craft stores.
4. The distance between the two arms of the inclined plane.
5. The pitch of the inclined plane.

Phenomenon Explained:

The center of mass is defined as the point in an object about which it's entire mass is equally distributed. The center of gravity refers to that point of an object about which there is a balance in the forces of gravity. When an object falls, its direction is related to the path of its center of mass, or center of gravity. Although the double-cone appears to defy gravity, it is actually not rolling uphill. In fact, the apparatus allows the center of mass to roll downhill. Unbalanced forces can cause objects to travel down angled surfaces, called inclined planes.

The force of gravity acts to bring the object towards a horizontal surface. The normal force acts in a direction perpendicular to the surface an object is upon. When we stand on the ground, the normal force acts in a direction opposite that of gravity. When an object is on an inclined plane, the normal force acts perpendicular to its angled surface. The normal force is always perpendicular to the surface the object is on.

The contact point on the ramp and the double-cone changes from the center of the cone to the outer edges due to the increasing width of the two tracks on the plane. The center of gravity of the double-cone lies along its central axis and in the middle of the cone. The axis of rotation passes through this center of gravity. The center of gravity of the cones at the bottom of the plane is higher than at the widest point of the plane. Since the plane widens, the center of gravity of the cone drops. The cone is, in fact, rolling downhill. You can see in the diagram below that the height of the center of gravity measured above the table when the cone is at the bottom of the plane is higher than when measured at its position when at the top of the plane. The center of gravity is lower when the cone is at the top of the ramp. The center of gravity has actually moved "downhill".

The double cone and plane

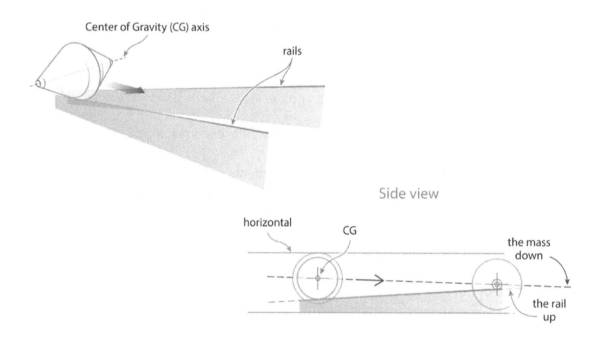

98

Standards Alignment:

Next Generation Science Standards (NGSS, Lead States 2013)

Disciplinary Core Ideas in Physical Science

PS2: Motion and Stability: Forces and Interactions

PS2.A: Forces and Motion

PS2.B: Types of Interactions

PS3: Energy

PS3.A: Definitions of Energy

PS3.B: Conservation of Energy and Energy Transfer

Acceleration Anomaly

<u>Concepts Illustrated:</u> Acceleration, velocity, Newton's first law of motion- the law of inertia, fluid dynamics, volume, density.

<u>Paradox:</u>

Students will be surprised to find that a ball *floating* in liquid and a ball *hanging* in liquid react differently to the same applied movement.

<u>Equipment:</u>

1. Two balls of equal volume. One ball (light) with a density less than that of water (1.0 g/ml) and one ball (heavy) with a density greater than water.
2. String, thread, or fishing line.
3. Either two standard Mason jars or two Polycarbonate Screw Cap Storage Bottle. If you use Mason jars, they must have lids. If Polycarbonate bottles are used, they should be 1000ml.

<u>Preparation:</u>

Let's assume you're using Polycarbonate bottles. Fill the bottles with water. Next, using a hot glue gun, attach the string or fishing line onto the lid of one bottle and the base of the other. Now, attach the less dense ball to the opposite end of the string that is connected to the base of the jar. Attach the denser ball to the opposite end of the string that is connected to the lid. Screw the lids onto the bottles. Both bottle should remain upright. In one bottle, the ball will **float** freely, anchored to the base. In the other bottle, the ball will **hang** freely, anchored to the lid.

Golf ball hangs in water

100

Ping-pong ball floats in water.

The Lesson:

Display both bottles to the students. The bottles should be sitting motionless on a table or desk. Explain the setup to them. They should understand that the bottles are filled with water and that the ball hanging in its jar is heavier than the lighter ball floating freely in its own jar. Now, ask students to predict how the balls will behave when the bottles are pushed to the left. Students can be prompted to recall any similar experiences they may have had, such as the way their own bodies react in a car that accelerates when a traffic light changes from red to green. Most will recall that if the car moves forward, their bodies are pushed backwards, into the seat. Virtually all students will predict that if the bottles are moved to the left, the balls will move to the right. Once students have made their predictions, move the bottles to the left, sliding them along the table. Students will observe that the **hanging** ball will move to the right, as expected. But, they will also observe the **floating** ball actually moves to the left- in the same direction in which it is being moved! The bottles can now be moved to the right to show that the balls behave in the same manner. The hanging ball will now move to the left. But, the floating ball will move to the right! The **hanging ball** will always move in the **opposite direction** as the motion of the jar, but the **floating ball** will always move in the **same direction** as the motion of the jar!

❖ The two bottles can also be placed on the same skateboard, which is pushed along the table top.

Possible Variables:

1. The length of the string.
2. Filling the bottles with a liquid that has a density other than water (1.0 g/ml).
3. Replacing the balls with objects of different shapes.
4. The viscosity of the liquid used.
5. The volume of liquid used.
6. Using balls of different diameters, other than that shown in the demonstration. Students might use the same diameters (different than shown in the demonstration) in both bottles, or they might mix and match diameters between the bottles. For example, they might try using larger and smaller diameter balls in each bottle.
7. Using a vessel of different shape. For example, if the demonstration is conducted using Polycarbonate bottles, students might want to investigate using Mason jars, or vice versa.
8. Using vessels of different volumes. For example, if the demonstration is conducted using 100ml Polycarbonate bottles, students might want to investigate using 500ml or 250ml bottles.
9. Replacing the balls with those made of different substances, having different densities. For example, they might want to use two lead, aluminum, brass, or tin balls in the bottles. Or, they may want to mix and match these balls of differing substances in each of the bottles. They may even want to investigate how these balls of differing densities behaves in bottles of differing volumes or shapes.
10. Consider how the class discussion can be strengthened by having one group investigate the balls of differing densities in the same volume or shape vessel, and another group investigating balls of differing densities in vessels of different volumes or shapes. You might think that even if there were no difference in the behavior observed between these two investigations, it might not be a valuable use of time. However, even a result of this nature reveals much, contributes to the class discussion, and strengthens an understanding for the nature of the phenomena.
11. In place of the balls, students might consider using a plastic vial that can be filled with liquid of varying densities, to investigate how these objects react in water. They can also investigate the behavior of the vial filled with liquids of varying densities when the jar is also filled with liquids of varying densities. Students could also use ping-pong balls that they fill with liquids by poking a hole on either end of the ball and plugging it with a small bead of putty, clay, or wax after filling.

Phenomenon Explained:

This demonstration illustrates Newton's first law of motion. Known as the law of inertia, it states that an object either at rest or in motion, remains at rest or in motion with the same speed and direction, unless acted upon by an unbalanced force. Inertia describes the property of matter to either maintain a state of rest or its velocity along a straight path, unless acted upon by an external force. The demonstration also serves to illustrate the principle of acceleration, defined as the rate at which an object changes its velocity. The rate at which an object travels from one place to another is known as its velocity.

As the bottles in this demonstration are moved, and experience acceleration, the lighter ball will always move in the same direction of motion, while the heavier ball will always move in the opposite direction of motion. If the jar is moved to the left, the inertia of the water moving to the right produces a slightly higher water pressure on the right of the lighter ball than on the left. This higher pressure on the right side of the ball pushes the ball to the left. It's essentially a force applied by a pressure. On the other hand, the inertia of the heavy ball causes it to lag. This is the same phenomena that occurs when you are pushed into your seat when the car accelerates forward.

Viscosity is defined as a fluid's resistance to flow. Think of it as the "thickness" of a fluid. Fluids such as honey, molasses, and engine oil are highly viscous. Students might choose to investigate the outcome when liquids of varying viscosities are employed.

Standards Alignment:

Next Generation Science Standards (NGSS, Lead States 2013)

Disciplinary Core Ideas in Physical Science

PS1: Matter and Its Interactions

PS1.A: Structure and Properties of Matter

PS1.B: Chemical Reactions

PS2: Motion and Stability: Forces and Interactions

PS2.A: Forces and Motion

Animated Art

Concepts Illustrated: Solubility, density, cohesion, adhesion, miscibility, properties of liquids, process of dissolving, water as a universal solvent, viscosity, polymers.

Paradox:

When water is poured onto a picture drawn with a dry erase marker, the picture suddenly becomes animated and moves around within the water!

Equipment:

1. A glossy clean surface, such as a pane of glass. A picture frame will work, but a glass dish or bowl can also be used.
2. A white sheet of paper to place behind the glass.
3. A dry erase marker. Any color can be used, but it should be a relatively new marker.
4. Beaker of water.
5. A straw is optional.

Preparation:

Be sure that the glass is clean prior to presenting this demonstration. If you place a white sheet of paper behind the glass, the drawings will be more easily seen.

The preferred method to present this demonstration would be for each student to have their own small glass square, dry erase marker, and small beaker of water. Students will then have these supplies to conduct their investigations. The *Lesson Procedure* will be explained using this method.

The alternative method of presentation is to either present the demonstration on a projector, or have students surround you.

Following the addition of water, the picture floats and becomes animated when blown on.

<u>The Lesson:</u>

Display a picture frame or glass surface. Now show the marker and point out that it is a dry erase marker. Draw a picture of a stickman on the surface of the glass and hold it up for everyone to see. Instruct students to use their marker and draw the same figure on their piece of glass.

Now, explain that they are going to pour enough water onto the stickman to completely cover him in a large "puddle." Ask students to predict what will happen. Most will predict that the ink will dissolve or that the drawing will break apart. Others will predict that the ink will cause the water to turn the same color.

Once the predictions have been shared, ask students to pour the water on their stickman figure. They should not pour directly over the stickman figure. Rather, they should pour to the side of the figure, until he is covered in water. Once a puddle forms, the stickman will loosen from the glass plate, his entire body floating in the puddle! He will begin to wiggle around and move around in the puddle! Instruct students to gently blow on the puddle of water. The stickman will become incredibly animated, moving arms and legs as he "swims" around in the puddle! Students love this!

Note that a straw can be used to blow into the puddle and animate the drawing.

<u>Possible Variables:</u>

1. Liquid other than plain water, such as saltwater, sugar water, water with food coloring, vegetable oil, etc.
2. The density of the liquid.
3. The viscosity of the liquid. This can involve honey, corn syrup, etc.
4. Temperature of the liquid. It can be warmed or chilled.
5. Type of marker.
6. Brand of marker.
7. Replace the marker with a crayon.
8. Using two different colors in the same drawing.
9. The shape and size of the drawing.
10. A drawing with more than one layer of ink.
11. The amount of pressure applied when drawing on the glass.
12. The surface drawn on, such as a plastic Petri dish.

<u>Phenomenon Explained:</u>

Adhesion is the force of attraction between different molecules. An acrylic polymer in permanent ink makes it extremely adhesive to the surface on which it is applied. On the other hand, dry erase marker ink does not adhere strongly to many surfaces, due to an oily silicone polymer ingredient. The ink also contains a release agent, which causes it to be easily wiped off most non-porous substances, such as whiteboards, glass, mirrors, and porcelain. When applied, the release agent settles underneath the ink pigments, forming a layer between the surface and the pigment.

Solubility is the characteristic property of one substance to dissolve in another. It is specifically the ability of a solute to dissolve in a solvent. The solute is the substance being dissolved and the solvent is the substance in which the solute is dissolved. Water is called the universal solvent because it is capable of dissolving more solutes than any other liquid. These distinct pigment/release agent layers arise because the two do not dissolve, or are insoluble, in one another. This is partly due to the oil-based silicone polymer. Oil and water are insoluble, or immiscible. As a result, the pigments do not come in direct contact with non-porous surfaces. This oil-based polymer is also insoluble in water, explaining why the dry erase ink does not dissolve when the water is poured onto it.

Density is another property involved in the success of this demonstration. Objects with a density less than water will float, while those denser than water will sink. The density of water is 1.0g/ml. Dry erase marker ink is less dense than water, explaining why the drawing will lift off the glass surface and float in the puddle of water.

Viscosity is defined as a fluid's resistance to flow. Think of it as the "thickness" of a fluid. Fluids such as honey, molasses, corn syrup, and engine oil are highly viscous. Students might choose to investigate the outcome when liquids of varying viscosities are employed.

The drawing maintains its shape due to the property of cohesion, or the force of attraction between like molecules. Dry erase ink particles exhibit strong cohesion. Because of this, the drawing keeps its shape and moves around in the water when blown on. The drawing will even remain intact when you push it around with your finger. Amazingly, you can actually pick the drawing up and pull it out of the water!

Finally, be aware that ceramic plates or dishes do not work very well. Keep in mind that not all dishes and markers will display this phenomenon. Dry erase marker ink can stain porous surfaces, so do not use any valuable dishes.

Standards Alignment:

Next Generation Science Standards (NGSS, Lead States 2013)

Disciplinary Core Ideas in Physical Science

PS1: Matter and Its Interactions

PS1.A: Structure and Properties of Matter

PS1.B: Chemical Reactions

PS2: Motion and Stability: Forces and Interactions

PS2.B: Types of Interactions

Disciplinary Core Ideas in Earth and Space Science

ESS2: Earth's Systems

ESS2.C: The Roles of Water in Earth's Surface Processes

Appearing Beaker

Concepts Illustrated: Density, reflection, refraction, refractive index, properties of liquids, volume, properties of light.

Paradox:

Students are shown a large beaker filled with a clear golden colored liquid. They are completely startled when a blue liquid is added and a smaller beaker magically appears within the larger beaker!

Equipment:

1. A 4000ml beaker.
2. A smaller beaker that fits inside the 4000ml beaker. A 1000 ml beaker works well, but a 600ml beaker can also be used. This beaker should not have any print on it.
3. A 600ml beaker.
4. Vegetable oil. Wesson oil works very well.
5. Corn syrup. This can also be substituted with honey, molasses, or salt water.
6. Food coloring.
7. A large, plastic funnel.
8. Either a ring stand or a funnel stand.

Preparation:

Set the 1000 ml beaker on the bottom of the 4000ml beaker. Fill the large beaker with between 2500 and 3000 ml of vegetable oil. The 1000 ml beaker will no longer be visible. If you are using a ring stand, the 4000ml beaker sits on it. If not, the funnel stand is nearby. The funnel should be plastic so that the stem is visible when lowered into the vegetable oil.

Fill the 600ml beaker with corn syrup. Add a few drops of food coloring and stir to mix well. The color should sharply contrast that of the vegetable oil. Blue, red or green work well. If molasses is used, no food coloring is necessary. Blue will be used in the explanation below.

The Lesson:

Show the 4000ml beaker and inform students that it is filled with vegetable oil. Then show the 600ml beaker and explain that it is filled with corn syrup colored with food coloring. Explain that you are about to pour the blue corn syrup into the vegetable oil. Further explain that you will use a funnel to do this. Place the funnel over the larger beaker. The stem of the funnel should be positioned directly above the small beaker, the stem entering that beaker. Ask students to predict what will happen when you pour the corn syrup into the vegetable oil. Some will predict that the colors will mix, resulting in a new color. Others will predict that the corn syrup will remain separated from the vegetable oil, either floating above or sinking below it.

Once students have shared their predictions, begin pouring the corn syrup into the funnel. The corn syrup will fill the 1000 ml beaker, causing it to suddenly appear- as if by magic!

Possible Variables:

1. Temperature of the liquids.

2. Using different colored food coloring. This could involve changing the color of the corn syrup so that it is closer to that of the vegetable oil. It could also involve adding food coloring to the vegetable oil.

3. Pouring the corn syrup into Pyrex glassware made of different shapes.

4. Using Pyrex glassware with sizes other than a 4000ml beaker.

5. Using glassware that is not Pyrex, such as plastic.

6. Different liquids including Johnson's baby oil, olive oil, Karo corn syrup, corn oil, saltwater, sugar water, etc.

7. Using differently colored glassware. These could be investigated with the original Wesson oil or they could be investigated with assorted colors of liquids using food coloring.

Phenomenon Explained:

There are a few different concepts illustrated in this demonstration. Let's begin with density. The blue liquid must have a density greater than the vegetable oil. Typically, vegetable oil has a density of between 0.91 and 0.93 g/ml, depending on the brand. Because corn syrup has a density of about 1.4 g/ml, it is a wonderful candidate to be used as the blue liquid. However, some other common liquids that are readily available include honey and molasses, each also having a density of about 1.4 g/ml. You can also mix salt and water to achieve a desired density that is greater than that of vegetable oil. When the corn syrup is poured into the vegetable oil, it sinks and remains in the 1000 ml beaker due to its greater density.

The outcome also relies on refraction. Light travels through space at about 300 million meters per second. Light travels through different mediums at different speeds. Its speed is affected as it travels from one transparent medium through another. When this happens, light can bend. That bend in light is called refraction. When there is a significant difference between the speed of light traveling through two media, there is a greater bend in the light, or a greater refraction.

Refraction is dependent on the medium through which the light passes. The index of refraction, or the refractive index, is a number that describes how light travels through a particular medium. The index of refraction measures the degree to which light bends. The larger the index, the slower the light travels through the medium. The index of refraction, or the refractive index, is a number that describes how light travels through a particular medium. When light travels through two mediums, both of which have the same refractive index, there is neither refraction nor reflection. The object will seem to "vanish". This happens to be the case with both Pyrex and Wesson oil. Both have a refractive index of 1.474. As a result, there is no refraction or reflection of the smaller Pyrex beaker when submersed in the oil filled larger Pyrex beaker, and the smaller beaker "vanishes". This explains why the smaller beaker is not visible in the oil at the beginning of the demonstration.

The blue-colored corn syrup has a much different refractive index than the vegetable oil. As a result, the corn syrup remains visible when poured into the vegetable oil.

If you happen to see a faint outline or "ghostly" image of the glassware immersed in the oil, it's due to internal strains within the glass which influences the refractive index.

Interestingly, the index of refraction changes with a change in temperature. If students investigate temperature as a variable, they would most likely notice that the visibility of the submerged test tube can be manipulated. In fact, if the beaker containing the oil and the submerged test tube was gradually heated on a hot plate, the test tube will gradually become increasingly visible, as if by magic!

Standards Alignment:

Next Generation Science Standards (NGSS, Lead States 2013)

Disciplinary Core Ideas in Physical Science

PS1: Matter and Its Interactions

PS1.A: Structure and Properties of Matter

PS4: Waves and Their Applications in Technologies for Information Transfer

PS4.A: Wave Properties

PS4.B: Electromagnetic Radiation

Archimedes' Paradox

Concepts Illustrated: Archimedes' principle, buoyancy, displacement, properties of liquids, viscosity, mass, volume, density.

Paradox:

Two clear, plastic disposable drinking glasses are shown and one is filled 3/4 to the top with water. Using a marker, a line is drawn on the cup to mark the level of water. Next, 1/3 of the water is poured into the second cup, which is lowered onto the surface of the water in the first cup. Surprisingly, students will find that the water in the first cup rises to its original mark. Now, 2/3 of the water is poured from the second into the first cup, which now contains only 1/3 of its original volume of water. The second cup is once again lowered onto the surface of the water in the first cup. Although most students will predict the water in the first cup to now rise above the original mark, their surprise grows when it rises to the original mark once again! Surprise leads to startled puzzlement when they realize that each time the cups are nested, the water levels in the first and second cups always meet!

Original water level- marked

1/3 water poured into second glass

Water level rises to original mark

| 2/3 water poured into second glass | Water level rises to original mark |

Equipment:

1. Two identical clear, plastic disposable drinking glasses.
2. Water.
3. Food coloring.
4. A marker.

The Lesson:

Inform students that they will be making a series of predictions during this demonstration. Begin by showing the clear glasses and fill one ¾ full of water. Using a non-washable marker, draw a line on the outside of this glass to mark the level of the water.

Show the second glass and explain that you will be setting this empty glass on top of the water in the first. Ask students to make two predictions. The first answers whether the empty glass will float or sink in the water. The second prediction addresses what will happen to the water level in the first glass. The level might rise, lower, or remain the same. Most will predict that the empty glass will float, and that the water level will remain the same. Once they have made their predictions, slowly lower the empty glass onto the surface of the water. Students will be excited to find that their predictions are accurate. The glass will float and the water level will be observed to remain the same.

Now lift the second glass from the water and set it aside. Pour about 1/3 of the original colored liquid into the second glass. Be sure to explain that you have poured about 1/3, so there is about 2/3 remaining in the first cup. There is "more" liquid in the first cup and "less" in the second. The water level in the first glass is now beneath the line drawn on the cup. Now add a few drops of food coloring to the water in each of the glasses. The food coloring will allow the water level to be more readily seen by students. You should specifically use a light color, such as yellow, in the first glass. Use a darker color, such as blue, in the second glass. This will allow the water in the second glass to be easily seen when it is nested into the first, but this should not be discussed with students. Explain that the food coloring is used to more easily observe the water level. Announce that you will once again nest the second glass, with less water, into the first glass, with more water. Ask students to make the same two predictions as before. Will the second glass now float or sink? And, what will happen to the level of the original yellow water? Again, the level might rise, lower, or remain the same. Most will predict that the second glass will still float, because it contains less water than the first glass. Most will also predict that the water level will rise, but will be below the line drawn on the glass. Once they have made their predictions, slowly lower the second glass onto the surface of the water. Students will observe that the glass does float, as most predicted. But the water level in the original glass will rise and stop directly on the line made at the beginning of the demonstration, surprising most. Students might also notice that the levels of water in each of the glasses meet. If so, act surprised as if you did not expect it. This will prevent students from thinking that this is the focus of the demonstration and simply guessing the same outcome in the next step. You don't want students to anticipate this outcome and predict it will happen because they are trying to "outsmart" the demonstration. Student predictions should be genuine. They should not be viewed as a game. If students do not notice that the level of the water in each of the glasses does meet, subtly point that out as if it's something you've not noticed before. By approaching it this way, the observation does not become the focus of the outcome. The water levels should be readily seen because of the colors used.

Next, pour more water from the first glass into the second. You want to end up with about 2/3 in the second glass and only about 1/3 in the first glass. The blue color in the second glass will become a little lighter, or might begin to change to green. This is still an ideal situation because it will still be darker than the yellow in the first glass. Be sure to point out the water levels in each of the glasses. There is now a lot more liquid in the second glass than the first. In fact, it should be made very clear that the two glasses now have the opposite amounts as they did in the previous trial.

Announce that, as before, you will once again nest the second glass, now with more water, into the first glass, now with less water. Students will address the same two questions as the last trial. Will the second glass float or sink? And, what will happen to the level of the original yellow water when the second glass is now rested onto the surface of the water. Again, the level might rise, lower, or remain the same. This is where discrepancies become clearly evident. Most students will feel that the second glass will sink, because it contains more water than the glass it is nested in. And, most will agree that the level will rise higher than the line drawn on the glass. This is because most will consider the water in the second glass to be much "heavier" than that in the first. Once they have made their prediction, slowly lower the second glass onto the surface of the water. Students will be surprised to find that the inner glass still floats, and that the water in the outer glass will once again rise only to the line drawn on it. Because it was just mentioned in the previous trial, students typically note that the two water levels once again meet- at the line drawn on the glass. If they do not readily comment, be sure to do so. Students will be amazed and puzzled at this repeated outcome!

Vessels wider than drinking glasses, such as a small tub, basin or Tupperware can also be used. The wider base on these vessels would limit the slight "tipping" that might occur with drinking glasses that have a narrow base.

<u>Possible Variables:</u>

1. The density of the liquid used. This can be easily accomplished by adding salt or sugar to the water. Density can be investigated two separate ways. In the first involves using the same liquid, with a different density than water, in both glasses. The second approach involves using two different liquids, with entirely different densities, in each of the glasses. This approach can also be extended to investigate whether the outcome would be different depending on which glass contained the liquid with the greater density. Each of these investigations involves density, but each is entirely different from one another.
2. The volume of liquid used.
3. The viscosity of the liquid. This can involve honey, corn syrup, etc.
4. The shape of the cups.

<u>Phenomenon Explained:</u>

This demonstration illustrates the concept of buoyancy and Archimedes' principle. Buoyancy is defined as the tendency for an object to float in a fluid. Liquids and gases are fluids. The upward force exerted by the molecules of the fluid is called the buoyant force. Archimedes' principle states that the upward buoyant force exerted on a body immersed in a fluid is equal to the weight of the fluid the body displaces, acting in an upward direction at the center of the mass of the displaced fluid. Because the mass of the plastic glasses is so small, no appreciable water is displaced when the empty glass floats on the surface of the water in the second glass. The water level is essentially unchanged. But on each of the subsequent trials, the volume of water poured into the second glass is always equal to the difference between the line drawn on the first glass and the resulting level when water is removed from it. As a result, the water in the first glass will always rise to its original level.

Students might choose to investigate the density of the liquid as a variable. The density of an object will determine whether it will float in a fluid. Density is determined by calculating the mass for a given volume, expressed in the formula g/ml, g/cm^3, or g/cc. Density is independent of the sample size, since it represents the mass per ml of the sample. A larger volume does not necessarily equate to a higher mass. Fewer molecules packed into a given volume will result in a lower density than many more molecules packed into the same volume, which would increase the density. Objects with a density less than water will float, while those denser than water will sink. The density of water is 1.0g/ml.

Viscosity is defined as a fluid's resistance to flow. Think of it as the "thickness" of a fluid. Fluids such as honey, molasses, and engine oil are highly viscous. Students might choose to investigate the outcome when liquids of varying viscosities are employed.

If the density of the liquid is altered by adding salt or sugar, discourse can include solutions, solubility, solutes, solvents, and concentration. Saltwater or sugar water is a mixture. One property of a mixture is that it is physically combined, not chemically, and it can be physically separated. For example, saltwater can be physically separated through the process of evaporation, or boiling the water away.

A solution is one in which a solute is dissolve in a solvent. The solute is the substance being dissolved and the solvent is the substance in which the solute is dissolved. Water is called the universal solvent because of its capability to dissolve more solutes than any other liquid. Solubility is the ability of a solute to dissolve in a solvent.

A concentrated solution is one which there are many dissolved particles of solute in the solvent. On the other hand, a dilute solution is one in which there are few dissolved particles of solute. A solution which contains all the dissolve particles it can possibly hold is called saturated.

Standards Alignment:

Next Generation Science Standards (NGSS, Lead States 2013)

Disciplinary Core Ideas in Physical Science

PS1: Matter and Its Interactions

PS1.A: Structure and Properties of Matter

PS2: Motion and Stability: Forces and Interactions

PS2.A: Forces and Motion

PS2.B: Types of Interactions

Atomic Trampoline

Concepts Illustrated: Alloys, molecular arrangement of crystals, potential energy, kinetic energy, plasticity, elastic deformation, first law of thermodynamics, properties of solids, physical changes, transfer of energy, amorphous solids, elements and compounds, density, mass, volume.

Paradox:

Three transparent tubes are shown. Each has a base made of a different material; stainless steel, titanium, and liquid metal. One small steel ball bearing is positioned at the top of each tube. The balls are simultaneously dropped. No one expects the outcome! The ball bearing dropped on the liquid metal continues to bounce at the same height for an unusually extended period of time, far longer than the other two.

Equipment:

9. Three transparent tubes
10. Three small steel ball bearings
11. One small circular base for each tube; one stainless steel, one titanium, and one liquid metal

The Lesson:

Three transparent tubes are shown. Each has a base made of a different material; stainless steel, titanium, and liquid metal. Students are now shown three small steel ball bearings, and one is positioned at the top of each tube. Explain that the balls will be dropped simultaneously in the three tubes. Students are asked to predict which ball bearing will bounce for a longer period of time when dropped. Most will predict that the ball bearing dropped on the liquid metal base will stop bouncing first. This is because of their past experiences with the nature of solid metals and liquids. Students will be surprised to find that the ball bearing dropped on liquid metal behaves quite differently than expected. First, the ball bearing dropped on the liquid metal will continue to bounce far longer than the other two. Second, the height of this bouncing ball bearing will not appear to diminish. It will appear to continue to bounce at the same height for a very long duration of time.

Possible Variables:

1. Ball bearings made of different substances, such as titanium, stainless steel, liquid metal, copper, brass, lead, aluminum, nickel, wood, plastic, etc. This would involve an investigation of the density of the spheres.
2. Ball bearings that are hollow, rather than solid. This can also include hollow ball bearings made of different substances.
3. Bases made of different materials.
4. The height from which the ball bearings are dropped.
5. The mass of the spheres.
6. The volume of the spheres.

The formula for Liquid metal is $Zr_{41.2}Ti_{13.8}Cu_{12.5}Ni_{10}Be_{22.5}$. Liquid metal is an amorphous alloy. It's essentially a frozen liquid, or a metallic glass. Conventional metals, such as stainless steel, are a crystalline substance. This means their molecular arrangement exists in regular, repeating patterns. Although the molecules in metallic glass don't move, as in conventional metals, they behave as a liquid in that they are not aligned in a uniform pattern. When the ball bearing is dropped on stainless steel, the substance undergoes plastic deformation. This occurs when a load is placed on a material and it deforms, causing the atoms to shift or slide past each other.

Plastic deformation, also known as plasticity, refers to the change in size of shape on an object resulting from a stress applied to it. It occurs in many materials, including metals, plastics, concrete, rocks, and even bones. In the case of rocks and bones, the cause is typically produced by high stress or slippage at micro cracks, resulting in fracture or rupture. Plastic deformation permanently alters the material. There is no recovery following the deformation. It does not return to its original shape. Consider stretching saltwater taffy, or bending a nail.

On the other hand, elastic deformation is reversible. The object may regain its original shape. In plastic deformation, the object initially undergoes elastic deformation. Those materials with a large plastic deformation range include soft thermoplastics and ductile metals, such as copper, steel, and silver. Materials with very small plastic deformation ranges include cast iron, crystals and ceramics.

Now, imagine bouncing a basketball in sand. The basketball loses energy as the sand absorbs energy from the basketball. Grains of sand are shifted, creating a pit in the sand. This is similar to what happens when the ball bearing in our demonstration hits the stainless steel plate at the base. When the ball bearing is held in place above the plate, it has potential energy. This is converted to kinetic energy when the ball bearing is released. When it hits the steel plate, some of the kinetic energy is used to shift atoms. On the other hand, the atoms of Liquidmetal are locked in place and very little energy is lost, or absorbed, when the ball bearing hits it. Rather the energy is conserved for the following rebound. This is similar to a basketball bouncing on a material such as concrete or asphalt.

Liquid metal can be purchased in quantity at http://www.liquidmetal.com/

Standards Alignment:

Next Generation Science Standards (NGSS, Lead States 2013)

Disciplinary Core Ideas in Physical Science

PS1: Matter and Its Interactions

PS1.A: Structure and Properties of Matter

PS2: Motion and Stability: Forces and Interactions

PS2.B: Types of Interactions

PS3: Energy

PS3.A: Definitions of Energy

PS3.B: Conservation of Energy and Energy Transfer

PS3.C: Relationship Between Energy and Forces

PS4: Waves and Their Applications in Technologies for Information Transfer

PS4.A: Wave Properties

Backwards Balloon

Concepts Illustrated: Newton's first law- the law of inertia, acceleration, properties of gas, fluid dynamics.

Paradox:

A balloon behaves in a puzzling manner. We know that our bodies are pulled backwards, into the seat, when the car we sit in accelerates. We also know that our bodies are pulled forward, away from the seat, when the moving car we sit in stops abruptly. Yet, in this demonstration, a balloon floating from a string secured to the bottom of an enclosed box, acting as the car, will behave in the exact opposite manner- moving in the same direction of the force. The balloon moves to the right when the box is pushed to the right! And, when the motion of the box moving to the right is abruptly stopped, the balloon moves to the left!

Equipment:

1. Cardboard box, or any other type of enclosure which students can see into.
2. Helium balloon.
3. String.
4. Saran Wrap, if a cardboard box is used.
5. Tape.

Preparation:

Cut the side wall out of a cardboard box. The box should be completely enclosed with the exception of this cut out side. Tie an inflated helium balloon to a string. Fasten the other end of the string to the center of the base of the cardboard box, so that it floats upward. The length of the string should allow the balloon to freely move about inside the box without hitting the top. The box should also be big enough so that the balloon has enough room to move freely from one side to the other as well.

Now encircle the box with Saran Wrap so that the cut out side is completely covered. The result is a completely enclose box whose inside is visible. The alternative is to use a plastic, transparent box, comprised of a base and a lid.

The Lesson:

Show students the box with the balloon floating inside. Suggest that in order to make the following prediction it might help to recall how our bodies react while we're sitting in a car when it accelerates and brakes quickly. The box should not be moved at all yet. Now, explain that in this demonstration the box represents the car, and the balloon represents a body resting inside. Tell students that you will push the box, sliding it to the right. Students should predict how the balloon will behave. Then, further explain that they should also explain how the balloon will react when the box stops sliding. Once they have made their predictions, push the box to show students that the balloon actually moves in the same direction as the box is moving and that it moves in the opposite direction when the box stops- counterintuitive to what they may have thought.

Lesson Variation:

Variation #1:

This version requires a large cardboard box with its side cut out for viewing. Saran Wrap covers the cut out. This version also uses two balloons, one filled with helium, the other filled with ordinary air. A string tied to the knot of the helium-filled balloon is fastened to the floor at the left side of the box. This balloon floats up, but does not touch the top of the box. A string tied to the balloon filled with normal air is tied to the roof of the box. This balloon hangs down, but does not touch the bottom of the box. These balloons could either be arranged to the left and right of the box, as explained, or positioned in the center, so that one hangs directly over the other. They should not be touching one another.

Push the box to the right. The helium balloon will swing to the right, in the direction the box is moving. But, the balloon filled with ordinary air will swing to the left, in the opposite direction the box is moving.

Variation #2:

This demonstration can also be presented by placing a toy car in the box along with the balloon. The toy car, resting on the floor of the box, will behave as most would expect. When the box is pushed to the right, the car will move to the left. And when the box is abruptly stopped while moving to the right, the car will move in the same direction- to the right. Students will observe that while the car and the balloon are in the same box, they both behave differently to the motion of the box!

Possible Variables:

1. Diameter of the balloon.
2. Shape of the balloon.
3. Length of the string.
4. Shape of the container (box).
5. Volume of the box.
6. Direction of movement of the box- moving in a circular pattern, for example.
7. Holes made in the box, in various locations.

Phenomenon Explained:

Gases and liquids are considered fluids. This demonstration illustrates Newton's first law of motion. Known as the law of inertia, it states that an object either at rest or in motion, remains at rest or in motion with the same speed and direction, unless acted upon by an unbalanced force. Inertia describes the property of matter to either maintain a state of rest or its velocity along a straight path, unless acted upon by an external force. The demonstration also serves to illustrate the principle of acceleration, defined as the rate at which an object changes its velocity. The rate at which an object travels from one place to another is known as its velocity.

The toy car obeys Newton's first law of motion and behaves as your body would in a moving car. When you are a passenger in a moving car, your body is moving at the same speed and direction as the car. When the car brakes, you continue at the same speed and direction in the car.

Events become more interesting when considering an object in the car that is less dense than its surroundings. An example would be the helium filled balloon. At Standard Temperature and Pressure (STP), helium has a density of about 0.00018 g/cm^3. The air surrounding the balloon consists of nitrogen, oxygen, argon, carbon dioxide, and other trace gases. At STP, air has a density of about 0.0012929 g/cm^3. Due to its composition, the air surrounding the balloon is denser than the helium within it. In its resting state, the air inside the box sinks to the bottom, while the gas inside the balloon is pushed upwards, because of their respective densities.

When the box is pushed to the right, the denser air molecules are pushed to the left of the box. This results in the less dense helium molecules being pushed in the opposite direction, to the right.

You can observe a similar phenomenon using a water filled bottle, resting on its side, producing an air bubble that floats up. The bottle lies parallel with the direction the box will be moved in. When the box is in motion, the water and the bubble move with the box. If the box abruptly stops, the water and air bubble continue moving forward. But, since the water is denser than the air bubble, it pushes the air to the back of the bottle as the water moves forward.

Standards Alignment:

Next Generation Science Standards (NGSS, Lead States 2013)

Disciplinary Core Ideas in Physical Science

PS1: Matter and Its Interactions

PS1.A: Structure and Properties of Matter

PS2: Motion and Stability: Forces and Interactions

PS2.A: Forces and Motion

PS3: Energy

PS3.C: Relationship Between Energy and Forces

Big Drip

Concepts Illustrated: Kinetic molecular energy, molecular motion of liquids, temperature, properties of liquids, heat, temperature, thermal energy, heat capacity, fluid dynamics, volume, viscosity.

Paradox:

Your students will be amazed to discover that hot water drips much faster than cold water!

Equipment:

1. Two identical cans or Styrofoam cups.
2. Ice water.
3. Hot water.
4. Stopwatch.
5. Two beakers.

Preparation:

Make a hole in the center of the bottom of two Styrofoam cups or metal cans. The hole must be identical diameters. This can be done with a simple straight pin if you're using Styrofoam cups.

You will also need to prepare cold and hot water. To prepare cold water, either place it in the refrigerator or freezer, or simply add ice. The ice should not be poured into the Styrofoam cup during the demonstration. To prepare hot water, you may either use hot tap water, or water can be heated in a portable hot pot.

The Lesson:

Show the two cans or cups to students. Point out that each has a hole in the base. Be certain to explain that each hole has the exact same diameter. Regardless of whether you're using cans or cups, place one on top of each beaker. The size of the cup or can will determine the size of the beaker you use. The can or cup should sit straight on top of the beaker. You may also use ring stands by positioning the can or cup on the ring assembly of the ring stand and placing a beaker under each cup. Assuming you're using cups, explain that you will add hot water to one cup and cold water to the other. The volume of water will be the same in each cup. The water will naturally drip out of the hole in the bottom of each cup.

Inform students that they will time the drips coming out of the bottom of each cup. After 2 minutes, you will add five drops of red food coloring to each cup of water. Then, the rate of drips coming from the bottom of each cup will once again be timed for two minutes.

Ask students to make two predictions. They should predict what will happen before and after the addition of the food coloring. In fact, the food coloring will not affect the rate of dripping from each cup. It is essentially intended to deter attention from a single variable of temperature. Without the food coloring added during the demonstration, most students will identify that the only difference between the two setups is one of temperature. This focused attention on temperature might then lead some to predict something unusual, even if they wouldn't have normally done so. With the addition of food coloring, focus on temperature is reduced slightly. Since they are asked to make two predictions before and after a key action in the demonstration, the addition of food coloring, their focus is on a change that might be observed before and after adding that food coloring.

Once students have recorded their two predictions, fill the cups with their appropriate water and use the stopwatch to time the rate that water drips out of each cup. Record these values on the board or easel paper for all to see. The patterns between the two cups will more easily be observed if the data remains in full view. Students won't necessarily find any difference that occurs following the addition of food coloring. But with a guided discussion, while referencing the recorded data, students will discover that the hot water drips at a much faster rate than the does the cold water.

If the cups containing the hot and cold water were clear, students would be able to see the different speeds at which the food coloring travels throughout each. This observation would be intended to become a part of the discussion following the demonstration. This visual representation of molecular activity, and the different rates of molecular activity between hot and cold water, could lead to a deeper understanding of the concept under study.

If you choose, a thermometer can also be used to measure the exact temperature of the water in each cup.

Possible Variables:

1. The temperature of the hot and the cold water.
2. Using liquids other than water. These liquids could have varying viscosities, such as vegetable oil, honey, molasses, different weights of engine oil, milk, etc.
3. Adding salt or sugar to the hot and cold water to change its density.
4. Placement of the hole in the bottom of the can or cup. This can mean a hole placed off-center in the bottom of the can, as well as a hole placed in the side of the can near the bottom.
5. The size of the can or cup.
6. The shape of the container that holds the water.
7. The number of holes placed in the can. This can mean more than one hole placed in either the bottom or the side, or holes placed in both locations at once.
8. The size of the hole placed in the can or cup.
9. The shape of the hole made in the bottom of the can. Different shapes could easily be cut in the bottom of Styrofoam or paper cups.
10. Adding food coloring to the water.
11. The volume of liquid in the cup.
12. Using metal cans in place of Styrofoam cups. One metal can could be chilled by placing it in the freezer, or in an ice bath. The other metal can would remain at room temperature. Then, the metal cans are filled with the same volume of water at the same temperature. This investigation would try to determine whether the temperature of the can would affect the drip rate. The investigation could also test whether heating one of the metal cans, either on a hot plate or in a hot water bath, would affect the drip rate. Be sure to use tongs or hot gloves when handling heated metal cans.

13. Investigations can involve a comparison of two cans with the same hole size, but differing fluid densities or viscosities, and two cans with the same fluid densities but differing hole sizes.

Phenomenon Explained:

This demonstration illustrates kinetic molecular energy. Molecules, including those of water, are in constant motion. But, there is a direct relationship between the motion of molecules and their temperature. The temperature of a substance is actually the average kinetic energy of its molecules. Molecules that have low average kinetic energy move slowly and have low temperatures in comparison to molecules with high kinetic energy, which move more quickly and have a higher temperature. Since the molecules of hot water are moving much more rapidly than the cold molecules, they flow out of the hole in the bottom of the can more often.

Heat is not the same as temperature. Essentially, heat is energy and temperature is a measure of it. Heat is a form of energy that can transfer from one medium to another, flowing from objects of higher temperature to those with lower temperature. When a cup of coffee feels hot, it is because energy from the cup is being transferred to your hand. On the other hand, a glass of iced tea feels cold because heat energy from your hand is flowing into the glass. This causes it to feel cold.

The temperature of a substance is a measure of the average kinetic energy of its molecules. All matter is composed of atoms or molecules that are in constant motion. The faster they move, the more kinetic energy they have. There is a direct relationship between the motion of molecules and their temperature. The greater the kinetic energy, the higher the temperature of the object. Molecules that have low average kinetic energy move slowly and have low temperatures in comparison to molecules with high kinetic energy, which move more quickly and have a higher temperature. The molecules of solids generally move very slowly, simply vibrating in place. Thermal energy is defined as the energy within an object or system due to the movement of the particles or molecules within.

Heat is the *total* kinetic energy in a substance or system. This is different than temperature which, as we have learned, is the *average* kinetic energy. Heat is dependent on the speed of the particles, the number of particles, and the type of particles in a substance. On the other hand, temperature is independent of the number and type of particles. A large tub of water could have the same temperature as a small cup of water, but the water in the large tub would possess more heat because it contains many more molecules, therefore more total kinetic energy.

The heat capacity of a substance is the amount of heat required to change its temperature by one degree Celsius. A large amount of matter will have a proportionally large heat capacity. Properties of a substance will affect heat capacity. For example, water has a much higher heat capacity than sand. In other words, much more energy is required to raise the temperature of water than sand. If you go to the beach, the sand will feel very cool in the morning, but hot in the afternoon. However, the water at the same beach may not seem to change much at all.

The effects of temperature on the motion of water molecules can be illustrated by filling two beakers with water. One should have very hot water and the other very cold water. Place a few drops of food coloring in each beaker. Use the same color and the same number of drops. Observe what happens. The food coloring will spread throughout the water in each beaker. But, the food coloring will travel through the hot water much more quickly than the cold water. As the water molecules move in their respective beakers, they carry the food coloring with them. There is more heat energy in the hot water, so it has more kinetic molecular energy and the molecules move much faster. The cold water will eventually become completely colored because the molecules are moving, but they move much more slowly.

If the density of the liquid is altered by adding salt or sugar, discourse can include solutions, solubility, solutes, solvents, and concentration. Saltwater or sugar water is a mixture. One property of a mixture is that it is physically combined, not chemically, and it can be physically separated. For example, saltwater can be physically separated through the process of evaporation, or boiling the water away.

Viscosity is defined as a fluid's resistance to flow. Think of it as the "thickness" of a fluid. Fluids such as honey, molasses, and engine oil are highly viscous. Students might choose to investigate the outcome when liquids of varying viscosities are employed.

Standards Alignment:

Next Generation Science Standards (NGSS, Lead States 2013)

Disciplinary Core Ideas in Physical Science

PS1: Matter and Its Interactions

PS1.A: Structure and Properties of Matter

PS2: Motion and Stability: Forces and Interactions

PS2.B: Types of Interactions

PS3: Energy

PS3.A: Definitions of Energy

Disciplinary Core Ideas in Earth and Space Science

ESS2: Earth's Systems

ESS2.C: The Roles of Water in Earth's Surface Processes

Block Toppler

<u>Concepts Illustrated:</u> Potential energy, kinetic energy, polymers, elasticity, coefficient of restitution, friction, mass, volume, transfer of energy, law of conservation of energy, mechanical energy, mass, volume, density, elements and compounds, properties of solids.

This novel twist to the Happy/Sad Balls elevates the traditional demonstration to one that delivers a powerful contradiction to student expectation! This version truly defies reason and elicits pure amazement! Furthermore, investigation of one particular variable can add additional surprise, compounding the shock of the original demonstration!

<u>Paradox:</u>

After observing the properties of two balls, one made entirely of clay and another of hollow rubber, students are astounded to discover which of the two will actually topple over a heavy wood block!

<u>Equipment:</u>

Note that this demonstration can certainly be conducted using the traditional set of Happy/Sad balls. This presentation is detailed in the Lesson Variation section. But, the demonstration will be initially presented using a rubber ball and a ball of clay, which I believe makes it a bit more impressive.

1. One large hollow rubber ball.
2. One large ball of clay. It should be made to be the same diameter as the hollow rubber ball.
3. Two eyehooks.
4. Happy/Sad Balls. As explained above, these are optional, depending on your choice of presentation. These balls are available at science supply stores, sold in a set.
5. String.
6. Ring stand with horizontal support bar. A meter stick can also be used.
7. One or two wooden blocks. They must be identical.

<u>Preparation:</u>

Two lengths of string will be needed. They appropriate length will depend on the height of the support bar from which you are swinging the balls. One end of the string will be tied to the support bar. The other ends are tied onto the eyehooks- one on each string.

The rubber ball should have a hole drilled into it. This hole will accommodate the screw end of the eyehook. Screw the eyehook into the hole. It should be a tight fit, so that the ball remains attached to the eyehook without falling off it.

As mentioned, the demonstration can very effectively be presented with the Sad/Happy Balls. Using hot glue, each ball would simply be attached to the end of a string. See the Lesson Variation section for presentation using the Sad/Happy Balls.

The Lesson:

Two balls of equal diameter are shown. Students are informed that one is a hollow rubber ball, while the other is made entirely of clay. It is explained that each has their own characteristic properties, which can be observed by simple manipulation of the balls.

This is illustrated by dropping each of the balls on the table. They should be dropped from the same height. Students will observe that the rubber ball bounces, while the other hits the table with a resounding "thud" and does not bounce at all. Each of the balls are now rolled across the table. Students will observe that the rubber ball rolls much further than the clay ball.

The wooden block is now introduced. Knock on it so that students can hear the solid sound this produces. Now, lay the block down on its side and drop each of the balls on the surface of the block, one at a time. Again, the rubber ball bounces off the block, while the clay ball hits it with a "thud." This is an important part of the demonstration. Students observe how each of the balls interact with the block upon impact. When they see the rubber ball bounce, students get the impression that this ball did not generate great "impact" on the block. On the other hand, when the clay ball hits the block with a solid "thud," students consider this as a strong or forceful impact. All the observations, especially this one, will lead most students to believe that the clay ball, hitting the block with a "thud" and not moving, will generate the impact to knock the block over.

The balls are now attached to the pendulum strings. One of the eyehooks at the end of the string is pushed into the clay ball. The other eyehook is screwed into the hole previously made in the rubber ball. They are each swung to show that they have free movement, and that they swing in the same manner. The wooden block is placed into position, standing upright. Lift the balls to illustrate the point from which they will be released. The demonstration works best when the balls are released from about 45^0 from the vertical. Explain that they will be released individually. Ask students to predict which ball, if any, will knock the wooden block over. For reasons mentioned earlier, most will predict that the clay ball will topple the block.

Note that you can position two identical blocks so that the balls can be released simultaneously. If you choose to do this, be sure that students understand they are identical.

If you are only using one wooden block, release the rubber ball first. This ball will bounce off the block, toppling it over! This generates surprise in most. But it sets students up for an even greater surprise in the next phase. Release the clay ball next. When it impacts the wooden block, it will hit with a "thud" and the block will remain standing! The expectations of most are contradicted in each phase of the demonstration. Students are surprised to find that the hollow rubber ball topples the block, but in their minds, this almost guarantees that the clay ball will as well. They are shocked when the actual outcome contradicts their expectation!

Lesson Variation:

This presentation uses a set of Happy/Sad balls. It follows the steps of the original presentation. After observing the properties of the two solid rubber balls, students are astounded to discover which of the two will actually topple over a heavy wood block!

Students should be able to clearly distinguish between the two balls, and tell one from the other, during the demonstration. For this reason, they could be spray painted two different colors, if you choose. But, this is certainly not necessary.

The two rubber balls are shown. Students are told that these rubber balls are actually made from different types of rubber. Each type of rubber has its own characteristic properties, which can be observed by simple manipulation of the balls.

This is demonstrated by first bouncing each of the balls on the table. They should be dropped from the same height. Students will observe that one of the balls bounces, while the other hits the table with a resounding "thud" and does not bounce much at all. Be sure that you do not mix them up from this point on. You want students to clearly know which is which throughout the rest of the demonstration. You could name them "happy" and "sad," or they could be labeled "A" and "B" for "bounce." Each of the balls are now rolled across the table. Students will observe that the happy ball not only bounces much higher, also rolls much further.

The wooden block is now introduced. Knock on it so that students can hear the solid sound this produces. Now, lay the block down on its side and bounce each of the balls on the surface of the block, one at a time. Again, the happy ball bounces off the block, while the unhappy ball hits it with a thud. This is an important part of the demonstration. Students observe how each of the balls interact with the block upon impact. When they see the happy ball bounce, students get the impression that this ball did not generate great "impact" on the block. On the other hand, when the unhappy ball hits the block with a solid "thud," students consider this as a strong or forceful impact. All the observations, especially this one, will lead most students to believe that the unhappy ball, hitting the block with a "thud" and not moving, will generate the impact to knock the block over.

The balls are now attached to the pendulum strings. They are each swung to show that they have free movement, and that they swing in the same manner. The wooden block is placed into position, standing upright. Lift the balls to illustrate the point from which they will be released. Explain that they will be released individually. Ask students to predict which ball, if any, will knock the wooden block over. For reasons mentioned earlier, most will predict that the unhappy ball will topple the block.

Note that you can position two identical blocks so that the balls can be released simultaneously. If you choose to do this, be sure that students understand they are identical. The demonstration works best when the balls are released from about 45^0 from the vertical.

If you are only using one wooden block, release the happy ball first. This ball will bounce off the block, toppling it over! This generates surprise in most. But it sets students up for an even greater surprise in the next phase. Release the unhappy ball next. When it impacts the wooden block, it will hit with a "thud" and the block will remain standing! The expectations of most are contradicted in each phase of the demonstration. Students are surprised to find that the happy ball topples the block, but in their minds, this almost guarantees that the unhappy ball will as well. They are shocked when the actual outcome contradicts their expectation!

The demonstration can also be conducted using a curved ramp in place of a pendulum. The wooden block would be positioned upright at the end of the ramp. The ball is released down the ramp and impacts the wooden block.

Possible Variables:

1. The temperature of the balls. They can be made colder by placing them in ice water, or into hot water to make them warmer. Freezing both balls presents a very interesting outcome. The properties of the two balls will reverse, setting the stage for great puzzlement and rich discourse.
2. The height from which the balls are released on the pendulum.
3. Solid vs hollow wooden blocks.
4. The substance that the blocks are made of, such as different types of wood and metals, Styrofoam, plastic, etc. This could effectively alter the density of the blocks.
5. The shape of the object the balls contact.
6. The size of the object the balls contact.
7. Using balls made of various substances, such as lead, iron, copper, tin, aluminum, etc. The sad/happy balls can even be substituted with golf balls.
8. The balls can be substituted with ping pong balls that can be filled with sand to alter their weight. A small hole can be place near the top of the balls so that sand can be added. The hole can be covered with a small amount of clay to contain the sand.
9. The mass of each ball.
10. The volume of each ball.
11. The balls can also be substituted with clay. This could allow for its mass to be varied.

Phenomenon Explained:

The different properties that these balls exhibit can be attributed to the characteristics of the materials they are made from. If you are using the Sad/Happy Balls, they are actually made of different polymers. A polymer molecule is composed of atoms bonded in a repeating pattern. The ball that bounces, or the happy ball, is typically made of conventional neoprene rubber. The one that does not bounce, or the sad ball, is commonly made from norbornene.

The happy ball, or hollow rubber ball, illustrates an elastic collision. It bounces well because it stores very little energy in collisions. It has a high-resolution elasticity, or coefficient of restitution. In other words, it exhibits a rapid return to its original shape following a deformation upon impact. It collides elastically, bouncing off the block and knocking it over. This ball requires a larger change in momentum to rebound from the wooden block than the clay ball does. It imparts a larger impulse, applying a larger force.

On the other hand, the sad ball, or the clay ball, illustrates an inelastic collision. It does not bounce well because it has a low-resolution elasticity, or coefficient of restitution. It absorbs most of its kinetic energy. When it impacts the wooden block, its kinetic energy is converted into deformation of the ball, heat, and sound.

When rolled across the table, the happy, or hollow rubber ball, rolls farther because it exhibits lower surface friction. The unhappy, or clay, ball has a greater coefficient of friction. As a result, it does not roll a great distance.

The system employed in this demonstration is a simple pendulum, consisting of a mass, or bob, attached to the end of a string swinging about a pivot point.

Mechanical energy is defined as the energy an object possesses due to its motion or position. There are two forms of mechanical energy, potential and kinetic. Potential energy is stored energy, while kinetic is the energy of motion. The law of conservation of energy states that energy can never be created or destroyed, although it can be converted from one form to another.

When the happy/sad balls, acting as bobs of a pendulum, are pulled back and lifted, they have potential energy. When released, the force of gravity works on the ball as it swings down, converting the potential energy to kinetic. As the ball swings and strikes the block, some energy from the ball is dissipated through friction and air resistance, while some energy is transferred to the block.

Standards Alignment:

Next Generation Science Standards (NGSS, Lead States 2013)

Disciplinary Core Ideas in Physical Science

PS1: Matter and Its Interactions

PS1.A: Structure and Properties of Matter

PS2: Motion and Stability: Forces and Interactions

PS2.A: Forces and Motion

PS2.B: Types of Interactions

PS3: Energy

PS3.A: Definitions of Energy

PS3.B: Conservation of Energy and Energy Transfer

PS3.C: Relationship Between Energy and Forces

Brachistochrone Problem

<u>Concepts Illustrated:</u> Acceleration, speed, momentum, velocity, conservation of energy, potential energy, kinetic energy, translational energy, rotational energy, elements and compounds, density.

This is a very well-known demonstration. Originally presented as a problem to solve, the solution is rather counterintuitive indeed!

<u>Paradox:</u>

A series of ramps with varying slopes are shown. A ball is placed at the top of each ramp and released simultaneously. Most students predict that the ball traveling the straight ramp will reach the bottom quickest. They are completely shocked when their observations harshly contradict that expectation. The straight ramp, the shortest distance between two points, does not get the ball to the bottom in the shortest period of time- it is the slowest!

<u>Equipment:</u>

1. A series of ramps, each with varying slopes. The demonstration typically employs four ramps. Although the demonstration will be described using the apparatus shown below, there are a number of different slopes that can be used. Two to four ramps are typically used. One should be a straight ramp.
2. A metal ball for each ramp in the apparatus. Our demonstration will use four. They should be identical in mass and volume.

<u>The Lesson:</u>

Display the ramps to students. Be sure to distinctly point out that the starting and ending point is the same for each ramp. Call attention to the different paths taken by each ramp to arrive at the same ending point.

Now show the metal balls. It should be made clear to students that each ball is identical in mass, volume, and substance. Place one ball at the top of each ramp and keep them in this position, at rest, by placing a ruler in front of them. Explain that you will simultaneously release the balls by lifting the ruler. Ask students to predict which ramp will get the ball to the bottom in the least amount of time.

Since the ramp providing the straight line also offers the shortest path, most students predict it will get the ball to the end in the shortest period of time. Count to three and release the balls simultaneously by lifting the ruler. Students will be surprised to discover that the straight line is not the quickest path to the end! The quickest path between two points is not always a straight line!

<u>Possible Variables:</u>

1. Density of the balls. This could involve the type of material the ball is made of, including steel, wood, cork, steel, glass, rubber, tin, aluminum, lead, copper, etc. This also includes golf balls, tennis balls, etc.

2. The slope of the ramps. Keep in mind that students do not need to set up four ramps when conducting their investigation.

3. Adjusting the straight ramp so that it has the same starting point as the other ramps, but lifting the end of the ramp. This would essentially be racing the ball on the straight ramp against any arbitrary section of the cycloid. The cycloid still wins.

Phenomenon Explained:

To begin, we should become familiar with the terms momentum, velocity, speed, and acceleration.

Momentum refers to a quantity of motion that an object has. The momentum of a moving object can be calculated using the following formula:

momentum = mass x velocity

The momentum of any moving object is dependent upon its mass and velocity. The terms speed and velocity are oftentimes mistakenly used interchangeably. Whereas speed refers to the measure of how fast an object moves, velocity measures how fast an object arrives at a certain point. They are different. Speed is defined as the rate of time that an object travels a distance. Velocity is defined as the rate of change in displacement with respect to time, or the rate that an object moves from one point to another. The formula for speed is:

Distance Traveled
time of travel

As a vector quantity, velocity involves both speed and direction. The formula for velocity is:

Displacement
Time

Consider a person walking two steps forward and two steps back, returning to the original starting position. Their speed of each step can be measured. But their velocity would be measured as zero.

Acceleration is defined as the rate at which an object changes its velocity.

When a ball is placed at the top of the incline, it has potential energy due to gravity. The amount of potential energy is dependent on the balls mass and the height to which it has been lifted. When the released to roll down the incline, its potential energy is converted into kinetic energy. Some energy will be lost to friction. In the case of a rolling object, as in this lesson, the kinetic energy is divided into two types of kinetic energy- translational and rotational. Translational energy refers to motion in a straight line, whereas rotational energy refers to the motion of spinning.

Mechanical energy is defined as the energy an object possesses due to its motion or position. There are two forms of mechanical energy, potential and kinetic. Potential energy is stored energy, while kinetic is the energy of motion. The law of conservation of energy states that energy can never be created or destroyed, although it can be converted from one form to another. That is exactly what happens in this demonstration. The energy involved is both potential and kinetic.

Students can investigate whether the density of the spheres affects the outcome. Density is determined by calculating the mass for a given volume, expressed in the formula g/ml, g/cm^3, or g/cc. Density is independent of the sample size, since it represents the mass per ml of the sample. A larger volume does not necessarily equate to a higher mass. Fewer molecules packed into a given volume will result in a lower density than many more molecules packed into the same volume, which would increase the density.

The shape of a cycloid can be illustrated by putting a dot on the outer edge of a circle and tracing the path the dot takes as the circle rolls along a horizontal surface.

Now let's imagine three ramps in our apparatus: straight, parabolic, and cycloid. Since the starting point is identical for each ball, they each have the same amount of potential energy. In this apparatus, the ball traveling the cycloid will arrive first, followed by the parabolic ramp, and finally the straight ramp. The straight ramp, the shortest distance between two points, is actually the slowest path!

The cycloid wins because the ball immediately travels steeply, picking up speed. The average speed along the cycloid is faster than the average speed on the straight ramp, making up for the extra distance the ball must travel. The cycloid presents the ideal balance between traveling a short distance and gaining speed from gravity early on the route. A quick internet search will give you the mathematical formulas that illustrate this idea.

Brachistochrone problem

A ball is released from the top of each ramp – all at the same time

Side view

The cycloid ramp is the fastest

Let's imagine two ramps, a straight ramp and a cycloid. Keeping the starting point the same height for each, lift the end of the straight ramp. Picture this straight ramp directly next to the cycloid. Adjusting the end of the straight ramp will essentially allow you to race the straight ramp against any arbitrary section of the cycloid. It does not matter which section of the cycloid the straight ramp is measured against. Any section of the cycloid will be a faster track than the corresponding straight line between those two points.

The shortest distance might be a straight line, but the quickest path is a cycloid ramp.

Standards Alignment:

Next Generation Science Standards (NGSS, Lead States 2013)

Disciplinary Core Ideas in Physical Science

PS1: Matter and Its Interactions

PS1.A: Structure and Properties of Matter

PS2: Motion and Stability: Forces and Interactions

PS2.A: Forces and Motion

PS3: Energy

PS3.A: Definitions of Energy

PS3.B: Conservation of Energy and Energy Transfer

Braess' Paradox

<u>Concepts Illustrated:</u> Spring constants, behavior of springs in series, behavior of springs in parallel, properties of spring systems, physical changes.

This counter-intuitive demonstration is truly amazing to observe. The behavior of the springs contradicts all expectation and is sure to elicit exclamations of "that's impossible" from your students.

Variations are included for those with limited supplies.

<u>Paradox:</u>

Two springs, hanging vertically, are connected in series by a short string. A mass hangs at the bottom of the springs. Everyone expects that the springs will lengthen when the string is cut. But amazingly, the opposite occurs. When the string connecting the two springs is cut, the springs actually shorten!

<u>Equipment:</u>

1. Two springs.
2. String.
3. Support to hang the springs from. This could be a ring stand with a horizontal rod.
4. Mass to attach to the bottom of the springs.
5. Scissors.
6. Meter stick.

<u>Preparation:</u>

The equipment should be set up prior to students entering the classroom. Hang one spring from the horizontal rod attached to the ring stand. Cut a short length of string and use it to attach the bottom of that string to one end of the other. The two springs should now be hanging vertically, connected by the short string. Connect a mass to the bottom of the lower spring. You can use either a hook or a piece of string to do this. Tie another piece of string from the rod, where the upper spring is connected, to the top of the lower spring. This "peripheral" piece of string should have slack in it. You should be able to pull the string a few inches to the side of the springs, without affecting the setup, to clearly show it to students during the demonstration. Now connect a third string from the bottom of the upper string to the mass. Again, this string should have enough slack to pull it to the side without affecting the setup.

If the small string that connects the two springs in series is a different color than the two strings with slack, students will more easily be able to distinguish between them.

Set the ring stand on the edge of a table so that the springs can freely hang to the side of the table, extending above the floor.

There are a variety of materials that can be used to set up this demonstration, depending on your available resources. Here are a few of them:

The mass can be a hooked mass used in the lab, but it can also be a small bucket connected by its handle to the lower spring. The bucket could contain sand, to add mass. During their investigations, students could simply adjust the mass by filling the bucket with the desired amount of sand. The mass can also be something as simple as a Ziploc baggie. This would also allow for its mass to be altered by adding or removing sand from it. A bag of rice or sugar can also be used. An empty plastic gallon jug, such as a milk container, can also be used. This would allow for water to simply be added to the jug to adjust its mass.

If you do not have springs, rubber bands can be used. Since rubber bands come in different lengths, this offers an alternative method of allowing student to investigate their lengths as a variable.

Finally, if ring stands are not available, the system can actually be constructed from K'Nex. This system will not support a great deal of mass hanging from it, but it will certainly allow for Ziploc baggies containing mass.

The Lesson:

Display and explain the entire setup to the students. Be sure that they understand the connections made by the three strings. Hold the two strings with slack out to the side, so that their role is understood. Now use a meter stick to measure the total length of the springs, from their connection to the rod to their connection at the mass below. Note that you can also measure the distance from the floor to the bottom of the mass, if the system hangs over the floor. Record this length on the chalkboard for all to see. Call attention to the small string connecting the two springs in series. Explain that you will cut this string. Ask students to predict what will happen to the total length of the springs when this happens. There will be a couple of students who might predict that the length will remain the same. But, just about every student will predict that the total length will increase- that the springs will stretch farther apart. It is completely counter-intuitive to think that the length will decrease.

Cut the connecting string to show that this is, in fact, exactly what happens! When you cut the string, the mass will rise by a very noticeable difference, shocking the students. Instead of hanging lower, the mass is dramatically pulled higher by the springs! Use the meter stick to once again measure the total length of the two strings. Record this measurement next to the original and compute the difference.

Possible Variables:

1. Springs of different compression strengths.
2. The amount of mass hanging from the springs.
3. Length of the springs. This could involve both two springs of equal lengths as well as two springs of different lengths.
4. If rubber bands are used, the lengths of the rubber bands could become a variable that is tested.
5. Length of the peripheral strings.

Phenomenon Explained:

Two or more springs are said to be in *series* when they are connected end to end. They are said to be in *parallel* when they are connected side by side. The spring constant refers to a ratio of the force applied to the spring and the displacement caused by it.

The springs are in series when the demonstration begins. The spring constant of the system is $k/2$, k representing the spring constant of the individual springs.

When the small string is cut, the system changes from series to parallel, increasing the spring constant of the system to $2k$.

Cutting the small string can be related to the removal of a link in a network, such as a traffic pattern. This is a common idea used when explaining Braess' Paradox. Cutting the string is analogous to removing a road in a particular route.

Standards Alignment:

Next Generation Science Standards (NGSS, Lead States 2013)

Disciplinary Core Ideas in Physical Science

PS2: Motion and Stability: Forces and Interactions

PS2.A: Forces and Motion

PS3: Energy

PS3.B: Conservation of Energy and Energy Transfer

Bricks in a Boat

Concepts Illustrated: Archimedes' principle, buoyancy, displacement, density, properties of liquids, solubility, solute, solvent, concentration, mass, volume.

Paradox:

Two large bricks are placed inside a plastic tub which is lowered into an aquarium of water. The water rises and its level is noted and marked. The bricks are removed from the tub and placed directly into the water, at the bottom of the aquarium. When it is once again noted, the water level is observed to have actually gone down!

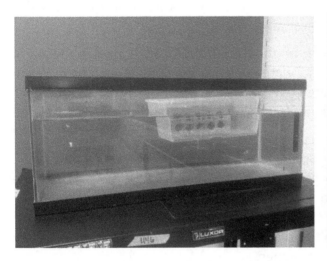
Bricks in boat- water level is marked.

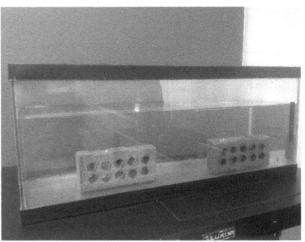
Bricks out of boat- water level has gone down.

A close-up view of the change in water level.

<u>Equipment</u>:

1. An aquarium or some other clear tank that can hold water.
2. A plastic tub, metal paint can, or even a plastic kitchen bowl.
3. Two bricks. A large rock can also be used.
4. A marker- to show the level of water. Use water soluble so that it can be wiped off later.

<u>Preparation</u>:

Fill the aquarium 1/2 - 2/3 full of water.

<u>The Lesson</u>:

Show the aquarium and explain that it contains plain water. Show the two bricks and place them in the plastic tub. Before placing the tub in the aquarium, ask students to note the water level and how it changes when the tub is lowered into the water. Now, place the tub in the aquarium as students pay careful attention to the water level. The water will rise. Mark this water level on the side of the tank using a marker or tape.

Explain that you are going to remove the bricks from the tub. The tub will remain in the water and the bricks will be lowered directly into the water and placed onto the bottom of the aquarium. Ask students to predict how the water level will react when this is done. The water level will either rise, remain the same, or lower from the level marked on the side of the aquarium. They should choose one.

You can relate this to a boat floating in a pond. Students can imagine that they are sitting in the boat. There is also a very large rock in the boat with them. Ask them to imagine throwing the rock out of the boat and allowing it to sink to the bottom of the pond. What does the water level in the pond do? Does the level rise, stay the same, or go down? Students will most likely predict that the water level will rise. You won't find too many students that predict the water level to go down. In fact, that is exactly what will happen.

Once they have predicted the outcome, remove the bricks from the tub and place them into the water, resting on the bottom of the aquarium. The tub should still be floating in the water. Students should once again pay careful attention to the water level. They will be surprised to find that the water level actually goes down! Mark this new level on the side of the tank using a marker or tape.

<u>Lesson Variation</u>:

The demonstration can be presented using a 500g mass and two beakers, one large and one small. Fill the larger beaker with water. Place the mass into the smaller beaker and then put it in the water. It will float on top. Note and mark the water level. Now remove the mass and place it into the water, at the bottom of the large beaker. The small beaker continues to float at the surface of the water. Note and mark the new water level. Attaching a string to the mass will allow you to safely lower it into the beaker without breaking the bottom of the beaker.

Rather than a plastic tub and two bricks the demonstration can be conducted using a metal can, such as a paint can, and a large rock. Place the rock into the paint can and float the whole assembly on top of the water. Then remove the rock and place it directly into the water, to the bottom of the tank while the remains floating at the surface of the water.

Note that plastic film canisters can also be used. These are readily accessible by most, and will fit into a beaker of smaller volume. They can also be easily filled with washers, nuts, and bolts to change their mass.

The same concept can be illustrated using a 100ml graduated cylinder, a syringe, and a 100g mass. Fill the graduated cylinder with about 60ml of water. Place the mass into the syringe and then lower the syringe into the graduated cylinder. Note the new level of the water in the graduated cylinder. Now, remove the mass from the syringe and put it in the water, allowing it to sink to the bottom of the graduated cylinder. Then put the syringe back into the water. Note this new level of the water. You'll find that it has decreased.

Another variation of this demonstration can elicit significant surprise. It uses a box, or any vessel, made of metal that will sink in water. This box should have a hole in its bottom that can be plugged somehow, such as with a cork. With the cork in place, put the box in the water-filled aquarium and observe that it floats. Note and mark the water level on the outside of the aquarium with a marker or tape. Then remove the cork and allow the box to sink to the bottom of the aquarium. When the box is fully submerged and resting on the bottom of the tank, note and mark the new water level. You will find that it has decreased.

Possible Variables:

1. Liquids with densities different than water. This can be entirely different liquid, or it can involve adding salt or sugar in order to change the density. If salt or sugar is added to water, it would allow you to control the density and investigate the outcomes from using liquids of several densities.
2. Depth of the tub.
3. Plastic tubs, cans, or any other vessel having different volumes.
4. Plastic tubs, cans, or any other vessel having different shapes.
5. In place of a brick, use weights of different masses.
6. In place of a brick, use weights of different densities.
7. An investigation of the effects when various volumes of liquids are combined with various sized tubs, as well as weight with various masses.
8. Instead of using one weight in the tub, use several that have a combined mass of the original. This keeps the mass constant, but changes the surface area. For example, in place of a 500g mass, use ten 50g masses.
9. Begin with two weights, one in the boat and one in the water. Then switch the two. The weight in the water goes into the boat, while the weight in the boat goes into the water. The weights could also be of equal or differing mass.
10. Put a shelf in the water. When the weight is removed from the tub it is placed in the water on the shelf. It is not placed at the bottom of the tank. Does the depth at which it is placed influence the outcome?

Phenomenon Explained:

This surprising demonstration illustrates the concept of buoyancy and Archimedes' principle. Buoyancy is defined as the tendency for an object to float in a fluid. Liquids and gases are fluids. The upward force exerted by the molecules of the fluid is called the buoyant force. Archimedes' principle states that the upward buoyant force exerted on a body immersed in a fluid, regardless of whether it is partially or fully submerged, is equal to the weight of the fluid that the body displaces. The volume of fluid that is displaced is equivalent to the volume of the entire object if it is fully immersed. If it is partially submerged, the volume of displaced fluid is equivalent to the volume of the portion of the object that is below the surface of the liquid.

When the bricks in the boat are floating, their weight in water is displaced. In the case of two bricks the weight is significant. However, when they are placed directly into the water, resting at the bottom of the aquarium, they displace their volume in water. This is much less water than their weight would displace. This is essentially because the density of each brick is much more than the density of water, which is 1.0 g/ml.

The density of an object will determine whether it will float in a fluid. Density is determined by calculating the mass for a given volume, expressed in the formula g/ml, g/cm^3, or g/cc. Density is independent of the sample size, since it represents the mass per ml of the sample. A larger volume does not necessarily equate to a higher mass. Fewer molecules packed into a given volume will result in a lower density than many more molecules packed into the same volume, which would increase the density. Objects with a density less than water will float, while those denser than water will sink. Again, the density of water is 1.0g/ml.

If the density of the liquid is altered by adding salt or sugar, discourse can include solutions, solubility, solutes, solvents, and concentration. Saltwater or sugar water is a mixture. One property of a mixture is that it is physically combined, not chemically, and it can be physically separated. For example, saltwater can be physically separated through the process of evaporation, or boiling the water away.

A solution is one in which a solute is dissolve in a solvent. The solute is the substance being dissolved and the solvent is the substance in which the solute is dissolved. Water is called the universal solvent because of its capability to dissolve more solutes than any other liquid. Solubility is the ability of a solute to dissolve in a solvent.

A concentrated solution is one which there are many dissolved particles of solute in the solvent. On the other hand, a dilute solution is one in which there are few dissolved particles of solute. A solution which contains all the dissolve particles it can possibly hold is called saturated.

Standards Alignment:

Next Generation Science Standards (NGSS, Lead States 2013)

Disciplinary Core Ideas in Physical Science

PS1: Matter and Its Interactions

PS1.A: Structure and Properties of Matter

PS1.B: Chemical Reactions

Disciplinary Core Ideas in Earth and Space Science

<u>ESS2: Earth's Systems</u>

ESS2.C: The Roles of Water in Earth's Surface Processes

Bubble Battle

Concepts Illustrated: Air pressure, surface area, Law of Laplace, properties of gas, molecular motion of gases, volume, fluid dynamics, physical changes, physical properties of matter, properties of surfactants, the respiratory system of fish, the human respiratory system.

Paradox:

Two balloons are connected onto opposite ends of a short tube. Although they are each blown up, one balloon is two times larger than the other. A clip prevents air from traveling from one balloon to the other. When the clip is removed, the results are shocking and completely illogical. Although students will predict that the large balloon will release air into the smaller until they both achieve the same size, the complete opposite occurs. When the clip is removed is opened, the smaller balloon will shrink and deflate as it blows up the larger balloon even more!

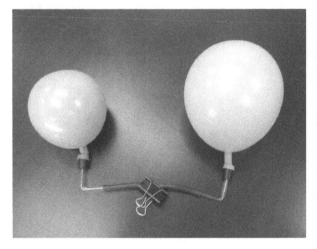 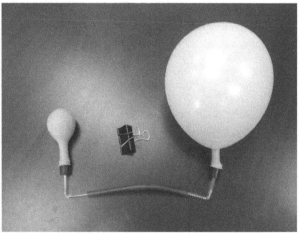

Binder clips hold air in balloons.   Binder clip removed allows air to flow freely.

The Lesson Variation section describes an interesting method involves soap bubbles in place of balloons.

Equipment:

1. Two balloons.
2. A short length of rubber tubing.
3. Two one-hole rubber stoppers.
4. Two glass angle bends.
5. One large spring binder clip.

Preparation:

First, insert a glass tubing onto each end of the rubber tubing. Then, push a rubber stopper on the other end of each glass tubing. Now attach the binder clip to the rubber tubing, at about the center. The balloons do not have to be attached prior to the demonstration. However, you may choose to do so. Read the Lesson section below, which will explain how to attach the balloons.

A variation of this setup involves attaching one balloon to each side of a glass stopcock, using rubber bands to hold the balloons in place.

It can also be made simply from a length of lab grade glass or plastic tubing with the balloons held in place by rubber bands and the air contained in each balloon using spring file clips. These clips can be removed to allow air flow between the balloons.

The setup can probably be assembled most simply by blowing up the two balloons and placing one on each end of a rigid straw. Squeeze the nozzles of the balloons shut with your fingers, and just let go of them when you are ready to allow air to flow between them.

There is another variation involving a thread spool. Blow up the balloons and keep the air trapped within each with a small spring file clamp, or even a twist tie, around each nozzle. Stretch the nozzle of the large balloon all the way over the end of the spool. Now stretch the nozzle of the smaller balloon completely around the other end of the spool, and over the nozzle of the first balloon already stretched on the spool. Now, unclip or untie the nozzles to allow air flow.

Finally, the necessary apparatus can be made by using the lift-top nozzles from two sports drink bottles, or bottles of water. These are the nozzle types that can be pulled up to drink from, then pushed down to close. They can even be found on some dishwashing liquid bottles. Remove the nozzle ends of the bottles. A small portion of the bottle should still be attached to the nozzle. Then, either hot glue or tape them together so that the nozzles are on opposite ends, facing away from one another. Slide one balloon over each nozzle.

The Lesson:

Show the rubber tubing setup to students. Fully inflate one balloon and slide the nozzle of the balloon over one of the rubber stoppers. You can let go of the balloon. Because of the binder clip, the air remains in the balloon. Now inflate the second balloon to about half the size of the first balloon. Slide the nozzle of this balloon over the second rubber stopper. Again, you can let go of this balloon. The air will remain in each balloon. Explain to students that the air within each is prevented from exiting the balloons because of the binder clip between them. Explain to students that you will remove this clip from the rubber tubing, which will allow the air inside the two balloons to flow freely between them. Ask students to predict what they think will happen to the diameter of the two balloons when this valve is opened. Most will predict that the air in the larger balloon will travel through the rubber tubing and blow up the smaller balloon, until they both reach the same size. Some might predict that nothing will happen. Once predictions have been shared, remove the binder clip. Hold the apparatus up when you do this, so that the balloons can be clearly seen by all. Be sure to hold the rubber tubing, not the balloons. If you hold the balloons during this, some students might think that pressure applied by your fingers caused the result. Students will be startled as the large balloon grows even larger, while the small balloon deflates!

<u>Lesson Variation:</u>

As mentioned earlier, this paradox could be shown using soap bubbles in place of balloons.

Using two glass funnels, attach a length of rubber tubing to the stem of each. Attach the opposite ends of the tubing to opposite ends of a t-tube. Another length of rubber tubing is attached to the third (center) stem of the t-tube. Let's call this section the air entry tube. Attach a clamp onto each section of rubber tubing. Now invert the funnels and lower them into soap solution. A soap film should form across the inverted, widest part of the funnel. Remove the clamp on one section of rubber tubing attached to a funnel. Then, remove the clamp from the air entry tube and blow into it. The soap film will expand and become a large bubble, still attached to the funnel. Reattach the clamp onto the funnel tubing to keep the air inside that bubble. Now, remove the clamp from the other funnel tubing. Repeat the process, but this time blow a much smaller bubble. Reattach the clamp on the air entry tube. The apparatus can be supported from a ring stand so that the funnels, and attached bubbles, are hanging down side by side. Remove the clamps on the funnel tubing to allow the air within each bubble to flow freely. The smaller bubble will shrink and collapse as the air inside blows up the large bubble even larger.

For a more visual effect, use bubble solution that will glow under black light. Lower the room lights, turn on the black light and watch the glowing bubbles do the impossible!

Another soap bubble setup involves two empty thread spools. Dip each into the bubble solution. Blow through the spool and keep the air in the bubble by covering the hole with a playing card. Put the two spools together and, when ready, remove the playing cards to allow the air in the bubbles to flow.

If you choose to use soap bubbles, adding glycerin to the soap solution will make the bubbles more durable and last longer.

<u>Possible Variables:</u>

1. Diameter of the balloons, or the volume of air in each balloon.
2. Length of the connecting tube between the balloons.
3. Diameter of the tubing between the balloons.
4. Shape of the balloons.
5. Different gases within the balloons.
6. Using water, or other liquids, instead of air.
7. Varying the temperature of the gas in the balloons. This could be accomplished by placing one or both of the balloons in a freezer or refrigerator. This could lead into variations, such as having the larger balloon warmer, the smaller balloon warmer, etc.
8. Different brands of soap or bubble solution, if using soap bubbles.
9. Different size funnels, if using soap bubbles.

<u>Phenomenon Explained:</u>

The unexpected results observed in this demonstration become easier to comprehend when you consider the force required to blow into a balloon and inflate it. It is much easier to inflate a balloon that is already inflated. On the other hand, there is much more force required to blow into and inflate a balloon that is deflated. You've probably also noticed that the change in diameter is much more obvious when you initially begin to blow up the balloon. But once the balloon has been blown up much larger, each breath you put into it does not show such an obvious increase in diameter.

The results of this demonstration actually make sense, mathematically. We can calculate the surface area for balloons filled with 1000cm^3, 2000cm^3, and 3000cm^3 of air. The radius of each balloon would be 6.20cm, 7.82cm, and 8.95cm respectively. The surface area of each balloon would then be 483cm^2, 768cm^2 and 1006cm^2 respectively. Now, let's assume that the small and large balloons used in our demonstration are filled with 1000cm^3 and 3000cm^3 of air. The total surface area for these two balloons would be 1489cm^2. And let's use the prediction that when the valve is opened, air would flow between the two balloons until they were both the same diameter. That would mean that each balloon would be filled with 2000cm^3 of air. But if that were to happen, the total surface area of the two balloons would become 1536cm^2. The total surface area would have had to increase- with the same volume of air!

The Law of Laplace can also help us understand the observed phenomena. This law explains the relationship between the radius, surface tension, and internal pressure of a vessel. It reveals a counterintuitive relationship between the balloon's radius and its internal air pressure. It might seem to make sense that the balloon which is more inflated would have a greater internal air pressure than the less inflated balloon. However, just the opposite is true. The smaller balloon actually has the greater internal air pressure. The pressure that a balloon exerts on the air content inside is decreased as the diameter of the balloon increases. The internal pressure of the balloon is inversely proportional to its radius. As a balloon is inflated, the internal pressure decreases. This explains why smaller soap bubbles are more spherical than much larger ones. It is also why very large soap bubbles are "wobbly," and have difficulty maintaining a steady spherical shape. Since the pressure is inversely proportional to the radius, a smaller balloon is capable of expanding a larger one.

This demonstration can also be used to demonstrate the results that would occur within the human body without pulmonary surfactant in the lungs. Surfactant plays a critical role in our bodies. Following the results of this demonstration, one would think that smaller alveoli would collapse, while the larger grow even larger. The reason this phenomenon does not occur in the lungs is because of surfactant, which is a phospholipid. It alters the surface tension of the alveoli as its radius changes, stabilizing the pressure between the alveoli of differing diameters.

Surfactant plays a critical role in our bodies. There is a thin layer of water that lines human lungs. This water is necessary for the gas exchange of carbon dioxide and oxygen to occur. These gases require a wet layer or surface for the exchange to take place. In fish, this exchange takes place in their gills. Since they are on the outside of the fish, gills have direct contact with water. Our lungs, on the other hand, are best able to be kept wet inside of our bodies. However, due to the properties of water, surface tension arises that can interfere with the expansion of our lungs as we breathe. Surfactant acts to reduce surface tension. This prevents alveoli, small air sacs in the lungs, from collapsing when we exhale. The most efficient oxygen-carbon dioxide exchange occurs in our lungs with the greatest alveoli surface area. By preventing the collapse of alveoli, surfactant helps to maximize the surface area available for the exchange of gases.

Differently colored balloons can also generate a conversation about the physical properties of matter. A physical property is a property of a substance that can be immediately observed without changing the identity of the substance. Color is a physical property of matter. It can be immediately observed and it can help identify a substance. When you refer to a yellow balloon, students will know which one you are pointing out. Other physical properties include hardness, shape, size, texture, odor, etc. A few of these can be included in the discussion as the balloons are referred to.

Standards Alignment:

Next Generation Science Standards (NGSS, Lead States 2013)

Disciplinary Core Ideas in Physical Science

PS1: Matter and Its Interactions

PS1.A: Structure and Properties of Matter

PS3: Energy

PS3.A: Definitions of Energy

Disciplinary Core Ideas in Life Science

LS1: From Molecules to Organisms: Structures and Processes

LS1.A: Structure and Function

Buoyancy Paradox

<u>Concepts Illustrated:</u> Archimedes' principle, Newton's third law, buoyancy, displacement, mass, volume, elements and compounds, density.

<u>Paradox:</u>

Students observe dramatically different outcomes when two objects hanging from a string are individually submerged in water.

<u>Equipment:</u>

1. A meter stick.
2. Water.
3. String.
4. Two construction nails.
5. Beaker.
6. Ring stand and horizontal support arm.
7. A Mass that will hang from the support arm.
8. Double pan balance.

The setup

<u>Preparation:</u>

The meter stick used in the first phase of the demonstration can either be hung from a string or attached to a device that mounts at the top of a ring stand support. These devices can be purchased at science supply stores. Tie a string to each end of the meter stick, then tie a hardware nail to the end of each string. The strings should be of equal length. A beaker, large enough to accommodate the nail, should be filled with water.

The balance can be set up during class, but setting it up before students enter the classroom will save time. Place the ring stand on one pan of the balance. The support arm extends over the pan on the other side of the balance. The arm is positioned over the outside edge of that pan. A string is tied to the arm and a mass is tied to the other end. The mass hangs freely above the edge of the pan. A beaker of water sits on the pan, the mass hanging directly to its side. The balance should be at equilibrium. The size, in grams, of the hanging mass is dependent on the weight of the other equipment on the balance.

<u>The Lesson:</u>

Begin by displaying the setup. Students are shown a meter stick hanging horizontally from a string tied at its center. A string hangs from each end of the meter stick. Two nails hang freely, one tied to the end of each string. Demonstrate that the meter stick can pivot on the string it hangs from, but the equal masses of the nails cause it to be in a horizontal position. Tug on one of the nails to show this. Now show the beaker and fill it with water. Place it under one of the hanging nails. Explain that there will be three predictions to make. The meter stick will be lowered in its horizontal position so that the nail hanging above the beaker is submerged into the water. Students are asked to predict what will happen. Some might predict that nothing will happen and the meter stick will remain in its horizontal position. Others might predict that the nail submerged in the water will sink, causing that end of the meter stick to lower. And others might predict that the nail will rise in the water, causing that end of the meter stick to raise. The meter stick is lowered and the end with the submerged nail rises.

Now introduce the balance. Explain the setup to students. Be sure to point out that the mass hangs over the pan with the beaker of water. It should also be distinctly pointed out that the system is at equilibrium. Inform students that you will be adjusting the mass, so that instead of hanging to the side of the water-filled beaker, it will hang *in* the water. Ask students to predict how the balance will respond. They can use the observations made in the previous demonstration to make their predictions. Based on those observations, most students will predict that the balance will respond in the same manner as the hanging meter stick. In the previous demonstration, the nail rose when submerged in water, causing the nail hanging on the opposite side of the stick to lower. Because of this, students will predict that the hanging mass also rise when submerged, causing the pan on the opposite side to lower. The counterintuitive outcome of this demonstration is visually powerful.

Lift the hanging mass and carefully lower it into the water. Be sure that your fingers do not enter the water. Use the string to lift and lower the mass. Do not move any other piece of equipment in the process. Students will be rather shocked to discover that this system behaves quite differently than the last one they observed. When the mass is lowered into the water, the pan on the opposite side rises!

Although this outcome provides a valuable discrepancy to launch meaningful investigations, it can be followed with a further paradox that will deepen the puzzle and increase the investigative paths to pursue. Ask students to predict how much mass needs to be added to the balance pan with the ring stand in order to achieve equilibrium. Most will predict that the mass added to the ring stand pan should equal that of the hanging mass to balance the two pans. You can tell the mass of the hanging object. If, for example, the hanging mass is 100g, most will predict that 100g should be added to the pan with the ring stand. Place a 100g mass on the pan to show that the balance is actually far from a state of equilibrium!

Mass hanging in water.

Brought to equilibrium.

Possible Variables:

1. The height of the mass, when hanging in the water. It could hang near the top, middle, or bottom of the beaker.
2. The density of the liquid.
3. The volume of liquid.
4. The shape of the hanging mass. It could be spherical, cylindrical, cube shaped, etc.
5. Using a solid or hollow hanging mass.
6. If, for example, the hanging mass was 100g, what would happen if there were two 50g masses hanging and one was allowed to hang in the water, while the other hung to its side?

7. The volume, mass, or density of the hanging ball. This could involve a hanging mass made of copper, aluminum, brass, tin, etc.

Phenomenon Explained:

Buoyancy is defined as the tendency for an object to float in a fluid. Liquids and gases are fluids. The upward force exerted by the molecules of the fluid is called the buoyant force. The upward force, or pressure, increases as depth in the fluid increases. Pressure at the bottom of a body of liquid is greater than near the top. So, there is greater pressure on the bottom of a submerged object than at its top. This difference in pressure creates a net upward buoyant force on the object.

Newton's third law tells us that for every action, there is an equal and opposite reaction. When objects interact, the force exerted by one object on another is equal in strength to the force exerted by the second object on the first, but in the opposite direction. In this demonstration, there is a downward force that is equal and opposite of the upward buoyant force. When the ball hangs in the beaker during the second phase of the demonstration, the buoyant force of the water supports some of the weight that was previously supported by the tension of the string when it hung freely. Because of the reduced tension in the string, the downward force causes the beaker to have more weight. Since the beaker is allowed to move up or down freely due to the balance it rests on, this downward force "pushes" the beaker pan down.

According to Archimedes principle, the upward buoyant force exerted on a body immersed in a fluid is equal to the weight of the fluid the body displaces. This explains why a mass placed on the ring stand pan that is equal to the hanging mass will not bring the balance to equilibrium. Rather, the mass required to balance the two pans is equal to the weight of the volume of liquid that the hanging mass displaces. In order to bring the system to equilibrium, the volume of the hanging object must first be determined, followed by the mass of liquid equal to that volume. The specific liquid used in these calculations refers to the liquid that the hanging mass is lowered into.

In the first phase of the demonstration the beaker is in a fixed position, unable to move, being "held in place" by the table it rests on. The buoyant force exerted on the nail acts to push the nail up. The table prevents the beaker from being "pushed" down as a response to the upward force on the nail.

Students might choose to investigate the density of the liquid as a variable. The density of an object will determine whether it will float in a fluid. Density is determined by calculating the mass for a given volume, expressed in the formula g/ml, g/cm^3, or g/cc. Density is independent of the sample size, since it represents the mass per ml of the sample. A larger volume does not necessarily equate to a higher mass. Fewer molecules packed into a given volume will result in a lower density than many more molecules packed into the same volume, which would increase the density. Objects with a density less than water will float, while those denser than water will sink. The density of water is 1.0g/ml.

Standards Alignment:

Next Generation Science Standards (NGSS, Lead States 2013)

Disciplinary Core Ideas in Physical Science

PS1: Matter and Its Interactions

PS1.A: Structure and Properties of Matter

PS2: Motion and Stability: Forces and Interactions

PS2.A: Forces and Motion

Candle Drop

<u>Concepts Illustrated:</u> The process of flammability, capillary action, convection, law of inertia, properties of fluids, chemical changes, physical changes, molecular motion of gases, heat, melting, phase changes, amorphous solids, volume, kinetic energy, physical characteristics of solids, laminar flow, turbulent flow, gravity, capillary action in the human body, chemical reactions, exothermic reactions.

This demonstration involves fire and is intended for upper level students only. It is not suitable for elementary level children. When allowing upper level students to conduct this investigation, be certain to follow all safety guidelines and necessary precautions. As always, supervision and student awareness for the rules of safety are critical when using fire.

<u>Paradox:</u>

A burning candle in an open jar with holes in its side is dropped and the candle is extinguished. But students will be surprised to find that when the burning candle is placed into a sealed jar and dropped, it also extinguishes!

<u>Equipment:</u>

1. One plastic jar with holes in its side. Do not use a glass jar.
2. One plastic jar with lid. Do not use a glass jar.
3. Candle.
4. Clay to secure candle in jar.

<u>Preparation:</u>

A peanut butter jar works nicely for this demonstration. Holes can be made in its side with a utility knife. A second peanut butter jar of equal size can be used in the second part of the demonstration.

Add a lump of clay to the base of the jars. Then insert a candle into each lump of clay.

If you do not have clay, a clothes pin can be used. Break the ends of the clothes pin so that it fits horizontally in the lid. Now put a piece of double-sided tape onto the lid. Put the candle into the clothes pin and press it into the tape. When presenting the demonstration, light the candle and screw the lid in place. The candle can either be dropped upright by holding the bottle upside-down, or the candle can be dropped upside-down by holding the bottle upright.

You can also stick a pushpin through the lid and then push the base of the candle into the pin.

<u>The Lesson:</u>

Show the jar with holes in its side. The candle is positioned firmly in the clay. Explain that you will light the candle, hold the bottle above your head, and drop it. Select one student to catch the jar, or use a large basket with a pillow inside to "catch" the jar. Ask students to predict what will happen to the burning candle when the jar is dropped. Dim the lights or turn them off, so that the flame is easily visible. Light the candle and drop the jar to show that the candle is extinguished. Discuss with the class why this happened. The will probably attribute the flame being snuffed to "wind" or the "rushing air" as the bottle falls.

Explain that you will repeat the process, but this time the candle will be dropped in a sealed jar to eliminate "wind" or "rushing air" from affecting the flame. Ask students to predict what will happen to the burning candle this time. Most will now predict that the candle will remain lit, in the absence of wind on the wick. Light the candle and drop the jar to show, to the amazement of students, that the flame is once again extinguished- even though the candle is in a sealed jar!

Possible Variables:

1. Size of the jar.
2. Shape of the jar.
3. Rolling the jar, rather than dropping it.
4. Moving the jar on a cart, skateboard, or simply sliding it along a flat surface like the floor or table.
5. Swinging the jar.
6. Replacing the candle with a match. This would show that the flame is not put out because of wax splashing on it.
7. Attaching the candle to the lid, so that it falls upside-down.
8. Size of the candle.
9. Candle brand.
10. Some may surmise that a lack of sufficient air or oxygen is causing the flame to extinguish. This can be investigated by timing the candle as it burns stationary in the sealed jar, and then again while dropping. You'll find that the flame will stay lit much longer when sitting stationary, showing that a lack of oxygen is not causing the flame to go out.

Phenomenon Explained:

There are two explanations that can help us understand why the flame is extinguished when the jar falls. To begin, we'll have to first understand how a candle burns.

As a candle burns it undergoes an exothermic reaction, defined as a chemical reaction that releases energy by light or heat. When water freezes it is an exothermic process. The wick of a candle is shrouded in a coating of paraffin wax. When you light the wick of a candle, the paraffin coating melts and then vaporizes. This wax vapor, combined with oxygen in the air, burns. As the candle burns, "cooler" air containing the oxygen necessary to keep it burning flows in from beneath the flame while the heated gases given off from the flame rise, through the process of convection. Through capillary action, more wax is drawn up the wick, and the flame continues to burn. Capillary action is the upward movement of liquid, against gravity. Capillary action allows liquid to flow without the assistance of, and even in opposition to, external forces such as gravity. We depend on capillary action to live. Proper blood circulation, for example, depends on capillary action. Our eyes also use capillary action to drain excess tears into the nasal passage. Plants also depend on capillary action for their survival. Water is transported from roots, through the stem of smaller plants and the trunks of trees, to leaves and branches, against the force of gravity, through capillary action.

But, this process is hampered as the bottle falls. When the bottle drops it's in free fall. Objects in free fall behave as if there were no net gravity force. Because of this, heated air does not rise; convection does not occur. As a result, the oxygen rich air is not drawn into the base of the flame, and the flame goes out. This is the first explanation.

To understand the second explanation, we must understand that the candle, the flame, and the hot gases surrounding the flame fall together. Newton's first law of motion, known as the law of inertia, states that an object either at rest or in motion, remains at rest or in motion with the same speed and direction, unless acted upon by an unbalanced force. Inertia describes the property of matter to either maintain a state of rest or its velocity along a straight path, unless acted upon by an external force. Because of inertia, when the jar is caught at the end of the fall, the cooler air positioned higher, at the top of the jar, continues to fall and rushes to the bottom of the bottle. This sudden rush of falling, cooler air can also extinguish the flame. However, it's important to note that this movement of air also delivers oxygen to the wick. It's possible for the wick to potentially re-ignite in the presence of this renewed oxygen.

Thermal energy involves energy that generates due to the movement of particles within an object or system. Since thermal energy results from particle or molecular movement, it is considered a type of kinetic energy, or energy due to motion. Thermal energy is responsible for temperature, which is a measure of the average motion of the particles within a substance. The candle has the property of flammability, it can burn. As it burns, it undergoes a chemical reaction resulting in a chemical change. During a chemical change, bonds within molecules are broken and atoms rearrange. The result of a chemical change is a new substance. The new substances formed from a burning candle include carbon dioxide and ash. But the candle also undergoes physical changes. As the solid wax melts, it forms liquid wax, which evaporates to form wax vapor. Melting and evaporation are phase changes, occurring as a substance changes from one phase of matter to another. Other phase changes include freezing, condensation, and deposition, as states of matter move between solid, liquid and gas.

A candle is an example of an amorphous solid, or a solid "without shape." Amorphous solids are those without rigidity or consistent defined shape. The atoms and molecules within an amorphous solid do not maintain an orderly arrangement or pattern. The molecular arrangement of these solids can be altered, typically by heating them. Amorphous solids exhibit the opposite characteristics of crystalline solids, with molecules that form well-defined lattice type arrangements. Other examples of amorphous solids include plastic, rubber, and glass.

In laminar flow, a fluid flows in a well-defined, orderly manner, with rather distinct paths. On the other hand, turbulent flow describes the random, chaotic flow. There is no order in turbulent flow. Instead, the fluid undergoes irregular fluctuations. Turbulent flow can be observed in streams used for whitewater rafting, where the water moves in random and erratic directions. Consider laminar flow as the opposite of turbulent flow. When a candle flame is extinguished, the smoke that rises straight up from the wick is in laminar flow. But, as it reaches some distance from the wick it begins to spread out, waver, and even curl around. This is turbulent flow. It is rather difficult, if not impossible, to predict the behavior of turbulent flow.

Standards Alignment:

Next Generation Science Standards (NGSS, Lead States 2013)

Disciplinary Core Ideas in Physical Science

PS1: Matter and Its Interactions

PS1.A: Structure and Properties of Matter

PS1.B: Chemical Reactions

PS2: Motion and Stability: Forces and Interactions

PS2.B: Types of Interactions

PS3: Energy

PS3.A: Definitions of Energy

PS3.B: Conservation of Energy and Energy Transfer

Disciplinary Core Ideas in Life Science

LS1: From Molecules to Organisms: Structures and Processes

LS1.A: Structure and Function

Disciplinary Core Ideas in Earth and Space Science

ESS2: Earth's Systems

ESS2.D: Weather and Climate

Candle Ladder

Concepts Illustrated: The process of flammability, density, properties of gas, heat flow, chemical changes, physical changes, heat, molecular motion of gases, fluid dynamics, melting, phase changes, amorphous solids, volume, kinetic energy, physical characteristics of solids, laminar flow, turbulent flow, physical properties of matter, thermal energy, thermodynamics, capillary action, chemical reactions, capillary action in the human body, convection, exothermic reactions.

This demonstration involves fire and is intended for upper level students only. It is not suitable for elementary level children. When allowing upper level students to conduct this investigation, be certain to follow all safety guidelines and necessary precautions. As always, supervision and student awareness for the rules of safety are critical when using fire.

Paradox:

Students might expect that a collection of lit candles will be extinguished when covered with a large jar. But, they will be amazed to see the flames go out according to the height of the candle- from the tallest to the shortest!

This demonstration is quite a curious spectacle. But contradiction can be amplified for your students if they are first introduced to the ideas that candle flames produce carbon dioxide, that carbon dioxide is denser than air and sinks, and that carbon dioxide extinguishes candle flames. Why doesn't the carbon dioxide produced from these burning candles sink in the jar and extinguish the shorter candle first? If you choose to present these ideas as an introduction to the Candle Ladder, a detailed explanation is provided in the Lesson Variation section.

Equipment:

1. Candles of varying lengths. They should be of the same brand and type.
2. Jar or beaker large enough to cover all the candles at once.
3. Tray or plate to place the candles onto.
4. Putty, clay, or hex nut to hold the candles upright.

Showing height differences. Presented to class initially as random, mixed heights.

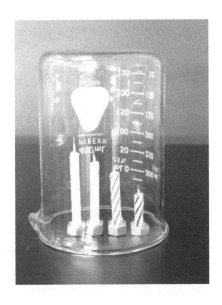

When lit, candles are extinguished by height- from tallest to shortest.

The Lesson:

To begin, the candles should be lying flat on the table. If they were upright, their differing heights would be visually glaring and draw immediate attention. Show the candles to the students, but don't call attention to their varying lengths.

Now show the jar. Explain that you will stand the candles upright and light them. Then you will cover them at once by putting the jar over all of them at the same time. Add "you probably know what will happen, but…", and ask students to write their prediction. The intent of this comment is to dissuade those who might be predicting some surprising event simply because they anticipate the demonstration must have one.

Push a small piece of putty onto the base of each candle and position them upright on the plate or tray in a random arrangement. Light the candles, then cover them with the jar. Focus on the candles. As they are being snuffed out, if no one recognizes the pattern, act surprised and explain that you do see one. Some students will have missed the pattern because of the random arrangement. Offer to present the demonstration one more time.

Lift the jar and reposition the candles so that they are in sequential order according to height. Light the candles once more and place the jar over them. Focus on the candles as the pattern is observed by all.

Lesson Variation:

As mentioned earlier, you can magnify the contradiction of expectation by first introducing some chemical properties of the substances involved. If you choose to pursue this method of presentation, students should understand three ideas. The first is that candles produce carbon dioxide gas. The second that carbon dioxide is denser than air, which causes it to sink. And the third idea is that carbon dioxide extinguishes candle flames. As I mentioned, there are a number of ways to illustrate these ideas to your students.

One way to prove that candle produce carbon dioxide when they burn involves limewater. In the presence of carbon dioxide, limewater turns cloudy. Burn a candle and place a large beaker over it. Let the candle burn as long as possible, allowing as much gas coming from the flame to be trapped in the beaker. Before the candle goes out, lift the beaker off of the candle and quickly turn it upright. Now pour some limewater into the beaker and swirl it around a bit. The limewater will turn cloudy, showing the presence of carbon dioxide.

Now, show that carbon dioxide is heavier than air and that it's a gas that will extinguish a candle flame by showing the following. In a beaker, mix vinegar and baking soda. It will bubble and produce carbon dioxide. Allow the reaction to continue for a bit. Then, pour the gas from this beaker into another. You don't want to pour any of the liquid. Now, pick up this beaker and pour it over a lit candle. The flame will be extinguished. Carbon dioxide is commonly used in fire extinguishers for this reason.

Another way to demonstrate the density of carbon dioxide is to combine baking soda and vinegar in an empty bucket, tub, or aquarium. Give it ample time to react and produce the gas, then blow bubbles into the container. The bubbles will float on the layer of carbon dioxide gas that hovers, due to its density, at the bottom of the container. Do not blow the bubbles directly into the container, as your breath might blow the carbon dioxide out. Instead blow the bubbles over the container so that they settle into it.

Possible Variables:

1. Candles of different colors.
2. Candles of different thicknesses.
3. Size of the jar.
4. Shape of the jar.
5. Candles of varying heights.
6. Brand of candles.

<u>Phenomenon Explained:</u>

As a candle burns it undergoes an exothermic reaction, defined as a chemical reaction that releases energy by light or heat. When water freezes it is an exothermic process. The wick of a candle is shrouded in a coating of paraffin wax. When you light the wick of a candle, the paraffin coating melts and then vaporizes. This wax vapor, combined with oxygen in the air, burns. s the candle burns, "cooler" air containing the oxygen necessary to keep it burning flows in from beneath the flame while the heated gases given off from the flame rise, through the process of convection. Through capillary action, more wax is drawn up the wick, and the flame continues to burn. Capillary action is the upward movement of liquid, against gravity. Capillary action allows liquid to flow without the assistance of, and even in opposition to, external forces such as gravity. We depend on capillary action to live. Proper blood circulation, for example, depends on capillary action. Our eyes also use capillary action to drain excess tears into the nasal passage. Plants also depend on capillary action for their survival. Water is transported from roots, through the stem of smaller plants and the trunks of trees, to leaves and branches, against the force of gravity, through capillary action.

As it burns, the candle uses oxygen and gives off carbon dioxide. Although this gas is naturally heavier than air, it has been heated by the flame and so its density changes. Because it is hot, the carbon dioxide gas becomes less dense as the molecules spread apart from one another. This heated carbon dioxide rises to the top of the overturned glass jar. The top of the jar continues to fill with this heated gas, forcing the other gases down. As more and more carbon dioxide accumulates and builds up, it takes up a larger volume of the jar. Eventually, it reaches the tallest candle and extinguishes it. It continues to fill the jar until it reaches the next tallest candle, which is extinguished. This continues until the shortest candle has been extinguished.

Thermal energy involves energy that generates due to the movement of particles within an object or system. Since thermal energy results from particle or molecular movement, it is considered a type of kinetic energy, or energy due to motion. Thermal energy is responsible for temperature, which is a measure of the average motion of the particles within a substance. Thermodynamics refers to the transfer of heat between different objects or systems, as occurs when the heat given off the flame causes to warm the bottle.

Heat is not the same as temperature. Essentially, heat is energy and temperature is a measure of it. The temperature of a substance is a measure of the average kinetic energy of its molecules. All matter is composed of atoms or molecules that are in constant motion. The faster they move, the more kinetic energy they have. There is a direct relationship between the motion of molecules and their temperature. The greater the kinetic energy, the higher the temperature of the object. Molecules that have low average kinetic energy move slowly and have low temperatures in comparison to molecules with high kinetic energy, which move more quickly and have a higher temperature.

The candle has the property of flammability, it can burn. As it burns, it undergoes a chemical reaction resulting in a chemical change. During a chemical change, bonds within molecules are broken and atoms rearrange. The result of a chemical change is a new substance. The new substances formed from a burning candle include carbon dioxide and ash. But the candle also undergoes physical changes. As the solid wax melts, it forms liquid wax, which evaporates to form wax vapor. Melting and evaporation are phase changes, occurring as a substance changes from one phase of matter to another. Other phase changes include freezing, condensation, and deposition, as states of matter move between solid, liquid and gas.

A candle is an example of an amorphous solid, or a solid "without shape." Amorphous solids are those without rigidity or consistent defined shape. The atoms and molecules within an amorphous solid do not maintain an orderly arrangement or pattern. The molecular arrangement of these solids can be altered, typically by heating them. Amorphous solids exhibit the opposite characteristics of crystalline solids, with molecules that form well-defined lattice type arrangements. Other examples of amorphous solids include plastic, rubber, and glass.

In laminar flow, a fluid flows in a well-defined, orderly manner, with rather distinct paths. On the other hand, turbulent flow describes the random, chaotic flow. There is no order in turbulent flow. Instead, the fluid undergoes irregular fluctuations. Turbulent flow can be observed in streams used for whitewater rafting, where the water moves in random and erratic directions. Consider laminar flow as the opposite of turbulent flow. When a candle flame is extinguished, the smoke that rises straight up from the wick is in laminar flow. But, as it reaches some distance from the wick it begins to spread out, waver, and even curl around. This is turbulent flow. It is rather difficult, if not impossible, to predict the behavior of turbulent flow.

Differently colored candles can also generate a conversation about the physical properties of matter. A physical property is a property of a substance that can be immediately observed without changing the identity of the substance. Color is a physical property of matter. It can be immediately observed and it can help identify a substance. When you refer to an orange candle, students will know which one you are pointing out. Other physical properties include hardness, shape, size, texture, odor, etc. A few of these can be included in the discussion as the candles are referred to.

Standards Alignment:

Next Generation Science Standards (NGSS, Lead States 2013)

Disciplinary Core Ideas in Physical Science

PS1: Matter and Its Interactions

PS1.A: Structure and Properties of Matter

PS1.B: Chemical Reactions

PS2: Motion and Stability: Forces and Interactions

PS2.B: Types of Interactions

PS3: Energy

PS3.A: Definitions of Energy

PS3.B: Conservation of Energy and Energy Transfer

Disciplinary Core Ideas in Life Science

<u>LS1: From Molecules to Organisms: Structures and Processes</u>

LS1.A: Structure and Function

Disciplinary Core Ideas in Earth and Space Science

<u>ESS2: Earth's Systems</u>

ESS2.D: Weather and Climate

Candy Palette

<u>Concepts Illustrated:</u> Solubility, miscibility, density, chromatography, solvent, solute, concentrated solutions, saturated solutions, properties of liquids, water as a universal solvent, fluid dynamics, physical changes, process of dissolving, physical properties of matter, properties of a mixture, viscosity, wavelengths of light, absorption and reflection of light, perception, visual interpretation of color, ocean currents.

<u>Paradox:</u>

When colorful candy is allowed to sit in water, their rainbow of colors dissolves and colors the water. But students are surprised to find the colors collide but do not mix, forming a perfectly plated palette! Expectations are further contradicted when the single color coating on each individual candy actually transitions through a spectrum of colors as it dissolves!

<u>Equipment:</u>

1. Gobstopper candy.
2. Shallow plate or petri dish.
3. Water. Use room temperature water.

<u>The Lesson:</u>

Show the Gobstopper candy to the students. Select three of each color of Gobstopper and group them together on the plate. Position the colors, in groups of three, around the perimeter of the dish. Introduce a beaker of water and explain that you're going to carefully pour the water into the plate, just enough to partially submerge the candies without disturbing their position. Ask students to predict what will happen. To help them form a prediction, you can encourage them to consider what might happen if the candies sat in their mouth for a period of time, which they have no doubt experienced. Most will predict the colors to dissolve and mix in the water, creating uniquely colored water.

Once they've generated their predictions, carefully pour the water into the dish. Observe them as they sit, undisturbed. Soon, the colors on the candy will begin to dissolve in the water. Many students may have predicted that the water would become colored from the dissolving candy. They'll be excited to find that their predictions are correct, because that's exactly what will happen. But if they continue to observe the dish, something very strange happens. The individual colors disperse and collide, but do not mix. Instead, they appear to be distinctly separated by an invisible wall!

Other students may have predicted that the color would "come off" each candy, leaving the candy colorless. They certainly won't expect that the candies will continue to change color during the dissolving process! And this is actually what happens. As students continue to carefully observe the demonstration, they will notice that each candy cycles through a spectrum of colors as it dissolves. This is truly surprising, as it would be expected that each candy has only one color coating.

Lesson Variation:

The demonstration can also be conducted by evenly spacing individual candies around the entire perimeter of a bowl or petri dish. Be sure to alternate colors. The result will be a pinwheel effect, with pie-shaped colors around the entire dish.

If you present this demonstration using a clear pan, students will be able to observe the colors from the side, as well as from above. With this added perspective, students will form more extensive observations, leading to a discussion based on a wider scope of details. A glass baking dish or pan works well.

Possible Variables:

1. Using a solvent other than water, such as vegetable oil, corn syrup, sprite, milk, vinegar, mouthwash, orange juice, soapy water, isopropyl alcohol, saltwater, sugar water, etc.
2. The amount of water covering the candies.
3. Candy other than Gobstoppers, such as M&M's, Skittles, Spree, Starlight mints, etc. When Starlight mints are used, the candy actually dissolves in stripes.
4. Once the candies have begun to color the water, differently colored candy can be placed into each section of colored water. So, a purple Gobstopper could be placed into a section filled with yellow colored water, etc.
5. Changing the density of water by adding salt or sugar before pouring it into the dish. This could also involve testing various concentrations of salt water or sugar water.
6. Varying the temperature of the water. It can be heated or chilled.
7. The shape of the dish or container.
8. Distance between each piece of candy.
9. Different colored candy touching one another in the dish.
10. Changing the pH of the liquid.
11. The number of Gobstoppers in each pile.
12. Positioning of the candy. There are numerous possibilities for creatively positioning the candies. For example, the piles can be closer together or the candies within each pile can be separated from one another. If three individual candies form a triangle in the center of the plate, a colored circle is formed.
13. The viscosity of the liquid. This could involve liquids such as honey, corn syrup, etc.

Phenomenon Explained:

This demonstration involves chromatography. This is a process of separating a mixture of solutes, oftentimes observed as pigments or colors in science experiments. A mixture is a combination of two or more substances, each retaining their own individual properties. One of the properties of a mixture, or what makes a mixture a mixture, is that it can be physically separated.

A solution is one in which a solute is dissolve in a solvent. The solute is the substance being dissolved and the solvent is the substance in which the solute is dissolved. Water is called the universal solvent because it is capable of dissolving more solutes than any other liquid. In our demonstration, the solute is the candy coating, and the solvent is water. Solubility is the ability of a solute to dissolve in a solvent. The colored sugar coating on a Gobstopper is soluble in water. As the color dissolves, it colors the water. If you observe the phenomenon from the side, such as in a Petri dish, you will notice that the sugar coating and its color sinks to the bottom of the dish. This is because the sugar solution is denser than the water it sits in.

Each Gobstopper candy is actually comprised of four layers of different colors. The manufacturer needs to ensure that these layers of colors don't mix during their production. This is accomplished by coating each color with a thin layer of wax. Because this wax is insoluble in water, the colors are inhibited from mixing in the bowl. As the Gobstoppers dissolve in the water, they are observed to transition through a series of changing colors as their colored dye dissolves one layer at a time.

The assorted colors will be observed to dissolve and spread in the water at about the same rates. This is because the coating on each candy has a similar amount of sugar. Any slight differences observed are due to the slight differences in molecular weight and polarity of the pigments.

The separation of colors as they dissolve is actually not a specific property of Gobstopper's. Students will find that M&M's and other sugar-coated candies will exhibit the same outcome. This is a characteristic property of colored sugar solutions. As mentioned, the sugar solution is denser than the water surrounding it. An object or solution that is less dense than water, will float. If it is denser than water it sinks. As the solution spreads, it pushes the less dense water aside until the differently colored denser solutions contact one another and the density driven current stops. The relatively slow molecular motion at room temperature contributes to the immiscibility, or the inability to mix. Conducting the experiment in warm or hot water illustrates the effect of increased molecular motion caused by the added energy. There is also enough energy to overcome the attraction between the sucrose molecules, and the sugar will dissolve at a faster rate. The one exception might be the chocolate component of the candy, such as in an M&M, which will not appear to dissolve as easily. This is because chocolate contains a relatively elevated level of fat, which is not as polar as sugar.

The candy coating will be observed to dissolve more slowly when placed in a sugar solution. This is due to concentration. A concentrated solution is one which there are many dissolved particles of solute in the solvent. On the other hand, a dilute solution is one in which there are few dissolved particles of solute. The more concentrated the sugar solution is, the denser it is. As a result, it becomes increasingly difficult for the coating to spread into this denser solution and less dissolves off the candy. Since the solution surrounding the candy is concentrated and already full of sugar, it does not readily dissolve more into it. A solution which contains all the dissolve particles it can possibly hold is called saturated.

A physical property is a property of a substance that can be immediately observed without changing the identity of the substance. Color is a physical property of matter. It can be immediately observed and it can help identify a substance. When you refer to the green

Gobstopper, students will know which one you are pointing out in the Petri dish. Other physical properties include hardness, shape, size, texture, odor, etc.

Absorption and reflection of wavelengths of light cause objects to display color. Light is made up of a spectrum of distinct wavelengths, each a particular color. Specifically, these are red, orange, yellow, green, blue, indigo, and violet. Objects around you appear to be particular colors because those colors, or wavelengths, are reflected from those objects. All other colors in the spectrum are absorbed. For example, when light hits a red Gobstopper it absorbs the entire spectrum of light except for red, which is reflected off the candy. Your retina perceives the color being reflected and transmits that information to the brain for processing. The Gobstopper appears red. Essentially, the colors that we see are those wavelengths that are reflected off the object.

Viscosity is defined as a fluid's resistance to flow. Think of it as the "thickness" of a fluid. Fluids such as honey, molasses, and engine oil are highly viscous. Students might choose to investigate the effects of solubility using a liquid more viscous than water.

The separated colored solutions exhibit a density gradient.

Standards Alignment:

Next Generation Science Standards (NGSS, Lead States 2013)

Disciplinary Core Ideas in Physical Science

PS1: Matter and Its Interactions

PS1.A: Structure and Properties of Matter

PS1.B: Chemical Reactions

PS2: Motion and Stability: Forces and Interactions

PS2.B: Types of Interactions

PS4: Waves and Their Applications in Technologies for Information Transfer

PS4.B: Electromagnetic Radiation

Disciplinary Core Ideas in Life Science

LS1: From Molecules to Organisms: Structures and Processes

LS1.A: Structure and Function

LS1.D: Information Processing

Disciplinary Core Ideas in Earth and Space Science

<u>ESS2: Earth's Systems</u>

ESS2.C: The Roles of Water in Earth's Surface Processes

Capsized Confusion

Concepts Illustrated: Buoyancy, density, mass, volume, Archimedes' principle, elements and compounds.

Paradox:

A flat Styrofoam block, with a metal block attached to its top, floats when placed into a tank of water. Its position at the surface of the water is noted and marked. The Styrofoam block is flipped over, so that the attached metal block is now underneath. Most expect that the metal block will pull the Styrofoam block deeper into the water. But, contradicting all expectation, the Styrofoam block now floats even higher at the surface of the water!

Equipment:

1. A block of Styrofoam that has a smaller block of aluminum fastened to one side.
2. Aquarium or tank of water.

Preparation:

The block of Styrofoam should be about 6 inches thick. If you can only find Styrofoam that is 3 inches thick, glue two pieces together to make a piece that is 6 inches in thickness. This block should be about 12 inches square. In our example, the metal block will be 8 inches square. It can be attached to the center of one side of the Styrofoam block by using glue or Velcro strips. This block should remain adhered to the Styrofoam block when it is inverted. Note that exact dimensions are not critical, but the aluminum block should be smaller than the Styrofoam block.

The tank should be filled to about ¾ with water.

Place the two connected blocks into the water, with the aluminum block on top. The Styrofoam block will be partially submerged, with about ½ of the block floating above the surface of the water. Mark the side of the Styrofoam block at the water line. Now remove the block from the water and extend this line completely around the edge of the block. When you place this block back into the water, the surface of the water should line up with this marking along the edge.

The Lesson:

Show the two connected blocks to the students. Explain that one is made of Styrofoam and the smaller one is metal. You should explain that the two blocks are connected.

Hold the blocks above the water, with the metal block on top. Ask students to predict what will happen when you lower the blocks into the water and let them go. You will hear a variety of responses, including the blocks will fully submerge, partially submerge, float entirely on top of the water, and sink to the bottom of the tank. Some will say that the block will flip over leaving the metal block underneath.

Once predictions have been recorded and shared, place the block onto the surface of the water. Students will observe that the Styrofoam block floats. It should be distinctly pointed out that the surface of the water aligns with the line drawn on the edge of the Styrofoam block.

Now ask student to make a second prediction. Explain that you are going to invert the connected blocks, so that the metal block is underneath, and place it back into the water. Students should predict whether the line around the edge of the block will once again line up with the surface of the water, sink below the water level, or rise above it. Most will predict that the weight of the metal block will pull the Styrofoam block deeper into the water, causing the line on the edge of the Styrofoam block to drop below the surface of the water.

Once predictions are recorded and shared, flip the connected blocks over and lower them onto the surface of the water. Students will be rather perplexed to find that the Styrofoam block now floats higher on the surface of the water! The line on the edge of the block is now well above the water level!

Lesson Variation:

This is a great presentation for students who have already learned about the concept of density. Before placing the blocks into the water, explain that the small block is made of aluminum. Then, with the help of the class, determine the density of aluminum. This can be done by either searching online, or measuring the volume and mass of a sample piece of aluminum to calculate the density. Students will find that the density of aluminum is about 2.7 g/cm3. Their knowledge of density will prompt most students to predict that the inverted block will sink below the marked line, since the density of the aluminum block is greater than the density of water. Since objects with a density greater than water will sink when placed into water, it will seem that the metal block would sink and pull the Styrofoam block deeper into the water. They will be surprised to find that the opposite occurs!

Possible Variables:

13. The size of the Styrofoam block. The length, width, and height can be manipulated.
14. The size of the small block.
15. The substance of the small block that sits on top of the Styrofoam block. For example, the block can be made of tin, copper, steel, iron, cork, wood, plastic, etc.
16. Density of the water. This can be easily accomplished by adding salt or sugar.
17. The orientation of the small block. Instead of lying "flat", or horizontally, it can stand up, vertically.

<u>Phenomenon Explained:</u>

This demonstration illustrates the concepts of buoyancy and density.

The density of an object will determine whether it will float in a fluid. Density is determined by calculating the mass for a given volume, expressed in the formula g/ml, g/cm^3, or g/cc. Density is independent of the sample size, since it represents the mass per ml of the sample. A larger volume does not necessarily equate to a higher mass. Fewer molecules packed into a given volume will result in a lower density than many more molecules packed into the same volume, which would increase the density. Objects with a density less than water will float, while those denser than water will sink. The density of water is 1.0g/ml.

Considering density alone, the Styrofoam block alone would float on water because its density is less than water. The metal block alone would sink because its density is greater than water. However, buoyancy also plays a significant role here.

Buoyancy is defined as the tendency for an object to float in a fluid. Liquids and gases are fluids. The upward force exerted by the molecules of the fluid is called the buoyant force. Archimedes' principle states that the upward buoyant force exerted on a body immersed in a fluid is equal to the weight of the fluid the body displaces, acting in an upward direction at the center of the mass of the displaced fluid.

In addition, the upward force, or pressure, increases as depth in the fluid increases. Pressure at the bottom of a body of liquid is greater than near the top. So, there is greater pressure on the bottom of a submerged object than at its top. This difference in pressure creates a net upward buoyant force on the object.

When the blocks are initially placed into the water, the density of the Styrofoam causes it to float. When the blocks are inverted, the density of the metal block will cause it to sink into the water. But in this situation, since the depth in the fluid has increased, so too has the buoyant force on the blocks. This force is so great that it causes the blocks to rise above the previous level in the water.

If the density of the liquid is altered by adding salt or sugar, discourse can include solutions, solubility, solutes, solvents, and concentration. Saltwater or sugar water is a mixture. One property of a mixture is that it is physically combined, not chemically, and it can be physically separated. For example, saltwater can be physically separated through the process of evaporation, or boiling the water away.

A solution is one in which a solute is dissolve in a solvent. The solute is the substance being dissolved and the solvent is the substance in which the solute is dissolved. Water is called the universal solvent because of its capability to dissolve more solutes than any other liquid. Solubility is the ability of a solute to dissolve in a solvent.

A concentrated solution is one which there are many dissolved particles of solute in the solvent. On the other hand, a dilute solution is one in which there are few dissolved particles of solute. A solution which contains all the dissolve particles it can possibly hold is called saturated.

Standards Alignment:

Next Generation Science Standards (NGSS, Lead States 2013)

Disciplinary Core Ideas in Physical Science

PS1: Matter and Its Interactions

PS1.A: Structure and Properties of Matter

PS1.B: Chemical Reactions

PS2: Motion and Stability: Forces and Interactions

PS2.A: Forces and Motion

Disciplinary Core Ideas in Earth and Space Science

ESS2: Earth's Systems

ESS2.C: The Roles of Water in Earth's Surface Processes

Centripetal Force Paradox

Concepts Illustrated: Centripetal force, centrifugal force, fluid dynamics, Newton's first law of motion- the law of inertia, properties of liquids, fluid dynamics, volume, viscosity, density.

Paradox:

Two upside-down glass jars filled with water are attached, opposite each other, to the outer edge of a rotating turntable. Each jar has a ping pong ball floating in it, attached to the lid with a string. Students expect that when the turntable is spun around, the ping pong balls will be pushed to the outside of the jars- away from the center of rotation. But, the result is just the opposite. When spun around, the ping pong balls move to the inside, or towards the center of rotation!

Disequilibrium intensifies when two more water-filled jars are introduced. In addition to the ping pong balls, each of these jars contains a golf ball, hanging from a string attached to the bottom of the upside-down jar. When the unit is rotated, each type of ball behaves differently! The ping pong ball is pushed towards the center of rotation, while the golf ball is pushed away from it. Contradicting all expectation, the ping pong ball leans inward while the golf ball in the same jar leans outward!

Equipment:

1. Two identical jars with lids. Mason jars work well.
2. 2 ping pong balls. Styrofoam balls, fishing bobbers, golf balls, or corks can also be used.
3. A rotating turntable. This unit can be a Lazy Susan, record player, or constructed apparatus.
4. String or fishing line.
5. Super Glue or similar cement.

Preparation:

Using a hot glue gun, attach the string or fishing line to the center of the Mason jar lid. Now, attach one ping-pong ball to the other end of each string. The string should be long enough so that when the lid is screwed into place, and the Mason jar is turned upside-down, the ping-pong ball will float freely in the water, anchored to the lid. Fasten the lids to the rotating unit using Super Glue. Be sure to allow them to dry thoroughly. Now, fill the Mason jars with water. Turn the rotating unit upside-down and screw the jars onto the lids. Turn the unit right-side up, so that the bottles are now upside-down.

The alternative is to Super Glue the bottom of the Mason Jars to the rotating unit. The string would be attached to the inside of the jar using a hot glue gun to fasten it to the bottom. The jars would be filled with water and the lids screwed on, without turning the rotating unit upside-down.

If using a Lazy Susan or record player, a board about 24" x 5" can be set on top the spinning device. This will create distance between the bottles, and a much larger diameter of rotation.

The board can be permanently glued or cemented to the Lazy Susan. If a record player is used, a hole can be drilled in the center of the board to snugly accommodate the spindle in the center of the turntable.

The Lesson:

Display the entire apparatus to the students. They should understand that the bottles can be spun around on the base they are attached to. While explaining this, it should be sitting motionless on the table. Be sure that they understand that the jars are filled with water and that the ping pong balls are freely floating in them. Now, ask students to predict what will happen to the ping pong balls if the jars were to be spun on the unit, in a circular motion. Prompt students to recall any similar experiences they may have had, such as the way their own bodies react in a car that turns a corner. Most will recall that in such a situation, their bodies are pushed outwards, away from the center of the car. Virtually all students will predict that when the jars are spun, the ping pong balls will be pushed outward, or away from the center of the rotating unit. Once students have made their prediction, spin the jars. Students will observe that the ping pong balls actually move to the inside- towards the center of the rotating unit!

Now introduce the two additional jars. Each jar has a golf ball and ping pong ball. If two additional jars are unavailable, the golf ball can be simply added to the original jars. While the ping pong balls float because they are less dense than water, the golf balls sink because they are denser than water. Ask students to predict how these balls will react when the table is rotated. Most will base their predictions in their previous observations. When the unit is spun, the two balls lean in opposite directions. The ping pong ball is pushed towards the center of rotation, or the inside wall of the jar, while the golf ball is pushed away from it, leaning outward. This outcome startles everyone!

Lesson Variation:

If resources are limited, the demonstration can be presented using only one ball in each jar. A golf ball would hang from the top of one jar, while a ping pong ball would float from the bottom of the other.

The demonstration can also be presented following a different sequence of events. For the first part of the demonstration, leave the jars empty. Fasten a ping pong ball to the end of a string and attach the other end to the bottom of the upside-down jar. Do this in each jar. Spin the apparatus and the ping pong balls will be observed to fly outward, *away* from the center of rotation. For the second part of the demonstration, remove the strings from the bottom of the jar and reattach them to the lids of the jars. Now fill the jars with water and screw the lids on. When the jars are affixed to the rotating unit, the ping pong balls are now floating upward in the water, due to their density. Most students will predict that the balls will still fly outward, but not as much as before, due to the water. Spin the apparatus and the ping pong balls will actually be observed to fly inward, the opposite direction as before, *towards* the center of rotation!

Another variation would involve hanging a ball under each jar. The ball would not be in the jar, but rather hanging outside of it from underneath.

Yet another variation would involve hanging a ball directly above each jar, from a rod attached to the top of each jar. The ball would not be in the jar, but rather hanging outside of it from above.

Possible Variables:

1. Jars of differing sizes. This can be two bottles of the same size, but different from those used in the original demonstration, or two bottles of different sizes. The jars can differ in height or width.
2. Jars of different shapes.
3. Liquids of varying densities.
4. The viscosity of the liquids.
5. Balls filled with liquids that have similar densities as the liquid in the bottles.
6. Balls filled with liquids that have different densities as the liquid in the bottles.
7. Diameter of balls.
8. Balls made of different substances, such as lead, copper, brass, tin, etc. This can involve using balls made of the same substances in each jar, or two balls made of different substances in each jar.
9. Length of thread attached to the balls, which changes their placement as they float or hang in the bottles.
10. Laying bottles on their sides as they spin.
11. Rather than balls, use objects of different shapes.
12. Filling each bottle by layering it with liquids of different densities (so that the upper and lower half of the bottle has a different density), then placing balls with different densities in each layer.
13. Position of jar on rotating arm; closer to the center, or farther away. The rotating arms could have a series of holes in them, so that the jars can be placed at different positions.
14. Balls with holes in them, like a whiffle ball or small ping pong ball with holes.
15. Balls of different substances can be used in the demonstration variations explained above. For example, could float a Styrofoam ball from a string inside the jar, while suspending a metal ball above or below the outside of the jar. A cork can also replace the floating ball. Different shapes or sizes of corks can also be studied.
16. Clockwise vs counter-clockwise rotation of the bottles.

Phenomenon Explained:

Some will confuse centrifugal force with centripetal force. Centrifugal force draws a rotating body away from the center of rotation. It is caused by inertia of the body. This is the force we experience when we turn a corner in a car. On the other hand, centripetal force acts on a body that is in a curvilinear motion. The force is directed toward the axis of rotation.

When we are riding in a car that makes a sharp turn, we feel as though we are being "pushed" outwards, sometimes pressed against the door next to us. This is centrifugal force. It describes the tendency of an object in a circular, or curved path, to be forced outwards, away from the center of the rotation. The force we are feeling arises due to inertia. Newton's first law of motion, known as the law of inertia, states that an object either at rest or in motion, remains at rest or in motion with the same speed and direction, unless acted upon by an unbalanced force. You are traveling forward, in a straight path, before the car makes its turn. According to the law of inertia, when the car turns, your body wants to keep going straight, and you are forced into the door. Centrifugal force is not really a "force," but rather an outcome of inertia.

As the unit spins, the water is forced to the outside of each jar due to inertia. As a result, there is greater water pressure against the outside of the jar. The water pressure increases with distance from the center of rotation. Essentially, this means that the force exerted on the liquid at the outside of the jar is greater than the force exerted on the fluid which is nearer the center of rotation. The circular motion of the unit requires a net force directed towards the center of rotation, causing the ping pong ball to move in that direction. The ping pong balls essentially move in the direction of the accelerating force.

Viscosity is defined as a fluid's resistance to flow. Think of it as the "thickness" of a fluid. Fluids such as honey, molasses, and engine oil are highly viscous. Students might choose to investigate the effects of solubility using a liquid more viscous than water.

Standards Alignment:

Next Generation Science Standards (NGSS, Lead States 2013)

Disciplinary Core Ideas in Physical Science

PS1: Matter and Its Interactions

PS1.A: Structure and Properties of Matter

PS2: Motion and Stability: Forces and Interactions

PS2.A: Forces and Motion

PS2.B: Types of Interactions

Cheese Puzzler

<u>Concepts Illustrated:</u> Surface area, heat, heat retention/loss and metabolism within organisms, volume, thermal energy, transfer of energy, microwave radiation, heat flow, conduction, physical changes, phase changes, melting, physical properties of matter, mass, volume, electromagnetism, thermodynamics.

This demonstration can serve as a springboard to a lesson on the diverse body sizes and shapes of organisms and how this might affect or influence heat retention/loss and metabolism.

Surface area: Students could be asked to calculate volume and surface area of the cubes. By calculating the surface area to volume ratio, students can begin to discover, among other ideas, that larger objects generally have smaller surface area to volume ratio.

This demonstration does involve a microwave oven. However, this does not mean that every student, or group of students, needs a microwave for their follow-up investigations. Three methods of investigation are presented, involving only one microwave. See the Possible Variables section for details on conducting the demonstration and the follow-up investigations with only one microwave oven.

<u>Paradox:</u>

When presented with a plate of differently sized cubes of cheese, most students will predict that the smaller cubes will melt first when placed in a microwave. The results are contradictory. When placed in the microwave, the larger cubes are observed to melt faster!

<u>Equipment:</u>

1. One block of cheese, cut into cubes that are small, medium, and large in comparison.
2. A microwave oven.
3. A dish to place the cheese onto.
4. Hot plates are optional for student investigations.

<u>Preparation:</u>

Cut a block of cheese into randomly sized cubes. Be sure that some cubes are distinctly larger than the rest, and that some are considerably smaller.

<u>The Lesson:</u>

Present the plate of cheese cubes to your students. Ask them to identify any characteristic differences between the cubes. Since all the cubes are cut from the same block of cheese, one of the most obvious differences will be their sizes. Be sure to point out that some are much larger than others, while some are much smaller in size. Ask students to predict what will happen to the cubes when heated in a microwave. After they've written their predictions, ask students to verbally share them. The majority will respond that the cheese will obviously melt. Ask how many wrote this prediction. All will probably have done so.

Remark that since most of the predictions were identical, you'll add a second prediction and "we'll see if we get similar answers once again." Add that "we probably will since we've all seen things melt before." This comment diminishes suspicion of any counterintuitive outcome and strengthens the probability that students will respond intuitively. Continue by asking students to predict the order in which the cubes will melt, by size. At this point, rearrange the cubes on the plate so that they are lined up in order of size, from smallest to largest. This will help focus the predictions and make the melting process more visually impactful. Ask students to verbally share predictions once again. You'll find consensus as most will respond that the smaller cubes will melt faster, while the larger cubes will take the longest to melt.

Place the plate in the microwave and turn it on. The window on the front of the microwave may not be large enough for all to comfortably see inside. So, stop the heating process midway and remove the plate so that all students can clearly see the larger cubes melting as the smaller cubes remain intact. Then place the plate back into the microwave to complete heating the cheese. Remove the plate to show that the larger cubes have fully melted- the smaller cubes still intact!

Possible Variables:

As mentioned earlier, there are three formats for the follow-up investigations.

In the first, students conduct investigations using hot plates. They compare findings and observations to one another, but also to those made in the microwave during the demonstration.

In the second format, the class decides on one follow-up investigation they would like to conduct with the microwave. A pair of students is chosen to conduct that investigation, using the microwave, while the other students in the class conduct their investigations using hot plates.

Finally, the third format involves a whole-class approach to the follow-up investigations. Once students have designed their research questions, the class chooses those they would like to pursue. Using the single microwave, the class collaboratively engages in those investigations. Discourse can follow each investigation and connections can be made as the investigations progress.

1. Sizes, or volumes, of the cheese cubes.
2. Surface area of the cheese cubes.
3. Placement in the microwave.
4. Temperature.
5. Tray that the cheese cubes rest on.
6. Type of cheese.
7. Brand of cheese.
8. Covering the cheese with a napkin or Tupperware lid.
9. Substances other than cheese, such as ice, chocolate, wax, crayons, etc.

<u>Phenomenon Explained:</u>

Heat is not the same as temperature. Essentially, heat is energy and temperature is a measure of it. Heat is a form of energy that can transfer from one medium to another, flowing from objects of higher temperature to those with lower temperature. When a cup of coffee feels hot, it is because energy from the cup is being transferred to your hand. On the other hand, a glass of iced tea feels cold because heat energy from your hand is flowing into the glass. This causes it to feel cold.

The temperature of a substance is a measure of the average kinetic energy of its molecules. All matter is composed of atoms or molecules that are in constant motion. The faster they move, the more kinetic energy they have. There is a direct relationship between the motion of molecules and their temperature. The greater the kinetic energy, the higher the temperature of the object. Molecules that have low average kinetic energy move slowly and have low temperatures in comparison to molecules with high kinetic energy, which move more quickly and have a higher temperature. The molecules of solids generally move very slowly, simply vibrating in place. Thermal energy is defined as the energy within an object or system due to the movement of the particles or molecules within.

Heat is the *total* kinetic energy in a substance or system. This is different than temperature which, as we have learned, is the *average* kinetic energy. Heat is dependent on the speed of the particles, the number of particles, and the type of particles in a substance. On the other hand, temperature is independent of the number and type of particles. A large tub of water could have the same temperature as a small cup of water, but the water in the large tub would possess more heat because it contains many more molecules, therefore more total kinetic energy.

Microwave ovens produce electromagnetic rays, found between radio and infrared waves. They are part of the electromagnetic spectrum, consisting of waves that do not require a medium to travel through. Food placed in a microwave will absorb the microwaves produced, causing water molecules in the food to vibrate and produce heat. Those foods with a higher water content will cook faster than those with lower water content. Those foods with little water content, or have thick outer layers, are heated on the outside, the heat traveling to the center through conduction. In conduction, energy is passed from one molecule to the next through molecular collisions, caused by the increased kinetic energy. Conduction is one of the three main methods of heat transfer.

A microwave heats food from the inside. The smaller cubes lose their heat more quickly than the larger cubes, which retain more heat and thus melt more quickly.

The process of melting cheese represents a physical change, or a change that does not alter the chemical composition of the substance. Unlike a chemical change, a physical change does not produce a new substance. Melting cheese simply changes the form of cheese from the solid phase to the liquid phase. When matter transitions from one phase to another, it is called a phase change.

Standards Alignment:

Next Generation Science Standards (NGSS, Lead States 2013)

Disciplinary Core Ideas in Physical Science

PS1: Matter and Its Interactions

PS1.A: Structure and Properties of Matter

PS1.B: Chemical Reactions

PS2: Motion and Stability: Forces and Interactions

PS2.B: Types of Interactions

PS3: Energy

PS3.A: Definitions of Energy

PS3.D: Energy in Chemical Processes and Everyday Life

PS4: Waves and Their Applications in Technologies for Information Transfer

PS4.B: Electromagnetic Radiation

Clanging Cans

<u>Concepts Illustrated:</u> Bernoulli's principle, air pressure, air current, aerodynamics, airplane flight, mass, volume, molecular motion of gases, fluid dynamics, properties of tornadoes, human anatomy of the vocal chords.

The materials involved in this counterintuitive demonstration present tremendous variety, depending on your focus, grade level, and availability of resources.

<u>Paradox:</u>

When students blow between two hanging empty soda cans, they expect them to swing apart from one another. The counterintuitive outcome defies reason when the cans actually move closer! The harder the students try to blow the cans apart, the more quickly they collide, banging into each other!

<u>Equipment:</u>

1. Two soda cans. The demonstration can also be presented using balloons, ping-pong balls, aluminum foil balls, paper cups, cotton balls, or a number of other objects. See the *"Possible Variables"* section below for further ideas.
2. String, thread, or fishing line.
3. Any horizontal rod to hang the soda cans from. A ring stand with a horizontal support rod works well.

<u>Preparation:</u>

Cut two equal lengths of string. 15-30 cm will do, but the length is insignificant. Secure one soda can to the end of each string. You can do this by either tying the string to the tab on top of the can, or by fastening the string to the can with a piece of tape or putty. Tie the other end of the string to the horizontal support rod of the ring stand. The two cans should hang at the same height, about 5-7 cm apart.

If you do not have a ring stand, stack two piles of textbooks on a table and place a meter stick across them. Tie the strings to the meter stick to hang the cans.

If you are using paper or Styrofoam cups, poke a hole in the bottom of each. Push the end of a length of string through the hole and tape it to the inside bottom of the cup. Attach the other end of the string to the ring stand or meter stick to hang the inverted cups. You can even tape the ends of the strings to the edge of a table or desk, the cups hanging off the edge of the table.

The Lesson:

Show the setup. Explain that the soda cans are empty and hang freely. Ask students to predict what will happen when you blow into the space between the two cans. Most students know from experience that objects are usually blown away from the source of the air flow. This will lead them to predict that the two cans will swing apart from one another, blown away by the force of the wind. Allow students to share the reasoning for their predictions. Many in the class will have shared experiences involving wind that will lead to a rich discussion. Now, gently blow directly between the two cans. Students will be amazed when the two cans are actually drawn closer, banging into each other!

Note that you can produce a rather intriguing discrepant event using just one soda can. Blowing against one side of the can will actually draw the can closer to the source of the air flow, rather than away from it. For example, blowing air on the right side of one can will cause it to swing to the right! This is very counterintuitive.

Note that a straw can be used to blow between the cans.

Lesson Variation:

Variation #1:

Rather than hanging the soda cans, the demonstration can be performed on a table. Remove about 8 straws from their wrappers and lie them on the table in rows, parallel to each other. Leave about 1 cm space between each. Now place the two cans upright on the straws, about 5-7 cm apart. Blow directly between the cans, without blowing at the table or the straws. They will glide along the straws towards each other and bang together.

You can actually place the cans about 20 cm apart and still observe the same outcome! With the cans in this position, blow a steady stream of air along the right side of the left can, while moving your head slowly to the right. The can will glide 20 cm and bang against the other!

<u>Variation #2:</u>

The demonstration can be accomplished using two hanging sheets of paper. Allow the sheets to hang freely about 3-5 cm from one another. Using a straw, blow air in between them. Most will expect the sheets to blow apart from one another. But instead, they will be drawn closer.

If you bend the bottom of each sheet, curling them out and away from one another, the demonstration can be used as a model to illustrate the mechanics of the human vocal folds. See the Phenomenon Explained section for an explanation.

<u>Variation #3:</u>

Press two lumps of clay, about 7 cm apart, onto a table or desk. Push one end of a straw into each. The straws will be upright. Press a small lump of clay onto each of two ping-pong balls. Now press the clay on the balls onto the top of upright straws. Each straw will now have a ping-pong ball affixed to its top. The balls should be at the same height. Wiggle the base of the straws a bit, so the straws have a little "play" and are able to move slightly. Blow between these ping-pong balls and they will be drawn together.

<u>Possible Variables:</u>

1. Replacing the hanging soda cans with other objects, such as balloons, paper cups, cotton balls, cork balls or stoppers, rubber stoppers, tennis balls, apples, billiard balls, rubber balls, ping-pong balls, empty liter soda bottles, aluminum foil balls, coffee cans, etc. Each of these can be paired with a like object of a different size. For example, a small and a large paper cup can be hung together. This small/large pairing can be investigated with any of the other objects.
2. Hanging objects of various shapes. These can be cutouts from construction paper, Styrofoam shapes, cork shapes, etc. Examples of shapes can include cubes, rectangles, diamonds, vertical or horizontal discs, stars, etc. This can also involve two of the same shape, or a different shape hanging from each string. If balloons are used, it would allow for balloons of varying shapes.
3. Balls of varying volumes and masses. This can involve both balls of the same volume, or differing volumes. The mass of each can also be the same or different. If ping-pong balls are used, they can be filled with sand or water to change their mass. Poke a hole near the top of the ball so that it can be filled. Coffee cans could also be filled with sand to adjust their weights. If balloons are used, they can be expanded to different volumes.
4. Distance between the cans.
5. Distance between the air source and the cans.
6. Speed of the air source. This can be controlled if using a blow dryer with settings.
7. Direction of the air flow.
8. Ping-pong balls with holes, or whiffle balls.
9. Replacing the soda cans with containers of different shapes, such as square pint size milk cartons or plastic water bottles.
10. Sucking air in through the straw, rather than blowing it out.
11. Altering the position of the cans so that one is hanging more forward than the other.
12. Dents in cans.

The following variables are specific to Lesson Variation #1:

1. The number of straws.
2. The diameter of the straws.
3. The distance between the straws.
4. Distance between the straws.
5. The mass of the cans. Water or sand can be added to change their mass.
6. The size of the cans.
7. Distance between the cans.
8. Dowel, pencils, or even paper rolls in place of straws.
9. Altering the position of the cans so that one is sitting more forward than the other.
10. The following variables are specific to Demonstration Variation #3:

The following variables are specific to Lesson Variation #2:

1. The size of the paper. This can involve two sheets of the same size, but different from that used in the demonstration. It can also involve two differently sized sheets of paper.
2. The type of paper. For example, construction paper, tissue paper, etc.
3. Holes in the paper. This can involve holes in one sheet, or both. It can also involve varying the placement of the hole in the sheet, as well as holes of various shapes and sizes.

The following variables are specific to Lesson Variation #3:

1. Adding more upright straws, in different positions relative to one another.
2. The diameter of the straws.
3. Putting the straws on angles, rather than upright.
4. Something other than straws, such as pipe cleaners, bamboo skewers, toothpicks, wood dowel, Popsicle sticks, or wire.
5. Direction of air flow. Students can blow on the ping-pong balls directly from above, from the side, or aimed up, from below.

Phenomenon Explained:

This demonstration presents a fun, interactive method of illustrating Bernoulli's principle. It states that when the velocity of a fluid increases, the pressure decreases. The faster a fluid, whether gas or liquid, moves over a surface, the less air pressure it exerts on that surface.

The lower air pressure between the cans causes the higher air pressure exerted on the outer sides of the cans to push them towards each other.

Blowing directly on the soda can will cause it to blow away from the air source, as we might expect. This is because air molecules hit the surface of the can, transferring kinetic energy to the can, pushing it away.

However, blowing between the two cans pushes air molecules away from this space, and they no longer exert pressure on the inner sides of the cans. This results in a lower pressure in that area. The air on the opposing sides of the cans maintains its pressure, which is now higher than that in the space between the cans. The higher air pressure on the outside of the cans essentially pushes them towards one another.

Counterintuitively, the faster the flow of air, the lower the pressure it exerts. This explains why the cans are drawn together faster, with a bigger bang, when you blow harder between them. It also explains the massive destruction caused by tornadoes. The incredible speed movement of air creates a tremendous decrease in pressure within a tornado. The stronger air pressure around the tornado throws nearby objects into it.

Bernoulli's principle explains, in part, how airplanes fly. Air flows over the upper surface of the wings faster than under them. This creates a reduced air pressure above the wings and a higher pressure under them. This generates lift. In addition, when the wing is tilted, air is deflected downward by both its upper and lower surface. Air flowing across the wing glides along the tilted direction of its surface. The air is entrained from the surroundings, resulting in a region of lower pressure above the wing. This also generates lift.

The Bernoulli principle and the lift of a wing

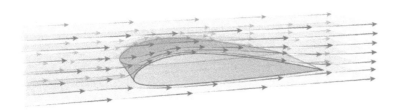

Side view

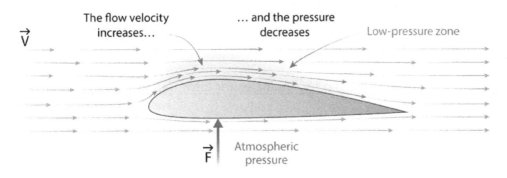

As mentioned in Variation #2, if you bend the bottom of each sheet, curling them out and away from one another, the demonstration can be used as a model to illustrate the mechanics of the human vocal folds. The diagram below illustrates the science behind the action.

The Bernoulli principle

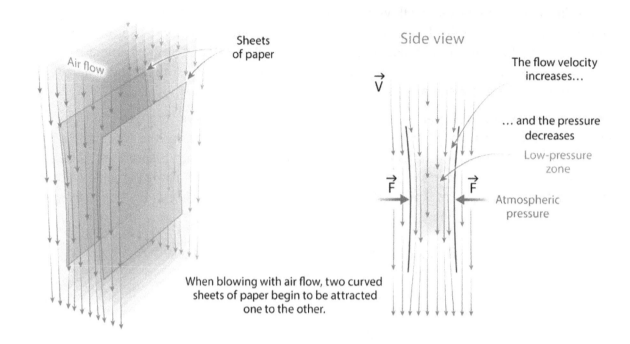

Sheets of paper

Air flow

Side view

The flow velocity increases...

... and the pressure decreases

Low-pressure zone

$\vec{V}$

$\vec{F}$ $\vec{F}$

Atmospheric pressure

When blowing with air flow, two curved sheets of paper begin to be attracted one to the other.

Standards Alignment:

Next Generation Science Standards (NGSS, Lead States 2013)

Disciplinary Core Ideas in Physical Science

PS1: Matter and Its Interactions

PS1.A: Structure and Properties of Matter

PS4: Waves and Their Applications in Technologies for Information Transfer

PS4.A: Wave Properties

Disciplinary Core Ideas in Life Science

LS1: From Molecules to Organisms: Structures and Processes

LS1.A: Structure and Function

Disciplinary Core Ideas in Earth and Space Science

ESS3: Earth and Human Activity

ESS3.B: Natural Hazards

The Climbing Ball

Concepts Illustrated: Density, buoyancy, miscibility, displacement, solutions, homogeneous solutions, solubility, solute, solvent, concentration, viscosity, elements and compounds.

Paradox:

A ball is shown to float in a beaker of liquid. In a second beaker of liquid it is shown to sink. The liquid that causes the ball to sink is added to the liquid in the first beaker, while the ball floats in it. But the behavior of the ball contradicts expectation by floating even higher in the liquid it was shown to sink in!

Ball "sinks" lower in vegetable oil than water. But when mixed, it floats higher in the layer of oil.

Equipment:

1. Two beakers. 600ml or 1000ml beakers work well.
2. One ball or sphere with a density less than water. It should float when placed in water.
3. Water.
4. Vegetable oil.

Preparation

The first beaker should be filled nearly halfway with water. The second is filled nearly halfway with vegetable oil. These two beakers sit on the desk. The ball is not in the liquid yet.

The Lesson:

Begin by drawing attention to the two beakers. Students can be told that one beaker contains water, while the other has vegetable oil. Explain to the students that in this demonstration they will be making some observations prior to making a prediction.

Begin by placing the ball in the beaker of water. The ball will be observed to float. Ask students to note exactly how much of the ball is submerged under water and how much is above water. You can ask students to share the percentage of the ball that is either sinking or floating. Now remove the ball from the water, dry it off, and place it in the beaker of vegetable oil. The ball will be observed to sink in this liquid. Again, ask students to share how much of the ball is now either sinking or floating.

Explicitly point out the water "causes the ball to float," while the vegetable oil "causes the ball to sink." These words have been deliberately chosen. First, they reinforce the observed behavior of the ball in each of the liquids. But more importantly, students will use these words when making their predictions in the next phase. The intent is to establish how each liquid "affects" the ball. When they make their predictions, students will recall that the vegetable oil "causes the ball to sink." This will lead most to predict that when it is added to the water it will again cause the ball to sink. This would seem to make sense.

Now remove the ball from the vegetable oil and dry it off. Place the ball in the beaker of water once again. It will float, as before. Now explain that you are going to slowly pour the vegetable oil, which caused the ball to sink, into the beaker of water. Ask students to predict how they think the ball will react when the vegetable oil is added. Some will predict that the ball will sink, as it previously behaved in the liquid. But most will predict that the ball will sink, but not as much, because the water will still cause it to float a bit. They will predict the ball to rest at a point somewhere midway between the observed level in the water and that in the vegetable oil.

Now, very carefully and slowly, pour the vegetable oil into the water. Pour near the side of the beaker. As you pour, students will observe the ball to rise higher and higher, eventually floating higher in the liquid than previously observed! The vegetable oil seems to have actually reversed its effect on the ball!

Possible Variables:

1. The substance that the ball is made of. For example, the ball could be wood, tin, aluminum, copper, etc. This could essentially be changing the density of the ball. The density could also be altered by using a ping pong ball which can be filled with varying amounts of sand or water. A small hole would allow sand or water to be added, which would then be plugged with putty.
2. Using a different object, such as a cork or rubber stopper, in place of the ball.
3. The density of the liquid. This could be changed by adding salt or sugar. It could also be changed by using entirely different liquids.
4. The diameter of the ball.

Phenomenon Explained:

The concepts of density, buoyancy, and miscibility contribute to the counterintuitive outcome of this demonstration. The ball floats in water because it is less dense than the water. Conversely, it is denser than vegetable oil, causing it to sink.

The density of an object will determine whether it will float in a fluid. Density is determined by calculating the mass for a given volume, expressed in the formula g/ml, g/cm^3, or g/cc. Density is independent of the sample size, since it represents the mass per ml of the sample. A larger volume does not necessarily equate to a higher mass. Fewer molecules packed into a given volume will result in a lower density than many more molecules packed into the same volume, which would increase the density. Objects with a density less than water will float, while those denser than water will sink. The density of water is 1.0g/ml.

Miscibility refers to the inability of two substances, typically two liquids, to mix and form a homogeneous solution. A solution that is homogeneous is the same throughout. When blended together, immiscible liquids will eventually separate into layers. The vegetable oil and the water are immiscible, they do not mix. Furthermore, the vegetable oil is less dense than the water. As a result, the oil floats on top of the water when it is slowly poured together. Pouring the oil into the water will help to ensure that it remains at the surface. If the two liquids were miscible, the outcome may be different. This is certainly one property to be investigated.

Buoyancy is defined as the tendency for an object to float in a fluid. Liquids and gases are fluids. The upward force exerted by the molecules of the fluid is called the buoyant force. When the two liquids are mixed, the oil exerts an additional buoyant force on the ball, because it is floating above the water. This causes the ball to rise even higher.

Viscosity is defined as a fluid's resistance to flow. Think of it as the "thickness" of a fluid. Fluids such as honey, molasses, corn syrup, and engine oil are highly viscous.

If the density of the liquid is altered by adding salt or sugar, discourse can include solutions, solubility, solutes, solvents, and concentration. Saltwater or sugar water is a mixture. One property of a mixture is that it is physically combined, not chemically, and it can be physically separated. For example, saltwater can be physically separated through the process of evaporation, or boiling the water away.

A solution is one in which a solute is dissolve in a solvent. The solute is the substance being dissolved and the solvent is the substance in which the solute is dissolved. Water is called the universal solvent because of its capability to dissolve more solutes than any other liquid. Solubility is the ability of a solute to dissolve in a solvent.

A concentrated solution is one which there are many dissolved particles of solute in the solvent. On the other hand, a dilute solution is one in which there are few dissolved particles of solute. A solution which contains all the dissolve particles it can possibly hold is called saturated.

Standards Alignment:

Next Generation Science Standards (NGSS, Lead States 2013)

Disciplinary Core Ideas in Physical Science

PS1: Matter and Its Interactions

PS1.A: Structure and Properties of Matter

PS1.B: Chemical Reactions

PS2: Motion and Stability: Forces and Interactions

PS2.A: Forces and Motion

Disciplinary Core Ideas in Earth and Space Science

ESS2: Earth's Systems

ESS2.C: The Roles of Water in Earth's Surface Processes

Color Wheel

Concepts Illustrated: The color spectrum, mechanics of the human eye, wavelengths of light, prisms, perception, visual interpretation of color, absorption and reflection of light.

Paradox:

When a multi-colored wheel is spun, the only color that can be seen is white!

Equipment:

1. White cardboard, construction paper, or even a paper plate.
2. Pencil (with an eraser).
3. Thumbtack.

Preparation:

Cut a circle out of the construction paper. You can use either a protractor, or even a cereal bowl or coffee can lid to create this circle. It should be about 10-12 cm in diameter. This should be a rigid piece of paper that will not bend too easily. If you use paper that will not readily keep its shape, such as a paper plate, then glue the paper onto a rigid piece of cardboard. Using a pencil, trace lines on the paper so that the circle is divided into eight equal sections. With seven differently colored markers, crayons, or paints, color seven of the eight sections with a different color. Ideally, these seven colors should be red, orange, yellow, green, blue, indigo, and violet (ROYGBIV). This is not a precise pattern. Don't worry if you can't find "indigo". The eighth section will not be colored. It will remain white. Push the thumbtack through the center of the disc and into the end of the pencil eraser. Don't push the tack in too hard. The wheel should be allowed to spin freely.

It is also possible to have the colored wheels prepared for students to assemble. Make one of the colored wheels on a computer, then print them off. Students will need to simply cut them out and affix them to the pencil. This would minimize time constraints, if this were a concern.

It's actually unnecessary to include a section of white in your color wheel! The phenomenon still works when all of the sections are colored. See the *Lesson Variation* section below for more details.

The Lesson:

Display the color wheel attached to the pencil. Turn the wheel a little to show that it can spin. Don't actually spin the wheel, but rather show that it *can* spin. Ask a student to name the different colors on the wheel. Now ask students to predict what color they might see when the wheel is spun fast. They will generally respond with a color that they envision might be a mix of the colors on the wheel. Now, holding the pencil horizontally, spin the wheel quickly. Students will be amazed to find that the only color they see is white! The entire face of the wheel appears white!

Rather than attach the wheel to a pencil, the effect can also be achieved using string. About 3 feet of kite string or yarn works well. Poke two small holes at the center of the colored wheel. Feed one end of the string through one of the holes, from the back (no color) to the front (colored) of the wheel. Then thread that same end into the other hole, now from the front to the back of the wheel. Tie the two ends of the string together so that it forms one continuous loop with the wheel threaded at its center. Now, hold the loop of string horizontally in front of you between both hands. There should be some slack in the string. Begin spinning the colored wheel around in a large circular motion by making the same motion with your hands in synch, similar to a jump rope. Once the wheel is in motion, pull on both ends of the string by spreading the hands apart from one another, making the string taught, and then releasing tension on the string by bringing the hands together. Repeat this action, pulling the hands apart and towards each other, and you'll cause the wheel to spin quite rapidly. Elementary students will especially have fun with this method when they conduct their own investigation.

The phenomenon can also be observed using a colored wheel that actually has no white sections in it. If the sections of the wheel were filled with all the colors of the rainbow, the same effect would be produced. The white section is really unnecessary.

Rather than segmented "pie" slices of different colors, the wheel can also be designed using colored rings. On a piece of cardboard, use a protractor or small cup as a template to outline two rings surrounding a circle in their center. Trace a line through the wheel to divide it in half. Color the wheel in blue, yellow, and red.

Possible Variables:

1. The size of the wheel.
2. The size of each colored area on the wheel.
3. The shape of each colored area on the wheel.
4. Different colors used on the wheel.
5. The number of colored sections on the wheel.
6. The position of the colors on the wheel.
7. A different colored design on the wheel.
8. A different shape other than a circular wheel, such as a star or square shape.

Phenomenon Explained:

Light is made up of a spectrum of distinct wavelengths, each a particular color. Specifically, these are red, orange, yellow, green, blue, indigo, and violet. Objects around you appear to be particular colors because those colors, or wavelengths, are reflected from those objects. All other colors in the spectrum are absorbed. For example, when light hits a red apple it absorbs the entire spectrum of light except for red, which is reflected off the apple. Your retina perceives the color being reflected and transmits that information to the brain for processing. Essentially, the colors that we see are those wavelengths that are reflected off the object.

The light that we perceive as white is actually comprised of the entire spectrum of colors. Look carefully at the wheel with the pie-shaped colors. You will notice all the colors of the spectrum, in order. This is the key to understanding why we see white as the wheel spins. The color wheel spins too quickly for the eye to identify and transmit each of the individual colors to the brain for processing. The retina is overwhelmed with the myriad of colors. As the wheel of pie-shaped colors spins, the colors essentially blend together to produce the white perceived by your eye.

Interestingly, the visual effect is different when the wheel is comprised of red, blue, and yellow colored rings. Obviously, this wheel does not contain the full spectrum of wavelengths. But, the colors on this wheel are a special group referred to as the primary colors of light. And when two primary colors are combined, the result is a secondary color. The secondary colors are purple, green, and orange. Once again, the wheel spins so quickly that your brain cannot process the individual primary colors of red, blue, and yellow. Instead, the colors blend to produce purple, green, and orange rings.

Standards Alignment:

Next Generation Science Standards (NGSS, Lead States 2013)

Disciplinary Core Ideas in Physical Science

PS4: Waves and Their Applications in Technologies for Information Transfer

PS4.B: Electromagnetic Radiation

Disciplinary Core Ideas in Life Science

LS1: From Molecules to Organisms: Structures and Processes

LS1.A: Structure and Function

LS1.D: Information Processing

Confused Balloons

<u>Concepts Illustrated:</u> Air pressure, density, buoyancy, volume, properties of gas, acceleration, gravitational force, fluid dynamics, molecular motion of gases.

The colors of the balloons used could lead into a discussion of absorption and reflection of light, wavelengths of light, perception, and visual interpretation of color.

<u>Paradox:</u>

Two balloons behave in a contradictory manner, despite being subjected to the same action. One balloon is suspended by a string secured to the top of an enclosed box. A second balloon floats in the same box, being secured by a string attached to the floor of the box. When the box is pushed to the right and slid on a table, the suspended balloon moves to the left, while the floating balloon moves to the right!

<u>Equipment:</u>

1. Cardboard box, or any other type of enclosure which students can see into.
2. 2 balloons- 1 must be filled with helium.
3. String.
4. Saran Wrap, if a cardboard box is used.
5. Tape.

<u>Preparation:</u>

Cut the side wall out of a cardboard box. The box should be completely enclosed, with the exception of this cut out side. Blow up a helium balloon and tie it to a string. Fasten the other end of the string to the center of the base of the cardboard box. The length of the string should be such that the top of the balloon floats just below half the height of the box. The balloon should be able to move freely.

Using your lungs, blow up the second balloon and tie it to a string. Fasten the other end of the string to the center of the top of the box, so that this balloon hangs directly above the helium balloon. The two balloons should be able to move freely without touching each other.

Now encircle the box with Saran Wrap so that the cut-out side is completely covered. The result is a completely enclose box who's inside is visible. The alternative is to use a plastic, transparent box, comprised of a base and a lid.

<u>The Lesson:</u>

Show students the box with the two balloons inside. The box should remain stationary. Explain that you will push the box, sliding it to the right on the table. Students should predict how the two balloons will behave. Once they have made their predictions, push the box to show students that the balloons actually react differently to the single force of pushing the box. The floating helium balloon will move in the same direction of motion as the box, while the balloon suspended from the ceiling of the box moves in the opposite direction of the force.

As an extension to the demonstration, you could ask students to predict how the balloons will behave when the box is abruptly stopped while moving. The floating balloon, which leans to the right when the box is pushed to the right, will be push to the left when abruptly stopped. The suspended balloon, which leans to the left when the box is moving to the right, will be pushed to the right when abruptly stopped.

Possible Variables:

1. Diameter of the balloons.
2. Shape of the balloons.
3. Length of the strings.
4. Shape of the container (box).
5. Volume of the box.
6. Direction of movement of the box- moving in a circular pattern.

Phenomenon Explained:

At Standard Temperature and Pressure (STP), helium has a density of about 0.00018 g/cm^3. The air in the box, surrounding the balloons, consists of nitrogen, oxygen, argon, carbon dioxide, and other trace gases. At STP, air has a density of about 0.0012929 g/cm^3. Due to its composition, the air surrounding the balloon is denser than the helium within it. In its resting state, the air inside the box sinks to the bottom, while the gas inside the helium balloon is pushed upwards, because of their respective densities.

When the box is pushed to the right, the denser air molecules are pushed to the left of the box. This results in the less dense helium molecules being pushed in the opposite direction, to the right.

The buoyant force generally acts in the opposite direction of the "local gravity," determined by combining the vectorial direction of gravity and acceleration. When the box is accelerated to the right, the direction of local gravity will be downward and to the left. As a result, the air-filled balloon will move downward in that direction, while the helium balloon floats upward, along that extended direction.

Buoyancy is defined as the tendency for an object to float in a fluid. Liquids and gases are fluids. The upward force exerted by the molecules of the fluid is called the buoyant force. Generally, a buoyant force that is greater than the force of an object due to its own mass will accelerate an object in the direction opposite to a force. When the box is pushed to the right, the helium balloon experiences both a gravitational force downwards as well as a force backwards, due to its acceleration forward. The buoyant force causes the balloon to accelerate upwards and forwards.

Light is made up of a spectrum of distinct wavelengths, each a particular color. Specifically, these are red, orange, yellow, green, blue, indigo, and violet. Objects around you appear to be particular colors because those colors, or wavelengths, are reflected from those objects. All other colors in the spectrum are absorbed. For example, when light hits a blue balloon it absorbs the entire spectrum of light except for blue, which is reflected off the balloon. Your retina perceives the color being reflected and transmits that information to the brain for processing. The balloon appears blue. Essentially, the colors that we see are those wavelengths that are reflected off the object.

Standards Alignment:

Next Generation Science Standards (NGSS, Lead States 2013)

Disciplinary Core Ideas in Physical Science

PS1: Matter and Its Interactions

PS1.A: Structure and Properties of Matter

PS2: Motion and Stability: Forces and Interactions

PS2.A: Forces and Motion

PS3: Energy

PS3.C: Relationship Between Energy and Forces

Cork Accelerometer

Concepts Illustrated: Acceleration, velocity, density, mass, volume, Newton's first law of motion- the law of inertia, fluid pressure, properties of liquids, fluid dynamics.

Paradox:

Students will be surprised to find that the movement of a cork floating in water behaves differently than expected!

Equipment:

1. A cork of any size or shape. You can also use a ping-pong ball in place of the cork.
2. String, thread, or fishing line.
3. Either a standard Mason jar, an Erlenmeyer flask, or a Polycarbonate screw cap storage bottle. If you use a Mason jar, it must have a lid. If an Erlenmeyer flask is used, it should be at least between 500-2000ml. It should also have a rubber stopper. If a Polycarbonate bottle is used, it should be 1000ml.

Preparation:

First, fill the Mason jar or Erlenmeyer flask with water. Next, using a hot glue gun, attach the string or fishing line to the center of the Mason jar lid, or Erlenmeyer flask rubber stopper. Now, attach the cork or ping-pong ball to the other end of the string. The string should be long enough so that when the lid or rubber stopper is put into place, and the jar or flask is turned upside-down, the cork or ping-pong ball will float freely, anchored to the lid or rubber stopper.

<u>The Lesson:</u>

Display the upside-down jar or flask to the students. It should be sitting motionless on a table or desk. Explain the setup to them. They should understand that the jar is filled with water and that the cork or ping-pong ball is freely floating in it. Now, ask them to predict what will happen to the cork if the jar were to be pushed and moved to the left. Students can be prompted to recall any similar experiences they may have had, such as the way their own bodies react in a car that accelerates when a traffic light changes from red to green. Most will recall that if the car moves forward, their bodies are pushed backwards, into the seat. Virtually all students will predict that if the jar is moved to the left, the cork will move to the right. Once students have made their prediction, move the jar to the left, sliding it along the table. Students will observe that the cork actually moves to the left- in the same direction in which it is being moved! The jar can now be moved to the right to show that the cork will again move in the same direction- to the right! The cork will always move in the same direction as the motion of the jar- not the opposite, as expected!

<u>Possible Variables:</u>

1. The length of the string.
2. Filling the jar with a liquid that has a density other than water (1.0 g/ml).
3. Viscosity of the liquid.
4. Using a cork of different shape, other than that shown in the demonstration.
5. Using a cork of different size, other than that shown in the demonstration.
6. Balls of varying volumes.
7. Balls of varying densities.
8. Using a vessel of different shape. For example, if the demonstration is conducted using an Erlenmeyer flask, students might want to investigate using Mason jars, or vice versa.
9. Replacing the cork with a different object, such as a Styrofoam ball or even a plastic washer. Students might also use plastic washers of different sizes. Students can also investigate Styrofoam balls of different diameters, as well as various Styrofoam shapes.
10. In place of the cork or ping-pong ball, students might consider using a plastic vial that can be filled with liquid of varying densities, to investigate how these objects react in water. They can also investigate the behavior of the vial filled with liquids of varying densities when the jar is also filled with liquids of varying densities. Students could also fill the ping-pong ball with liquids by poking a hole on either end of the ball and plugging it with a small bead of putty, clay, or wax after filling.

<u>Phenomenon Explained:</u>

This demonstration illustrates Newton's first law of motion. Known as the law of inertia, it states that an object either at rest or in motion, remains at rest or in motion with the same speed and direction, unless acted upon by an unbalanced force. Inertia describes the property of matter to either maintain a state of rest or its velocity along a straight path, unless acted upon by an external force. The demonstration also serves to illustrate the principle of acceleration, defined as the rate at which an object changes its velocity. The rate at which an object travels from one place to another is known as its velocity.

The demonstration uses an accelerometer, which is simply a device that measures acceleration, to illustrate Newton's first law of motion. Known as the law of inertia, it states that an object either at rest or in motion, remains at rest or in motion with the same speed and direction, unless acted upon by an unbalanced force. As the jar or flask is moved, and experiences acceleration, the cork moves in the direction of that acceleration. If the jar is moved to the left, the inertia of the water moving to the right produces a slightly higher water pressure on the right of the cork than on the left. This higher pressure on the right side of the cork pushes the cork to the left. It's essentially a force applied by a pressure.

Viscosity is defined as a fluid's resistance to flow. Think of it as the "thickness" of a fluid. Fluids such as honey, molasses, corn syrup, and engine oil are highly viscous. Students might choose to investigate the outcome when liquids of varying viscosities are employed.

The density of an object will determine whether it will float in a fluid. Density is determined by calculating the mass for a given volume, expressed in the formula g/ml, g/cm^3, or g/cc. Density is independent of the sample size, since it represents the mass per ml of the sample. A larger volume does not necessarily equate to a higher mass. Fewer molecules packed into a given volume will result in a lower density than many more molecules packed into the same volume, which would increase the density. Objects with a density less than water will float, while those denser than water will sink. The density of water is 1.0g/ml.

Standards Alignment:

Next Generation Science Standards (NGSS, Lead States 2013)

Disciplinary Core Ideas in Physical Science

PS1: Matter and Its Interactions

PS1.A: Structure and Properties of Matter

PS2: Motion and Stability: Forces and Interactions

PS2.A: Forces and Motion

PS3: Energy

PS3.C: Relationship Between Energy and Forces

Defying Gravity

Concepts Illustrated: Cohesion, adhesion, air pressure, surface tension, properties of water, properties of gas, properties of mixtures, viscosity, solutions, solubility, solutes, solvents, concentration, saturated solutions, properties of surfactants, the respiratory system of fish, the human respiratory system, process of dissolving, air pressure within the human body, the effects of air pressure on the human body (lungs, ears, sinuses), the influence of air pressure on ailments, barometric pressure.

Paradox:

Jaws will drop as students believe they are witnessing real magic when a bottle full of water, covered with a mesh screen, is tipped over- and no water falls out!

Equipment:

1. A Mason jar works is preferred, due to the construction of its lid.
2. Mesh screen.
3. A square piece of stiff construction paper.
4. Water.
5. A sink or tub. A sink is best, but not necessary.
6. A toothpick is optional.

Preparation:

The Mason jar lid is composed of two parts. Remove the flat center portion of the lid, leaving you with the lid "ring" that screws onto the top of the jar. Discard the flat center piece. It is not used in the demonstration.

Cut a small square out of the mesh screen. It should be large enough to fit over the mouth of the Mason jar.

You will also need to cut a square piece of stiff construction paper. It should fit over the mouth of the jar with a couple of inches extending. If this piece is laminated, you will be able to reuse it.

The Lesson:

Display the empty Mason jar. Then hold up the mesh screen so that students are looking through it. Explain that this screen is similar to one they might see in a window or door of a house, full of tiny holes. Although they may not be able to easily see them from a distance, you can demonstrate the presence of these holes. Hold the screen horizontally underneath the faucet of the sink. Turn the faucet on and allow water to pass through the screen. This is a very important step that is oftentimes overlooked. It proves to students that water can, in fact, pass through this screen. The image of water seen to easily pass through the screen now, generates great cognitive conflict when no water passes through it later in the demonstration.

Place the screen over the mouth of the jar and screw the lid ring onto it, over the screen. Now turn the faucet on once again and fill the jar. This is another important step. Students observe the water entering the jar through the screen, so they naturally assume that water can exit through the screen as well. The jar should be filled to the top of the jar. Allow the water to spill out of the jar as you are filling it. Place the construction paper square over the mouth of the jar.

Now, holding the paper firmly in place over its mouth, invert the jar over the sink or tub. Ask students to predict what will happen when you remove your hand away from the paper. Appear to be very nervous about doing this. Once predictions have been made, slowly and cautiously remove your hand to build suspense. Be sure to hold the jar upright, without tipping it. The card will remain in place over the mouth of the jar!

This is shocking, primarily to elementary and middle level students. But, what happens next will shock them and created a most powerful, and effective, counter-intuitive experience. While in this position, explain that there are some very cool properties and concepts at work here, and that they will be the focus of the follow-up investigations. Most students will attribute this shocking moment to the mesh screen, trying to imagine how it causes this phenomenon. Now nonchalantly add that "we all know what will happen when I remove the paper". Having believed they have already observed the highlight of the demonstration, all will acknowledge that the water will fall out, of course! Now act very nervous, as if you are expecting water to splash everywhere. Slowly and dramatically slide the paper away. You will see jaws drop when no water falls out of the jar!

If you have a toothpick, hold it upright under the mouth of the inverted jar. Keep the jar upright, without tipping it. Now insert the toothpick into one of the squares in the screen and release it. The toothpick will enter the jar and float up through the water until it hits the bottom of the jar!

As a climax to the demonstration, suggest that it looks "really cool" up close. Hold the jar up, still over the sink, and tilt it a little bit as you try to peek underneath. Then, snap your fingers as you continue to tilt just a tiny bit more. The water will come rushing out into the sink. It will appear as though by snapping you fingers you magically caused the water to be released! Of course, this is actually another important part of the demonstration that should become part of the investigations and the discourse that follows. You can also cause the water to fall from the jar without tipping it simply by touching a finger to the screen. Using the hand holding the jar upright, secretly sneak one of those fingers under the jar as you speak. Time this so with the snap of your fingers and the water rushes out of the upright jar!

Lesson Variation:

The demonstration can be shown using a Mason jar that is only half-filled with water. Some students will suspect that the same outcome cannot be achieved if the jar is completely full, leading to some valuable investigations.

To a certain extent, the phenomena can be illustrated using an Erlenmeyer flask and a one-hole rubber stopper. Fill the flask with water. You can add a few drops of food coloring so that the liquid is easily seen. Insert the rubber stopper. Invert the flask and no water will escape the flask. However, you can insert toothpicks into the hole of the rubber stopper. The toothpick will float up through the water until it hits the bottom of the flask.

Possible Variables:

1. Density of the liquid. The density of water can be changed simply by adding salt or sugar.
2. The viscosity of the liquid.
3. The number and size of the holes can be altered by using Saran Wrap and aluminum foil which can be poked with a toothpick to create holes.
4. Liquids of varying densities can be combined with different number of holes.
5. Adding soap to the water. This can lead to an investigation of different brands and different amounts of soap or detergent. Soap acts as a surfactant, affording the opportunity for class discourse to expand learning to the life sciences.
6. Mesh screens with holes of various sizes and shapes. This can include common screens as well as plastic produce net bags, stockings, cheesecloth, or gauze.
7. The amount of liquid in the jar.
8. The size of the jar. Soup or vegetable cans with differing diameters and heights can be used.

9. The shape of the jar. This can even involve soda bottles, graduated cylinders or an Erlenmeyer flask. If the flask is used, rubber stoppers with different numbers of holes can be investigated.
10. The width of the mouth of the jar.
11. The temperature of the water. It can be warmed or chilled.
12. Replacing the jar with a Styrofoam or paper cup. This will also for investigation after holes are made in the bottom or sides of the cup.

Phenomenon Explained:

The combined effects of air pressure with certain properties of water, namely surface tension and cohesion, provide the "magic" in this demonstration.

Cohesion is the attraction of like molecules to one another. Water molecules have a very strong cohesive attraction for one another. Imagine a glass of water. There are powerful cohesive forces between the molecules in that glass. The water molecules at the surface do not have any water molecules above them. As a result, they are strongly attracted to those neighboring water molecules at their sides and to those below, which draws them in towards the liquid. This strong attraction to the molecules around and underneath creates what is known as surface tension.

Adhesion is the property of unlike molecules to be attracted to one another. When the construction paper is held over the mouth of the jar, it comes into contact with the water that fills it. This results in an adhesive force between the water and the paper. When you release your hand away from the paper covering the inverted jar, it is held in place by this adhesive "seal" and the air pressure underneath the jar.

Air pressure exerted on the paper also contributes to the paper remaining in place when the jar is inverted. Atmospheric pressure is a force exerted by the weight of air in the atmosphere. It is determined by the amount of air directly above a person or object. Rarely are we aware of its immense force. This is because the pressure of air is exerted on us uniformly, all our lives. But, consider that all the air molecules above you have weight. The combined weight actually creates a pressure equivalent to about 10,000kg/square meter. At sea level, this translates to about 1000kg/0.1 square meter, or about 14.7lbs/square inch or PSI! This means there is about a ton of weight on each of us! Of course, this number varies slightly depending on the altitude you happen to be. Air pressure is exerted on all of us. The air pressure in our bodies, our lungs, stomachs, ears, fluids, etc., "balances" the pressure outside of our bodies. Our internal pressure is essentially the same as the outside pressure- we are at equilibrium. This prevents us from being crushed by the outside air pressure. In this demonstration, the effective downward pressure of the water is actually less than the atmospheric pressure outside the jar.

The human body is capable of being affected by low pressure weather systems, that can cause effects such as headaches, motion sickness, and distension in the sinuses. Effects such as these can be influenced by the difference between pressure within the body's cavities, such as lungs, ears, and sinuses, and the atmospheric pressure surrounding the body. This also explains why our ears pop in an airplane, or driving through hills or mountains. The ears essentially try to equalize the pressure within its cavities with the atmospheric pressure. Even those who suffer from arthritis or bursitis might experience increased joint pain as swelling occurs due to a decrease of pressure on the body.

The small amount of water within each of the tiny holes in the mesh, creates tiny pockets of surface tension. This surface tension is strong enough to overcome the force of gravity. This, in addition to the air pressure, prevents the water from falling out of the jar when the paper is pulled away. When the jar is tilted, surface tension decreases and is overcome by the force of gravity.

The toothpick is able to enter the jar due to cohesion and adhesion. Adhesive forces attract the water to the toothpick, forming a "membrane" around it as it passes through the screen.

Tipping the jar, or touching the screen with a finger, disrupts the cohesion of the water and the surface tension that results. The air outside of the jar is pushed into the jar due to air pressure and displaces the water inside the jar, which flows out.

The addition of soap as a variable broadly expands the scope of topics covered in class discourse. Soap is a surfactant. Surfactants play a critical role in our bodies. There is a thin layer of water that lines human lungs. This water is necessary for the gas exchange of carbon dioxide and oxygen to occur. These gases require a wet layer or surface for the exchange to take place. In fish, this exchange takes place in their gills. Since they are on the outside of the fish, gills have direct contact with water. Our lungs, on the other hand, are best able to be kept wet inside of our bodies. However, due to the properties of water, surface tension arises that can interfere with the expansion of our lungs as we breathe. Surfactant acts to reduce surface tension. This prevents alveoli, small air sacs in the lungs, from collapsing when we exhale. The most efficient oxygen-carbon dioxide exchange occurs in our lungs with the greatest alveoli surface area. By preventing the collapse of alveoli, surfactant helps to maximize the surface area available for the exchange of gases.

Viscosity is defined as a fluid's resistance to flow. Think of it as the "thickness" of a fluid. Fluids such as honey, molasses, and engine oil are highly viscous. Students might choose to investigate the outcome when liquids of varying viscosities are employed.

If the density of the liquid is altered by adding salt or sugar, discourse can include solutions, solubility, solutes, solvents, and concentration. Saltwater or sugar water is a mixture. One property of a mixture is that it is physically combined, not chemically, and it can be physically separated. For example, saltwater can be physically separated through the process of evaporation, or boiling the water away.

A solution is one in which a solute is dissolve in a solvent. The solute is the substance being dissolved and the solvent is the substance in which the solute is dissolved. Water is called the universal solvent because it is capable of dissolving more solutes than any other liquid. Solubility is the ability of a solute to dissolve in a solvent.

A concentrated solution is one which there are many dissolved particles of solute in the solvent. On the other hand, a dilute solution is one in which there are few dissolved particles of solute. A solution which contains all the dissolve particles it can possibly hold is called saturated.

Standards Alignment:

Next Generation Science Standards (NGSS, Lead States 2013)

Disciplinary Core Ideas in Physical Science

PS1: Matter and Its Interactions

PS1.A: Structure and Properties of Matter

PS1.B: Chemical Reactions

PS2: Motion and Stability: Forces and Interactions

PS2.B: Types of Interactions

Disciplinary Core Ideas in Life Science

LS1: From Molecules to Organisms: Structures and Processes

LS1.A: Structure and Function

Disciplinary Core Ideas in Earth and Space Science

ESS2: Earth's Systems

ESS2.C: The Roles of Water in Earth's Surface Processes

Directional Acceleration

Concepts Illustrated: Newton's first law of motion- the law of inertia, fluid dynamics, center of rotation, density, acceleration, properties of liquids, viscosity, solutions, solubility, solutes, solvents, concentration, saturated solutions, process of dissolving.

Paradox:

A ball floating inside a clear tube filled with water responds to the directional movement of the tube in very surprising and unexpected ways!

Equipment:

1. One ping pong ball.
2. A clear tube, about 1.5-2 ft in length. The ends of the tube should have caps, so that the tube will not leak when filled with water. The diameter of the tube should allow the ping pong ball to freely move within the walls of the tube. This tubing is available at stores such as Home Depot and Lowes. Rubber caps for chair legs can also be found there and can be used as caps on the ends of the tube.

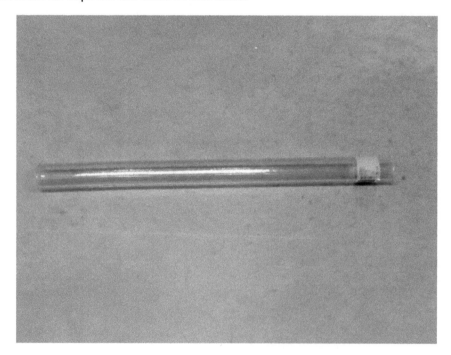

Preparation:

Remove the cap on one end of a clear tube. Put the ping pong ball into the tube and fill the tube with water. Replace the cap. The tube should now be able to be moved about freely without any water leaking out.

<u>The Lesson:</u>

Display the water-filled tube to the students. It should be sitting motionless on a table or desk. Explain the setup to them. They should understand that the jar is filled with water and that the ping-pong ball is freely floating in it. Now, explain to students that you will perform two actions with the tube. They are to predict what will happen when each of these actions is carried out. First, ask them to predict what will happen to the ball if the tube were to be quickly pushed and moved to the left. Students can be prompted to recall any similar experiences they may have had, such as the way their own bodies react in a car that accelerates when a traffic light changes from red to green. Most will recall that if the car moves forward, their bodies are pushed backwards, into the seat. Virtually all students will predict that if the tube is quickly pushed to the left, the ball will move to the right. Next, students are to predict what will occur if the tube is quickly spun on the desk, rotating in a clockwise fashion. Once again, students can consider the movement of their own bodies in an amusement ride that moves in a circular path. They will recall that their bodies are "pushed" outward, towards the outside of the circular path, during the ride. Most students will predict that when the tube is spun in a circular, clockwise direction, the ball will be "pushed" to the end of the tube.

Once students have written both predictions, begin by first pushing the tube to the left, quickly sliding it along the table. Students will observe that the ball actually moves to the left- in the same direction in which the tube is being moved! The tube can now be moved to the right to show that the ball will again move in the same direction- to the right! When the tube is pushed in a linear direction, the ball will always move in the same direction as the tube- not the opposite, as expected!

Now, perform the second action and spin the tube in a clockwise direction. Students will be surprised to find that the ball moves to the center of the tube- not the end as expected! The tube can actually be spun in the opposite direction as well, with the same results.

<u>Possible Variables:</u>

1. Filling the bottles with a liquid that has a density other than water (1.0 g/ml).
2. Viscosity of the liquid.
3. Replacing the ping pong ball with objects of different shapes.
4. Using a ball of a different diameter than the ping pong ball.
5. Using a vessel of different shape. For example, students might want to replace the clear tube with a Mason jar or 2 Liter soda bottle.
6. The volume of liquid in the tube.
7. Replacing the ping pong ball with one made of a different substance, and a different density. For example, they could use lead, aluminum, brass, or a tin ball. Students might also investigate the behavior of these balls in differing volumes of liquid.
8. In place of the balls, students might consider using a plastic vial that can be filled with liquid of varying densities, to investigate how these objects react in water. They can also investigate the behavior of the vial filled with liquids of varying densities when the jar is also filled with liquids of varying densities. The vial can also be filled with various amounts of sand, washers, nuts and bolts, etc. Students could also alter the density of the ping-pong ball by poking a hole on either end of the ball, filling it with a liquid, and

plugging it with a small bead of putty, clay, or wax. The ping pong balls could be filled with materials such as sand, cooking oil, salt water, or sugar water, for example.

9. Consider how the class discussion can be strengthened by having one group investigate balls of differing densities in the same volume of liquid, while another group investigates balls of differing densities in a tube filled with different volumes of liquid. You might think that even if there were no difference in the behavior observed between these two investigations, it might not be a valuable use of time. However, even a result of this nature reveals much, contributes to the class discussion, and strengthens an understanding for the nature of the phenomena.

Phenomenon Explained:

The tube acts as an accelerometer, a device that measures acceleration, to illustrate Newton's first law of motion. Known as the law of inertia, it states that an object either at rest or in motion, remains at rest or in motion with the same speed and direction, unless acted upon by an unbalanced force. As the tube is accelerated linearly, the ping pong ball, being less dense than water, will always move in the same direction of the acceleration. If the tube is pushed to the left, the inertia of the water moving to the right produces a slightly higher water pressure on the right of the side of the ball than on the left. This higher pressure on the right side of the ball pushes the ball to the left. It's essentially a force applied by a pressure. On the other hand, if the ball were made to be denser than the water, the inertia of this ball would cause it to lag behind. This is the same phenomena that occurs when you are pushed into your seat when the car accelerates forward. When the tube is rotated in a clockwise fashion, the ping pong ball moves toward the center of rotation.

Viscosity is defined as a fluid's resistance to flow. Think of it as the "thickness" of a fluid. Fluids such as honey, molasses, corn syrup, and engine oil are highly viscous. Students might choose to investigate the outcome when liquids of varying viscosities are employed.

If the density of the liquid is altered by adding salt or sugar, discourse can include solutions, solubility, solutes, solvents, and concentration.

A solution is one in which a solute is dissolve in a solvent. The solute is the substance being dissolved and the solvent is the substance in which the solute is dissolved. Water is called the universal solvent because it is capable of dissolving more solutes than any other liquid. Solubility is the ability of a solute to dissolve in a solvent.

A concentrated solution is one which there are many dissolved particles of solute in the solvent. On the other hand, a dilute solution is one in which there are few dissolved particles of solute. A solution which contains all the dissolve particles it can possibly hold is called saturated.

Standards Alignment:

Next Generation Science Standards (NGSS, Lead States 2013)

Disciplinary Core Ideas in Physical Science

PS1: Matter and Its Interactions

PS1.A: Structure and Properties of Matter

PS1.B: Chemical Reactions

PS2: Motion and Stability: Forces and Interactions

PS2.A: Forces and Motion

Disciplinary Core Ideas in Earth and Space Science

ESS2: Earth's Systems

ESS2.C: The Roles of Water in Earth's Surface Processes

Distance Winner

<u>Concepts Illustrated</u>: Kinetic energy, potential energy, mass, volume, density, diameter, moment of inertia, conservation of energy, velocity, acceleration, Newton's first law of motion- the law of inertia, elements and compounds, Newton's second law, rotational energy, translational energy.

This is a rather simple demonstration to set up that will expose a widely-held misconception- that as the length of a ramp increases, the ball traveling on it will have greater speed and travel a farther distance from its end.

<u>Paradox</u>:

Two ramps are shown. They are elevated to the same height, but one is twice the length of the other. The end of each ramp is at the edge of the table. A metal ball is placed at the top of each ramp and released simultaneously. They roll off the ramp, and the edge of the table. Contradicting student expectation, each ball lands the same distance from the table!

<u>Equipment</u>:

1. Two ramps. One must be twice the length of the other.
2. Two spheres. They can be metal balls or marbles. They must be identical in mass and volume.
3. A wide tray or box is optional.
4. Sand is also optional.

<u>Preparation</u>:

The ramps can be elevated using books or blocks. It is important that they are both at the same height. They should be positioned on the table so that the end of the ramp lines up with the edge of the table. When the ball rolls off the end of the ramp, they should be traveling horizontally, and should not contact the table at all.

It is certainly not necessary, but a wide tray, bucket or box can be placed on the floor, positioned to catch the balls when they roll off the ramp. The sand serves to mark the impact of the balls. If it is used, the area of this "sandbox" should be large, even though the balls will land the same distance from the edge of the table. This is because a small sandbox might "tip" the results before conducting the demonstration. If sand is not used, it is easy enough to observe the where the balls land.

<u>The Lesson</u>:

Show the two ramps. Explain that although their heights are the same, one ramp is twice the length of the other. Now show the two balls. Be sure that students understand they are identical in diameter and substance. Place one ball at the top of each ramp, but do not release them yet. Explain that you will be releasing these balls simultaneously. The ball on the longer track will obviously travel twice as long as the other ball before it reaches the end of the ramp. They will both be allowed to roll off their ramps and land on the floor. Ask students to predict which ball will land farthest from the end of the ramp. You will find that most students will predict that the ball traveling down the longer ramp will land farthest. These students typically believe that if the ball has the opportunity to travel down a longer ramp, it will also have the opportunity to travel faster. They believe that if the ball is traveling faster, it will land a greater distance from the other ball. The idea is that the other ball has not had the opportunity to travel as far and gain as much speed.

If you are using a box or tray to catch the balls, put it into position now. Be sure that you have waited for students to make their predictions. Now release the balls simultaneously. Most will be shocked to find that the balls land the same distance from the end of the ramp!

Possible Variables:

1. A wide variety of ramp designs, for example, adding a steep incline to one of the tracks.
2. The diameter of the spheres.
3. Spheres of various substances, such as tin, aluminum, wood, cork, lead, copper, etc. This could involve changing the density of the sphere.
4. The mass of the spheres. This would be investigated by changing diameters and substances.
5. Solid spheres vs hollow spheres.

Phenomenon Explained:

There are two terms we should become familiar with before discussing this demonstration. The first is velocity, defined as the rate that an object moves from one point to another. Being a vector quantity, it involves both speed and direction. The second term is acceleration, defined as the rate at which an object changes its velocity.

When an object is placed at the top of the incline, it has potential energy due to gravity. The amount of potential energy is dependent on the mass of the object and the height to which it has been lifted. When the object is released to roll down the incline, its potential energy is converted into kinetic energy. Ignoring loss by friction, the total amount of energy is conserved. In the case of a rolling object, as in this lesson, the kinetic energy is divided into two different types of kinetic energy- translational and rotational. Translational energy refers to motion in a straight line, whereas rotational energy refers to the motion of spinning.

Although the ramps in our demonstration differ in length, the top of the ramps are at the same height. When the two balls sit at the top of the ramp, at rest, they each have the same amount of potential energy, due to gravity. When released from this position they will accelerate at different rates, as potential energy is converted to kinetic. The balls kinetic energy at the end of the track is directly related to the potential energy it had at the top, before its release. Since they are released from the same height, they will have the same amount of kinetic energy at the bottom of the ramp. They will also have the same final velocity as they leave the ramp, again because they are released from the same height. As a result, they will land the same distance from the end of the ramp.

The demonstration can be used to illustrate Newton's first law of motion. Known as the law of inertia, it states that an object either at rest or in motion, remains at rest or in motion with the same speed and direction, unless acted upon by an unbalanced force.

Standards Alignment:

Next Generation Science Standards (NGSS, Lead States 2013)

Disciplinary Core Ideas in Physical Science

PS1: Matter and Its Interactions

PS1.A: Structure and Properties of Matter

PS2: Motion and Stability: Forces and Interactions

PS2.A: Forces and Motion

PS3: Energy

PS3.A: Definitions of Energy

PS3.B: Conservation of Energy and Energy Transfer

Dizzy Directions

<u>Concepts Illustrated:</u> Bernoulli's principle, Magnus effect, fluid dynamics, Newton's first law- the law of inertia, elements and compounds, viscosity.

There are two versions of this demonstration. Although they appear to be different demonstrations, each exhibits the same phenomenon. One critical distinction lies in the resources necessary to conduct them. One setup requires more equipment, while the other is incredibly simplistic, using limited resources available to most. The two versions are differentiated for particular grade levels. The variation involving more equipment is fruitful for middle to high school students, while the less complex version presents itself as an invaluable component to an elementary curriculum.

<u>Paradox:</u>

#1. A solid cylinder is rolled down a ramp and into a tub of water. Once in the water, students are amazed to find the trajectory of the cylinder follows a very unexpected path. Upon impact, the cylinder abruptly changes direction, spinning far behind its entry point into the water!

#2. A ramp is positioned so that its end is at the edge of a table. A paper tube is rolled down the ramp and allowed to roll off the edge of the table. Most will predict that the tube will either continue forward in its trajectory path, or fall straight down due to gravity. Yet, students will be surprised to find that when the tube rolls off the edge of the ramp, it changes course and spins in a reverse direction- opposite its path down the ramp!

<u>Equipment:</u>

Paradox #1:

1. A solid metal cylinder. It should be composed of a substance that is denser than water, so that it will sink in the water and land on the bottom of the tank.
2. A ramp. This can be as simple as a piece of wood, or even a book, held in place with a clamp on a ring stand.
3. A tub or tank to hold the water. The sides must be clear so that students can easily observe the cylinder after it enters the water. A small aquarium works well.

Paradox #2:

1) A ramp. It can be as simple as a book supported at an angle, a couple of rulers positioned side by side, or a ramp on a ring stand.
2) A paper tube. It can be a piece of rolled up construction paper or a paper towel tube.

<u>Preparation:</u>

Prior to the demonstration, the tub or tank should be filled with water. The ramp and cylinder nearby.

When selecting your ramp, be sure that the cylinder will roll freely in its path to the water. It is not advisable to have side walls on the ramp. You don't want the cylinder to hit side walls and deviate from a straight roll into the water. You also want a ramp that is wide enough so that the cylinder will not roll off the sides.

As explained in the *Equipment* section, the ramp is held in place with a clamp on a ring stand. However, the ramp can also be wide, extending over the tank as well as the table at its side. In this case, you might need two ring stands to support the ramp. See the picture below for reference. The choice between a narrow or wide ramp will be discussed in the Demonstration Procedure section.

When investigating, students can use much smaller tubs. The larger tub is necessary for demonstration to ensure that all students can clearly see the cylinders motion in the water. During their investigations, there could potentially be only two students observing the cylinder. A small tube will work, as long as it allows for the cylinder to complete its path in the water.

<u>The Lesson:</u>

Draw attention to the tank of water. Be sure to point out that it contains plain water. Show the cylinder.   Before rolling the cylinder into the water, ask students to observe the cylinders motion as it rolls down the ramp and onto the table. Let them know that this observation will help them to make their prediction as the demonstration moves forward. Now, if you are using a narrower ramp, move it into position in front of the tank. Essentially, at this point you want the cylinder to roll down the ramp and onto the table- not in the water. Explain that you are about to roll the cylinder down the ramp and students should pay specific attention to the path the cylinder takes when it rolls off of the ramp, as well as the point at which it lands on the table. Now release the cylinder, allowing it to land on the table. Immediately place something on the table, where it was impacted by the cylinder. Restate what just happened. "We just saw the cylinder travel in this direction," using your finger to follow the trajectory through the air, "and we saw it land here." Point to the landing spot.

Now, slide the ramp into position above the tank of water. If you are using a wide ramp, there is no need to move the ramp. The cylinder is simply rolled down the ramp either over the table, or over the water. Explain to students that they have had a chance to see the cylinder roll down the ramp and travel through the air. They will now observe the same cylinder rolling down the ramp and through the water. They should predict where the cylinder will land at the bottom of the tank. They are given four choices, labeled A, B, C, and D. The first point of impact will be the same distance from the ramp as when the cylinder travelled through the air. Mark this point on the front of the tank with a small piece of tape. This piece of tape should be aligned with the point of impact previously observed on the table. The next point is marked directly below the edge of the ramp. This would signify the cylinder rolling straight down into the water. Mark this point on the front of the tank. The third point is midway between the first two. Mark this point on the front of the tank. The final point is behind the ramp. It should be about the same distance behind the ramp as the distance of the first point from the edge of the ramp. Now label these points A, B, C, and D from the first point to the last. A is the first point you labeled.

Ask students to predict where the cylinder will land at the bottom of the tank. They can choose either A, B, C, or D. Most students will choose point B, thinking that the cylinder will be slowed down a bit by the water. Some will choose point C, thinking the cylinder will be stopped completely upon impact and just fall straight down. You will find that others will choose point A, thinking the water will make no difference to the path of the cylinder. Very rarely will a student choose point D.

Release the cylinder down the ramp into the water. Students will be quite surprised to see the cylinder travel "backwards" once it hits the surface of the water. It will land at point D!

Possible Variables:

1. The angle of the ramp.
2. The length of the cylinder.
3. The diameter of the cylinder.
4. The height from which the cylinder is released on the ramp.
5. Cylinders made of various substances, such as brass, copper, tin, aluminum, lead, steel, iron, wood, plastic, etc.
6. The distance between the ramp and the surface of the water.
7. The surface of the ramp. This can involve laying a piece of felt, sandpaper, etc. on the ramp.
8. A hollow cylinder, rather than a solid one.
9. The viscosity of the liquid.

Phenomenon Explained:

The principle at work here is called the Magnus effect, discovered by Gustav Magnus in 1852. The Magnus effect describes the force generated by a spinning or rotating object through a fluid medium, either liquid or gas. It employs principles from the Bernoulli equation which, in effect, states that if the velocity of a moving fluid increases, the pressure decreases.

In our demonstration, when the cylinder enters the water, its top surface is moving forward with the spin. This spinning creates a circular motion of the water around the cylinder, pulling the water around it. The rotation of the cylinder as it travels through the water causes the water on one side of the cylinder to take a longer path, as it is deflected in the direction of the spin.

The water on one side of the cylinder is now flowing with a lower speed than the other. The side with the greater speed has less pressure. The pressure differential causes a force on the cylinder that is perpendicular to its path, and the direction of the water, as shown in the diagram. The same is true in the case of a paper tube rolling off a ramp. This force, termed the Magnus effect, causes the cylinder to change its directory.

The Magnus effect

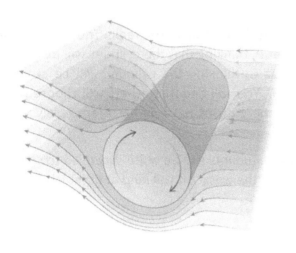

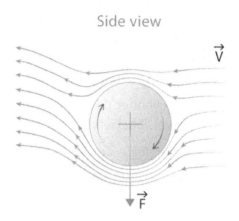

Side view

The demonstration can also be used to illustrate Newton's first law of motion. Known as the law of inertia, it states that an object either at rest or in motion, remains at rest or in motion with the same speed and direction, unless acted upon by an unbalanced force.

Viscosity is defined as a fluid's resistance to flow. Think of it as the "thickness" of a fluid. Fluids such as honey, molasses, and engine oil are highly viscous. Students might choose to investigate the outcome when liquids of varying viscosities are employed.

Standards Alignment:

Next Generation Science Standards (NGSS, Lead States 2013)

Disciplinary Core Ideas in Physical Science

PS2: Motion and Stability: Forces and Interactions

PS2.A: Forces and Motion

PS2.B: Types of Interactions

Drips and Drops

<u>Concepts Illustrated:</u> Density, phase change, solubility, solute, solvent, concentration, saturated solutions, process of dissolving, miscibility, surface tension, cohesion, viscosity, properties of a mixture, properties of liquids, properties of water, phase changes, molecular motion of solids, molecular motion of liquids, freezing, melting.

<u>Paradox:</u>

Students discover amazing behavior of substances in liquid and solid form when combined!

<u>Equipment:</u>

1. Vegetable oil.
2. Water.
3. 3 Beakers.
4. Food coloring.

<u>Preparation:</u>

Into one 400ml beaker, pour 75ml of water. Into another, pour 250ml of vegetable oil. Color the water by adding a dark food coloring, such as blue. This will contrast the golden yellow color of the oil.

Vegetable oil ice cubes can be made by simply pouring the oil into an ice cube tray and allowing it to freeze overnight. The cubes will not become a firm solid. Use the paddle end of a stirring rod, or the flat handle on a lab scoop, to remove the oil cube from the tray. The consistency of the cube will be more like soft jello. The cubes will leave a slight film on the ice cube tray, so it might be a good idea to use a tray that will be dedicated to make only vegetable oil cubes for future labs. These cubes should remain in the freezer until the moment they are needed. Once they are removed from the freezer, they will begin to soften and become a liquid again.

<u>The Lesson:</u>

Begin by showing one beaker of vegetable oil and another of water. When presenting these beakers, be sure to tip them slightly to show their viscosities. Distinctly point out that there is only 75ml of water, but 250ml of vegetable oil. Ask students to predict what will happen when the two liquids are poured together.

Some will predict that vegetable oil will float on water, having seen this occur in their kitchens at home. But, because there is such a greater volume of oil than water, a number of these students, and others, will predict the oil to sink. Sometimes, students assume that a larger volume also means a larger mass. They are led to think that the larger mass makes the oil "heavier" than the smaller volume of water. Believing this could alter the outcome, they predict the oil will sink. Even those students who might surmise that vegetable oil will float might change their minds when faced with this situation. Others will focus solely on the viscous property of the oil, making it "heavy" and causing the "lighter" water to float on top of it. Yet, others will predict the two will mix and become one new liquid. The responses will vary depending on the student's grade level and their experiences with vegetable oil. Once predictions have been shared, add the two liquids together. Because of the food coloring, both liquids will be easily identifiable. Some will be surprised to find that the oil floats on water.

Explain that the next phase of the demonstration will involve vegetable oil ice cubes. Explain that these ice cubes are made entirely of frozen vegetable oil. Ask students to predict, based on the previous observations, what will happen if you place one of these cubes into a beaker of water. They have just seen oil float on water, so most will predict the cube to float. Once they have shared predictions, scoop a vegetable oil cube out of the tray and place it in a beaker of water. Students will observe that the cube does float, as most expect. As the cube melts, the oil continues to float, forming a layer on top of the water.

Now, introduce the next phase. Show a beaker of vegetable oil. Explain that you are going to place an ice cube in it. As before, students should base their predictions on previous observations. They have consistently observed, in every phase, that water sinks below oil. As a result, most will predict that the ice cube will sink. There will be others who will predict the ice to float, because they have consistently observed this behavior every time they have put ice in liquid. Once they have made their predictions, drop the ice cube in the oil. It will float, contradicting the predictions of most. But surprise awaits everyone as the ice cube begins to melt and the liquid water drops sink to the bottom of the beaker!

There are essentially two discrepant events occurring here. For those who incorrectly predicted ice to sink, they are faced with explaining how it floats. For those who correctly predicted ice to float, they are now faced with explaining why it sinks as it melts.

Lesson Variation:

This version looks bizarre and has to be seen to be truly appreciated. In it, water is replaced with mineral oil. Baby oil works well. Begin by adding vegetable oil to a 400 or 600 ml beaker until it is half full. Then fill the remainder of the beaker with baby oil. The two liquids will not mix, forming two layers. Vegetable oil is denser, so it will settle below the baby oil. If the oils used have roughly the same color, the line separating them will be invisible. The beaker will appear to hold one liquid. Now gently drop an ice cube into the liquid. It will float in the middle of the beaker, where vegetable oil meets baby oil. This looks very mysterious. The melting ice cube slowly releases drops, which eventually fall free and sink to the bottom of the beaker.

Another variation involves food coloring. The ice cube can be colored with food coloring, as in the original demonstration, or food coloring can be added to the bottom of the beaker prior to adding any liquid. When vegetable oil is poured on top of the food coloring, they are immiscible and do not mix. But when the drops fall from the melting ice, they land on the food coloring, absorbing and mixing with the food coloring. Each drop falls as clear liquid, but suddenly changes into a color upon landing.

<u>Possible Variables:</u>

1. Placing the cubes in liquid other than water, such as saltwater, sugar water, honey, corn syrup, maple syrup, etc. This would comprise an investigation on density or viscosity.
2. Ice cubes made of saltwater or sugar water. These could be placed into beakers of plain water, saltwater, sugar water, honey, corn syrup, etc.
3. Adding food coloring to the ice cubes.
4. Could make the ice out of various liquids. These different kinds of ice cubes could be used together in different combinations with various liquids.
5. Could layer liquids of various densities to observe how the ice and the drops react as they travel through each liquid. Could use different kinds of ice cubes together with the layered liquids.
6. Temperature of the water or vegetable oil.

<u>Phenomenon Explained:</u>

The density of an object will determine whether it will float in a fluid. Density is determined by calculating the mass for a given volume, expressed in the formula g/ml, g/cm^3, or g/cc. Density is independent of the volume of liquid, since it represents the mass per ml of the sample. A larger volume does not necessarily equate to a higher mass. Fewer molecules packed into a given volume will result in a lower density than many more molecules packed into the same volume, which would increase the density.

Ice will float in water, as well as vegetable oil. Most students are familiar with ice floating in water, but do not truly appreciate the unusual nature of this behavior. Generally, most liquids will contract and their density will increase when frozen. However, water is unusual in that it behaves in an opposite manner. When liquid water cools, it contracts and becomes denser. But when its temperature reaches about 4^0C it expands and become less dense, until it reaches the freezing point. Frozen water is less dense than liquid water, which is why ice floats in it.

Vegetable oil floats on water because it is less dense than water. The density of vegetable oil is 0.91-0.93g/ml, while that of water is 1.0g/ml. Vegetable oil will freeze, but it must get colder than your freezer will allow. For this reason, the oil will thicken until it reaches the consistency of lard or very soft jello. When taken out of the freezer, the density of the frozen vegetable oil cube has increased, but not enough to alter its behavior in water. It will still float. However, when placed in liquid vegetable oil, the frozen oil cube will sink! This is because the density of the frozen cube is greater than that of liquid vegetable oil.

As explained, when the ice is placed into the oil it floats and will eventually begin to melt. As the frozen water goes through the melting phase change, it changes into liquid water, which has a higher density than either the ice or the oil. This causes the liquid drops to sink to the bottom of the oil. It is a rather amazing process to observe. Water and oil are immiscible, they do not combine to form a homogenous mixture. As a result, the liquid water drops form individual beads that settle on the bottom of the beaker. If the ice is colored with food coloring, these beads retain their color. Since food coloring is water-based, it does not spread into the oil. Large colored water drops will continue to accumulate at the beakers bottom, maintaining a generally spherical shape for three reasons.

The first is due to cohesion, which refers to the attraction of like, or similar, molecules towards one another. Water molecules have a very strong cohesive attraction for one another. This cohesive property forms from the attraction of the hydrogen atoms, with positive charges, in one water molecule to the oxygen atoms, with negative charges, of another molecule.

Cohesion is also a contributing property behind the phenomena of surface tension. Cohesion allows water to resist external forces, exhibiting the appearance of an elastic membrane across its surface. This is referred to as surface tension. The properties of both cohesion and surface tension becomes apparent as the drop maintains its beaded, dome shape on the bottom of the beaker. Droplets of water will tend to be pulled into a spherical shape, due to cohesive forces on the outer membrane. The shape is the result of water molecules attracting to one another in an optimal shape, minimizing surface area to volume ratio. This is also what soap bubbles do.

Cohesive forces and surface tension are also significantly decreased with an increase in temperature. Students investigating this variable will discover the drops that fall to the bottom of the beaker will be able to maintain their shape for shorter periods of time.

When using baby oil in place of water, the vegetable oil will settle below the baby oil when the two are mixed. This is because baby oil is less dense than vegetable oil. The density of baby oil is about 0.83 g/ml, while vegetable oil has a density of about 0.92 g/ml. When an ice cube is lowered into the combined liquid, it will hover mysteriously at the point where vegetable oil meets baby oil. Ice, with a density of about 0.91 g/ml, is denser than baby oil, but slightly less dense than vegetable oil. So, the ice will sink to the bottom of the baby oil layer and float on top of the vegetable oil layer. As the ice cube melts, the liquid water drops that fall from it have a density of 1.0 g/ml. This is denser than vegetable oil, so they sink to the bottom of the beaker and accumulate. Note that water can actually replace vegetable oil. If baby oil and water are used, their densities still allow for baby oil to float above water and the ice cube to still float at the point where the two meet.

The density of baby oil is 0.83, vegetable oil is 0.92, water is 1.0, and an ice cube is 0.916.

If the density of the liquid is altered by adding salt or sugar, discourse can include solutions, solubility, solutes, solvents, and concentration. Saltwater or sugar water is a mixture. One property of a mixture is that it is physically combined, not chemically, and it can be physically separated. For example, saltwater can be physically separated through the process of evaporation, or boiling the water away.

A solution is one in which a solute is dissolve in a solvent. The solute is the substance being dissolved and the solvent is the substance in which the solute is dissolved. Water is called the universal solvent because it is capable of dissolving more solutes than any other liquid. Solubility is the ability of a solute to dissolve in a solvent.

A concentrated solution is one which there are many dissolved particles of solute in the solvent. On the other hand, a dilute solution is one in which there are few dissolved particles of solute. A solution which contains all the dissolve particles it can possibly hold is called saturated.

The process of melting ice represents a physical change, or a change that does not alter the chemical composition of the substance. Unlike a chemical change, a physical change does not produce a new substance. Melting ice simply changes the form of water from the solid phase to the liquid phase. When matter transitions from one phase to another, it is called a phase change.

Standards Alignment:

Next Generation Science Standards (NGSS, Lead States 2013)

Disciplinary Core Ideas in Physical Science

PS1: Matter and Its Interactions

PS1.A: Structure and Properties of Matter

PS1.B: Chemical Reactions

PS2: Motion and Stability: Forces and Interactions

PS2.B: Types of Interactions

PS3: Energy

PS3.A: Definitions of Energy

Disciplinary Core Ideas in Earth and Space Science

ESS2: Earth's Systems

ESS2.C: The Roles of Water in Earth's Surface Processes

Drop Kick

Concepts Illustrated: Velocity, gravity, Newton's second law, elements and compounds, acceleration, mass, volume, density.

This well-known demonstration is presented here in two phases, uniquely structured intentionally to compound the disequilibrium, and the shock, that student's experience.

Note that there is a wonderful variation of this demonstration which involves resources that are readily available to most- simply an index card and three pennies. Details are included below.

Paradox:

Two identical metal balls are placed into a device that will release them simultaneously. When released, one ball is dropped to the floor *vertically*, while the other is ejected *horizontally*. Students are amazed to find that they both hit the floor at the same time!

In the second phase of the demonstration, the ball that drops vertically is replaced with one double the mass of the ball ejected horizontally. Students are shocked to discover that although the ball dropping straight to the floor has double the mass, both balls still hit the floor at the same time!

If you do not have metal spheres available, one variation of the demonstration can be presented using pennies. The demonstration involves a device simply constructed out of an index card. These materials make the demonstration, as well as the student investigations, readily accessible to all.

Equipment:

1. A release device from which to drop the balls. These can be purchased from science supply stores, or constructed from a 3"x5" index card. The construction of this device is explained in the Preparation section.
2. Two metal balls. It is not necessary that they are made of metal. They can be made of wood, plastic, etc. But, they must both be made of the same substance. They must also have the same diameter. 1" diameters work well. If spheres are not available, they can be substituted with two marbles.
3. Although the second phase is optional, if it is presented, one additional ball is required. This ball should have more mass, preferably double, than the other.
4. An index card and three pennies, if this variation is presented.

Preparation:

The release device can either be purchased from science supply stores or it can be constructed. Those purchased at supply stores can either be mounted on the edge of a table or on a ring stand. If you use this device, you will need metal spheres.

However, as mentioned earlier, you can use a 3"x5" index card to create your own simple release device. First, fold the card in half lengthwise. Then lay the card on its side with the open end facing you. Bend the open end up so that it meets the top and put a crease in it. Flip the card over and do the same on the other side. If you look at the card from the end, it should look like a "V" with "wings." Attach a piece of tape to each end of the "fin" section of the device, so that the two sides stay together and don't spread apart. To double the mass, for the second phase of the demonstration, simply use a glue stick to temporarily stick two of the pennies together. Students can investigate the mass as a variable by sticking numbers of pennies together.

Construction of the device.

In position to release the pennies.

The Lesson:

Show the release device and the balls, or pennies, to students. Explain that the balls will be placed into this device, which will rest flatly on the edge of a table. Demonstrate this and show how the balls, or the pennies, are held in the device. If you are using pennies, hold the index card so that the "wings" are flat on the table, but ¾ of the card is actually extending beyond the edge of the table. The pointed ridge of the card should be aimed upward. Place one coin on each wing.

Explain further that this device will allow you to cause the balls to simultaneously be released. Now, detail exactly *how* the balls will be released. Do not release the balls, but illustrate using your index finger as you outline the path each ball will take. Be very clear when you explain that one ball will fall straight down, in a vertical motion. Illustrate the motion with your finger. The other will be ejected horizontally before falling to the floor. Again, illustrate the horizontal path with your finger. It will travel about 4ft away from the device. Point out that the ball projected horizontally will have a greater distance to travel before hitting the floor. Ask students to predict which will hit the floor first.

Most students will predict that the ball dropping vertically will reach the floor first. Others might reason that the ball being ejected horizontally will hit the floor first, because it is being hit with force and has more energy. Once they have made their predictions, release the balls from the device. If you are using an index card, flick the top of the pointed ridge to the side. This will cause one of the pennies to be launched away from you, while the other drops straight to the floor. Listening carefully, students will be able to hear the balls or pennies as they hit the floor. Students will not expect it, but they both hit the floor simultaneously!

Possible Variables:

1. The substance and density that the balls are made of. This can include tin, aluminum, copper, steel, iron, wood, cork, golf balls, ping pong balls, etc. Marbles can also be used.
2. The diameter of the balls. This can involve using two balls of the same diameter, or two balls of differing volumes. This can also be extended to include balls of the same diameter but made of different substances, or balls of different diameters but made of the same substance.
3. Balls that have holes drilled through their centers. This could also involve two balls, each with a hole, or only one ball with a hole. The idea can also be extended to using balls of different metals, with and without holes.
4. The mass of the balls.
5. Using objects of different shapes. For example, a spherical object, such as a marble, can be paired with a flat object such as a coin. Other objects, such as jacks can be used as well.
6. The mass of the pennies. As mentioned earlier, the mass can be adjusted simply by gluing pennies together using a glue stick.

Phenomenon Explained:

Newton's second law describes the relationship between force, mass, and acceleration.

Students will clearly observe that while one ball is traveling vertically through its entire path to the floor, the other follows a curved path. They are both accelerated downward, due to the force of gravity. If it were possible to draw a line from the center of one ball to the center of the other, we would observe the line to be horizontal through their entire paths. The centers of both balls would be at the same height, vertically, from the floor through their entire flight. As they fall, the change in vertical position is identically the same for each ball. This shows that the horizontal motion of the ejected ball does not affect its vertical motion. Because of this, their average vertical velocities are also the same. Although they follow different trajectories, the ball projected horizontally falls at the same rate as the one falling vertically. Both balls experience the same force of gravity that accelerates them downward. Interestingly, this means that the downward acceleration is the same, even if the balls have different masses. Vertical and horizontal motion are independent of one another.

Standards Alignment:

Next Generation Science Standards (NGSS, Lead States 2013)

Disciplinary Core Ideas in Physical Science

PS1: Matter and Its Interactions

PS1.A: Structure and Properties of Matter

PS2: Motion and Stability: Forces and Interactions

PS2.A: Forces and Motion

PS2.B: Types of Interactions

PS3: Energy

PS3.C: Relationship Between Energy and Forces

PS4: Waves and Their Applications in Technologies for Information Transfer

PS4.A: Wave Properties

Drowning Candles

Concepts Illustrated: Air pressure, chemical changes, physical changes, molecular motion of gases, process of flammability, melting, condensation, phase changes, amorphous solids, volume, kinetic energy, physical characteristics of solids, properties of gas, fluid dynamics, properties of gas, heat flow, condensation, capillary action, capillary action in the human body, laminar flow, turbulent flow, chemical reactions, exothermic reactions.

This fundamental demonstration illustrates how a seemingly elementary phenomenon can be investigated through a diverse number of approaches.

This demonstration involves fire and is intended for upper level students only. It is not suitable for elementary level children. When allowing upper level students to conduct this investigation, be certain to follow all safety guidelines and necessary precautions. As always, supervision and student awareness for the rules of safety are critical when using fire.

Paradox:

A candle is placed upright in the center of a pie tin that is filled with colored water. The candle is lit and covered with an inverted beaker. As the flame is extinguished, the colored water rises dramatically into the jar!

Equipment:

1. A pie pan.
2. One or two candles.
3. Matches or lighter.
4. Room temperature water in a beaker.
5. Food coloring (optional).
6. A tall glass, jar, beaker, or flask. An Erlenmeyer flask works very well.

Preparation:

If the candle does not stand up of its own accord without tipping, it should be fixed to the bottom of the pie tin. This can either be done while students look on, or prior to the lesson. If the candle topples over because it is too thin or its base is uneven, you would affix it to the pie tin using its own wax. Light the candle. Once it begins to melt, tip it over so that the wax drips into the center of the empty pie tin. Once you have a few drops in place, blow out the candle and immediately place the base of the candle into the hot wax. Hold the candle in place for a few seconds. The candle will now remain upright when you let it go. A smaller candle can be inserted into a hex nut, acting as the base to support it upright.

The water will be more visible to students if it is colored. If food coloring is available, add a few drops to the beaker of water and stir. If food coloring is unavailable, the demonstration still works without it.

Students are shown the materials used in this demonstration. Place the candle upright in the center of the pie tin, or affix it using melted wax, if this has not already been done (see the Preparation section). Pour the water into the pie tin. The water level should almost reach the top of the tin. Now light the candle. Show the tall jar or beaker and invert it, so the mouth is at the bottom. Explain that you are going to slowly lower the jar over the candle and set it down in the pie tin. Ask students to predict what will happen. Most will expect the candle to go out. Some might say the jar will fill with smoke. Lower the jar slowly over the candle, without hitting it. Set the jar directly onto the bottom of the tin. The flame will be extinguished as the liquid dramatically rises into the jar!

Lesson Variation:

A tea candle can be used in place of an upright candle. First fill the pie tin with the colored water, almost to the rim. Then place the tea candle in the center of the tin. The candle will float on the water. Light the candle and cover it with the jar. The water will rise. But because the candle is floating on the water, it will rise along with it.

Possible Variables:

1. The number of candles under the jar. Water will rise higher when more candles are used.
2. The height of the candle. If you do not have candles of varying heights, the candle can be placed on small wood blocks to raise it up. Taller candles will typically extinguish before shorter ones. This is due to rising carbon dioxide, a byproduct of combustion, which engulfs the flame of the taller candle. It will be discussed more in the section that follows.
3. The diameter of the candle.
4. Shape of bottle or jar.
5. The height of the bottle or jar.
6. The width of the jar.
7. Creating a gap between the pie tin and the jar. This can be accomplished by placing rubber stoppers in the tin. The jar sits on the rubber stoppers, lifting it off the tin.
8. Different liquids other than water, such as milk, corn syrup, salt water, sugar water, carbonated liquid, dish soap added to the water, etc.
9. The level of liquid in the pie tin.
10. Wick length of the candle.
11. Matchstick instead of a candle. This could be accomplished by sticking the bottom of a wooden matchstick into a tea candle. A teepee can also be made using three wooden matchsticks stuck into the tea candle. As additional matches are used, the water and tea candle rise higher.
12. Temperature of the liquid.
13. Temperature of the bottle, either chilled or warmed. This does slightly affect the observations.

14. Put the candle upside down or sideways, glued to either the bottom or the side of the jar.

Phenomenon Explained:

As a candle burns it undergoes an exothermic reaction, defined as a chemical reaction that releases energy by light or heat. The wick of a candle is shrouded in a coating of paraffin wax. When you light the wick of a candle, the paraffin coating melts and then vaporizes. This wax vapor, combined with oxygen in the air, burns. As the candle burns, "cooler" air containing the oxygen necessary to keep it burning flows in from beneath the flame while the heated gases given off from the flame rise, through the process of convection. Through capillary action, more wax is drawn up the wick, and the flame continues to burn. Capillary action is the upward movement of liquid, against gravity. Capillary action allows liquid to flow without the assistance of, and even in opposition to, external forces such as gravity. We depend on capillary action to live. Proper blood circulation, for example, depends on capillary action. Our eyes also use capillary action to drain excess tears into the nasal passage. Plants also depend on capillary action for their survival. Water is transported from roots, through the stem of smaller plants and the trunks of trees, to leaves and branches, against the force of gravity, through capillary action.

When the inverted jar is initially placed over the candle, the flame heats up the air in the jar. As air molecules become heated, they spread out and move faster, increasing the pressure within the jar. This can be observed in the water, as bubbles are pushed out of the mouth of the jar. In fact, if the jar is lowered very quickly, more bubbles will be observed. When the jar is slowly lowered, the pressure in the jar has already increased greatly by the time it touches the water. The flame diminishes and is eventually extinguished, due to oxygen deficiency. This causes the air under the jar to cool and contract. This reduces the air pressure in the jar. Some of this air pressure is also reduced as the heat under the jar is transferred to the glass jar and its surroundings. There is now greater air pressure on the water outside of the jar than there is inside. This pressure gradient forces water into the jar, until the pressure is at equilibrium.

The decrease in air pressure under the jar can also be attributed to a slight decrease in the number of gas molecules under the jar. There are two reasons for this. The first concerns the chemical composition of candle wax, which is a hydrocarbon. It is made of hydrogen and carbon. As the candle burns, oxygen and carbon atoms bond to form carbon dioxide. Some of the oxygen atoms combine with hydrogen, to form water vapor. Some of this vapor condenses, to form liquid water. You might observe this as water droplets forming on the inner wall of the jar. This condensation results in slightly fewer gas molecules under the jar. The second reason for the slight decrease in the number of gas molecules under the jar is because some escape in the form of bubbles. If dish soap is added to the water, students will more readily observe these bubbles escaping from under the jar.

Thermal energy involves energy that generates due to the movement of particles within an object or system. Since thermal energy results from particle or molecular movement, it is considered a type of kinetic energy, or energy due to motion. Thermal energy is responsible for temperature, which is a measure of the average motion of the particles within a substance. The candle has the property of flammability, it can burn. As it burns, it undergoes a chemical

226

reaction resulting in a chemical change. During a chemical change, bonds within molecules are broken and atoms rearrange. The result of a chemical change is a new substance. The new substances formed when a candle burns include carbon dioxide and ash. But the candle also undergoes physical changes. As the solid wax melts, it forms liquid wax, which evaporates to form wax vapor. Melting, evaporation, and condensation are phase changes, occurring as a substance changes from one phase of matter to another. Other phase changes include freezing and deposition, as states of matter move between solid, liquid and gas.

A candle is an example of an amorphous solid, or a solid "without shape." Amorphous solids are those without rigidity or consistent defined shape. The atoms and molecules within an amorphous solid do not maintain an orderly arrangement or pattern. The molecular arrangement of these solids can be altered, typically by heating them. Amorphous solids exhibit the opposite characteristics of crystalline solids, with molecules that form well-defined lattice type arrangements. Other examples of amorphous solids include plastic, rubber, and glass.

In laminar flow, a fluid flows in a well-defined, orderly manner, with rather distinct paths. On the other hand, turbulent flow describes the random, chaotic flow. There is no order in turbulent flow. Instead, the fluid undergoes irregular fluctuations. Turbulent flow can be observed in streams used for whitewater rafting, where the water moves in random and erratic directions. Consider laminar flow as the opposite of turbulent flow. When a candle flame is extinguished, the smoke that rises straight up from the wick is in laminar flow. But, as it reaches some distance from the wick it begins to spread out, waver, and even curl around. This is turbulent flow. It is rather difficult, if not impossible, to predict the behavior of turbulent flow.

Results differ between a tall and short candle. When using a tall candle, the water rises quickly before the flame is extinguished. Most of the change in water level will occur before the flame is extinguished. However, a short candle exhibits different behavior. The water rises slowly until the flame is extinguished. Then the water rises quickly.

Results will also differ between tall and short jars, even those of the same volume. You will observe that the duration of time the candle remains lit will change depending on the height of the bottle.

Differently colored candles can also generate a conversation about the physical properties of matter. A physical property is a property of a substance that can be immediately observed without changing the identity of the substance. Color is a physical property of matter. It can be immediately observed and it can help identify a substance. When you refer to a purple candle, students will know which one you are pointing out. Other physical properties include hardness, shape, size, texture, odor, etc. A few of these can be included in the discussion as the candles are referred to.

Standards Alignment:

Next Generation Science Standards (NGSS, Lead States 2013)

Disciplinary Core Ideas in Physical Science

PS1: Matter and Its Interactions

PS1.A: Structure and Properties of Matter

PS1.B: Chemical Reactions

PS2: Motion and Stability: Forces and Interactions

PS2.B: Types of Interactions

PS3: Energy

PS3.A: Definitions of Energy

PS3.B: Conservation of Energy and Energy Transfer

Disciplinary Core Ideas in Life Science

LS1: From Molecules to Organisms: Structures and Processes

LS1.A: Structure and Function

Disciplinary Core Ideas in Earth and Space Science

ESS2: Earth's Systems

ESS2.D: Weather and Climate

Elastic Steel

Concepts Illustrated: Magnetism, elasticity, properties of solids, momentum, velocity, kinetic energy, elements and compounds, conservation of momentum.

Although this demonstration can lead to tremendous learning opportunities at the elementary level, it is also well-suited, and can lead to equally rewarding learning opportunities at the middle school level.

Paradox:

Two steel balls are individually shown to be magnetically attracted to a bar magnet. However, when the magnet is brought near the balls which are touching each other, the ball farthest from the magnet shoots away!

Equipment:

1. A bar magnet or cow magnet.
2. Two steel balls. They could be the same diameter or different.

The Lesson:

Show the two steel balls to students. Then introduce the magnet. Bring each steel ball, one at a time, next to the magnet. Be sure to show that each ball is attracted to the magnet, and that the attraction is strong enough that each ball will individually cling to the magnet. Now place the two steel balls on a table with a smooth surface. They should be separate from one another by about 6 inches. Explain to students that there will be several parts to this demonstration and that they can expect to make a few predictions. First you'll ask students to predict what will happen to each ball as the magnet is drawn closer to it. Most students will predict that the ball will roll towards the magnet and then cling to it. Once they've predicted, show them that this is actually what happens. Now place the steel balls on the table, separated this time by a distance of about 2-3 inches. Explain that you will once again bring the magnet close to one of the balls. Students should predict what will happen. Some will predict that only the ball closest to the magnet will attract to it, while the second ball does nothing. Others will predict that once the closest ball has been attracted to the magnet, the second ball will then be attracted to the first.

Move the magnet towards one of the balls. This ball will be attracted to the magnet. The magnetic force will pull the second ball towards the first, resulting in both balls attracted to the magnet and touching each other. Some students will be surprised by this. Now place the balls on the table again, but this time make sure they are touching one another. Explain that once again you will bring the magnet close to one of the balls. Ask students to make their predictions. You should not tell students that this is the final prediction of the demonstration. If they know this is the final piece to the presentation, they might guess some strange outcome, anticipating a surprise result. Instead, you want students to ground their predictions from expectations based on observations of the two previous actions. If students are truly making predictions based on their observations up to this point, they will either say that both balls will be attracted to the magnet together, or that the ball closest will be initially attracted to the magnet, followed by the second ball. Bring the magnet towards the two balls to show a most surprising outcome that none of your students will really expect. Although both balls will be attracted by, and pulled towards the magnet, at the moment of contact the ball farthest from the magnet will instantly propel away.

There are a couple of reasons that cause this demonstration to be discrepant. The first is that most students will expect that a magnet and a metallic object will always behave by attracting and "clinging" together. They won't expect that a metallic object will be repelled away from a magnet. The second reason that this demonstration creates a discrepant experience lies in the way it is presented. You'll notice that the presentation involves three different observations. The first two establish the discrepancy of the third. In the first, students observe that each individual ball will attract to, and cling to, the magnet. The ball does not "bounce" off the magnet. In the second observation, students observe that even when the balls are separated by a distance they still behave in the same manner. After the first ball attracts to, and clings to, the magnet, the second ball does the same. Even though they are separated, and the second ball is "slamming" into the first with great force, it does not "bounce" off the magnet. These two observations establish a pattern in the minds of the observer. The balls behave by attracting to, and clinging to, the magnet- regardless of their position. And if the second ball does not bounce off the first after being "pulled" towards it from a distance, then it certainly isn't going to bounce off of it if they are pulled towards the magnet together- while continuously touching. Yet, that is exactly what happens!

Possible Variables:

1. The number of steel balls.
2. Using balls other than steel, such as aluminum, bronze, tin, brass, iron, glass, or even rubber. This could also involve placing the balls in various sequences. For example, the glass ball could be positioned between two steel balls, but it could also be placed first or third in the sequence.
3. The diameter of the balls. This idea could also include various positions of balls of differing diameters within a sequence. For example, an investigation could involve three steel balls- one a smaller diameter than the other two. But, then the smaller ball could be positioned in the first, second, or third position within the sequence of three balls. Another investigation could involve one larger ball than the other two. Again, the various positions of this ball within the sequence of three could be investigated.
4. Investigations could also involve balls made of different substances, with differing diameters.
5. Size of the magnet.
6. Type of magnet.
7. The distance between balls.
8. The surface that the balls rest on.
9. Direction of the magnet.

Phenomenon Explained:

Although it may appear that the ejected steel ball is repelled from the magnet, this is not at all what is happening. We must appreciate two important ideas in order to understand the cause of the outer ball's ejection.

First, there is an elasticity to steel. Elasticity is defined as the property of solids to return to their original shape upon removal of deforming forces. At the moment of collision, this elasticity of the outer steel ball causes it to "bounce" off of the one closest to the magnet.

Second, as the ball rolls away from the magnet it also moves out of its magnetic field. The magnetic attraction becomes weaker as the ball rolls farther away from the magnet. If the magnet used is too strong, the steel ball might not roll out of the magnetic field.

Standards Alignment:

Next Generation Science Standards (NGSS, Lead States 2013)

Disciplinary Core Ideas in Physical Science

PS1: Matter and Its Interactions

PS1.A: Structure and Properties of Matter

PS2: Motion and Stability: Forces and Interactions

PS2.A: Forces and Motion

PS2.B: Types of Interactions

PS3: Energy

PS3.A: Definitions of Energy

PS3.B: Conservation of Energy and Energy Transfer

PS3.C: Relationship Between Energy and Forces

Fickle Flame

Concepts Illustrated: Air pressure, air current, chemical changes, fluid dynamics, aerodynamics, Coanda effect, process of flammability, properties of gas, heat flow, chemical changes, physical changes, heat, temperature, molecular motion of gases, melting, phase changes, amorphous solids, physical characteristics of solids, laminar flow, turbulent flow, physical properties of matter, thermal energy, kinetic energy, thermodynamics, capillary action, chemical reactions, capillary action in the human body, exothermic reactions, turbulence, airplane flight, dynamics of tornadoes, atmosphere on distant planets.

This demonstration involves fire and is intended for upper level students only. It is not suitable for elementary level children. When allowing upper level students to conduct this investigation, be certain to follow all safety guidelines and necessary precautions. As always, supervision and student awareness for the rules of safety are critical when using fire.

Paradox:

The flame of a candle is observed to first lean away, but then lean *towards* the source of air flow!

Equipment:

1. A candle that will independently stand upright.
2. A water bottle.
3. An index card.

Preparation:

The index card should be taller than the candle when held upright, in front of it. The flame of the candle should not extend above the index card, which can be stood on end.

Practice this demonstration before class, so that you can appreciate the optimal distance between the index card, the bottle and you from the candle.

The Lesson:

Show the candle and light it. Inform students that they will be making three predictions. They will first predict the behavior of the flame when you gently blow on it from the side. Some will predict that the flame will bend away from you. Others that it will simply flicker, and others will predict that it will be extinguished. Blow slowly towards the flame, from the side. Students should observe the flame to lean away from you and the direction of air flow.

Now hold the index card vertically, about 6 cm in front of the candle. The students should be looking from the side, so that they can see the card and the candle. Explain that you are going to blow directly at the face of the index card. Ask students to predict the behavior of the flame. There will be several responses, but most will say that the flame will remain unaffected. Blow directly at the index card. There will be great surprise when the flame leans *towards* the index card!

Now, set the index card aside and place the bottle upright in front of the candle. Explain that you are now going to blow directly against the side of the bottle. Again, students should be observing from the side. Ask students to predict how the flame will behave in this situation. Some will predict the flame to lean either away or towards the bottle. Others will predict that in this scenario it will remain unaffected. Once predictions have been shared, blow directly against the side of the bottle. Amazingly, the flame is extinguished!

Note that if you do not have a bottle, you can roll the index card and hold it upright in front of the candle.

Lesson Variation:

If several bottles are lined up in front of the candle, you can still blow the candle out. The candle can be 3-4 feet away. When you blow against the first bottle, the air continues forward, wrapping around each bottle, until it reaches the candle flame. This is the Coanda Effect, explained below.

Bernoulli's principle can be easily demonstrated with a candle and a straw. Light the upright candle. Now, place the end of the straw directly to the side of the flame and blow into the straw. Although many will predict the flame to lean away from the straw, the flame will actually lean *towards* the straw.

This version leads to a highly unexpected outcome. Light a candle. Hold a funnel so that the wide end is directed at the candle. Blow into the stem, blowing air directly at the candle through the funnel. The most expected outcomes include either a flame that leans away from the funnel or the candle being blown out. Instead, the flame moves *towards* the funnel!

Possible Variables:

1. Height and width of the bottle.
2. Size of the index card.
3. Index card cut with shapes cut into sides.
4. Size of candle, both in height and diameter.
5. Shape of bottle, for example cylinder or square.
6. Distance between the card, the bottle and your lips, from the candle.
7. Angle or direction that you blow from.
8. Using two or more bottles instead of one.
9. Using two index cards instead of one.
10. Different number of candles. This can also involve various positions relative to one another.
11. Using a candle with different numbers of wicks or flames.
12. The shape of the index card. For example, it can be curved either horizontally or vertically.
13. Holding the index card on the opposite side of the candle so that the air blows back at it. This can then include various positions relative to the candle. It can also involve using differently shaped cards.

14. Cutting the index card into various shapes.

Phenomenon Explained:

As a candle burns it undergoes an exothermic reaction, defined as a chemical reaction that releases energy by light or heat. When water freezes it is an exothermic process. The wick of a candle is shrouded in a coating of paraffin wax. When you light the wick of a candle, the paraffin coating melts and then vaporizes. This wax vapor, combined with oxygen in the air, burns. As the candle burns, "cooler" air containing the oxygen necessary to keep it burning flows in from beneath the flame while the heated gases given off from the flame rise, through the process of convection. Through capillary action, more wax is drawn up the wick, and the flame continues to burn. Capillary action is the upward movement of liquid, against gravity. Capillary action allows liquid to flow without the assistance of, and even in opposition to, external forces such as gravity. We depend on capillary action to live. Proper blood circulation, for example, depends on capillary action. Our eyes also use capillary action to drain excess tears into the nasal passage. Plants also depend on capillary action for their survival. Water is transported from roots, through the stem of smaller plants and the trunks of trees, to leaves and branches, against the force of gravity, through capillary action.

Thermal energy involves energy that generates due to the movement of particles within an object or system. Since thermal energy results from particle or molecular movement, it is considered a type of kinetic energy, or energy due to motion. Thermal energy is responsible for temperature, which is a measure of the average motion of the particles within a substance. Thermodynamics refers to the transfer of heat between different objects or systems, as occurs when the heat given off the flame causes to warm the bottle.

Heat is not the same as temperature. Essentially, heat is energy and temperature is a measure of it. The temperature of a substance is a measure of the average kinetic energy of its molecules. All matter is composed of atoms or molecules that are in constant motion. The faster they move, the more kinetic energy they have. There is a direct relationship between the motion of molecules and their temperature. The greater the kinetic energy, the higher the temperature of the object. Molecules that have low average kinetic energy move slowly and have low temperatures in comparison to molecules with high kinetic energy, which move more quickly and have a higher temperature.

The candle has the property of flammability, it can burn. As it burns, it undergoes a chemical reaction resulting in a chemical change. During a chemical change, bonds within molecules are broken and atoms rearrange. The result of a chemical change is a new substance. The new substances formed from a burning candle include carbon dioxide and ash. But the candle also undergoes physical changes. As the solid wax melts, it forms liquid wax, which evaporates to form wax vapor. Melting and evaporation are phase changes, occurring as a substance changes from one phase of matter to another. Other phase changes include freezing, condensation, and deposition, as states of matter move between solid, liquid and gas.

A candle is an example of an amorphous solid, or a solid "without shape." Amorphous solids are those without rigidity or consistent defined shape. The atoms and molecules within an amorphous solid do not maintain an orderly arrangement or pattern. The molecular arrangement of these solids can be altered, typically by heating them. Amorphous solids exhibit the opposite characteristics of crystalline solids, with molecules that form well-defined lattice type arrangements. Other examples of amorphous solids include plastic, rubber, and glass.

In laminar flow, a fluid flows in a well-defined, orderly manner, with rather distinct paths. On the other hand, turbulent flow describes the random, chaotic flow. There is no order in turbulent flow. Instead, the fluid undergoes irregular fluctuations. Turbulent flow can be observed in streams used for whitewater rafting, where the water moves in random and erratic directions. Consider laminar flow as the opposite of turbulent flow. When a candle flame is extinguished, the smoke that rises straight up from the wick is in laminar flow. But, as it reaches some distance from the wick it begins to spread out, waver, and even curl around. This is turbulent flow. It is rather difficult, if not impossible, to predict the behavior of turbulent flow.

In the first phase of the demonstration, blowing directly on the candle flame will cause it to blow away from the air source, as we might expect. This is because air molecules hit the flame directly, pushing it away. The next two phases reveal unexpected outcomes that illustrate Bernoulli's principle and the Coanda Effect.

Bernoulli's principle, which describes a phenomenon observed in moving fluids, either liquid or gas, is illustrated in the second phase of the demonstration involving the index card. The principle states that as the speed of a fluid increases, the pressure within it decreases. Fast moving air essentially creates a region of low pressure. The faster a fluid, whether gas or liquid, moves over a surface, the less air pressure it exerts on that surface. When blowing against the index card, the air impacts the face of the card and flows towards the outer edges. When it meets the sharp edges, the flow of air glides off the edge and continues away from the card, spreading outward a bit. This creates a region of low air pressure behind the card. Higher air pressure now exists on the opposite side of the flame. This higher air pressure essentially pushes the flame towards the area of lower air pressure, towards the card. If you blow incredibly hard at the index card, you could possibly blow out the candle. This occurs because of swirling air, or turbulence.

The Coanda Effect is illustrated in the third phase of the demonstration involving the bottle. The Coanda Effect describes how a fluid, in this case air, forms a stream that follows the contour of the convex surface of an object. When blowing against the bottle, the air current divides, wraps around the bottle, converges on the other side, hits the flame and extinguishes it.

Bernoulli's principle and the Coanda Effect explain, in part, how airplanes fly. Air flows over the upper surface of the wings faster than under them. This creates a reduced air pressure above the wings and a higher pressure under them. This generates lift. In addition, when the wing is tilted, air is deflected downward by both its upper and lower surface. Air flowing across the wing glides along the tilted direction of its surface. The air is entrained from the surroundings, resulting in a region of lower pressure above the wing. This also generates lift.

Counter intuitively, the faster the flow of air, the lower the pressure it exerts. This explains the massive destruction caused by tornadoes. The incredible speed movement of air creates a tremendous decrease in pressure within a tornado. The stronger air pressure around the tornado throws nearby objects into it.

Differently colored candles can also generate a conversation about the physical properties of matter. A physical property is a property of a substance that can be immediately observed without changing the identity of the substance. Color is a physical property of matter. It can be immediately observed and it can help identify a substance. When you refer to an orange candle, students will know which one you are pointing out. Other physical properties include hardness, shape, size, texture, odor, etc. A few of these can be included in the discussion as the candles are referred to.

Standards Alignment:

Next Generation Science Standards (NGSS, Lead States 2013)

Disciplinary Core Ideas in Physical Science

PS1: Matter and Its Interactions

PS1.A: Structure and Properties of Matter

PS1.B: Chemical Reactions

PS2: Motion and Stability: Forces and Interactions

PS2.B: Types of Interactions

PS3: Energy

PS3.A: Definitions of Energy

PS3.B: Conservation of Energy and Energy Transfer

Disciplinary Core Ideas in Life Science

LS1: From Molecules to Organisms: Structures and Processes

LS1.A: Structure and Function

Disciplinary Core Ideas in Earth and Space Science

ESS3: Earth and Human Activity

ESS3.B: Natural Hazards

Flipped

Concepts Illustrated: Optics, convex lenses, refraction of light, properties of light, characteristic properties of liquids, viscosity, symmetry, Snell's law, mechanics of the human eye, visual perception.

In this lesson, the demonstration is individually conducted by each student, allowing them to personally initiate and more closely observe the startling phenomenon. A few wonderful approaches for elementary level students are included.

Paradox:

Amazed at the prospect they might possess magical powers, students won't believe their eyes when some images observed through water appear unchanged while others reverse and flip!

Equipment:

1. A test tube.
2. A rubber stopper.
3. Water.
4. Objects to observe through the water.
5. Index card.
6. A large beaker or tank. A 4000ml beaker works well.

Preparation:

Fill a test tube with water and insert a rubber stopper. Try to add enough water to avoid a large air bubble.

Although there are a multitude of objects that can be viewed, the *Lesson* explained below will use two printed images. The first is a black arrow. The image below is the exact size that works well with a test tube.

Print a sheet of these arrows and cut them out so that each is on its own 4x4 inch square cutout. Glue or tape one arrow cutout to a 3x5 inch index card. The arrow should point up. You will need a class set of these index cards with an arrow pasted on one side. Each student will get their own index card.

You will also want to choose and print a word that will be pasted to the other side of the index card. A collection of suggestions can be found in the *Concept Explained* section. We will use the word "WOW". This word will be spelled out vertically. It must be capitalized and printed in black ink. Again, Times New Roman typeface with a font size of 14-16 works well. This word is pasted on the index card, on the opposite side of the arrow. The arrow and the word are both vertical on opposite sides of the card. If the card is flipped over, side to side, both images would be vertical.

Finally, you will also want to choose and print a phrase that will be pasted onto a second index card. The exact phrase can vary. Again, a collection of ideas for this phrase can be found in the *Concept Explained* section that follows. The phrase we will use here is: SMART CHOICE. These letters must be capitalized. The word "SMART" is printed in red ink, whereas the word "CHOICE" is in black. Times New Roman typeface with a font size of 14-16 works well. As before, cut each phrase out of a printed sheet and paste the cutout onto an index card. Each student will get one of these cards.

All text and images should be printed by computer. Those written and drawn by hand will contain irregularities that reveal flipped images when you do not necessarily want them to be revealed.

Every student will also need a test tube filled with water and capped with a rubber stopper. Students can either assemble their own in class, or you can have them prepared in advance.

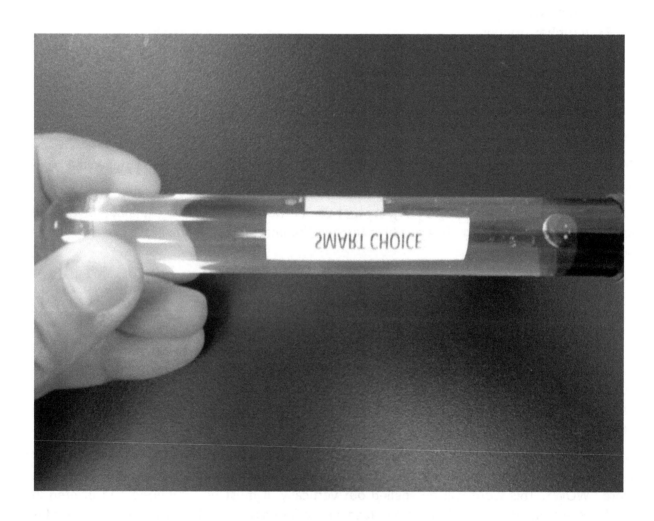

<u>The Lesson:</u>

A large beaker of water is shown. Explain that you are going to submerge your hand under the water. Ask students to predict what will happen to the image of your hand when placed in the water. I have heard many different answers to this question. Depending on the age you present to, some might predict that your hand will appear larger, smaller, or that there will be no change. Others might predict that the underwater image will be offset, angled away from the point of entry into the water. Submerge your hand into the water to show that your hand appears to grow in size. This can be observed from any angle.

Now ask students to predict what happens to the image of an object when it is placed *behind* the water, but still viewed *through* it. Again, there will be many different answers including no change, it decreases in size, and that it appears larger than when *in* the water.

Because this must be observed directly from the front, students will be given their own equipment. If you have not already prepared them, ask students to prepare a test tube (tt) by filling it almost to the top with water and placing a rubber stopper on it. There should be some space at the top of the tt so that water will not splash out when the stopper is put in place. The tt should be in a tt rack, for safety.

Give each student an index card with the image of an arrow on one side and the word "WOW" on the other. The class should follow the next steps together. The index card is on the table, the side with the arrow is face up and the arrow points up. Ask students to hold the tt above the arrow, parallel to it. They will be looking through the side wall of the tt at the arrow on the other side. The arrow should appear unchanged. Depending on the distance between the tt and the arrow, it might appear smaller.

Now, explain that we will be observing text instead of pictures. Ask students to predict what the image will look like if we view text through the tt. Some might predict the text will remain unchanged, others might think the image will change somehow because it is text. After flipping over the index card, so that the text vertically reads "WOW", students will view the text while holding the tt parallel above it. The text will appear to be unchanged. Collect these index cards.

Inform students that they will now observe text printed horizontally and in differently colored ink. Ask them to predict what will happen to the image this time. Hand each student an index card with the phrase "SMART CHOICE" on it. Once again, they should align the tt parallel with the phrase. But, because the text is printed horizontally, the tt is held in a in a different position. Each trial the tt is held parallel to the table. For the previous two trials, the tt was held away from the student. In this trial, it is held from left to right. Students will be shocked to discover that the word "CHOICE" remains unchanged, while the word "SMART" is flipped!

These three trials are intended to cause the student to question specific characteristics of each that might cause the phenomenon. At this point, most will consider that words printed in black ink do not flip, while some other colors do. Some might think that the position of the tt causes the letters to flip.

As the concept is developed through discourse, students can be provided index cards, beakers, or test tubes to allow them to observe the concepts and phenomena as it is discussed. In this way, the development of the concept is guided by individual experiments.

<u>Lesson Variation:</u>

Another rather startling method to observe this phenomenon is by positioning the object behind the beaker and filling the beaker with water while looking through it. The image will visibly reverse itself as the water level passes through it. However, when executed in this manner, the object must be placed at the appropriate distance from the beaker to cause the flip.

Another strategy is to place the image directly against the beaker and then move it back until it is seen to flip. For example, fill a beaker with water and lean a $1 bill against it. The long edge of the bill is on the table. The front of the bill faces the beaker. Look through the water to see the image of the bill on the other side. The president's picture on the front of the bill faces right. Slowly pull the bill away from the beaker, and continue to look through it. When the bill reaches a distance about four inches away from the beaker, the president's face suddenly turns and faces left.

One method of presentation for those with limited resources, or for elementary level students, involves newspaper, eyedroppers, and transparent plastic wrap, such as Saran Wrap. Each student is given a page or section from the newspaper and a piece of plastic wrap. They lay the piece of plastic wrap on top of the newspaper. Then, using an eyedropper, they place a drop of water on the plastic wrap. The image of the newspaper text is observed through the water drop. By moving the plastic wrap around on the paper, students can observe pictures and text of varying fonts. An investigation can involve the outcome when food coloring is added to the water and when using a liquid other than water.

There are two wonderful versions for elementary level students. The first involves drawing two squares or triangles side by side on a piece of paper, each filled with a different color. They will appear to switch places when viewed through the water. This occurs in a tt if it is held in a left to right position. Holding the tt in a direction facing away from you will not cause the colors to reverse, but if the tt is slowly rotated, the colors suddenly trade places!

In the second version for the elementary level, students are given a beaker of water and an index card with a green image on it. They hold the card behind the beaker and pull it away slowly until it reverses. Then they are given an index card with two words- one green and one red- one above the other. They hold the card behind the beaker again and discover that the green image once again reverses, but not the red one! Students will predict that green ink flips.

<u>Possible Variables:</u>

1. The distance between the test tube or beaker, and the object being observed.
2. Various pictures, instead of words.
3. Different liquids, such as vinegar, vegetable oil, dish soap, corn syrup, sugar/salt water, etc.

4. Viscosity of the liquid.
5. Shape of the glass viewing through.
6. Size of the letters or symbols.
7. Colored water- add food coloring.
8. Type of glass viewing through, such as glass stirring rods or empty bottles.
9. Thickness of the glass viewing through.
10. Colored glass.
11. Using colored letters or symbols with colored water.
12. Placing the letters or symbols *in* the water, rather than behind it.
13. The number of test tubes or glasses of water viewing through. Look through two or three test tubes of water. This could also involve varying the distances between them.
14. Viewing through flat piece of glass, such as a plastic box filled with water.
15. Diameter of the test tube or beaker.
16. Volume of liquid viewing through. This would involve partially filled test tubes.
17. Angle of viewing.
18. Lower and uppercase letters in the phrase.
19. Viewing through an empty test tube or beaker.
20. Viewing through plastic tubing, rather than glass. The tubing can be empty, or filled with water. This can also involve plastic soda bottles, or graduated cylinders.

Phenomenon Explained:

Light can bend when it changes speed as it passes from one medium into another. This bend is called refraction. The degree of bending is dependent on the indices of refraction for each medium. Snell's law is used to quantitatively describe the refraction.

Refraction is the phenomenon that causes image formation by the eye. About 80% of the refraction occurs at the surface of the cornea, as light passes from air into the cornea. Another 20% occurs in the inner crystalline lens.

Refraction also accounts for the misaligned image of an object, such as a straw, pencil, or your hand when a portion is above and another below the water. The portion observed underwater is shifted, causing a distorted or broken appearance.

To fully understand the phenomenon observed in this demonstration, we need to understand the mechanics of convex lenses. Eyeglasses, cameras, telescopes, magnifying glasses, and many other optical instruments employ convex lenses. A convex lens is thicker at the center than at the edges. When light rays enter a convex lens parallel to its principal axis, they refract, or bend, towards one another and converge on the opposite side. The point at which they converge and cross paths is called the focal point. The refraction of the light, as it passes through the curvature of the lens, produces an inverted image of the object being viewed. A convex lens will reverse an image.

The water-filled test tube or beaker act as a convex lens, inverting the images that pass through it. If you were to observe the printed arrow through an empty beaker, the light from the room bounces off the arrow and travels directly into your eye. This explains why you see the arrow head on the side it was drawn. However, the path of light bends, or refracts, when it enters the boundary between the water in the beaker and the air around it.

Imagine looking through a beaker of water at the image of an arrow on the other side, the arrow pointing to the right. When the light bouncing off the arrow head hits the right side of the beaker, it refracts to the left. Conversely, when light bounces off the tail of the arrow, it hits the left side of the beaker and bends to the right. On the other side of the beaker, the light will converge at the focal point. Their new paths continue and the light rays that entered the beaker on the left side end up hitting your eye on the right, while the light ray entering the beaker on the right side hits your eye on the left.

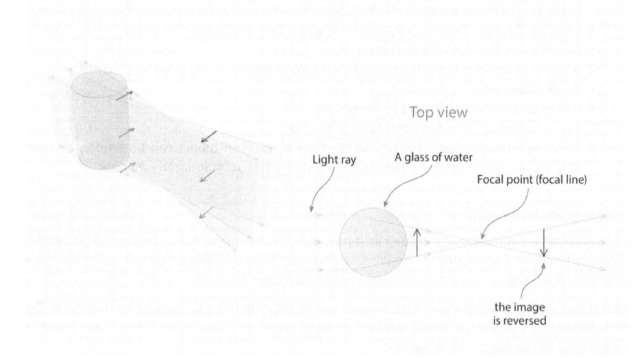

Top view

Light ray   A glass of water

Focal point (focal line)

the image
is reversed

The greater the angle that the light strikes the water, the greater the refraction. As a result, the distance from the beaker that causes the image to flip is dependent on the diameter of the beaker and the size of the image or text you're viewing. It can range from 3-18 inches. It's best to try this out for yourself first. The angle of refraction produced is also a characteristic property of the liquid. When student investigations involve various liquids, the results lead to rich discussion and learning.

Although some words appear unchanged, all the words observed through the test tube flip. But, due to their symmetry, sometimes the flip is not recognizable. Words, and the letters that make them up, can exhibit two types of symmetry: horizontal and vertical. Words with horizontal symmetry have letters which are mirror images of themselves. If you draw a horizontal line through the middle of the word, the top would be a mirror image of the bottom. They will appear unchanged when viewed through a tt held parallel to the word. Turn the tt perpendicular and the words flip from left to right. The following words have horizontal symmetry:

242

CHOICE, COOKBOOK, DIOXIDE, HIDE, ICEBOX, EXCEEDED, DECIDED, CODEBOOK, CHECKBOOK

These letters can be used to construct words with horizontal symmetry: B, C, D, E, H, I, K, O, X

In vertical symmetry, the left and right sides of letters with a vertical line bisecting them will be mirror images of themselves. In this lesson, writing these words vertically will cause them to appear unchanged when viewed through a tt held parallel to them. Turn the tt perpendicular and the words flip from top to bottom. The following words have vertical symmetry:

TOOT, MAAM, TOT, TUT, AHA!, WOW!, MOM, HAH!, MAMMOTH, TOMATO, WITHOUT, YOUTH

These letters can be used to construct words with vertical symmetry: A, H, I, M, O, T, U, V, W, X, Y

If the word "WOW" is written vertically and viewed through a parallel tt, it will flip to read "MOM" when the tt is spun to a perpendicular position.

An arrow pointing upward will appear unchanged when viewed through a tt held parallel to it. The arrow is actually flipping but, due to its vertical symmetry, will not appear flipped. It will reverse and point downward when the tt is held perpendicular. This is due to the orientation of the curvature of the tt. Spinning the tt from parallel to perpendicular while looking through it, is rather startling, as the arrow actively flips in the process. Another startling method of observing this involves an arrow pointing left. Hold a tt perpendicular to it and slowly glide the tt over the arrow. It will be seen to actively flip and point right. In addition, if you tip the tt, allowing the air bubble inside to travel from one end of the tube to the other, the arrow will flip as the bubble passes over. Finally, the arrow will diminish in size when the distance between the test tube and the image increases.

Viscosity is defined as a fluid's resistance to flow. Think of it as the "thickness" of a fluid. Fluids such as honey, molasses, corn syrup, and engine oil are highly viscous. Students might choose to investigate the outcome when liquids of varying viscosities are employed.

Standards Alignment:

Next Generation Science Standards (NGSS, Lead States 2013)

Disciplinary Core Ideas in Physical Science

PS1: Matter and Its Interactions

PS1.A: Structure and Properties of Matter

PS2: Motion and Stability: Forces and Interactions

PS2.B: Types of Interactions

<u>PS4: Waves and Their Applications in Technologies for Information Transfer</u>

PS4.A: Wave Properties

PS4.B: Electromagnetic Radiation

Disciplinary Core Ideas in Life Science

<u>LS1: From Molecules to Organisms: Structures and Processes</u>

LS1.A: Structure and Function

LS1.D: Information Processing

Floating Fruit

Concepts Illustrated: Density, buoyancy, displacement, physical properties of matter, absorption and reflection of light, visual interpretation of color.

This demonstration produces quite a discrepant outcome for elementary level students.

Paradox:

Students will be rather amazed to find that when dropped in water, the largest fruit floats while the smallest sinks!

Equipment:

1. A clear tank or aquarium. See the Demonstration Variation section for a version using beakers. A large tub can also be used.
2. Pieces of fruit. The demonstration will be explained using several types of fruit. There is actually a wide selection of fruit to choose from.
3. Water.

Preparation:

Fill the tank, beakers, or bowl with water. Leave enough room at the top to allow for your hands and the fruit to be put into the water without spilling over the rim.

The pieces of fruit are lined up on the desk in the following order: Pumpkin, grapefruit, orange, apple, lemon, lime, strawberry, and grape. Note that this is in order of size, from largest to smallest. Try to select pieces that clearly display this. Students should distinctly recognize that each piece of fruit is progressively smaller from pumpkin to grape.

The Lesson:

Call attention to the fruit lined up on the desk. Ask if anyone recognizes a pattern amongst the fruit. This is a critical step of the demonstration. You want to be certain students identify that each piece of fruit decreases in size from pumpkin to grape, or increases in the reverse order. When lined up in successive order, students are apt to more easily recognize this.

Display the tank and explain that it is filled with plain water. Explain that you will place each piece of fruit into the water, one at a time. Tell them that you will begin with the grape. Pick it up and casually show it. Inform them that you will test each piece of fruit in their successive order on the table, ending with the pumpkin. When you say this, pick up the pumpkin. Be a little dramatic as you do. Struggle with it as you pick it up, reinforcing the stark difference in mass from grape to pumpkin. In comparison to the grape, it is very heavy. Although mass does play a role here, many students think that heavy objects naturally sink while lighter objects float. Ask students to predict whether each piece floats or sinks.

Place the grape into the water. Most students predict that the grape floats, because it is small and light. They are surprised to find that it actually sinks! Many will now think that if the grape sank, the larger pieces of fruit that follow will also sink. But again, they are surprised to find that the strawberry which is a little larger than the grape floats! This presents a conflict. Why does the smaller grape sink, while the larger strawberry floats? The contradictions and questions continue with the next pieces of fruit.

The next two pieces of fruit tested present a discrepancy as well. The lime is shown to sink. But the lemon, which is a bit larger than the lime, floats. Even if they are very close in size, most students predict both to float. They are surprised to find that the lime sinks. Many do predict apples to float, and they do. But many then predict oranges, and especially grapefruit, to sink. Yet, they float! The demonstration culminates with the most discrepant observation. Almost all will predict the massive pumpkin to sink. There is great surprise when it floats! The sight of it floating in water is actually rather startling!

<u>Lesson Variation:</u>

The demonstration can be extended by peeling the orange, lemon, and lime. This can serve to launch student investigation, or it can be left entirely to investigation. Students might consider that the rind causes these fruits to sink or float. After removing the rind from each, drop them in water. The outcome surprises most. The lime continues to sink, the lemon continues to float, but the orange now sinks! This phenomenon can lead into some "fruitful" student-led investigation!

The demonstration can also be presented using just limes and lemons. In this case, one 4000ml beaker can be used, or one of each fruit can be separately dropped into two large beakers. A very large bowl could also be used. Select pieces of fruit that are very close in size. When presented with just these two pieces of fruit, most students will predict they both float. They are surprised to find that only the lemon floats, while the lime sinks!

Bananas provide a number of variables to investigate. Use either one half or one third of it in the demonstration. Students will question whether using the whole piece of fruit will affect the outcome. They might also question whether peeling it or removing the stem plays a role in the outcome.

Your demonstration could include a number of other fruit choices. Be creative!

<u>Possible Variables:</u>

1. Different types of fruit.
2. Using fruit slices. This can extend to studying slices of varying thickness.
3. Cutting the pieces of fruit in half.
4. Using wedges cut into various shapes.
5. Removing the rind.

<u>Phenomenon Explained:</u>

The density of an object will determine whether it will float in a fluid. Density is determined by calculating the mass for a given volume, expressed in the formula g/ml, g/cm^3, or g/cc. Density is independent of the sample size, since it represents the mass per ml of the sample. A larger volume does not necessarily equate to a higher mass. Fewer molecules packed into a given volume will result in a lower density than many more molecules packed into the same volume, which would increase the density. Objects with a density less than water will float, while those denser than water will sink. The density of water is 1.0g/ml. Whether the pieces of fruit float or sink when placed into water is dependent on their density.

The density of each piece of fruit can be calculated by massing it and then finding the volume by placing it into an overflow can, collecting and measuring the water that spills out. Students will discover the densities to be close. Yet their densities do explain why one floats and the other sinks. The density of a lemon is approximately 1.02 g/ml, while the lime is about 1.12 g/ml. Since the density of water is 1.0 g/ml, it makes sense the lemon floats while the lime sinks.

Students might think that differences in the rind cause limes to sink, while lemons and oranges float. Yet when they investigate this by removing the rind from each, they will be surprised. As mentioned, the orange will behave differently once the rind is removed. Air pockets within the rind cause the orange to float. When the rind is removed, the orange sinks. When they see this, most students assume that removing the rinds from the lemon and lime will change their outcome as well. However, their expectations are contradicted when the rinds are removed and the outcomes do not change! The lemon still floats and the lime still sinks!

Since fruits of different colors can be used, the lesson presents the opportunity for a rich discussion regarding the absorption and reflection of light, as well as the visual interpretation of color. Light is made up of a spectrum of distinct wavelengths, each a particular color. Specifically, these are red, orange, yellow, green, blue, indigo, and violet. Objects around you appear to be particular colors because those colors, or wavelengths, are reflected from those objects. All other colors in the spectrum are absorbed. For example, when light hits a green lime it absorbs the entire spectrum of light except for green, which is reflected off the lime. Your retina perceives the color being reflected and transmits that information to the brain for processing. The lime appears green. Essentially, the colors that we see are those wavelengths that are reflected off the object.

Differently colored fruits can also generate a conversation regarding the physical properties of matter. A physical property is a property of a substance that can be immediately observed without changing the identity of the substance. Color is a physical property of matter. It can be immediately observed and it can help identify a substance. When you refer to a yellow lemon, students will know which one you are pointing out. Other physical properties include hardness, shape, size, texture, odor, etc. A few of these can be included in the discussion as the pieces of fruit are referred to.

Standards Alignment:

Next Generation Science Standards (NGSS, Lead States 2013)

Disciplinary Core Ideas in Physical Science

PS1: Matter and Its Interactions

PS1.A: Structure and Properties of Matter

PS3: Energy

PS3.D: Energy in Chemical Processes and Everyday Life

Disciplinary Core Ideas in Life Science

LS1: From Molecules to Organisms: Structures and Processes

LS1.A: Structure and Function

LS1.C: Organization for Matter and Energy Flow in Organisms

LS1.D: Information Processing

Floating Letters

Concepts Illustrated: Solubility, solute, solvent, chromatography, solutions, viscosity, density, process of dissolving.

Paradox:

They won't believe their eyes when students place M&M's in water and the letters printed on the candies detach and float, completely intact, on the surface of the water!

Equipment:

1. M&M's.
2. A Petri dish or shallow dish or bowl. A glass bowl allows the phenomena to be easily observed from all angles, but a paper or Styrofoam plate will also work.
3. Water.

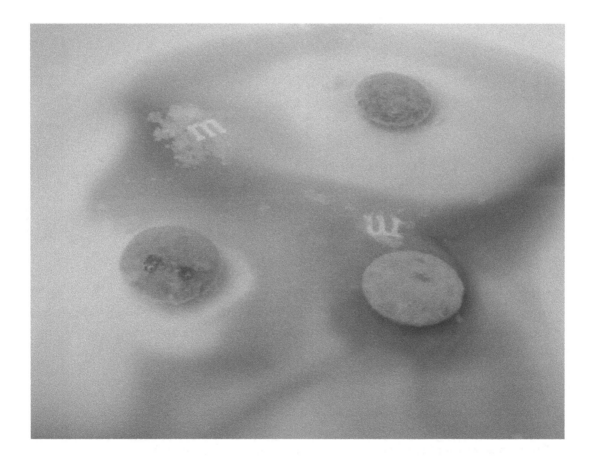

<u>The Lesson:</u>

Place several M&M's into the bottom of the bowl. Be sure that the M&M logo printed on the candies are face up. Explain to students that you're going to pour room temperature water into the bowl to cover the candies. Ask students to predict what will happen. Many will predict that the candy will dissolve. Some will predict that the colors of the candy will color the water. But no one will predict what will actually happen. Once students have predicted, carefully pour the room temperature water into the bowl. The water should completely cover the candies at the bottom. Pour slowly so that the candies do not flip over.

The first thing your students will observe is that the colored food dye will begin to change the color of the surrounding water. The water will begin to turn blue around the blue M&M's, red around the red M&M's, green around the green M&M's, and so on. The different colors will begin to mix and make swirling rainbow patterns. Those students who predicted this outcome will begin to get excited over their accurate predictions. Eventually, all the color will dissolve off the candies and they will become white. But, continue to watch the candies.

The surprise follows, as the M&M logo suddenly lifts off each individual piece of candy and floats up to the surface of the water, fully intact!

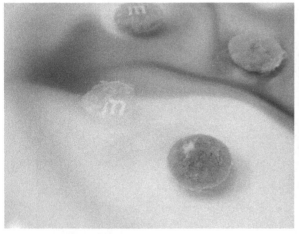 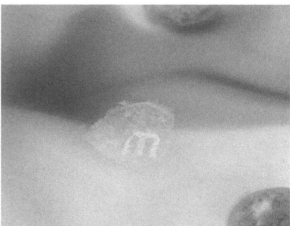

<u>Possible Variables:</u>

1. Using a liquid other than water, such as vinegar, vegetable oil, corn syrup, soda, milk, soapy water, alcohol, sugar water, salt water, etc. If sugar water or salt water is explored, their concentrations can be manipulated and the outcomes studied.
2. The density of the liquid.
3. The viscosity of the liquid.
4. The pH of the liquid.
5. Type of candy such as Skittles, or any other candy with a printed coating.
6. Placing M&M's in the bowl with their letters facing down.
7. The temperature of the water. It can be heated or chilled with ice.

Phenomenon Explained:

This demonstration involves chromatography. This is a process of separating a mixture of solutes, oftentimes observed as pigments or colors in science experiments.

If the density of the liquid is altered by adding salt or sugar, discourse can include solutions, solubility, solutes, solvents, and concentration.

A solution is one in which a solute is dissolve in a solvent. The solute is the substance being dissolved and the solvent is the substance in which the solute is dissolved. Water is called the universal solvent because it is capable of dissolving more solutes than any other liquid. Solubility is the ability of a solute to dissolve in a solvent.

The first observation students make will be that the colored food dye is seen to dissolve off the candies and color the surrounding water. This occurs because the water, acting as the solvent, dissolves the coating of sugar, or the solute, on the M&M's. The colored food dye is soluble, so it dissolves into the water surrounding the candy, coloring it. But the M&M logo on each piece of candy is actually made of edible paper that doesn't dissolve in water. Sugar holds this insoluble logo onto the candy. When the sugar is dissolved off the candy, the letters that form the M&M logo are free to peel away. The letters float to the surface of the water because they are less dense than water. It will take between 5-15 minutes for this to occur.

Standards Alignment:

Next Generation Science Standards (NGSS, Lead States 2013)

Disciplinary Core Ideas in Physical Science

PS1: Matter and Its Interactions

PS1.A: Structure and Properties of Matter

PS1.B: Chemical Reactions

PS2: Motion and Stability: Forces and Interactions

PS2.B: Types of Interactions

Disciplinary Core Ideas in Earth and Space Science

ESS2: Earth's Systems

ESS2.C: The Roles of Water in Earth's Surface Processes

Fountain Phenomenon

<u>Concepts Illustrated:</u> Air pressure, fluid dynamics, gravity, displacement, viscosity, density, solutions, solubility, solutes, solvents, concentration, saturated solutions, properties of mixtures, process of dissolving.

<u>Paradox:</u>

Two 1-liter plastic soda bottles are connected at their openings, one inverted over the other. The lower bottle is filled with colored water, while the upper bottle is empty. Two straws pass between them. As expected, when the bottles are turned over as one unit, the water now in the upper bottle travels through the one straw into the empty bottle below. But, suddenly the water shoots upward, through the other straw and into the bottle on top- creating a continuous spraying fountain that defies expectation and gravity!

<u>Equipment:</u>

1. Two 1-liter bottles.
2. Water.
3. Food coloring.
4. Two straws. Rigid plastic tubing can also be used.
5. A connector that secures the two 1-liter bottles together. The connector is constructed so that plastic tubing or straws can be inserted into each side. These connectors can be found at science supply stores.
6. A thumbtack or nail.

<u>Preparation:</u>

The contents of the bottles should be completely visible to students during the demonstration. For this reason, you should remove any labels on the outside of the bottles. Fill one of the bottles about ¾ full of water. Then, add some food coloring to it. The food coloring allows the water to be more readily visible to all students. If you use a color like green or yellow, the bottle will be translucent, allowing students to also see the straws. You don't want to "hide" anything in the bottle. The phenomenon can only begin to be understood by observing all the parts involved.

<u>The Lesson:</u>

In preparation for this demonstration, all the pieces of equipment involved should be laid out and visible. The device should be assembled as students look on. Ask students to observe the assembly of the device that will be used in the demonstration to follow as you direct their attention to all the individual parts. Begin by showing the 1-liter bottle filled with colored water. Explain that this liquid is simply water that has had food coloring added to it.

Show the two straws. Using the thumbtack, push three holes into each straw. The holes should be about two or three inches from one end. Now show the connector and insert the straws into it, one from each side of the connector. Next, show how the connector screws onto the bottle top by attaching it to the top of the bottle filled with the colored water. Then attach the empty bottle to the top of the connector, so that this bottle is inverted over the water-filled bottle. Make sure that students appreciate that the straw in the lower bottle extends into the liquid.

Explain that you will simply turn the entire apparatus over, so that the water-filled bottle is on top of the empty bottle. Ask students to predict what will happen. Then turn over the device, allowing the fountain to spray into the upper bottle.

Possible Variables:

1. Volume of liquid.
2. Viscosity of the liquid.
3. Liquids with different densities. This could involve one liquid at a time in the bottles. It could also involve two different liquids in the bottles at the same time, each with different densities. Density could be manipulated by adding salt or sugar to the water. If two liquids were investigated, food coloring could also be used to observe the movement of each liquid.
4. Length of the straws. This could also be studied with the volume of liquid used. For example, small volume of liquid with a long straw or large volume of liquid with a shorter straw.
5. Width of the straws or tubes in the bottles.
6. Volume of the bottles.
7. Shape of the bottles.
8. Cutting off the bottom half of the top bottle and pouring liquid directly into that bottle.
9. Size of the holes placed into the sides of the straws.
10. Number of holes placed into the sides of the straws.
11. No holes in the straws.
12. Straws bent into different shapes. Crazy Straws can also be used.

Phenomenon Explained:

This demonstration illustrates the principle of the Hero Fountain, named from its discovery by Hero of Alexandria. The device uses air pressure to lift water to a point higher than its origin. When the bottles are inverted, gravity causes the water to flow through one straw and into the lower bottle. As the liquid is emptied from the upper bottle there is a reduction of pressure in that bottle. The air that filled the lower bottle is compressed and displaced, being pushed up the opposite straw and into the upper bottle.

The straws actually have tiny holes very close to the connector. Water leaking into the upper straw through those tiny holes is pushed upward by the air being displaced and pushed into the upper bottle. This creates the erupting fountain effect.

Viscosity is defined as a fluid's resistance to flow. Think of it as the "thickness" of a fluid. Fluids such as honey, molasses, corn syrup, and engine oil are highly viscous. Students might choose to investigate the outcome when liquids of varying viscosities are employed.

If the density of the liquid is altered by adding salt or sugar, discourse can include solutions, solubility, solutes, solvents, and concentration. Saltwater or sugar water is a mixture. One property of a mixture is that it is physically combined, not chemically, and it can be physically separated. For example, saltwater can be physically separated through the process of evaporation, or boiling the water away.

A solution is one in which a solute is dissolve in a solvent. The solute is the substance being dissolved and the solvent is the substance in which the solute is dissolved. Water is called the universal solvent because it is capable of dissolving more solutes than any other liquid. Solubility is the ability of a solute to dissolve in a solvent.

A concentrated solution is one which there are many dissolved particles of solute in the solvent. On the other hand, a dilute solution is one in which there are few dissolved particles of solute. A solution which contains all the dissolve particles it can possibly hold is called saturated.

Standards Alignment:

Next Generation Science Standards (NGSS, Lead States 2013)

Disciplinary Core Ideas in Physical Science

PS1: Matter and Its Interactions

PS1.A: Structure and Properties of Matter

PS1.B: Chemical Reactions

PS2: Motion and Stability: Forces and Interactions

PS2.A: Forces and Motion

PS2.B: Types of Interactions

Disciplinary Core Ideas in Earth and Space Science

ESS2: Earth's Systems

ESS2.C: The Roles of Water in Earth's Surface Processes

Free Fall

<u>Concepts Illustrated:</u> Velocity, acceleration, mass, momentum, speed, gravity, free fall, density.

<u>Paradox:</u>

A string with identical weights attached at distinctly unevenly spaced intervals is dropped by holding one end of the string, allowing it to hang vertically from the fingertips, into a metal wastebasket. Even though the weights are placed at various, random points along the string, they are heard to hit the wastebasket at evenly spaced time intervals.

A second string with identical weights attached at evenly spaced intervals is now dropped in the same manner and allowed to fall into the metal wastebasket. This time, even though the weights are evenly spaced, they are heard to hit the wastebasket at uneven time intervals.

<u>Equipment:</u>

1. String.
2. A number of identical weights that can be attached to the string. Metal washers can be used.
3. Stopwatch.
4. Meter stick or ruler.
5. A metal wastebasket. If a metal wastebasket is unavailable, a large metal tray or pan can be used instead.

<u>The Lesson:</u>

Begin by showing students the string with weights attached. Hold the string, or lay it on the floor or counter and ask a student to measure the distances between each of the weights. As these distances are measured, they are recorded on the board or easel paper for all to see. The weights should be spaced at intervals that clearly show their randomness and differences. There shouldn't be any pattern. Now, ask students to predict how much time it would take for the weights to hit the metal pan when the string is held above it and dropped. Hold the string up to demonstrate this, but do not release it yet. Let them know that the event will be timed with a stopwatch. Once they've made predictions, ask one student to control the stopwatch. Everyone else is asked to simply listen to the spacing of the sounds made when the weights hit the metal pan. Release the string. The sounds of the weights hitting the metal pan will occur at regularly spaced intervals. This will be evident to all listening. It will be supported by the stopwatch data.

You'll find that students will predict times that match the spacing of the weights. For example, the time predicted for weights spaced far apart will be longer than the time predicted for weights spaced more closely together.

You can repeat this procedure using a second string with evenly spaced identical weights.

When using a string with unevenly spaced weights, students will generally draw weights that are evenly spaced along the string. In their drawings, the distance between weights might vary from student to student, but the intervals will exhibit uniformity along each string. The opposite will generally be true when using a string with evenly spaced weights. In this case, student drawings will generally show weights that are unevenly spaced.

Lesson Variation:

In an alternate method of presentation, no stopwatch is used. The string is not shown to students prior to the drop, so students do not know the spacing of the weights. Instead, students are told that there are weights attached to the string and that you will be holding the string out, hanging above the metal pan before dropping it onto the pan. Ask them to listen carefully to the sound of the weights as they hit the pan. Before dropping the string, ask students to draw a line on their paper that represents the string. Once the string is dropped and they have had a chance to listen to the weights hit the pan, they will be asked to draw the weights, and their approximate placement on the string. Make it clear that they will not be asked to predict the shape of these weights- only their placement on the string. Now, ask students to close their eyes so that they can focus solely on the sound. Once all students have closed their eyes, hold the string above the pan and drop it. They can now open their eyes and, without discussing, they are asked to draw the weights on the string with specific placements based on the sounds they made when they hit the pan. Once they've completed their drawings, reveal the string used to show that the actual position of the weights does not align with their predictions.

In one final method, a string can be displayed with unevenly spaced weights, as shown below:

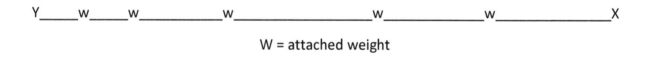

W = attached weight

When this string is dropped from end X, it will result in sounds that occur in unequal intervals. However, when dropped from end Y, the result will be sounds that occur in equal intervals.

Possible Variables:

1. The same number of weights on the string, but using weights made of a different substance and density from the original weights.
2. The same number of weights, but using weights made of varying substances and densities on the same string.
3. If metal washers are used as weights, differently sized washers can be tested.

Phenomenon Explained:

To begin, we should become familiar with the terms momentum, velocity, speed, and acceleration.

Momentum refers to a quantity of motion that an object has. The momentum of a moving object can be calculated using the following formula:

momentum = mass x velocity

The momentum of any moving object is dependent upon its mass and velocity. The terms speed and velocity are oftentimes mistakenly used interchangeably. Whereas speed refers to the measure of how fast an object moves, velocity measures how fast an object arrives at a certain point. They are different. Speed is defined as the rate of time that an object travels a distance. Velocity is defined as the rate of change in displacement with respect to time, or the rate that an object moves from one point to another. The formula for speed is:

distance traveled
time of travel

As a vector quantity, velocity involves both speed and direction. The formula for velocity is:

displacement
time

Consider a person walking two steps forward and two steps back, returning to the original starting position. Their speed of each step can be measured. But their velocity would be measured as zero.

Acceleration is defined as the rate at which an object changes its velocity.

When the weights are evenly spaced along the string, they travel the same distance before hitting the metal pan. But, each successive weight actually hits the pan in a shorter time interval. This means that the velocity, or speed, of the string is increasing. This rate of change of velocity per unit of time is called acceleration. If the string was falling with uniform velocity, or speed, we would hear equally spaced sounds. This would be because each weight would be traveling the same distance in the same time. An object is accelerating if it is changing its velocity.

Imagine two baseballs, one dropped from a height of one meter, and the other dropped from a height of 1000 meters. The concept of acceleration explains why we would easily consider catching the ball dropped from a distance of one meter, but might think twice about catching the one dropped from 1000 meters.

Free fall describes the motion of a falling object that is acted upon by gravity alone, and no other forces.

Students could choose to investigate the density of the weights dropped. Density is determined by calculating the mass for a given volume, expressed in the formula g/ml, g/cm^3, or g/cc. Density is independent of the sample size, since it represents the mass per ml of the sample. A larger volume does not necessarily equate to a higher mass. Fewer molecules packed into a given volume will result in a lower density than many more molecules packed into the same volume, which would increase the density.

The demonstration can also show that energy can be transferred as sound.

Standards Alignment:

Next Generation Science Standards (NGSS, Lead States 2013)

Disciplinary Core Ideas in Physical Science

PS1: Matter and Its Interactions

PS1.A: Structure and Properties of Matter

PS2: Motion and Stability: Forces and Interactions

PS2.A: Forces and Motion

PS2.B: Types of Interactions

PS3: Energy

PS3.A: Definitions of Energy

PS3.B: Conservation of Energy and Energy Transfer

PS4: Waves and Their Applications in Technologies for Information Transfer

PS4.A: Wave Properties

Disciplinary Core Ideas in Life Science

LS1: From Molecules to Organisms: Structures and Processes

LS1.D: Information Processing

Frightened Pepper

Concepts Illustrated: Density, cohesion, properties of water, surface tension, viscosity, solutions, solubility, solutes, solvents, concentration, saturated solutions, process of dissolving, hydrophobic molecules, hydrophilic molecules, properties of mixtures, properties of surfactants, the respiratory system of fish, the human respiratory system.

Paradox:

The contradictions begin when pepper placed into water sinks as a whole kernel, but floats when ground up! But expectations are sharply contradicted with the addition of a drop of dishwashing liquid. Although most students expect the ground pepper to sink, it is instantly driven away from the drop of soap, shooting quickly to the edge of the bowl!

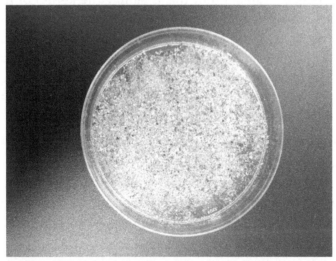

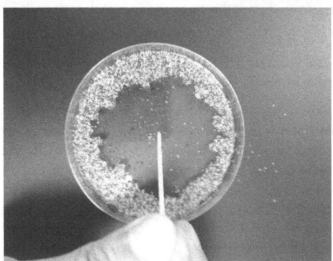

<u>Equipment</u>:

1) Toothpick.
2) Dishwashing liquid.
3) Wide bowl. A pie tin works well.
4) Ground pepper.
5) Whole pepper kernel.

<u>The Lesson</u>:

Allow students to observe you fill the pie tin with water. Show one whole pepper kernel to the students. Ask them to predict what will happen when you drop the kernel into the water. Some will predict it will float, other that it sinks, and some that it will break apart. Drop the kernel into the water and students will observe that it sinks.

Now show the ground pepper. Explain that this is simply the kernel of pepper ground up. It is the same substance, just in a different form. Inform them that you are going to sprinkle some of this pepper over the water. Ask them to predict what will happen. Because it is the same substance, some will predict it will behave the same way and sink. Others will predict just the opposite. They expect a different outcome than the kernel of pepper. Sprinkle a generous amount of ground pepper onto the surface of the water, until there is a layer of pepper on the entire surface. It will float. This contradicting outcome surprises most.

Now, put a drop of dishwashing liquid onto one of your fingertips. Dip the end of a toothpick into the drop of dishwashing liquid. Make sure students understand that there is soap on the end of the toothpick. Ask them to predict what they think will happen when you touch the surface of the water with the end of the toothpick with soap on it. Most will now think that the soap will cause the floating pepper to sink. What happens is much more visually alarming!

Slowly touch the end of the toothpick to the surface of the water, in the center. The pepper will be instantly driven away from the toothpick, pushed up against the edge of the bowl.

<u>Lesson Variation</u>:

This phenomenon can be dramatically presented by using a petri dish on top of an overhead projector, or by projecting its image on a visualizer, such as an Elmo.

You can also use a shallow paper plate. Fill the plate with water. Place two or three beads onto the surface of the water, at the center of the plate, about two inches apart from one another. Now dip the toothpick into the soap and then into the water, directly in the center of the bead formation. The beads will quickly race away from the center of the dish, towards the edge. Using the same plastic beads, you could place them in the water in two or three groups of three or four beads per group. These groups can be arranged in a circular pattern near the center of the dish. When the soap covered toothpick is placed in the center of this arrangement, the groups will stay together while moving towards the edge of the dish.

The demonstration can also be done with a thread loop. Tie the ends of a small piece of thread to form a loop. Place this loop onto the surface of the water in the center of the dish. Place the soap covered toothpick into the center of this piece of thread and it will immediately expand outwards, forming a complete circle around the toothpick.

Q-Tips, or even the tip of your finger, can be used in place of a toothpick.

Possible Variables:

1. Different liquids other than water, such as vegetable oil, olive oil, vinegar, etc.
2. Density of the liquid. Adding salt or sugar to the water will change its density.
3. Viscosity of the liquid.
4. Different spices other than pepper.
5. Different dish soaps.
6. Different amounts of pepper.
7. Assorted brands of ground pepper.
8. Shampoo instead of dish soap.
9. Width of container- this can involve testing the distance the pepper travels compared to the amount of soap or the brand of soap.
10. Temperature of the water.
11. Temp of the soap.
12. Substances other than ground pepper, such as flour, baby powder, coconut shavings, cinnamon, corn kernels, plastic beads, small Styrofoam balls, or even cracked pepper.
13. Thread or string of various thickness.

Phenomenon Explained:

Water molecules are strongly attracted to one another due to cohesion, the force of attraction that holds like molecules together. Those molecules at the surface do not have any water molecules above them. Thus, they are strongly attracted to those below. The strong attraction to the molecules around and underneath create a surface tension, a film-like layer of water at the surface, almost like an "elastic skin." This is one of the reasons that the pepper floats on the surface of water. The other involves density.

The density of an object will determine whether it will float in a fluid. Density is determined by calculating the mass for a given volume, expressed in the formula g/ml, g/cm^3, or g/cc. Density is independent of the sample size, since it represents the mass per ml of the sample. A larger volume does not necessarily equate to a higher mass. Fewer molecules packed into a given volume will result in a lower density than many more molecules packed into the same volume, which would increase the density. Objects with a density less than water will float, while those denser than water will sink. The density of water is 1.0g/ml.

The density of pepper is greater than the density of water. This explains why the whole kernel sinks. But the density of pepper does not change, whether it is whole or ground up. So why does the ground pepper float? Because the small particles are light enough to be held up by the strong surface tension at the surface of the water.

Soap is a surfactant, a compound that reduces surface tension. Although the cohesive force between the water molecules in direct proximity to the soap is weakened, the force between water molecules farther away is still strong. These stronger forces pull the more weakly held water molecules towards them. As those water molecules move, they bring the pepper with them.

If consecutive investigations are conducted, the bowl or tray will need to be thoroughly rinsed to remove any soap film or residue from the previous trial.

Soap molecules are bipolar. That is, each molecule has two ends. One is a non-polar "tail" and the other a polar "head." The polar end is hydrophilic, it *likes* water and dissolves in it. The non-polar end is hydrophobic, meaning it doesn't *like* water.

Viscosity is defined as a fluid's resistance to flow. Think of it as the "thickness" of a fluid. Fluids such as honey, molasses, corn syrup, and engine oil are highly viscous. Students might choose to investigate the outcome when liquids of varying viscosities are employed.

If the density of the liquid is altered by adding salt or sugar, discourse can include solutions, solubility, solutes, solvents, and concentration. Saltwater or sugar water is a mixture. One property of a mixture is that it is physically combined, not chemically, and it can be physically separated. For example, saltwater can be physically separated through the process of evaporation, or boiling the water away.

A solution is one in which a solute is dissolve in a solvent. The solute is the substance being dissolved and the solvent is the substance in which the solute is dissolved. Water is called the universal solvent because of its capability to dissolve more solutes than any other liquid. Solubility is the ability of a solute to dissolve in a solvent.

A concentrated solution is one which there are many dissolved particles of solute in the solvent. On the other hand, a dilute solution is one in which there are few dissolved particles of solute. A solution which contains all the dissolve particles it can possibly hold is called saturated.

Surfactants play a critical role in our bodies. There is a thin layer of water that lines human lungs. This water is necessary for the gas exchange of carbon dioxide and oxygen to occur. These gases require a wet layer or surface for the exchange to take place. In fish, this exchange takes place in their gills. Since they are on the outside of the fish, gills have direct contact with water. Our lungs, on the other hand, are best able to be kept wet inside of our bodies. However, due to the properties of water, surface tension arises that can interfere with the expansion of our lungs as we breathe. Surfactant acts to reduce surface tension. This prevents alveoli, small air sacs in the lungs, from collapsing when we exhale. The most efficient oxygen-carbon dioxide exchange occurs in our lungs with the greatest alveoli surface area. By preventing the collapse of alveoli, surfactant helps to maximize the surface area available for the exchange of gases.

Standards Alignment:

Next Generation Science Standards (NGSS, Lead States 2013)

Disciplinary Core Ideas in Physical Science

PS1: Matter and Its Interactions

PS1.A: Structure and Properties of Matter

PS1.B: Chemical Reactions

PS2: Motion and Stability: Forces and Interactions

PS2.B: Types of Interactions

Disciplinary Core Ideas in Life Science

LS1: From Molecules to Organisms: Structures and Processes

LS1.A: Structure and Function

Disciplinary Core Ideas in Earth and Space Science

ESS2: Earth's Systems

ESS2.C: The Roles of Water in Earth's Surface Processes

Fruit Blast

<u>Concepts Illustrated:</u>   Hydrocarbons, color as a physical property, atoms, molecules and compounds.

<u>Paradox</u>:

Students will be startled, then shocked, when a small orange peel squeezed next to a balloon causes it to suddenly burst! They are further puzzled when only specific colors of balloons seem to pop!

In this lesson, you will find two outstanding variations of this bewildering phenomenon. Select the presentation that best suits your curriculum and resources. Each delivers quite a discrepant event.

<u>Equipment</u>:

1. Balloons. You will need two different types of balloons- vulcanized and non-vulcanized rubber. The balloons we are most familiar with are made of vulcanized rubber. Most water balloons are made of non-vulcanized rubber.
2. An orange.
3. A lemon and a lime, if you are presenting the second lesson variation.

<u>The Lesson:</u>

Begin by showing three balloons. These balloons should be made of vulcanized rubber, but this fact is not shared with students yet. The balloons we are most familiar with are made of vulcanized rubber. You'll find more about this in the Phenomenon Explained section. You should point out that they are "regular" balloons. There should also be three different colors. For our purposes, we'll say they are blue, yellow, and orange. Inflate the balloons and tie a knot in them, to hold the air. Now show the orange and peel a bit of the rind from it. Inform the students that you are about to squeeze the rind over each balloon. Some may have peeled an orange and experienced orange juice squirting from it. Ask them to predict what will happen. Most likely, there will be two predominate predictions. Some students think the balloons will pop. Others think nothing will happen. Once predictions have been shared, position the balloons in a row on the table. Squeeze the rind over each balloon, one at a time. No balloons will pop. Students who predicted that nothing would happen, will cheer.

Now show three more balloons. They are also blue, yellow, and orange. But, although two of these balloons are made of vulcanized rubber, the orange balloon is made of non-vulcanized rubber. This is not explained to students yet. Explain that you'd like to try a different kind of demonstration now- one they "may have seen before." Line these balloons in a row on the table. Tell the students that you are going to touch balloons of the same color together. Ask them to predict what will happen. Several students might predict that they will "cling" or "stick" together. This explains why you previously included the statement that they may have seen something like this before. Depending on the age group, some students have experienced the static attraction of balloons. You are not trying to "trick" them. Rather, you want students to draw from past experience- something they are familiar with- something they expect. Experiences with balloons and statics will most likely be introduced into the discussion as predictions are shared. Others might recall similar experiences.

Touch the blue balloons together. They might be attracted a bit. Touch the yellow balloons together. They also might be attracted. Next touch the orange balloons together. Be sure that the orange spray on the first balloon comes into direct contact with the second. The second orange balloon will pop! This is startling!

The presentation can end here, or it can be extended to a second phase. If you choose to continue, act surprised over the outcome and exclaim that you want to do it again! You will need six more balloons- two of each color again. The first three that you squeeze the rind over are vulcanized, once again. But this time, the blue balloon from the second set is made of non-vulcanized rubber. The yellow and orange are made of vulcanized rubber. When you touch these balloons together, as you did before, students will expect the orange balloon to pop again. But this time, the blue balloon pops!

Again, you can choose to end the presentation here, or continue with a third and final phase. The scenario is the same. You will conduct the exact same actions. But, the yellow balloon from the second set is made of non-vulcanized rubber. Contradicting the first two experiences, the yellow balloon now pops!

Lesson Variation:

In addition to an orange, you will also need a lemon and a lime for this version of the demonstration. We will once again use three balloons. But, this time they should be orange, yellow, and green. And, the green balloon is made of non-vulcanized rubber, while the other two are made of vulcanized rubber. As in the original version, you will inflate the three balloons. Then show the lime. Explain that you are going to peel some of the rind from the lime and squirt it on each balloon. Ask students to predict what will happen. Squeeze the lemon rind over each balloon to find that the green balloon pops, but not the other two.

Exclaim that you'd like to conduct the experiment again, but this time you'd like to squeeze a lemon rind over the balloons. Use a new set of balloons for this trial. Explain that you don't want to mix the juices on the balloon because contamination could affect the results. Once again, you will use a yellow, orange, and green balloon. But this time, only the yellow balloon is made of non-vulcanized rubber. The other two are vulcanized rubber. When you squeeze the lemon rind over these balloons, the yellow balloon pops.

Conduct one more trial of the demonstration. This time you will squeeze an orange rind over three new balloons with the same colors as before. Now, only the orange balloon will be made of non- vulcanized rubber. In this trial, the orange rind pops the orange balloon.

Possible Variables:

1. Differently colored balloons could be used. They could be mixed and matched in various combinations.
2. Using the rind of fruit other than lemons, oranges, and limes.
3. The area of the balloon that the rind juice is squirted on.
4. The brand of balloon.
5. The type of balloon.

Phenomenon Explained:

To fully understand the entire demonstration, we'll need to discuss the fruit as well as the balloons. Each plays a role here.

Citrus fruits contain a compound called limonene. A molecule of limonene is a hydrocarbon, meaning it is composed of only carbon and hydrogen atoms. Limonene is responsible for the aroma of the fruit. It can also be found as a solvent in cleaning products.

Balloons are made primarily from rubber, composed of strands of polymer molecules. In "common" balloons, long strands of polymer molecules are easily separated from one another, causing the balloon to pop. Just like limonene, balloons are constructed of molecules of hydrocarbon. Hydrocarbons are non-polar molecules. They dissolve well in one another. Since both balloons and limonene are hydrocarbons, when they contact one another, some of the rubber balloon weakens, dissolves, and pops.

The balloons we are most familiar with undergo a process called vulcanization that connects polymer strands in a cross-link manner. The effect is that it becomes more difficult to separate the molecules of vulcanized rubber from one another. This makes vulcanized rubber difficult to dissolve. The balloons we are most familiar with are made of vulcanized rubber, so that they don't easily pop. But, most water balloons are made of non-vulcanized rubber, so that they are generally easily broken. Due to these differences, most water balloons will pop when squirted with limonene or the peel of some citrus fruits.

Some might think that it is the citric acid found in citrus fruits that causes the balloons to pop. However, if you place some citric acid solution on the balloons, they will not pop. This is true for both vulcanized and non-vulcanized balloons.

Note that you could conduct the demonstration by simply touching the non-vulcanized balloons with your fingertip, if you have some of the juice from the fruit on your finger.

Standards Alignment:

Next Generation Science Standards (NGSS, Lead States 2013)

Disciplinary Core Ideas in Physical Science

PS1: Matter and Its Interactions

PS1.A: Structure and Properties of Matter

PS1.B: Chemical Reactions

Interrupted Pendulum

Concepts Illustrated: Law of conservation of energy, mechanical energy, potential energy, speed, kinetic energy, mass, volume, density.

Paradox:

A bob is swung on a pendulum and the height it reaches on each side of the arc is noted. A bar is put in place so that at the bottom of its path the string strikes it, causing it to swing in a much smaller arc. But, the bob still reaches the same height at each end of its swing!

Equipment:

1. A simple pendulum. This can be comprised of equipment as simple as a ring stand and string. There must be two bars. One horizontal suspension bar at the top of the ring stand. The pendulum string will hang from this bar. A second bar, the interrupting bar, attaches midway along the ring stand to act as the stop. The interrupting bar should be easily detachable.
2. A bob to hang from the pendulum string.
3. Large construction paper or dry erase board, used as a backdrop to the pendulum so that the height of the arc can be marked.

Preparation:

Prior to the demonstration the pendulum should be fully assembled, with the exception of the interrupting bar. This bar will be attached to the ring stand as the students look on.

A meter stick can also serve as a reference for the height of the bob.

The Lesson:

Display the pendulum to the students. Demonstrate that the mass can swing freely from the suspension bar. Now, on the backdrop, mark the point from which the bob will be released. As the bob swings, note and mark the height attained at each side of the arc. Attach the interrupting bar and explain that you will once again swing the pendulum. You will begin at the same release point. Further explain that the string will hit the interrupting bar as it swings, causing it to swing in a smaller arc. Ask students to predict the new height achieved by the bob at each side of the arc, once it has struck the interrupting bar. Their answer should relate this new height to the previously marked height, when the pendulum swung without the interrupting bar in place. In other words, will the bob achieve a height at, above, or below the previous mark?

Most students will believe this new height will be lower than the previous height. Swing the bob, being sure to begin at the same release point as before. Direct students to focus on the end point of the bob at each side of the arc. Note and mark the new height achieved at each end of the arc. Students will find that the height is exactly the same as before, even though the interrupting bar caused a much smaller arc. The bob still reaches the same elevation from which it was released!

Possible Variables:

1. The length of the string.
2. The mass of the bob.
3. The shape of the bob.
4. The volume of the bob.
5. The density of the bob.
6. The placement of the interrupting bar.
7. The release point of the bob.

Phenomenon Explained:

The system employed in this demonstration is a simple pendulum, consisting of a mass, or bob, attached to the end of a string swinging about a pivot point.

Mechanical energy is defined as the energy an object possesses due to its motion or position. There are two forms of mechanical energy, potential and kinetic. Potential energy is stored energy, while kinetic is the energy of motion. The law of conservation of energy states that energy can never be created or destroyed, although it can be converted from one form to another.

This demonstration illustrates the conservation of mechanical energy. The potential energy at the release point is converted to kinetic energy as the bob reaches the bottom of its swing. Upon its release, the bob gains speed as it falls. As it continues to fall, and lose height, it also loses potential energy. However, it also gains speed and kinetic energy. As stated in the law of conservation of energy, the total energy is conserved for both potential and kinetic combined. The same amount of kinetic energy is required to reach the highest point on the other side of the swing.

Note that if the interrupting bar is positioned too low, the bob achieves a lower maximum height at the end of its arc, requiring some kinetic energy. As a result, the bob will wrap around the interrupting bar. Prior to demonstrating before students, be sure of where you will place the interrupting bar so that this does not happen during the actual demonstration.

Students could choose to investigate the density of the bob. Density is determined by calculating the mass for a given volume, expressed in the formula g/ml, g/cm^3, or g/cc. Density is independent of the sample size, since it represents the mass per ml of the sample. A larger volume does not necessarily equate to a higher mass. Fewer molecules packed into a given volume will result in a lower density than many more molecules packed into the same volume, which would increase the density.

Standards Alignment:

Next Generation Science Standards (NGSS, Lead States 2013)

Disciplinary Core Ideas in Physical Science

PS1: Matter and Its Interactions

PS1.A: Structure and Properties of Matter

PS2: Motion and Stability: Forces and Interactions

PS2.A: Forces and Motion

PS3: Energy

PS3.A: Definitions of Energy

PS3.B: Conservation of Energy and Energy Transfer

PS3.C: Relationship Between Energy and Forces

Inverted Straw

Concepts Illustrated: Air pressure, cohesion, adhesion, properties of water, surface tension, viscosity, solutions, solubility, solutes, solvents, concentration, saturated solutions, process of dissolving, properties of mixtures, properties of surfactants, the respiratory system of fish, the human respiratory system, density, gravity, air pressure within the human body, the effects of air pressure on the human body (lungs, ears, sinuses), the influence of air pressure on ailments, barometric pressure.

Paradox:

A small ball of clay is pressed firmly in place at the bottom of a large beaker full of colored water. A straw is positioned upright in the water with one end stuck into the clay. When the beaker is quickly overturned, above a sink or bucket, all of the water is dumped out of the beaker- except for the water in the straw… and it's upside-down!

Equipment:

1. One beaker. This can be any size beaker, but a larger beaker is most impressive. A 400ml beaker can be used, with a straw cut short. A 1000ml beaker can be used with a much longer straw and more water. The larger beaker, more water, and longer straw make the phenomena more visible to students.
2. A straw
3. Small piece of clay.
4. Food coloring

Preparation:

Before presenting this demonstration, push a small lump of clay onto the inside bottom of the beaker. Cut the straw at a length that will allow it to fit completely in the beaker. When the water is added, the straw should be completely submerged under the water and not protrude above it. Fill the beaker with water and add food coloring. Colored water is used so that it can be clearly seen inside the straw after the water has been dumped out of the beaker.

Clay at bottom of beaker

The Lesson:

Display the beaker of colored water to students. Explain to them that it is just colored water. Now, clearly show them the straw and insert one end into the clay. Lower the straw into the water and push the clay into the bottom of the beaker, so that the straw remains upright. Ask students to predict what will happen when you turn the beaker over and dump the all of the water out. Once predictions have been made, quickly turn the beaker over, above a sink or bucket. Make sure that students can clearly observe that the colored water remains in the upside-down straw!

Straw placed upright in the liquid.

Liquid remains in straw when inverted.

Possible Variables:

1. Width of straw.
2. Length of straw.
3. Density of the liquid. Density can be manipulated by adding salt to the water.
4. Volume of liquid in beaker.
5. Viscosity of the liquid.
6. Size of beaker.
7. Container other than beaker, with a different shape.
8. Add lid to jar so that the water remains in jar when tipped over, but straw is no longer in the water because of its length.
9. Shape of the straw- bend the straw into different shapes- crazy straw.
10. Temperature of the water.
11. Putting a hole in the straw. Also, the placement of the hole in the straw and the number of holes in the straw.
12. Speed of pouring the liquid out of the jar.
13. Positioning of the straw in the jar- center vs off-center.
14. Adding the straw to the jar before or after filling with water.
15. Attaching straw to the side of the beaker, rather than the bottom.

16. Put straw in place, add water, followed by straw, and then add food coloring- does the food coloring get into the straw?
17. Straw is long enough that when placed in the beaker, the end of the straw sticks out of the water and is not fully submerged.
18. Adding soap to the water. This can lead to an investigation of different brands and different amounts of soap or detergent. Soap acts as a surfactant, affording the opportunity for class discourse to expand learning to the life sciences.

Phenomenon Explained:

The combined effects of air pressure with certain properties of water, namely surface tension and cohesion, provide the "magic" in this demonstration.

Cohesion is the attraction of like molecules to one another. Water molecules have a very strong cohesive attraction for one another. Imagine a glass of water. There are powerful cohesive forces between the molecules in that glass. The water molecules at the surface do not have any water molecules above them. As a result, they are strongly attracted to those neighboring water molecules at their sides and to those below, which draws them in towards the liquid. This strong attraction to the molecules around and underneath creates what is known as surface tension. The property of cohesion occurs at the surface of the water in the straw. Adhesion describes the force that attracts different molecules to one another. In our demonstration, water molecules are attracted to the inner walls of the straw through adhesion. This force of attraction is strong enough to keep the water in the straw, even when inverted.

Air pressure also contributes to the water remaining in the straw when inverted. Atmospheric pressure is a force exerted by the weight of air in the atmosphere. It is determined by the amount of air directly above a person or object. In this demonstration, the effective downward pressure of the water in the straw is less than the atmospheric pressure outside of it. When the straw is upside-down, the atmospheric pressure against the water in it is greater than the force of gravity.

Air pressure is exerted on all of us. Rarely are we aware of its immense force. This is because the pressure of air is exerted on us uniformly, all our lives. But, consider that all the air molecules above you have weight. The combined weight actually creates a pressure equivalent to about 10,000kg/square meter. At sea level, this translates to about 1000kg/0.1 square meter, or about 14.7lbs/square inch or PSI! This means there is about a ton of weight on each of us! Of course, this number varies slightly depending on the altitude you happen to be. The air pressure in our bodies, our lungs, stomachs, ears, fluids, etc., "balances" the pressure outside of our bodies. Our internal pressure is essentially the same as the outside pressure- we are at equilibrium. This prevents us from being crushed by the outside air pressure.

The human body is capable of being affected by low pressure weather systems, that can cause effects such as headaches, motion sickness, and distension in the sinuses. Effects such as these can be influenced by the difference between pressure within the body's cavities, such as lungs, ears, and sinuses, and the atmospheric pressure surrounding the body. This also explains why our ears pop in an airplane, or driving through hills or mountains. The ears essentially try to equalize the pressure within its cavities with the atmospheric pressure. Even those who suffer from arthritis or bursitis might experience increased joint pain as swelling occurs due to a decrease of pressure on the body.

Soap is a surfactant, a compound that acts to lower the surface tension of water. It does this by weakening the attractive forces between the water molecules. The addition of soap alters the surface tension and affects the ability of the water to remain in the inverted straw.

The addition of soap as a variable broadly expands the scope of topics covered in class discourse. Surfactants play a critical role in our bodies. There is a thin layer of water that lines human lungs. This water is necessary for the gas exchange of carbon dioxide and oxygen to occur. These gases require a wet layer or surface for the exchange to take place. In fish, this exchange takes place in their gills. Since they are on the outside of the fish, gills have direct contact with water. Our lungs, on the other hand, are best able to be kept wet inside of our bodies. However, due to the properties of water, surface tension arises that can interfere with the expansion of our lungs as we breathe. Surfactant acts to reduce surface tension. This prevents alveoli, small air sacs in the lungs, from collapsing when we exhale. The most efficient oxygen-carbon dioxide exchange occurs in our lungs with the greatest alveoli surface area. By preventing the collapse of alveoli, surfactant helps to maximize the surface area available for the exchange of gases.

Viscosity is defined as a fluid's resistance to flow. Think of it as the "thickness" of a fluid. Fluids such as honey, molasses, corn syrup, and engine oil are highly viscous. Students might choose to investigate the outcome when liquids of varying viscosities are employed.

If the density of the liquid is altered by adding salt or sugar, discourse can include solutions, solubility, solutes, solvents, and concentration. Saltwater or sugar water is a mixture. One property of a mixture is that it is physically combined, not chemically, and it can be physically separated. For example, saltwater can be physically separated through the process of evaporation, or boiling the water away.

A solution is one in which a solute is dissolve in a solvent. The solute is the substance being dissolved and the solvent is the substance in which the solute is dissolved. Water is called the universal solvent because it is capable of dissolving more solutes than any other liquid. Solubility is the ability of a solute to dissolve in a solvent.

A concentrated solution is one which there are many dissolved particles of solute in the solvent. On the other hand, a dilute solution is one in which there are few dissolved particles of solute. A solution which contains all the dissolve particles it can possibly hold is called saturated.

Standards Alignment:

Next Generation Science Standards (NGSS, Lead States 2013)

Disciplinary Core Ideas in Physical Science

PS1: Matter and Its Interactions

PS1.A: Structure and Properties of Matter

PS1.B: Chemical Reactions

PS2: Motion and Stability: Forces and Interactions

PS2.B: Types of Interactions

Disciplinary Core Ideas in Life Science

LS1: From Molecules to Organisms: Structures and Processes

LS1.A: Structure and Function

Disciplinary Core Ideas in Earth and Space Science

ESS2: Earth's Systems

ESS2.C: The Roles of Water in Earth's Surface Processes

Invisible Soda

Concepts Illustrated: Properties of mixtures, density, chemical changes, physical changes.

Paradox:

Students will be stunned to discover that when milk is added to a clear bottle of Coke, the mixture becomes transparent!

Equipment:

1. A clear bottle of Coke, or any other cola.
2. 2% milk

Preparation:

Remove the label from a bottle of soda so that students have an unobstructed view of the contents.

The Lesson:

Open a new bottle of Coke, or any other type of brown cola. Show students a pitcher of milk and explain that you'll be pouring the milk into the Coke, until the bottle is filled to the top. Ask them to predict what will happen when you do so. Then, slowly pour the milk into the bottle of soda until the mixture fills the bottle. You'll only need to pour a small volume of milk. The soda might fizz up and a little might flow out of the bottle. Screw on the bottle cap. The transformation will take time and patience. Put the bottle in a safe place in the classroom where it will remain untouched until the next time the class meets. In the following class, unveil the bottle to show that the contents are now transparent!

Possible Variables:

1. Varying volumes and ratios of milk and soda.
2. Different bottle shapes.
3. Shaking the bottle or stirring the liquids.
4. Changing the temp of either the milk, the soda, or both.
5. Assorted brands of soda.
6. Diet vs regular soda.
7. Club soda in place of soda.
8. Non-carbonated (flat) soda.
9. Assorted brands of milk.
10. Adding drops of food coloring to either the soda, the milk, or the mixture.
11. 2%, 1%, non-fat, powdered, condensed, evaporated, chocolate, soy, coconut, almond milk and heavy cream.
12. Replacing milk with other colloids.
13. Pour soda into milk rather than milk into soda.

14. Keep the bottle cap off the bottle after mixing.
15. Volume of air in the bottle after capped.
16. Set bottle on its side after mixing liquids- maybe roll the bottle slowly after reaction takes place.
17. Turn bottle upside down once reaction has taken place.

Phenomenon Explained:

The surprising result in this demonstration occurs due to a reaction between phosphoric acid and milk. When the phosphoric acid molecules bind to the milk molecules, their density increases. This increase in density causes these molecules to sink to the bottom of the bottle, separating them from the rest of the liquid, which is less dense.

Standards Alignment:

Next Generation Science Standards (NGSS, Lead States 2013)

Disciplinary Core Ideas in Physical Science

PS1: Matter and Its Interactions

PS1.A: Structure and Properties of Matter

PS1.B: Chemical Reactions

Jittery Coin

Concepts Illustrated: Phase changes, physical changes, kinetic energy, air pressure, ideal gas law, heat, temperature, Gay-Lussac's law, Charles' law, properties of gas, kinetic molecular theory, molecular motion of gases, properties of water, cohesion, adhesion, conduction of heat, relationship between temperature and pressure of gases, heat transfer, human body heat, catalyst in action.

Paradox:

A coin is placed on top of an open glass soda bottle. You hold the bottle and the coin begins to mysteriously vibrate and rattle!

Equipment:

1. Empty soda bottle- this can be glass or plastic
2. Coin

The Lesson:

Show students the empty soda bottle and the coin. Lay the coin flat over the opening at the top of the bottle. Now place a few drops of water around the edge of the coin, between the coin and the bottle. Ask students to predict what will happen when you simply wrap your hands around the bottle. Then, firmly wrap your hands around the body of the bottle. Focus your attention on the coin and soon the coin will begin to rattle!

I would suggest asking students "what will happen when I squeeze the bottle with two hands?" This is different than asking "what will happen when I put my hands around the bottle?" When students imagine "squeezing" hands around the bottle, they are led to think that nothing will result because they know that the bottle can be squeezed and nothing happens. Squeezing draws attention away from the coin and what *it* might do, and brings focus on the bottle itself, because it is the object being squeezed. It also dissuades students from predicting movement from the coin, because the focus shifts to the action of "squeezing" rather than "wrapping hands" around the bottle.

Lesson Variation:

The phenomena can also be observed by placing the bottle into a hot water bath. This eliminates the need to place your hands on the bottle to generate heat.

Possible Variables:

Note that each of the variables listed below can be tested as a function of time to make the coin dance. This data can also be graphed.

1. The temperature of the soda bottle. It can be chilled or heated.
2. Putting a few drops of liquid other than water, such as cooking oil, on the coin.
3. Coins of varying sizes.
4. Coins of varying denominations.

5. Coins of varying masses.
6. Bottles of varying volumes
7. Bottles of varying shapes.
8. Rubbing hands together to generate more heat.
9. The number of coins stacked on top of the bottle.
10. Number of hands on the bottle.
11. Palms only on the bottle, rather than wrapping the entire hands around it.
12. Fingers only on the bottle.
13. Temperature of water bath that bottle is placed into.

Phenomenon Explained:

This demonstration illustrates the relationship between pressure and temperature, which are directly proportional to each other. This relationship, known as the Gay-Lussac's law, makes up part of the ideal gas law. It states if the volume of a container remains constant as the temperature of a gas inside increases, so too does its pressure.

As described by Charles' law, the volume of gases tends to expand when heated. Conversely, when cooled, the volume of a gas will decrease. As the gas within the bottle continues to heat, the motion of the particles, increase, and the volume of the gas increases. As the speed and volume of space these particles take up increases, so too does the pressure, or the force at which they hit the inside of the bottle. The gas particles, trapped inside the bottle by the coin on top, continue to move faster, thereby increasing the pressure of the gas within the bottle. The movement of particles is known as kinetic energy. Those which move faster have greater kinetic energy. The kinetic molecular theory summarizes all of this by stating that as heat rises, the particles of a gas move faster and spread out, resulting in increased pressure.

In humans, mitochondria which control metabolism by regulating most intracellular production, will produce most of our body heat. Heat is essentially the release of energy. Warm hands wrapped around the bottle act as the catalyst that adds energy to the system. Heat moves in predictable ways, flowing from warmer objects towards cooler ones, until both reach equilibrium at the same temperature. In this demonstration, when hands are wrapped around the bottle, heat energy is transferred from the hands to the bottle, and then to the gas molecules within the bottle. This acts to warm the air in the bottle, increasing the motion of the gas molecules, and the pressure within the bottle. Eventually, this gas pressure becomes so great that it begins to push on and rattle the coin.

Conduction is one of the three types of heat transfer. It occurs when the kinetic energy of molecules increases, causing them to move faster, collide with neighboring molecules. When they do so, heat energy is passed along from one molecule to the next.

Water acts to form a "seal" between the coin and the mouth of the bottle. This seal forms because of cohesion and adhesion. Cohesion is the attraction of like molecules to one another. Water molecules have a very strong cohesive attraction for one another. Adhesion is a force that attracts different molecules to each other. In this demonstration, adhesion is the force that attracts the water molecules to the mouth of the bottle. The water molecules are attracted to one another, as well as to the mouth of the bottle.

The layer of water between the coin and the bottle acts to hold the air in the bottle as the gas inside heats up and expands. Eventually it expands to create enough pressure on the coin to lift it, and some gas escapes. Without the water, some gas would escape between the coin and the mouth of the bottle without actually lifting the coin.

Heat is not the same as temperature. Essentially, heat is energy and temperature is a measure of it. Heat is a form of energy that can transfer from one medium to another, flowing from objects of higher temperature to those with lower temperature. When a cup of coffee feels hot, it is because energy from the cup is being transferred to your hand. On the other hand, a glass of iced tea feels cold because heat energy from your hand is flowing into the glass. This causes it to feel cold.

The temperature of a substance is a measure of the average kinetic energy of its molecules. All matter is composed of atoms or molecules that are in constant motion. The faster they move, the more kinetic energy they have. There is a direct relationship between the motion of molecules and their temperature. The greater the kinetic energy, the higher the temperature of the object. Molecules that have low average kinetic energy move slowly and have low temperatures in comparison to molecules with high kinetic energy, which move more quickly and have a higher temperature. The molecules of solids generally move very slowly, simply vibrating in place. Thermal energy is defined as the energy within an object or system due to the movement of the particles or molecules within. Thermodynamics refers to the transfer of heat between different objects or systems.

Heat is the *total* kinetic energy in a substance or system. This is different than temperature which, as we have learned, is the *average* kinetic energy. Heat is dependent on the speed of the particles, the number of particles, and the type of particles in a substance. On the other hand, temperature is independent of the number and type of particles. A large tub of water could have the same temperature as a small cup of water, but the water in the large tub would possess more heat because it contains many more molecules, therefore more total kinetic energy.

Standards Alignment:

Next Generation Science Standards (NGSS, Lead States 2013)

Disciplinary Core Ideas in Physical Science

PS1: Matter and Its Interactions

PS1.A: Structure and Properties of Matter

PS2: Motion and Stability: Forces and Interactions

PS2.B: Types of Interactions

PS3: Energy

PS3.A: Definitions of Energy

PS3.B: Conservation of Energy and Energy Transfer

PS3.D: Energy in Chemical Processes and Everyday Life

PS4: Waves and Their Applications in Technologies for Information Transfer

PS4.A: Wave Properties

Disciplinary Core Ideas in Life Science

LS1: From Molecules to Organisms: Structures and Processes

LS1.A: Structure and Function

LS1.D: Information Processing

Disciplinary Core Ideas in Earth and Space Science

ESS2: Earth's Systems

ESS2.D: Weather and Climate

Laser Water

Concepts Illustrated: Reflection of light, total internal reflection, refractive index, properties of water, fiber optics, properties of light, density.

Paradox:

As water streams out of a hole in the side of a 2 Liter bottle, a laser pointer is directed at the hole from the opposite side of the bottle. The path of the laser light astonishes everyone as it travels within the stream, following its curved path into a receptacle below!

Equipment:

1. A 2 Liter soda bottle.
2. Water.
3. A laser pen.
4. A bowl to place under the stream of water. A clear, glass bowl is the most effective.
5. A piece of foam display board to place as an intended laser target.

Preparation:

The 2 Liter soda bottle must be prepared by making a hole in its side. Use an awl or small nail and carefully punch a hole about 8 cm from the bottom. Cover the hole with a piece of tape. This will allow the bottle to hold the water until you remove the tape. Now fill the bottle with water. The cap does not have to be screwed in place. However, if you do screw the cap onto the bottle, you'll be able to remove the tape without any water escaping. In presentation, you would unscrew the cap to allow water to begin streaming from the hole.

Prepare the foam display board by holding it upright along the side of the bottle with the hole. Make a bold "X" on the display board where the hole is. The X should be aligned with the hole. Prop the board in this upright position about 12" from the side of the bottle with the hole.

Place the bowl between the bottle and the display board.

The Lesson:

Display all of the equipment to the students. Everything should be set into position to execute the demonstration. Point out the hole in the side of the bottle. Explain that the bottle is filled with water. Be sure to explain that the X on the display board is perfectly aligned with the position of the hole in the side of the bottle. Now, show the laser pointer. You can demonstrate the laser by shining it onto the display board, but do not shine it at the bottle or through the water. You don't want students to observe how the laser behaves before making predictions.

Explain that you are about to remove the tape from the hole, allowing the water to escape and stream out. Further explain that the bowl will be used to catch the falling water. Now hold the laser pointer in position on the side of the bottle opposite the hole, but do not turn it on. Hold the pointer horizontal, about 3-4" from the side of the bottle. Explain that while the water is streaming out of the bottle, you will hold the laser pointer in this position, aimed directly at the hole on the opposite side of the bottle, and turn it on. Students are asked to predict where they think the laser light will "hit" the display board on the other side. Be sure that students understand they have a number of choices. They might predict the light will shine straight through, directly hitting the X on the board. However, they might predict that the trajectory of the light will "bend" and hit a different location. It might hit above, below, or to the left or right of the X. They might even say that the light will hit upper right, upper left, lower right, or lower left. There are many choices. Be sure to verbalize these choices. Using the display board as a "target" and providing possible target locations on the board establishes student expectation that highly contradicts the actual outcome. Students observe the demonstration with focus and anticipation of where the light will hit the board, which actually doesn't happen at all. The observed outcome is elevated to a higher level of surprise.

Once students have made their predictions, lower the lights in the room, remove the tape (or unscrew the cap), and shine the laser at the hole from the opposite side of the bottle. Be sure to hold the laser pointer horizontal and parallel with the hole. Students will be shocked to find that the light is carried in the stream of water as it descends into the bowl below. If you use a shallow glass bowl, the light will actually light up the water in the bowl!

This is a great demonstration to follow a lesson on refraction in water, the behavior of light in water, and how it affects the visual perception of objects within the water. When students begin to understand that light can "bend" as it travels through liquid, they commonly predict that the laser light will "bend" as it travels through the liquid in the bottle. They also believe that the falling stream of water will further "bend" the light so that it hits the display board in unexpected places- quite the opposite of what actually occurs.

Possible Variables:

1. Shape of the bottle.
2. The color of the water. Food coloring can be used to investigate this.
3. Adding dish soap to the water. This can lead into various brands of dish soap.
4. The density of the liquid in the bottle. This can involve liquids other than water, or it can be achieved by adding sugar to the water in various amounts.
5. Using liquids other than water. Tonic water is effective due to the quinine it contains.
6. The position of the hole on the side of the bottle.
7. The angle at which the laser is directed at the hole.
8. Size of the hole in the bottle.
9. Different colors of laser light.
10. The substance that the bottle is made of- plastic or glass.
11. Might investigate whether movement of the liquid will affect the outcome. This can be achieved by placing a magnetic stirrer in the bottle.
12. Placing the bottle in a horizontal position.
13. Shining the laser up, through the bottom of the glass bowl, and into the descending stream of water. This is essentially aiming the laser in the opposite direction, at the end of the stream rather than at its beginning.
14. Adding a colloid, such as milk, to the water. This is actually quite effective.

Phenomenon Explained:

Light travels through space at about 300 million meters per second. Light travels through different mediums at different speeds. Its speed is affected as it travels from one transparent medium through another. When this happens, light can bend. That bend in light is called refraction. The process is dependent on the medium through which the light passes. The index of refraction, or the refractive index, is a number that describes how light travels through a particular medium. The index of refraction measures the degree to which light bends. The larger the index, the slower the light travels through the medium.

Reflection describes how a wave, such as light, alters direction when it strikes a surface. The phenomena observed in this demonstration is due to the principle of total internal reflection. The same principle is employed in optical fibers, which essentially transport light. An optical fiber is comprised of a core of flexible glass or plastic fibers, with a glass or plastic coating that has a lower index of refraction than the fibers within. Light entering one end of the optic fiber essentially reflects and "bounces" between the walls of the coating, through the internal fibers, until it exits the opposite end.

In this demonstration, the stream of water acts as an optic fiber would, carrying the light through it. The light is totally internally reflected within the stream of water. There is no "outer coating" for the light to reflect and bounce off of, as in the case of fiber optics. However, the light does reflect off the boundary between the outer edge of the stream and the air that surrounds it. This is due, in part, to the difference in density between the two mediums, the water being denser than the air that surrounds it. It also occurs because the water has a higher index of refraction than the air. As a result, light can actually be transmitted through the stream of water with very little loss of energy. However, the molecules of water do reflect small amounts of the light out of the water. This is the light that you see.

Standards Alignment:

Next Generation Science Standards (NGSS, Lead States 2013)

Disciplinary Core Ideas in Physical Science

PS3: Energy

PS3.A: Definitions of Energy

PS3.B: Conservation of Energy and Energy Transfer

PS4: Waves and Their Applications in Technologies for Information Transfer

PS4.A: Wave Properties

PS4.B: Electromagnetic Radiation

Lava Lamp

Concepts Illustrated: Density, volume, solubility, solute, solvent, concentration, saturated solutions, process of dissolving, miscibility, chemical changes, properties of gases, properties of liquids, viscosity, fluid dynamics, molecular motion of gases, convection currents, properties of mixtures.

Paradox:

Students will be surprised and excited when drops of food coloring vigorously dance and circulate through vegetable oil following the addition of an Alka-Seltzer tablet!

Equipment:

1. A clear bottle of any type. Any labels, like those found wrapped around soda bottles, should be removed.
2. Beaker or clear drinking glass.
3. Alka-Seltzer tablets.
4. Vegetable oil. Baby oil can be substituted.
5. Food coloring.
6. Water.
7. Glitter and/or sequins are optional.

The Lesson:

Show the bottle and fill it about ¾ full of vegetable oil. Explain that you are going to fill the remainder of the bottle with water. Ask students to predict what will occur. Many predict that the two liquids will remain separated, with the water above the oil. From their experience with it, these students think vegetable oil is "heavy" or "thick" and so it will naturally sink to the bottom. Others will think that the vegetable oil will remain at the bottom of the bottle because there is so much more of it than the water. Once they have made and shared predictions, add the water. Students will be surprised to find that water actually sinks below the vegetable oil. When adding the water, be sure to leave space at the top of the bottle to allow for the bubbling reaction that will occur later in the demonstration.

Explain that you are going to add food coloring to the liquids. Ask students to predict what will happen when you do that. Again, from experience most students will predict that the liquid in the bottle will become colored. Add several drops of food coloring. Students will be amazed once again when the drops of food coloring remain as spherical drops, traveling through the vegetable oil until they rest on the surface of the water below. They will sit at the layer separating the two liquids, as spherical drops!

Now, introduce the Alka-Seltzer. Some students may not know what this is. It should be explained that this is a product which can be purchased at most grocery stores. Add some water to the beaker and allow students to observe the reaction that occurs when Alka-Seltzer is placed in water. Do not explain the reaction and avoid using the word "bubbles". Simply allow students to observe for themselves. This observation will guide their predictions in the next phase of the demonstration. You can say "as you can see, when we add Alka-Seltzer to water it creates quite a reaction- agitating and stirring up the water".

Inform students that you are going to place a tablet of Alka-Seltzer into the bottle. Ask them to predict what will happen. Based on the chemical reaction in the beaker of water, and the "stirring up" motion observed, many will predict that the two separated liquids will become all "stirred up" and mix together. No one will predict the actual reaction that takes place.

Drop a tablet of Alka-Seltzer into the bottle. You may want to cap the bottle, or screw on the lid, so that the liquid does not overflow. The spherical drops of food coloring will burst, releasing their color through the water. Then, colored drops or "bubbles" will vigorously rise through the vegetable oil to the surface, where they will sink back to the water below. This hypnotic, vibrant action repeats with many colored drops quickly rising and sinking, circulating vigorously!

The bottle and its contents are entirely reusable. The bubbling action will eventually slow and stop when the Alka-Seltzer is used up. But, you only need to drop in another tablet to "revive" the bottle and set the contents into motion once again.

Lesson Variation:

As mentioned earlier, glitter and/or sequins are optional. These can be added to the bottle at any point. When the Alka-Seltzer is added, the glitter and sequins will circulate through the liquids.

Glow sticks can also be activated and added to the bottle, creating a glowing lava lamp.

The bottle can also be placed above a flashlight or demo light box to illuminate its contents.

Possible Variables:
1. The temperature of the vegetable oil or the water. This could involve both liquids at the same or different temperatures.
2. The viscosity of the liquid.
3. The brand of vegetable oil or baby oil.
4. The density of the liquid. This can be manipulated by adding salt or sugar to either the water, vegetable oil, or baby oil.
5. Adding food coloring after the Alka-Seltzer.
6. Adding a third liquid to the bottle.
7. Adding two or more different colors of food coloring. Will they mix or remain as individually colored drops?
8. Adding water to the bottle first, then adding vegetable oil.
9. Replacing vegetable oil with another liquid, such as liquid hand soap or dish detergent.

Phenomenon Explained:

When water is added to vegetable oil, the two remain separated because they are immiscible, or do not mix together. Vegetable oil is hydrophobic and so it does not mix with water. Vegetable oil is also less dense than water and so it will always float above it.

Food coloring is water-based. Because of this it sinks through the vegetable oil and does not mix as it travels through.

Alka-Seltzer will only react with water. When it does, it produces carbon dioxide gas, which rises in the form of bubbles. As they rise, these bubbles carry some of the colored water with them. When the bubble reaches the surface of the vegetable oil, the gas is released and the colored water drop sinks. Because it is immiscible in vegetable oil, the colored water drop does not mix as it travels to the bottom of the bottle. Density and miscibility certainly play a role in the reaction.

Viscosity is defined as a fluid's resistance to flow. Think of it as the "thickness" of a fluid. Fluids such as honey, molasses, corn syrup, and engine oil are highly viscous. Students might choose to investigate the outcome when liquids of varying viscosities are employed.

If the density of the liquid is altered by adding salt or sugar, discourse can include solutions, solubility, solutes, solvents, and concentration.

A solution is one in which a solute is dissolve in a solvent. The solute is the substance being dissolved and the solvent is the substance in which the solute is dissolved. Water is called the universal solvent because it is capable of dissolving more solutes than any other liquid. Solubility is the ability of a solute to dissolve in a solvent.

A concentrated solution is one which there are many dissolved particles of solute in the solvent. On the other hand, a dilute solution is one in which there are few dissolved particles of solute. A solution which contains all the dissolve particles it can possibly hold is called saturated.

Standards Alignment:

Next Generation Science Standards (NGSS, Lead States 2013)

Disciplinary Core Ideas in Physical Science

PS1: Matter and Its Interactions

PS1.A: Structure and Properties of Matter

PS1.B: Chemical Reactions

PS2: Motion and Stability: Forces and Interactions

PS2.B: Types of Interactions

PS4: Waves and Their Applications in Technologies for Information Transfer

PS4.B: Electromagnetic Radiation

Disciplinary Core Ideas in Earth and Space Science

ESS2: Earth's Systems

ESS2.C: The Roles of Water in Earth's Surface Processes

Leaky Cup Tumble

<u>Concepts Illustrated</u>: Air pressure, gravity, properties of liquids, acceleration, free fall, fluid dynamics.

<u>Paradox</u>:

Using a pencil, a hole is poked into the side of a Styrofoam cup, near its bottom. With a finger over the hole, the cup is filled with water. When the finger is removed, water streams out of the hole as expected. But, students do not expect that when the cup is dropped, the water stops streaming from it as it falls through the air!

Your finger is removed from the hole and water begins to stream out of the cup. Release the cup. Students will observe that as the cup is falling towards the bucket, the water stops streaming from it!

<u>Equipment</u>:

1. Styrofoam or paper cup. A 2L bottle can also be used.
2. Wide bucket or tub.

<u>The Lesson</u>:

Show students the Styrofoam or paper cup. Push the pointed end of a pencil into the side of the cup, near its bottom. Then, fill the cup with water while plugging the hole by holding a finger over it. While holding the cup over a sink or bucket, remove your finger from the hole to show water streaming from it. You should distinctly point out a few observations. The first is that the water flows freely from the hole. Secondly, you should ask students to observe the shape of the arc of the stream coming from the cup. Finally, students should be asked to observe the distance that the stream flows away from the cup. These should become noteworthy features of the demonstration by drawing focus to them. With these as a focus, more students are apt to predict they will exhibit some type of change later in the demonstration.

Now, add more water to the cup to be sure it is full. Hold the cup a few meters above a wide bucket. Explain that you will now remove your finger from the hole and immediately drop the cup in an upright position, allowing it to fall into a bucket below. Ask students to predict what will happen. Some might predict that the stream will flow closer to, or farther away from, the cup. Others will predict that the stream will flow up, trailing behind the cup as it falls. But no one will expect what actually occurs. While standing on a chair, or on a ladder, release the cup. Students will observe that the water does not come out of the cup while it's falling!

<u>Lesson Variation:</u>

The phenomena can also be illustrated using a 2L soda bottle. If you have the cap on the bottle, it can be used to control the stream flow. Make a hole in the center of the cap. Fill the bottle with water and screw the cap in place. Now, by covering the hole in the cap with your finger, you will prevent any water from streaming out of the hole in the side of the bottle.

<u>Possible Variables:</u>

1. Placement of the hole on the side of the cup.
2. Altering the shape of the holes.
3. Volume of water in the cup.
4. The number of holes in the cup (two or several). This could then involve the placement of those holes in the cup. It could also involve the size of the holes. They could all be the same size or differing sizes.
5. Diameter of the hole in the cup.
6. Size of the cup.
7. The height of the drop.
8. The density of the liquid in the cup (this could include using a liquid such as oil, honey, or even adding sugar or salt to the water).
9. Viscosity of the liquid.
10. Making a row of holes in the cup. This could involve the number of holes in the row, changing the diameter of the holes within the row, and horizontal vs vertical rows.
11. Shape of the cup.
12. Placing holes under cup rather than on the sides.
13. Putting a lid on the cup.
14. Adding holes to the lid. This could involve the placement of those holes, the number of them, and their diameter.
15. Holes placed in lid and bottom of cup at once.
16. Dropping the cup upside down with a lid on it.
17. Replacing the water with sand or salt.

<u>Phenomenon Explained:</u>

When the cup is held stationary, the water inside is pulled down by the force of gravity. When your finger is removed, water streams out because of the pressure created from this downward pull of the liquid at the hole. When the cup falls, the water accelerates at the same rate as the cup. As a result, there is no pressure at the hole and the water does not stream from it.

Free fall describes the motion of a falling object that is acted upon by gravity alone, and no other forces.

Viscosity is defined as a fluid's resistance to flow. Think of it as the "thickness" of a fluid. Fluids such as honey, molasses, corn syrup, and engine oil are highly viscous. Students might choose to investigate the outcome when liquids of varying viscosities are employed.

Standards Alignment:

Next Generation Science Standards (NGSS, Lead States 2013)

Disciplinary Core Ideas in Physical Science

PS1: Matter and Its Interactions

PS1.A: Structure and Properties of Matter

PS2: Motion and Stability: Forces and Interactions

PS2.A: Forces and Motion

PS2.B: Types of Interactions

Leaping Liquid

Concepts Illustrated: Properties of liquids, the Kaye Effect, viscosity, fluid dynamics.

Paradox:
Pouring a stream of dishwashing liquid into a pan produces liquid streams that launch up and shoot away in bizarre manners from the point of impact!

Equipment:
1. A bottle of dishwashing liquid, liquid hand soap, or shampoo.
2. A plate, tray, or clear container.

The Lesson:
Show the bottle of dishwashing liquid or shampoo to students. Assure them that it was purchased from the grocery store and has not been altered in any way. Tell them that you're simply going to turn the bottle upside down and squirt a stream onto the plate. Ask them to predict how the liquid will behave when you do so. Then, hold the bottle about 20 cm above the plate and squirt a thin stream onto it. Be sure that the stream is consistently channeled into the same place within the pile of liquid as it collects and forms on the plate. The liquid will shoot out, arcing, twisting, and circling about in strange and surprising behaviors.

Dawn dishwashing liquid works very well for this demonstration. There is no need to continue to purchase bottles of Dawn, because the liquid can simply be reused. The dishwashing liquid can be drizzled into a pan or receptacle from which it can be poured directly back into the original container for reuse. You can purchase the smaller sized dishwashing bottles and reuse them, or purchase the dishwashing liquid in a bulk size and fill smaller bottles for students to use.

The optimum situation that will cause the phenomena to occur more persistently, pour the stream onto a tilted or sloping surface at a height of about 20 cm with a stream thickness of about 0.4 mm.

Possible Variables:
1. Different brands of dishwashing liquid.
2. Liquids other than dishwashing liquid, such as honey, shampoo, liquid hand soap, maple syrup, ketchup, or even water, etc.
3. Mixing two liquids together.
4. Height from which the stream is dropped.
5. Stream diameter.
6. Angle of landing surface (tilting the plate).
7. Shape of stream landing surface, such as using a bowl or into the peak of an upside-down pyramid shaped container.

8. Various landing surfaces, such as wood, plastic, rubber, materials with different textures, etc.
9. Varying the pressure put on bottle to squeeze liquid out.
10. Altering the density, or viscosity, of the liquid used. This can be done by simply adding salt or sugar to the liquid. The addition of sand to the liquid might be an interesting investigation.
11. Temperature of the soap or dishwashing liquid.
12. Changing the temp of the landing surface, for example using a cold or hot plate.

Phenomenon Explained:

The principle behind this phenomenon is called the Kaye Effect. It occurs in liquids that display shear-thinning behavior, or when the viscosity of a liquid decreases as it flows. As you begin to squirt a stream of the liquid at the same point on a flat surface such as a plate, it will begin to form a heap. Eventually, once the heap is large enough, the stream slides down the side of this heap. This stream will not mix with the heap because one of the properties of the shear-thinning liquid is that it acts as a lubricant. As the viscous heap builds, it also forms dimples on its surface. Because it is prevented from mixing with the heap due to its lubricating property, the stream hits one of the formed dimples on the surface and launches up from it.

Viscosity is defined as a fluid's resistance to flow. Think of it as the "thickness" of a fluid. Fluids such as honey, molasses, corn syrup, and engine oil are highly viscous. Students might choose to investigate the outcome when liquids of varying viscosities are employed.

Standards Alignment:

Next Generation Science Standards (NGSS, Lead States 2013)

Disciplinary Core Ideas in Physical Science

PS1: Matter and Its Interactions

PS1.A: Structure and Properties of Matter

PS2: Motion and Stability: Forces and Interactions

PS2.B: Types of Interactions

PS3: Energy

PS3.C: Relationship Between Energy and Forces

Lift-Off

<u>Concepts Illustrated:</u> Bernoulli's principle, properties of gases, air pressure, fluid dynamics, air pressure within the human body, the effects of air pressure on the human body (lungs, ears, sinuses), the influence of air pressure on ailments, aerodynamics, airplane flight, mechanics of bird flight, barometric pressure.

<u>Paradox:</u>

The teacher is seen to blow on top of a piece of paper held at the mouth. Expectations are contradicted when, rather than blowing the paper down, it rises into the air!

<u>Equipment:</u>

1. Paper

<u>Preparation:</u>

This demonstration will require one full sheet of paper and a strip, cut from the same type of paper. The strip can be about 2" in width.

The demonstration can also be presented by bending a sheet of paper around a pencil and taping the ends of the paper together. Hold the pencil on the ends and allow the curved, rounded end of the paper to hang on the pencil, with the taped ends hanging down.

The Lesson:

Begin the demonstration by showing students a thin strip of paper. Describe that you are about to hold the paper in a specific position at your lips. Demonstrate by holding the paper near your lips so that it hangs down and away from the mouth to demonstrate that position. Then, explain that while the paper is in this position, you will blow air over the top surface of the paper. Ask students to predict how the paper will behave when you do this. Some students will predict that the strip will be blown down, closer to the floor. Others will expect the strip to extend away from your face. Once students have made their predictions, blow over the strip to show that it lifts up towards your face.

Then show the full sheet of paper. Explain that you will now repeat the procedure with this larger, heavier piece of paper. Ask students to predict what will happen this time. Some might think nothing will happen, even after observing the strip of paper rise, because they feel that the full sheet will be too heavy. Students will be surprised to find that when you blow across the full sheet it also rises!

Lesson Variation:

Place two textbooks flat on the table, side by side, about 6 cm apart. Now, lay a sheet of paper across the books, so that it covers the space between them. Ask students to blow into the space, under the paper. They can either blow directly into the space, or use a straw. Most students will expect that the paper will be blown upwards and lift off the textbooks. They will be quite surprised to find that the paper actually pushes downward, into the space!

The air over the paper is stationary. The air that is moving under the paper creates reduced air pressure in that space. The air pressure above the paper exerts a greater force than that below. The greater pressure above pushes the paper down, into the space between the books.

The same idea can be achieved without the need for textbooks. Fold the opposite ends of an index card to make 1 cm flaps. Place the index card on a desk, flaps facing down. The flaps will keep the card about 1 cm above the desk.

Blowing under the index card will reduce the air pressure in that region, leaving a higher air pressure above. The greater air pressure above the card will push it down against the desk.

Possible Variables:

1. Width of the paper.
2. Length of the paper.
3. Thickness of paper.
4. Type of paper.
5. Force of air blown.
6. Distance between paper and mouth.
7. Number of sheets of paper used at once.
8. Wet paper.
9. Shape of the paper.
10. Putting wrinkles in the paper. This can lead to even more variables, including the shape and direction of the wrinkles.
11. Blowing under the paper.
12. Paper is held straight out instead of hanging down.
13. Put holes and tears in the paper. This can lead to even more variables, including the number of holes, their position, and their shapes.
14. Tape small masses to the paper. This can lead to even more variables, including the positioning of these masses on the paper and the amount of mass used.
15. Folding certain parts of the paper. For example, putting folds in the sides or the end away from the mouth. This can lead to even more variables, including the shape of the fold, its specific position on the paper, and the number of folds.

Phenomenon Explained:

Aerodynamics is the study of how air moves around objects. In terms of flight, we say that the more aerodynamic an object is, the better it will fly. An object that is not aerodynamically shaped will encounter drag, or friction between the moving object and air. This is commonly referred to as air resistance. Bernoulli's principle is a contributing factor when considering the aerodynamics of an object. Any object that flies using wings take advantage of Bernoulli's principle, including birds and airplanes.

Bernoulli's principle states that the faster a fluid flows across a surface, the less pressure it exerts on that surface. Fluids can be either gases or liquids. In our demonstration, the fluid is air. Imagine a cross-sectional view of an airplane wing. This shape is called an airfoil. Air approaching from the front is "split" across the top and bottom of the wing, rejoining at the back. The upper surface of the wing is not flat, but rather curved upward. Because of this, air moves faster across the top than across the bottom of the wing. The faster flow of air creates lower pressure along the top of the wing. The resulting greater air pressure along the bottom of the wing produces lift.

The Bernoulli principle and the lift of a wing

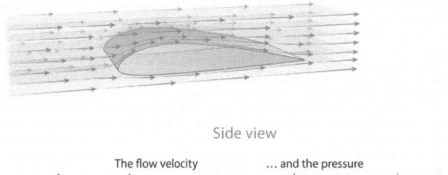

Side view

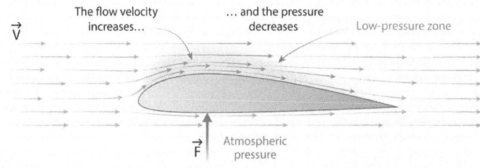

The air blowing over the paper moves faster than the air under it. As a result, the air under the paper has higher pressure than the decreasing air pressure above. Because the pressure is lower above the paper, the higher pressure below it lifts the paper.

Air pressure, or atmospheric pressure, is exerted on all of us. It is calculated by the weight of air in the atmosphere, or the amount of air directly above us. Rarely are we aware of its immense force. This is because the pressure of air is exerted on us uniformly, all our lives. But, consider that all the air molecules above you have weight. The combined weight actually creates a pressure equivalent to about 10,000kg/square meter. At sea level, this translates to about 1000kg/0.1 square meter, or about 14.7lbs/square inch or PSI! This means there is about a ton of weight on each of us! Of course, this number varies slightly depending on the altitude you happen to be. The air pressure in our bodies, our lungs, stomachs, ears, fluids, etc., "balances" the pressure outside of our bodies. Our internal pressure is essentially the same as the outside pressure- we are at equilibrium. This prevents us from being crushed by the outside air pressure.

The human body is capable of being affected by low pressure weather systems, that can cause effects such as headaches, motion sickness, and distension in the sinuses. Effects such as these can be influenced by the difference between pressure within the body's cavities, such as lungs, ears, and sinuses, and the atmospheric pressure surrounding the body. This also explains why our ears pop in an airplane, or driving through hills or mountains. The ears essentially try to equalize the pressure within its cavities with the atmospheric pressure. Even those who suffer from arthritis or bursitis might experience increased joint pain as swelling occurs due to a decrease of pressure on the body.

Standards Alignment:

Next Generation Science Standards (NGSS, Lead States 2013)

Disciplinary Core Ideas in Physical Science

PS1: Matter and Its Interactions

PS1.A: Structure and Properties of Matter

Disciplinary Core Ideas in Life Science

LS1: From Molecules to Organisms: Structures and Processes

LS1.A: Structure and Function

Magic Jelly Beans

Concepts Illustrated: Density, mass, volume, buoyancy, friction, physical properties of matter, transfer of energy.

This demonstration is typically presented using a solid metal ball and a ping pong ball placed in a jar of beans. However, most observers are quick to identify the difference in mass between these two objects. As a result, they predict the "heavy" ball to sink and the "light" ball to rise. This does not lead to any contradiction because it is precisely what occurs. More importantly, this leads students to erroneously attribute the outcome to weight or mass. This version of the demonstration diverts attention towards color and size. The result is a contradiction of expectation for almost all!

Although this traditional version is included, the highlight of the description provided here is a newly designed variation.

Paradox:

When a bottle full of jelly beans and differently sized spheres or cubes are shaken, their newly settled positions contradict all predictions!

Equipment:

1. Jelly Beans- roughly 500g if you use a 1.5L beaker. Two distinctly different colored jelly beans are required. There should be enough of each to fill half the jar. A number of substitutes can be made, and will be explained in the sections that follow.
2. Two large beakers to hold the separated jelly beans.
3. Large transparent jar or bottle to hold the mixed jelly beans. A 1- 1.5L beaker will work, but some beans might spill out the spout when being shaken.
4. Ten spheres or cubes of two different colors and sizes. See the Preparation section for specific details.
5. One large beaker to hold the spheres or cubes.

Preparation:

The specific size of the spheres or cubes is not critical, but they should be distinctly different. Students should be able to identify them as large and small. There should be five of each. The large spheres or cubes must be less dense than the small. They can all be made of metal by choosing materials such as tin for the large and iron for the small. However, they can also be made of plastic and metal, for the large and small respectively. Check the website *phenomenadriveninquiry.com* for information to obtain these objects.

The masses and densities of the spheres or cubes should never be discussed prior to the demonstration. These items should be identified and described as simply "large and small."

The colors of the spheres or cubes should match those of the jelly beans. The larger items should match the color of the smaller jelly beans. It is not necessary, but if each sphere or cube has the same single letter printed on its sides, it will provide a very "magical" ending to the demonstration. If you want to include this optional ending, the five large items should have the letters M, A, G, I, and C printed on them- one letter on each. The five small spheres or cubes can have any random letters printed on them.

Prior to the demonstration, the jelly beans should be separated by color into two different beakers. The large bottle is empty. The cubes are randomly placed together into a beaker.

The Lesson:

Although jelly beans of any colors will suffice, the demonstration will be explained using blue and yellow jelly beans. It will also be explained using cubes, although spheres can be substituted.

Display the empty bottle to students. Show the jelly beans and the cubes. The cubes should be randomly displayed. It should be clearly pointed out that there are two sizes of cubes, as well as two colors that happen to match those of the jelly beans. Pull a few of each color and size randomly from the beaker and set them on the table. Then, pour the remainder out onto the table in a haphazard manner. The letters printed on the cubes are casually shown in the process. You can say that you happen to find some that were plastic, and others metal, to use.

Now, pour all the blue jelly beans into the bottle. Then, randomly scatter the cubes- both large and small- across the surface of them. Explain that this layer of cubes will act as a barrier between the blue and yellow jelly beans. Illustrate this by pouring all the yellow jelly beans on top of the layer of cubes. Screw the lid onto the bottle. Hold the bottle in your hands and ask students to predict what will happen to the contents of the bottle when it is vigorously shaken. The word "content" is deliberately chosen here. It does not draw focus to any one component within the bottle and does not "tip off" that one particular component will behave in a special way.

Some students will predict that nothing will happen because the cubes will act as an effective barrier. Basing their prediction on size, many will predict that the large cubes will sink. And others will add that the small cubes will rise. If the cubes are all made of metal, some will predict they will all sink to the bottom of the bottle. Some will predict that all the cubes will collectively either sink to the bottom or rise to the surface, while other predict that the blue and yellow cubes will separate into the jelly beans of matching color. And others will predict that the yellow and blue beans will switch places.

Shake the bottle vigorously. You will be able to see when the results have appeared. The large cubes will be seen to "pop" up above the surface of the yellow jelly beans. Stop shaking. The blue and yellow jelly beans will mix. If you are surrounded by the students as you shake the bottle, they will also be able to observe this. Students will immediately key in on this result.

Point this out and act surprised. Now lift the bottle and curiously peek underneath. Act surprised that some have also sunk to the bottom. Allow students to observe these by holding the bottle up for them. Unscrew the lid and take out the cubes on top, placing them on the desk. As you line them up on the desk, students will begin to notice that they are all large cubes. Join in their surprise. How did all the larger cubes rise? Point out that all the small cubes have sunk to the bottom of the bottle! Now, act amazed as you recognize something even stranger. Hold the large cubes up one at a time, showing the letters printed on them. Students will shout with disbelief to discover that the letters spell- "MAGIC"!

This outcome contradicts the expectations of all. As mentioned, many predicted that nothing will occur. Others did not predict the cubes to separate at all. The jelly beans did not switch places, as some predicted. Others who predicted the cubes to separate by color did not see this happen either. Finally, the larger cubes did not fall to the bottom of the bottle. In fact, just the opposite occurred. Discovering that the large cubes spell "magic" is an added surprise!

Do not have a discussion regarding the volume, mass or density of the cubes. Given the same set of cubes, students will mix them in various groupings according to color, size, and letter. A balance should be available during student investigations. When they are able to handle and manipulate the cubes on their own, students will begin to slowly discover the difference in mass among them. The objective is that as students mix and match these cubes, mass them, and observe the outcomes of their sizes upon shaking, the collective findings will provide a rich discussion to develop an understanding for the concepts at hand.

Lesson Variation:

Variation #1:

The demonstration can certainly be made to have a more "magical" feel by resting the large blue cubes are placed in the bottom of the empty bottle. As you do this, explain that these will serve to remind us of where the blue jelly beans will be placed. Illustrate this by pouring all the blue jelly beans into the bottle, over the blue cubes. Now, pour all the yellow jelly beans over the blue ones. The yellow cubes are layered on top of the yellow jelly beans, again to remind us of where the yellow jelly beans are located in the bottle. Show the students that they can see the yellow cubes from above, by looking down into the open bottle, and the blue cubes from below, by holding the bottle up and allowing them to see the blue cubes resting on the bottom of the bottle. When asked to predict, many students will think that the blue and yellow jelly beans will switch places, while the blue and yellow cubes remain in place due to their sizes. When the bottle is shaken, students will observe a magical looking switch as the small cubes sink below the surface and the large cubes pop up.

Variation #2:

It will look like magic to your students when you shake a beaker full of beans and the metal ball sitting on top of the beans is suddenly replaced by the ping pong ball previously buried at the bottom!

This is the traditional version of the demonstration. It would make an effective presentation for students at the elementary level. Differently colored jelly beans are not necessary here.

Unpopped popcorn kernels or uncooked beans, such as lima, kidney or pinto for example, can be substituted.

A metal ball and a ping pong ball will work well for this demonstration. Any metal ball can be used, as long as it is denser than the popcorn or beans. A sphere 4cm in diameter will be clearly visible to students.

Display the beaker to students. Place the ping pong ball at the bottom of the beaker. Fill the beaker with the beans, covering the ping pong ball. Now, show the metal ball and place it on top of the beans. Make sure that students know this ball is metal. Ask students to predict what will happen when you shake the beaker vigorously. Shake the beaker from side to side. The metal ball will sink beneath the beans, while the ping pong ball will rise to the top.

This can also be accomplished using blue and yellow jelly beans, as explained in the previous variations. But you could also use a blue ping pong ball at the bottom of the bottle, covered by the blue jelly beans. Pour the yellow jelly beans on top of the blue and add a yellow metal ball on the top. Students can be told these balls act as markers, identifying where the yellow and blue jelly beans reside in the jar.

You can also use letters made of plastic and metal. The plastic letters are placed at the bottom of the bottle and rise to the top upon shaking. Those made of metal begin at the top and sink to the bottom.

You might also choose to cover the beaker with a cloth before shaking. It will startle many when you remove the cloth to show the ping pong ball now resting on top of the beans, where the metal ball had just been seen a moment ago.

For a very simplistic version of the demonstration, the phenomena can also be observed using a drinking glass filled with rice. Place a marble at the bottom of the glass before filling it with the rice. Rest the bottom of the glass against one palm, and place the other palm on top of the glass. Shake the glass between your hands.

Note that each lesson variation can show that some of the energy put into the system, when shaking, is transferred as sound.

Possible Variables:

1. Rice, corn, beads, sand, sawdust, flour, salt, oatmeal, sunflower seeds, sugar, pasta, frozen peas, unpopped popcorn kernels, or other subtance in place of beans. Can also fill the jar with particles of differing shapes, such as pebbles, mixed nuts, and mixtures of substances, such as corn and frozen peas.
2. Cubes of various sizes, masses, and substances.
3. Beans of different varieties can be tested, such as pinto, lentil, etc.
4. Instead of cubes, balls of differing densities, such as tin, lead, copper, brass, plastic, cork, glass, rubber, wood, super ball, marble, etc. Balls that can be filled with liquids, or even sand, can also be tested. This idea can also be expanded to include an investigation of balls made of certain substances, such as copper, that are both solid and hollow. Students can also put a solid ball within a hollow ball.

5. Objects with different shapes other than spheres can also be used, such as cubes, diamonds, rods, etc. Different densities within these shapes can also be tested.
6. In place of a metal ball, use steel nuts or fishing sinkers.
7. In place of a ping pong ball, use plastic push pins, foam peanuts, or fishing bobbers.
8. Balls with different textures on their surface. This can also be coupled with different substances in the jar, such as rice, corn, etc.
9. Can use different brands of golf balls.
10. Adding water so that the spaces between the beads or beans are filled with water instead of air spaces. Liquids of varying densities can also be tested.
11. Balls of different diameters, but with the same densities.
12. The shape of the container, including a flatter, wider bowl rather than a taller, cylindrical jar.
13. Shaking the bottle from side to side, rather than up and down.
14. Gluing the metal ball to the ping pong ball.

Phenomenon Explained:

The density of both a fluid and the object placed in that fluid will determine whether the object sinks or floats. The differing densities between the metal sphere, the ping pong balls, and the beans they are placed into, causes the outcome observed in this demonstration.

Typically, density is demonstrated in the classroom by placing objects of various densities into water. Objects with a density lower than water will float when place into it, while those with a density higher than water will sink. Density is determined by calculating the mass for a given volume, expressed in the formula g/ml, g/cm^3, or g/cc. Density is independent of the sample size, since it represents the mass per ml of the sample. A larger volume does not necessarily equate to a higher mass. Fewer molecules packed into a given volume will result in a lower density than many more molecules packed into the same volume, which would increase the density.

In this demonstration, the water is replaced by beans, which act as the fluid. If the density of the metal ball is greater than that of the beans, it should sink. Conversely, if the density of the ping pong ball is less than that of the beans, it should "float," or rise to the top. But if you place the metal ball on top of the beans and bury the ping pong ball at the bottom of the beans, they don't simply sink and rise of their own accord. This is explained by friction. That's because the beans have too much friction between them to allow the balls to do so. This frictional force is reduced when the beans are shaken and put into motion. Shaking the jar moves the beans around, reducing the friction between the individual beans, allowing the objects to more easily sink or rise between them.

Friction is described as the force occurring at the surface of an object when another object moves against it. Believed to result from the electromagnetic attraction between the particles of the two substances, friction acts to resist the movement of one object relative to the other. Friction can occur between the molecules of any phase of matter. The amount of friction produced between two objects depends on the substance the objects are made of. There are two types of friction. Static friction occurs between the surfaces of two objects that are not moving, while kinetic friction occurs between objects in motion.

Buoyant forces are also at work here. Buoyancy is defined as the tendency for an object to float in a fluid. Liquids and gases are fluids. The upward force exerted by the molecules of the fluid is called the buoyant force. Archimedes explained that buoyancy is an upward force exerted by a fluid on an object. If you throw a brick into a pond, the brick will sink. The water in the pond is exerting an upward force, but this force is not greater than the weight of the brick. The brick sinks. Conversely, if you throw a piece of Styrofoam into the pond it will float. If you push the Styrofoam down below the surface of the water and let it go, it will quickly rise to the top. This is because the buoyant force is greater than the weight of the Styrofoam.

In our demonstration, the beans also exert a buoyant force. It is the same force that particles of either liquid or gas exert on objects placed within them. When the jar of beans is motionless, the frictional force between the beans is greater than the buoyant force exerted by the beans. As mentioned, when the beans are shaken the frictional force is reduced enough that the buoyant force is now greater. This buoyant force allows causes the ping pong ball to rise to the surface.

Differently colored jelly beans can also generate a conversation about the physical properties of matter. A physical property is a property of a substance that can be immediately observed without changing the identity of the substance. Color is a physical property of matter. It can be immediately observed and it can help identify a substance. When you refer to the purple jelly beans, students will know which ones you are pointing out. Other physical properties include hardness, shape, size, texture, odor, etc. A few of these can be included in the discussion as the jelly beans are referred to.

Standards Alignment:

Next Generation Science Standards (NGSS, Lead States 2013)

Disciplinary Core Ideas in Physical Science

PS1: Matter and Its Interactions

PS1.A: Structure and Properties of Matter

PS2: Motion and Stability: Forces and Interactions

PS2.B: Types of Interactions

PS3: Energy

PS3.A: Definitions of Energy

PS3.B: Conservation of Energy and Energy Transfer

Measured Chaos

Concepts Illustrated: Density, properties of solids, mass, volume, characteristics properties of substances, properties of mixtures, transfer of energy.

This discrepant event lends itself very well to a number of rewarding different presentation approaches. Several variations are included. Read these variations with your particular grade level in mind. You will find that some are more suited for elementary, and others for secondary, grade levels. The presentation can also be chosen according to the resources available. The type of presentation you choose will also direct students toward specific investigations. Choose the presentation that aligns with the path you would like students to follow. Each presentation will lead to exciting investigations and rewarding learning outcomes for your students. Read each variation to select the demonstration that best suits your curriculum, grade level, and availability of resources.

Paradox:

Students are shown a bottle containing red and yellow spheres of differing diameters. The yellow are clearly larger in diameter than the red. When massed individually, the yellow is shown to have greater mass than the red. Students are asked to predict what will happen when the bottle is shaken. Most predict that the larger yellow spheres will sink below the red because they are larger and heavier. The bottle is shaken and students are shocked to discover that the larger, heavier yellow spheres rise above the smaller red spheres with less mass!

Equipment:

1. Any sphere or bead. However, they must align with certain densities that allow for the intended outcome of the demonstration. Specifics are provided in the explanation of the concept.
2. An empty large bottle or jar. A 2L soda bottle or a standard Mason jar will work well. There should also be a cap or lid for the bottle/jar used.

Preparation:

The spheres should be in the bottle prior to the demonstration. They should be mixed together. They should not appear layered. One of each color is out of the jar, ready to be massed. This is because you don't want to drop the spheres into the jar as students look on. Because of their densities, the sound created when they are dropped in might provide clues to the outcome. The jar should be about half filled. You want to ensure that the spheres can freely mix together when shaken.

The Lesson:

Display the bottle containing the red and yellow spheres to the students. Be careful not to shake them yet. Set the bottle down and pick up the individual spheres. These should already have been set aside (see the Preparation section). Mass each of the spheres individually. Be sure that students are all able to see that the yellow sphere has more mass than the red one. It should also be directly pointed out that the yellow sphere has a much larger diameter. Now drop these two spheres into the bottle and screw the lid onto it. Explain that you will shake the bottle and that students should predict how these spheres will behave. Instruct students to use the data just observed, and past experience, when making their predictions. The bottle can be shaken either in a vertical or horizontal position. Students will be alarmed to find that the yellow spheres, with greater diameter and mass than the red, actually rises above the red!

Lesson Variations:

Variation #1:

Students are shown a bottle containing red and yellow spheres of two different diameters. Mass one of each to show that the larger, yellow sphere has more mass than the red. Ask students to predict what will happen when they are shaken. Most will predict that the larger yellow sphere with more mass will sink below the red. Shake them and the yellow spheres do sink below the red. Now introduce green spheres that have even greater diameter and mass than the yellow. They are added to the bottle and students predict what will now happen when the bottle is shaken. Relying on the results of the previous trial, most students will predict that the green will sink below the yellow, which would be below the red. Yet when shaken, the green rises to the top- above the yellow, *and* the red!

Variation #2:

In this demonstration, students are led to become confident in their assumption that the spheres with the larger diameter and mass will sink below the others when they observe this to actually happen. But they are shocked to find that this does not happen in the second half of the demonstration!

Students are shown a bottle that contains red and yellow spheres of differing diameters. The yellow are clearly larger in diameter than the red. Students are asked to predict how the spheres will behave when the bottle is shaken. In this demonstration, students are also asked to include an explanation for that behavior. Most will predict the yellow to sink because they are larger and weigh more. Even though the spheres have not been massed, students will assume that since the yellow are larger than the red, they must also weigh more. When shaken, students find their prediction to be correct- the yellow does sink below the red. Students are now asked to share their written explanations for this behavior. Most will explain the yellow spheres must weigh more. The yellow spheres sink because they are "heavier" than the red. The teacher reacts in agreement. The idea here is that she makes it seem that students have correctly "figured out" the observed results from shaking the jar. She responds "Great! Now let's make a prediction of how much you think they actually do weigh." The teacher wants students to think that they have basically observed the entire demonstration, but that they will conclude with a game to see who can guess the closest mass of the red and yellow spheres.

Students are asked to predict the mass of a single red sphere. Students will be eager and excited to find if they have guessed closer than others. Then, they are asked to predict the mass of the yellow sphere. It is suggested that they might consider the mass of the red spheres when predicting the mass of the yellow ones. Because they observed the yellow to sink below the red, most will now predict the mass of the yellow to be greater than that of the red. Students will once again be eager and excited to find who had the closest guess to the actual mass. However, they are shocked to find that they are not even close and that, in fact, the mass of the yellow spheres are actually less than the red spheres! Here, cognitive dissonance does not occur from the initial observed results, but rather from the alarming contradiction of expected data and student reasoning. When the observed results align with their expectations, students become quite confident that their reasoning must also be correct. This cultivated confidence establishes fertile ground for a rather powerful discrepant expectation when the spheres are massed.

Variation #3:

This variation is amenable to any grade level. Note the first half can provide valuable perplexity to elementary grade levels.

Students are shown a bottle containing yellow and red spheres of the *same* diameter. In this demonstration, the spheres are actually layered in the bottle prior to the start of the demonstration. The yellow should be the upper layer. Students do not know that the yellow spheres are actually denser than the red. They are asked to predict what will happen when the bottle is shaken. Most will predict that they will become well-mixed. Yet, when shaken, the yellow sinks below the red- in effect, the two layers switch their original positions!

The demonstration can end here for elementary levels, or continue on with middle level grades.

In this second half to the demonstration, additional yellow and red spheres are introduced. These spheres have the same diameter, but are larger in diameter than the original spheres. They are added to an empty bottle, in mixed fashion. If you don't have a second bottle, dump out the original spheres and add the larger spheres to this empty bottle. Students will recall the first part of the demonstration, when spheres of equal diameter resulted in the yellow below the red. Students are now asked to predict what will happen to these spheres when the bottle is shaken. Most will now predict the same outcome. These new spheres are larger, but since they are both the same diameter, they will predict the same outcome as previously observed. Shake the bottle and students will be startled to find that this time the red spheres sink. This is surprising because when the two colors were the same small size the yellow sank, but when the two colors were the same large size, the red sank!

Note that when presenting to secondary grade level students, all of the spheres could be mixed in the second half of the demonstration. Students could be asked to predict the layers that will form. The correct series of layers, from bottom to top will be: red large, yellow small, red small, yellow large.

<u>Variation #4:</u>

This variation is specifically directed towards elementary grade levels.

The first demonstration involves two spheres of the *same* diameter, red and yellow. Once students have made their predictions, the bottle is shaken. The yellow is observed to sink below the red. Students are asked why they think this happened. Most will claim that the yellow sinks because it is heavier.

A second bottle is shown with spheres of differing diameters, *large* yellow and *small* red spheres. One of each sphere is individually massed. The yellow sphere is observed to have greater mass than the red. Once students predict the outcome, the bottle is shaken. Yet this time, the red sinks!

<u>Variation #5:</u>

This variation is specifically directed towards elementary grade levels, specifically with limited resources.

A bottle is shown to contain spheres with two different diameters and colors. Yellow spheres are larger than the red. Most students will predict the larger yellow spheres will sink to the bottom of the pile, below the red, when the jar is shaken. But in fact, the larger diameter sphere is actually less dense than the sphere of smaller diameter. Most will be surprised to find that the larger yellow sphere will rise above the smaller red sphere when the bottle is shaken!

<u>Variation #6:</u>

This is a wonderful adaptation of the previous variation for an elementary level classroom with limited resources.

As in the previous variation, a bottle is shown to contain spheres with two different diameters and colors. The yellow have greater diameter than the red. Most students predict the larger yellow spheres will sink to the bottom of the pile when the jar is shaken. In this version, the larger spheres actually do, in fact, sink. Now students are asked to guess the mass of each color sphere. They will naturally guess that the larger, yellow sphere has more mass. They are surprised to find that the larger, yellow sphere actually has less mass than the red!

<u>Variation #7:</u>

This variation is also specifically directed towards elementary grade levels.

Two bottles are shown to students. The first contains small yellow spheres and large blue squares. The second contains small blue squares and larger yellow spheres. Most students will predict larger objects to sink below smaller ones. Yet, in each bottle it is the smaller object that sinks below the larger!

<u>Lesson Extension:</u>

The following extension can be added to the end of any of the previous demonstrations. Finishing with this extension generates a bit more wonder, and serves to create more diverse investigations.

Use spheres of two different diameters, but made of the same substance. Students do not know they are made of the same substance. In this case, students might predict the sphere of larger diameter to sink, but they actually do not separate at all. They remain mixed after being shaken.

Possible Variables:

1. Spheres made of wood, plastic foam, Styrofoam, copper, lead, tin, iron, stainless steel, brass, cork, ping pong balls, etc.
2. Differently shaped objects in place of spheres, such as cubes, cylinders, "jacks," etc.
3. Shape of the bottle.
4. The manner in which the bottle is shaken.
5. Filling the bottle with water.
6. Students can be provided spheres of various diameters, substances, and densities to investigate.
7. Students could be provided ping pong balls and sand to construct their own spheres. See Concept Explained, the following section, to fully understand and appreciate the reasoning and potentially rewarding learning opportunities presented with this approach.
8. Objects with different textures on their surfaces.

Phenomenon Explained:

Note that each lesson variation can show that some of the energy put into the system, when shaking, is transferred as sound.

When the objects are shaken together, they form a mixture. One property of a mixture is that it is physically combined, not chemically. Therefore, it can be physically separated.

Differently colored objects can also generate a conversation about the physical properties of matter. A physical property is a property of a substance that can be immediately observed without changing the identity of the substance. Color is a physical property of matter. It can be immediately observed and it can help identify a substance. When you refer to the blue cubes, students will know which ones you are pointing out. Other physical properties include hardness, shape, size, texture, odor, etc. A few of these can be included in the discussion as the various objects are referred to.

Density causes the sorting of spheres into layers. Upon shaking, friction occurs between the spheres, but those with the least density will rise above those with greater density. The shape or size of the objects used are irrelevant to the outcome. In this demonstration, sorting relies entirely on the density of the objects. Through their investigations, and the class discourse that follows, students discover that density causes the objects to separate when the bottle is shaken, irrespective of shape or size.

The density of an object is defined as its mass per unit volume. Density is determined by calculating the mass for a given volume, expressed in the formula g/ml, g/cm^3, or g/cc. Density is independent of the sample size, since it represents the mass per ml of the sample. A larger volume does not necessarily equate to a higher mass. Fewer molecules packed into a given volume will result in a lower density than many more molecules packed into the same volume, which would increase the density. Density is essentially a measure of how closely packed the molecules are in an object. The more closely packed the molecules are, the greater its density.

It is an important note that the density of the spheres is never calculated or referred to during the demonstration. Students may question whether density plays a role. Encourage investigation, but do not reveal that density does produce the separation.

In this demonstration, spheres made of varying substances can be obtained from science supply stores. Density is a physical characteristic property of each substance. We have learned that the density of a substance remains the same, regardless of the size or volume of the substance. A large piece of iron has the same density as a small piece. The density of each particular substance, and the combinations used in the bottle, will determine the sorting that occurs upon shaking. For example, the density of tin is about 7.3 g/cm^3 and the density of lead is about 11.3 g/cm^3. If spheres of these metals were put into the bottle and shaken, the lead spheres would sink below those made of tin. This is because lead is denser than tin. See the Possible Variable section for ideas on other substances that can be used.

Spheres of certain densities can actually be created using ping pong balls. Keep in mind that you will have to use ping pong balls of differing diameters, as the volume is critical to the density. Puncture a hole into the ping pong ball and fill the ball with sand until the desired density is achieved. Once you have discovered how much sand is necessary to achieve the desired density with the first ball, then you only need to measure that much sand to fill into the remaining balls. Once you have filled the ping pong balls with the appropriate amount of sand, plug the hole with either a very small piece of tape, or a small amount of putty. The density of sand is dependent on the specific type of sand you are using. If you choose to make your own spheres using ping pong balls and sand, here are some examples, and a bit more explanation, for each of the demonstration variations:

Original Lesson Explanation:

When asked to predict the outcome of shaking the bottle, most students will predict the yellow to sink below the red for two reasons. The first is that it is larger in diameter- it is "bigger" in appearance. The second is that it has more mass.

Although the yellow spheres have a much greater diameter and mass, they are less dense than the red spheres. As a result, when the bottle is shaken, the denser red spheres will sink below the yellow ones. Here are two examples that show how the spheres can be constructed to make this happen:

Example A: red- 100g/20ml= 5 g/ml or 5 g/cm^3 yellow- 200g/100ml= 2 g/ml or 2 g/cm^3

In Example A, the diameter of the red sphere is 20ml, while the yellow is 100ml. You can see that the mass of the red is 100g per sphere, while the yellow is 200g per sphere.

Example B: red- 100g/10ml= 10 g/ml or 10g/cm^3 yellow- 200g/50ml= 4 g/ml or 4 g/cm^3

In each of these examples, the yellow sphere is less dense than the red.

Lesson Variation #1 Explanation:

These are the physical requirements for the spheres used in this demonstration:

Green- must have the largest diameter and mass (greater diameter and mass than yellow). They must also be the least dense of the three spheres.

Yellow- must have a larger diameter and mass than the red spheres. They must also be the most dense of the three spheres.

Here is an example of how these spheres can be constructed:

green- 250g/250= 1 g/ml   red- 75g/50ml= 1.5 g/ml   yellow- 200g/100ml= 2 g/ml

Lesson Variation #2 Explanation:

In this variation, the yellow spheres have greater volume, but less mass than the red.   For example:

red- 200g/20ml= 10 g/ml or 10 g/cm^3 yellow- 100g/100ml= 1 g/ml or 1 g/cm^3

Lesson Variation #3 Explanation:

The red and yellow spheres used in the first part of this demonstration must have the same diameter. The yellow spheres are denser than the red, so they must have greater mass. For example:

red- 50g/100ml= 0.5 g/ml or 0.5 g/cm^3 yellow- 200g/100ml= 2 g/ml or 2 g/cm^3

Spheres used in the second part of this demonstration follow the same rules. These spheres are simply larger in diameter, but they are the same diameter. The yellow must also be denser than the red. A simple way to achieve this is to double the measurements of the spheres used in the first part.

red- 100g/200ml= 0.5 g/ml or 0.5 g/cm^3 yellow- 400g/200ml= 2 g/ml or 2 g/cm^3

Lesson Variation #4 Explanation:

In the first part of this demonstration, the red and yellow spheres have the same diameter. The yellow have more mass, and so they have a greater density. For example:

red- 50g/100ml= 0.5 g/ml or 0.5 g/cm^3 yellow- 200g/100ml= 2 g/ml or 2 g/cm^3

In the second part of the demonstration, the yellow spheres are larger in diameter and mass than the red. But, this time the red have greater density, causing them to sink below the yellow. For example:

red- 100g/20ml= 5 g/ml or 5g/cm^3 yellow- 200g/100ml= 2 g/ml or 2 g/cm^3

Lesson Variation #5 Explanation:

In this variation, the yellow spheres have greater volume, but more mass. They are less dense than the red. For example:

red- 100g/20ml= 5 g/ml or 5 g/cm^3 yellow- 200g/100ml= 2 g/ml or 2 g/cm^3

Lesson Variation #6 Explanation:

In this variation, the yellow spheres are larger in diameter than the red, but they have less mass. As a result, the yellow spheres are less dense than the red. For example:

red- 200g/20ml= 10 g/ml or 10 g/cm^3 yellow- 100g/100ml= 1 g/ml or 1 g/cm^3

Lesson Variation #7 Explanation:

This variation does not use spheres, but rather objects with two different shapes and sizes. The larger objects have less mass than the smaller objects. As a result, the larger objects are less dense. For example:

small objects- 200g/20ml= 10 g/ml or 10 g/cm^3 large objects- 100g/100ml= 1 g/ml or 1 g/cm^3

Lesson Extension Explanation:

Here, the spheres used are all made of the same substance. They can be painted to look different. Since they are made of the same substance, the spheres have the same density, regardless of their size difference. This would also be true if you used small spheres/large cubes, small spheres/large "jacks", large spheres/small cubes, large spheres/small cylinders, etc. Again, the shape of the object is no concern to its density.

Standards Alignment:

Next Generation Science Standards (NGSS, Lead States 2013)

Disciplinary Core Ideas in Physical Science

PS1: Matter and Its Interactions

PS1.A: Structure and Properties of Matter

PS2: Motion and Stability: Forces and Interactions

PS2.B: Types of Interactions

PS3: Energy

PS3.A: Definitions of Energy

PS3.B: Conservation of Energy and Energy Transfer

Melting Blocks

Concepts Illustrated: Phase changes, physical changes, melting, heat, volume, heat transfer, conduction, properties of solids, properties of liquids, temperature, endothermic reactions, thermal energy, conductors, insulators, kinetic energy, molecular motion of solids and liquids, the human body's perception of heat.

Paradox:

Although students expect that ice will be melted more quickly when set upon a warm block rather than a cold one, the exact opposite is observed. Two blocks are shown- one warm and one cold. Ice is set on top of each. The ice on the cold block melts noticeably faster than the ice resting on the warm block!

Equipment:

1. Two melting blocks. These can be purchased from science supply stores. They can also be constructed rather simply, as explained in the Phenomenon Explained section.
2. Ice.

The Lesson:

Students are shown the two blocks. Allow students to feel the top of each block. They will discover that one feels very cold, while the other feels very warm. The difference is easily noticeable. Explain that you will put an ice cube of similar size on top of each block. Ask students to predict which ice cube will melt faster, the one on the cold block or the one on the warm block? Without hesitation, most students will predict that the warm block will melt the ice faster. Place an ice cube on each block. The ice cube on the warm block seems to be almost unaffected while the ice cube on the cold block rapidly melts. The difference is unmistakable and quite remarkable. The ice cube on the warm block will have barely begun to melt by the time the ice cube on the cold block has completely melted!

Possible Variables:

1. The amount of ice.
2. The size of the ice cube. This could also involve putting a larger cube on the cold block and a smaller cube on the warm block.
3. Ice made with food coloring added.
4. Ice made from salt water.
5. Ice made from sugar water.
6. Thickness of the blocks.
7. Different types of metals and foam.
8. Objects other than blocks, such as black Teflon pans and white ceramic bowls.
9. The surface area of the blocks. Smaller and larger blocks could be investigated.
10. Substance other than ice, such as butter, lard, a Popsicle, candle wax, or chocolate.
11. Shape of the ice. This could also involve crushed ice.

12. Adding water of varying temperature to the top of the block, then putting the ice on it.
13. Using one block with a split surface of metal and foam. A larger piece of ice could be laid across the top so that it is in contact with both substances at once.
14. Blocks of various substances, such as steel, plastic, cardboard, tin, aluminum foil, or even different types of wood to compare. Aluminum foil can also be used as a "flat" piece, or "crumpled."

Phenomenon Explained:

One of the blocks is made of aluminum, while the other is a high density foam. These blocks can either be purchased as a kit, or they can be made by cutting the blocks out yourself. They should be the same thickness and size. As a kit, they are painted black to conceal the identity of the substances. If you make them, they could remain as unpainted blocks. But, this would allow students to clearly identify them as two different materials. When making their predictions, students would most likely take this information into consideration, basing their predictions on the type of substance. When painted black, student predictions will tend to focus on their perceptions of the relative temperatures of the blocks by touching them. The most rewarding learning strategy would be to initially direct student focus on the perceived temperature of the blocks. The identity of the substances would be introduced as the class discussion develops.

Heat is not the same as temperature. Essentially, heat is energy and temperature is a measure of it. Heat is a form of energy that can transfer from one medium to another, flowing from objects of higher temperature to those with lower temperature. When a cup of coffee feels hot, it is because energy from the cup is being transferred to your hand. On the other hand, a glass of iced tea feels cold because heat energy from your hand is flowing into the glass. This causes it to feel cold.

The temperature of a substance is a measure of the average kinetic energy of its molecules. All matter is composed of atoms or molecules that are in constant motion. The faster they move, the more kinetic energy they have. There is a direct relationship between the motion of molecules and their temperature. The greater the kinetic energy, the higher the temperature of the object. Molecules that have low average kinetic energy move slowly and have low temperatures in comparison to molecules with high kinetic energy, which move more quickly and have a higher temperature. The molecules of solids generally move very slowly, simply vibrating in place. Thermal energy is defined as the energy within an object or system due to the movement of the particles or molecules within.

Heat is the *total* kinetic energy in a substance or system. This is different than temperature which, as we have learned, is the *average* kinetic energy. Heat is dependent on the speed of the particles, the number of particles, and the type of particles in a substance. On the other hand, temperature is independent of the number and type of particles. A large tub of water could have the same temperature as a small cup of water, but the water in the large tub would possess more heat because it contains many more molecules, therefore more total kinetic energy.

In this demonstration, the two blocks actually have the same temperature. Using an infrared thermometer, students can confirm this. There are also smart phone apps that can act as thermal cameras, which can be used to indicate the level of thermal heat being produced from each block. A search for "thermal cameras" should provide a few different app choices. By viewing each block through the camera, any difference in thermal temperature can be immediately observed. Self-adhesive liquid crystal thermometers can also be used to clearly show the thermal temperatures of the blocks. These types of thermometers are commonly used in terrariums and aquariums. They can be found at most pet stores for minimal cost. A liquid crystal thermometer could be stuck to the back of each block.

Materials that are poor conductors of heat are called insulators. Although the two blocks have the same temperature, the aluminum block is a better conductor of heat than foam. The aluminum block will absorb and transfer heat from its surroundings more readily. When you touch this block, it absorbs and conducts heat away from your hand, causing it to feel cold to the touch. In this example, foam is a better insulator than the block of aluminum.

When ice melts it undergoes an endothermic process. In an endothermic reaction, the reactants absorb energy from their surroundings. When ice melts, the energy absorbed is heat. Since the aluminum block is a good conductor, it absorbs thermal energy from the air and readily transfers that heat energy to the ice. This is why a larger aluminum block would melt the ice more quickly.

The foam block, on the other hand, acts as an insulator. As an insulator, it will not readily lose heat to its surroundings. Heat does not conduct through it as easily as the aluminum block. As a result, thermal energy is not readily absorbed from the surrounding air and the heat energy of the foam block is not readily transferred to the ice. In this case, most of the energy melting the ice comes directly from the air in the room.

The human body's senses may not always be accurate in their perception of heat. When two objects come into contact with one another, heat will always travel from the warmer to the cooler object. When metal touches your hand, your hand is the warmer object. Heat travels from your hand, causing the metal to feel cold to the touch. However, when metal comes into contact with ice, the metal is now the warmer object. In this case heat flows from the metal to the ice, and the ice melts.

The process of melting ice represents a physical change, or a change that does not alter the chemical composition of the substance. Unlike a chemical change, a physical change does not produce a new substance. Melting ice simply changes the form of water from the solid phase to the liquid phase. When matter transitions from one phase to another, it is called a phase change.

Standards Alignment:

Next Generation Science Standards (NGSS, Lead States 2013)

Disciplinary Core Ideas in Physical Science

PS1: Matter and Its Interactions

PS1.A: Structure and Properties of Matter

PS1.B: Chemical Reactions

PS2: Motion and Stability: Forces and Interactions

PS2.B: Types of Interactions

PS3: Energy

PS3.A: Definitions of Energy

PS3.B: Conservation of Energy and Energy Transfer

Disciplinary Core Ideas in Life Science

LS1: From Molecules to Organisms: Structures and Processes

LS1.D: Information Processing

Meniscus Magic

<u>Concepts Illustrated:</u> Meniscus, cohesion, adhesion, buoyancy, density, properties of water, surface tension, viscosity, solutions, solubility, solutes, solvents, concentration, saturated solutions, process of dissolving, properties of mixtures, properties of surfactants, the respiratory system of fish, the human respiratory system.

<u>Paradox:</u>

There are two surprising outcomes in this demonstration. The first occurs when three ping pong balls are placed into a bowl of water and they immediately migrate to the perimeter of the bowl. The second occurs when water is added, bring the water level to its brim, and the ping pong balls move towards each other, collecting at the center!

<u>Equipment:</u>

1. One wide bowl.
2. Three ping pong balls.
3. Water.

<u>The Lesson:</u>

Show the bowl and add water to about one inch below the rim. Instruct students that they'll be making two predictions. First, you will place three ping pong balls into the water and students should predict what will happen. Then explain that you will add water until it becomes level with, and even rises a little bit above, the rim. Students are to predict how the ping pong balls will then behave. They should make both of those predictions before you place the ping pong balls into the water.

Now place the ping pong balls into the water. Once everyone has seen the balls move to the edge of the bowl, add water to the rim and the balls will move and collect at the center.

The outcome of this demonstration is definitely more surprising when presented in this manner and students are asked to make both predictions before the demonstration begins. Provided the foresight of all the steps involved in the demonstration, students will generally predict that when the balls are initially placed into the water they will float near the center, but when water is added they will spread out to the edge of the bowl, and maybe even go over the edge. Exactly the opposite of what will actually happen! But if the balls are placed into the water after students have made only the first prediction, they will observe the balls moving to the edge before making the second prediction. When they do make the second prediction, some will predict that when water is added the balls will go over the edge, but many will predict that the balls will move to the center. Asking students to make both predictions at the outset of the demonstration will cause more students to be surprised.

Lesson Variation:

The demonstration can also be conducted using miniature Styrofoam balls in a glass of water. Fill the glass ¾ full of water. Drop one of the Styrofoam balls onto the surface of the water and it will immediately be pulled to the edge of the glass. If you drop a number of these balls onto the surface, they will all be pulled to the edge of the glass, forming a ring of balls around the edge.

Now fill the water to over the edge of the glass. Drop one of the miniature balls onto the surface of the water, near the edge of the glass, and it will be drawn to the center. Continue to add balls, one at a time, near the edge of the glass. One by one, they will be pulled to the center. These balls will migrate together. If you push this floating collection of balls to the edge of the glass, the entire collection will move as one back to the center.

You can now carefully remove some water from the glass using an eyedropper. As you do, the balls will migrate towards the edge of the glass. This can be done with either one ball, or a collection of them.

Possible Variables:
1. Liquids with different densities. This could involve adding salt or sugar to change the density of the water. It could also involve using an entirely different liquid, such as vegetable oil, honey, or even milk.
2. The viscosity of the liquid.
3. Balls of different masses. This would involve balls of varying diameters.
4. Balls of different densities. This could involve using balls of the same diameter and filling them with liquid or sand to alter their densities.
5. Shape of the container, such as square-shaped.

6. Objects that float, other than ping pong balls. For example, corks, plastic beads, Styrofoam balls, cereal pieces, corn kernels, erasers, wooden balls, pith balls, small whiffle balls, etc.
7. Temperature of the water.
8. Objects with different shapes, such as Styrofoam squares or triangles. This could also involve investigating squares and triangles of various heights.
9. Placing the balls into the bowl before adding water.

Phenomenon Explained:

The density of an object will determine whether it will float in a fluid. Density is determined by calculating the mass for a given volume, expressed in the formula g/ml, g/cm^3, or g/cc. Density is independent of the sample size, since it represents the mass per ml of the sample. A larger volume does not necessarily equate to a higher mass. Fewer molecules packed into a given volume will result in a lower density than many more molecules packed into the same volume, which would increase the density. Objects with a density less than water will float, while those denser than water will sink. The density of water is 1.0g/ml. Ping-pong balls have a density less than 1.0g/ml, and so they float in water. This is one of the reasons that the ping-pong balls float on the surface of the water. The other involves surface tension. The behavior exhibited by the ping-pong balls can also be attributed to meniscus.

Cohesion is the attraction of like molecules to one another. Water molecules have a very strong cohesive attraction for one another. Imagine a glass of water. There are powerful cohesive forces between the molecules in that glass. The water molecules at the surface do not have any water molecules above them. As a result, they are strongly attracted to those neighboring water molecules at their sides and to those below, which draws them in towards the liquid. This strong attraction to the molecules around and underneath creates what is known as surface tension. The strong attraction to the molecules around and underneath create a surface tension, a film-like layer of water at the surface, almost like an "elastic skin."

Adhesion describes the force that attracts different molecules to one another. In our demonstration, water molecules are attracted to inner wall of the bowl through adhesion. This force of attraction causes the water to "climb up" the wall of the bowl, enough to form a slight curve around the perimeter. This curved surface of the water is known as a meniscus.

Buoyancy, which also plays a role in this demonstration, is defined as the tendency for an object to float in a fluid. Liquids and gases are fluids. The upward force exerted by the molecules of the fluid is called the buoyant force.

When the water is filled to about 1" from the top of the bowl it forms a concave meniscus. The combined forces of adhesion, cohesion, and buoyancy play significant roles. Adhesion causes the perimeter of the water to "climb" up the wall of the bowl. Because of cohesion, the water molecules are strongly attracted to one another even as they are drawn up the side of the bowl. As a result, the surface of the water acquires a meniscus, a concave shape, curved and lifted where it meets the bowl. The water is at its highest point at the edge of the bowl. The buoyant force on floating objects acts to push them towards the highest point possible. Since the water in this part of the demonstration is highest at the outer edge, the ball is pulled there.

The water can actually be filled above the rim of the bowl due to the strong force of attraction between the water molecules. This force creates a surface tension that allows the water to take the shape of a dome, or convex meniscus, at the surface without spilling over the edge of the bowl. This convex meniscus is sometimes referred to as a *reverse meniscus*.

These same properties are at play when water rises above the rim of the bowl. The large dome, or convex meniscus, that the water forms above the rim of the bowl is due to these properties of water. The cohesive forces are so great that the molecules can resist the external force of gravity. The force of adhesion attracts the water molecules to the rim of the bowl. Because of these two forces, the water resists spilling over the rim of the bowl, even when the level rises above the rim.

Again, the buoyant force on the balls pushes them upward, towards the highest point. But, the highest point on the surface of the water is now in the center of the bowl. As a result, the ping pong balls migrate towards this highest point, at the center of the bowl.

If the density of the liquid is altered by adding salt or sugar, discourse can include solutions, solubility, solutes, solvents, and concentration. Saltwater or sugar water is a mixture. One property of a mixture is that it is physically combined, not chemically, and it can be physically separated. For example, saltwater can be physically separated through the process of evaporation, or boiling the water away.

A solution is one in which a solute is dissolve in a solvent. The solute is the substance being dissolved and the solvent is the substance in which the solute is dissolved. Water is called the universal solvent because it is capable of dissolving more solutes than any other liquid. Solubility is the ability of a solute to dissolve in a solvent.

A concentrated solution is one which there are many dissolved particles of solute in the solvent. On the other hand, a dilute solution is one in which there are few dissolved particles of solute. A solution which contains all the dissolve particles it can possibly hold is called saturated.

The addition of soap as a variable broadly expands the scope of topics covered in class discourse. Soap is a surfactant. Surfactants play a critical role in our bodies. There is a thin layer of water that lines human lungs. This water is necessary for the gas exchange of carbon dioxide and oxygen to occur. These gases require a wet layer or surface for the exchange to take place. In fish, this exchange takes place in their gills. Since they are on the outside of the fish, gills have direct contact with water. Our lungs, on the other hand, are best able to be kept wet inside of our bodies. However, due to the properties of water, surface tension arises that can interfere with the expansion of our lungs as we breathe. Surfactant acts to reduce surface tension. This prevents alveoli, small air sacs in the lungs, from collapsing when we exhale. The most efficient oxygen-carbon dioxide exchange occurs in our lungs with the greatest alveoli surface area. By preventing the collapse of alveoli, surfactant helps to maximize the surface area available for the exchange of gases.

Viscosity is defined as a fluid's resistance to flow. Think of it as the "thickness" of a fluid. Fluids such as honey, molasses, corn syrup, and engine oil are highly viscous. Students might choose to investigate the outcome when liquids of varying viscosities are employed.

Note that beakers will not work in this demonstration. Because of their spout, water will spill over the rim.

Standards Alignment:

Next Generation Science Standards (NGSS, Lead States 2013)

Disciplinary Core Ideas in Physical Science

PS1: Matter and Its Interactions

PS1.A: Structure and Properties of Matter

PS1.B: Chemical Reactions

PS2: Motion and Stability: Forces and Interactions

PS2.B: Types of Interactions

Disciplinary Core Ideas in Life Science

LS1: From Molecules to Organisms: Structures and Processes

LS1.A: Structure and Function

Disciplinary Core Ideas in Earth and Space Science

ESS2: Earth's Systems

ESS2.C: The Roles of Water in Earth's Surface Processes

Milk Fireworks

Concepts Illustrated: Solubility, solute, solvent, surface tension, properties of mixtures, fluid dynamics, density, properties of surfactants, cohesion, polarity, hydrophobic molecules, hydrophilic molecules, molecular motion of liquids.

Paradox:

A few drops each from several different colors of food coloring are added to a bowl of milk. When just a couple drops of dish soap are added, the food coloring reacts wildly, resembling colorful exploding fireworks!

Equipment:

1. Whole milk.
2. Recessed bowl- a dinner or soup bowl works fine.
3. Food coloring- 4 different colors works well.
4. Dish soap- Dawn brand works very well.
5. Cotton swabs.

The Lesson:

Pour enough milk in the bowl to completely cover the bottom, at least ¼" deep. Be sure that students know this is regular milk that they might find in their refrigerator. Now add one drop of each of the four colors of food coloring. Mentally divide the bowl into four quarters and place one drop into each quarter, close to the center of the bowl. Show the dish soap and the cotton swabs. Explain that you will first touch the tip of a cotton swab to the milk in the center of the bowl. Then you will dip the tip of the cotton swab into the dish soap and touch it once again to the milk in the center of the bowl. Ask students to predict what will happen when you perform each of those actions. They will make two predictions.

Carefully touch the tip of the dry cotton swab to the milk in the center of the bowl without stirring the milk at all. There shouldn't be any reaction. Now add a drop of dish soap to the tip of the cotton swab. Touch the soapy tip of the swab to the milk in the center of the bowl and hold it in place. There will be an eruption of colors as the food coloring swirls and churns, forming beautiful patterns. Hold the cotton swab still and the food coloring will continue to explode outward! The colors should continue to disperse and swirl even after the swab is removed from the milk!

Be sure to use a well rinsed plate or bowl. Any dish soap residue from previous demonstrations could affect the observed behaviors when the food coloring is added to the milk.

Lesson Variation:

Use Elmer's glue, add the soap to produce the colorful patterns, and allow it to harden. Once it is completely hardened, lift the Elmer's glue out of the plate for a wonderful art project that has preserved the beautiful patterns within. In fact, you can also shine a light through these pieces of art for a unique look at them.

Using buttermilk produces a crystallizing type of reaction that looks similar to growing ice crystals.

Possible Variables:

1. Placement of the soapy tip of the cotton swab in the bowl of milk.
2. Placement and proximity of food coloring to each other, and to the soap.
3. Using liquids other than milk, such as water, juice, or Kool-Aid, etc.
4. The type of milk, such as skim, 1%, 2% , whole milk, half and half, buttermilk, heavy cream, powdered milk, chocolate milk, and even Elmer's glue.
5. Putting substances other than dish soap on the tip of the cotton swab, such as vinegar, lime juice, orange juice, water, rubbing alcohol, or even soda.
6. Adding drops of dish soap directly into the milk, without the use of the cotton swab.
7. The temperature of the milk. Could heat it or chill it with ice.
8. Brand of dish soap.
9. Volume of milk.
10. Volume of dish soap used. This could involve comparing the effects observed dependent on the ratio of dish soap to food coloring, or dish soap to milk.
11. Using a soap other than dish soap, such as shampoo, hand soap, or even laundry detergent.
12. The material that the bowl is made of, such as plastic, glass and aluminum pie plates.
13. Number of cotton swabs simultaneously dipped into the milk. This could also involve using a different brand of soap on each of the swabs, or the same on each swab.
14. Size of bowl or pie tin.
15. Temperature of the food coloring. Could heat it or chill it with ice. This could also involve an investigation of the temperature of the food coloring vs the temperature of the milk.
16. The density of the liquid used. This could involve adding sugar or salt to the milk or water.
17. Brand of food coloring.
18. Using an eyedropper to deliver the soap, the effects of specific numbers of drops can be studied.

Phenomenon Explained:

There are two reasons that the food coloring floats at the surface of the milk. The first is that it is less dense than milk. The density of an object will determine whether it will float in a fluid. Density is determined by calculating the mass for a given volume, expressed in the formula g/ml, g/cm^3, or g/cc. Density is independent of the sample size, since it represents the mass per ml of the sample. A larger volume does not necessarily equate to a higher mass. Fewer molecules packed into a given volume will result in a lower density than many more molecules packed into the same volume, which would increase the density.

Food coloring also floats on the surface of milk because of surface tension caused, in part, by cohesion. Cohesion refers to the attraction of like molecules towards one another. Water molecules have a very strong cohesive attraction for one another. Milk consists of about 87% water. At the surface, there is a strong cohesive force that attracts water molecules that are next to one another. Those molecules at the surface do not have any water molecules above them. Thus, they are strongly attracted to those water molecules below. Since there are no water molecules above those directly at the surface, these water molecules are pulled outwards, towards those around them. The strong attraction to the molecules around and underneath create a surface tension, a "flexible skin" across the surface of the water. In doing so, water minimizes its surface area. This is surface tension.

Soap is a surfactant, a compound that reduces surface tension. When soap contacts the surface, it disrupts the cohesive property of water and reduces the surface tension. Although the force inwards towards the drop of soap is broken, the force between water molecules directed away from the drop of soap is still very strong. Since this force outward is now much stronger than the force inward, the molecules are pulled outward, away from the center. As we have learned, milk is made of mostly water. So, when soap is added and the water molecules in the milk are pulled outward, the food coloring at the surface is pulled along with them. When the food coloring is pulled outward, toward the edge of the bowl, you're actually watching the molecular action of the surface tension when it is broken.

But what about the continuous churning activity observed when soap is added to the milk. That can be explained by the interaction between soap molecules and the fat molecules found in milk. Soap molecules are bipolar. That is, each molecule has two ends. One is a non-polar "tail" and the other a polar "head." The polar end is hydrophilic, it *likes* water and dissolves in it. The non-polar end is hydrophobic, meaning it doesn't *like* water.

Fat molecules are non-polar. The entire molecule is hydrophobic. As a result, fat molecules don't dissolve in water. When soap is added to milk, the non-polar ends of the soap molecules attach themselves to the non-polar fat molecules in the milk. This is actually how soap cleans your dishes. Soap molecules attach to fat globules from food on the dish, which are then washed away.

In this demonstration, when the soap is added, the soap molecules "whip around" trying to align and attach themselves to the fat molecules. The food coloring is pushed and carried along amidst this activity, causing the continuous churning motion observed. As the milk churns and swirls, you're actually observing molecules in motion. As the soap becomes evenly mixed through the milk, the reaction slows down.

The rate at which the colors swirl is affected by the fat content in the milk used. For example, colors swirl faster when whole milk is used. In contrast, the swirling motion slows down when milk with lower fat content is used.

If you conduct the experiment with water, you will also be able to see the surface tension broken. When the cotton swab is dipped in, food coloring molecules can be seen quickly spreading out from the center of the plate. But, once the molecules have spread out from the center, they will not continue to move. And you won't see the churning, swirling movements.

By testing different types of milk, you're basically investigating the reactions that occur from different levels of fats. The milk with the greatest fat content will produce the most amazing reactions.

Elmer's glue is a polyvinyl acetate, a polymer composed of bipolar molecules. The food coloring fireworks can be observed in it. But, mixing a solution of Elmer's glue and water produces unique reactions, different from using the Elmer's glue alone.

Standards Alignment:

Next Generation Science Standards (NGSS, Lead States 2013)

Disciplinary Core Ideas in Physical Science

PS1: Matter and Its Interactions

PS1.A: Structure and Properties of Matter

PS1.B: Chemical Reactions

PS2: Motion and Stability: Forces and Interactions

PS2.B: Types of Interactions

Misbehaving Bubble

Concepts Illustrated: Newton's first law of motion- the law of inertia, density, solutions, solubility, solutes, solvents, concentration, saturated solutions, process of dissolving, properties of mixtures, fluid dynamics, properties of gases, viscosity, properties of fluids.

Paradox:

An air bubble inside a bottle partially filled with water behaves in a puzzling manner. Based on our personal experiences, we know that our bodies are pulled backwards, into the seat, when the car we sit in accelerates. We also know that our bodies are pulled forward, away from the seat, when the moving car we sit in stops abruptly. Yet in this demonstration, the air bubble inside of a horizontal bottle of water will behave in the exact opposite manner- moving in the same direction as the force applied. The air bubble moves to the right when the bottle is pushed to the right! And, when the motion of the bottle moving to the right is abruptly stopped, the bubble moves to the left!

Equipment:

1. 2 L soda bottle. The bottle needs a cap and the label on the bottle should be removed.
2. Water.
3. Food coloring is optional.

Preparation:

Prepare the bottle by partially filling it with about 2/3 water. You might choose to add food coloring so that the liquid can be easily seen by all students. Screw the cap onto the bottle.

The Lesson:

Begin by showing students the bottle. The bottle should be upright, in a vertical position. Point out that the liquid inside is water. Be sure to also point out that the bottle is not completely filled, so there is some air trapped above the liquid. Suggest that in order to make the following prediction it might help to first recall how our bodies react while we're sitting in a car when it accelerates and brakes quickly. The bottle should not be moved at all yet. Now tip the bottle over into a horizontal position, so that students are looking at its side. The bottle cap is on your left. Point out that the air bubble is still above the water, but that its position has changed with respect to the bottle.

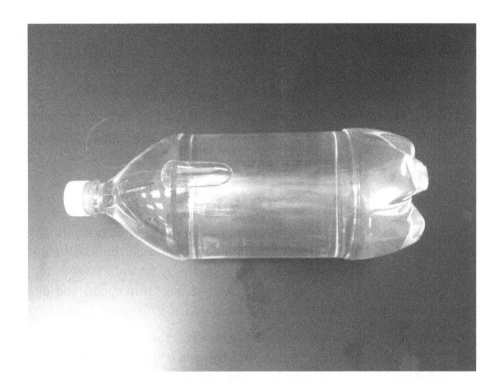

Explain that in this demonstration the bottle represents the car, and the air bubble represents a body resting inside. Tell students that you will push the bottle, quickly sliding it to their right- in the direction of the cap. Students should predict how the bubble will behave. Then, further explain that they should also explain how the bubble will react when the bottle is abruptly stopped. Once they have made their predictions, push the bottle to show students that the air bubble actually moves in the same direction as the bottle is moving and that it moves in the opposite direction when the bottle stops- counterintuitive to what most predict.

Lesson Variation:

This demonstration could become even more surprising by placing the bottle on a strong piece of cardboard. The bottle should be glued to the cardboard. A toy car is placed in front of the horizontal bottle on the cardboard, but is not glued in place. The piece of cardboard is pushed, along with the bottle and toy car on it. The toy car will behave as most would expect. When the cardboard is pushed to the right, the car will move to the left. And when the box is abruptly stopped while moving to the right, the car will move in the same direction- to the right. Students will observe that while the car and the bottle lie on the same piece of cardboard, they both behave differently to the same directional motion!

Possible Variables:

1. Size of the bottle.
2. Shape of the bottle.
3. Volume of liquid in the bottle.

4. The density of the liquid. Density can be manipulated by adding salt or sugar, or other liquids can be used.
5. Viscosity of the liquid.
6. Direction of movement of the cardboard- moving in a circular pattern, for example.
7. Placing an object in the bottle that replaces the air bubble. This could be a cork, piece of Styrofoam, etc. Different shapes of these objects could also be investigated.

Phenomenon Explained:

The toy car obeys Newton's first law of motion and behaves as your body would in a moving car. Known as the law of inertia, it states that and object in motion remains in motion with the same speed, and in the same direction, unless acted upon by an unbalanced force. When you are a passenger in a moving car, your body is moving at the same speed and direction as the car. When the car brakes, you continue at the same speed and direction in the car.

Events become more interesting when considering an object in the car that is less dense than its surroundings. An example would be the air bubble in our bottle. The bottle represents the car, while the air bubble represents a body in the car. But, when you sit in the car you are surrounded by air. The air bubble is surrounded by water. You are denser than the air around you. But, the air bubble is less dense than the water that surrounds it. These density differences result in the observed behavior of the air bubble.

When the bottle is pushed to the right, the denser water is pushed to the left. This results in the less dense air bubble being pushed in the opposite direction, to the right.

The density of an object will determine whether it will float in a fluid. Density is determined by calculating the mass for a given volume, expressed in the formula g/ml, g/cm^3, or g/cc. Density is independent of the sample size, since it represents the mass per ml of the sample. A larger volume does not necessarily equate to a higher mass. Fewer molecules packed into a given volume will result in a lower density than many more molecules packed into the same volume, which would increase the density. Objects with a density less than water will float, while those denser than water will sink. The density of water is 1.0g/ml.

When the bottle is abruptly stopped, its contents continue moving. Both the water and the bubble attempt to continue in the same direction as the bottle is moving- to the right. But as the denser water pushes to the right, it essentially pushes the air bubble to the left.

If the density of the liquid is altered by adding salt or sugar, discourse can include solutions, solubility, solutes, solvents, and concentration. Saltwater or sugar water is a mixture. One property of a mixture is that it is physically combined, not chemically, and it can be physically separated. For example, saltwater can be physically separated through the process of evaporation, or boiling the water away.

A solution is one in which a solute is dissolve in a solvent. The solute is the substance being dissolved and the solvent is the substance in which the solute is dissolved. Water is called the universal solvent because it is capable of dissolving more solutes than any other liquid. Solubility is the ability of a solute to dissolve in a solvent.

A concentrated solution is one which there are many dissolved particles of solute in the solvent. On the other hand, a dilute solution is one in which there are few dissolved particles of solute. A solution which contains all the dissolve particles it can possibly hold is called saturated.

Viscosity is defined as a fluid's resistance to flow. Think of it as the "thickness" of a fluid. Fluids such as honey, molasses, corn syrup, and engine oil are highly viscous. Students might choose to investigate the outcome when liquids of varying viscosities are employed.

Standards Alignment:

Next Generation Science Standards (NGSS, Lead States 2013)

Disciplinary Core Ideas in Physical Science

PS1: Matter and Its Interactions

PS1.A: Structure and Properties of Matter

PS1.B: Chemical Reactions

PS2: Motion and Stability: Forces and Interactions

PS2.A: Forces and Motion

PS2.B: Types of Interactions

Disciplinary Core Ideas in Earth and Space Science

ESS2: Earth's Systems

ESS2.C: The Roles of Water in Earth's Surface Processes

Naked Eggs

Concepts Illustrated: Osmosis, hypotonic, hypertonic, isotonic, semi-permeable membrane, selectively permeable membrane, concentration, diffusion, active transport, passive transport, osmotic pressure, solutions, solubility, solute, solvent, equilibrium, properties of water, physical changes, chemical changes, gaseous exchange in the lungs, osmosis and diffusion in the human body, fluid exchange in cells, biology of blood vessels, biological development of eggs.

This demonstration has a few variations, each strikingly amazing. Be sure to check out the Glowing Egg variation- a spectacular twist that fascinates students!

Paradox:

Students will be astounded to find that when placed in vinegar, an egg completely loses its shell and becomes a see-through egg with a rubbery membrane!

Equipment:

1. A beaker
2. White vinegar
3. A raw egg

The Lesson:

Show the egg to students. Be sure they understand that it is a raw egg. Place the egg into a beaker. Then show the bottle of vinegar. Explain that you are going to pour the vinegar into the beaker until the egg is completely covered. Then, the beaker will be set aside for one week. Ask students to predict what will happen to the egg after a one-week period. There will be a number of different ideas, but no one will predict what actually happens!

Pour the vinegar into the beaker until it completely covers the egg. Now place the beaker in a safe place where it will remain undisturbed. Keep in mind that you should check on the egg periodically. Do not remove it from the vinegar. Through the beaker, students will observe the shell slowly "vanishing" over time. They will see bubbles rising off the surface of the shell. Remnants of the shell will be observed floating on the surface of the vinegar. You may have to add vinegar as the week progresses to keep the egg submerged.

At the end of one week, carefully pour the vinegar out of the beaker, remove the egg, and pat it with a towel to dry it off. The shell should be completely dissolved. Note that if the shell is not completely dissolved from the egg, you can carefully remove it from the vinegar and wipe the remnants of the shell off the membrane beneath it. You will be left with a raw egg encased only by a transparent, "rubbery" membrane. The yolk should be visible within. When compared to a raw egg with a shell, this naked egg will be noticeably larger. That's because some vinegar is absorbed into it.

You can gently squeeze the naked egg without breaking it to show its new physical characteristics. The egg can even be dropped from a few inches above a table so that students can see it "bounce." The membrane will not break when the egg is dropped from a several inches off the table.

In dramatic fashion, if you shine a light from behind the egg, making the egg transparent. Students will be able to easily observe the yolk inside. Even the light from the "flashlight" app on a cell phone can be used to do this. You can also accomplish this by shining a laser light through the egg. If the laser light is colored, the transparent egg will display this color, but the dense yolk will still remain visible inside. Any color of light will cause the egg to "glow" in that color.

The demonstration can be rather dramatically ended by dropping the egg a couple of feet off the table. From this distance, the egg will break apart and splatter when it hits the table. The membrane will remain in one piece. Pick it up and show it to students. It has great strength and can be stretched to show its elasticity. Of course, this is an optional ending to the demonstration.

Lesson Variation:

Variation #1:

This variation can either be used as its own independent demonstration, as an extension to the original demonstration, or it can be a student-led investigation following the original demonstration.

Students become very excited with this variation. They often choose to investigate variations of this "glowing egg" demonstration. The demonstration is conducted the same as the original demonstration, with one exception. Prepare the vinegar by first carefully disassembling a highlighter and removing the ink tube inside. Now as students look on, put the tube into a large beaker and pour some vinegar onto it. Once the tube is completely covered, squeeze the tube with your fingers, releasing the ink inside. The ink will begin to mix with the vinegar in the beaker. Get as much of the ink out of the tube as possible. Discard the tube and pour additional vinegar into the beaker. This mixture will be poured over the egg. First, ask students to predict what will happen after this mixture is poured over the egg and allowed to sit for a couple of days. If you do not want to create this mixture while students observe, you can certainly prepare it in advance. It is important that students are aware that highlighter ink was added to the vinegar. Most students will predict that the highlighter ink will become "stuck" onto the shell of the egg and cause it to glow. No one will predict that the outer shell of the egg will dissolve and that the egg will absorb the ink, causing it to grow and glow! Pour the mixture over the egg and, after a couple of days, carefully remove it from the beaker. The egg will not appear to be "glowing." But, if you turn a black light onto the egg, it will begin to glow in the color of the highlighter used. Students can then be asked to predict whether the inside of the egg also glows. Drop the egg from a height above the table that causes it to break. Do this while the black light is aimed on it. When the egg splatters, students are excited to find that the entire egg does, in fact, glow!

If you have any available, Luminol can also be used in place of highlighter liquid.

Variation #2:

Intended as an extension to the original Demonstration Procedure, in this variation students discover and learn about osmosis.

Once students have observed the shell dissolved from the egg you can also choose to continue with a demonstration of osmosis, the movement of water across a permeable membrane. Place the naked egg into a beaker and pour enough corn syrup into the beaker to completely cover the egg. Karo Syrup works well. After about 24 hours the egg will be shriveled. This is caused by the different concentrations of water between the inside of the egg and the syrup that surrounds it. The egg white inside the membrane is about 90% water. The corn syrup surrounding it is about 25% water. This gradient different causes the water to move from an area of higher concentration to one of a lower concentration- osmosis. The water inside the egg moves out, through the membrane, and into the corn syrup.

The membrane, which actually consists of two membranes, surrounding the naked egg is selectively permeable, meaning it allows some molecules to pass through, but not others. It allows water to pass through, but larger molecules such as the sugar in corn syrup cannot pass through. So, if you now place this shriveled naked egg into a beaker of water, it will regain its plump appearance. Water will once again move from an area of high to low concentration, moving from the syrup outside the egg, to the inside of the egg. The naked egg will return to its original state.

Variation #3:

You could begin the original demonstration with two eggs in vinegar. When you have two naked eggs, you could place one in a beaker of corn syrup and the other in a beaker of water. Ask students to predict what will happen in each beaker. After a few days, the naked egg in the water will have grown in size, but the one in corn syrup will shrink. If you add food coloring to the liquids, you will be able to see the color enter the naked egg in water.

Possible Variables:

1. Different brands of vinegar.
2. Strength of vinegar, such as diluted or concentrated.
3. Different types of vinegar, such as balsamic, apple cider, etc.
4. A different acid in place of vinegar, such as lemon juice.
5. Temperature of the vinegar. It can either be cooled or warmed.
6. Submerging only half of the egg in vinegar.
7. Different brands of eggs.
8. Brown eggs instead of white.
9. Food coloring added to the vinegar. Students can study whether the membrane absorbs the food coloring by ultimately breaking the egg, as in the demonstration, and inspecting the membrane.
10. Using a dyed egg. What happens to the dye absorbed into the shell?
11. Organic vs free-range eggs.
12. Using a hardboiled egg.
13. Temperature of the egg. For example, it can be chilled in the refrigerator or freezer.

14. Different colors of highlighter ink.
15. Using other liquids or solutions with varying densities and viscosities. These could include maple syrup (which will cause the egg to shrink), Kool-Aid (this will cause the egg to grow in size), cooking oil, honey, salt water, sugar water, etc.
16. Placing one or more small holes in the eggshell using a pin.
17. Investigations might question the density of liquid that most effectively passes through the membrane and enters the egg. Students would have to determine the method of measurement used to answer the question.

Phenomenon Explained:

A solution is one in which a solute is dissolve in a solvent. The solute is the substance being dissolved and the solvent is the substance in which the solute is dissolved. Water is called the universal solvent because it is capable of dissolving more solutes than any other liquid. Solubility is the ability of a solute to dissolve in a solvent.

A concentrated solution is one which there are many dissolved particles of solute in the solvent. On the other hand, a dilute solution is one in which there are few dissolved particles of solute. A solution which contains all the dissolve particles it can possibly hold is called saturated.

Osmosis refers to the process in which the molecules of a solvent, typically water, pass through a semipermeable membrane until the concentration of solutes in the solvent is equal on both sides of the membrane. In osmosis, the water flows in the direction of lower to higher solute concentration. When the concentration of solutes is at equilibrium, or equal on both sides of the membrane, the condition is called *isotonic*.

When the concentration of solutes is lower outside a cell and higher inside, it is known as *hypotonic*. In this condition, more water will flow into the cell than out. The cell will swell in size. Conversely, when the concentration of solutes is higher outside a cell and lower inside, it is called *hypertonic*. In this condition, water will flow out of the cell. The cell will shrivel.

Osmosis is an example of diffusion, occurring when the motion produced by the kinetic energy of the molecules causes them to distribute evenly within a space. Diffusion does not require a semipermeable membrane. A semipermeable membrane is a type of biological membrane that allows certain molecules to pass through by diffusion, but not others. It is generally permeable to the solvent, but not the larger solute molecules. The rate of osmosis is dependent on concentration, temperature, electrical charge of the solute, electric potential of the membrane, the permeability of the membrane, and osmotic pressure.

Osmotic pressure refers to the amount of pressure necessary to stop the flow of liquid across the membrane. The concentrations of the solutions on either side of the membrane generally determines the osmotic pressure. An isotonic solution has the same osmotic pressure on either side of the membrane. Osmotic pressure is a critical component of transport in living organisms.

Diffusion and osmosis are both forms of *passive transport*, meaning no energy is required. But, in diffusion both solvent and solute particles are free to move. Osmosis is a special type of diffusion in which only the solvent moves. *Active transport* involves the movement of molecules from areas of lower to higher concentration. The process requires chemical energy because the movement is against the concentration gradient. This is a critical function of cells.

Osmosis and diffusion are processes that our bodies consistently undergo. To live, we depend on the ability of our cells to maintain certain concentrations of solutes. Osmosis and diffusion occurs in our lungs, kidneys, intestines, and even our skin.

The vinegar reacts with the egg shell, made of calcium carbonate. The vinegar breaks the calcium carbonate down. The bubbles observed are one of the visible products of the reaction. They are filled with carbon dioxide. Vinegar is about 5% acetic acid and 95% water. Some of the vinegar does enter the egg through the process of osmosis. This causes the naked egg to be larger than a raw egg with a shell. Once the shell has dissolved, the underlying "rubbery" membrane becomes its outermost layer. This membrane actually consists of two membranes, called the inner and outer membrane. These membranes serve to protect the contents of the egg from bacteria. They also limit the volume of liquid content that leaves the egg. These membranes are composed, in part, from keratin, a protein also found in human hair. This protein adds to the strength of the membrane, which is why it can be gently squeezed without breaking.

When placed in corn syrup, the concentration of water inside the egg is greater than that outside. Water moves out of the egg and it shrinks. However, when placed in water, the concentration gradient is reversed. There is more water outside the egg, than inside. As a result, water moves into the egg and it swells in size.

Standards Alignment:

Next Generation Science Standards (NGSS, Lead States 2013)

Disciplinary Core Ideas in Physical Science

PS1: Matter and Its Interactions

PS1.A: Structure and Properties of Matter

PS1.B: Chemical Reactions

PS2: Motion and Stability: Forces and Interactions

PS2.A: Forces and Motion

PS2.B: Types of Interactions

PS3: Energy

PS3.D: Energy in Chemical Processes and Everyday Life

PS4: Waves and Their Applications in Technologies for Information Transfer

PS4.B: Electromagnetic Radiation

Disciplinary Core Ideas in Life Science

LS1: From Molecules to Organisms: Structures and Processes

LS1.A: Structure and Function

LS1.B: Growth and Development of Organisms

LS1.C: Organization for Matter and Energy Flow in Organisms

LS2: Ecosystems: Interactions, Energy, and Dynamics

LS2.A: Interdependent Relationships in Ecosystems

Disciplinary Core Ideas in Earth and Space Science

ESS2: Earth's Systems

ESS2.C: The Roles of Water in Earth's Surface Processes

Newton's Cradle

<u>Concepts Illustrated:</u> Potential energy, kinetic energy, law of conservation of momentum, law of conservation of energy, transfer of energy, mechanical energy, inelastic collisions, friction, magnetism, momentum, velocity, mass, volume, density, elements and compounds.

This very well-known demonstration is incredibly effective at the elementary level.

<u>Paradox:</u>

Whatever number of balls is swung on one end of the Newton's Cradle will move the same number of balls on the opposite end!

<u>Equipment:</u>

1. Newton's Cradle.

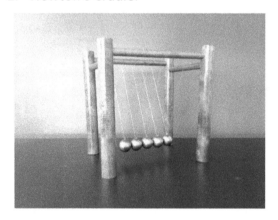 

<u>The Lesson:</u>

This lesson is best suited for elementary level students.

Display the Newton's Cradle and explain that each of the balls can be swung individually. Tell students that you will lift and release one ball from the end of the unit. Then you will lift and release two balls on one end simultaneously. Finally, you will lift and release three balls simultaneously on one end. You simply would like them to predict what will happen when you perform each of these actions. Then, execute these actions and allow students to observe the reactions that occur.

Students are entranced by this demonstration. The variables that can be investigated produce truly intriguing outcomes. Among them are using five balls and lifting three to drop and impact the other two. Another exciting effect is produced when using three balls and lifting the outer two, releasing them simultaneously to hit the center ball at the same time. And yet another particularly intriguing effect can be seen when removing the center ball in a sequence of five, leaving two sets of two balls with a space between them. Lift the outer two balls together and release them simultaneously to produce an outcome that thrills students!

Lesson Variation:

This demonstration could also be performed by rolling balls on a simple curved track. It can be made by slightly bending and curving a small piece of metal track. But it can also be made of plastic tubing that can easily be shaped into the desired curve, and cut to any length. Tubing like this is readily available at stores such as Home Depot or Lowes. You'll find a picture of this tubing below. Place 3-5 balls on the track, or in the tube. Roll another ball into these and observe that one ball on the end is ejected. As in a traditional Newton's Cradle, roll two balls to show that two will move on the opposite end. Do the same with three balls. Friction does come into play here.

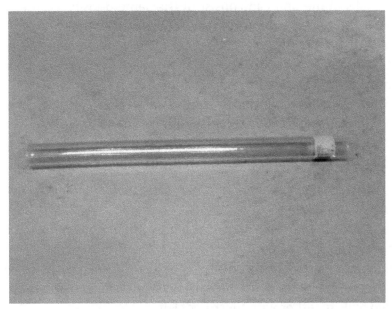

The same idea can be done on a flat track with a ramp on one end. The colliding ball is released from its position on the ramp, rolling down to the flat track. The height of this ramp can also be adjusted as a variable to investigate. Once again, friction will come into play in this version.

The concept can also be illustrated using a plastic ruler and some marbles. Place the marbles in the groove of the ruler. They should all be touching. Now place one marble at the end of the ruler in the groove and roll it towards the row of marbles. You can also roll two or three marbles down the groove as well. It would also be easy to separate the row of marbles from one another to investigate the outcome when the sequence of marbles is not touching.

Finally, two magnets can be hung from the Newton's Cradle to show that momentum is conserved even in the absence of physical contact. Hang the magnets so that the two like poles face each other with about 1cm separation between them. Lift and release one magnet. It will stop prior to hitting the other magnet, which will repel and be pushed away with the same speed as the magnet dropped. The demonstration can then be extended using a sequence of magnets to observe the outcome of swinging two at once.

Possible Variables:

1. Balls made of varied materials, such as aluminum, copper, wood, plastic, lead, etc.
2. Each of the balls in the unit can be made of the same material, or they can be mixed. For example, in a Newton's Cradle of 4 balls, 3 balls can be made of one material such as steel, while the fourth ball is made of a different material such as aluminum. Additionally, this "odd" ball could be placed within different sequential positions within the group. So, it could be on the end, second from the end, or third from the swinging end.
3. Balls of varying densities. This can be done by either using solid balls made from different substances with different densities, or the balls can be filled with varied materials, such as sand, water, corn syrup, etc.
4. Each of the balls in the unit can consist of the same density, or they can be mixed. For example, in a Newton's Cradle of 4 balls, 3 balls can consist of one density while the fourth ball consists of an entirely different density. Additionally, this "odd" ball could be placed within different sequential positions within the group. So, it could be on the end, second from the end, or third from the swinging end.
5. Removing one of balls in the middle of the sequence. This could be accomplished by simply lifting individual balls out of the sequence.
6. Adjusting the space or distance between balls. This could involve modifying the distance between only two of the balls, or between every ball.
7. Using balls made of the same material that sequentially increase in diameter along the hanging row.
8. Using balls made of the same material whose diameters differ, and so their masses differ, but are in no specific pattern.
9. Using magnetic spheres. This could involve an entire row of magnetic spheres, or replacing just one, or more, of the balls in the sequence with one that is magnetic.
10. Securing two balls together with Velcro or clay.

Phenomenon Explained:

The Newton's Cradle is a classic, elegant demonstration of the law of conservation of momentum and the law of conservation of energy, among the most fundamental laws of physics and mechanics.

Mechanical energy is defined as the energy an object possesses due to its motion or position. There are two forms of mechanical energy, potential and kinetic. Potential energy is stored energy, while kinetic is the energy of motion. The law of conservation of energy states that energy can never be created or destroyed, although it can be converted from one form to another. That is exactly what happens in this demonstration. The energy involved is both potential and kinetic.

Let's assume we have five balls in our Newton's Cradle. When they are all at rest they have zero potential energy because gravity cannot cause it to move down any further from its current position. They also have zero kinetic energy because they are not in motion. If we lift one of the balls on the end, it continues to have zero kinetic energy, as long as it is held in place. But, it now has greater potential energy because gravity can cause it to fall further than its current position.

Once the ball is released, this potential energy is converted into kinetic energy while in motion. Once the ball has reached the lowest point of its swing, its potential energy is now zero. But, its kinetic energy is greater. Don't forget that energy cannot be destroyed. This means that the ball's maximum potential energy is now equal to its maximum kinetic energy. When this ball hits the next ball in the sequence, it is abruptly stopped, causing both its potential and kinetic energy to be zero once again. All the energy that this ball had is not transferred into the next ball in the sequence, the one that it hits. This ball compresses a bit, due to the impact. But it immediately hits the third ball, which also compresses due to the impact. This impact transfers energy from the second to the third ball. The same happens as this ball hits the fourth, and the fourth hits the fifth. Because energy is conserved throughout the process, the fifth ball has the same amount of kinetic energy as the first ball. As a result, the fifth ball swings out since it has no other ball in its path. When this ball reaches its maximum height in the swing, gravity acts to pull the ball downward and the cycle continues.

Momentum plays a role in the Newton's Cradle. Momentum refers to a quantity of motion that an object has. The momentum of a moving object can be calculated using the following formula:

$$momentum = mass \times velocity$$

The momentum of any moving object is dependent upon its mass and velocity. The terms speed and velocity are oftentimes mistakenly used interchangeably. Whereas speed refers to the measure of how fast an object moves, velocity measures how fast an object arrives at a certain point. They are different.

The law of conservation of momentum states that when a collision occurs between two objects in an isolated system, the total momentum of the two before the collision must equal the total after. Any momentum "lost" by one object must be equal to the momentum gained by the other.

In this demonstration, momentum and energy are transferred in a series of collisions. The momentum of the first ball dropped carries the energy through each of the balls in the sequence in the same direction that the first ball traveled. If all the balls are identical in mass and size, however, many balls are swung into the hanging row will move the same number of balls on the opposite end. The momentum and energy are transferred from one ball to the next in each collision.

Eventually, friction will play a role in slowing and stopping the movement of the balls. Friction is described as the force occurring at the surface of an object when another object moves against it. Believed to result from the electromagnetic attraction between the particles of the two substances, friction acts to resist the movement of one object relative to the other. Friction can occur between the molecules of any phase of matter. The amount of friction produced between two objects depends on the substance the objects are made of. There are two types of friction. Static friction occurs between the surfaces of two objects that are not moving, while kinetic friction occurs between objects in motion.

In the Newton's Cradle, friction comes from air resistance as well as from the balls. When one ball collides with another, friction between these two balls converts some of the kinetic energy into heat, while some kinetic energy is transferred to the surrounding air in the form of vibrations that we hear- the clicking noise made when one ball hits another. The system represents inelastic collisions, in which the kinetic energy after the collision is less than before it.

Using balls of different densities will also change the way the energy is transferred through them. The density of an object will determine whether it will float in a fluid. Density is determined by calculating the mass for a given volume, expressed in the formula g/ml, g/cm^3, or g/cc. Density is independent of the sample size, since it represents the mass per ml of the sample. A larger volume does not necessarily equate to a higher mass. Fewer molecules packed into a given volume will result in a lower density than many more molecules packed into the same volume, which would increase the density.

When using a ball that is has less mass than the others in the system, a complete transfer of momentum and energy does not transfer to the next ball. The outcome will not be the same as when using identical balls.

Standards Alignment:

Next Generation Science Standards (NGSS, Lead States 2013)

Disciplinary Core Ideas in Physical Science

PS1: Matter and Its Interactions

PS1.A: Structure and Properties of Matter

PS2: Motion and Stability: Forces and Interactions

PS2.A: Forces and Motion

PS2.B: Types of Interactions

PS3: Energy

PS3.A: Definitions of Energy

PS3.B: Conservation of Energy and Energy Transfer

PS3.C: Relationship Between Energy and Forces

PS4: Waves and Their Applications in Technologies for Information Transfer

PS4.A: Wave Properties

Newton's Nightmare

Concepts Illustrated: Magnetism, properties of metals, Lenz's law, eddy currents, mass, volume, density, gravity, gravitational acceleration, momentum, velocity, speed, physical properties of matter, elements and compounds.

Paradox:

A magnet is placed next to a copper tube to show there is no visible effect. The copper tube is not drawn to the magnet. As a result, students expect that when the magnet is dropped into the center of the upright tube, it will fall straight through- uninterrupted. Holes in the side of the tube show the magnet as it is dropped in. Students will be excited and stunned to discover the outcome. When the magnet is dropped into the tube, it can be seen hovering and slowly moving down the length of the tube, floating all the way down in a very eerie manner! This, even though there was no magnetic reaction or affect observed between the copper and the magnet. Eventually, the magnet falls from the bottom of the tube. This is an astonishing demonstration!

Equipment:

Additional details regarding equipment are provided in the *Preparation* section.

1. A hollow copper or aluminum tube.
2. A magnet, small enough to fit inside the tube. Spherical magnets are most effective.
3. A wooden sphere, small enough to fit inside the tube.
4. A plastic sphere, small enough to fit inside the tube.
5. A watch or stopwatch.

Preparation:

Ideally, the copper, plastic and wooden objects used to drop into the tube should be spheres of differing diameters. The most fruitful demonstration will occur when the magnet has the largest diameter of the spheres. However, these are not necessary conditions. They do not affect the success of the demonstration. But they do affect student perception and, more importantly, surprise impact from the outcome. The most valuable presentation of this phenomena occurs when students are focusing on the size of the objects dropped into the tube rather than the substance they are made of. This will become clearer in the Demonstration Procedure section.

Although one of the spherical objects must be a magnet, the others do not have to be made of wood and plastic. Any non-magnetic substance will work. For example, they could be aluminum, tin, glass, or lead. But the three spheres should be made of three different substances.

Although we will refer to a tube made of copper in the *Lesson Procedure*, it can also be made of aluminum. This is also a non-magnetic metal that interacts with the magnet in a similar way as copper. It is not necessary for this tube to have holes in its side, but it certainly makes the demonstration more dramatic by allowing the spheres to be visible through their entire path. Another alternative is to fasten a magnetic strip along the length of the tube. This actually makes the path of the magnet visible as it travels down the tube.

Be sure to use caution when working with Neodymium magnets. A Neodymium magnet is a rare earth magnet. Larger Neodymium magnets are quite powerful. If you are handling two at once, they can pinch your fingers if you are not careful. If students do handle them, smaller Neodymium magnets are safer and will still produce the desired effects. When students are performing their investigations, they should be instructed to only handle one magnet at a time. There really is no need to handle more than one, but caution cannot be overstated. As long as students are handling one magnet in their investigation, there really is not too much need for concern.

<u>The Lesson:</u>

Begin by asking students if they believe that copper, plastic, or wood is magnetic. Ask them to make a prediction for each. Once they have done so, introduce a sphere of each substance, as well as a spherical magnet. First, show that the magnet will attract metal by holding it next to a metallic object that it will be attracted to. Now, one at a time, hold the magnet next to each sphere. Students will not observe any attraction. Each of the spheres can be placed next to one another to show that none of them are actually attracted to one another.

Next, introduce the copper tube and show it to be hollow. Point out the holes in the side of the tube. Explain that you will drop each sphere into the tube, one at a time. Hold the tube upright as you explain, to show exactly how you will execute the demonstration. Ask students to predict how long each sphere will take to exit the bottom of the tube once it has been dropped in. Show the stopwatch and explain that the descent will be timed. They should make a prediction for each sphere. Before they predict, be sure to point out two things. The first is that the magnet is not attracted to the copper tube. Place the magnet on the side of the copper tube to confirm that there is no attraction. Secondly, be sure that students have clearly seen and compared the different diameters of each sphere. This is what students will focus on. They have already seen that magnetic forces do not exist between the substances involved. This will lead them to base their predictions on the different diameters, and the different masses of each sphere. Most will predict the largest sphere to exit the tube more quickly than the others. As previously discussed, this should be the magnet.

Once students have each made three predictions, drop the spheres into the tube, saving the magnet for last. Ask a student to time the descent of each sphere. Be sure to hold the tube so that the holes face students, allowing them to see the sphere as it travels down the tube. As each of the first two spheres are dropped into the tube, students will be comparing their predictions to the observed time. Since they should not be considering magnetic force, most students will predict the magnetic sphere to exit most quickly. Because it has the largest diameter of the spheres, it will also be perceived to have the largest mass. When you drop this sphere into the tube, students will think you are performing a magic trick! This sphere will not only take a considerably longer period of time to exit the tube, its eerily slow movement as it floats down the tube will elicit gasps!

<u>Possible Variables:</u>

1. The length of the tube.
2. The wall thickness of the tube.
3. The substance that the tube is made of, such as copper, aluminum, brass, tin, PVC, etc.
4. The shape of the magnet, such as spherical, cylindrical, cube, and rod shaped.
5. The size of the magnet. This could involve magnets of the same size and magnetic strength and magnets of the same size, but different magnetic strengths. This could also involve "attaching" more than one magnet together.
6. They type of magnet, such as Neodymium, standard, or cow magnet.

<u>Phenomenon Explained:</u>

Copper is magnetic. However, it is so weakly magnetic that it cannot readily be observed in normal situations or using common magnets that we might be accustomed to in our everyday lives. You can confirm this by trying to pick up, or move, a penny with a magnet.

However, although copper is not readily observed to be magnetic, it does interact with magnets in rather fascinating ways. The principle of Lenz's law is at work behind the bizarre interaction observed in this demonstration. The law states that an electric current induced by a force such as a changing magnetic field will create a counterforce that opposes the force inducing it. Essentially, this means that the magnet is weakly repelled by the copper tube. As seen in this demonstration, the effects can almost seem to be magical.

When the magnet is placed next to copper, it creates an eddy current. An eddy current is an electrical current that is induced by an alternating magnetic field. When a current is induced in a conductor, such as the tube used in our demonstration, the current flows in small circles. The currents resemble the swirling water currents observed in streams, known as eddies. The current is strongest at the surface, only able to penetrate a very short distance into the substance inducing it.

The eddy current essentially has a magnetic field that is in the opposite direction as the field around the magnet. As a result, the eddy current essentially repels the magnet as it travels down the tube. It is this repulsion that slows the movement of the magnet. Looking down into the tube, you will see the magnet floating, without hitting or contacting the walls of the tube.

The thickness of the tube walls, the lengths of the tubes, and the substance the tubes are made of will affect the rate at which the magnet falls through. Thicker, longer tubes will increase the falling time.

The momentum of the magnet can also be studied. Momentum refers to a quantity of motion that an object has. The momentum of a moving object can be calculated using the following formula:

$$momentum = mass \times velocity$$

The momentum of any moving object is dependent upon its mass and velocity. The terms speed and velocity are oftentimes mistakenly used interchangeably. Whereas speed refers to the measure of how fast an object moves, velocity measures how fast an object arrives at a certain point. They are different. Speed is defined as the rate of time that an object travels a distance. Velocity is defined as the rate of change in displacement with respect to time. The formula for speed is:

$$\frac{\text{distance traveled}}{\text{time of travel}}$$

While the formula for velocity is:

$$\frac{\text{displacement}}{\text{time}}$$

Consider a person walking two steps forward and two steps back, returning to the original starting position. Their speed of each step can be measured. But their velocity would be measured as zero.

Standards Alignment:

Next Generation Science Standards (NGSS, Lead States 2013)

Disciplinary Core Ideas in Physical Science

PS2: Motion and Stability: Forces and Interactions

PS2.B: Types of Interactions

PS3: Energy

PS3.A: Definitions of Energy

PS3.C: Relationship Between Energy and Forces

Paper Ball Puzzler

<u>Concepts Illustrated:</u> Surface tension, density, cohesion, properties of water, solutions, solubility, solutes, solvents, concentration, saturated solutions, process of dissolving, properties of mixtures, properties of surfactants, the respiratory system of fish, the human respiratory system.

This demonstration exhibits an unexpected outcome that excites elementary level students. It is constructed in a way for students to question several attributes that might cause the surprising results.

<u>Paradox:</u>

When one paper ball is dropped into a beaker of water and another into a beaker of soapy water, they behave quite differently. One floats, while the other sinks!

<u>Equipment:</u>

1. Two differently sized beakers.
2. Water.
3. Liquid dish soap.
4. Food coloring.
5. Differently colored paper.

<u>The Lesson:</u>

Add water to the two beakers. The volumes of water should be strikingly different between them. The level of water should be distinctly higher than the other. Be sure to point this out. To the beaker with a higher water level, add about 25-30ml of liquid dish soap. Stir this solution gently, to avoid creating bubbles. Add food coloring to each beaker. To the beaker with dish soap, add a color that most closely matches the color of the soap. For example, if you used blue dish soap, add blue food coloring. If you used yellow dish soap, add yellow food coloring. The food coloring added to the other beaker should sharply contrast the first. Now show two differently colored paper squares. Although they are both the same type of paper, one is clearly larger than the other. Again, be sure to point this out. The color of the larger paper square should closely match that of the dish soap/ food coloring solution. For example, if that solution is blue, use blue paper. The color of the smaller piece of paper should contrast the food coloring in the beaker of plain water. For example, if that beaker has red food coloring, use yellow paper. Now crumple the paper squares, so that they are as close to the same size as possible. Now explain that you are simply going to drop one into each beaker. Be sure to show which colored paper ball will go into each beaker. Ask students to predict what will happen. Once the predictions have been made, drop the paper balls into their appropriate beakers. Students will be greatly surprised to find that the paper ball in plain water remains floating, while the paper ball in the dish soap solution will unravel slightly and sink!

Due to the design of the demonstration, students will attribute various causes to the behavior of the two paper balls. There will be some who will attribute the sinking behavior to the dish soap. But some will think that because its color matched the components of the dish soap solution, that paper ball sank. Other students will think the paper ball sank because it was placed in a low level of water or that it was in a smaller beaker. And there will be some students who attribute the sinking behavior to the larger size of that piece of paper. Each of these ideas lead to some very fruitful investigations.

Possible Variables:

1. The amount of soap in the beaker.
2. The brand of soap used.
3. The type of paper.
4. The temperature of the water. It can be warmed or chilled.
5. Adding food coloring to the water.
6. The color of the paper.
7. The size of the paper.
8. Paper of different shapes that are not crumpled into balls.
9. The volume of water.
10. Density of the water. Density can be manipulated by adding salt or sugar to the water.

Phenomenon Explained:

Cohesion refers to the attraction of like molecules towards one another. Water molecules have a very strong cohesive attraction for one another. Those molecules at the surface do not have any water molecules above them. Thus, they are strongly attracted to those water molecules below. The strong attraction to the molecules around and underneath creates surface tension, a "flexible skin" across the surface of the water. Cohesion and surface tension are two contributing factors that cause one of the paper balls to float.

Soap is a surfactant, a compound that acts to lower the surface tension of water. It does this by weakening the attractive forces between the water molecules. With the addition of soap, there is no longer enough surface tension to keep the paper ball suspended, and it sinks.

Another concept at play here is density. The density of an object will determine whether it will float in a fluid. Density is determined by calculating the mass for a given volume, expressed in the formula g/ml, g/cm^3, or g/cc. Density is independent of the sample size, since it represents the mass per ml of the sample. A larger volume does not necessarily equate to a higher mass. Fewer molecules packed into a given volume will result in a lower density than many more molecules packed into the same volume, which would increase the density. Objects with a density less than water will float, while those denser than water will sink. The density of water is $1.0 g/ml$.

We have already learned that the paper ball will sink when the surface tension of the water is lowered. As it sinks, the surface area of the paper contacts more water. The paper is porous and can absorb water. As more water contacts the paper, more is absorbed. This causes the density of the paper to rise. Eventually it will become denser than the solution it sits in, and it will sink.

If the density of the liquid is altered by adding salt or sugar, discourse can include solutions, solubility, solutes, solvents, and concentration. Saltwater or sugar water is a mixture. One property of a mixture is that it is physically combined, not chemically, and it can be physically separated. For example, saltwater can be physically separated through the process of evaporation, or boiling the water away.

A solution is one in which a solute is dissolve in a solvent. The solute is the substance being dissolved and the solvent is the substance in which the solute is dissolved. Water is called the universal solvent because it is capable of dissolving more solutes than any other liquid. Solubility is the ability of a solute to dissolve in a solvent.

A concentrated solution is one which there are many dissolved particles of solute in the solvent. On the other hand, a dilute solution is one in which there are few dissolved particles of solute. A solution which contains all the dissolve particles it can possibly hold is called saturated.

The addition of soap as a variable broadly expands the scope of topics covered in class discourse. Soap is a surfactant. Surfactant plays a critical role in our bodies. There is a thin layer of water that lines human lungs. This water is necessary for the gas exchange of carbon dioxide and oxygen to occur. These gases require a wet layer or surface for the exchange to take place. In fish, this exchange takes place in their gills. Since they are on the outside of the fish, gills have direct contact with water. Our lungs, on the other hand, are best able to be kept wet inside of our bodies. However, due to the properties of water, surface tension arises that can interfere with the expansion of our lungs as we breathe. Surfactant acts to reduce surface tension. This prevents alveoli, small air sacs in the lungs, from collapsing when we exhale. The most efficient oxygen-carbon dioxide exchange occurs in our lungs with the greatest alveoli surface area. By preventing the collapse of alveoli, surfactant helps to maximize the surface area available for the exchange of gases.

Standards Alignment:

Next Generation Science Standards (NGSS, Lead States 2013)

Disciplinary Core Ideas in Physical Science

PS1: Matter and Its Interactions

PS1.A: Structure and Properties of Matter

PS1.B: Chemical Reactions

PS2: Motion and Stability: Forces and Interactions

PS2.B: Types of Interactions

Disciplinary Core Ideas in Life Science

LS1: From Molecules to Organisms: Structures and Processes

LS1.A: Structure and Function

Disciplinary Core Ideas in Earth and Space Science

ESS2: Earth's Systems

ESS2.C: The Roles of Water in Earth's Surface Processes

Pendulum Wave

Concepts Illustrated: Oscillation, pendula waves, amplitude, phase, mechanical energy, kinetic energy, potential energy, mass, volume.

Paradox:

A set of pendula with varying lengths, hanging in consecutive series, exhibits amazing and startling motion that simply stuns students, transitioning from snake-like movements to swinging in unison!

Equipment:

1. A device consisting of consecutive pendula in series, with bobs hanging at incrementally decreasing lengths. The device can be purchased at science supply stores, or easily constructed.
2. A release board. This can simply be a length of sturdy cardboard.

The Lesson:

The pendulum device is shown to students, who should understand that the spheres, or bobs, can each swing individually. Show the release board and demonstrate how it is used without actually releasing the pendulum. Push all the bobs backwards simultaneously with the release board. Holding the bobs in this raised position and explain that you plan to release the bobs simultaneously by quickly withdrawing the release board. Impress the idea that every bob will be raised to the same height, and all will be released at the exact same time. Ask students to predict how the pendulum will behave when the release board is removed. Now slowly lower the release board so that the bobs return to their original resting position without swinging, while students record their predictions. Once those predictions have been made, push the bobs backwards with the release board as explained earlier. Then, quickly withdraw the release board. None of your students will predict the mesmerizing behavior that follows, as the pendula exhibits a wide range of completely unexpected and fascinating waves and oscillations.

The pendula can be observed facing the front of the device or facing the end of it. Each should be explored. First, demonstrate the behavior of the pendula from the front. Then, spin the device so that its end faces your students and demonstrate the action once again. Your students will be astounded when observing from the front of the unit. But, even after observing the action from the front, expect them to be completely stunned when they observe the same hypnotic action from the end of the device!

<u>Lesson Variation:</u>

<u>Variation #1:</u>

Present this demonstration by setting the pendulum wave on a standard overhead projector for an incredibly visual demonstration.

<u>Variation #2:</u>

The system can be constructed using empty plastic soda bottles, suspended by strings tied around the bottom of each cap. The soda bottle acts as the bob. This setup allows for the mass of each bottle, or bob, to be manipulated by filling the bottles with water to desired volumes. Student investigations can include the density of the bobs by filling the bottles with liquids of varying densities.

<u>Possible Variables:</u>

1. Changing the mass of the bobs. This can involve two different investigations. The first would involve changing all of the bobs to be the same new mass. Students would study the effect, if any, on bobs that all have greater mass or less mass. The second investigation would involve changing individual bobs for those that have either greater or less mass. Any number of bobs, and in any pattern or sequence, can be changed.
2. Using bobs made of different materials, such as cork, wood, aluminum, brass, copper, tin, etc. Hex nuts can also be used. This would allow investigation of various sizes. This could be extended to all the same size, but different from those used in the demonstration, or assorted sizes used at one time on the device. Hex nuts can also be used as bobs. This would be a very easy system to set up that would also allow for the investigation of nuts of assorted sizes and masses.
3. Bobs could be filled with liquid. This would allow bobs to be partially filled. All of the bobs could be partially filled with liquid, or any number of bobs, in any pattern or sequence. Different liquids with different densities could also be investigated. Liquid could be added to ping-pong balls with holes cut in their tops.
4. Density of the bobs. This could be investigated using bobs of various substances, but could also be investigated using soda bottles, as explained in Lesson Variation #2. Density could be easily manipulated by adding salt or sugar to the water in the bottles. Investigations could include changing the density of one bob, several, or all of them.
5. Adjusting the length of the pendula strings.
6. Removing one of the bobs from the sequence.

<u>Phenomenon Explained:</u>

The pendula system employed in this demonstration produces a dynamic transverse wave that repeatedly transitions from chaos to uniformity.

Mechanical energy is defined as the energy an object possesses due to its motion or position. There are two forms of mechanical energy, potential and kinetic. Potential energy is stored energy, while kinetic is the energy of motion. The energy involved is both potential and kinetic.

When the pendula are initially pulled back and held in place, at the beginning of the demonstration, they have potential energy. When released and set into motion, they begin to swing or oscillate. The force of gravity works on the pendula as they swing down, converting the potential energy to kinetic. The pendula alternate between potential energy, at rest, to kinetic energy, in motion.

The system consists of a series of pendula, each with successively shorter lengths. Because of these differences in length, each successively shorter pendulum executes an additional oscillation per period. Their phases, relative to one another, continuously change due to their sequentially increasing periods of oscillation. It's this that produces the effect of a wave when they are released. As the wavelength diminishes, the pendula appear quite chaotic. But eventually, the pendula reach phase with one another due to their sequential lengths along the series, swinging in unison once again. The pattern then repeats.

The amplitude can be described as the maximum displacement of points on a wave. Eventually, the energy from the pendula system dissipates through friction encountered in air resistance, amplitude diminishes, and they will stop swinging.

Students could choose to investigate the density of the bobs. Density is determined by calculating the mass for a given volume, expressed in the formula g/ml, g/cm^3, or g/cc. Density is independent of the sample size, since it represents the mass per ml of the sample. A larger volume does not necessarily equate to a higher mass. Fewer molecules packed into a given volume will result in a lower density than many more molecules packed into the same volume, which would increase the density.

Standards Alignment:

Next Generation Science Standards (NGSS, Lead States 2013)

Disciplinary Core Ideas in Physical Science

PS1: Matter and Its Interactions

PS1.A: Structure and Properties of Matter

PS2: Motion and Stability: Forces and Interactions

PS2.A: Forces and Motion

PS3: Energy

PS3.A: Definitions of Energy

PS3.B: Conservation of Energy and Energy Transfer

PS3.C: Relationship Between Energy and Forces

PS4: Waves and Their Applications in Technologies for Information Transfer

PS4.A: Wave Properties

Penny Plunge

<u>Concepts Illustrated:</u> Properties of water, cohesion, surface tension, viscosity, meniscus, volume, density, viscosity, solutions, solubility, solutes, solvents, concentration, saturated solutions, process of dissolving, properties of mixtures, properties of surfactants, the respiratory system of fish, the human respiratory system.

This demonstration is especially effective for elementary level students.

<u>Paradox:</u>

Students will be astounded to discover the number of pennies that can be added to a glass full of water without the water spilling over the edge! The number far exceeds all expectations!

<u>Equipment:</u>

1. A glass or plastic cup. A paper or Styrofoam cup may also be used. A transparent cup is not necessary, but is more visually appealing.
2. Water.
3. Pennies. Paperclips can be substituted.

<u>Preparation:</u>

Only a few of the pennies should be visible to students at the start of the demonstration. If students saw a large pile of pennies, they may begin to suspect the number that will actually go into the water without spilling.

<u>The Lesson:</u>

Display the cup and fill it to the brim with water. The level of water should be even with the top of the cup. Make sure that students understand this objective. It should be an exciting part of the demonstration, becoming increasingly suspenseful as the water approaches the rim of the cup. Now show only a few of the pennies. Explain that you are going to carefully begin adding pennies into the water. Students are asked to simply predict how many pennies will be added to the water before it begins to spill over the rim of the cup.

Once their predictions have been made, and shared with the class, begin to slowly and carefully add pennies, one by one. Each penny should develop a suspenseful moment. Do not drop the pennies from a distance above the water. Avoid splashing water by carefully inserting the edge of each penny into the water before releasing it. Be sure that your fingers do not dip into the water when placing the penny in. To add drama, the class can count aloud with you as each penny is added.

Students will be quite amazed to find how many pennies or paperclips can be added to the cup before any water spills out. Even more startling than the number of pennies added are the visual observations made of the water. It should be imperative that students are able to deliberately look closely and carefully at the cup from the side. They will observe a large bubble, or dome, above the rim of the cup. The water level will actually rise rather high above the rim of the cup without overflowing!

Possible Variables:

1. Adding soap to the water.
2. Dipping the pennies into soap before placing them into plain water.
3. Shape of cup or container that pennies are dropped into.
4. Volume of water used.
5. Type of cup used, such as glass, plastic, paper, or Styrofoam.
6. The type and size of coins used, such as dimes, nickels, and quarters.
7. Using objects that are shaped differently than coins, such as marbles, hex nuts, etc.
8. Using liquids of different densities and viscosities.
9. The temperature of the water. It can be heated or chilled.

Phenomenon Explained:

Cohesion is the attraction of like molecules to one another. Water molecules have a very strong cohesive attraction for one another. There are powerful cohesive forces between the molecules in the glass of water used in this demonstration. The water molecules at the surface do not have any water molecules above them. As a result, they are strongly attracted to those neighboring water molecules at their sides and to those below, which draws them in towards the liquid. This strong attraction to the molecules around and underneath creates what is known as surface tension. Adhesion describes the force that attracts different molecules to one another. In our demonstration, water molecules are attracted to the rim at the top edge of the glass. These two forces act to prevent the water from spilling over the edge, even while rising above it.

The properties of cohesion and adhesion cause water to form a meniscus in the glass. Add some water to a glass, not to the rim, and you will observe a meniscus. You will be able to observe it more clearly in a thin glass or cylinder, such as a thin, glass graduated cylinder. Adhesion causes the perimeter of the water to "climb" up the wall of the glass. Because of cohesion, the water molecules are strongly attracted to one another even as they are drawn up the side. As a result, the surface of the water acquires a meniscus, a concave shape, curved and lifted where it meets the glass.

These same properties are at play when water rises above the rim of the glass following the addition of the pennies. The large dome, or convex meniscus, that the water forms above the rim of the cup is due to these properties of water. The cohesive forces are so great that the molecules can resist the external force of gravity. The force of adhesion attracts the water molecules to the rim of the glass. Because of these two forces, the water resists spilling over the rim of the cup, even when the level rises above the rim.

Eventually, the water will spill over the rim of the cup when the force of gravity is greater than the cohesive and adhesive forces at the surface.

Soap is a surfactant, a compound that acts to lower the surface tension of water. It does this by weakening the attractive forces between the water molecules. Water will spill over the rim of the glass sooner once soap has been added.

The addition of soap as a variable broadly expands the scope of topics covered in class discourse. Surfactants play a critical role in our bodies. There is a thin layer of water that lines human lungs. This water is necessary for the gas exchange of carbon dioxide and oxygen to occur. These gases require a wet layer or surface for the exchange to take place. In fish, this exchange takes place in their gills. Since they are on the outside of the fish, gills have direct contact with water. Our lungs, on the other hand, are best able to be kept wet inside of our bodies. However, due to the properties of water, surface tension arises that can interfere with the expansion of our lungs as we breathe. Surfactant acts to reduce surface tension. This prevents alveoli, small air sacs in the lungs, from collapsing when we exhale. The most efficient oxygen-carbon dioxide exchange occurs in our lungs with the greatest alveoli surface area. By preventing the collapse of alveoli, surfactant helps to maximize the surface area available for the exchange of gases.

Viscosity is defined as a fluid's resistance to flow. Think of it as the "thickness" of a fluid. Fluids such as honey, molasses, corn syrup, and engine oil are highly viscous. Students might choose to investigate the outcome when liquids of varying viscosities are employed.

If the density of the liquid is altered by adding salt or sugar, discourse can include solutions, solubility, solutes, solvents, and concentration. Saltwater or sugar water is a mixture. One property of a mixture is that it is physically combined, not chemically, and it can be physically separated. For example, saltwater can be physically separated through the process of evaporation, or boiling the water away.

A solution is one in which a solute is dissolve in a solvent. The solute is the substance being dissolved and the solvent is the substance in which the solute is dissolved. Water is called the universal solvent because it is capable of dissolving more solutes than any other liquid. Solubility is the ability of a solute to dissolve in a solvent.

A concentrated solution is one which there are many dissolved particles of solute in the solvent. On the other hand, a dilute solution is one in which there are few dissolved particles of solute. A solution which contains all the dissolve particles it can possibly hold is called saturated.

Standards Alignment:

Next Generation Science Standards (NGSS, Lead States 2013)

Disciplinary Core Ideas in Physical Science

PS1: Matter and Its Interactions

PS1.A: Structure and Properties of Matter

PS1.B: Chemical Reactions

PS2: Motion and Stability: Forces and Interactions

PS2.B: Types of Interactions

PS4: Waves and Their Applications in Technologies for Information Transfer

PS4.A: Wave Properties

Disciplinary Core Ideas in Life Science

LS1: From Molecules to Organisms: Structures and Processes

LS1.A: Structure and Function

Disciplinary Core Ideas in Earth and Space Science

ESS2: Earth's Systems

ESS2.C: The Roles of Water in Earth's Surface Processes

Pitch Paradox

<u>Concepts Illustrated:</u> Properties of sound, pitch, vibration, mass, volume, acoustic waves, properties of liquids, solids, and gases, solutions, solubility, solutes, solvents, concentration, saturated solutions, process of dissolving, properties of mixtures, temperature, mechanics of human vocal chords, sound energy, transfer of energy, kinetic energy, molecular arrangement and motion of solids, liquids and gases.

<u>Paradox:</u>

Students discover that vibrations created in bottles containing liquid produce surprising, unexpected pitches!

<u>Equipment:</u>

1. Three to six identical glass bottles. Students should be able to see levels of liquids placed within.
2. Ruler.
3. Water.

<u>The Lesson:</u>

Display the bottles to students. Fill the first bottle with a small volume of water. Then, fill each of the other bottles with a steadily increasing volume of water. Line them up in sequential order, from least to greatest volume of water. Ask students to predict which of the bottles will have the lowest and highest pitch when you produce vibrations within them by tapping them and blowing into them.

Don't make an emphatic distinction between the two. You don't want students to consider two separate outcomes simply because you've emphasized a difference in your explanation. If they do predict two separate outcomes, you want this to be derived independent of any influence on your part.

Once they've made predictions, lift each bottle one at a time with two fingers by the neck. Begin with the bottle that contains the smallest volume of liquid. Hit the side of each bottle with the edge of a ruler, or a pencil, allowing students to listen carefully to the pitch. Progress to the bottle with the largest volume of liquid. Students will recognize a pattern. The bottle with the smallest volume of water will have the highest pitch. The bottle with the largest volume of water will have the lowest pitch. When five or six bottles are used, the progressive change in pitch is clearly heard. Some students may have predicted this accurately.

Point out that tapping the bottle is just one way to create vibrations within the bottle. Explain that vibrations can also be generated by blowing over the top of the bottle. Some students will share that they have done this before. Emphasize that both actions, tapping the bottle with a ruler and blowing over the top of the bottle, both produce vibrations in the bottle. You want to emphasize this, because it will make a stronger, more pronounced cognitive disruption when the discrepancy in pitch is heard in the next phase of the demonstration. Announce that you will demonstrate this alternate method of generating vibrations. Again, emphasize the term *alternate*.

Begin once again with the bottle that contains the smallest volume of water. Blow over the mouth of the bottle by placing your lower lip on the rim and blowing a stream of air across the top of the bottle. This time, the bottle will produce a very low pitch. Act surprised. Move directly to the bottle with the largest volume of water. Blow over the top of this bottle in the same manner. It will now produce a very high pitch. Act surprised once again. You can blow over the top of each bottle, in successive order from least volume of water to most volume of water. Students will now observe a distinctly different pattern than heard when tapping the bottles. The pitch will now progressively change from lowest pitch to highest pitch- the reverse of the previous observations.

You can also demonstrate this difference in a very clear manner by first tapping and then blowing over the top of the same bottle. Choose the bottle with the least volume of water. Tap it, and then immediately blow over the top of it. Then, do the same for the bottle with the greatest volume of water. The differences will be very noticeable.

Lesson Variation:

The bottles can be hung from a horizontal rod or meter stick suspended between two tables or ring stands. Tie one end of a piece of string around the neck of each bottle and the other end around the rod or meter stick. Hang the bottles in succession, from the least volume of water to the most. Hanging the bottles allows you to avoid picking them up while tapping them.

Another variation involves placing one end of a straw into a glass of water and blow across the top of the straw as you did with the bottles. Now, raise and lower the straw in the water as you continue to blow across the top. You'll find that the pitch changes. When the straw is lowered deep into the water, the pitch becomes higher. Conversely, when the straw is lifted high in the water, the pitch is lower. When the column of air above the water in the straw is shorter, the pitch is higher. When the column of air is increased, the pitch becomes lower.

Possible Variables:

1. Differently shaped bottles. This can involve all bottles of the same shape, but different from the original bottles. It can also involve bottles that each have a different shape.
2. Bottles of varying volumes. This could involve all bottles of the same shape and volume, but different from the original bottles. It could also involve bottles that each have the same shape, but a different volume.
3. The volume of liquid in the bottles.
4. Liquids of varying densities. This can also involve varying the volumes of these liquids. For example, all of the bottles could have the same volume of the same liquid with a density different from the liquid used in the demonstration. It could also involve bottles with different volumes of the same liquid with a density different from that used in the demonstration. Or, it could involve bottles with the same volume of different liquids with different densities. Density can be manipulated simply by adding salt or sugar to the water.

5. Viscosity of the liquid.
6. The temperature of the liquds.

Phenomenon Explained:

Although vibrations are caused by tapping the bottle as well as blowing over the top, the medium that is vibrating is different in each case. When tapping the bottle, it is the glass and the liquid that are vibrating. However, when blowing over the top of the bottle, it is the air within the bottle that vibrates.

A smaller mass of substance will produce a higher pitch than a larger mass, which produces a lower pitch. The bottle that has the greatest volume of liquid also contains the least mass of air. Blowing over this bottle vibrates that air and produces the highest pitch. However, when this bottle is tapped, the liquid and glass is vibrating. Since the greatest mass of this bottle is found in the liquid and glass, tapping the bottle produces a low pitch.

The bottle with the greatest mass of liquid will produce the lowest pitch when tapped and the highest pitch from blowing over its top. Conversely, tapping the bottle with the least mass of liquid produces the highest pitch, while blowing over it results in the lowest pitch.

Sound is essentially a pressure disturbance that travels through a medium such as solid, liquid, or gas in the form of mechanical energy. This occurs through "compression," as the atoms and molecules in the medium are caused to move or vibrate, in turn "bumping into" and exerting a force on adjacent molecules. This continues throughout the medium. This movement is basically a transfer of energy, showing that some of the energy put into the system is transferred as sound. Our vocal chords produce this energy as they vibrate when we speak. In space, where there is no atmosphere, there are too few molecules to transfer sound energy.

The molecules in a solid are packed very closely together. Liquid molecules are spaced farther apart, and gases have the greatest space between molecules. The distance between molecules affects how quickly energy can be transferred between them. Generally speaking, the closer the molecules, the easier for them to bump into one another and transfer energy. Molecular spacing allows sound to travel much faster through a solid than a liquid, and faster yet through a gas. For example, the distance and speed is about four times faster in water than in air and about fourteen times faster in wood than in air. Since kinetic energy and molecular speed increases with an increase in temperature, sound will travel faster when the medium is heated. The molecules collide much more frequently than in a cooler medium. Warming the liquid in the bottles could have an influence on the sound perceived by students.

If the density of the liquid is altered by adding salt or sugar, discourse can include solutions, solubility, solutes, solvents, and concentration. Saltwater or sugar water is a mixture. One property of a mixture is that it is physically combined, not chemically, and it can be physically separated. For example, saltwater can be physically separated through the process of evaporation, or boiling the water away.

A solution is one in which a solute is dissolve in a solvent. The solute is the substance being dissolved and the solvent is the substance in which the solute is dissolved. Water is called the universal solvent because of its capability to dissolve more solutes than any other liquid. Solubility is the ability of a solute to dissolve in a solvent.

A concentrated solution is one which there are many dissolved particles of solute in the solvent. On the other hand, a dilute solution is one in which there are few dissolved particles of solute. A solution which contains all the dissolve particles it can possibly hold is called saturated.

Viscosity is defined as a fluid's resistance to flow. Think of it as the "thickness" of a fluid. Fluids such as honey, molasses, corn syrup, and engine oil are highly viscous. Students might choose to investigate the outcome when liquids of varying viscosities are employed.

Standards Alignment:

Next Generation Science Standards (NGSS, Lead States 2013)

Disciplinary Core Ideas in Physical Science

PS1: Matter and Its Interactions

PS1.A: Structure and Properties of Matter

PS1.B: Chemical Reactions

PS3: Energy

PS3.A: Definitions of Energy

PS3.B: Conservation of Energy and Energy Transfer

PS4: Waves and Their Applications in Technologies for Information Transfer

PS4.A: Wave Properties

Disciplinary Core Ideas in Life Science

LS1: From Molecules to Organisms: Structures and Processes

LS1.A: Structure and Function

LS1.D: Information Processing

Disciplinary Core Ideas in Earth and Space Science

ESS2: Earth's Systems

ESS2.C: The Roles of Water in Earth's Surface Processes

Pouring Underwater

<u>Concepts Illustrated</u>: Properties of liquid, properties of gases, density, displacement, immiscibility, air pressure, molecular arrangement of gases, volume, air pressure within the human body, the effects of air pressure on the human body, the influence of air pressure on ailments, barometric pressure.

This is a unique demonstration with variations that serve to engage students in different scientific concepts. Be sure to read each, to appreciate the sense of wonder generated by the phenomenon in each.

<u>Paradox</u>:

While submerged underwater, two differently colored liquids, in two different glasses, switch places- each being transferred to the other glass, "poured" while underwater!

<u>Equipment</u>:

1. An aquarium or other transparent tank.
2. Two clear, tall glasses.
3. Water.
4. Vegetable oil.
5. Food coloring.
6. A sturdy square of construction paper, or laminated paper. It must be wide enough to cover the mouth of one of the tall glasses.

<u>Preparation</u>:

Fill about ¾ of the tank with water. You do not want to fill it completely because it will overflow when you submerge the glasses into it. Add yellow food coloring and mix well.

Fill one of the glasses about ¾ full of vegetable oil. Add blue food coloring and mix well.

<u>The Lesson</u>:

Show the aquarium tank containing the yellow liquid and explain that it is regular water, colored yellow with food coloring. Show the two tall glasses, one empty and the other filled with blue liquid. You can explain that this liquid is vegetable oil. The empty glass is submerged into the tank and fills with the yellow water. The glass is inverted and set on the bottom of the tank. The mouth of the second glass, filled with blue liquid, is covered with the laminated square. The glass is inverted, lowered into the water, and set on the bottom of the tank. The laminated square is pulled away from the glass and set aside. The blue contents remain inside this glass because it sits inverted on the bottom of the tank. The two submerged glasses now sit side by side, submerged, one filled with yellow liquid, the other with blue.

Now explain that in a moment you are going to lift both glasses straight up from the bottom of the tank. You will hold them at about the middle of the tank, side by side. Then you will tip the mouths towards each other. Mimic these actions with your hands for students. Ask students to predict what will happen. Most will predict that the two colors will mix, producing a green color under the glasses. Some will predict that the vegetable oil will sink to the bottom of the tank, perhaps changing to a green color. Others might event predict the liquid in each glass will turn green. Almost every student will focus on the colors, expecting some type of change.

Once predictions have been made, lift the glasses and hold them side by side. The blue vegetable oil will remain in the inverted glass. Tip the glasses slightly towards one another, but hold the glass containing the vegetable oil a little lower and almost under the rim of the other glass. The blue vegetable oil will "pour" out of the glass as it is tipped. But the liquid will rise. If the glasses are properly placed, the blue liquid will rise directly into the glass filled with yellow liquid. Continue to hold the glasses tipped towards one another and the blue liquid will travel entirely to the other glass, filling it. As it does, the yellow liquid will move into the glass that held the blue liquid. It will appear as though the two glasses are exchanging liquids each transferred to the other glass!

Lesson Variation:

Variation #1:

This variation is slightly different from the original demonstration, but illustrates a different scientific concept.

One of the drinking glasses does contain colored vegetable oil and the other is empty. The difference is that when the empty glass is submerged, it is not allowed to fill with water. Keep the glass straight and inverted as it is submerged and it will remain full of air. When the glass containing the vegetable oil is tipped towards the other, the oil will rise into the empty glass, filling it. Students will observe the empty glass being filled with the colored liquid, as it is "poured" into it.

Variation #2:

In this variation, one of the glasses can be substituted for a beaker. The glass is filled to the top with colored water. Begin by picking up the glass and explaining that it is filled with water colored with food coloring. Place the construction paper over the mouth of the glass and, while firmly holding the paper in place, invert the glass. Lower this inverted glass into the water, while holding the paper in place. Carefully set the glass on the bottom of the tank. Slide the laminated paper away. The glass remains full of colored water.

Pick up the empty beaker, invert it and explain that in a moment you are going to lower the beaker into the water. Hold the beaker over the water as you explain, but do not put it in the water yet. Further explain that once the beaker is underwater you will quickly pick the glass up from the bottom of the tank and hold the two side by side. Mimic this action with your hands so that students can visualize what you will do. Explain that then you will tip the inverted beaker slightly towards the glass. Mimic the tipping motion. Ask students to predict what will happen. Most will focus on the colored water, predicting that it will move from the glass to the beaker. Very few will expect what actually does occur.

Once predictions have been made, lower the inverted beaker into the water, holding it about midway down. Quickly pick the glass up from the bottom of the tank and hold the two side by side. The colored water will start to mix with the rest of the water in the tank. Now slowly tip the beaker towards the glass. The air trapped in the beaker will move to the glass as air bubbles, which will rise into the glass and push the water out. The air will actually be transferred under water, from the beaker to the glass!

Possible Variables:

1. Using a differently shaped inverted receptacles, such as a test tube, etc.
2. Using liquids with varying densities. This can be accomplished by adding salt or sugar. This could involve liquids of two different densities in the two glasses, or the same densities, that are either the same or different from the liquid in the tank. This could also involve layering liquids of differing densities in one glass or both.
3. The temperature of the liquids.

Phenomenon Explained:

The original demonstration occurs due to density. The density of an object will determine whether it will float in a fluid. Density is determined by calculating the mass for a given volume, expressed in the formula g/ml, g/cm^3, or g/cc. Density is independent of the sample size, since it represents the mass per ml of the sample. A larger volume does not necessarily equate to a higher mass. Fewer molecules packed into a given volume will result in a lower density than many more molecules packed into the same volume, which would increase the density. Objects with a density less than water will float, while those denser than water will sink. The density of water is 1.0g/ml.

Vegetable oil is less dense than water. It will not fall out of the inverted glass because it is less dense than the water that surrounds it. As this glass is tipped, the vegetable oil will naturally rise to the surface of the water. If this glass is held slightly under the one with yellow water, the oil will rise into this glass. It will rise to the bottom of the inverted glass. As it does, it will displace the yellow water, or push it out of the glass. This action is not really seen, since the surrounding water is also yellow. The glass will appear to just be filling up with the blue liquid. This blue liquid will not change color because oil does not "mix" with the water- the two are immiscible.

As the blue liquid is "poured" out of its glass, the surrounding yellow water moves in to take the place of the space that was previously occupied by the blue liquid. The yellow liquid is not really being "poured" into this glass from the other one. It is actually just being filled with the yellow water that surrounds it.

When the two glasses are held side by side and tipped, it creates the illusion that the two liquids are being transferred between the two glasses. In fact, the blue liquid is, but it is then simply replaced by the water in the tank.

In the demonstration variations, the inverted glass remains full of air and does not fill with water. As in the original demonstration, density also plays a role here. But this variation also works because the molecules of air inside the empty beaker occupy space. The water molecules cannot occupy the same space. As long as the inverted beaker is not tipped, to release some of the air molecules, the air inside is trapped and prevents water from entering.

Furthermore, the air inside the inverted glass exerts pressure. Atmospheric pressure is a force exerted by the weight of air in the atmosphere. Rarely are we aware of its immense force. This is because the pressure of air is exerted on us uniformly, all our lives. But, consider that all the air molecules above you have weight. The combined weight actually creates a pressure equivalent to about 10,000kg/square meter. This translates to about 1000kg/0.1 square meter, or about 14.7lbs/square inch! This means there is about a ton of weight on each of us! Of course, this number varies slightly depending on the altitude you happen to be. The air pressure in our bodies, our lungs, stomachs, ears, fluids, etc., "balances" the pressure outside of our bodies. Our internal pressure is essentially the same as the outside pressure- we are at equilibrium. This prevents us from being crushed by the outside air pressure.

The human body is capable of being affected by low pressure weather systems, that can cause effects such as headaches, motion sickness, and distension in the sinuses. Effects such as these can be influenced by the difference between pressure within the body's cavities, such as lungs, ears, and sinuses, and the atmospheric pressure surrounding the body. This also explains why our ears pop in an airplane, or driving through hills or mountains. The ears essentially try to equalize the pressure within its cavities with the atmospheric pressure. Even those who suffer from arthritis or bursitis might experience increased joint pain as swelling occurs due to a decrease of pressure on the body.

When the inverted beaker is submerged, the air pressure within prevents the water from entering. But because the liquid and the air cannot occupy the same space, the air is displaced, or pushed out of the beaker, as the colored liquid moves in.

Note that drinking glasses are used for those receptacles that sit on the bottom of the tank, because beakers will not work. Because of their spout, they will not sit flat on the bottom and liquid can "leak" out.

Standards Alignment:

Next Generation Science Standards (NGSS, Lead States 2013)

Disciplinary Core Ideas in Physical Science

PS1: Matter and Its Interactions

PS1.A: Structure and Properties of Matter

Powerful Cork

Concepts Illustrated: Surface tension, cohesion, properties of water, properties of gases, mass, volume, density, molecular arrangement of liquids and gases, air pressure, air pressure within the human body, the effects of air pressure on the human body, the influence of air pressure on ailments, barometric pressure.

This novel variation of a well-known demonstration will confound students at any grade level. Two variations are presented, each highly effective at generating cognitive conflict in any classroom. This is a phenomenon that will surprise students of all ages.

Paradox:

A large tank or beaker of water is shown. A cork floats on the surface of the water. A second beaker is inverted over the cork. It is dramatically, slowly pushed deep into the water until it is fully submerged. Students are quite surprised to find that the water never enters the inverted beaker and the cork never rises into it- remaining at the mouth of the inverted beaker!

The power in this variation lies in the equipment, specifically the cork. When asked to predict, students imagine several scenarios involving the cork. Some predict that when the water enters the inverted beaker it will fill the beaker until the cork is submerged. Some will add that when that happens, the cork will sink to the bottom of the large beaker. And others will predict that the water will rise until the cork hits the bottom of the inverted beaker, preventing the water from rising any further. These are all wonderfully creative responses. But because they are focused on the cork, very few predict that the water will not even enter the inverted beaker!

Equipment:

1. A large transparent tub, tank, or large beaker.
2. A small transparent beaker or glass. It must fit inside the large tub or beaker.
3. Water.
4. A cork.
5. Another variation, described below, will require paper towel, a sponge, a small toy stuffed animal, or any other object that will remain in the small beaker when inverted.

Preparation:

Fill about ¾ of the large tub or beaker with water. You do not want to fill it completely because it will overflow when you submerge the inverted beaker into it. If you do not have access to a transparent tank or tub, a 1000ml beaker will work, but a 4000ml beaker will work better.

Students can use 600ml or 1000ml beakers when they conduct their investigations.

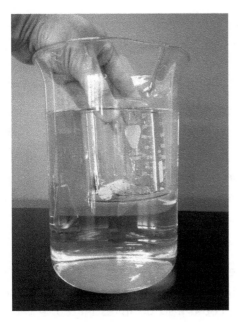

Cork floats at mouth of inverted beaker.   A close-up view.

The Lesson:

The lesson will be explained using a 4000ml beaker to hold the water and a 1000ml inverted beaker.

Show the 4000ml beaker of water and explain that it is ordinary tap water. Introduce the cork and place it in the water. Students will observe that it floats. Now show the 1000ml beaker, invert it, and hold it over the cork floating on the surface of the water. Explain that you are about to push this beaker into the water, capturing the cork as you do, until the beaker is at the bottom of the water. Ask students to predict what will happen when you do this. Reponses will range from the water will rise in the inverted beaker until the cork is submerged, water will rise until the cork hits the bottom of the inverted beaker and then no more water will enter, the cork will sink to the bottom of the water, and the cork will "pop" out from under the inverted beaker. Dramatically push the inverted beaker down, very slowly. Give students the opportunity to experience the anticipation for the outcome, which very few will predict. The cork provides a wonderful point of focus, clearly showing that no water is entering the inverted beaker. The cork remains at the mouth of the inverted beaker throughout!

Lesson Variation:

This is the traditional method of presentation, a wonderfully effective variation for the elementary level:

A large amount of dry paper towel is stuffed into a small beaker. The beaker is inverted and fully submerged in a larger beaker of water. When the inverted beaker is removed from the water, students are quite surprised to find that the paper towel has remained dry!

Show the 4000ml beaker of water and explain that it is ordinary tap water. Rip off a rather significant amount of paper towel and stuff it into the 1000ml beaker. Explain that you are about to push this beaker into the water. Illustrate this as you speak by inverting the beaker and holding it over the water. Ask students to predict what will happen when you do this.

Lift the inverted beaker straight up and out of the water. Do not tip this beaker because water on its outside could drip inside and wet the paper towel. Reach inside, from underneath, and pull out the dry paper towel, using a dry hand.

Note that in this variation, the inverted beaker can be replaced with any cup- even a paper cup. It is not necessary that it is transparent, but this allows students to "observe the effects" of air pressure.

Possible Variables:

1. Using a differently shaped inverted receptacle, such as a test tube.
2. Placing a hole in the inverted beaker, which would be replaced by a paper cup. The number of holes, as well as their placement, could also be investigated. A tack or nail can be used to make the hole(s) in the paper cup.
3. Using an overflow can as the inverted beaker. The nozzle on the side of the can introduces the variable.
4. Putting the inverted beaker in place first, then adding water.
5. The density of the water. This can be accomplished by adding salt or sugar.
6. Placing a piece of mesh or screen over the top of the beaker. This could also be extended to placing this mesh covered beaker into the water inverted and upright.

Phenomenon Explained:

The phenomenon occurs primarily because the molecules of air occupy space and the water molecules cannot occupy the same space. As long as the inverted beaker is not tipped, to release some of the air molecules, the air inside is trapped and prevents water from entering.

The air inside the inverted glass exerts pressure. Atmospheric pressure is a force exerted by the weight of air in the atmosphere. Rarely are we aware of its immense force. This is because the pressure of air is exerted on us uniformly, all our lives. But, consider that all the air molecules above you have weight. The combined weight actually creates a pressure equivalent to about 10,000kg/square meter. At sea level, this translates to about 1000kg/0.1 square meter, or about 14.7lbs/square inch! This means there is about a ton of weight on each of us! Of course, this number varies slightly depending on the altitude you happen to be. The air pressure in our bodies, our lungs, stomachs, ears, fluids, etc., "balances" the pressure outside of our bodies. Our internal pressure is essentially the same as the outside pressure- we are at equilibrium. This prevents us from being crushed by the outside air pressure. When the inverted beaker is submerged, the air pressure within prevents the water from entering.

The human body is capable of being affected by low pressure weather systems, that can cause effects such as headaches, motion sickness, and distension in the sinuses. Effects such as these can be influenced by the difference between pressure within the body's cavities, such as lungs, ears, and sinuses, and the atmospheric pressure surrounding the body. This also explains why our ears pop in an airplane, or driving through hills or mountains. The ears essentially try to equalize the pressure within its cavities with the atmospheric pressure. Even those who suffer from arthritis or bursitis might experience increased joint pain as swelling occurs due to a decrease of pressure on the body.

The surface of the water remains level, even as the inverted beaker is submerged, due to surface tension. Cohesion is the attraction of like molecules to one another. Water molecules have a very strong cohesive attraction for one another. The water molecules at the surface do not have any water molecules above them. As a result, they are strongly attracted to those neighboring water molecules at their sides and to those below, which draws them in towards the liquid. This strong attraction to the molecules around and underneath creates what is known as surface tension, a film-like layer of water at the surface, almost like an "elastic skin". This is one of the reasons that the cork floats on the surface of water. The other involves density.

The density of an object will determine whether it will float in a fluid. Density is determined by calculating the mass for a given volume, expressed in the formula g/ml, g/cm^3, or g/cc. Density is independent of the sample size, since it represents the mass per ml of the sample. A larger volume does not necessarily equate to a higher mass. Fewer molecules packed into a given volume will result in a lower density than many more molecules packed into the same volume, which would increase the density. Objects with a density less than water will float, while those denser than water will sink. The density of water is 1.0g/ml. The cork floats on the surface of water because it is less dense than water.

Standards Alignment:

Next Generation Science Standards (NGSS, Lead States 2013)

Disciplinary Core Ideas in Physical Science

PS1: Matter and Its Interactions

PS1.A: Structure and Properties of Matter

PS2: Motion and Stability: Forces and Interactions

PS2.B: Types of Interactions

Pressure Point

<u>Concepts Illustrated:</u> Density, volume, air pressure.

<u>Paradox:</u>

A large 4000ml beaker is filled about ¾ full of water. A clear cylindrical tube, with open ends, is introduced. A playing card is held against one end of the tube. This end is lowered vertically into the water until at least half of the tube is immersed. When the playing card is released, it remains in place on the end of the tube. Now water is poured into the open end of the tube. The card supports all the weight of the water poured onto it- only falling off the end of the tube when the water level inside the tube meets the water level in the beaker!

<u>Equipment:</u>

1. 4000ml beaker. An aquarium or other clear demonstration tank can also be used.
2. Glass or plastic tube with open ends. The size can vary, but should be around 3-4cm in diameter and 12-18cm in length.
3. A playing card or a stiff piece of plastic that will not readily dissolve in water.
4. A beaker used to pour water into the tube. A 600ml beaker works well.
5. Water.
6. A piece of strong thread is optional to hold the playing card in place over the end of the tube.
7. Food coloring is also optional.

<u>Preparation:</u>

The only preparation necessary for this demonstration would be optional. The 600ml beaker can be filled with water and food coloring could be added to it prior to the start of class. The food coloring makes the water more visible to students as it is poured into the cylindrical tube. Without the food coloring it might be difficult for students to see the level of the water poured into the tube.

<u>The Lesson:</u>

When performing this demonstration, be sure that students have eye level at the large beaker. You want them to recognize that the playing card falls off the tube at the precise moment that the water level within the tube meets the water level in the large beaker. This is most recognizable at eye level.

Show the 4000ml beaker and fill it about ¾ full of water. Next, introduce the cylindrical tube and the playing card. Show that the tube is open on both ends. Explain that you will hold the playing card on one end of the tube, lower it into the water vertically, and let go of the playing card. Demonstrate this for students. Allow them to see that the playing card remains in place. Some students will be astonished at this. Don't explain the science behind this right now.

Rather, include it in the discussion that follows the investigations. The card will easily stay in place. But when you release it, act as thought you are being extremely careful because you're worried it will fall off. If you make it look as though the card might fall off now, students will later tend to think that only a little bit of water poured onto the card will be necessary to make it fall off. The card will also make a water tight seal on the tube and no water from the beaker will enter. Continue to hold the tube in place in the water, and with your free hand show the beaker of colored water. Explain that you are going to pour this water directly into the open end of the tube and onto the playing card. Ask students to predict how much water will be poured into the tube before the playing card falls off. Tell students that there is currently 600ml of water in the beaker, so you'll be able to measure how much was poured into the tube after the card falls off. Once students have predicted, begin pouring water into the tube. Pour very slowly so that the impact or force of the water on the card does not cause it to fall off. The playing card will fall off as soon as the water level inside the tube meets the water level in the large beaker. Do not point this out. Allow students to identify it on their own. Some might at this point. If not, it's okay. Stop pouring immediately, as soon as the card falls off. Then, measure how much colored water is remaining in the 600ml beaker. This will tell how much was poured into the tube.

Now tell students that you're going to repeat the same procedure, but this time the tube will be lowered more deeply into the water. You may have to replace the water in the large beaker because the food coloring was just released into it. You may also need to add some water to the smaller beaker. Lower the tube with the card into the water again. But this time, make sure that when the tube is submerged students can plainly see that much more of it is underwater than the previous time. Students are to predict, since much more of the tube is underwater, how much water can be added before the card falls off. Most students will alter their original prediction, thinking that the depth of the tube will affect the volume of water that will cause the card to fall off. Repeat the procedure. Students will begin to recognize the relationship between the water level inside the tube and inside the beaker with respect to when the card falls off. If not, comment that you are noticing something strange. Guide students towards it, but don't tell them what it is. Then execute the demonstration one more time, drawing attention to the water levels.

The thread is optional and may be used to hold the playing card in place without having to submerge your hands in the water. Tape one end of the thread to the center of the playing card. Hold the card over the vertical tube and allow the thread to lower into the tube. The thread should be long enough to hang out the end of the tube opposite the playing card. Grasp the free end of the thread hanging out of the tube and turn the tube over, end to end. You can now hold the playing card in place on the end of the tube by pulling slightly on the thread. Once you've lowered the tube into the water, you can release the thread and the playing card will remain in place.

Possible Variables:

1. Width of the tube.
2. Length of the tube.
3. Tubes with different shapes. Funnels of different sizes can also be used.

4. Density of the liquid used. This can be accomplished by adding salt to the water, or by simply using liquids with densities other than water. The same liquid can be used in the large beaker and poured into the tube. Or, two different liquids with different densities can be used- one in the beaker and the other poured into the tube. The liquid with the larger density can be in the large beaker, while the lower density liquid is poured into the tube- or vice versa.
5. The depth that the tube is lowered into the water.
6. The card used can be made of varying card stock and materials, such as glass, plastic, tin, etc. Various sizes of cards made out of each of the materials can also be investigated.
7. Diameters of the beaker. This idea can be combined with the diameter of the cylinder. For example, there could be large diameter beaker/ small diameter cylinder, small diameter beaker/large diameter cylinder, and both large or both small.

Phenomenon Explained:

When the tube is initially lowered into the water, there is a pressure differential on each side of the playing card. Air pressure is on one side of the card, water pressure on the other. The water pressure forces exerted upward hold the playing card in place. When the water level in the tube meets the water level in the beaker, the water pressure is the same on both sides of the card and it drops from the tube. This shows that the water pressure is dependent on depth, not volume. When the water level in the tube meets that in the beaker, the volume of water in the tube does not equal the volume of water in the beaker. But, the pressures are equal. Without a net upward force to hold the card in place, it drops from the tube.

If the liquid poured into the tube has a lower density than the liquid in the large beaker, the liquid level in the tube will rise above the level in the beaker before the card falls off. Conversely, if the liquid poured into the tube has a higher density than the liquid in the beaker, the card will fall off before the level in the tube reaches that in the beaker.

Standards Alignment:

Next Generation Science Standards (NGSS, Lead States 2013)

Disciplinary Core Ideas in Physical Science

PS1: Matter and Its Interactions

PS1.A: Structure and Properties of Matter

Racing Pendula

Concepts Illustrated: Potential energy, kinetic energy, conservation of mechanical energy, gravity, rotational acceleration, density, volume, mass, radius of gyration.

Paradox:

Two identical rods, suspended from a horizontal bar, swing independently of one another. A large weight is attached to the end of one of these rods. The ends of both rods are lifted to an equal horizontal position. They are simultaneously released. The outcome shocks students. The rod without the weight actually reaches the bottom first!

Equipment:

1. A ring stand.
2. A horizontal support bar attached to the ring stand.
3. Two identical metal rods that will hang freely from the horizontal bar.
4. A weight that can be attached to the end of one of the metal rods. Details are provided in the Preparation section.

Preparation:

The apparatus should be set up prior to the demonstration. he weight should not be attached to the rod. The weight, and its construction, can vary. It can be as sophisticated as a cylinder with a hole in its center, so that it can be slid on the rod. A hole in the side of the cylinder can accommodate a thumbscrew which, when turned, will tighten the cylinder onto the rod.

But, the weight can be as simple as a mass of clay that is "stuck" onto the end of the rod. This is a setup that includes equipment readily accessible to most. It also the manipulation of variables easier for students during their investigations.

The Lesson:

Show the apparatus to students. Demonstrate that each of the rods can swing independently of one another, as a pendulum. Lift each rod, one at a time, to a horizontal position and release it. Allow students to observe the swinging motion of each.

Inform students that they will be asked to make two predictions. Lift both rods at the same time, to a horizontal position. They should be held side by side. A ruler can be used to hold them in place. They can be labeled A and B for clarity. For example, B can be the rod closest to the ring stand support. Explain that you will remove the ruler, releasing the rods simultaneously. Ask students to predict from the following choices:

a) Rod A will arrive at the bottom first.
b) Rod B will arrive at the bottom first.
c) Both rods will arrive at the bottom simultaneously.

Most will predict choice C, that they will reach the bottom at the same time. Remove the ruler, releasing the rods. Students will observe that the rods do reach the bottom together.

Now show the weight. Students can be told the mass of this weight. Attach the weight to the end of rod A. Once again, lift both rods to the same horizontal position, side by side. A ruler holds them in place, as before. Explain that you will once again remove the ruler and allow the rods to swing. Students will predict from the same choices:

a) Rod A will arrive at the bottom first.
b) Rod B will arrive at the bottom first.
c) Both rods will arrive at the bottom simultaneously.

Just about every student will predict choice A, that the rod with the weight will reach the bottom first. Remove the ruler, releasing the rods. Students will be quite shocked to find that rod B, the rod without the weight, actually reaches the bottom first! A counterintuitive outcome for almost every student.

Possible Variables:

1. The position of the weight along the rod.
2. The mass of the weight attached to the rod.
3. Multiple weights attached to the rod, at different positions. This could also involve using weights of varying metals, densities, or masses, at different positions.
4. The height from which the pendula are released.
5. Using string in place of metal rods.
6. The substance that the rods are made of. This could change its mass or density. For example, one rod could be aluminum while the other is steel. Or, they could both be made of the same substance. There are a number of combinations.

Phenomenon Explained:

Mechanical energy is defined as the energy an object possesses due to its motion or position. There are two forms of mechanical energy, potential and kinetic. Potential energy is stored energy, while kinetic is the energy of motion.

This demonstration illustrates the conservation of mechanical energy. The potential energy at the release point is converted to kinetic energy as the bob reaches the bottom of its swing. Upon its release, the bob gains speed as it falls. As it continues to fall, and lose height, it also loses potential energy. However, it also gains speed and kinetic energy. As stated in the law of conservation of energy, the total energy is conserved for both potential and kinetic combined. Mechanical energy is conserved.

These physical pendula demonstrate a wonderfully counterintuitive phenomenon. Most students will think that the weight will pull rod A down faster and it will reach the bottom first. However, rod B, without a weight attached, accelerates faster and reaches the bottom first.

The angular speed at which the pendulum swings is a function of the mass distributed along it. The perpendicular distance from the axis point of rotation to the mass is called the radius of gyration. The moment of inertia of a body with a complex shape can be determined by applying its radius of gyration to the formula, $I=mk^2$. In this formula, inertia (I) is equal to the mass of the weight x the radius of gyration (k). When the weight is attached to rod A, it increases its radius of gyration, thereby slowing its rotational acceleration.

Standards Alignment:

Next Generation Science Standards (NGSS, Lead States 2013)

Disciplinary Core Ideas in Physical Science

PS1: Matter and Its Interactions

PS1.A: Structure and Properties of Matter

PS2: Motion and Stability: Forces and Interactions

PS2.A: Forces and Motion

PS2.B: Types of Interactions

PS3: Energy

PS3.A: Definitions of Energy

PS3.B: Conservation of Energy and Energy Transfer

Resonant Rods

Concepts Illustrated: Resonance, oscillation, resonant frequency, natural frequency, vibration, mass, volume, elements and compounds, amplitude, simple harmonic motion, kinetic energy, sympathetic resonance, transfer of energy.

Paradox:

Students are shown a sequence of upright rods of varying heights. Each rod has a mass attached to its upper end. When one rod is agitated and caused to sway back and forth, the rod of equal height amongst the group is observed to sway back and forth as well. Whichever rod is wiggled, the only rod within the group that will respond by also moving is the rod of equal height, regardless of its position among the group!

Equipment:

1. Steel rods of varying lengths secured upright on a base. Each rod has an identical mass attached to its upper end.

The Lesson:

Show students the apparatus. Explain that you will pluck or wiggle each rod individually so that, one by one, they sway back and forth. Ask students to predict what will happen when you do so. Then agitate the rods singly and allow students time to observe any outcomes. Once the moving rod has stopped swaying, agitate another rod and cause it to sway. This should be done in no particular order. Allow for comments and discussion that can lead to an identification of the swaying pattern. Students should eventually recognize that rods of similar length will always sway together.

Once the class has begun to discuss this patterned swaying movement, reposition the rods so that they are aligned in a line, according to height. The tallest rods are on the ends and the height tapers to the shortest rods in the center.

Then, repeat the demonstration with the rods arranged this way. This will allow for a much more recognizable pattern of swaying. In this arrangement, students will more easily observe that rods of equal lengths sway in unison.

When the rods are arranged in a sequential pattern showing their incrementally increasing height, students might be more inclined to predict that the pairs of heights will lead to some particular outcome. I would encourage a setup in which the rods are not in sequential order arranged by height.

Possible Variables:

1. Altering the pattern of the upright rods. They could be repositioned so that they are aligned in a row, or various other patterns could also be investigated.

2. Adding weights to other positions on the rods. For example, adding an additional weight midway on some rods. This can also involve varying the mass of those weights.
3. Instead of the weights at the top of each rod being the same mass, they can have different masses. Rods of equal length can have weights of different mass.
4. Repositioning the base to be either upside-down, so that the rods are upside-down, or turning the base vertical, so that the rods are now horizontal.
5. Rods of different materials and densities, such as aluminum, copper, tin, etc.

Phenomenon Explained:

The equipment involved resembles a system of inverted pendula. The demonstration illustrates resonant motion between pendula of equal length.

All objects have a *natural frequency* at which they can vibrate following the introduction of energy from an external source. Resonance occurs when one object vibrates in phase with the same natural frequency of an applied oscillatory force. In our demonstration, this occurs between the rods of varying lengths. Vibrations develop in one rod, transferred from repeated impulses of another with a matching natural frequency in the system. The length of each rod is associated with a particular natural frequency. Those that are longest have the lowest natural frequency, the shortest rods have the highest natural frequency.

Rods of identical length will vibrate, or oscillate, at identical resonant frequencies. When one rod is set into motion it vibrates at the same natural frequency as another rod of equal length, and the two will vibrate in unison. The result is known as sympathetic resonance, or sympathetic vibration, a phenomenon that occurs when a vibration produced in one body causes similar vibrations in a passive, neighboring body of similar frequency.

On the other hand, rods of differing lengths will oscillate at different resonant frequencies. So, rods that differ in length from the one that vibrates will remain motionless.

Simple harmonic motion is described as a periodic movement in which the restoring force is proportional to the displacement, generally in the opposite direction of the displacement. Our simple pendula system behaves like a harmonic oscillator. However, the period is determined by the pendulum length, not the mass of the bob. They system involves kinetic energy, or the energy of movement and gravitational potential energy.

Standards Alignment:

Next Generation Science Standards (NGSS, Lead States 2013)

Disciplinary Core Ideas in Physical Science

PS1: Matter and Its Interactions

PS1.A: Structure and Properties of Matter

<u>PS3: Energy</u>

PS3.A: Definitions of Energy

PS3.B: Conservation of Energy and Energy Transfer

<u>PS4: Waves and Their Applications in Technologies for Information Transfer</u>

PS4.A: Wave Properties

Rolling Racers

Concepts Illustrated: Mass, volume, density, diameter, potential energy, kinetic energy, moment of inertia, rotational energy, translational energy, angular acceleration about a rotational axis, velocity, Newton's first law of motion- the law of inertia, Newton's second law, center of gravity, force, elements and compounds, momentum, acceleration.

This demonstration is chock full of variation and potential methods to show discrepancy and initiate cognitive disequilibrium. As explained below, the demonstration has three phases producing a series of increasingly discrepant outcomes and surprises. The final phase has two additional variations to choose from. There is also an absolutely fantastic variation involving only one set of ring and disk, if resources are limited. Each method of demonstration offers a tremendous variety of investigative pathways, due to countless variables that can be studied. Discrepancies and surprises will persist throughout the incredibly rich student-led investigations.

Paradox:

Phase 1: Students are shown a metal ring and a solid wooden disk. They are both shown to have the same diameter. Students are asked to determine which will roll farthest when simultaneously pushed with equal force on a flat surface. Most will predict the ring to continue to roll farther. This is actually the behavior observed. When given a push, the ring is shown to roll farther.

Phase 2: An inclined plane is shown. Students are asked to determine which will reach the bottom first when they are released simultaneously from the same height on the inclined plane. Most will once again expect the ring to reach the bottom first. But, to their surprise, students will observe the disk to now reach the bottom first!

They are massed and the ring is shown to have a greater mass than the disk! This surprise serves to contradict the observations from Phase 1, but does seem to illustrate that on an inclined plane, the lighter object travels quicker.

Phase 3: To confirm the previous results, a ring with a significantly greater diameter than the disk is now shown. But the smaller disk is now shown to have a greater mass than the ring. In addition, the ring is much narrower than the disk, which is noticeably wider. Most will now predict the ring to win the race- for a variety of reasons. Some will base their prediction on the observations from the previous phase, claiming the ring to win due to its lighter mass. Others predict the ring to win due to its diameter, thinking it will require fewer spins to reach the bottom of the inclined plane. And yet others will predict the ring to win because they will feel that the wider disk creates greater surface area in contact with the plane, causing increased friction, slowing the disk down. They are released down the plane. To the amazement of every student, the disk wins once again, contradicting all expectations!

<u>Equipment:</u>

1. A ring and disk. A second set will be necessary for Phase 3, but it is optional. This is explained in the demonstration procedure below.
2. Inclined plane.
3. A ruler.
4. A balance to measure the mass of the ring and disk.

<u>Preparation:</u>

All of the equipment should be readily accessible, but the ring/disk sets should not both be visible to students at the outset of the demonstration. The first set can be visible prior to the demonstration, but the second set should be hidden. This is to avoid student anticipation for upcoming phases.

<u>The Lesson:</u>

Note that Phase 3 is optional if you only have one ring and disk set. An alternate handling is included for a demonstration involving only Phases 1 and 2 with one set of ring/disk. See the Demonstration Variation section below for details. As you will see, only one set is actually necessary to generate a great deal of discrepancy. If you have additional ring/disk sets to conduct Phase 3, it will allow the discrepancy to deepen.

In the beginning of the demonstration, inform students that there will be three parts to this demonstration and that they will be making predictions for each. For those who anticipate discrepancy, they might expect the first two phases to produce "conventional" results, but the third to produce the discrepancy. In fact, discrepancies arise throughout the demonstration.

Phase 1 serves to instill confidence in student's cognitive schema, albeit misaligned. Deliberately uncovering this misconception and drawing awareness to it at this point in the demonstration directly leads to its subsequent investigation. Most feel that the ring will roll farther. It will, but their reasoning is ill-founded. Most reason that the ring rolls farther because it is lighter, or has less mass, than the solid disk. Yet, this is not why it does roll farther than the disk. The perception appears to be "verified" to students in this phase, establishing a powerful discrepancy in Phase 2, ultimately sparking curiosity and a focus of investigation.

Begin Phase 2 saying "based on the observations you just made (referring to phase 1)..." The objective should be for students to base their predictions on previous observations and experiences. Grounding Phase 2 predictions on their observations from Phase 1, most will predict the ring to once again win the race. But, since the outcome does not rely on which object is lighter, their predictions are incorrect and a discrepancy arises. Phase 2 observations contradict the schema, and expectation, of most.

Most students feel that the lighter object will travel down the inclined plane quicker. They are first surprised to find that the disk reaches the bottom first, because they assume the ring is lighter. They base this assumption on its appearance. Another surprise awaits when they find that the disk actually has less mass than the ring. Its appearance contradicts this reality. This knowledge also serves to generate perplexity, as it seems to contradict observations from Phase 1. Why did the heavier object roll farther in Phase 1? Yet, it does seem to explain the results of Phase 2. Point out that although the heavier object rolled farther on flat ground, the lighter object did roll faster on the inclined plane. Students remain content that the Phase 2 observations align with their schema. The lighter object did, in fact, roll faster down the inclined plane. However, all of this reasoning remains ill-founded. The total mass does not play a role in determining which object wins the race. All of this deepens the contradiction and the puzzle that awaits.

Begin Phase 3 by introducing a ring that has a significantly greater diameter than the disk. This small disk is shown to be considerably wider and have greater mass than the ring. Although almost every student will predict the ring to win the race, they will submit a variety of reasons supporting this outcome. Most will predict the ring will win because of its lighter mass. But there will be some who feel that the ring will win the race because of a different reason- because of its larger diameter. They feel that the ring will not have to roll as many times to reach the bottom of the plane, whereas the disk will have to spin many more times before it reaches the bottom due to its significantly smaller diameter. And others will ground their prediction in friction. They will surmise that the wider disk, having more surface area in contact with the plane, will cause "drag" and slow it down. When they are raced, the disk wins once again, establishing contradiction with all expectation!

It should be explained to students that although the disk used in Phase 3 looks very different from the original, much narrower disk used in the previous phases, it is still a disk, nonetheless. They should begin to understand that this "wide" disk is called a "cylinder." The inclusion of a cylinder introduces an additional variable to investigate. The demonstration ends with a tremendous variety of potential investigative pathways to follow.

There are two methods to show the ring and disk to have the same diameter. The first is to simply superimpose them, lying one against the other. The other is to actually measure them. The choice can be made according to available resources, time, and age level of the students.

Note that when racing objects, the points at which the objects come in contact with the plane should be at the same height on the plane. Inclined planes of one meter long are optional. If the angle of the plane is too large, object could potentially slide, rather than roll. It is important to ensure that objects are rolling down the plane. Practice with your setup first, to be certain that everything is properly positioned and in working order.

Lesson Variation:

When only one set of ring and disk is available:

As previously mentioned, there is an incredibly powerful alternate method of presentation if you only have one set of ring and disk. Presenting Phases 1 and 2 alone will generate a remarkable amount of cognitive conflict. However, if presented in this manner, both objects must have equal mass. This is not pointed out to students in Phase 1. The mass is shown at the completion of Phase 2. Initially, students will perceive the ring to be "lighter" than the disc. They also believe the lighter object will travel farther. The results from Phase 1 strengthen their confidence in this idea. This confidence is carried into Phase 2, where students further predict that the lighter object will travel faster down the inclined plane. They are surprised when the results of Phase 2 contradict their expectation. Their cognitive disequilibrium is compounded when they discover that the ring and disk actually have equal mass. Their expectation that the ring has less mass is based on its appearance. But, the discrepancy adds another layer of disbelief as students are forced to wrestle with this new knowledge. If both objects had the same diameter and mass, why didn't they reach the bottom of the inclined plane together? What caused the disk to reach the bottom first? This is just a tremendous method of presentation that raises a variety of student questions, variables, and investigative pathways.

Each of the following variations can replace Phase 3 of the demonstration:

Variation #1:

A new ring and disk are introduced. Once again, they have the same diameter. But they are now shown to also have the same mass. Students are asked to predict which will reach the bottom of the inclined plane when released simultaneously. They will most likely now predict that they will reach the bottom at the same time. Yet, once again, the disk reaches the bottom first!

Variation #2:

A new ring and disk are introduced. As in Phases 1 and 2, they have the same diameter. But the band that makes up the disk is now significantly wider than the disk. Each are shown to have the same mass. Students are asked to predict which of these objects will reach the bottom of the inclined plane when released simultaneously. Some will expect they reach the bottom at the same time. Others will expect the wider disk to generate friction that slows it down, resulting in the ring to win the race. Yet, when they are release, it is the disk that once again reaches the bottom first!

Possible Variables:

1. Angle of the inclined plane.
2. Different types of surfaces along the outer edge of both ring and disk.
3. Different types of surfaces on the inclined plane.
4. The ring and the disk can each be made from different substances, such as aluminum, brass, rubber, glass, plastic, cork, steel, lead, tin, wood, copper, etc. Investigation can involve comparing results when the disk and ring are made of the same substance, or when they are made of different substances.
5. The ring and disk can be made of the same substance, but have differing diameters.
6. The ring and disk can be made of different substances, but have the same diameters.
7. The width of the ring and disk. This would essentially involve cylinders.
8. Students might choose to investigate rings of various materials against one another.

9. Students might choose to investigate disks of various materials against one another.
10. Rings, disks and cylinders can be mixed and matched for investigations.
11. Each variable listed here can also be measured against distance traveled.

Phenomenon Explained:

To begin, we should become familiar with the terms momentum, velocity, speed, and acceleration.

Momentum refers to a quantity of motion that an object has. The momentum of a moving object can be calculated using the following formula:

$$momentum = mass \times velocity$$

The momentum of any moving object is dependent upon its mass and velocity. The terms speed and velocity are oftentimes mistakenly used interchangeably. Whereas speed refers to the measure of how fast an object moves, velocity measures how fast an object arrives at a certain point. They are different. Speed is defined as the rate of time that an object travels a distance. Velocity is defined as the rate of change in displacement with respect to time, or the rate that an object moves from one point to another. The formula for speed is:

$$\frac{distance\ traveled}{time\ of\ travel}$$

As a vector quantity, velocity involves both speed and direction. The formula for velocity is:

$$\frac{displacement}{time}$$

Consider a person walking two steps forward and two steps back, returning to the original starting position. Their speed of each step can be measured. But their velocity would be measured as zero.

Acceleration is defined as the rate at which an object changes its velocity.

The Rolling Racers demonstration illustrates a principle called the Moment of Inertia, or Rotational Inertia. The principle describes angular acceleration about a rotational axis. It is a measure of an objects resistance to changes in its state of rotational motion. Rotational inertia of and object does, in fact, depend on its mass. But, it specifically depends on the distribution of that mass relative to the axis of rotation.

Let's begin by considering the general nature of a disk and a ring. All the mass of the disk is uniformly distributed, with respect to a central geometric axis. But, all the mass of the ring is in the periphery. Although they may both have the same total mass, the distribution of that mass differs between the two.

When the mass moves farther from the axis of rotation, or to the periphery of the body, as in the ring, it becomes difficult to alter the rotational velocity of the body. The farther the mass is distributed from the point of rotation, the higher the rotational inertia. The mass of the ring is in its periphery, far from the point of rotation- the center. Since the mass of the disk is uniformly distributed, a disk and a ring of the same mass do not have the same rotational inertia. The ring will have a greater rotational inertia than the disk.

As a result, when the ring and disk have the same diameter, the disk reaches the bottom of the inclined plane first. If a disk of smaller diameter is used, it will reach the bottom of the inclined plane before the larger ring. And if the disk has a larger diameter than the ring, the disk is the first to reach the bottom once again. Essentially, any disk will always reach the bottom of the inclined plane before any ring. All disks beat all rings.

Students might think that the solid disk always beats the ring because it is heavier. But, if they race a disk against a ring with greater mass, it is the disk that will reach the bottom of the plane first. And, if they race a brass disk against an aluminum one, they will find that they both reach the bottom at the same time. These results show that the total mass of the object is irrelevant to the outcome.

When rolling objects down the inclined plane, the object reaching the bottom of the plane last has the greater rotational inertia. This object has a greater resistance to a change in its state of rotational motion. As a result, it has a smaller rotational acceleration rolling down the plane. In Phase 1 of the demonstration, the ring will roll farther on the flat surface because of its *greater* moment of inertia. In Phase 2, the disk reaches the bottom of the inclined plane first due to its *lesser* moment of inertia.

A solid cylinder is essentially a *disk* with a long axis. A hollow cylinder is a *ring* with a long axis. When a hollow and solid cylinder, each made of the same substance, are raced against one another, the solid cylinder wins. The hollow cylinder will always lose, independent of its mass, diameter, or length.

A solid cylinder behaves the same as our other disks. If a solid cylinder were raced against a ring with a larger diameter, the cylinder reaches the bottom first. When a hollow cylinder and a disk of smaller diameter is raced, the disk wins. When the cylinder is raced against a larger disk, the disk wins once again. Again, since the cylinder is a wide disk, it will always reach the bottom of the plane before any ring does.

If two solid cylinders of the same diameter and length rolled down the inclined plane, they would both reach the bottom at the same time. This is regardless of their mass. If one were brass and the other aluminum, even though their masses would be very different, the outcome would not change. They would both reach the bottom of the plane together. Two cylinders made of the same substance could differ remarkably in their masses, diameter, and lengths, will still both arrive at the bottom of the inclined plane at the same time.

Consider two solid cylinders with the same diameter, each made of the same substance, but one with a greater length than the other. Some might consider that the cylinder with the greater length would have more surface area touching the plane, thus creating more friction, causing it to roll slower and reach the bottom of the plane last. Yet they would still both reach the bottom of the plane together.

Now consider two cylinders, one made of aluminum and one of copper. The aluminum cylinder has a diameter far greater than that of the copper cylinder. Many would predict the larger diameter to reach the bottom of the plane first because it has to roll significantly fewer times to reach the bottom than does the smaller diameter cylinder. Yet they both reach the bottom of the plane together.

Regardless of the substance, mass, length, or diameter, all cylinders will reach the bottom of the ramp at the same time.

If they investigate spheres, students will discover they always reach the bottom of the inclined plane before rings. Spheres will also reach the bottom before disks. When the three are rolled simultaneously, the sphere will always reach the bottom first, followed by the disc, and finally the ring. The exception would be hollow spheres. The hollow sphere will always lose to the disk. If spheres were introduced, or available for students to investigate, there should be access to spheres of differing diameters- large medium and small. Students will find that all spheres roll alike. In fact, a basketball and a tennis ball will reach the bottom of the ramp together. However, you may see some minor differences between the two, due to friction and air resistance. This becomes evident when rolling a basketball and a ping-pong ball. A slight difference will also be observed when rolling solid spheres against hollow. Solid spheres, such as a marble, will roll faster than a hollow sphere, like a basketball. The solid sphere should always roll faster than the hollow sphere, regardless of their diameters. For these reasons, students should have access to spheres of differing substances, with both the same and different diameters. Spheres can be tested against other spheres, disks or rings.

A solid object will consistently roll down the ramp faster than a hollow object of identical shape, whether it is a sphere or cylinder, regardless of mass or volume.

When an object is placed at the top of the incline, it has potential energy due to gravity. The amount of potential energy is dependent on the mass of the object and the height to which it has been lifted. When the object is released to roll down the incline, its potential energy is converted into kinetic energy. Ignoring loss by friction, the total amount of energy is conserved. In the case of a rolling object, as in this lesson, the kinetic energy is divided into two different types of kinetic energy- translational and rotational. Translational energy refers to motion in a straight line, whereas rotational energy refers to the motion of spinning.

The demonstration can also be used to illustrate Newton's first law of motion. Known as the law of inertia, it states that an object either at rest or in motion, remains at rest or in motion with the same speed and direction, unless acted upon by an unbalanced force.

Students might opt to investigate the outcome when manipulating the density of the spheres. The density of an object will determine whether it will float in a fluid. Density is determined by calculating the mass for a given volume, expressed in the formula g/ml, g/cm^3, or g/cc. Density is independent of the sample size, since it represents the mass per ml of the sample. A larger volume does not necessarily equate to a higher mass. Fewer molecules packed into a given volume will result in a lower density than many more molecules packed into the same volume, which would increase the density.

Standards Alignment:

Next Generation Science Standards (NGSS, Lead States 2013)

Disciplinary Core Ideas in Physical Science

PS1: Matter and Its Interactions

PS1.A: Structure and Properties of Matter

PS2: Motion and Stability: Forces and Interactions

PS2.A: Forces and Motion

PS3: Energy

PS3.A: Definitions of Energy

PS3.B: Conservation of Energy and Energy Transfer

Salt Water Surprise

Concepts Illustrated: Phase changes, physical changes, melting, process of dissolving, volume, density, properties of mixtures, solutions, solutes, solvents, concentration, solubility, elements and compounds, temperature, convection currents, ocean currents, characteristic properties of solids, salinity, homogenous solutions, properties of water, saturated solutions, molecular motion of solids and liquids, fluid dynamics, weather patterns.

Purposefully constructed in two phases, this is an incredibly simple demonstration establishing powerful contradiction.

Paradox:

Since salt is used to melt ice on roads, student predictions are initially confirmed when a beaker of salt and ice melts more quickly than a beaker of plain ice. However, they encounter quite a cognitive dilemma when the ice in a beaker of saltwater melts much more slowly than the ice in a beaker of plain water!

Equipment:

1. Salt (NaCl- sodium chloride).
2. Four beakers. 250ml beakers work well.
3. Water.
4. Ice cubes.
5. A stirring rod.
6. Two stopwatches or timers.

Preparation:

Fill two beakers with water and allow them to sit until they have reached room temperature. The salt used in the demonstration is common table salt, sodium chloride (NaCl). Although other salts can be studied in the investigations that follow. But, since students are most familiar with common table salt (NaCl), it should be used in the demonstration. The beakers should be placed on a table that students can surround during the demonstration.

The Lesson:

Begin by showing two empty beakers. Explain that you will add the same number of ice cubes to each beaker and then sprinkle a tablespoon of salt onto the ice cubes in one. Ask students to predict whether the salted or plain ice will melt faster. Be sure to share out predictions and explanations. There may be a student who will explain that since salt is used to melt ice on roads, the ice with salt will melt faster than the plain ice. Those who live in snowy climates have most likely seen salt trucks spreading salt in an effort to de-ice roads. If not, knowledge of this practice should be shared during class discussion prior to the demonstration, so that all students become aware of it.

Students should surround the table holding the beakers, to clearly observe the melting process. Although it is an option, it is not necessary to wait until the ice in once beaker fully melts. Students will be able to observe that the ice with salt will melts faster than the ice without by measuring the water that forms in the bottom of the beakers. The graduated measurements on the beakers will allow for the accumulated water to be easily measured. If you do observe the ice until all melts in one beaker, stopwatches could be used. Select two students and give each a stopwatch. Be sure that students understand how to use them prior to placing the ice cubes in the beakers. Each student should focus on only one beaker.

Now add the same amount of ice to each beaker and immediately sprinkle the salt onto the ice in one. The results will confirm that salt does cause ice to melt faster. Students will clearly recognize that the ice with salt added melts more quickly than the plain ice. This observation establishes the foundation for a rather strong discrepancy in the next phase of the demonstration.

Begin the next phase by introducing the two beakers of water. Be sure to inform students that the water in each beaker is at room temperature. Now add a heaping teaspoon of salt to one beaker and stir the solution. Explain that you will place one ice cube in each beaker. Ask students to predict which beaker of ice will melt more quickly, adding that they should base their predictions on their knowledge of salt/ice mixtures. You can also add that they "probably know what will happen based on the observations just made." Most will now predict that the ice in the beaker of saltwater will melt faster than the ice in the plain water. Once those predictions have been shared, students should once again surround the table holding the beakers, to clearly observe the melting process.

Select two students and give each a stopwatch. As in the first phase, each student should focus on only one beaker. Place one ice cube into each beaker and ask the students to begin timing how long it takes for each cube to melt. The difference will be very noticeable. Students will clearly recognize that the ice cube in the saltwater will now dissolve much more slowly than the one in the plain water! After a brief period, the ice cube in saltwater will only be partially dissolved, while the cube in plain water will be fully dissolved! These observations completely contradict those made earlier!

Lesson Variation:

The melting process, and the convection currents that form, can become visual by using ice cubes made with food coloring. The more concentrated, the more visual these processes will become. Food coloring also allows the process to be observed from a greater distance. It is recommended that the addition of food coloring be investigated by the students, because it vividly shows the activity of the water, minimizes the mystery, and limits exploration leading towards an understanding of the observed behavior. As a component of discourse following the investigations, the addition of food coloring can lead to rich, collaborative construction of the concept and processes involved.

A thermal imaging camera can also be used to observe the contents of each beaker.

Possible Variables:

1. Volume of water.
2. Temperature of the water.
3. Amount of salt added. Does concentration affect melting point?
4. Size of the ice cube.
5. Shape of the ice cube.
6. Ice cubes made with saltwater. This could also involve varying the amounts of salt in the ice cube. It could also involve investigating the ratio of salt in the ice cube to that of the water in the beaker.
7. Replacing salt with sugar. This could also expand into an investigation involving various amounts of sugar added to the ice cubes and the water in the beaker.
8. Type of salt, such as kosher salt, Epsom salt, rock salt, etc.
9. Adding food coloring to the ice cubes. This would allow the convection current to be observed.
10. Adding food coloring to the water in the beaker.
11. Ice cubes made of different liquids other than water, such as vegetable oil, canola oil, corn syrup, etc.
12. Replacing water with another liquid.

Phenomenon Explained:

The process of melting represents a phase change, occurring when there is a transition from one state of matter to another. A phase change does not alter the chemical composition of a substance. All phase changes are physical changes, unlike a chemical change, which will produce a new substance. In our demonstration, the phase change occurs when water transitions from the solid to liquid states of matter. Under normal conditions, ice begins to melt at $0^{\circ}C$ or $32^{\circ}F$. The molecules in frozen water are packed very tightly together and vibrate in place, characteristic of most solids. Molecules of a liquid have more space between them, and move about more freely and quickly than those in a solid.

In the first phase of the demonstration, the ice with salt melts more quickly than the plain ice because salt acts to lower the freezing point of ice. The melting point of ice is the same as its freezing point. Ice will begin to melt or freeze at $0^{\circ}C$. Since salt lowers the freezing point, or the point at which it *begins* to freeze, it also lowers its melting point, or the point at which it *begins* to melt. It begins to melt at a lower temperature.

The density of an object will determine whether it will float in a fluid. Density is determined by calculating the mass for a given volume, expressed in the formula g/ml, g/cm^3, or g/cc. Density is independent of the sample size, since it represents the mass per ml of the sample. A larger volume does not necessarily equate to a higher mass. Fewer molecules packed into a given volume will result in a lower density than many more molecules packed into the same volume, which would increase the density. Objects with a density less than water will float, while those denser than water will sink. The density of water is 1.0g/ml.

The second phase of the demonstration seems to contradict this concept, as the ice in saltwater melts more slowly than the ice in plain water. As the ice cube in plain water melts, the cold water that drips off it is denser than the warmer water it is surrounded by. Because of its greater density, the cold water dripping from the ice cube sinks. This acts to push the warmer, less dense, water up towards the top of the beaker. As the warm water rises, it surrounds the ice cube, causing it to melt even more. The cycle continues, serving to accelerate the melting process.

On the other hand, the addition of salt increases the density of water in the second beaker. As in the beaker of plain water, cold water drips from the ice cube in this beaker. However, in this beaker the dripping cold water is less dense than the denser saltwater that surrounds it. Because it is less dense, the cold water does not sink. Instead, it floats at the top of the beaker and surrounds the ice cube. There is no convection current established in this beaker. Warm water is not pushed up. The water immediately surrounding the ice cube remains cold, and the ice cube melts more slowly. Contradicting the expectations of most students, salt actually prevents the ice cube from melting quickly.

The addition of salt or sugar can expand discourse to include solutions, solubility, solutes, solvents, and concentration. Saltwater or sugar water is a mixture. One property of a mixture is that it is physically combined, not chemically, and it can be physically separated. For example, saltwater can be physically separated through the process of evaporation, or boiling the water away.

A solution is one in which a solute is dissolve in a solvent. The solute is the substance being dissolved and the solvent is the substance in which the solute is dissolved. Water is called the universal solvent because of its capability to dissolve more solutes than any other liquid. Solubility is the ability of a solute to dissolve in a solvent.

A concentrated solution is one which there are many dissolved particles of solute in the solvent. On the other hand, a dilute solution is one in which there are few dissolved particles of solute. A solution which contains all the dissolve particles it can possibly hold is called saturated.

The dynamic process whereby fluid sinks and rises due to its density, establishes what is known as a convection current. When food coloring is added to the ice cubes, the convection current is quite evident. In the beaker of saltwater, the melting ice cube forms a distinct layer of colored water that remains at the surface. In the beaker of plain water, water dripping from the melting cube sinks visibly sinks to the bottom of the beaker.

The process of convection currents can serve to illustrate the dynamics of ocean currents and the thermohaline circulation. Winds can drive ocean currents in about the upper 100 meters of the ocean. However, deeper ocean currents, thousands of meters below the surface, are driven by the density of the water. Both temperature and salinity can affect the waters density. The process is known as thermohaline circulation. "Thermo" refers to temperature and "haline" refers to salinity, or the concentration of dissolved salts in the water. The convection currents occurring in the upper 100 meters and those thousands of meters below act to provide constant motion in the ocean, known as a global ocean conveyor belt.

The phenomenon can also be used to illustrate weather patterns and the movement of Earths heat. Lake effects can cause the land to warm faster than a nearby body of water during the day, while the opposite occurs at night. Convection in the atmosphere can affect the formation of thunderstorms, the wind chill effect, and the formation of fog layers.

Elements are the basic building blocks of matter. An element is defined as the simplest form of matter, unable to be broken down any further by normal chemical means. A compound is formed from two or more elements bonded in a definite proportion. For example, water is a compound. Each molecule of water is composed of two hydrogen atoms and one oxygen atom, giving the formula H_2O. The table salt used in this demonstration is also a compound. Each molecule of table salt is composed of one atom of sodium and one atom of chlorine, giving the formula NaCl.

Standards Alignment:

Next Generation Science Standards (NGSS, Lead States 2013)

Disciplinary Core Ideas in Physical Science

PS1: Matter and Its Interactions

PS1.A: Structure and Properties of Matter

PS1.B: Chemical Reactions

PS2: Motion and Stability: Forces and Interactions

PS2.B: Types of Interactions

PS3: Energy

PS3.A: Definitions of Energy

PS3.B: Conservation of Energy and Energy Transfer

Disciplinary Core Ideas in Earth and Space Science

ESS2: Earth's Systems

ESS2.C: The Roles of Water in Earth's Surface Processes

Shocking Sand

Concepts Illustrated: Mass, volume, diameter, kinetic energy, heat energy, conservation of energy, transfer of energy, force, friction, shock wave, shock wave propagation.

Paradox:

Using a rubber band, a tissue covers the end of a small paper tube. The tube is held vertically, with the tissue at the bottom. A wooden dowel, acting as a plunger, is dropped into tube, ripping the tissue upon contact. A new tissue is affixed to the end of the tube. Sand is now poured into the tube, adding weight on top of the tissue below. The plunger is again dropped into the tube and onto the sand below. Contradicting all expectation, students are amazed to find that the tissue rips with only a little sand on it, but when a lot of sand is added to the tube, the tissue does not rip!

Equipment:

1. Paper tube. A paper towel tube works well.
2. A wooden dowel. Its diameter should fill much of the tube, but should move freely in the tube. When dropped into the tube, its width should not prevent it from falling freely down the length of the tube. It should have enough mass to rip the tissue when dropped onto it.
3. Tissue.
4. Rubber band.
5. Sand. Rice can also be used as a substitute for sand.

The Lesson:

Show students the paper tube and the dowel. Hold the tube upright, placing your open palm below it. Demonstrate that the dowel will fit into the tube. Place the dowel above the tube and drop it into the tube, catching it with your open palm below. Be sure that students can see the dowel freely falling out the bottom of the tube. Now, using a rubber band, affix a tissue to one end of the tube. Now inform students that they will be making a series of predictions. Explain that you will drop the dowel into the empty tube, on top of the tissue. Students are to predict the outcome. Now show the sand. Explain that you will then replace the tissue with a new one, if necessary. You will pour a light layer of sand on the tissue paper and drop the dowel into the tube in the same manner, so that it lands on top of the sand sitting on the tissue. Students should predict the outcome. Further explain that you will again replace the tissue if necessary and add enough sand to fill the tube about ¼ full. Again, you will drop the dowel onto the sand. You will repeat this procedure two more times, filling the tube ½ full of sand and ¾ full of sand each time. Students should predict the outcome for each trial. They should further predict which trial(s), if at all, they think the tissue will rip. Once they have made these predictions, conduct each trial. Most will predict that the chance of the tissue ripping will increase as more sand is added to the tube. In fact, the outcome will be exactly opposite. More sand actually *prevents* the tissue from ripping!

As mentioned in the Equipment section, rice makes a terrific substitute if sand is unavailable.

Possible Variables:

1. Different brands of tissue.
2. Paper tubes of varying diameters.
3. Using a square tube rather than a circular one.
4. Replacing the sand with another substance such as rice, flour, salt, sugar, etc.
5. Using more than one tissue. This involves studying the outcome using different layers of tissue.
6. The diameter of the dowel used.
7. The length of the paper tube, which would alter the height from which the dowel is dropped.
8. The substance that the dowel is made of. This could change its density.
9. The mass of the dowel.

Phenomenon Explained:

A shock wave is a type of propagating disturbance caused by a violent change in pressure. It can propagate through either solid, liquid, gas, or plasma. The shock wave carries energy as it propagates. Essentially, the shock impulse is absorbed and dissipated by converting kinetic energy into another form of energy. Typically, it is converted into heat energy.

Sand is an excellent shock absorber. When the dowel is dropped, it applies pressure to the sand. The energy created from this pressure is dispersed. When the dowel makes impact, some of the grains of sand at the top of the pile are thrown upwards, while others are pressed against the inside of the paper tube. The movement of these grains of sand creates friction, converting kinetic energy, or the energy of motion, into heat energy. The law of conservation of energy states that energy can never be created or destroyed, although it can be converted from one form to another.

More sand in the tube allows for more dissipation through it. When there is more sand there are more grains to be thrown up and press against the sides of the tube. The tissue will not rip, as long as there is enough sand to dissipate the energy. However, with fewer grains of sand, the energy is transferred to the tissue, causing it to tear.

Standards Alignment:

Next Generation Science Standards (NGSS, Lead States 2013)

Disciplinary Core Ideas in Physical Science

PS2: Motion and Stability: Forces and Interactions

PS2.B: Types of Interactions

PS3: Energy

PS3.A: Definitions of Energy

PS3.B: Conservation of Energy and Energy Transfer

PS3.C: Relationship Between Energy and Forces

PS4: Waves and Their Applications in Technologies for Information Transfer

PS4.A: Wave Properties

Soap Powered Boat

<u>Concepts Illustrated:</u> Surface tension, properties of surfactants, cohesive property of water, hydrophobic molecules, hydrophilic molecules, polarity, Newton's third law of motion, polar molecules, solubility, the respiratory system of fish, the human respiratory system, properties of water.

The phenomenon observed in this demonstration is surprising to most. Elementary level students are especially excited to investigate further. Disequilibrium is generated when students observe an object to move forward in the absence of an obvious force.

<u>Paradox:</u>

A paper boat placed into water, propelled by nothing more than a drop of soap, speeds forward!

<u>Equipment:</u>

1. Index card.
2. Scissors.
3. Toothpick or eyedropper.
4. Liquid soap detergent.
5. Water.
6. Wide bowl, at least 2-3cm deep. A pie tin or foam food tray works well.
7. Food coloring.

<u>Preparation:</u>

An index card is used in this demonstration because of its stiffness. Cut the boat design out of the index card. The design is of your choice, but you should test the design prior to the demonstration. A simple triangle "house shape" with a section cut out for the "door" works well.

The designs are endless. Another would be the shape of a rocket with a notch cut out of its base.

If you are concerned about younger students using scissors, templates of boats could be prepared ahead of time. They could choose the design they would like to investigate.

The bowl can either be filled with water prior to the demonstration, or it can be filled as students look on.

Food coloring is not necessary for the demonstration to work. It is used for two reasons. The first is that it adds a dimension to the outcome that is not typically observed. This will be explained in the Demonstration Procedure. The second is that it leads to richer investigations because students do not know whether the food coloring played a role in the outcome.

Be sure that the bowl has been cleaned prior to the demonstration. You do not want any soap film or residue remaining in the bowl from any practice trials. This will affect surface tension and the outcome.

The Lesson:

Show the shape cut out of the index card. Don't refer to it as a boat, as that will "tip" expected results. Instead, explain that you cut out a random shape. Further explain that in a moment you will place this object into the water. Demonstrate by dropping it squarely onto the surface of the table. You don't want to get the boat wet until students have made their predictions.

After informing students that they will be expected to make two predictions, show the food coloring. With the boat still on the table, demonstrate how you will place one drop of food coloring in the cut-out triangle. Tip the bottle of food coloring with the cap on, so that none is released yet. Then show the liquid soap. Students should be told what this is. Then show an eyedropper. If students do not know how it works, demonstrate the use of the eyedropper with the water. Then explain that you are going to place a drop of soap in the same spot that you placed the food coloring. Students should predict what will happen when you add food coloring and when you add soap.

There will be a variety of predictions. Some students predict that when the food coloring is added it will spread and surround the boat, but when the soap is added it will push the food coloring away from the boat. Others predict that adding the soap will cause the food coloring to spread quickly away from the boat. And others predict that the food coloring will initially spread, but the addition of soap will cause the food coloring to regroup to its original placement in the cut-out area of the boat. Some will predict that the paper will sink, but the food coloring and soap will cause it to rise.

Uncap the bottle of food coloring and fill the eyedropper with soap, in preparation. You want to add food coloring and soap shortly after placing the boat into the water. Now drop the boat squarely into the water, placing it at the outer edge of the bowl, engine closest to the outer edge. Place a drop of food coloring into the engine area. The food coloring will begin to spread a little, but will basically remain within the confines of the engine area for a bit. Now place one drop of soap onto the food coloring, in the engine area. The boat will immediately jet forward across the surface of the water! As it travels, it will leave behind a trail of food coloring!

Lesson Variation:

The soap can also be placed onto the engine area of the boat before placing it in the water. Dip the toothpick into the soap and then "apply" it to the back of the boat. Wipe the soap onto the sides of the cut-out engine area. Then drop the boat squarely onto the surface of the water. It will immediately jet forward!

The toothpick dipped in soap can also be dipped into the water at the engine.

If you do not have food coloring available, the demonstration works without it. Simply add the soap to the engine of the boat to cause it to propel forward.

As an extension to the demonstration, place another boat in a second bowl of water. Lower a sugar cube into the water and the boat will float towards the cube! This happens because the sugar is porous. It draws water inwards, pulling the boat towards it. Matchsticks can also be used in place of the paper boat.

Possible Variables:
1. The design of the boat. Ranging from simplistic to intricate, the possible designs are endless. This includes using three dimensions. Edges can be bent up. Tiers and extra components can be added as well.
2. The size of the boat. This would involve keeping the same shape, but changing its size.
3. The number of engines added to the boat.
4. Size of the engine.
5. Brands of soap.
6. Types of soap, such as hand soap, shampoo, body wash, etc.

7. Placing soap at a different location or more than one location of the boat.
8. The type of material the boat is made of. This can include aluminum foil and even a foam grocery or lunch tray. Aluminum foil would allow for 3 dimensional shapes.
9. The weight of the boat. Masses, such as tiny washers, can be added to the boat.
10. Using a boat without an engine cut out.
11. Adding salt or sugar to the water. This changes the density of the water, but students can also investigate any affect through interaction of soap and salt/sugar.
12. Adding salt or sugar to the soap.
13. Using a liquid other than water, such as vegetable oil, milk, or carbonated beverages.
14. Using soapy water.
15. The temperature of the water. It can be warmed or chilled with ice.
16. The temperature of the soap.
17. Placing the soap on the boat before placing it into the water.
18. The amount of soap used. Will more soap cause the boat to travel further?

Phenomenon Explained:

Cohesion refers to the attraction of like molecules towards one another. Water molecules have a very strong cohesive attraction for one another. Those molecules at the surface do not have any water molecules above them. Thus, they are strongly attracted to those water molecules below. The strong attraction to the molecules around and underneath create a surface tension, a "flexible skin" across the surface of the water. These cohesive forces surround the boat when placed in the water. The molecules at the surface pull the boat on all sides with equal force.

Soap is a surfactant, a compound that reduces surface tension. The addition of soap disrupts the cohesive property of the water where the engine is, at the back of the boat. The cohesive forces and surface tension around the boat are no longer equal and consistent. Less cohesive force in the back, and more towards the front, cause the boat to be pulled forward. The boat is not actually "pushed", rather it is "pulled". As it does, the soap in the engine area continues to act as a surfactant through each new area of water it encounters. This keeps the boat moving.

If consecutive investigations are conducted, the bowl or tray will need to be thoroughly rinsed to remove any soap film or residue from the previous trial.

The addition of soap as a variable broadly expands the scope of topics covered in class discourse. Surfactants play a critical role in our bodies. There is a thin layer of water that lines human lungs. This water is necessary for the gas exchange of carbon dioxide and oxygen to occur. These gases require a wet layer or surface for the exchange to take place. In fish, this exchange takes place in their gills. Since they are on the outside of the fish, gills have direct contact with water. Our lungs, on the other hand, are best able to be kept wet inside of our bodies. However, due to the properties of water, surface tension arises that can interfere with the expansion of our lungs as we breathe. Surfactant acts to reduce surface tension. This prevents alveoli, small air sacs in the lungs, from collapsing when we exhale. The most efficient oxygen-carbon dioxide exchange occurs in our lungs with the greatest alveoli surface area. By preventing the collapse of alveoli, surfactant helps to maximize the surface area available for the exchange of gases.

Soap molecules are bipolar. That is, each molecule has two ends. One is a non-polar "tail" and the other a polar "head." The polar end is hydrophilic, it *likes* water and dissolves in it. The non-polar end is hydrophobic, meaning it doesn't *like* water.

If the density of the liquid is altered by adding salt or sugar, discourse can include solutions, solubility, solutes, solvents, and concentration. Saltwater or sugar water is a mixture. One property of a mixture is that it is physically combined, not chemically, and it can be physically separated. For example, saltwater can be physically separated through the process of evaporation, or boiling the water away.

A solution is one in which a solute is dissolve in a solvent. The solute is the substance being dissolved and the solvent is the substance in which the solute is dissolved. Water is called the universal solvent because it is capable of dissolving more solutes than any other liquid. Solubility is the ability of a solute to dissolve in a solvent.

A concentrated solution is one which there are many dissolved particles of solute in the solvent. On the other hand, a dilute solution is one in which there are few dissolved particles of solute. A solution which contains all the dissolve particles it can possibly hold is called saturated.

Standards Alignment:

Next Generation Science Standards (NGSS, Lead States 2013)

Disciplinary Core Ideas in Physical Science

PS1: Matter and Its Interactions

PS1.A: Structure and Properties of Matter

PS1.B: Chemical Reactions

PS2: Motion and Stability: Forces and Interactions

PS2.A: Forces and Motion

PS2.B: Types of Interactions

Disciplinary Core Ideas in Life Science

LS1: From Molecules to Organisms: Structures and Processes

LS1.A: Structure and Function

Disciplinary Core Ideas in Earth and Space Science

ESS2: Earth's Systems

ESS2.C: The Roles of Water in Earth's Surface Processes

Spinner

Concepts Illustrated: Thermal energy, convection, heat conductivity, thermodynamics, density, molecular movement of gases, temperature, exothermic reactions, chemical changes, transfer of energy, convection, first law of thermal dynamics, second law of thermodynamics.

This demonstration involves a heat source and is intended for upper level students only. It is not suitable for elementary level children. When allowing upper level students to conduct this investigation, be certain to follow all safety guidelines and necessary precautions. As always, supervision and student awareness for the rules of safety are critical when using fire.

Paradox:

A paper cup is lined with liquid crystal, a laminated sheet of temperature sensitive plastic. When suspended over a heat source, students expect that the paper will change color. But they do not expect that as the heat rises, the cup will spin wildly!

Equipment:

1. A ring stand and horizontal support rod.
2. A paper cup. A tall paper cup works best.
3. Thread.
4. An alcohol burner, candle, hot plate, or mobile light bulb.
5. Liquid Crystal sheets. Readily available, these are temperature sensitive, plastic laminated sheets that can be cut with scissors. These sheets are black, but when exposed to heat they will display the visible spectrum of colors. They have self-adhesive backing and can be found, rather inexpensively, at science supply stores.

Preparation:

Three or four rectangular flaps must be cut out of the side of the paper cup. The number depends on the size of the cup. Using a utility knife, carefully cut three sides of each rectangular flap- one long side and the two ends. The flaps should be evenly spaced around the cup. Each of the ends should be cut about 1 inch from the top and bottom of the cup. The same side should remain uncut on each flap. Bend the flaps open, hinged on each uncut side.

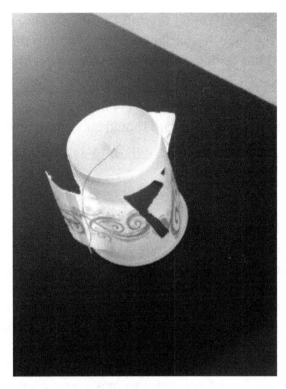

The design of the cup

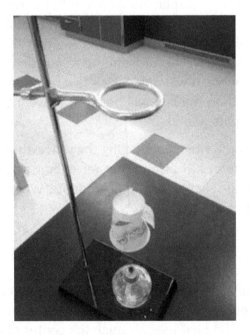

The setup

Close-up view

Now line the inside of each flap with Liquid Crystal. This is very easy to do. Cut the paper to the size of the flaps. Then peel the adhesive backing and press it onto the inside of each flap. Liquid Crystal will change color within a temperature range between 77-110°F.

Poke a hole in the bottom of the cup and insert one end of a piece of thread through the hole. Tape the thread to the inside bottom of the cup. It will eventually be used to hang the cup from a horizontal support on the ring stand. The cup should hang straight- it should not be tipped.

The cup will not spin very much if string is used to support it. Use sewing thread and the cup is more easily able to rotate. It will spin wildly!

The Lesson:

When the lesson begins, the cup is not yet hanging from the ring stand. Show the cup first. It should be made distinctly clear that the inside of each flap on the cup is lined with Liquid Crystal. Students should understand the properties of this material. Demonstrate its sensitivity to temperature by placing it on your open palm. The heat from your palm will cause the color of the Liquid Crystal to change within seconds. You can then also place a finger on the inside of one of the flaps to show the color change. Students should understand that when exposed to increased heat, the inside of the flap will change color. Explain that the open flaps will allow a clear view into the cup while it is hanging. Without the flaps, it will be difficult to observe the inside of the cup. This is an important comment to make, as it gives a purpose to the flaps that draws attention away from any other intended purpose. Most students will not initially imagine their purpose as anything other than to offer a clear view to all observers.

Now, hang the cup from the support rod so that it is suspended over the hot plate or alcohol burner positioned next to the ring stand. Inform students that you will turn the hot plate on, or light the alcohol burner. Ask them to predict what will occur. Most will say that the flaps will change color. Some will predict that the color change will occur from top to bottom on the flap, especially if a tall cup is used. Initiate the heat source. It will only take a few seconds before the inside of each flap is seen to change color. But then the cup will begin to move a bit. To the surprise of most, it will gradually rotate, until it spins wildly!

Note that students can use candles as a heat source when conducting their investigations. This may meet the needs of those with limited resources, if alcohol burner or hot plates are not available. Of course, this would not be advised for elementary level students. When using fire, all safety measures and rules should be enforced.

Lesson Variation:

The paper cup in this demonstration can be replaced with a spiral cut out of a sheet of Liquid Crystal. This spiral is suspended over the heat source. Again, students will expect that the Liquid Crystal will change color, from top to bottom, as the heat rises through the center of the spiral. But, they do not expect the spiral to wildly spin!

The phenomenon can still be observed without the use of Liquid Crystal. Beginning at the center of a paper plate or piece of construction paper, draw a spiral. If using a paper plate, the spiral should expand to its full diameter. Then cut the spiral out and tape a piece of thread to the center point. Hold the thread and the spiral will hang down.

Possible Variables:

1. The size of the flaps. This could mean that each flap is the same size, but different from those used in the demonstration. It could also mean that each flap has a different size.
2. The shape of the flaps. Each flap could have the same shape, or each could have a different shape.
3. Placing the Liquid Crystal on the outside of the flaps.
4. No Liquid Crystal used on the flaps.
5. The number of flaps.
6. The placement of the flaps.
7. The shape of the open edge of the flaps.
8. A hole in the bottom of the cup. This could also involve multiple holes.
9. A hole, or multiple holes, placed in the side of the cup. This could also involve various placements of these holes.
10. The size of the cup.
11. The distance between the cup, or spiral, and the heat source.
12. A spiral made of paper, rather than Liquid Crystal.
13. The width of the spiral.
14. Thickness of the paper used to make the spiral.
15. The length of the spiral.
16. The angle of the flaps.

Phenomenon Explained:

Heat is not the same as temperature. Essentially, heat is energy and temperature is a measure of it. Heat is a form of energy that can transfer from one medium to another, flowing from objects of higher temperature to those with lower temperature. When a cup of coffee feels hot, it is because energy from the cup is being transferred to your hand. On the other hand, a glass of iced tea feels cold because heat energy from your hand is flowing into the glass. This causes it to feel cold.

The temperature of a substance is a measure of the average kinetic energy of its molecules. All matter is composed of atoms or molecules that are in constant motion. The faster they move, the more kinetic energy they have. There is a direct relationship between the motion of molecules and their temperature. The greater the kinetic energy, the higher the temperature of the object. Molecules that have low average kinetic energy move slowly and have low temperatures in comparison to molecules with high kinetic energy, which move more quickly and have a higher temperature. The molecules of solids generally move very slowly, simply vibrating in place. Thermal energy is defined as the energy within an object or system due to the movement of the particles or molecules within. Thermodynamics refers to the transfer of heat between different objects or systems. Stated as the law of conservation of energy, the first law of thermodynamics tells us that energy can never be created or destroyed, although it can be converted from one form to another.

Heat is the *total* kinetic energy in a substance or system. This is different than temperature which, as we have learned, is the *average* kinetic energy. Heat is dependent on the speed of the particles, the number of particles, and the type of particles in a substance. On the other hand, temperature is independent of the number and type of particles. A large tub of water could have the same temperature as a small cup of water, but the water in the large tub would possess more heat because it contains many more molecules, therefore more total kinetic energy. As the alcohol burner beneath the cup burns, it undergoes an exothermic reaction, defined as a chemical reaction that releases energy by light or heat.

This demonstration wonderfully illustrates the process of convection. The process of convection is one of the three types of heat transfer. Convection can only occur in liquids and gases. In convection, heated air rises because it is less dense than cooler air, which sinks and pushes the heated air molecules up. As the heat rises, the air molecules just above the hot plate gain kinetic energy and move faster. The increased movement causes them to spread apart from one another, making that portion of air less dense. As these molecules rise, they "hit" the flaps on the cup. This force causes the cup to rotate.

Liquid Crystal sheets are formed from layers of very small, micron sized, crystals. The color changes observed are caused when these layers twist as they are warmed.

Standards Alignment:

Next Generation Science Standards (NGSS Lead States 2013)

Disciplinary Core Ideas in Physical Science

PS1: Matter and Its Interactions

PS1.A: Structure and Properties of Matter

PS1.B: Chemical Reactions

PS3: Energy

PS3.A: Definitions of Energy

PS3.B: Conservation of Energy and Energy Transfer

Disciplinary Core Ideas in Earth and Space Science

ESS2: Earth's Systems

ESS2.D: Weather and Climate

Spinning Glitter Paradox

Concepts Illustrated: Properties of mixtures, physical changes, density, properties of liquids, fluid dynamics, viscosity, solutions, solubility, solutes, solvents, concentration, saturated solutions, process of dissolving, laminar flow, turbulent flow, global weather patterns, atmosphere of distant planets, vascular system of the human body.

Special thanks to Bruce Yeager for his generosity and willingness to share this demonstration.

Paradox:

A mixture of differently colored glitter is poured into an Erlenmeyer flask that has some water in it. The flask is vigorously shaken and all the glitter collects in a dome-shaped pile in the center. The flask is once again shaken to spread the glitter across its base. Now it is next placed on a Lazy Susan and spun. This time the glitter collects in a ring around the perimeter of the base. But, incredibly, the glitter separates by color in donut-shaped rings at the bottom of the flask!

Equipment:

1. Large Erlenmeyer flask or beaker.
2. Glitter of different colors.
3. Water.
4. Lazy Susan.
5. Double-sided tape.

Preparation:

Place a piece of double-sided tape in the center of the Lazy Susan. When the Erlenmeyer flask is set on it, the Lazy Susan can be spun without the risk of the flask being thrown from it.

The Lesson:

Begin by showing students the mixture of differently colored glitter. Make sure they recognize that the mixture contains differently colored glitter particles. Now fill 1/3 of the Erlenmeyer flask with water. Pour the glitter into the flask. Shake the flask, just a little, so that the glitter forms a thick layer across the entire bottom. Tell students that there will be few steps to this demonstration. To begin, they should predict what will happen to the glitter when the flask is shaken. When students are told that there are a series of steps to the demonstration, they might predict that a surprising event might happen at the end, but not necessarily at this early step. The impact of the surprising outcome at this step becomes stronger. Most will predict here that the glitter will float in the water, or that it will become completely mixed up.

Holding the flask firmly by its neck, shake it vigorously in a swirling, circular motion. All the glitter should be clearly seen mixed and swirling around in the liquid. Set the flask down on a table and as the swirling subsides, the glitter will collect into a dome-shaped pile in the center at the bottom. This is the first surprising outcome. Now, be sure to reiterate that all you did was shake the flask. Some students will explain the outcome by saying that you swirled in a circular motion. If they don't add this detail in discussion, you should introduce it. You want to plant the notion that perhaps this outcome was due to the spinning, circular motion of the flask. This will make the outcome of the next phase even stronger. Explain that you can generate a more "precise" spinning, circular motion on a Lazy Susan, eliminating any subtle hand motions that might affect contents in the flask. You want to express the idea that you'll produce the exact same spinning motion, just on the Lazy Susan rather than in the hands. Show the Lazy Susan and spin it, so that all students know how the device operates. When expressed in this way, most students will predict that the dome-shaped pile will be more "perfectly" shaped. Lightly shake the flask once again so that the glitter forms a thick layer across the entire bottom. Place the flask in the center of the Lazy Susan. Explain that they probably will know what will happen here, but they should now predict what the outcome might be on the Lazy Susan.

Spin the Lazy Susan. The outcome is strikingly different than observed in the previous step. This time the glitter collects in a ring around the perimeter of the base. But, it also separates the different colored glitter into their own individual rings!

Lesson Variation:

Instead of holding the flask at the neck and shaking it in a circular motion, you could simply keep the flask on the desk and stir it with a stirring rod. This will result in the same outcome.

This demonstration can also be done by suspending the flask in the air and spinning it. This method adds another level of discrepancy. Tie a strong string or monofilament around the neck of the flask. Tie the other end of the string around a rod or meter stick suspended between two ring stands. With the water and glitter in the flask, spin the flask in a circular motion. The glitter will be observed to be pushed to the outside perimeter of the flask. However, when the flask reverses its direction, at the end of its initial spin, the glitter will be pulled into the center!

Finally, the phenomenon can be illustrated by placing some marbles into a large beaker full of water. Use a stirring rod to stir the water in a circular motion. The marbles will push to the outside perimeter of the beaker as they spin around in the water. Now, place some tea leaves into another beaker full of water. Again, stir the water in the same manner as before. The outcome here will be surprisingly different. The tea leaves will be pulled inward and form a pile in the center of the beaker.

Possible Variables:

1. Instead of glitter use beads. This can involve beads that all have the same shape, but have different colors. Beads of different shapes can also be tested. Another investigation can involve differently colored beads, each color having a different shape.
2. Beads that are hollow and beads that are solid. Investigations can involve all hollow beads, all solid beads, or a combination of them.
3. Mix and match differently shaped beads that are both hollow and solid. This can involve a multitude of combinations.
4. Beads that are filled with liquids of varying densities. All beads can contain liquid of the same density, or beads can contain liquids of differing densities. Again, there are many

combinations of events to study here. A simple investigation could involve different densities of salt or sugar water.

5. Temperature of the water that the beads are placed into. This can also be coupled with beads filled with liquids of different densities.
6. Density of the liquid. This can be manipulated by simply adding salt or sugar to the water. This could also be coupled with beads that are also filled with different densities of salt or sugar water.
7. Viscosity of the liquid.
8. Speed of rotation of the flask.
9. Objects other than glitter, such as small pebbles. This will allow for pebbles of different sizes and shapes. This can also involve pebbles of all the same size, or different sizes mixed together. Another investigation could involve Skittles, M & M's, or any other candy.
10. Direction of rotation of the flask.
11. Using sand instead of glitter. This can involve different color sand, placed at different locations within the beaker.
12. Shape of container, such as square, rectangle, round as in a Florence flask, etc.
13. Placement of the beaker on the Lazy Susan. Instead of in the center, place it at the outer edge.
14. In place of glitter, marbles can be used. This would allow for marbles of different diameters as well.

Phenomenon Explained:

The density of an object will determine whether it will float in a fluid. Density is determined by calculating the mass for a given volume, expressed in the formula g/ml, g/cm^3, or g/cc. Density is independent of the sample size, since it represents the mass per ml of the sample. A larger volume does not necessarily equate to a higher mass. Fewer molecules packed into a given volume will result in a lower density than many more molecules packed into the same volume, which would increase the density. Objects with a density less than water will float, while those denser than water will sink. The density of water is 1.0g/ml.

If the density of the liquid is altered by adding salt or sugar, discourse can include solutions, solubility, solutes, solvents, and concentration. Saltwater or sugar water is a mixture. One property of a mixture is that it is physically combined, not chemically, and it can be physically separated. For example, saltwater can be physically separated through the process of evaporation, or boiling the water away.

A solution is one in which a solute is dissolve in a solvent. The solute is the substance being dissolved and the solvent is the substance in which the solute is dissolved. Water is called the universal solvent because of its capability to dissolve more solutes than any other liquid. Solubility is the ability of a solute to dissolve in a solvent.

A concentrated solution is one which there are many dissolved particles of solute in the solvent. On the other hand, a dilute solution is one in which there are few dissolved particles of solute. A solution which contains all the dissolve particles it can possibly hold is called saturated.

To fully understand the phenomenon exhibited in this demonstration, we must understand two principles of fluid dynamics, namely laminar flow and turbulent flow. In laminar flow, the fluid flows in a well-defined, orderly manner, with rather distinct paths. On the other hand, turbulent flow describes random, chaotic flow. There is no order in turbulent flow. Instead, the fluid undergoes irregular fluctuations. Turbulent flow can be observed in streams used for whitewater rafting, where the water moves in random and erratic directions. Consider laminar flow as the opposite of turbulent flow.

We actually observe laminar flow in many facets of our lives. One example is blood flow through capillaries. Each particle in the fluid flows in a smooth path, never interfering with one another. As a result, the velocity of the fluid is constant at any point in the flow. Another example can be seen when a candle flame is extinguished. The smoke that rises straight up from the wick is in laminar flow. But, as it reaches some distance from the wick it begins to spread out, waver, and even curl around. This is turbulent flow. It is rather difficult, if not impossible, to predict the behavior of turbulent flow. Turbulent flow can be the cause of murmurs in the heart and larger arteries. Recent research on turbulent flow continues to provide new insights into global weather patterns, as well as the atmosphere of distant planets.

When the flask is swirled, it exhibits laminar flow. In fluid dynamics, the term "drag" refers to a force, essentially viscous friction, that opposes the motion of a moving object, with respect to a surrounding fluid. In this demonstration, a viscous drag is exerted on those objects within the fluid. Drag forces are dependent on velocity. In laminar flow, drag force is proportional to it. In turbulent flow, it is the squared velocity. Frictional force will accelerate the fluid against the direction of the flow, or backwards. But, these same forces will accelerate the objects in the same direction of the flow, or forwards. In addition, the viscous drag is linearly increased along with the speed of the fluid.

When the water is stirred by grasping the flask and spinning it in a circular motion, the sides and bottom of the beaker produce a viscous effect, which steadily slows the water. This creates a pressure gradient that pulls the glitter towards the center of the beaker, partly due to the low mass of the particles.

Pressure gradients can cause fluids to accelerate. When the beaker is spun on the Lazy Susan, rather than slowing it down, the viscous effects of the jar accelerate the water. The pressure gradient is reversed and the glitter is pushed to the outside perimeter of the flask. The drag force decreases the velocity of the fluid, relative to the object in the fluid flow.

Replacing water with a fluid of greater viscosity causes a higher degree of laminar flow.

Viscosity is defined as a fluid's resistance to flow. Think of it as the "thickness" of a fluid. Fluids such as honey, molasses, corn syrup, and engine oil are highly viscous. Students might choose to investigate the outcome when liquids of varying viscosities are employed.

Standards Alignment:

Next Generation Science Standards (NGSS, Lead States 2013)

Disciplinary Core Ideas in Physical Science

PS1: Matter and Its Interactions

PS1.A: Structure and Properties of Matter

PS1.B: Chemical Reactions

PS2: Motion and Stability: Forces and Interactions

PS2.B: Types of Interactions

Disciplinary Core Ideas in Life Science

LS1: From Molecules to Organisms: Structures and Processes

LS1.A: Structure and Function

Disciplinary Core Ideas in Earth and Space Science

ESS2: Earth's Systems

ESS2.C: The Roles of Water in Earth's Surface Processes

Straight Path, Short Path

<u>Concepts Illustrated:</u>   Potential energy, kinetic energy, mass, volume, density, acceleration, speed, momentum, velocity, elements and compounds, horizontal and vertical motions are independent of one another, conservation of energy, mechanical energy, translational energy, rotational energy.

There are countless variations of this counterintuitive demonstration, commonly called High Road, Low Road. A number of these variations, involving equipment and investigative class structure, allow for flexibility of resources and presentation.

<u>Paradox:</u>

Students discover that the shortest distance between two points is not necessarily the fastest! Two metal balls are released from rest at equal heights on their own tracks. They each have the same initial velocities and travel the same horizontal distance. However, after traveling down a short ramp, one ball travels a straight, flat path while the other encounters a number of hills before finally reaching the end of the track. Although everyone believes the ball traveling the shortest possible path, the straight track, will reach the end first, their expectations are contradicted when the ball taking the longest path actually reaches the end first!

<u>Equipment:</u>

1. Two identical metal balls.
2. High Road, Low Road track.

<u>Preparation:</u>

There is plenty of choice when constructing the tracks. Construction can range from very intricate to very simple. Shelving track in a number of styles, widths, and materials can be found at most hardware or home supply stores. Clear, plastic flexible tubing is another choice. The balls would travel through this tubing, but would remain visible.

<u>The Lesson:</u>

Display the tracks to students. Show the two metal balls and explain that they are identical. They are made of the same metal, with equal mass and diameter. Illustrate what you will do by placing the balls on their individual tracks, at the top of the incline. Do not release the balls. Explain that you will be releasing the balls to travel down their respective tracks. They will be released simultaneously. Distinctly point out that the initial ramps are identical in height and angle, and the final heights are also the same. It should also be made clear that the balls will travel the same horizontal distance.

However, one ball will be traveling a shorter path than the other. After rolling down the short ramp, this ball will travel a straight line to the end of the track. On the other hand, after rolling down its ramp, the other ball will encounter a series of hills that will make its path to the end much longer. Ask students to predict, based on their experiences, which ball will reach the end of the track first.

Most will certainly predict the ball traveling the shortest road will finish first. It appears to be the most sensible answer. Some might predict that they will reach the end of the track together. Once predictions have been made and shared, set the balls on the track and release them simultaneously. Hold a ruler or piece of cardboard in front of the balls to keep them in place. Then lift the ruler to release the balls. Students are always amazed when they observe the ball traveling the longest path to reach the end of the track first!

Lesson Variations:

Foam pipe insulation, offered at most hardware stores, can also be made into a track. It can be found in many lengths- commonly six feet- and is available in a variety of diameters. This track is pre-sliced on one side. You only need to make a slice in the opposite side of the insulation, effectively cutting its diameter into half a circle. This will actually give you two six foot lengths of track that can be easily formed into many designs.

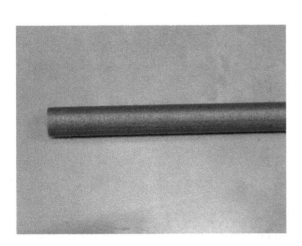

This extension to the demonstration contradicts expectations of those who might begin to surmise that the ball traveling the longer distance is winning due to the conversion of potential into kinetic energy. Explain that you will conduct the experiment one more time, releasing the balls simultaneously. But, you will allow the balls to continue to roll along their respective tracks. Students are asked to predict which ball will stop rolling first. Most will predict that the ball encountering hills will continue to roll longer, because of its ability to convert potential to kinetic at each hill. Surprisingly, this is the ball that stops rolling first. The ball traveling the straight path continues to roll longer!

The phenomenon can be conducted as a series of demonstrations. Each employ one straight track. But, the number of hills on the other track increases in each successive demonstration. In the first demonstration, the other track has a dip followed by a flat section and an incline to the end. Students feel that if a "hill" was place in the center of this flat track, it would slow the ball down enough so that the ball on the straight track will win. After observing it does not, they feel that two hills will surely slow the ball. Again, it does not. Finally, it can be shown that this ball wins even when encountering three hills.

Possible Variables:

1. Diameter of the balls. This can involve two balls of the same diameter, or different diameters.
2. Balls of varying substances, masses, and densities, such as bocce balls, billiard balls, marbles, golf balls, tennis balls, or those made of glass, wood, copper, aluminum, steel, lead, iron, tin, plastic, rubber, etc.
3. The number of hills on the track.
4. The placement of the hills on the track.
5. The slope of the initial ramp.
6. The length of the tracks.
7. A hill or dip on each track, but in different locations along the track.
8. Placement of the plateau on the track.
9. Number of plateaus on the track.
10. The height at either end of the track(s). This can be accomplished by supporting the ends on ring stands, or by using blocks to adjust their heights. An investigation can involve two inclined tracks, one straight and the other "hilly".
11. Rather than balls or spheres, using an object with wheels, such as a toy car.

Phenomenon Explained:

To begin, we should become familiar with the terms momentum, velocity, speed, and acceleration.

Momentum refers to a quantity of motion that an object has. The momentum of a moving object can be calculated using the following formula:

$$momentum = mass \times velocity$$

The momentum of any moving object is dependent upon its mass and velocity. The terms speed and velocity are oftentimes mistakenly used interchangeably. Whereas speed refers to the measure of how fast an object moves, velocity measures how fast an object arrives at a certain point. They are different. Speed is defined as the rate of time that an object travels a distance. Velocity is defined as the rate of change in displacement with respect to time, or the rate that an object moves from one point to another. The formula for speed is:

$$\frac{\text{distance traveled}}{\text{time of travel}}$$

As a vector quantity, velocity involves both speed and direction. The formula for velocity is:

$$\frac{\text{displacement}}{\text{time}}$$

Consider a person walking two steps forward and two steps back, returning to the original starting position. Their speed of each step can be measured. But their velocity would be measured as zero.

Acceleration is defined as the rate at which an object changes its velocity.

When a ball is placed at the top of the incline, it has potential energy due to gravity. The amount of potential energy is dependent on the balls mass and the height to which it has been lifted. When the released to roll down the incline, its potential energy is converted into kinetic energy. Some energy will be lost to friction. In the case of a rolling object, as in this lesson, the kinetic energy is divided into two types of kinetic energy- translational and rotational. Translational energy refers to motion in a straight line, whereas rotational energy refers to the motion of spinning.

Mechanical energy is defined as the energy an object possesses due to its motion or position. There are two forms of mechanical energy, potential and kinetic. Potential energy is stored energy, while kinetic is the energy of motion. The law of conservation of energy states that energy can never be created or destroyed, although it can be converted from one form to another. That is exactly what happens in this demonstration. The energy involved is both potential and kinetic.

When released, both balls have the same initial horizontal velocity as they approach the flat section just after the ramp. The ball traveling the straight path moves at a constant speed the entire distance. The hills encountered by the other ball serve to accelerate it to a higher velocity as potential energy is converted to kinetic. Each downward slope allows the ball to gain speed, increasing its velocity and momentum along the horizontal portions of the track. It is the conversion of potential into kinetic energy that allows the ball traveling the longer distance to travel faster. It is able to more quickly travel the same distance as the other ball due to this higher rate of speed. Even though the ball travelling the straight path does convert some potential energy into kinetic at the initial ramp, the average speed of the ball on the longer track is greater than the one on the straight track. The ball traveling the longer path is capable of converting more of its potential energy to kinetic, providing enough velocity to reach the end faster.

Students can investigate whether the density of the spheres affects the outcome. Density is determined by calculating the mass for a given volume, expressed in the formula g/ml, g/cm^3, or g/cc. Density is independent of the sample size, since it represents the mass per ml of the sample. A larger volume does not necessarily equate to a higher mass. Fewer molecules packed into a given volume will result in a lower density than many more molecules packed into the same volume, which would increase the density.

High road low road track race

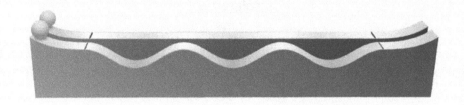

Side view

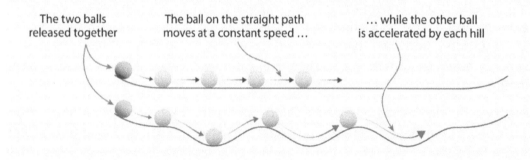

The two balls released together

The ball on the straight path moves at a constant speed …

… while the other ball is accelerated by each hill

Standards Alignment:

Next Generation Science Standards (NGSS, Lead States 2013)

Disciplinary Core Ideas in Physical Science

PS1: Matter and Its Interactions

PS1.A: Structure and Properties of Matter

PS2: Motion and Stability: Forces and Interactions

PS2.A: Forces and Motion

PS3: Energy

PS3.A: Definitions of Energy

PS3.B: Conservation of Energy and Energy Transfer

Stubborn Ping-Pong Ball

<u>Concepts Illustrated:</u> Air pressure, air current, Bernoulli's principle, Coanda effect, fluid dynamics, mass, volume, aerodynamics, airplane flight, dynamics of tornadoes, molecular motion of gases.

Several construction designs and demonstration variations of this demonstration offer a range of equipment and presentation choices to suit available resources.

<u>Paradox:</u>

No matter how hard they try, students discover they are unable to blow a ping pong ball farther than a couple of inches into the air!

<u>Equipment:</u>

Each student should use their own device. For sanitary reasons, they should not share them.

1. A bendable or flex straw.
2. A 1 or 2L plastic soda bottle and its cap.
3. A ping-pong ball.
4. Ruler.
5. Timer is optional.
6. Long-stem funnel is optional.
7. Tubing is optional.

<u>Preparation:</u>

Three construction designs will be described here. The first is the model that will be used for the *Lesson Procedure* explanation.

1. The device is constructed by first drilling a hole in the bottle cap. A hammer and nail can also be used to make this hole. The diameter of this hole should be the same as the straw. When pushed into this hole, the straw should fit as snugly as possible. Push the short end of the bent straw into the hole. It should be pushed in far enough so that when the ping-pong ball rests in the cap, the straw contacts it. To determine the most accurate position, hold the long end of the straw horizontally with the short end bent vertically. Place the ping-pong ball in the cap and blow through the long end of the straw. If the straw is not pushed into the cap far enough, the ball will spin but not lift into the air. If this occurs, push the straw up a bit into the cap. If the ball falls off the cap when you blow into the straw, the straw is pushed in too far. If this occurs, pull the straw out of the cap a bit. When the ping-pong ball hovers over the bottle cap when you blow into the straw, it is in the desired position. Now using a hot glue gun, put a bead of glue around the straw at the hole in the bottle cap.

Be sure to practice this demonstration several times before you present to the class. Blow a slow, steady stream of air. If you blow with too much force, the ball will fly out of the stream of air and away from the device.

2. This simplistic design involves just a straight straw. Using a hole puncher, make a hole in one end of the straw, about two inches from the end. There will be a hole through both sides of the straw. Put a piece of tape over a hole on one side. Now pinch that end of the straw and tape the end shut. Blow into the opposite end of the straw with the open hole on top and the sealed hole underneath. Place the ping-pong ball in the air stream above the straw and it will be held in place.
3. With practice, the ball will hover in mid-air using just a flex-straw. Bend the short end up, blow into the long end and place the ball in the upward stream.
4. The device can also be constructed by cutting off the top of a plastic water bottle or soda bottle. Using a box cutter or utility knife, cut the bottle where the sloped top meets the straight side wall. Drill a hole, or drive a nail, into the center of the plastic bottle cap. Screw the cap onto the bottle top and insert the short end of the straw into the cap. Match the nail to the width of the straw and it will form a fairly tight seal. That's it! Using this model, place the ball on the stream of air after you have begun blowing into the straw. Blow as hard as you can. The ball remains firmly in the stream of air.

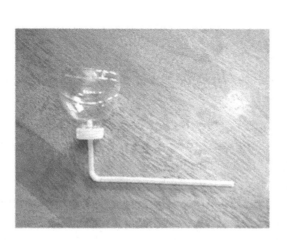

Construction of the device.   With ping-pong ball in place.

The Lesson:

Show the device and hold it in position with the long end of the straw horizontally and the cap upright. Now place the ping-pong ball into the cap. Explain that you are going to blow into the straw. You will use a ruler to measure how high the ping-pong ball will lift into the air, away from the cap. Hold the ruler at the cap, vertically. When the ball lifts off the cap it will rise along the ruler. There will be many different predictions. Now, blow into the straw while holding the ruler in place at the cap. Students will be quite surprised that their teacher cannot blow the ping-pong ball more than a few inches from the cap. They will be very surprised to find that the ball hovers in mid-air over the cap without being blown away from it! Students will be excited to try this for themselves, to prove they can blow hard enough to blow the ball completely away from the cap.

The demonstration can be extended, if you choose. Still holding the straw horizontally, rotate the cap so that it is now facing downward. Explain that while holding the straw 12 inches above the desk, you will hold the ping-pong ball in the cap. You will blow into the straw and then release the ball. Ask students to predict how long it will take for the ball to hit the desk. Charge one student to be the timekeeper, giving her a timer or asking her to watch the clock. Again, there will be many different predictions. But no one will predict what actually occurs. Hold the ball in place and begin to blow into the straw. Slowly release the ball. The ball will hover just under the cap, remaining suspended in the air without falling! This is rather startling to observe!

Lesson Variation:

This variation of the demonstration is conducted in the same manner as the previously described procedure, except that it employs a funnel in place of a straw. It should be unused and clean. Display the funnel and a ping-pong ball. Now place the ping-pong ball into the funnel, with the stem down. Lift the funnel up into the air, above your head, and blow into the stem. Hold the ruler in position to measure the height that the ball is thrown into the air. But, the ping-pong ball remains firmly in place!

Now invert the funnel so that the stem is upright. Place the ping-pong ball in the funnel, holding it in place so that it doesn't fall out. Explain that you will begin to blow into the stem and then release the ball. As in the previous demonstration, ask students to predict the time it takes for the ball to hit the desk once you begin blowing into the funnel. Once they've predicted, blow into the stem. Release the ball to show that it remains in place and does not fall out of the funnel!

A straw that slides over the stem of the funnel could also be used to blow into.

Flexible plastic tubing could also be pushed onto the stem of the funnel. This would allow for the length of the stem to be manipulated. It would also allow for the shape of the stem to be tested. Finally, it would allow students to use different funnels while simply reusing their plastic tubing.

Finally, a balloon could be used by students who do not want to blow into the tube or stem. Blow up the balloon and clip its neck to prevent the air from being released. Then, attach the neck of the balloon to the stem of the funnel. Remove the clip, allowing the balloon to deflate and the air inside to blow through the stem.

Possible Variables:

1. The length of the horizontal section of the straw.
2. The length of the vertical section of the straw.

3. The diameter of the straw. This can be investigated with balls of different diameters, as well.
4. The volume of the ball.
5. Balls with holes in them. The number of holes can also be investigated.
6. Balls of varying mass and density. The mass of the ping-pong ball can be adjusted by poking a hole in it, filling it with sand or water, and plugging it with a small bead of putty, clay, or wax.
7. Replacing the ping-pong ball with a ball of another substance, such as a cork, Styrofoam ball, or cotton ball. Students might also use different diameters of these balls. They can also investigate Styrofoam balls of various shapes.
8. Using the straw without a cap.
9. The number of balls placed into the stream of air.
10. Length of funnel stem. This can be adjusted by attaching tubing or a straw to the stem.
11. Angle that the device is held.

Phenomenon Explained:

This demonstration is a rather startling method of presenting Bernoulli's principle, which describes a phenomenon observed in moving fluids, either liquid or gas. It states that as the speed of a fluid increases, the pressure within it decreases. Fast moving air essentially creates a region of low pressure. The faster a fluid, whether gas or liquid, moves over a surface, the less air pressure it exerts on that surface.

When the ball is initially placed into the cap used in the original demonstration, gravity holds it in place. When you blow into the straw, air pressure pushes the ball against gravity. This is enough pressure to overcome the force of gravity and the ball is lifted. The air is traveling fastest at the cap, where it first contacts the ball. This creates an area of high pressure. After hitting the ball, the air travels around it, evenly distributed. The air curves around the ball, but continues on a straight path on the opposite side. A pocket of low pressure is created on this side of the ball. This creates a pressure gradient with more air pressure below the ball, and less above it. The atmospheric pressure above the ball is now greater than the air pressure blowing around it. The higher atmospheric pressure "pushes" the ball down, towards the cap, holding it in place. When the force upward is balanced with the force of atmospheric pressure and gravity, the ball will remain rather securely suspended in the stream of air.

When the device is held upside-down, the higher atmospheric pressure exerted on the opposite side of the ball is great enough to oppose the force of gravity, and the ball does not fall.

In the lesson variation, a current of fast moving air is created on the side of the ball where the stem meets the funnel. This results in reduced air pressure at that point and lower pressure on the opposite side of the ball, where the higher atmospheric pressure prevents the ball from being ejected from the funnel. In fact, the harder one blows into the stem, the lower the pressure, and the more difficult it becomes to blow the ping-pong ball out of the funnel.

The Coandă effect

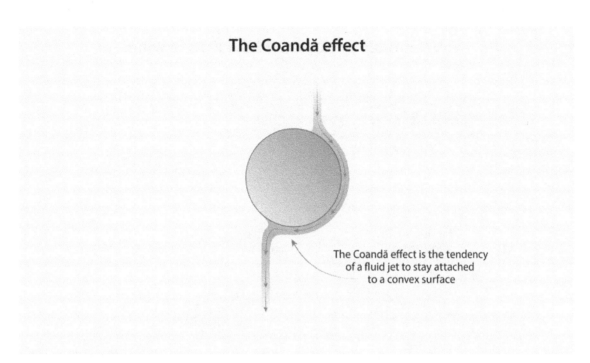

The Coandă effect is the tendency of a fluid jet to stay attached to a convex surface

The behavior of the air blown into the funnel also exhibits the properties of the Coanda effect. It describes the tendency of a streaming fluid to follow along a curved surface it encounters, given the angle of the curvature is not too sharp. When the air hits the ping-pong ball, the current divides, wraps around the ball, and converges on the other side.

Bernoulli's principle and the Coanda Effect explain, in part, how airplanes fly. Air flows over the upper surface of the wings faster than under them. This creates a reduced air pressure above the wings and a higher pressure under them. This generates lift. In addition, when the wing is tilted, air is deflected downward by both its upper and lower surface. Air flowing across the wing glides along the tilted direction of its surface. The air is entrained from the surroundings, resulting in a region of lower pressure above the wing. This also generates lift.

The Bernoulli principle and the lift of a wing

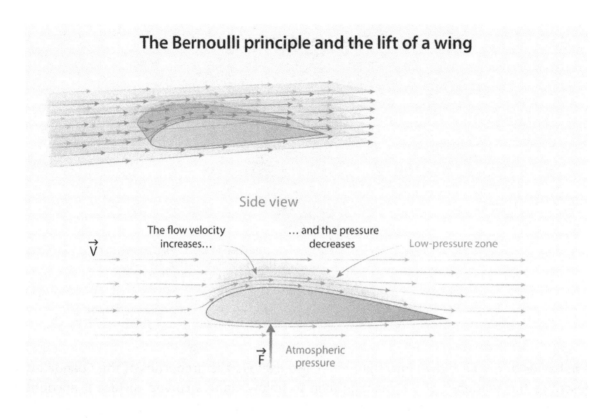

Counter intuitively, the faster the flow of air, the lower the pressure it exerts. This explains the massive destruction caused by tornadoes. The incredible speed movement of air creates a tremendous decrease in pressure within a tornado. The stronger air pressure around the tornado throws nearby objects into it.

Standards Alignment:

Next Generation Science Standards (NGSS, Lead States 2013)

Disciplinary Core Ideas in Physical Science

PS1: Matter and Its Interactions

PS1.A: Structure and Properties of Matter

Disciplinary Core Ideas in Earth and Space Science

ESS3: Earth and Human Activity

ESS3.B: Natural Hazards

Surprise Rise

Concepts Illustrated: Phase changes, properties of gases, boiling, condensation, air pressure, heat, temperature, volume, molecular kinetic energy, thermal energy, molecular movement of gases, molecular movement of liquids, air pressure within the human body, the effects of air pressure on the human body (lungs, ears, sinuses), the influence of air pressure on ailments, fluid dynamics, properties of water, physical changes.

Paradox:

A smaller beaker is inverted and submerged in a larger beaker filled with water. The water is heated and when the large beaker is removed from the heat, the water rushes in and fills the inverted beaker!

Equipment:

1. Two beakers- one large and one small.
2. Hot plate, alcohol burner, or Bunsen burner.
3. Hot gloves or tongs.
4. Food coloring (optional).
5. Mass to place on top of the inverted beaker.

The Lesson:

Fill about half of the large beaker with water. Invert the small beaker and lower it into the water. You do not want the small beaker to fill with water, so be sure to carefully place it straight down into the water. Place a mass on top of it to hold it in place and prevent it from tipping. Now place the large beaker on a hot plate, or above a Bunsen burner or alcohol burner. Explain to students that you are going to heat the water until it boils and ask them to predict what they think will happen. Heat the water until it begins to boil. Once it begins to boil, allow it to boil for about two additional minutes. Ask students to comment on their observations. They will conclude that other than water boiling, or maybe the smaller beaker "steaming up," nothing else has really happened. Once they have shared these observations, ask them to predict what will happen if you remove the setup from the heat. Once they have shared these predictions, remove the large beaker from the hot plate without disrupting the small beaker inside. Be sure to use hot gloves. Maintain the focus of the discussion on what has happened and is happening- not what will happen. Do not direct students to watch for an amazing outcome. Instead, casually remove the beaker from the hot plate while discussing the observations. Maintain a direct focus on the beaker while addressing those observations. Be sure that students are focused on the beaker as the water cools. At about 30-45 seconds after removing the beaker from the hot plate, the water will suddenly rush into the small inverted beaker, completely filling it!

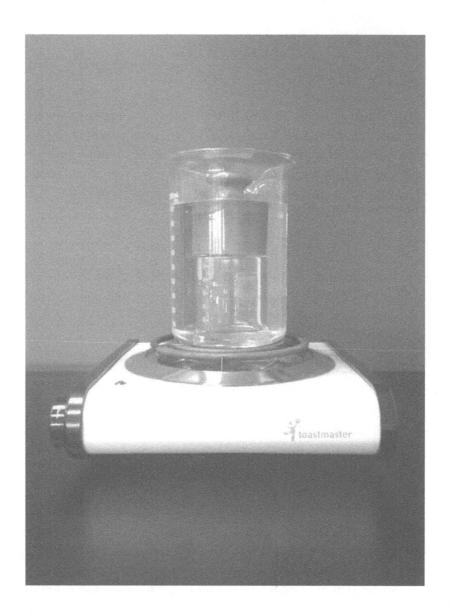

<u>Lesson Variation:</u>

Food coloring can be used to make the water more visible when it rises into the smaller beaker. You can also add a few drops of cold water, or a few chunks of ice, on top of the small beaker after being removed from the heat. This will speed the cooling process, and the movement of the rising water.

<u>Possible Variables:</u>

1. Size of the beakers.
2. Shape of the inverted beaker.
3. Using an inverted cylinder or container that has a hole in it. This can involve a hole in its base, on its side near the base, or both.
4. The temperature to which the water is heated.

5. Putting ice into the water when removed from the heat. This can involve measuring the rate or volume of liquid that enters the inverted beaker dependent of the amount of ice placed in the water or on top of the inverted beaker.

Phenomenon Explained:

The process of boiling water represents a physical change, or a change that does not alter the chemical composition of the substance. Unlike a chemical change, a physical change does not produce a new substance. Boiling water involves the addition of heat and simply changes the form of water from the liquid phase to the gas phase, as water vapor. When matter transitions from one phase to another, it is called a phase change. Phase changes do not produce new substances.

Another phase change is observed in the latter half of the demonstration, as water vapor cools and condenses. Condensation is the phase change from gas to liquid. It involves the removal of heat. Again, no new substance is formed as water vapor simply changes to liquid water.

As the water boils, hot water vapor rises into the small beaker, replacing the air that was under it. When the beaker is removed from the heat, this water vapor cools and condenses. This reduces the pressure within the beaker, creating a pressure differential between the inside of the small beaker and the atmospheric room pressure. The higher pressure outside of the large beaker pushes water into the small beaker.

Air pressure, or atmospheric pressure, is exerted on all of us. It is calculated by the weight of air in the atmosphere, or the amount of air directly above us. Rarely are we aware of its immense force. This is because the pressure of air is exerted on us uniformly, all our lives. But, consider that all the air molecules above you have weight. The combined weight actually creates a pressure equivalent to about 10,000kg/square meter. At sea level, this translates to about 1000kg/0.1 square meter, or about 14.7lbs/square inch or PSI! This means there is about a ton of weight on each of us! Of course, this number varies slightly depending on the altitude you happen to be. The air pressure in our bodies, our lungs, stomachs, ears, fluids, etc., "balances" the pressure outside of our bodies. Our internal pressure is essentially the same as the outside pressure- we are at equilibrium. This prevents us from being crushed by the outside air pressure.

The human body is capable of being affected by low pressure weather systems, that can cause effects such as headaches, motion sickness, and distension in the sinuses. Effects such as these can be influenced by the difference between pressure within the body's cavities, such as lungs, ears, and sinuses, and the atmospheric pressure surrounding the body. This also explains why our ears pop in an airplane, or driving through hills or mountains. The ears essentially try to equalize the pressure within its cavities with the atmospheric pressure. Even those who suffer from arthritis or bursitis might experience increased joint pain as swelling occurs due to a decrease of pressure on the body.

Heat is not the same as temperature. Essentially, heat is energy and temperature is a measure of it. Heat is a form of energy that can transfer from one medium to another, flowing from objects of higher temperature to those with lower temperature. When a cup of coffee feels hot, it is because energy from the cup is being transferred to your hand. On the other hand, a glass of iced tea feels cold because heat energy from your hand is flowing into the glass. This causes it to feel cold.

The temperature of a substance is a measure of the average kinetic energy of its molecules. All matter is composed of atoms or molecules that are in constant motion. The faster they move, the more kinetic energy they have. There is a direct relationship between the motion of molecules and their temperature. The greater the kinetic energy, the higher the temperature of the object. Molecules that have low average kinetic energy move slowly and have low temperatures in comparison to molecules with high kinetic energy, which move more quickly and have a higher temperature. The molecules of solids generally move very slowly, simply vibrating in place. Thermal energy is defined as the energy within an object or system due to the movement of the particles or molecules within.

Heat is the *total* kinetic energy in a substance or system. This is different than temperature which, as we have learned, is the *average* kinetic energy. Heat is dependent on the speed of the particles, the number of particles, and the type of particles in a substance. On the other hand, temperature is independent of the number and type of particles. A large tub of water could have the same temperature as a small cup of water, but the water in the large tub would possess more heat because it contains many more molecules, therefore more total kinetic energy.

Standards Alignment:

Next Generation Science Standards (NGSS, Lead States 2013)

Disciplinary Core Ideas in Physical Science

PS1: Matter and Its Interactions

PS1.A: Structure and Properties of Matter

PS3: Energy

PS3.A: Definitions of Energy

Disciplinary Core Ideas in Earth and Space Science

ESS2: Earth's Systems

ESS2.C: The Roles of Water in Earth's Surface Processes

ESS2.D: Weather and Climate

Sympathetic Pendula

Concepts Illustrated: Resonance, resonant frequency, oscillation, simple harmonic motion, potential energy, kinetic energy, amplitude, mass, volume, density, Hooke's law, sympathetic resonance, mechanical energy, law of conservation of energy, transfer of energy, elements and compounds.

There are a remarkable number of variations to this intriguing demonstration, each incredibly captivating! There are also countless potential variables, providing a wealth of rewarding investigations and rich discourse.

Paradox:

Students are amazed to discover that two pendulum bobs pass their energy and their motion back and forth, between one another!

Equipment:

The materials employed in this demonstration can vary greatly, presenting a tremendous breadth of investigation for students. Each of these variations will be described and explained in the sections that follow. Their setups range from quite simplistic to rather intricate. Ultimately, the materials used will be chosen by the method you personally prefer, the resources available, and your curriculum. There are four essential components, common to all variations. They are:

1. Two upright supports. Ring stands would work well.
2. String, thread, or fishing line that is connected horizontally between the two upright supports.
3. String, thread, or fishing line to use as a pendulum.
4. Four bobs. There are many objects that can be used, ranging from hooked weights or masses to simple washers. Two of the bobs should be identical.

Preparation:

The preparation will be explained using ring stands and washers as bobs, but, as you will discover, there are many objects that can be used in their place.

Set the two ring stands about 50-100cm apart. The distance between them is not critical. Tie a length of string between the two. The string should be near the top of the ring stand post and it should be tied at the same height on each. Now cut two lengths of string, one about 20cm long and the other about 10cm. Tie one end of each string to the horizontal string between the ring stand posts. Slide each of these so they are at opposite ends of the horizontal string, close to the ring stand posts. The distance between them is not critical. Tie one washer to the other end of each string. These will act as the bobs. They should be distinctly different sizes. For the sake of description, let's consider the setup from the student's perspective. The large washer, hanging from the 20cm string, will be to the right. The small washer, hanging from the 10cm string, is to the left.

Cut two additional lengths of string. These will vary in length. One should be 20cm long, the second longer. A specific length is not required. A length of 25-30cm will be good. I will refer to it as the 30cm string in the next section. Now tie one washer on the end of each string. The washer tied to the 20cm string should be identical in size to the washer currently hanging on the 20cm string in the setup. These two strings are not yet tied to the horizontal string between the ring stands.

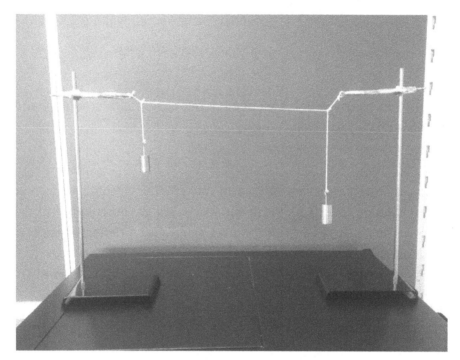

Showing the setup using masses as bobs.

The Lesson:

Display and explain the setup to students. Do not swing the washers yet, but you should certainly explain that they are able to swing freely under the influence of gravity and acquired momentum. You should also distinctly point out the difference in length of these two strings. This will become important to students when they begin to make predictions. Explain to students that they will be asked to make a series of predictions throughout this demonstration. Begin by explaining that you are about to swing the longer pendulum, at their right. Ask them to predict what will happen. Many will predict that the swinging motion will subside after some time. Some will predict that the perturbance of the string will cause the pendulum at their left to swing. Swing the 20cm pendulum. Acknowledge that the swinging motion does, in fact, slow down over time. If any students predicted that the second pendulum to swing, point out that did not occur.

424

Now stop the motion of the 20cm pendulum. Explain that you will now do the same with the pendulum of shorter length. Because of the difference in length, many will now predict that the motion will slow down either faster or slower than the first pendulum. Others will predict the arc to be larger or smaller. Set this pendulum into motion and acknowledge the differences in arc and slowed movement.

At this point, students should be considering these differences to be the focus of the demonstration. Your acknowledgement of these differences as the demonstration progresses helps to convince students of this. This approach establishes the conditions for a more intense cognitive disequilibrium later in the demonstration.

Explain that you have another pendulum that differs in length from the first two. This is the 30cm string. Show the string and tie it onto the horizontal string, close to the 10cm pendulum on their left. There are now three pendula of differing lengths. Once again ask students to predict what will happen when you set this newly added pendulum into motion. And, once again, they will most likely relate the arc or slowing motion to the other two. Swing this pendulum and, as before, acknowledge comparisons and differences.

Show the final length of string to be added and ask students to make another prediction, as they had before. This is the 20cm string. It will be attached next to the pendulum of similar length, on their right. Draw attention to the fact that this newly added string is the same length as the pendulum directly next to it. When students are now asked to make their predictions, they will most likely respond that the new pendulum will have identical arc and slowing motion as the pendulum of equal length. Their focus on these properties will heighten the unexpected nature of the actual resulting behavior.

Set this pendulum into motion. You are certain to see looks of disbelief as the 20cm pendulum that is hanging still, suddenly begins to move. It will increase speed and amplitude with each swing. As this movement intensifies, the pendulum initially set into motion slows. Eventually this pendulum stops swinging completely, while the pendulum next to it swings instead. Disbelief turns to shock as the movements reverse. The pendulum at their right begins to slow as the initial pendulum now begins to swing. Again, the pendulum at the right stops, as the other pendulum fully swings. This behavior will continue. The two pendulums will take turns swinging, one remaining motionless while the other swings fully.

Explain that you will now switch the places of the two pendula in the center, bringing the 30cm pendula, closest to the 10cm string, next to the 20cm string. If you word it as such, most students will think that whichever pendulum is hanging next to the 20cm string will also swing. So, some students will predict that the two pendula to their right will now transfer their swinging behavior between one another. Explain that you will set the 20cm pendulum into motion and ask students to make their predictions. No one will expect that the two 20cm pendula will actually trade their swinging motion, while the pendulum hanging between them remains completely motionless!

<u>Lesson Variation:</u>

If you do not have ring stands available, tie string between two chairs or desks that you can then hang pendula from.

Very interesting variations of this demonstration can be observed with "coupled pendula", a system created by coupling, or connecting, pendula. Typically, connections are formed using either springs or strings between pendula, but a solid rod can also be used. The connection can be made between the strings of the pendula, or the bobs themselves. Holding one bob stationary and pull the other bob either away from it, either along the length of the horizontal support string, or perpendicular to it, and then release them. In this manner, bobs can also be shown to "trade" movement.

<u>Possible Variables:</u>

1. The distance between the ring stands.
2. The distance between the pendula.
3. The mass of the bobs. Unlimited combinations are possible.
4. Substance the bob is made of, such as aluminum, tin, lead, glass, steel, plastic, etc.
5. The shape of the bob. For example, cubes, triangles or small rods. Will the outcome change if a sphere and a rod act as bobs on two pendula of equal length? What if they each had a rod? What if the rods had different masses? Clay can easily be molded into many shapes.
6. Too numerous to list here is the object used as a bob. These can include, but are certainly not limited to, tennis balls, golf balls, billiard balls, standard masses, washers and steel nuts and bolts of all sizes, fishing sinkers, and even apples or sneakers. Balls of various substances can also be purchased from science supply stores with hooks attached. In addition, if paper cups or film canisters are used as bobs, they can be easily filled with sand, buttons, or coins to change their mass. Poke a hole in the lid of a film canister to attach the pendulum string. Soda cans can also be used as bobs, attached to the pendulum string by their tabs. They can also be filled with sand or water. Ping pong balls with a small hole cut into them can also be filled with any amount of sand or clay to change the mass. Liquids can also fill the ping pong balls for a unique investigation. Clay can also be used as a bob. Easily attached to the end of the pendulum, the mass and volume could be changed by simply adding or taking clay away. Connecting paper clips to the end of the pendula will allow for pennies to be wedged into the paper clip. This setup allows for investigation of differently sized coins.
7. The density of the bobs. This can involve changing the density of one bob, several, or all.
8. Lifting the horizontal string between the pendula, so that it is no longer horizontal.
9. Putting the horizontal support string on a slight angle.
10. The pendula length. Again, the patterns imagined are endless.
11. The number of pendula.
12. Swinging the bob from side to side, along the length of the horizontal string it hangs from, rather than a front to back direction. This will cause the other bob to swing in the same direction.

13. Thickness of the strings used. This can include horizontal and pendula strings of different thickness, the horizontal different from the pendula strings, or each pendula string of different thickness.
14. Replacing the horizontal string with a piece of solid rod or dowel.
15. Replacing the pendulum string with other materials, such as ribbon, shoelace, yarn, or rubber band.
16. Replacing the pendulum string with a piece of solid rod. Coat hanger wire can be used as a pendulum by bending the ends into hooks and hanging them on the horizontal string.
17. The tautness of the horizontal supporting string.
18. Swinging the pendula of equal length together.
19. Attaching two bobs to the same pendulum. This can also involve varying the heights of those bobs and changing their mass in numerous combinations. If the upper bob has greater mass than the lower, setting the upper bob in motion will cause the smaller mass to oscillate with a much larger amplitude. More bobs can be added to the system. If those bobs have progressively less mass from top to bottom of the pendulum, the amplitude of each becomes successively greater from top to bottom.

Phenomenon Explained:

The phenomenon of resonance is wonderfully illustrated in this demonstration. Resonance occurs when large vibrations develop from repeated impulses whose frequency matches the natural frequencies of one of the pendula in the system. Each pendulum has a natural or resonant frequency. This is the number of times the pendulum will swing back and forth per second, or oscillate. A shorter pendulum has a greater frequency, longer pendula have lower frequencies. Pendula of equal length have the same natural frequency.

When the driver pendulum is set into motion, it begins to swing or oscillate. Each oscillation tugs on the horizontal supporting string above, creating vibrations. The energy produced from the vibration of each oscillation is transferred to the other pendula hanging in the system. Each tug from the driver pendulum occurs at the same natural frequency in a pendulum of equal length. The result is known as sympathetic resonance, or sympathetic vibration, a phenomenon that occurs when a vibration produced in one body causes similar vibrations in a passive, neighboring body of similar frequency.

The second pendulum begins to swing, out of phase with the driver pendulum. This means they are not swinging in tandem. When one is at the height of its swing, the second pendulum might be somewhere in the middle of its swing. Each swing of the second pendulum tugs on the first pendulum. The timing of these tugs causes the driver pendulum to slow down and eventually be brought to rest. To understand this, consider pushing a child on a playground swing. Pushing the swing at the right moment will cause the child to swing higher. But, pushing at the wrong moment causes the swing to slow down.

When all its energy has been transferred to the second pendulum, the driver pendulum stops swinging. But now the situation is reversed and the oscillations from the second pendulum begin to tug on the driver. In this manner, energy from the vibrations of their oscillations continues to be exchanged between the two pendula of similar frequency.

When the bob of a pendulum is pulled back and held in place it has potential energy. When released, the force of gravity works on the bob as it swings down, converting the potential energy to kinetic. The pendula alternate between potential energy, at rest, to kinetic energy, in motion. Eventually, the energy from the pendula system dissipates through friction and air resistance and they both stop swinging.

Pendula that are not the same length do not have the same frequency. As a result, the phenomenon is not observed.

Mechanical energy is defined as the energy an object possesses due to its motion or position. There are two forms of mechanical energy, potential and kinetic. Potential energy is stored energy, while kinetic is the energy of motion. The law of conservation of energy states that energy can never be created or destroyed, although it can be converted from one form to another.

This demonstration illustrates the conservation of mechanical energy. The potential energy at the release point is converted to kinetic energy as the bob reaches the bottom of its swing. Upon its release, the bob gains speed as it falls. As it continues to fall, and lose height, it also loses potential energy. However, it also gains speed and kinetic energy. As stated in the law of conservation of energy, the total energy is conserved for both potential and kinetic combined.

Simple harmonic motion is described as a periodic movement in which the restoring force is proportional to the displacement, generally in the opposite direction of the displacement. Our simple pendula system behaves like a harmonic oscillator. However, the period is determined by the pendulum length, not the mass of the bob. They system involves kinetic energy, or the energy of movement and gravitational potential energy.

Standards Alignment:

Next Generation Science Standards (NGSS, Lead States 2013)

Disciplinary Core Ideas in Physical Science

PS1: Matter and Its Interactions

PS1.A: Structure and Properties of Matter

PS2: Motion and Stability: Forces and Interactions

PS2.A: Forces and Motion

PS3: Energy

PS3.A: Definitions of Energy

PS3.B: Conservation of Energy and Energy Transfer

PS3.C: Relationship Between Energy and Forces

PS4: Waves and Their Applications in Technologies for Information Transfer

PS4.A: Wave Properties

Termite Trails

Concepts Illustrated: Pheromones, insect behavior, insect anatomy, entomology.

This is a rather remarkable phenomenon that continues to be researched and understood. Termites exhibit fascinating behavior that present fruitful investigative opportunity. Student reactions occur in two phases during this demonstration. First, there is sheer surprise and excitement when students discover that termites will follow trails made by pen ink- a phenomenon no one expects! But then there is puzzlement when students cannot explain why the termites follow some trails, but not others!

Paradox:

Only through investigation will students begin to explain the startling and unexpected behavior of termites encountering shapes drawn on paper!

Equipment:

1. Worker termites. They are not dangerous and can be purchased at science supply stores.
2. Colored pens and pencils.
3. Paper or paper plates.
4. Soft-bristle, thin art brushes.
5. Petri dishes.
6. Magnifying lenses.

Preparation:

In the explanation that follows, a demonstration will provide the students initial observations. However, these observations can be made as an introductory investigation, conducted by pairs of students. Since it allows students to observe proper handling of termites and equipment, it is advised that initial observations be made through demonstration. When presenting the demonstration, allow room for students to surround the demonstration area for optimal viewing.

Forceps are sometimes used to move termites, but this is not suggested. Termites should not be "picked up" using forceps. Students oftentimes have difficulty grasping the termites without injuring them. If forceps are used, they should only be used to gently "push" the termites towards a specific direction. It is also not advised to pick the termites up with fingers. Again, they can oftentimes be injured in the process. It is best to use very thin, soft-bristle art brushes.

Worker termites can be kept in a closed container, such as Tupperware, with damp or moist corrugated cardboard. They will feed on the cardboard. Do not soak the paper, or they could drown. Instead, mist the cardboard with a water bottle. Termites should be prepared in advance by placing 5-10 in a petri dish with a bit of moistened cardboard. Each group will be given one of these Petri dishes.

<u>The Lesson:</u>

Prior to the demonstration, students should understand that they will be working with living organisms. They should be given a brief background of termites. Students should understand that termites are delicate. They should be aware of the safe and ethical way to handle them. Expectations should be very clear and direct. All termites are expected to be returned unharmed after the investigations. The demonstration provides a wonderful opportunity for students to observe the proper handling of termites in the lab.

Show students a piece of white paper and two colored pens, one red and one green. The green should be Papermate or Bic brand, while the red is any other brand that termites do not respond to, such as a felt-tip or rollerball pen. Using the red pen, draw an octagon on the paper. Now draw a circle using the green pen. The shapes should be about the same size and should not overlap. Next, draw a square in red ink around the perimeter of the page. Now, within the perimeter of that square, draw another in green ink.

Explain that you are simply going to place one or two termites into each shape drawn. Ask students to predict how the termites will behave. Some might predict that the termites will explore the entire page, regardless of the drawn shapes, but will not leave the page. Because of the colors used, others will predict that the termites placed into the red shape will not leave its confines, while those in the green circle will venture out. Some of these students imagine that the colors they associate with "stop" and "go" will somehow translate into termite behavior. Other students will recognize that the shape drawn in red resembles the shape of traffic stop signs. Others will predict that the termites will leave the shapes, travel towards the edges of the paper, but will not cross the red square.

Using the art brush, gently push one or two termites into each shape. Students will observe that those in the green circle will not leave its confines, but will travel the green ink as if they are following a path! They will also observe that those termites within the octagon shape will venture out of that enclosure. Those termites might find and travel the path of the green ink as if they were trains on a track, either on the circle or the square around the perimeter of the page!

Using the art brush, model the care taken with the termites by gently guiding and pushing them back into their original Petri dish.

<u>Lesson Variation:</u>

To limit the area that the termites travel and to keep them from straying, students can cut a piece of paper that fits inside of a Petri dish. Paper plates or small bins can also be used.

To more carefully observer behavior and anatomy of termites, students can use magnifying lenses when conducting their investigations.

<u>Possible Variables:</u>

1. The shapes and designs drawn on the paper. The ideas are limitless.
2. The thickness of the lines drawn.
3. Straight and wavy lines drawn with dashes or dots.

4. The brand of paper used to draw the design on.
5. The thickness of the paper used.
6. The color of the paper used.
7. The texture of the paper used.
8. Different brands of pens, markers, and pencils. This can include scented ink.
9. Differently colored pens and pencils.
10. Making an indentation on the paper using the pen cap- no ink. Are termites following a depression in the paper, or are they following the ink?
11. If students understand that the ink is actually composed of various colors, they might investigate whether a certain component is attractive to the termites. To investigate this, they could conduct a chromatography lab to separate the different colors, and then cut those colors out of the chromatography paper to test individually.

Phenomenon Explained:

Termites have a hierarchical structure within their colonies. Worker termites, used in this demonstration, lack compound eyes. As a result, their behavior is not influenced by the recognition of ink color. Since they live underground, sight is of little use to them. This explains why pheromones play such a significant role in their lives. Pheromones are scent chemicals released by the termites. They provide a type of communication or signal. Different pheromones convey different messages or information. They have a variety of purposes, including the location of food, finding mates, warning others of danger, and even returning home. Certain brands of ballpoint pen ink, particularly Papermate brand pens, resemble specific pheromones that the termites recognize as "trail" pheromones. When they encounter a line drawn with a pen containing this ink, they will orientate to it and follow that line. They will not follow felt-tip and rollerball pen ink.

It should not be the goal for students to discover this, but current research leads to a volatile compound found in the ink, known as 2-phenoxyethanol, as the source of the phenomenon. This chemical is not present in all ink.

Standards Alignment:

Next Generation Science Standards (NGSS, Lead States 2013)

Disciplinary Core Ideas in Life Science

LS1: From Molecules to Organisms: Structures and Processes

LS1.A: Structure and Function

LS1.D: Information Processing

LS2: Ecosystems: Interactions, Energy, and Dynamics

LS2.D: Social Interactions and Group Behavior

Thirsty Coin

Concepts Illustrated: Cohesion, adhesion, surface tension, properties of water, viscosity, volume, density, heat, temperature, solubility, solute, solvent, concentration, saturated solutions, process of dissolving, properties of mixtures, properties of water, properties of surfactants, the respiratory system of fish, the human respiratory system.

Data collected during this experiment can be reported and shared through a variety of methods, allowing students to learn and practice the construction of box and whisker plots, stem and leaf plots, etc.

Paradox:

Students will be amazed to discover the number of drops of water that can be placed onto a coin without falling off its edge!

Equipment:

1. A coin.
2. Water.
3. Eyedropper or pipette.
4. Beaker.

Preparation:

Be sure that all students have a close, and very clear, view of the penny. Demonstrate this on a table in the center of the classroom, surrounded by your students. You could also place the penny under a projector, such as an Elmo, allowing you to zoom into the penny and project the image for all to clearly see.

<u>The Lesson:</u>

Show the coin, beaker of water, and eyedropper or pipette. Some students are unfamiliar with eyedroppers. For this reason, you should demonstrate how it is used. Show how water can be introduced into the eyedropper, then squeeze a few drops back into the beaker of water. Make sure that students understand that you can control the eyedropper so that only one drop comes out at a time. Lay the coin flat on the table. Explain that you're about to begin putting drops of water onto the flat surface of the coin. Ask students to predict how many drops of water they think will be placed onto the coin before water begins to fall off its edge. Begin to add drops of water onto the penny. Ask students to count aloud with you as each drop of water falls onto the penny. The drop that causes the water to fall over the edge of the coin should not be counted. Students will be amazed to discover exactly how many drops will build up without falling over the edge of the coin!

Due to the ease of setup and cleanup, students can conduct multiple trials. An example data table can look something like this:

Liquid	Trial 1	Trial 2	Trial 3	Trial 4	Trial 5
Water					
Other					

<u>Lesson Variation:</u>

Once you have completed the demonstration, you can perform it a second time using vegetable oil. Because of its viscous appearance, students will often predict that more drops of vegetable oil will stay on the penny than water. The outcome will surprise them once again when they discover that just the opposite is true. Without this extension, vegetable oil can become one of the variables chosen by students to investigate.

<u>Possible Variables:</u>

1. Different types of coins.
2. Heads vs tails side of coin.
3. Lincoln or wheat penny. Does the particular engraving affect the volume of water held?
4. Different liquids, including liquids of different densities, such as Karo syrup, vegetable oil, etc.
5. Soapy water. This can also involve testing different amounts of soap, as well as different brands or even types of soap, such as dish soap, hand soap, laundry soap, etc.
6. Dipping the penny in soapy water before adding plain water drops to it.

7. Density of the liquid. Density can be manipulated by simply adding salt or sugar to the water. This can also involve testing different amounts of salt or sugar.
8. Temperature of the water.
9. Height that the eyedropper is held above the coin.
10. Angle that the eyedropper is held above the coin.
11. Dipping penny into soapy water, or other liquids, before placing drops of water on it.
12. The method of placing the water on the coin.
13. The rate at which the drops are placed onto the coin.
14. The year of the coin. This would involve the same type of coin, for example a dime, but a different year that it was issued.
15. Using a clean vs a dirty coin.
16. The temperature of the coin.

Phenomenon Explained:

There are a few properties of water that are involved in this phenomenon. Cohesion is the attraction of like, or similar, molecules towards one another. Water molecules have a very strong cohesive attraction for one another. Imagine a glass of water. There are powerful cohesive forces between the molecules in that glass. This cohesive property forms from the attraction of the hydrogen atoms, with positive charges, in one water molecule to the oxygen atoms, with negative charges, of another molecule. The water molecules at the surface do not have any water molecules above them. As a result, they are strongly attracted to those neighboring water molecules at their sides and to those below, which draws them in towards the liquid. This strong attraction to the molecules around and underneath creates what is known as surface tension. The phenomenon allows water to resist external forces, exhibiting the appearance of an elastic membrane across its surface.

Adhesion describes the force that attracts different molecules to one another. In our demonstration, adhesion is the force that attracts water molecules to the surface of the coin. This force of attraction is strong enough to prevent the water from spilling over the edge.

The forces of cohesion and adhesion contribute to the observed phenomenon. The water molecules at the bottom of the bubble, or closest to the penny, hold the water to the penny due to adhesion. The water molecules on the surface of the bubble create surface tension. Each of these properties of water contribute to the stability of the water drop on the coin.

The forces of cohesion and adhesion, as well as the property of surface tension, cause the growing bubble of water to maintains its beaded, dome shape. A droplet of water will tend to be pulled into a spherical shape, due to cohesive forces on the outer membrane. The shape is the result of water molecules attracting to one another in an optimal shape, minimizing surface area to volume ratio. This is also what soap bubbles do.

Soap is a surfactant, a compound that acts to lower the surface tension of water. It does this by weakening the attractive forces between the water molecules. With the addition of soap, fewer water drops can be placed on the penny before water spills over the edge.

The addition of soap as a variable broadly expands the scope of topics covered in class discourse. Surfactants play a critical role in our bodies. There is a thin layer of water that lines human lungs. This water is necessary for the gas exchange of carbon dioxide and oxygen to occur. These gases require a wet layer or surface for the exchange to take place. In fish, this exchange takes place in their gills. Since they are on the outside of the fish, gills have direct contact with water. Our lungs, on the other hand, are best able to be kept wet inside of our bodies. However, due to the properties of water, surface tension arises that can interfere with the expansion of our lungs as we breathe. Surfactant acts to reduce surface tension. This prevents alveoli, small air sacs in the lungs, from collapsing when we exhale. The most efficient oxygen-carbon dioxide exchange occurs in our lungs with the greatest alveoli surface area. By preventing the collapse of alveoli, surfactant helps to maximize the surface area available for the exchange of gases.

Cohesive forces and surface tension are significantly decreased with an increase in temperature. Students investigating this variable will discover that fewer drops can be added to the coin before the water bead falls off the edge.

Surprisingly, a penny can actually hold about 36 drops of water on average. An average drop of water is about 50,000 Nano liters.

Students might choose to investigate whether the density of the liquid will affect the outcome. The density of an object will determine whether it will float in a fluid. Density is determined by calculating the mass for a given volume, expressed in the formula g/ml, g/cm^3, or g/cc. Density is independent of the sample size, since it represents the mass per ml of the sample. A larger volume does not necessarily equate to a higher mass. Fewer molecules packed into a given volume will result in a lower density than many more molecules packed into the same volume, which would increase the density.

If the density of the liquid is altered by adding salt or sugar, discourse can include solutions, solubility, solutes, solvents, and concentration. Saltwater or sugar water is a mixture. One property of a mixture is that it is physically combined, not chemically, and it can be physically separated. For example, saltwater can be physically separated through the process of evaporation, or boiling the water away.

A solution is one in which a solute is dissolve in a solvent. The solute is the substance being dissolved and the solvent is the substance in which the solute is dissolved. Water is called the universal solvent because of its capability to dissolve more solutes than any other liquid. Solubility is the ability of a solute to dissolve in a solvent.

A concentrated solution is one which there are many dissolved particles of solute in the solvent. On the other hand, a dilute solution is one in which there are few dissolved particles of solute. A solution which contains all the dissolve particles it can possibly hold is called saturated.

Viscosity is defined as a fluid's resistance to flow. Think of it as the "thickness" of a fluid. Fluids such as honey, molasses, corn syrup, and engine oil are highly viscous. Students might choose to investigate the outcome when liquids of varying viscosities are employed.

Students might also choose to investigate the effects of changing the temperature of the water. Heat is not the same as temperature. Essentially, heat is energy and temperature is a measure of it. Heat is a form of energy that can transfer from one medium to another, flowing from objects of higher temperature to those with lower temperature. When a cup of coffee feels hot, it is because energy from the cup is being transferred to your hand. On the other hand, a glass of iced tea feels cold because heat energy from your hand is flowing into the glass. This causes it to feel cold.

The temperature of a substance is a measure of the average kinetic energy of its molecules. All matter is composed of atoms or molecules that are in constant motion. The faster they move, the more kinetic energy they have. There is a direct relationship between the motion of molecules and their temperature. The greater the kinetic energy, the higher the temperature of the object. Molecules that have low average kinetic energy move slowly and have low temperatures in comparison to molecules with high kinetic energy, which move more quickly and have a higher temperature. The molecules of solids generally move very slowly, simply vibrating in place. Thermal energy is defined as the energy within an object or system due to the movement of the particles or molecules within. Thermodynamics refers to the transfer of heat between different objects or systems.

Heat is the *total* kinetic energy in a substance or system. This is different than temperature which, as we have learned, is the *average* kinetic energy. Heat is dependent on the speed of the particles, the number of particles, and the type of particles in a substance. On the other hand, temperature is independent of the number and type of particles. A large tub of water could have the same temperature as a small cup of water, but the water in the large tub would possess more heat because it contains many more molecules, therefore more total kinetic energy.

Standards Alignment:

Next Generation Science Standards (NGSS, Lead States 2013)

Disciplinary Core Ideas in Physical Science

PS1: Matter and Its Interactions

PS1.A: Structure and Properties of Matter

PS1.B: Chemical Reactions

PS2: Motion and Stability: Forces and Interactions

PS2.B: Types of Interactions

Disciplinary Core Ideas in Life Science

<u>LS1: From Molecules to Organisms: Structures and Processes</u>

LS1.A: Structure and Function

Disciplinary Core Ideas in Earth and Space Science

<u>ESS2: Earth's Systems</u>

ESS2.C: The Roles of Water in Earth's Surface Processes

Toothpick Star

<u>Concepts Illustrated:</u> Adhesion, cohesion, capillary action, properties of water, density, fluid dynamics, properties of mixtures, heat, temperature, molecular motion of liquids, solutions, solubility, solutes, solvents, concentration, saturated solutions, capillary action in the human body, process of dissolving.

<u>Paradox:</u>

Broken toothpicks are placed onto a plate or tray. When a few drops of water are added to the toothpicks, they become animated, moving to ultimately assemble into the shape of a star!

<u>Equipment:</u>

1. Toothpicks.
2. Small beaker of water.
3. Eyedropper or straw.
4. Plate or tray.

<u>The Lesson:</u>

Show five wooden toothpicks. Snap them in half, just enough to break the wood but not enough to actually break it in two separate pieces. Fold each toothpick into a "V" shape. Place them on the plate or tray, in a circle. The vertices, or the broken edges, should be close together and touching, like a wheel with spokes. Now, introduce the eyedropper and the beaker of water. Be sure that your students understand what an eyedropper is and how it is used. Ask them to predict what will happen when you place a few drops of water in the center of the circle, using the eyedropper. Then place enough drops in the center of the circle, so that each vertex is in contact with water. The "V" shaped toothpicks will become animated, spreading out and forming a five-pointed star.

You can use a straw in place of the eyedropper. Lower the straw into water, put your thumb over the top of the straw, then lift the straw out of the water while keeping your thumb on top. Now hold the straw over the toothpicks and release your thumb from the straw. The water will fall out of the straw.

Possible Variables:

1. Shape of toothpick: round or flat.
2. Surface that the toothpicks lie on.
3. Number of toothpicks.
4. Positioning of the toothpicks. What new shapes will result?
5. Different liquids.
6. Density of the water. Density can be manipulated simply by adding salt or sugar to the water.
7. Viscosity of the liquid.
8. Temperature of the liquid. The water can be warmed or chilled.

Phenomenon Explained:

The properties involved here are adhesion, cohesion, and capillary action. Cohesion is the attraction of like, or similar, molecules to one another. Water molecules have a very strong cohesive attraction for one another. Adhesion refers to the force of attraction between different molecules. Capillary action is the ability of a liquid to flow without the assistance of, and even in opposition to, external forces such as gravity. We depend on capillary action to live. Proper blood circulation, for example, depends on capillary action. Our eyes also use capillary action to drain excess tears into the nasal passage. Plants also depend on capillary action for their survival. Water is transported from roots, through the stem of smaller plants and the trunks of trees, to leaves and branches, against the force of gravity, through capillary action.

In our demonstration, the adhesive force between the water and wood molecules pulls the water molecules into the narrow spaces within the wood. The cohesive force between the water molecules causes the water molecules to follow one another. Via capillary action, the water flows through the porous spaces in the wood.

When the toothpick is broken, the wood at the break is compressed. As the wood absorbs more water, the wood swells, causing these bent fibers to expand. As these expanding fibers push against one another, it forces the opening of the toothpicks where they are broken.

Students might choose to investigate whether the density of the liquid will affect the outcome. The density of an object will determine whether it will float in a fluid. Density is determined by calculating the mass for a given volume, expressed in the formula g/ml, g/cm^3, or g/cc. Density is independent of the sample size, since it represents the mass per ml of the sample. A larger volume does not necessarily equate to a higher mass. Fewer molecules packed into a given volume will result in a lower density than many more molecules packed into the same volume, which would increase the density.

If the density of the liquid is altered by adding salt or sugar, discourse can include solutions, solubility, solutes, solvents, and concentration. Saltwater or sugar water is a mixture. One property of a mixture is that it is physically combined, not chemically, and it can be physically separated. For example, saltwater can be physically separated through the process of evaporation, or boiling the water away.

A solution is one in which a solute is dissolve in a solvent. The solute is the substance being dissolved and the solvent is the substance in which the solute is dissolved. Water is called the universal solvent because of its capability to dissolve more solutes than any other liquid. Solubility is the ability of a solute to dissolve in a solvent.

A concentrated solution is one which there are many dissolved particles of solute in the solvent. On the other hand, a dilute solution is one in which there are few dissolved particles of solute. A solution which contains all the dissolve particles it can possibly hold is called saturated.

Students might also choose to investigate the effects of changing the temperature of the water. Heat is not the same as temperature. Essentially, heat is energy and temperature is a measure of it. Heat is a form of energy that can transfer from one medium to another, flowing from objects of higher temperature to those with lower temperature. When a cup of coffee feels hot, it is because energy from the cup is being transferred to your hand. On the other hand, a glass of iced tea feels cold because heat energy from your hand is flowing into the glass. This causes it to feel cold.

The temperature of a substance is a measure of the average kinetic energy of its molecules. All matter is composed of atoms or molecules that are in constant motion. The faster they move, the more kinetic energy they have. There is a direct relationship between the motion of molecules and their temperature. The greater the kinetic energy, the higher the temperature of the object. Molecules that have low average kinetic energy move slowly and have low temperatures in comparison to molecules with high kinetic energy, which move more quickly and have a higher temperature. The molecules of solids generally move very slowly, simply vibrating in place. Thermal energy is defined as the energy within an object or system due to the movement of the particles or molecules within. Thermodynamics refers to the transfer of heat between different objects or systems.

Heat is the *total* kinetic energy in a substance or system. This is different than temperature which, as we have learned, is the *average* kinetic energy. Heat is dependent on the speed of the particles, the number of particles, and the type of particles in a substance. On the other hand, temperature is independent of the number and type of particles. A large tub of water could have the same temperature as a small cup of water, but the water in the large tub would possess more heat because it contains many more molecules, therefore more total kinetic energy.

Viscosity is defined as a fluid's resistance to flow. Think of it as the "thickness" of a fluid. Fluids such as honey, molasses, corn syrup, and engine oil are highly viscous. Students might choose to investigate the outcome when liquids of varying viscosities are employed.

Standards Alignment:

Next Generation Science Standards (NGSS, Lead States 2013)

Disciplinary Core Ideas in Physical Science

PS1: Matter and Its Interactions

PS1.A: Structure and Properties of Matter

PS1.B: Chemical Reactions

PS2: Motion and Stability: Forces and Interactions

PS2.B: Types of Interactions

Disciplinary Core Ideas in Life Science

LS1: From Molecules to Organisms: Structures and Processes

LS1.A: Structure and Function

Disciplinary Core Ideas in Earth and Space Science

ESS2: Earth's Systems

ESS2.C: The Roles of Water in Earth's Surface Processes

Tricky Temperature

Concepts Illustrated: Heat, temperature, heat transfer, conduction, properties of solids, thermal energy, conductors, insulators, kinetic energy, molecular motion of solids, the human body's perception of heat, wavelengths of light, heat capacity, radiant energy, thermodynamics, color absorption and reflection.

Paradox:

One thermometer is wrapped in wool, another in cotton, and a third in silk. They are allowed to remain wrapped and untouched until the following class. Most students will predict that the thermometer wrapped in wool will read the highest temperature. In fact, when the thermometers are read in the following class, each thermometer shows the exact same temperature reading!

Equipment:

1. Three thermometers.
2. Three pieces of fabric: wool, cotton, and silk. Each should be large enough to completely wrap a thermometer.

The Lesson:

Display three thermometers to the class. Ask a student to read the current temperatures on each thermometer. Point out to the class that the temperatures read indicate the room temperature. You should also point out that this is an indication that the thermometers appear to be "working" properly. Now show the three pieces of fabric. Show the piece of wool and say "this is a piece of wool, like from a wool sweater that you might wear in the winter." This prompts students to recall that wool sweaters are used to stay warm in the cold months. Show the piece of cotton and say "this is a piece of cotton, such as from a T-shirt." Again, this prompts students to consider when cotton is worn. Finally, show the piece of silk and say "this is a piece of silk, like from a man's tie or a woman's dress." Here you are prompting students to recall that silk is not necessarily worn for warmth.

Explain that you will completely wrap each of the three thermometers in their own piece of fabric, one in wool, the second in cotton, and the third in silk. Further explain that they will be set on a shelf, or your desk, where they will remain until the next class. They will be together, but not touching one another. As students look on, wrap each thermometer. Position them in the designated area and remind students that they will remain there, without being touched, until the next class. Tell them that in the next class each thermometer will be unwrapped and read. Ask them to predict which of the thermometers will read the highest temperature.

In the next class, be sure to remind students that the thermometers have not been touched in any way since the last class. Unwrap each thermometer, but be sure to handle them as little as possible. You don't want students to think that your hands, or the manner in which the thermometers were handled, affected the temperature readings. When the thermometer is unwrapped, do not hold the thermometer directly with your hands. Instead, keep it lying down on the fabric that was used to wrap it. Ask a student to read each thermometer as it is individually unwrapped. You don't want two thermometers to be exposed to the room temperature while reading the first. As each thermometer is read, and the temperature announced aloud to the class, record the number on the chalkboard for all to see. Students will be rather amazed to find that all three thermometers read the exact same temperature.

<u>Possible Variables:</u>

1. Various materials to wrap around the thermometers.
2. Double wrapping thermometers.
3. Environments that are colder or warmer. Could put the equipment under a heat lamp. Could also put it in a refrigerator, freezer, or even outside in cold weather, for some allotted time.

<u>Phenomenon Explained:</u>

Heat is not the same as temperature. Essentially, heat is energy and temperature is a measure of it. Heat is a form of energy that can transfer from one medium to another, flowing from objects of higher temperature to those with lower temperature. When a cup of coffee feels hot, it is because energy from the cup is being transferred to your hand. On the other hand, a glass of iced tea feels cold because heat energy from your hand is flowing into the glass. This causes it to feel cold.

Energy from the sun is called radiant energy, or solar energy. Placing the thermometers in a source of heat, such as the sun, might show a difference from other thermometers placed in a room away from the heat source. This can also be shown using a heat lamp. This is because light energy can be converted into heat energy. The first law of thermodynamics states that energy cannot be created or destroyed, but it can be converted from one form to another. A black object *absorbs* all wavelengths of light and converts them into heat. The object gets warmer. On the other hand, a white object *reflects* all wavelengths of light, so the light is not converted into heat. The temperature of the object might increase very little.

The degree to which an object is light or dark will affect how much heat it absorbs. A dark object absorbs more photons than a light object, even if they are the same color. The darker object will absorb more heat, and eventually be warmer than the light object.

Different wavelengths of light contain different amounts of energy. Red, on one end of the spectrum, contains less energy than violet, on the other end. A red object, such as an apple, will absorb the wavelengths other than red. It will reflect red, or perhaps some wavelengths near it. This causes the apple to appear red.

The temperature of a substance is a measure of the average kinetic energy of its molecules. All matter is composed of atoms or molecules that are in constant motion. The faster they move, the more kinetic energy they have. There is a direct relationship between the motion of molecules and their temperature. The greater the kinetic energy, the higher the temperature of the object. Molecules that have low average kinetic energy move slowly and have low temperatures in comparison to molecules with high kinetic energy, which move more quickly and have a higher temperature. The molecules of solids generally move very slowly, simply vibrating in place. Thermal energy is defined as the energy within an object or system due to the movement of the particles or molecules within. Thermodynamics refers to the transfer of heat between different objects or systems.

Heat is the *total* kinetic energy in a substance or system. This is different than temperature which, as we have learned, is the *average* kinetic energy. Heat is dependent on the speed of the particles, the number of particles, and the type of particles in a substance. On the other hand, temperature is independent of the number and type of particles. A large tub of water could have the same temperature as a small cup of water, but the water in the large tub would possess more heat because it contains many more molecules, therefore more total kinetic energy.

The heat capacity of a substance is the amount of heat required to change its temperature by one degree Celsius. A large amount of matter will have a proportionally large heat capacity. Properties of a substance will affect heat capacity. For example, water has a much higher heat capacity than sand. In other words, much more energy is required to raise the temperature of water than sand. If you go to the beach, the sand will feel very cool in the morning, but hot in the afternoon. However, the water at the same beach may not seem to change much at all.

In this demonstration, the thermometers were kept in the same environment. Heat from the room atmosphere affects the fabrics equally, and is conducted to the thermometer. So, regardless of whether the temperature of the environment changed, the thermometers were affected in the same way. The temperature remains the same regardless of the material wrapping the thermometers.

The materials that wrap the thermometers are not producing, or giving off, any heat. An exothermic reaction is defined as a chemical reaction that releases energy by light or heat. When water freezes it is an exothermic process. Neither the wool, cotton, or silk are producing or releasing any heat, so this is not an example of an exothermic reaction. The wool, cotton, and silk actually have the same temperature. Using an infrared thermometer, students can confirm this. There are also smart phone apps that can act as thermal cameras, which can be used to indicate the level of thermal heat being produced from each block. A search for "thermal cameras" should provide a few different app choices. By viewing each block through the camera, any difference in thermal temperature can be immediately observed.

Standards Alignment:

Next Generation Science Standards (NGSS, Lead States 2013)

Disciplinary Core Ideas in Physical Science

PS1: Matter and Its Interactions

PS1.A: Structure and Properties of Matter

PS1.B: Chemical Reactions

PS3: Energy

PS3.A: Definitions of Energy

PS3.B: Conservation of Energy and Energy Transfer

PS4: Waves and Their Applications in Technologies for Information Transfer

PS4.B: Electromagnetic Radiation

Disciplinary Core Ideas in Life Science

LS1: From Molecules to Organisms: Structures and Processes

LS1.D: Information Processing

Twin Tracks

Concepts Illustrated: Acceleration, speed, velocity, momentum, mass, density, volume, diameter, potential energy, kinetic energy, rotational energy, translational energy, Newton's first law of motion- the law of inertia, elements and compounds, Newton's second law, tautochrone curve.

Paradox:

Students are shown two identical ramps, positioned side by side, and two identical steel balls. Contradicting all expectation, students are shocked to discover that when released simultaneously from different points on the ramp, the balls will always reach the bottom at the same time!

Equipment:

1. Two identical curved tracks, alongside each other, with letters indicating various positions along the track.
2. Two identical steel balls.

The Lesson:

Begin by showing students the device and the two steel balls. Point out the positions of the letters on the ramp. Make sure they are aware that the steel balls are identical in every way. Note: do not specifically use the words volume, substance, diameter or mass. Using these words in the demonstration could directly provide students with variables for their expected investigation. Instead, allow students to think of these variables on their own. Simply explain that the balls and the ramps are identical.

Inform students that they will be making several predictions. Place the balls side by side, one on each track, at point A. Ask students to predict which ball will hit the wooden plate at the bottom of the ramp first. They should also predict the difference, in seconds, between the times it takes each ball to hit the plate. This is prediction #1. They will most likely predict both balls to reach the stop at the same time, with zero second's difference. Do not release the balls yet. Now place both balls at position G. Students should answer the same two questions. When released, which hits the plate first, and how many seconds' difference will there be? This is prediction #2. The balls are now placed at positions G and F. Again, ask them to predict which ball, when released, will hit the wooden plate at the end of the ramp and the difference in seconds. Remind them that you'll be releasing the balls at the same time. They will most likely predict that ball F will arrive at the plate first. This is prediction #3. For prediction #4, students answer which would arrive at the wooden stop, and the difference in seconds, when releasing the balls from points G and D. Stress upon them that the distance between the balls is increasingly greater than in the previous trials. Students will most likely predict that ball D will hit the stop first. The difference in seconds will vary. Hold the balls at positions F and C. Students should make the same two predictions- which hits first and how many seconds' difference? This is prediction #5. Finally, for prediction #6, hold that balls at positions G and A as students answer the same two questions. Everyone will predict that A will hit the plate first, but difference in seconds will again vary.

Once these predictions are complete, release the balls as explained for each trial. Students will be shocked to discover that in every trial, the balls reach the plate at the same time!

Lesson Variation:

The same effect can be shown using pendulums. Arrange two pendulums side by side. These can be hung from a horizontal rod attached to a ring stand. Position the setup in front of a chalkboard or easel paper. Imagining a clock, label points A, B, and C, at times 7, 8, and 9 o'clock on the board or paper. Now hold one pendulum bob in each hand and draw them back to show the different release points. First release them both from point A. Then hold one at point B and the other at point C. Release them simultaneously. Finally, release them simultaneously from points C and A. In each trial, the bobs will complete one swing and return to their original release points at the same time. Your hands can release them and await their return, to grasp them when they do. You can release the bobs from any combination of positions and achieve the same outcome.

If you have limited resources, student investigations can involve just one ramp. The ball can be released from different positions on the ramp and a stopwatch can be used to time how long it takes to reach the bottom.

Possible Variables:

1. Spheres made of different substances and densities, such as iron, lead, wood, plastic, aluminum, tin, etc. Spheres with varying densities can also be achieved by filling the ping pong balls with various liquids with differing densities.
2. Spheres made of the same substance, but with different diameters.
3. Rolling the spheres on substances of varying textures, such as felt, sandpaper of various grits, etc. This is accomplished by placing these surfaces directly on a ramp without tracks.
4. Solid vs hollow spheres.
5. Spheres that have holes, similar to a whiffle ball.

Phenomenon Explained:

The principle involved in this demonstration was discovered by Galileo using pendulums, as in the Lesson Variation. He found that regardless of the pendulums starting position, it would always take the same amount of time for them to swing through one complete movement. The oscillations take equal times no matter the amplitude. Similarly, a sphere placed at any point on the ramp in our demonstration, rolls to the bottom of the ramp in the same length of time. Known as a tautochrone or isochrone curve, the ramp is a cycloid upon which spheres released at any point will descend to the lowest point in the same amount of time.

To begin, we should become familiar with the terms momentum, velocity, speed, and acceleration.

Momentum refers to a quantity of motion that an object has. The momentum of a moving object can be calculated using the following formula:

$$momentum = mass \times velocity$$

The momentum of any moving object is dependent upon its mass and velocity. The terms speed and velocity are oftentimes mistakenly used interchangeably. Whereas speed refers to the measure of how fast an object moves, velocity measures how fast an object arrives at a certain point. They are different. Speed is defined as the rate of time that an object travels a distance. Velocity is defined as the rate of change in displacement with respect to time, or the rate that an object moves from one point to another. The formula for speed is:

<u>distance traveled</u>
time of travel

As a vector quantity, velocity involves both speed and direction. The formula for velocity is:

<u>displacement</u>
time

Consider a person walking two steps forward and two steps back, returning to the original starting position. Their speed of each step can be measured. But their velocity would be measured as zero.

Acceleration is defined as the rate at which an object changes its velocity.

Mechanical energy is defined as the energy an object possesses due to its motion or position. There are two forms of mechanical energy, potential and kinetic. Potential energy is stored energy, while kinetic is the energy of motion. The law of conservation of energy states that energy can never be created or destroyed, although it can be converted from one form to another.

When an object is placed at the top of the incline, it has potential energy due to gravity. The amount of potential energy is dependent on the mass of the object and the height to which it has been lifted. When the object is released to roll down the incline, its potential energy is converted into kinetic energy. Ignoring loss by friction, the total amount of energy is conserved. In the case of a rolling object, as in this lesson, the kinetic energy is divided into two different types of kinetic energy- translational and rotational. Translational energy refers to motion in a straight line, whereas rotational energy refers to the motion of spinning.

The ball that is lifted to a higher position on the ramp has greater acceleration. A ball placed at point G has a greater distance to travel, but greater acceleration than a ball placed at point A. A ball beginning at a higher point on the ramp has more potential energy than a ball starting lower on the ramp. The ball that begins higher has further to travel, but travels faster. The ball at point A does not have far to travel before it hits the stop, but it does not have much acceleration. This explains why both balls will reach the stop simultaneously.

The two balls reach the bottom of the ramp together

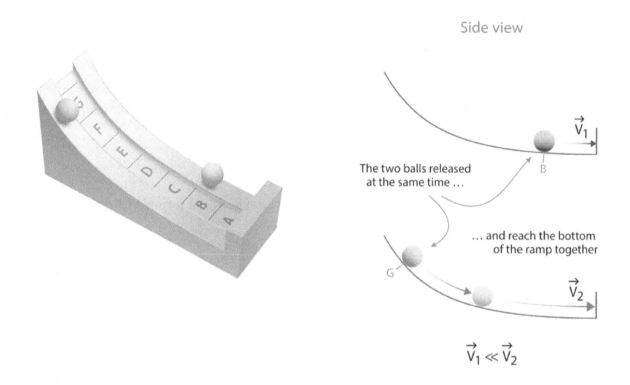

Side view

The two balls released at the same time ...

... and reach the bottom of the ramp together

$$\vec{V_1} \ll \vec{V_2}$$

To demonstrate this idea, attach a horizontal bar to a ring stand, as in the Lesson Variation. Hang a pendulum bob directly in front of the ramp, and aligned with it. You can release the bob from any point on the ramp behind it, and the bob will always hit the stop at the bottom of the ramp in the same amount of time. This is also a counterintuitive outcome that will shock most!

The outcome would be much different of the side by side tracks were on a straight inclined plane. Balls released from two different points on these tracks, would reach the bottom of the plane at different times. This is because the balls have the same acceleration as they travel down the track. They will remain the same distance apart as they travel down the inclined plane and will never reach the bottom together.

The demonstration can also be used to illustrate Newton's first law of motion. Known as the law of inertia, it states that an object either at rest or in motion, remains at rest or in motion with the same speed and direction, unless acted upon by an unbalanced force. Newton's second law of motion describes the relationship between force, mass, and acceleration.

Students might opt to investigate the outcome when manipulating the density of the spheres. The density of an object will determine whether it will float in a fluid. Density is determined by calculating the mass for a given volume, expressed in the formula g/ml, g/cm^3, or g/cc. Density is independent of the sample size, since it represents the mass per ml of the sample. A larger volume does not necessarily equate to a higher mass. Fewer molecules packed into a given volume will result in a lower density than many more molecules packed into the same volume, which would increase the density.

Standards Alignment:

Next Generation Science Standards (NGSS, Lead States 2013)

Disciplinary Core Ideas in Physical Science

PS1: Matter and Its Interactions

PS1.A: Structure and Properties of Matter

PS2: Motion and Stability: Forces and Interactions

PS2.A: Forces and Motion

PS3: Energy

PS3.A: Definitions of Energy

PS3.B: Conservation of Energy and Energy Transfer

Vanishing Beaker

<u>Concepts Illustrated:</u> Refraction, reflection, refractive index, properties of liquids, properties of water, properties of light, volume, Snell's law.

This demonstration is truly shocking to the observer. It looks like real magic! There are several demonstration variations presented, each involving a different approach and different equipment, but each offering an incredibly valuable method to launch into investigations.

<u>Paradox:</u>

Students will think that magic is real when glass objects vanish before their eyes as they are lowered into a beaker of vegetable oil! This truly looks like magic!

<u>Equipment:</u>

The following equipment is used in the *Lesson,* explained below.

1. 4000ml Pyrex beaker. The demonstration can be conducted using a 1000ml beaker.

2. Canola oil. Wesson brand oil works wonderfully. Glycerin can be used in place of vegetable oil.
3. Colored beads. These are optional, but they make for an absolutely startling demonstration.
4. Three additional Pyrex beakers. The size of these beakers can vary. If using a 4000ml beaker, these three beakers should be 250 or 400ml in size. However, if using a 1000ml beaker, these three beakers can be 50, 100 and 250ml, or 100, 250 and 400ml in size. These beakers should not have any print on them.

    a. As mentioned earlier, there are several presentation variations to follow, involving various glass objects made of Pyrex. These can include objects such as test tubes, glass stirring rods, and beakers. These objects should fit inside the largest beaker. The specific objects you use will depend on the presentation method you choose.

Preparation:

In addition to the 4000ml beaker, the demonstration strategy explained below uses three smaller beakers of different sizes- 250ml, 400ml, and 600ml. This strategy also involves a collection of three colorful beads. These beads should be identical. They only differ in color. One of those colors should match the color of the canola oil as closely as possible, a yellow/gold color. The other two colors should be strikingly different, such as blue and red. Fill each of the smaller beakers with a different color bead. One beaker is filled with the red beads, the second with blue, and the 600ml beaker is filled with yellow/gold beads. In our explanation below, red beads fill the 250ml beaker and the blue beads fill the 400ml beaker. It is not essential to use three differently sized beakers. They can all be 250 or 400ml.

The Lesson:

I think this is the most powerful and effective method of presentation.

Show students the 4000ml beaker and mention its size. Then show the Canola oil and ask students to observe as you pour the oil into the beaker. Pour between 2500 and 3000ml of oil and be sure to mention this volume. Now display the three bead-filled beakers and explain that you will lower each beaker into the oil, one at a time. Mention that you will begin with the beaker of red beads, followed by the beaker of blue, and finally the gold. Each will be removed before the next is lowered in. Ask students to predict what will happen when each of these beakers are submerged in the canola oil.

Using three or more beakers whose sizes are clearly different strengthens the demonstration, as attention is immediately directed towards the physical differences of the equipment involved. When three differently sized beakers are used in conjunction with three differently colored beads, student predictions will focus on one of these two features of the demonstration. Their predictions will focus on either displacement of the oil or visibility of the beads. Most will expect that the level of the oil will rise, but will displace different volumes of oil when submerged. Students may predict that the smaller beaker will raise the liquid only slightly, while the largest beaker will raise the level of oil much more, perhaps spilling over the rim.

Others will focus on the color of the beads, since that is the only other perceived variable. Many will predict that the yellow/gold beads will be difficult to see, or "disappear" because they match the color of the canola oil. They'll think that the red and blue beads will be easily visible because of their contrast in color to the canola oil. Ask students to share their ideas.

Once students have shared their ideas, lower the three bead-filled beakers into the oil. As they are lowered in, do not allow them to fill with oil. Both beaker and beads will remain visible. When you submerge the gold bead-filled beaker, allow it to fill with oil. No one will be expecting this beaker to vanish, leaving the beads to appear floating in the oil! The beaker will vanish and jaws will drop!

Lesson Variation:

As mentioned in the equipment list, glycerin can be used in place of vegetable oil. Whereas vegetable oil has a gold-yellow tint to it, glycerin is a colorless liquid.

There is what some may consider to be an even more startling approach to this demonstration. With your students watching, fill a large beaker halfway with water. Then, slowly and carefully pour oil into this beaker. The oil is less dense than water, which is in itself a discrepancy for most students. As a result, the oil will float on top of the water. Continue to add oil until the beaker is full. Clear water will fill the lower half of the beaker while the golden yellow oil fills the upper half of the beaker. Because of the difference in color, two distinctly different layers of liquid will be visible in the beaker. For the next part of the demonstration use a glass stirring rod that when placed into the beaker will protrude far above the top of the beaker. Lower the stirring rod into the beaker and its middle section will appear to disappear. The parts of the stirring rod protruding above the beaker and submerged in the water will be seen, but the middle portion within the oil will be invisible. The glass stirring rod will appear to be missing its middle!

Glass rod vanishes in vegetable oil.   Close-up view.

You can also use three layers of liquids for a very unique visual. First pour glycerin into a beaker. Then slowly pour water into the beaker. Because water is less dense than glycerin, it will float above the glycerin. Now, slowly pour Wesson oil. Since it is less dense than water, it will float above it. You now have three layers. When the Pyrex stirring rod is lowered into this layered liquid, it will vanish from the oil and glycerin layers. It will only remain visible in the water- the middle layer of liquid!

One additional feature that you can add to the demonstration is to hold a pencil horizontally behind the beaker as you fill it with oil. The pencil should be long enough so that students can see its ends protruding from each side of the large beaker. Before pouring the oil in, students will see the small beaker inside the larger. They will also see the entire pencil behind the large beaker. Now pour the oil into the large beaker. The small beaker will vanish, but the entire pencil will still be seen. Looks very mysterious!

There are a number of presentation strategies for this demonstration. Several are presented here. Choose the one that you think would be most engaging for your students and fits your teaching style.

The first variation involves a Pyrex glass beaker, test tube, and stirring rod. As in the previous demonstration, students will most likely expect that the level of the oil will rise, or be displaced, when the objects are lowered in. Students will focus on the different shapes and sizes of the three objects. They may predict that the smaller objects will raise the liquid only slightly, while larger objects will raise the level of oil much more, perhaps spilling over the rim. When students see the differently sized objects that you intend to lower into the oil, their attention is immediately directed towards their physical sizes.

Once a prediction is made for all three objects, ask students to share their ideas. Now, begin by lowering the test tube into the oil. In order for it to "vanish," it must be filled with oil. So, lower it into the beaker far enough so that the oil flows into it. Students will actually see the test tube until it fills with the oil. Students will watch in disbelief as the test tube vanishes before their eyes! This truly looks like real magic as the test tube appears to vanish from the bottom to its top. This is incredibly powerful! You'll hear shrieks! Once you've allowed time for students to react to this visual, remove the test tube. As it is drawn out, it will seem to appear as if by magic from the oil.

Next, lower in the glass stirring rod. As it dips below the surface of the oil, it visually vanishes! Allow as much of the rod as possible to be immersed in the oil, even if the entire rod fits. Remove the stirring rod from the beaker and it will seem to appear, as if by magic, from the oil as it is pulled out.

Finally, lower the beaker into the oil. It will also need to be filled with oil in order to vanish. The beaker will be visible until it fills with oil and disappears!

Another approach is to begin the demonstration by lowering the test tube into the oil-filled beaker. Do not allow the test tube to fill with oil. It will remain visible to the students, who will likely focus on the volume of oil that rises in the beaker. When the beaker is lowered into the oil next, tip it so that it immediately begins to fill with oil. It will vanish as it is lowered into the oil. The shock will have even more impact because this did not happen when the test tube was just immersed. You would finish the demonstration by lowering the glass rod into the oil, causing it to vanish as well.

Yet, in another approach you would lower the test tube and beaker into the oil only up to their rim, so that they don't fill with oil. They will remain visible. Save the glass stirring rod for last. Now, as you lower it into the oil it vanishes. The classroom will become electric! You have a couple of choices at this point. You could lower either the test tube or beaker into the oil, as a seemingly unplanned act. As students yell out comments, they might actually ask you to do this. When they see the beaker vanish, students may realize that allowing the beakers to fill with oil causes them to "vanish". But, you could also choose to end the demonstration with the stirring rod. Provide each group of students with beakers, test tubes, and stirring rods and allow them to discover the vanishing glassware on their own. When students discover this independently, the energy in the classroom is palpable!

A similar strategy would be to present the demonstration using only a series of differently sized beakers. These could be 50ml, 100ml, 250ml, 400ml, and 600ml. Before you begin the demonstration, they should be displayed on your desk in order of decreasing size. Ask students to predict what will happen when you lower each beaker, one at a time, into the 1000ml beaker filled with liquid. Make it clear that each beaker will be lowered upright, up to its rim and then removed. Students will recognize the pattern of the beakers laid out before them and will most likely predict that a decreasing volume of liquid will be displaced when each successively smaller beaker is lowered into the 1000ml beaker. Now, begin with the larger beaker. Lower it into the 1000ml beaker. Someone will probably announce that the liquid has risen. Acknowledge this observation and follow it up by reading off the new level of the oil displaced by the beaker. The beaker will not vanish because you did not allow it to fill with the oil. Remove the beaker and repeat this with each successively smaller beaker. Don't allow any to fill with oil. Each beaker will remain visible and students will focus on the volume of displaced water. Some might announce that their observations match their predictions. They will fall into a "relaxed" patter wherein they focus on the displaced oil, until the smallest beaker is lowered in. As with all the other beakers, lower it up to its rim. Do not allow the beaker to fill with oil. Read the level of displaced oil. Then, act as if you accidentally dropped the beaker. Tip it slight to the side as you do this, allowing oil to enter it. Then tip it more and release it as you act as though it were accidental. Your students will be startled as the beaker falls through the oil and vanishes! Act as shocked as they are. Act as though you have no idea what or how this just happened. Grab a pair of large tongs, reach into the oil, and pull the small beaker out. It will become visible as it is pulled from the oil. Now, you've got them! Allow the energized discussion to flow. Students will yell out. Eventually, someone will recognize and announce that this beaker is the only one to fall into the oil. They'll ask you to drop it in again, and to eventually drop in one of the larger beakers, allowing it to become fully submerged. Once they see that each beaker disappears when fully submerged, the demonstration takes on an entirely new life and direction.

An entirely different presentation would involve small bottles, such as Tabasco bottles, instead of beakers. Each could be filled with a different colored liquid before the demonstration begins. But, one bottle is filled with canola oil. Color the liquid in each bottle using food coloring, except for the bottle filled with canola oil. Do not add any food coloring to this bottle. Each bottle is lowered into the larger canola filled beaker, one bottle at a time. The last bottle lowered in is the one filled with canola oil, which vanishes.

Another approach enhances the unexpected vanish when you begin with a large beaker of water. Begin the demonstration by asking students to predict what will happen when you put your entire hand into the water. When you do so, students will recognize that your hand becomes magnified and appears larger than normal. Now ask students to predict what will happen when you place a test tube into the beaker of water. Then lower the test tube into the water, where it also appears slightly magnified. Now act as though you've just come up with an idea. Communicate to your students that you want to try a different kind of liquid. Then say that you'd like to try cooking oil, since it's "thicker" than water. Ask them to predict what they think will happen when lowering the test tube into a beaker of cooking oil rather than water Then submerge the test tube in the cooking oil to cause it to vanish.

This final presentation is especially effective for elementary students. In this strategy you would place a 250ml beaker into an empty 1000ml beaker. Then explain that you will pour vegetable oil directly into the 250ml beaker until it overflows and spills into the larger beaker that it sits in. Ask students to predict what will happen. There will be a number of diverse predictions. But, elementary students are apt to predict that the small beaker will float when it becomes surrounded by the oil. Begin pouring the oil into the smaller beaker. Eventually it will overflow into the larger beaker and begin to fill that beaker. As the oil surrounds the smaller beaker and rises around it, this beaker slowly vanishes.

Possible Variables:

1. In the demonstration involving a beaker half full of oil and half full of water, food coloring could be added to either the oil, the water, or both.
2. Temperature of the liquids.
3. Using different colored food coloring in the large beaker of oil.
4. Could fill the small beaker with cooking oil prior to lowering it into the large beaker. Then investigate many variations of colors used in the oil of both the small and large beakers. This could include using different colors of liquids in the larger and smaller beakers simultaneously.
5. Pyrex glassware made of different shapes and sizes lowered into the oil filled large beaker.

6. Size or shape of the large Pyrex glass beaker.

7. Glassware that is not Pyrex, such as plastic or other types of glass.

8. Different liquids including Johnson's baby oil, olive oil, Karo corn syrup, corn oil, etc.

9. Using differently colored glassware. These could be investigated with the original Wesson oil or they could be investigated with different colors of liquids through the use of food coloring.

Phenomenon Explained:

Light travels through space at about 300 million meters per second. Light travels through different mediums at different speeds. Its speed is affected as it travels from one transparent medium through another. When this happens, light can bend. That bend in light is called refraction. When passing from air into another substance which slows it down, such as water, light will bend towards a line drawn perpendicular to the surface of the water. This line is known as the normal line. This explains why your hand, or a pencil, placed half in and half out of water will appear to be bend. Refraction is dependent on the medium through which the light passes. The index of refraction, or the refractive index, is a number that describes how light travels through a particular medium. The index of refraction measures the degree to which light bends. The larger the index, the slower the light travels through the medium. The angle of refraction measures the angle between the refracted ray and the normal line.

Snell's law describes how light refracts when it travels through two different mediums with two different indices of refraction. The law provides a formula used to quantitatively describe this behavior. When the two media involved have great differences in the speed of the light traveling through them, there is a greater bend in the light, or a greater refraction. Light will both refract and reflect off the surface of transparent objects, such as glass beakers, making them visible to us. The large beaker that holds the Wesson oil remains visible throughout the demonstration because light reflects off it. Reflection describes how a wave, such as light, alters direction when it strikes a surface. Reflection causes the smaller beaker to vanish, while reflection causes the large beaker to remain visible.

When light travels through two mediums, both of which have the same refractive index, there is neither refraction nor reflection. The object will seem to "vanish" as the refractive indices of the mediums involved approach one another. This happens to be the case with both Pyrex and canola oil. Both have a refractive index of 1.474. As a result, there is no refraction or reflection of the smaller Pyrex beaker when submersed in the canola oil filled larger Pyrex beaker. As a result, the smaller beaker "vanishes."

If you happen to see a faint outline or "ghostly" image of the glassware immersed in the oil, it's due to internal strains within the glass which influences the refractive index.

Interestingly, the index of refraction changes with a change in temperature. If students investigate temperature as a variable, they would most likely notice that the visibility of the submerged test tube can be manipulated. In fact, if the beaker containing the oil and the submerged test tube was gradually heated on a hot plate, the test tube will gradually become increasingly visible, as if by magic!

<u>Standards Alignment:</u>

<u>Next Generation Science Standards (NGSS, Lead States 2013)</u>

Disciplinary Core Ideas in Physical Science

<u>PS1: Matter and Its Interactions</u>

PS1.A: Structure and Properties of Matter

<u>PS4: Waves and Their Applications in Technologies for Information Transfer</u>

PS4.A: Wave Properties

PS4.B: Electromagnetic Radiation

Vanishing Marbles

<u>Concepts Illustrated:</u> Hydrophilic molecules, hydrophobic molecules, polymers, refraction, refractive index, properties of liquids, properties of water, properties of light, Snell's law, polar molecules, volume.

This is absolute eye candy! Students will be convinced they are witnessing magic! Along with this is unique method of presentation are two equally impactful variations for those who have limited resources.

<u>Paradox:</u>

Students believe they are watching a magic trick when water marbles vanish before their eyes!

<u>Equipment:</u>

1. Water marbles. These can be obtained from science supply stores. Although they may have different names, they are still the same product.
2. 2 beakers. 400ml beakers work well.
3. Water.
4. Laser pen.
5. Construction paper.
6. A burner stand is optional.

<u>Preparation:</u>

When you obtain the marbles, they appear to be small crystals. You will need to place them in a beaker and then fill the beaker with water. The crystals will absorb the water and expand. It takes a few hours for their full expansion. The absorption and subsequent increase in volume of the marbles is a surprising effect, and can certainly be studied. However, it is not the focus of this demonstration. Instead, we will be focusing on the refractive index of the marbles. To maintain focus on this objective, we will need the marbles fully expanded when they are introduced to students at the beginning of the demonstration.

Create a sleeve from construction paper that will slide over the outside of the beaker. Do this by cutting a band from the paper that matches the height of the beaker. Wrap the band around the beaker and tape the ends together. Now cut two holes out of the paper. They should be on opposite sides of one another when the sleeve is on the beaker. One hole should be about 1cm in diameter. The other should be about 4-5cm in diameter.

You will need to draw a "bullseye" on either an easel paper, or the chalkboard. There should be two or three concentric circles around the center circle. It is not necessary that it be any particular size. This is what the laser light will be directed towards.

One of the beakers should be filled with water. The other holds the marbles.

<u>The Lesson:</u>

When you begin, the marbles fill about ¾ of the beaker without water. The paper sleeve is not yet wrapped around it.

Show the fully expanded water marbles to students. Explain that they are filled with water. Handle the marbles so that students can get a sense for their "spongy" characteristic. Drop a couple on the table to illustrate this, as well. At this point, students will be very eager and excited to handle the marbles themselves. Let them know that soon they will be able to.

Show the sleeve to students and point out the two holes. Slide the sleeve over the beaker and freely show that the holes are opposite one another. Now place the beaker in position in front of the bullseye. It can be set on top of a couple of textbooks, or a burner stand. The beaker and the bullseye must be positioned so that the holes in the paper sleeve are aligned with the center of the bullseye. Point out that the bullseye is on the direct opposite side of the beaker and that the holes in the sleeve align with the center of the bullseye. Show the laser pen. Explain that you will shine the laser light into the smaller hole of the paper sleeve. The light will, of course, hit the marbles inside. Ask students to predict where the light will hit the bullseye target as it exits the hole on the opposite side. They can choose either the center of the bullseye, or any of the concentric rings surrounding it.

Once predictions are made, shine the laser light into the small hole. Dim the room lights so that the laser light can be more clearly seen. The light will actually be diffused through the marbles. Very little will escape the other side, if any. Ask students to share predictions. Now, explain that you will show everyone what is actually occurring inside the beaker when the light enters. Remove the paper sleeve, reposition the beaker in front of the bullseye, and shine the light into the beaker. Allow students to observe the behavior of the light.

Now, replace the sleeve over the beaker. Discuss the behavior of the light just observed and ask students to use those observations as a point of reference when making the next prediction. Explain that you will add water to the beaker and once again shine the laser light into it, as you had before. Ask students to predict the behavior of the light. Will any light escape the hole on the other side? If so, what section of the bullseye will it hit? The lights should be dim. With the beaker of marbles in position, pour water into it from the second beaker. The marbles should be completely covered with water. Students should not be able to see inside the beaker. Shine the light into the beaker and it should be observed hitting the center of the bullseye on the other side. Ask students to share predictions. Explain that, as before, you will remove the paper to show the behavior of the light inside the beaker. Hold the beaker up in the air by grasping the top from above. Grab the sleeve from below and slide it down and off of the beaker. Prepare for gasps, screams, and shrieks when students see only a beaker of water!

Although this does look like a magic trick, the illusion is exposed as a natural phenomenon. When students question and demand an explanation that answers where the marbles are, and how you got them out of the beaker, explain that they are still inside. Of course, they will not believe you. Prove it to them by slowly pouring the water out of the beaker, into the beaker that originally held the water. Now ask students to observe as you pour water back over the marbles. Pour the water back into the beaker of marbles and allow students to observe them vanish before their eyes!

Lesson Variation:

One alternate demonstration would be to simply ask students to predict what will happen when you place the marble in a beaker of water. Most students will predict that it might sink or float. But no one will predict that it will vanish!

In another variation you could place the marbles into a beaker after showing them to students. Then, ask them to predict what will happen when you pour warm water over them. Students might predict that the marbles will "melt" or "dissolve" after observing their physical characteristics. Again, no one will expect them to vanish!

Possible Variables:

Investigations for the following variables can involve massing the water marbles or timing their absorption rates.

1. Adding fluorescent dye or highlighter ink to the water before placing the marbles in. They will actually absorb the dye, become fluorescent, and glow.
2. Adding food coloring to the water before placing the marbles.
3. The temperature of the water. Warmer water speeds the absorption rate.
4. The type of water. This can include distilled water, salt water, sugar water, or bottled water.
5. Liquids other than water, such as vegetable oil, corn syrup, honey, vinegar, soda, etc. Soaking the marbles in tonic water will cause them to "glow" under black light because of its quinine content.
6. The pH of the water. This can involve adding vinegar, lime juice, baking soda, etc.
7. Placing the water marbles in saltwater or a solution of water and sugar.

Phenomenon Explained:

We should begin by understanding the terms hydrophobic and hydrophilic molecules. A hydrophobic molecule is one that repels, tends not to combine with, or is insoluble in water. Some examples are oils, waxes, and fats. Hydrophobic molecules are non-polar, meaning they do not have a charge. As such, they are incapable of interacting with water molecules through charges. Water molecules are polar, containing both positive and negative charges. This allows them to potentially interact with any molecule that has a charge, such as hydrophilic molecules. A hydrophilic substance is one that easily takes up water.

Water marbles wonderfully illustrate the properties of hydrophilic polymers as their attraction to water allows them to absorb an astounding 300 times their weight in water. Water marbles are composed of a specific type of polyacrylamide polymer.

Light travels through space at about 300 million meters per second. Light travels through different mediums at different speeds. Snell's law describes how light refracts when it travels through two different mediums with two different indices of refraction. The law provides a formula used to quantitatively describe this behavior. The speed of light is affected as it travels from one medium through another. When this happens, light can bend. That bend in light is called refraction. When passing from air into another substance which slows it down, such as water, light will bend towards a line drawn perpendicular to the surface of the water. This line is known as the normal line. This explains why your hand, or a pencil, placed half in and half out of water will appear to be bend.

Refraction is dependent on the medium through which the light passes. The index of refraction, or the refractive index, is a number that describes how light propagates through a particular medium. The index of refraction measures the degree to which light bends as it passes from one medium into another. The larger the index, the slower the light travels through the medium. The angle of refraction measures the angle between the refracted ray and the normal line. We can see a piece of glass in water because the light is slowed down and bent as it passes from the water through the glass. The amazing phenomenon observed in this lesson is caused by the refractive index of the substances involved.

When light travels through two mediums, both of which have the same refractive index, there is neither refraction nor reflection. The object will seem to "vanish" as the refractive indices of the mediums involved approach one another. This happens to be the case with both water and water marbles. As a result, there is no refraction or reflection of the water marbles when submersed in the water, and the water marbles "vanish."

The marbles are filled with water. When placed in water, they become virtually invisible due to their refractive index, which is almost identical to that of water. Because of this, light rays are not bent as they travel through. Light passes from the water to the marble without no refraction, or bend. The light is diffracted in the beaker of marbles because it is traveling through the air between the marbles. The refractive index of air is much different than that of water. The refractive index of air is about 1.0003, while that of water is about 1.3.

Interestingly, the index of refraction changes with a change in temperature. If students investigate temperature as a variable, they would most likely notice that the visibility of the water marbles can be manipulated. In fact, if the beaker containing the water marbles is gradually heated on a hot plate, the water marbles will gradually become increasingly visible, as if by magic!

Note that water marbles are reusable. Allow them to sit for several days and they will regain their original size.

Standards Alignment:

Next Generation Science Standards (NGSS, Lead States 2013)

Disciplinary Core Ideas in Physical Science

PS1: Matter and Its Interactions

PS1.A: Structure and Properties of Matter

PS1.B: Chemical Reactions

PS2: Motion and Stability: Forces and Interactions

PS2.B: Types of Interactions

PS4: Waves and Their Applications in Technologies for Information Transfer

PS4.A: Wave Properties

PS4.B: Electromagnetic Radiation

Visible Sound

<u>Concepts Illustrated:</u> Sound waves, resonant mode, standing waves, nodes, anti-nodes, harmonics, natural frequency, properties of sound, transfer of energy, vibration.

<u>Paradox:</u>

Sand is sprinkled onto a metal plate. When a violin bow is drawn across the edge of the plate, the sand creates spectacular patterns, complex and symmetrical- one of the most breathtaking ways to "visualize sound!"

<u>Equipment:</u>

1. A metal plate. Any type of metal can be used. It can be either round or square, although the dimensions are not critical. A plate about 12" square or in diameter works well.
2. A wooden dowel, used as a handle to grip the metal plate.
3. A violin bow.
4. Sand. The procedure will be explained using sand. But if sand is unavailable you may also use sugar or salt. These are actually listed as possible variables which can be investigated by students.

<u>Preparation:</u>

The metal plate should not be held directly in the hands while conducting this demonstration. Drill a small hole into the center of the plate. One end of the wooden dowel is held against this hole, while a screw is driven into it from the other side of the metal plate. The dowel must be screwed in tightly so that the metal plate does not "wiggle" when held by the dowel.

<u>The Lesson:</u>

Display the metal plate to students by holding it from the dowel. Tip the plate forward, so that everyone can see its surface. Then hold it with the dowel upright, so that the surface of the plate is horizontal. Sprinkle sand onto the plate, covering the surface with a light coating. Now, introduce the bow. Explain that you are going to simply draw the bow across the edge of the plate two or three times. Demonstrate the motion without actually touching the plate. Ask students to predict what will happen. Some students will predict that the action will produce a noise. Others will predict that the sand will "shake," "dance around on the plate," or "form a pile." Now, draw the bow across its entire length on one edge of the plate. After one complete pass along the edge, move it off the plate and draw it across the edge again in the exact same manner. Each time you do this, the patter formed in the sand will become increasingly distinct. No one would have predicted the amazing patterns that form in the sand!

You could immediately draw the bow in a different place on the edge and the pattern previously created will shift and transform into a new, geometric design.

It's important to ensure that all students have a birds-eye view of the surface of the plate during the demonstration. If you do not have a projector to show the surface of the plate to the entire class, then the demonstration should be presented either sitting or kneeling, while the students stand around you and look down.

Be sure to use rosin on the bow.

Possible Variables:

1. The shape of the metal plate. It can be oval, rectangular, diamond, star-shaped, etc.
2. The thickness of the metal plate.
3. The size of the metal plate. This can involve the same type of metal, but in different diameters, or simply different metals of different diameters.
4. The type of metal that the plate is made of, such as brass, aluminum, tin, copper, bronze, etc.
5. Using stiff cardboard as the plate, in place of metal.
6. Gripping the plate between finger and thumb. This can also involve the location at which the plate is gripped.
7. The number of times that the bow is drawn across the edge of the plate.
8. Drawing the bow along different places along the edge of the plate.
9. Drawing two bows at once along the edge of the plate.
10. Using different substances other than sand, such as sugar, salt, pepper, baby powder, seeds, popcorn kernels, small beads, candy sprinkles, etc.
11. Using liquid in place of sand. This can also be an investigation involving liquids with varying viscosities.

Phenomenon Explained:

All objects have a *natural frequency* at which they can vibrate following the introduction of energy from an external source. The energy transmitted disturbs particles and generates a wave that travels through the medium. Resonance occurs when the object vibrates in phase with the applied oscillatory force. These resonance vibrations generate standing waves. Each natural frequency is associated with its own characteristic standing wave pattern, caused from a vibration from an external source. Standing wave patterns occur when the vibrational frequency from an external source causes reflected waves from the medium to interfere with incident waves from the source. The specific frequencies of vibration that produce standing wave patterns are known as harmonic frequencies, or simply harmonics.

Chladni plates display standing wave patterns. In our demonstration, drawing the bow across the edge of the plate causes it to vibrate at a specific frequency. Waves travel outward from the center of the plate, and then back towards the center once they have reached the edge of the plate. The waves traveling outward *from* the center and those traveling inward *toward* the center "interfere" with one another, resulting in standing wave patterns. In a standing wave, some points appear to remain in a fixed position- called nodes, while others display maximum amplitude- called antinodes. When the bow is drawn along the edge of the plate, the sand vibrates and aligns into formations comprised of geometric lines. These lines represent nodes.

The sand has essentially migrated to the nodal lines of the standing wave pattern. You'll notice that the sand vibrates wildly in the areas outside of the geometric lines. These are the antinodes. The sand essentially vibrates away from the antinodes and gather at the nodes. With higher frequencies, nodes become closer together, and the patterns on the metal plate become more intricate. The pattern formed by the sand represents the standing wave pattern associated with the natural frequency of the plate.

The vibrations that occur in the plate are governed by the shape of the plate, its thickness, size, the substance the plate is made of, and the specific point at which the bow is drawn. As a result, there are countless variations of designs that can be observed.

Standards Alignment:

Next Generation Science Standards (NGSS, Lead States 2013)

Disciplinary Core Ideas in Physical Science

PS3: Energy

PS3.A: Definitions of Energy

PS3.B: Conservation of Energy and Energy Transfer

PS4: Waves and Their Applications in Technologies for Information Transfer

PS4.A: Wave Properties

Disciplinary Core Ideas in Life Science

LS1: From Molecules to Organisms: Structures and Processes

LS1.D: Information Processing

Water Centrifuge

<u>Concepts Illustrated:</u> Centrifugal force, Newton's first law of motion- the law of inertia, fluid dynamics, viscosity, solutions, solubility, solutes, solvents, concentration, saturated solutions, process of dissolving, properties of mixtures, density.

<u>Paradox:</u>

Amazingly, a collection of objects will separate and group together inside of a water filled soda bottle when spun on its side!

<u>Equipment:</u>

1. Empty 2 Liter soda bottle, with cap.
2. Cork balls- at least two.
3. Marbles- at least two.
4. Water.

<u>Preparation:</u>

Place the cork balls and marbles into an empty soda bottle. Fill the bottle with water and screw the cap on top.

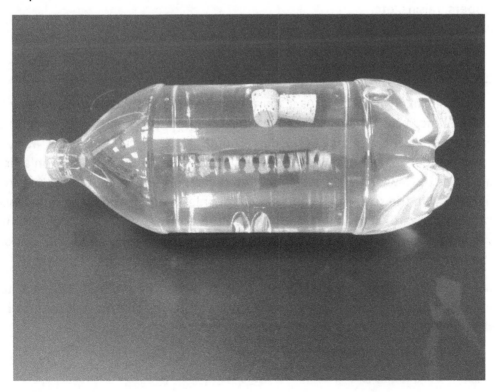

The Lesson:

Display the soda bottle to the students. Point out that it is filled with water and there are four balls inside- two are cork and two are marbles. Inform students that you will place the bottle on its side and spin with enough force that it rotates several times before coming to a stop of its own accord. Ask students to predict what they think will happen. Then, spin the bottle. You want to ensure that it will spin a few times. Allow it to stop spinning on its own. The cork balls will move to the center of the bottle, while the marbles will migrate to the ends!

Possible Variables:

1. Volume of water in the bottle.
2. Shape of the bottle.
3. The number of cork balls and marbles.
4. Density of the liquid that fills the soda bottle. This can be entirely different liquids, or simply adding salt or sugar to water to alter its density.
5. Balls of different substances and densities. This can include objects such as ping pong balls, rubber super balls, steel, aluminum, brass, copper, tin balls, etc. This can also involve using balls that can be filled with different amounts of liquid or sand to alter the density. This can also be extended to involve testing the volume of the liquid in the ball when placed into liquids of varying densities that fill the bottle. It can further involve testing various densities of liquids within the balls against varying densities of liquids in the bottle.
6. Balls with different diameters.
7. Replacing spherical cork balls and marbles with irregular objects, such as rubber stoppers, raisins, etc.
8. Viscosity of the liquid.

Phenomenon Explained:

When we are riding in a car that makes a sharp turn, we feel as though we are being "pushed" outwards, sometimes pressed against the door next to us. This is centrifugal force. It describes the tendency of an object in a circular, or curved path, to be forced outwards, away from the center of the rotation. The force we are feeling arises due to inertia. Newton's first law of motion, known as the law of inertia, states that an object either at rest or in motion, remains at rest or in motion with the same speed and direction, unless acted upon by an unbalanced force. You are traveling forward, in a straight path, before the car makes its turn. According to the law of inertia, when the car turns, your body wants to keep going straight, and you are forced into the door. Centrifugal force is not really a "force," but rather an outcome of inertia.

The marble used in our demonstration will sink in a centrifugal field. When rotated, the centrifugal field is directed towards the ends of the bottle. The marble will tend to behave as you would if you were a passenger in a car making a turn.

In our demonstration, the marble also sinks in the water due to density, another property involved in the outcome of this demonstration. The density of an object will determine whether it will float in a fluid. Density is determined by calculating the mass for a given volume, expressed in the formula g/ml, g/cm^3, or g/cc. Density is independent of the sample size, since it represents the mass per ml of the sample. A larger volume does not necessarily equate to a higher mass. Fewer molecules packed into a given volume will result in a lower density than many more molecules packed into the same volume, which would increase the density. Objects with a density less than water will float, while those denser than water will sink. The density of water is 1.0g/ml.

On the other hand, the cork will float up to the surface when placed in water. This is because it is less dense than water. Objects with a density less than water will float, while those denser than water will sink. The density of water is 1.0g/ml. The cork behaves in the same manner in a centrifugal field, floating towards the zero-centrifugal field. When the bottle spins, this is at the center of the bottle. Students might choose to investigate the density of the liquid as a variable.

If the density of the liquid is altered by adding salt or sugar, discourse can include solutions, solubility, solutes, solvents, and concentration. Saltwater or sugar water is a mixture. One property of a mixture is that it is physically combined, not chemically, and it can be physically separated. For example, saltwater can be physically separated through the process of evaporation, or boiling the water away.

A solution is one in which a solute is dissolve in a solvent. The solute is the substance being dissolved and the solvent is the substance in which the solute is dissolved. Water is called the universal solvent because of its capability to dissolve more solutes than any other liquid. Solubility is the ability of a solute to dissolve in a solvent.

A concentrated solution is one which there are many dissolved particles of solute in the solvent. On the other hand, a dilute solution is one in which there are few dissolved particles of solute. A solution which contains all the dissolve particles it can possibly hold is called saturated.

Viscosity is defined as a fluid's resistance to flow. Think of it as the "thickness" of a fluid. Fluids such as honey, molasses, corn syrup, and engine oil are highly viscous. Students might choose to investigate the outcome when liquids of varying viscosities are employed.

Standards Alignment:

Next Generation Science Standards (NGSS, Lead States 2013)

Disciplinary Core Ideas in Physical Science

PS1: Matter and Its Interactions

PS1.A: Structure and Properties of Matter

PS1.B: Chemical Reactions

PS2: Motion and Stability: Forces and Interactions

PS2.A: Forces and Motion

PS2.B: Types of Interactions

Disciplinary Core Ideas in Earth and Space Science

ESS2: Earth's Systems

ESS2.C: The Roles of Water in Earth's Surface Processes

Concepts Illustrated

The lessons included in this book provide opportunity for discourse and development of the following concepts, principles, and laws:

1. Acceleration
2. Acoustic waves
3. Adhesion
4. Aerodynamics
5. Air pressure within the human body
6. Airplane flight
7. Alloys
8. Amorphous solids
9. Archimedes' principle
10. Atmosphere on distant planets
11. Barometric pressure
12. Bernoulli's principle
13. Buoyancy
14. Capillary action
15. Catalysts
16. Center of gravity
17. Center of mass
18. Centrifugal force
19. Centripetal force
20. Charles' law
21. Chemical changes
22. Coanda effect
23. Cohesion
24. Color absorption and reflection
25. Concentrated solutions
26. Conduction
27. Conductors
28. Convection Currents
29. Density
30. Diamagnetism
31. Diameter
32. Displacement
33. Dynamics of tornadoes
34. Effects of air pressure on the human body (lungs, ears, sinuses, etc.)
35. Elastic deformation
36. Elements and compounds
37. Endothermic reactions
38. Entomology

39. Exothermic reactions
40. Fiber optics
41. Flammability
42. Fluid dynamics
43. Free fall
44. Friction
45. Gay-Lussac's law
46. Global weather patterns
47. Gravity
48. Heat
49. Heat capacity
50. Heat of fusion
51. Heat of vaporization
52. Heterogeneous solutions
53. Homogeneous solutions
54. Hydrocarbons
55. Ideal gas law
56. Inclined planes
57. Inertia
58. Influence of air pressure on physical ailments
59. Insect anatomy
60. Insect behavior
61. Insulators
62. Kinetic energy
63. Kinetic molecular theory
64. Laminar flow
65. Law of conservation of energy
66. Magnetism
67. Mass
68. Mechanical energy
69. Mechanics of bird flight
70. Mechanics of the human eye
71. Mechanics of the human vocal chords
72. Miscibility
73. Molecular motion of liquids, gases, and solids
74. Momentum
75. Newton's first law of motion- the law of inertia
76. Newton's second law
77. Normal force
78. Ocean currents
79. Perception of heat in the human body
80. Phase changes: melting, vaporization (evaporation and boiling), condensation, and freezing
81. Pheromones

Phenomena-Driven Inquiry

Cross-Reference #1: DCI to Lessons

PS1: Matter and Its Interactions

PS1.A: Structure and Properties of Matter

- A Twist in Time
- Acceleration Anomaly
- Animated Art
- Appearing Beaker
- Archimedes' Paradox
- Atomic Trampoline
- Backwards Balloon
- Big Drip
- Block Toppler
- Brachistochrone Problem
- Bricks in a Boat
- Bubble Battle
- Buoyancy Paradox
- Candle Drop
- Candle Ladder
- Candy Palette
- Capsized Confusion
- Centripetal Force Paradox
- Cheese Puzzler
- Clanging Cans
- Climbing Ball
- Confused Balloons
- Cork Accelerometer
- Defying Gravity
- Directional Acceleration
- Distance Winner
- Drips and Drops
- Drop Kick
- Drowning Candles
- Elastic Steel
- Fickle Flame
- Flipped
- Floating Fruit
- Floating Letters
- Fountain Phenomenon
- Free Fall
- Frightened Pepper
- Fruit Blast
- Interrupted Pendulum
- Inverted Straw
- Invisible Soda
- Jittery Coin
- Lava Lamp
- Leaky Cup Tumble
- Leaping Liquid
- Lift-Off
- Magic Jelly Beans
- Measured Chaos
- Melting Blocks
- Meniscus Magic
- Milk Fireworks
- Misbehaving Bubble
- Naked Eggs
- Newton's Cradle
- Paper Ball Puzzler
- Pendulum Wave
- Penny Plunge
- Pitch Paradox
- Pouring Underwater
- Powerful Cork
- Pressure Point
- Racing Pendula

- ➤ Resonant Rods
- ➤ Rolling Racers
- ➤ Salt Water Surprise
- ➤ Soap Powered Boat
- ➤ Spinner
- ➤ Spinning Glitter Paradox
- ➤ Straight Path, Short Path
- ➤ Stubborn Ping-Pong Ball
- ➤ Surprise Rise
- ➤ Sympathetic Pendula
- ➤ Thirsty Coin
- ➤ Toothpick Star
- ➤ Tricky Temperature
- ➤ Twin Tracks
- ➤ Vanishing Beaker
- ➤ Vanishing Marbles
- ➤ Water Centrifuge

PS1.B: Chemical Reactions

- ➤ A Twist in Time
- ➤ Acceleration Anomaly
- ➤ Animated Art
- ➤ Bricks in a Boat
- ➤ Candle Drop
- ➤ Candle Ladder
- ➤ Candy Palette
- ➤ Capsized Confusion
- ➤ Cheese Puzzler
- ➤ Climbing Ball
- ➤ Defying Gravity
- ➤ Directional Acceleration
- ➤ Drips and Drops
- ➤ Drowning Candles
- ➤ Fickle Flame
- ➤ Floating Letters

- ➤ Fountain Phenomenon
- ➤ Frightened Pepper
- ➤ Fruit Blast
- ➤ Inverted Straw
- ➤ Invisible Soda
- ➤ Lava Lamp
- ➤ Melting Blocks
- ➤ Meniscus Magic
- ➤ Milk Fireworks
- ➤ Misbehaving Bubble
- ➤ Naked Eggs
- ➤ Paper Ball Puzzler
- ➤ Penny Plunge
- ➤ Pitch Paradox
- ➤ Salt Water Surprise
- ➤ Soap Powered Boat
- ➤ Spinner
- ➤ Spinning Glitter Paradox
- ➤ Thirsty Coin
- ➤ Toothpick Star
- ➤ Tricky Temperature
- ➤ Vanishing Marbles
- ➤ Water Centrifuge

PS2: Motion and Stability: Forces and Interactions

PS2.A: Forces and Motion

- ➤ Abandoning Gravity
- ➤ Acceleration Anomaly
- ➤ Archimedes' Paradox
- ➤ Backwards Balloon
- ➤ Block Toppler
- ➤ Brachistochrone Problem
- ➤ Braess' Paradox
- ➤ Buoyancy Paradox

- Capsized Confusion
- Centripetal Force Paradox
- Climbing Ball
- Confused Balloons
- Cork Accelerometer
- Directional Acceleration
- Distance Winner
- Dizzy Directions
- Drop Kick
- Elastic Steel
- Fountain Phenomenon
- Free Fall
- Interrupted Pendulum
- Leaky Cup Tumble
- Misbehaving Bubble
- Naked Eggs
- Newton's Cradle
- Pendulum Wave
- Racing Pendula
- Rolling Racers
- Soap Powered Boat
- Straight Path, Short Path
- Sympathetic Pendula
- Twin Tracks
- Water Centrifuge

PS2.B: Types of Interactions

- Abandoning Gravity
- Animated Art
- Archimedes' Paradox
- Atomic Trampoline
- Big Drip
- Block Toppler
- Candle Drop
- Candle Ladder

- Candy Palette
- Centripetal Force Paradox
- Cheese Puzzler
- Defying Gravity
- Dizzy Directions
- Drips and Drops
- Drop Kick
- Drowning Candles
- Elastic Steel
- Fickle Flame
- Flipped
- Floating Letters
- Fountain Phenomenon
- Free Fall
- Frightened Pepper
- Inverted Straw
- Jittery Coin
- Lava Lamp
- Leaky Cup Tumble
- Leaping Liquid
- Magic Jelly Beans
- Measured Chaos
- Melting Blocks
- Meniscus Magic
- Milk Fireworks
- Misbehaving Bubble
- Naked Eggs
- Newton's Cradle
- Newton's Nightmare
- Paper Ball Puzzler
- Penny Plunge
- Powerful Cork
- Racing Pendula
- Salt Water Surprise
- Shocking Sand

- Soap Powered Boat
- Spinning Glitter Paradox
- Thirsty Coin
- Toothpick Star
- Vanishing Marbles
- Water Centrifuge

PS3: Energy
PS3.A: Definitions of Energy
- Abandoning Gravity
- Atomic Trampoline
- Big Drip
- Block Toppler
- Brachistochrone Problem
- Bubble Battle
- Candle Drop
- Candle Ladder
- Cheese Puzzler
- Distance Winner
- Drips and Drops
- Drowning Candles
- Elastic Steel
- Fickle Flame
- Free Fall
- Interrupted Pendulum
- Jittery Coin
- Laser Water
- Magic Jelly Beans
- Measured Chaos
- Melting Blocks
- Newton's Cradle
- Newton's Nightmare
- Pendulum Wave
- Pitch Paradox
- Racing Pendula

- Resonant Rods
- Rolling Racers
- Salt Water Surprise
- Shocking Sand
- Spinner
- Straight Path, Short Path
- Surprise Rise
- Sympathetic Pendula
- Tricky Temperature
- Twin Tracks
- Visible Sound

PS3.B: Conservation of Energy and Energy Transfer
- Abandoning Gravity
- Atomic Trampoline
- Block Toppler
- Brachistochrone Problem
- Braess' Paradox
- Candle Drop
- Candle Ladder
- Distance Winner
- Drowning Candles
- Elastic Steel
- Fickle Flame
- Free Fall
- Interrupted Pendulum
- Jittery Coin
- Laser Water
- Magic Jelly Beans
- Measured Chaos
- Melting Blocks
- Newton's Cradle
- Pendulum Wave
- Pitch Paradox

- ➤ Racing Pendula
- ➤ Resonant Rods
- ➤ Rolling Racers
- ➤ Salt Water Surprise
- ➤ Shocking Sand
- ➤ Spinner
- ➤ Straight Path, Short Path
- ➤ Sympathetic Pendula
- ➤ Tricky Temperature
- ➤ Twin Tracks
- ➤ Visible Sound

PS3.C: Relationship Between Energy and Forces

- ➤ Atomic Trampoline
- ➤ Backwards Balloon
- ➤ Block Toppler
- ➤ Confused Balloons
- ➤ Cork Accelerometer
- ➤ Drop Kick
- ➤ Elastic Steel
- ➤ Interrupted Pendulum
- ➤ Leaping Liquid
- ➤ Newton's Cradle
- ➤ Newton's Nightmare
- ➤ Pendulum Wave
- ➤ Shocking Sand
- ➤ Sympathetic Pendula

PS3.D: Energy in Chemical Processes and Everyday Life

- ➤ Cheese Puzzler
- ➤ Floating Fruit
- ➤ Jittery Coin
- ➤ Naked Eggs

PS4: Waves and Their Applications in Technologies for Information Transfer

PS4.A: Wave Properties

- ➤ Appearing Beaker
- ➤ Atomic Trampoline
- ➤ Clanging Cans
- ➤ Drop Kick
- ➤ Flipped
- ➤ Free Fall
- ➤ Jittery Coin
- ➤ Laser Water
- ➤ Newton's Cradle
- ➤ Pendulum Wave
- ➤ Penny Plunge
- ➤ Pitch Paradox
- ➤ Resonant Rods
- ➤ Shocking Sand
- ➤ Sympathetic Pendula
- ➤ Vanishing Beaker
- ➤ Vanishing Marbles
- ➤ Visible Sound

PS4.B: Electromagnetic Radiation

- ➤ Appearing Beaker
- ➤ Candy Palette
- ➤ Cheese Puzzler
- ➤ Color Wheel
- ➤ Flipped
- ➤ Laser Water
- ➤ Lava Lamp
- ➤ Naked Eggs
- ➤ Tricky Temperature
- ➤ Vanishing Beaker
- ➤ Vanishing Marbles

Disciplinary Core Ideas in Life Science

<u>LS1: From Molecules to Organisms: Structures and Processes</u>

LS1.A: Structure and Function

- ➢ A Twist in Time
- ➢ Bubble Battle
- ➢ Candle Drop
- ➢ Candle Ladder
- ➢ Candy Palette
- ➢ Clanging Cans
- ➢ Color Wheel
- ➢ Defying Gravity
- ➢ Drowning Candles
- ➢ Fickle Flame
- ➢ Flipped
- ➢ Floating Fruit
- ➢ Frightened Pepper
- ➢ Inverted Straw
- ➢ Jittery Coin
- ➢ Lift-Off
- ➢ Meniscus Magic
- ➢ Naked Eggs
- ➢ Paper Ball Puzzler
- ➢ Penny Plunge
- ➢ Pitch Paradox
- ➢ Soap Powered Boat
- ➢ Spinning Glitter Paradox
- ➢ Termite Trails
- ➢ Thirsty Coin
- ➢ Toothpick Star

LS1.B: Growth and Development of Organisms

- ➢ Naked Eggs

LS1.C: Organization for Matter and Energy Flow in Organisms

- ➢ Floating Fruit
- ➢ Naked Eggs

LS1.D: Information Processing

- ➢ Candy Palette
- ➢ Color Wheel
- ➢ Flipped
- ➢ Floating Fruit
- ➢ Free Fall
- ➢ Jittery Coin
- ➢ Melting Blocks
- ➢ Pitch Paradox
- ➢ Termite Trails
- ➢ Tricky Temperature
- ➢ Visible Sound

<u>LS2: Ecosystems: Interactions, Energy, and Dynamics</u>
LS2.A: Interdependent Relationships in Ecosystems

- ➢ Naked Eggs

LS2.D: Social Interactions and Group Behavior

- ➢ Termite Trails

Disciplinary Core Ideas in Earth and Space Science

<u>ESS2: Earth's Systems</u>
ESS2.C: The Roles of Water in Earth's Surface Processes

- ➢ A Twist in Time
- ➢ Animated Art

- ➤ Big Drip
- ➤ Bricks in a Boat
- ➤ Candy Palette
- ➤ Capsized Confusion
- ➤ Climbing Ball
- ➤ Defying Gravity
- ➤ Directional Acceleration
- ➤ Drips and Drops
- ➤ Floating Letters
- ➤ Fountain Phenomenon
- ➤ Frightened Pepper
- ➤ Inverted Straw
- ➤ Lava Lamp
- ➤ Meniscus Magic
- ➤ Misbehaving Bubble
- ➤ Naked Eggs
- ➤ Paper Ball Puzzler
- ➤ Penny Plunge
- ➤ Pitch Paradox
- ➤ Salt Water Surprise
- ➤ Soap Powered Boat
- ➤ Spinning Glitter Paradox
- ➤ Surprise Rise
- ➤ Thirsty Coin
- ➤ Toothpick Star
- ➤ Water Centrifuge

ESS2.D: Weather and Climate
- ➤ A Twist in Time
- ➤ Candle Drop
- ➤ Candle Ladder
- ➤ Drowning Candles
- ➤ Jittery Coin
- ➤ Spinner
- ➤ Surprise Rise

ESS3: Earth and Human Activity
ESS3.B: Natural Hazards

- ➤ Clanging Cans
- ➤ Fickle Flame
- ➤ Stubborn Ping-Pong Ball

Cross-Reference #2: Concepts to Lessons

1. Acceleration
   - Acceleration Anomaly
   - Backwards Balloon
   - Brachistochrone Problem
   - Confused Balloons
   - Cork Accelerometer
   - Directional Acceleration
   - Distance Winner
   - Drop Kick
   - Free Fall
   - Leaky Cup Tumble
   - Rolling Racers
   - Straight Path, Short Path
   - Twin Tracks
2. Active/Passive Transport
   - Naked Eggs
3. Adhesion
   - Animated Art
   - Defying Gravity
   - Inverted Straw
   - Jittery Coin
   - Meniscus Magic
   - Thirsty Coin
   - Toothpick Star
4. Aerodynamics
   - Clanging Cans
   - Fickle Flame
   - Lift-Of
   - Stubborn Ping-Pong Ball
5. Air Current
   - Clanging Cans
   - Fickle Flame
   - Stubborn Ping-Pong Ball
6. Air Pressure
   - Bubble Battle
   - Clanging Cans
   - Confused Balloons
   - Defying Gravity
   - Drowning Candles
   - Fickle Flame
   - Fountain Phenomenon
   - Inverted Straw
   - Jittery Coin
   - Leaky Cup Tumble
   - Lift-Off
   - Pouring Underwater
   - Powerful Cork
   - Pressure Point
   - Stubborn Ping-Pong Ball
   - Surprise Rise

16. Air Pressure Within the Human Body
   - Defying Gravity
   - Inverted Straw
   - Lift-Off
   - Pouring Underwater
   - Powerful Cork
   - Surprise Rise

17. Airplane Flight
   - Clanging Cans
   - Fickle Flame
   - Lift-Off
   - Stubborn Ping-Pong Ball

9. Alloys
   - Atomic Trampoline

10. Amorphous Solids
   - Atomic Trampoline
   - Candle Drop
   - Candle Ladder
   - Drowning Candles
   - Fickle Flame

11. Amplitude
   - Pendulum Wave
   - Resonant Rods
   - Sympathetic Pendula

492

Bibliography

Alvermann, D. E., & Hague, S. A. (1989). Comprehension of counterintuitive science text: Effects of prior knowledge and text structure. *Journal of Educational Research,* 82, 197-202.

American Association for the Advancement of Science. (1993). *Science for all Americans: Project 2061.* New York: Oxford University Press.

Anderson, C. W., & Roth, K. J. (1989). Teaching for meaningful and self-regulated learning of science. In J. Brophy (Ed.). *Advances in research on teaching* (pp. 265-309). Greenwich, CT: JAI Press.

Appleteon, K. (1993). Using theory to guide practice; Teaching science from a constructivist perspective. *School Science and Mathematics*, 93(5), 269-274.

Atkin, J.M., & Karplus, R. (1962). Discovery or invention? The Science Teacher, 29(5), 45-51.

Baddeley, A. D. (2000). The episodic buffer: A new component of working memory? *Trends in Cognitive Sciences*, 4(11), 417-423.

Baddock, M. & Bucat, R. (2008). Effectiveness of a classroom chemistry demonstration using the cognitive conflict strategy. *International Journal of Science Education*, 30(8), 1115- 1128.

Beall, H. (1996). Report on the WPI Conference "Demonstrations as a Teaching Tool in Chemistry: Pro and Con". *Journal of Chemical Education*, 73(7), 641.

Beasley, W. (1982). Teacher demonstrations: The effect on student task involvement. *Journal of Chemical Education*, 59(9), 789-790.

Bereiter, C., & Scardamalia, M. (1992). Cognition and curriculum. In P. W. Jackson (Ed.), *Handbook of research on curriculum* (pp. 517-542). New York: Macmillan.

Bianchi, H., & Bell, R. (2008). The many levels of inquiry. *Science and Children*, 46 (2), 26-29.

Bielaczyc, K., Pirolli, P. L., & Brown, A. L. (1995). Training in self-explanation and self-regulation strategies: Investigating the effects of knowledge acquisition activities on problem solving. *Cognition and Instruction,* 13, 221-252.

Bodner, G.M. (2001). Why lecture demonstrations are 'exocharmic' for both students and their instructors. *University Chemical Education*, 5, 31-35.

Botvinick, M.M., Carter, C.S., Braver, T.S., Barch, D.M., & Cohen, J.D. (2001). Conflict monitoring and cognitive control. *Psychological Review*, 108(3), 624-652.

Brown, J. S., Collins, A., & Duguid, P. (1989). Situated cognition and the culture of learning. *Educational Researcher*, 18(1), 32-42.

Buncick, M. C., Betts, P. G., & Horgan, D. D. (2001). Using demonstrations as a contextual road map: enhancing course continuity and promoting active engagement in introductory college physics. International Journal of Science Education, 23(12), 1237-1255.

Bybee, R. W. (2000). Teaching science as inquiry. In J. Minstrell & E. H. van Zee (Eds.), Inquiry into inquiry learning and teaching in science (pp. 20-42). Washington, DC: American Association for the Advancement of Science.

Callan, J.P., Crouch, C.H., Fagen, A.P., & Mazur, E. (2004). Classroom demonstrations: Learning tools or entertainment? *American Journal of Physics*, 72(6), 835-838.

Carey, S. (1986). Cognitive science and science education. *American psychologist,* 41(10), 1123-1130.

Champagne, A. N., Gunstone, R. F., & Klopfer, L. E. (1985). Effecting changes in cognitive structures among physics students. In L. H. T. West &A. L. Pines (Eds.), *Cognitive structures and conceptual change* (pp. 163-187). Orlando, FL: Academic.

Champagne, A.B., Klopfer, L.E., & Anderson, J.H. (1980). Factors Influencing the learning of classical mechanics. *American Journal of Physics*, 48, 1074-1079.

Chan, C., Burtis, J., & Bereiter, C. (1997). Knowledge building as a mediator of conflict in conceptual change. *Cognition and Instruction*, 15(1), 1–40.

Chi, M. T. H., De Leeuw, N., Chiu, M. H., & LaVancher, C. (1994). Eliciting self-explanation improves understanding. *Cognitive Science,* 18, 439-477.

Chinn, C. A., & Malhotra, B. A. (2002). Epistemologically authentic inquiry in schools: A theoretical framework for evaluating inquiry tasks. *Science Education*, 86(2), 175 218.

Clark, R.L., Clough, M.P., & Berg, C.A. (2000). Modifying cookbook labs. *The Science Teacher*, 67(7), 40-43.

Colburn, A., & Clough, M.P. (1997). Implementing the learning cycle. *The Science Teacher*, 64(5), 30-33.

Corder, G., & Slykhuts, J. (2011). Shifting to an inquiry-based experience. *Science and Children*, 48(9), 60-63.

Crouch, C.H., Fagen, A.P., Callan, J.P. & Mazur E. (2004). Classroom demonstrations: learning tool or entertainment? *American Journal of Physics*, 72, 835-838.

Dreyfus, A., Jungwirth, E., & Eliovitch, R. (1990). Applying the "cognitive conflict" strategy for conceptual change. Some implications, difficulties and problems. *Science Education,* 74, 555-569.

Driver, R., & Bell, B. (1986). Students' thinking and the learning of science: A constructivist view. *The School Science Review*, 67, 443-456.

Driver, R., & Oldham, V. (1986). A constructivist approach to curriculum development in science. *Studies in Science Education,* 13(1), 105-122.

Driver, R., Asoko, H., Leach, J., Mortimer, E., & Scott, P. (1994). Constructing scientific knowledge in the classroom. *Educational Researcher*, 23(7), 5-12.

Dykstra, D. I., Boyle, C. F., & Monarch, I. A. (1992). Studying conceptual change in learning physics. *Science Education*, 76(6), 615-652.

Eylon, B., & Linn, M. C. (1988). Learning and instruction: An examination of four research perspectives in science education. *Review of Educational Research,* 58, 251-301.

Festinger, L. (1957). A theory of cognitive dissonance. Stanford, CA: Stanford University Press.

Fredricks, J.A., Blumenfeld, P.C., & Paris, A.H. (2004). School engagement: Potential of the concept, state of the evidence. *Review of Educational Research*, 74(1), 59-109.

Freier, G. (1981). The use of demonstrations in physics teaching. *The Physics Teacher*, 19(6), 384-386.

Friedl, A.E. (1991). Teaching science to children: An integrated approach. New York: McGraw Hill.

Furtak, E. M. (2009). Formative assessment for secondary science teachers. Thousand Oaks, CA: Corwin Press.

Gick, B., & Derrick, D. (2009). Aero-tactile integration in speech perception. *Nature,* 462(7272), 502-504.

Glaser, R., & Bassok, M. (1989). Learning theory and the study of instruction. *Annual Review of Psychology,* 40, 631-666.

Glasson, G. E. (1989). The effects of hands-on and teacher demonstration laboratory methods on science achievement in relation to reasoning ability and prior knowledge. *Journal of Research in Science Teaching*, 26(2), 121-131.

Guzzetti, B. (1990). The effects of text and reader-based instructional manipulations on concept acquisition. *Reading Psychology,* 11, 49-62.

Guzzetti, B. J., Snyder, T.E., Glass, G. V., & Gamas, W.S. (1993). Promoting conceptual change in science: A comparative meta-analysis of instructional interventions from reading education and science education. *Reading Research Quarterly,* 28(2), 116-159.

Heath, C., & Heath, D. (2007). Made to Stick. New York: Random House.

Hewson, P. W., & Thorley, N. R. (1989). The conditions of conceptual change in the classroom. *International Journal of Science Education*, 11, 541-553.

Hidi, S., & Harackiewicz, J. (2000). Motivating the academically unmotivated: A critical issue for the 21st century. *Review of Educational Research*, 70, 151-179.

Hilton, W. (1981). Demonstrations as an aid in the teaching of physics. *The Physics Teacher*, 19(6), 389-390.

Huff, K.L., & Bybee, R.W. (2013). The practice of critical discourse in science classrooms. *Science Scope*, 36(9), 29-34.

Hynd, C. R., & Alvermann, D. E. (1989). Overcoming misconceptions in science: Am on-line study of prior knowledge activation. *Reading Research and Instruction,* 28(4), 12-26.

Johnson, D.W., & Johnson, R.T. (2009). Energizing learning: The instructional power of conflict. *Educational Researcher*, 38(1), 37-51.

Kang, H.K., Scharmann, L.C., Kang, S., & Noh, T. (2010). Cognitive conflict and situational interest as factors influencing conceptual change. *International Journal of Environmental & Science Education*, 5(4), 383-405.

Kang, S., Scharmann, L.C., & Noh, T. (2004). Reexamining the role of cognitive conflict in science concept learning. *Research in Science Education,* 34, 71-96.

Kelly, S. (2007). Classroom discourse and the distribution of student engagement. *Social Psychology of Education*, 10, 331-352.

Kur, J., & Heitzmann, M. (2008). Attracting student wonderings. *Science and Children*, 45(5), 28-32.

Lawler, R.W. (1981). The progressive construction of mind. *Cognitive Science*, 5, 1-30.

Lawson, A. E. (2000). Managing the inquiry classroom: Problems & Solutions. *The American Biology Teacher*, 62(9), 641-648.

Lawson, A., Abraham, M., & Renner, J. (1989). *A theory of instruction: Using the learning cycle to teach science concepts and thinking skills*. Manhattan, KS: National Association for Research in Science Teaching (NARST).

Leslie, I. (2014). Curious. New York: Basic Books.

Liem, T.L. (1981). Invitations to Science Inquiry. Gin Press.

Limon, M. (2001). On the cognitive conflict as an instructional strategy for conceptual change: A critical appraisal. *Learning and Instruction,* 11, 357-380.

Limon, M., & Carretero, M. (1997). Conceptual change and anomalous data; A case study in the domain of natural sciences. *European Journal of Psychology of Education*, 12(2), 213- 230.

Llewellyn, D. (2007). Inquiry within: Implementing inquiry-based science standards in grades 3–8. 2nd ed. Thousand Oaks, CA: Corwin Press.

Loewenstein, G. (1994). The psychology of curiosity: A review and reinterpretation. *Psychological Bulletin*, 116(1), 75-98.

Luna, T., & Renninger, L. (2015). Surprise. New York: Penguin Group.

Lynch, M. J., & Zenchak, J. J., (2002, January). Use of scientific inquiry to explain counterintuitive observations. Paper presented at the Proceedings of the Annual International Conference of the Association for the Education of Teachers in Science, Charlotte, NC.

MacBeth, D. (2000). On an apparatus for conceptual change. *Science Education*, 84(2), 228-264.

Manaf, E. B. A., & Subramaniam, R. (2004, June). Use of chemistry demonstrations to foster conceptual understanding and cooperative learning among students. Paper presented at the International Association for the Study of Cooperation in Education, Singapore.

Maria, K., & MacGinitie, W. (1987). Learning from texts that refute the reader's prior knowledge. *Reading Research and Instruction,* 26, 222-238.

Mason, L. (2001). Responses to anomalous data on controversial topics and theory change. *Learning and Instruction*, 11, 453-483.

McDermott, L. C. (2001). Physics education research- the key to student learning. *American Journal of Physics*, 69(11), 1127-1137.

Meyer, L. S., Schmidt, S., Nozawa, F., & Paneee, D. (2003). Using demonstrations to promote student comprehension in chemistry. *Journal of Chemical Education*, 80(4), 431-435.

Milne, C., & Otieno, T. (2007). Understanding engagement: Science demonstrations and emotional energy. *Science Education*, 91(4), 523- 53.

National Research Council. (1996). National Science Education Standards. Washington, DC: National Academies Press.

National Research Council. (2000). *Inquiry and the national science education standards: A Guide for Teaching and Learning*. Washington, DC: The National Academies Press.

National Research Council. (2007). *Taking science to school: Learning and teaching science in grades K-8*. Washington, DC: The National Academies Press.

National Research Council. (2012). *A Framework for K-12 Science Education: Practices, Crosscutting Concepts, and Core Ideas*. Washington, DC: The National Academies Press.

National Science Teachers Association. (1998). NSTA position statement- The national science education standards: A vision for the improvement of science and learning. *Science Scope*, 65(5), 32-34.

National Science Teachers Association. (2004, October). NSTA Position Statement: Scientific Inquiry. Retrieved from http://www.nsta.org/about/positions/inquiry.aspx

NGSS Lead States. (2013). Next Generation Science Standards: For States, By States. Washington, DC: The National Academies Press.

O'Brien, T. (1991). The science and art of science demonstrations. *Journal of Chemical Education*, 68(11), 933-936.

Palincsar, A. S. (1989). Less charted waters. *Educational Researcher*, 18(4), 5-7.

Palmeri, A. (2009). Making sense of data. *Science and Children*, 47(2), 30-33.

Parr, B. (2004). Captivology. New York: Harper Collins Publishers.

Piaget, J. (1964). Development and Learning. *Journal of Research in Science Teaching*, 2, 176- 186.

Piaget, J. (1970). Science of Education and the Psychology of the Child. New York: Orion Press.

Pintrich, P.R., & Schunk, D.H. (1996). Motivation in education: Theory, research, and applications. Englewood Cliffs, NJ: Merrill/Prentice Hall.

Pintrich, P.R., Marx, R.W., & Boyle, R.A. (1994). Beyond cold conceptual change: The role of motivational beliefs and classroom contextual factors in the process of conceptual change. *Review of Educational Research,* 63 (2), 167-199.

Posner, G.J., Strike, K.A., Hewson, P.W., & Gertzog, W.A. (1982). Accommodation of a scientific conception: Toward a theory of conceptual change. *Science Education,* 66, 211-227.

Roadruck, M.D. (1993). Chemical demonstrations: Learning theories suggest caution. *Journal of Chemical Education, 70* (12), 1025.

Roth, W-M., & Lucas, K. (1997). From "truth" to "invented reality": A discourse analysis of high school physics students' talk about scientific knowledge. *Journal of Research in Science Teaching*, 34, 145-179.

Roth, W-M., McRobbie, C. J., Lucas, K. B., & Boutonne, S. (1997). Why may students fail to learn from demonstrations? A social perspective on learning in physics. *Journal of Research in Science Teaching*, 34, 509-533.

Schauble, L., Glaser, R., Duschl, R., Schulze, S., & John, J. (1995). Students' understanding of the objectives and procedures of experimentation in the science classroom. *Journal of the Learning Sciences*, 4(2), 131-166.

Schraw, G., & Lehman, S. (2001). Situational interest: A review of the literature and directions for future research. *Educational Psychology Review*, 13(1), 23-52.

Schutzwohl, A. (1998). Surprise and schema strength. *Journal of Experimental Psychology*, 24(5), 1182-1199.

Scott, P.H., Asoko, H.M., & Driver, R.H. (1991). Teaching for conceptual change: A review of strategies. Research in Physics Learning: Theoretical Issues and Empirical Studies. Proceedings of an International Workshop.

Scribner-MacLean, M. (2012). More than just guessing. *Science Scope*, 35(8), 37-40.

Seel, N. M. (2001). Epistemology, situated cognition, and mental models: 'Like a bridge over troubled water'. *Instructional Science*, 29, 403-427.

Sharkawy, A. (2010). A quest to improve. *Science and Children*, 48(4), 32-35.

Shepardson, D. P., Moje, E. B., & Kennard-McClelland, A. M. (1994). The impact of a science demonstration on children's understanding of air pressure. *Journal of Research in Science Teaching*, 31(3), 243-258.

Stahl, A., & Feigenson, L. (2015). Observing the unexpected enhances infants' learning and exploration. Science, 348(6230), 91-94.

Strayer, D.L., & Johnston, W.A. (2000). Novel popout is an attention-based phenomenon: An ERP analysis. *Perceptions & Psychophysics*, 62(3), 459-470.

Strike, K.A., & Posner, G.J. (1992). A revisionist theory of conceptual change. In R.A. Duschl & R.J. Hamilton (Eds.), *Philosophy of Science, Cognitive Psychology and Educational Theory and Practice*. Albany, NY: State University of New York Press.

TED. (2009, October 8). Beau Lotto: Optical illusions show how we see [Video file]. Retrieved from https://www.youtube.com/watch?v=mf5otGNbkuc

Tillema, H.H., & Knol, W.E. (1997). Promoting student teacher learning through conceptual change or direct instruction. *Teaching and Teacher Education*, 13(6), 579-595.

Vosniadou, S., Ioannides, C., Dimitrakopoulou, A., & Papademetriou, E. (2001). Designing learning environments to promote conceptual change in science. *Learning and Instruction*, 11, 381-419.

Wang, T. Y., & Andre, T. (1991). Conceptual change text versus traditional text and application questions versus no questions in learning about electricity. *Contemporary Educational Psychology,* 16, 103-116.

Weaver, G.C. (1998). Strategies in K-12 science instruction to promote conceptual change. *Science Education*, 82, 455-472.

West, L. H., & Pines, A. L. (Eds.). (1985). *Cognitive structure and conceptual change.* Orlando, FL: Academic Press.

Willingham, D. (2008-09). What will improve a student's memory? *American Educator*, 32(4), 17-44.

Willis, J. (2009). What you should know about your brain. *Educational Leadership*, 67(4), 1-3.

Windschitl, M., & Buttemer, H, (2000). What Should the Inquiry Experience Be for the Learner? *The American Biology Teacher*, 62(5), 346-350.

Wright, E.L. & Govindarajan, G. (1995). Discrepant event demonstrations: Motivating students to learn science concepts. *The Science Teacher*, 62(1), 25- 28.

Zenchak, J., & Lynch, M.J. (2011). What's the next step. *Science and Children*, 48(6), 50-54.

Vince Mancuso, Ed.D., has been a middle school science teacher for 19 years. He earned his doctorate in Teaching and Curriculum from the University of Rochester, Warner School of Education. His research focuses on discrepant event phenomena in the science classroom and inquiry-based reform, specifically the development of inquiry-grounded curriculum and effective inquiry practices that enrich traditional classrooms. He developed and shaped Phenomena-Driven Inquiry and the POQIE model through fifteen years of extensive research and field testing that began with his Master's work, carried through his doctoral studies, and continued through several years of post-doctoral action research. He can be contacted at vince_mancuso@bcsd.org and followed on Twitter @discrepantevent.

To book Dr. Mancuso for professional development, please visit - phenomenadriveninquiry.com.

Continue your professional development journey!

Dr. Mancuso is dedicated to helping educators advance their practice and curriculum. His professional development services include custom workshops and keynote presentations that concern his research.

Contact him to bring any of the following exciting opportunities to your school or district:

- Phenomena-Driven Inquiry & the POQIE Model: Its design and implementation into the science curriculum. Discover a powerful approach to learning!

- Discrepant Event Demonstrations That Captivate: Discover discrepant events as you've never seen before. Add wonder to your curriculum and classroom!

- Effective Inquiry in the Science Classroom: The development and implementation of a rewarding inquiry-based, student-centered curriculum.

- Igniting Wonder and Passion for Learning!

Deliver the wonder, ignite the spark!

Visit phenomenadriveninquiry.com for more info and availability.

CPSIA information can be obtained
at www.ICGtesting.com
Printed in the USA
LVHW03s1502070618
579960LV00006B/356/P

9 780998 933009